QUANTITATIVE RESEARCH METHODS
for Communication

QUANTITATIVE RESEARCH METHODS

for Communication

A HANDS-ON APPROACH

FOURTH EDITION

Jason S. Wrench
State University of New York at New Paltz

Candice Thomas-Maddox
Ohio University, Lancaster

Virginia Peck Richmond
University of Alabama at Birmingham

James C. McCroskey
University of Alabama at Birmingham

New York   Oxford
OXFORD UNIVERSITY PRESS

Oxford University Press is a department of the University of Oxford.
It furthers the University's objective of excellence in research, scholarship,
and education by publishing worldwide. Oxford is a registered trade mark of
Oxford University Press in the UK and certain other countries.

Published in the United States of America by Oxford University Press
198 Madison Avenue, New York, NY 10016, United States of America.

For titles covered by Section 112 of the US Higher Education Opportunity
Act, please visit www.oup.com/us/he for the latest information about
pricing and alternate formats.

Library of Congress Cataloging-in-Publication Data

Names: Wrench, Jason S., editor.
  Title: Quantitative research methods for communication : a hands-on approach
    / Jason S. Wrench, State University of New York at New Paltz ; Candice
    Thomas-Maddox, Ohio University, Lancaster ; Virginia Peck Richmond,
    University of Alabama at Birmingham ; James C. McCroskey, University of
    Alabama at Birmingham.
  Description: Fourth edition. | New York : Oxford University Press, [2019]
  Identifiers: LCCN 2018018850 | ISBN 9780190861063 (pbk.)
  Subjects: LCSH: Communication—Research—Methodology. |
    Communication—Statistical methods.
  Classification: LCC P91.3 .Q36 2019 | DDC 302.2/072—dc23
  LC record available at https://lccn.loc.gov/2018018850

Brief Contents

Preface   xxvii

CHAPTER 1   An Introduction to Communication Research   1

CHAPTER 2   Empirical Research   17

CHAPTER 3   Research Ethics   39

CHAPTER 4   Searching for Previous Research and American Psychological Association Style   81

CHAPTER 5   Research Structure and Literature Reviews   131

CHAPTER 6   Variables   171

CHAPTER 7   Measurement   217

CHAPTER 8   Reliability and Validity   248

CHAPTER 9   Survey Research   280

CHAPTER 10   Content Analysis   319

CHAPTER 11   Experimental Design   336

CHAPTER 12   Sampling Methods   368

CHAPTER 13   Hypothesis Testing   391

CHAPTER 14   Descriptive Statistics   417

CHAPTER 15   Chi-Square (χ^2) Test of Independence   445

CHAPTER 16   Independent Samples t Tests   471

CHAPTER 17   One-Way Analysis of Variance   492

CHAPTER 18   Correlation   517

CHAPTER 19   Regression   539

CHAPTER 20   Presenting Research   561

APPENDIX A   Qualitative Research (Available online https://oup-arc.com/wrench)

APPENDIX B   Textbook Questionnaire (Available online: https://oup-arc.com/wrench)

APPENDIX C   Free and Open-Source Statistical Software (Available online: https://oup-arc.com/wrench)

APPENDIX D   Big Data (Available online: https://oup-arc.com/wrench)

APPENDIX E   Advanced Statistical Procedures (Available online: https://oup-arc.com/wrench)

Glossary   595

Index   607

Contents

Preface   xxviii

CHAPTER 1   An Introduction to Communication Research   1

The History of the Social Sciences   **2**

Ancient Greece   2

Sir Isaac Newton   3

Charles Darwin   4

Late 1800s to Early 1900s   4

James A. Winans and Everett Lee Hunt   4

Social Sciences After World War I   5

Social Sciences During World War II   5

Carl Hovland and Post–World War II Research   6

Social Sciences in Communication Today   6

The Nature of Communication   **9**

Modeling Communication   9

Source   10

Receiver   10

Message   10

Channel   11

Understanding the Book's Format   **12**

Research Outside the Walls of Academia   **15**

Conclusion   **15**

CHAPTER 2   Empirical Research   17

Ways of Knowing   **18**

Epistemology   18

How Does One Analyze Knowledge and Justification?   18

What Sources of Knowledge Does One Use?   18

What Is the Importance and Use of Skepticism?   19

Epistemology and This Book   19

Ordinary Versus Scientific Ways of Knowing   20

Ordinary Sources of Information   20

Problems with Ordinary Knowledge   21

Ordinary Knowledge Versus Science   21

The Scientific Approach to Communication Research   **23**

Scientific Method   23

Theories   24

Describe the Natural Phenomenon   24

Predict the Future   26

Falsification   26

Predictions/Hypotheses   27

Observations   29

Empirical Observations   30

Objective Observations   30

Controlled Observations   31

Empirical Generalizations   31

Common Problems with Generalizations   33

Generalizations Help Refine Theory   34

Research Outside the Walls of Academia   **34**

Conclusion   **35**

CHAPTER 3   Research Ethics   39

Ethical Scenarios   **40**

Tuskegee Syphilis Study   41

Liquor Store Burglary Study   42

Anonymous Sex Study   42

Wichita Jury Study   42

Stanford Prison Study   43

Milgram Study   43

Adolescent Alcohol Consumption Project   43

Professor Goes to School Undercover Study   44

Facebook Newsfeed Manipulation Study   44

Dr. Diederik Stapel's Inconsistent Data   45

Defining Ethics   **45**

Good Means–Good End: Ethical Behavior   46

Bad Means–Bad End: Unethical Behavior   46

Bad Means–Good End: Machiavellian Ethic   46

Good Means–Bad End: Subjective Ethic   46

The Belmont Report's Effect on Research Ethics   **47**

Informed Consent   47

Principle of Beneficence   48

Justice   49

Institutional Review Boards   **49**

IRB Basics   50

Research Participant   50

Paid Participation   51

Anonymity, Privacy, and Confidentiality   51

Informed Consent   54

Common Parts of a Consent Document   54

Do Consent Documents Really Work?   59

Waiver of Consent   60

Handling Deception During the Consent Process   61

IRB Processes   61

Basic IRB Functions   62

Levels of IRB Review   64

Specific Ethical Issues for Research   **71**

Data Accuracy   71

Data Sharing   72

Duplicate Data Publication   72

Post Hoc Hypothesis Revision   73

Participant Identity Protection   73

Authorship Credit   73

Conflict of Interest   74

Plagiarism   74

Source-Not-Cited Types of Plagiarism   75

Source-Cited Types of Plagiarism   76

Research Outside the Walls of Academia   **77**

Conclusion   **78**

CHAPTER 4   Searching for Previous Research and American Psychological Association Style   81

Step 1: Identifying the Topic   **82**

Why Are You Doing the Research?   83

What Interests You?   83

Three Possible Sources for Topics   84

Personal Experiences   84

Reviewing the Literature   85

Theoretically Driven Questions   85

Step 2: Clarifying the Research Question and Generating Key Terms   **86**

Stating the Topic in the Form of a Research Question   87

Identifying Key Terms and Synonymous Terms   89

Step 3: Locating Sources of Information   **91**

Primary Versus Secondary Sources   91

Primary Sources   91

Secondary Sources   91

Types of Information Sources   93

Locating Information Sources   95

Handbooks and Subject Encyclopedias   98

Electronic Databases   100

The World Wide Web   105

Other Online Research Databases   107

Evaluating Web Sources   109

Accuracy   110

Authority   110

Currency   110

Objectivity   110

Step 4: Organizing and Evaluating Information   **111**

Step 5: Citing Sources of Information Using the APA Format   **114**

What Information Must Be Referenced?   114

Citing Sources of Information   116

Parenthetical Citations   119

Quotations and Paraphrases   120

APA Paper Formatting   **122**

Creating a Title Page   122

Running Heads   122

Paper Titles   124

Author Name(s) and Affiliation(s)   124

Creating an Abstract   124

Creating the First Page   126

Creating the Reference Page   126

Conclusion   **128**

CHAPTER 5   Research Structure and Literature Reviews   131

The Abstract   **132**

The Introduction   **135**

Attention-Getter   135

Using Statistics or Claims   135

Posing a Rhetorical Question   137

Using an Acknowledged Fact   137

Using a Story or Illustration   137

Quoting or Acknowledging a Source   138

Link to the Topic   138

Significance of the Topic   139

Espousal of Credibility   139

Thesis   139

Preview   140

Literature Review   **140**

    Five Reasons for Literature Reviews   140

        Explaining Vocabulary   140

        Placing a Study in Historical Context   141

        Explanation and Rationalization for Variables   141

        Previous Findings and Research Needed   142

        Establishing Your Argument   142

    Previous Research   143

        Chronological   143

        Cause-and-Effect   144

        Compare-and-Contrast   145

        Problem–Cause–Solution   145

        Psychological   146

        Categorical/Topical   146

        An Example Literature Review   147

Study Rationale   **149**

Method Section   **150**

    Participants   150

    Apparatus   151

    Procedure   151

    Instrumentation   151

Results Section   **154**

Discussion Section   **156**

    Discussion of the Results   156

    Limitations   157

    Future Directions for Research   158

The Conclusion   **159**

References and End Materials   **160**

    References   160

    End Materials   160

        Footnotes   160

        Tables   161

        Figures   162

Reading and Critiquing Academic Literature   **162**

Preparing a First Draft of a Literature Review   **163**

    Step 1: Identify Your General Topic   163

    Step 2: Determine the Type of Study You Are Conducting   163

    Step 3: Determine What Variables You Will Examine   164

    Step 4: Search for Primary Sources   164

    Step 5: Obtain Full Text References   164

Step 6: Look for Other References in Obtained Materials   164

Step 7: Narrow Your List of References   164

Step 8: Organize References by Major Topics and Subtopics   165

Step 9: Look for Gaps in Your References   165

Step 10: Find References to Fill Gaps   165

Step 11: Create a Literature Review Outline   166

Step 12: Write   167

Research Outside the Walls of Academia   **167**

Conclusion   **168**

CHAPTER 6   Variables   171

How Are Research Projects Developed?   **172**

Variables   **172**

Units of Analysis   **173**

Individuals   173

Dyads   173

Groups   173

Organizations   174

Generalizations and Inferences   174

Aspects of Variables   **174**

Variable Attributes   174

Variable Values   174

Understanding Relationships and Differences   175

Relationships   175

Differences   177

Types of Variables   **179**

Independent and Dependent Variables   179

Intervening Variables   180

Antecedent Variables   180

Variable Levels   **181**

Nominal Variables   181

Ordinal Variables   182

Interval Variables   183

Likert Scale   183

Semantic Differential Scale   184

Staple Scale   185

Scalogram   186

Ratio Variables   187

Communication Variables   **189**

Nominal Variables   189

Biological Sex   189

Political Affiliation   189

Ordinal Variables   190

University Classification   190

Time Spent Online   190

Interval Variables   191

Common Interval Variable Measures   191

Traits and Communication   192

A Communication Trait Continuum   193

Communication Apprehension   194

Trait CA   196

Contextual CA   196

Situational CA   196

Ethnocentrism   197

Humor Assessment   197

Nonverbal Immediacy   200

Sociocommunicative Orientation   203

Assertiveness   203

Responsiveness   203

Sociocommunicative Orientation and Style   204

Willingness to Communicate   205

Beliefs and Attitudes   208

Generalized Belief Scale   208

Generalized Attitude Measure   208

Beliefs Versus Attitudes   209

Ratio Variables   209

Writing Up Scales Using APA Style   **210**

Participants   210

Apparatus   211

Procedures   211

Instrumentation   211

Conclusion   **214**

CHAPTER 7   Measurement   217

Defining the Term   **218**

Measuring a Line   218

Measurement Procedures and Rules   219

Numbers and Things   **219**

Review of Measurement Levels   **220**

Nominal   220

Ordinal   220

Interval   221

Ratio   222

A History of Measurement   **222**

Charles Darwin and Francis Galton   222

James McKeen Cattell   223

Alfred Binet and the Rise of Intelligence Tests   223

Robert Woodworth and the Creation of Personality Tests   224

Emory S. Bogardus's Social Distance Scale   224

Likert Scales   225

Semantic Differential Scale   227

Measuring Communication   **228**

Personality Traits/States   229

Beliefs and Attitudes   230

Knowledge   230

Cognitive Knowledge   231

Perceived Knowledge   231

The Process of Creating a New Measure   **232**

The Germinal Idea   233

Conceptualization   233

Operationalization   233

Putting People into Groups   234

Observing Existing Records/Asking People   234

Interviews and Surveys   234

Constructing Questions   **235**

1. Start with Twice as Many Items as You Will Need   235

2. Every Item Should Reflect the Construct   236

3. Use Concise, Clearly Worded, Unambiguous Items   236

4. Construct Relatively Short Items   236

5. Pay Attention to Terminology in the Item   237

6. Avoid Emotionally Charged Items   237

7. Avoid Leading Items   237

8. Avoid Loaded Items   237

9. Avoid Double Questions   238

10. Avoid Questions with False Premises   238

11. Avoid Using the Words "Always" and "Never"   238

12. Avoid Double Negatives/Positives   238

13. Avoid Hypothetical Questions   238

14. Avoid Ambiguous Pronoun References   239

15. Consider Recall Issues for Certain Types of Items   239

One Measure, Multiple Factors **239**

Measurement and Statistical Analysis **243**

Research Outside the Walls of Academia **244**

Conclusion **244**

CHAPTER 8 Reliability and Validity **248**

Reliability **248**

Scalar Reliability **249**

Test–Retest Reliability **252**

Alternate Forms Reliability **252**

Split-Half Reliability **252**

Cronbach's Alpha Reliability **253**

APA Discussion **259**

Alpha Reliabilities from this Book **260**

Alpha Reliabilities in the Real World **262**

Improving Reliability of Measurement **263**

Validity **265**

Face or Content Validity **268**

Criterion Validity **268**

Predictive or Prospective Validity **269**

Concurrent Validity **269**

Retrospective Validity **270**

Construct Validity **270**

Relying on Theory **270**

Measuring Known Groups **270**

Factorial Validity **271**

Which Approach to Use? **271**

Validity Threats **272**

Inadequate Preoperational Explication of Concepts **272**

Mono-Operation Bias **272**

Interaction of Different Treatments **272**

Interaction of Testing and Treatment **273**

Restricted Generalizability Across Constructs **273**

Confounding Constructs and Levels of Constructs **273**

Social Threats to Validity **274**

Problems with Measurement **274**

Coefficients **274**

Basic Measurement Problems **275**

Faking **275**

Response Set 276

Bad Measurement Items 277

Research Outside the Walls of Academia **277**

Conclusion **278**

CHAPTER 9 Survey Research 280

Surveys, Questionnaires, and Interview Schedules **280**

Survey 281

Descriptive Survey 281

Analytical or Explanatory Survey 281

Questionnaire 281

Interview Schedule 281

When to Use a Survey **282**

Do You Know What You Want to Ask? 282

Do You Really Need to Collect New Data? 282

Do Your Participants Know Anything, and Will They Tell You If They Do? 283

Does Your Goal Have Generalizability? 284

How to Conduct Survey Research **284**

Step 1: Picking Your Questions 285

Nominal Level Questions 285

Ordinal Level Questions 286

Interval Level Questions 287

Ratio Level Questions 288

Open-Ended Questions 288

Step 2: Creating Clear Instructions 289

Step 3: Study Design 289

Cross-Sectional Survey Design 290

Longitudinal Survey Design 290

Step 4: Data Processing and Analysis 292

Step 5: Pilot Testing 292

Use Actual Survey Population Members 293

Anticipate Survey Context 293

Test Parts of the Survey 293

Determining a Pilot Sample Size 293

Ask Questions After Someone Completes the Survey 293

Disseminating Your Surveys **294**

Surveying Techniques 294

Face-to-Face Surveying 294

Telephone Surveying 295

Self-Administration   296

　Mass Administration   296

　Mailed Administration   297

　Internet Administration   297

　Advantages and Disadvantages of Self-Administration   298

Problem Areas Associated with Survey Research   **299**

　Response Rate   299

　　Unit Nonresponse   300

　　Item Nonresponse   301

　　Effects of Nonresponse   303

　Improving Response Rates   303

Translating Surveys into Other Languages   **304**

　Issues of Equivalence   305

　　Semantic Equivalence   305

　　Conceptual Equivalence   305

　　Normative Equivalence   305

　Methods of Translation   307

　　Simple Direct Translation   307

　　Modified Direct Translation   307

　　Translation/Backtranslation   307

　　Parallel Blind Technique   308

　　Random Probe   308

Using the Research Project Worksheet   **308**

　Question   310

　Design   311

　Setting   311

　Participants   312

　　Specific Characteristics   312

　　Recruitment   312

　　Consent   312

　Variables   312

　　Independent Variables   312

　　Dependent Variables   312

　Hypotheses/Research Questions   313

　Statistical Testing   313

　Tentative Study Title   313

　Principal Researcher(s)   313

Research Outside of the Walls of Academia   **316**

Conclusion   **316**

CHAPTER 10   Content Analysis   319

Defining the Term   **319**

Conducting a Content Analysis   **321**

Theory and Rationale   322

Conceptualization   322

Operationalization   323

Coding Schemes   324

Sampling   326

Training and Pilot Reliability   326

Introduction to the Codebook and the Coding Form   327

Sample Coding   327

Coding of Initial Data   327

Initial Reliability   327

Retraining   331

Final Coding   331

Final Reliability   332

Tabulation and Reporting   332

Conclusion   **333**

CHAPTER 11   Experimental Design   336

What Are Experiments and Why Do We Do Them?   **338**

Rationale for Experimental Research   338

Determining Causal Relationships   338

Ruling Out Alternative Explanations   339

Determining the Influence of Intervening and Antecedent Variables   339

Determining Cause or Chance   339

Aspects of Experimental Design   **340**

Random Assignment   340

Manipulation of the Independent Variable   342

Example of Manipulating the Independent Variable   343

Ways to Manipulate an Independent Variable   344

Factorial Experimental Designs   346

Measurement of the Dependent Variable   347

Control of the Experiment   348

Threshold Effects   348

Experimenter Effects   348

The Hawthorne Effect   349

Extraneous Variables   349

Conducting an Experiment   **351**

Introduce the Experiment and Obtain Consent   351

Random Assignment of Participants   351

Manipulate the Independent Variable   351

Measure the Dependent Variable   352

Debrief the Participants   352

Threats to Experimental Validity   **353**

Historical Flaw   353

Maturation   353

Testing Flaw   354

Regression to the Mean   354

Selection Threat   354

Attrition   355

Other Threats to Experimental Validity   355

Common Experimental Designs   **356**

Preexperimental Designs   357

One-Shot Case Study Design   357

One-Group Pretest–Posttest Design   357

Static Group Comparisons Design   358

Quasi-Experimental Designs   358

Pretest–Posttest Design   358

Time-Series Design   359

Multiple Time-Series Design   359

Switching Replications Design   360

True Experimental Designs   361

Pretest–Posttest Design   361

Two-Group Posttest-Only Design   362

Randomized Switching Replications Design   362

Solomon Four-Group Design   363

Final Thoughts on Experiments   **364**

Limited Number of Variables   364

Generalizability Problems   365

Overreliance on College Students   365

Overreliance on Laboratory Settings   365

Low in Mundane Realism   365

Enhancing Generalizability   365

Conclusion   **366**

CHAPTER 12   Sampling Methods   368

Why Use a Sample?   **369**

Population   369

Sample   369

The Sampling Process **370**

Identifying the Theoretical Population   370

Identifying the Potential Participants   370

Selecting the Sample   371

Selecting a Sample Design   **371**

Probability Sampling   372

Simple Random Samples   373

Stratified Random Samples   375

Cluster Samples   376

Systematic Samples   377

Sampling Error   378

Nonprobability Samples   378

Convenience Samples   379

Volunteer Samples   380

Purposive Samples   380

Quota Samples   381

Network Samples   382

Determining Sample Size   **383**

Common-Sense Sample Recruiting   **385**

Know Your Target Population   385

Approaches to Recruitment   386

Face-to-Face   386

Advertisement   386

Letter   386

E-Mail   387

Snowball   387

Purchasing Samples   388

Ethical Recruitment   388

Conclusion   **389**

CHAPTER 13   Hypothesis Testing   391

Defining the Terms   **391**

Hypotheses   391

One-Tailed Hypotheses   393

Two-Tailed Hypotheses   393

Choice of One-Tailed Versus Two-Tailed Hypotheses   394

Research Questions   394

Directional Research Questions   395

Nondirectional Research Questions   395

Alternative and Null Hypotheses   395

Hypothesis Testing Case Study   **397**

    Case Study Introduction   398

    Hypothesis Testing in the Case Study   398

From Random Samples to a Whole Population   **399**

    Sampling Error   399

    95% Confidence   400

    Confidence Levels Across Research Fields   401

Testing for Significance   **401**

    Step 1: Set the Probability Level   402

    Step 2: Conduct a Statistical Test   403

    Step 3: Compare Calculated and Critical Values   403

Testing for Power   **406**

Effect Sizes   **408**

Understanding Error   **409**

    The Confidence Interval   411

    Power   413

    Type I Error   413

    Type II Error   413

    Minimizing Error   414

Conclusion   **414**

CHAPTER 14   Descriptive Statistics   417

The Benefits of Statistics   **418**

Descriptive Versus Inferential Statistics   **419**

Measures of Central Tendency   **421**

    Mean   421

    Median   422

    Mode   424

    Choosing a Measure of Central Tendency   425

    Frequency Distributions   426

        SPSS and Frequency Distributions   427

        Frequency Distributions and Charts   428

    Skewness and Kurtosis   433

Measures of Variability   **435**

    Range   435

    Sum of Squares   435

    Variance   437

    Standard Deviation   437

    SPSS and Measures of Variability   439

Dataset Variability **441**

Conclusion **443**

CHAPTER 15 Chi-Square (χ^2) Test of Independence **445**

Case Study Introduction **446**

Chi-Square Background Information **447**

Chi-Square Assumptions 447

Chi-Square and Statistical Significance 448

Chi-Square Formula 448

Step-by-Step Approach to the Chi-Square Test of Independence **449**

Step 1 449

Step 2 449

Step 3 450

Step 4 450

Step 5 451

Step 6 452

Computer Printouts of the Chi-Square Test of Independence **453**

SPSS and Chi-Square 454

Cramér's Phi (Φ) 457

APA Write-Up 459

Discussion of Findings 460

Post Hoc APA Write-Up 465

Biological Sex and Book Edition **466**

APA Write-Up 466

Discussion 466

Discussion of Brummans and Miller's Article **468**

Article Purpose 468

Methodology 468

Results 468

Research Outside the Walls of Academia **469**

Conclusion **469**

CHAPTER 16 Independent Samples *t* Tests **471**

Case Study Introduction **472**

Independent Samples *t* Test Background Information **472**

t Test Assumptions 473

t Test Formula 473

Step-by-Step Approach to the Independent *t* Test **474**

Step 1 474

Step 2 475

Step 3   476

Step 4   477

Step 5   477

Step 6   477

Step 7   478

Step 8   478

Step 9   478

Step 10   479

Computer Printouts of the Independent *t* Test   **480**

SPSS and *t* Tests   480

Interpreting SPSS Results   482

APA Write-Up   484

Discussion of Findings   484

Biological Sex and Communication Apprehension   **485**

APA Write-Up   485

Discussion   486

Calculating Effect Sizes   **486**

Step 1   486

Step 2   487

Discussion of the Weber, Fornash, Corrigan, and Neupauer Article   **487**

Article Purpose   488

Methodology   488

Results   488

Paired *t* Tests   **490**

Research Outside the Walls of Academia   **490**

Conclusion   **490**

CHAPTER 17   One-Way Analysis of Variance   492

Case Study Introduction   **493**

One-Way ANOVA Background Information   **493**

One-Way ANOVA Assumptions   494

One-Way ANOVA Formula   495

Step-by-Step Approach to the One-Way ANOVA   **495**

Step 1   495

Step 2   496

Step 3   496

Step 4   497

Step 5   497

Step 6   498

Step 7   499

Step 8   499

Step 9   499

Step 10   499

Step 11   500

Computer Printouts of the One-Way ANOVA   **501**

Multiple Comparison Tests   **507**

APA Write-Up (Without Chart)   510

APA Write-Up (With Chart)   510

Discussion of Findings   510

Political Affiliation and Humor Assessment   **511**

APA Write-Up   511

Discussion   511

Discussion of the Boiarsky, Long, and Thayer Article   **513**

Article Purpose   513

Methodology   513

Results   513

Research Outside the Walls of Academia   **514**

Conclusion   **515**

CHAPTER 18   Correlation   517

Case Study Introduction   **518**

Correlation Background Information   **518**

Types of Relationships   518

Correlation Not Causation   520

Correlation Assumptions   522

Correlation Formula   522

Step-by-Step Approach to the Pearson Product-Moment Correlation   **522**

Step 1   523

Step 2   524

Step 3   524

Step 4   525

Step 5   525

Step 6   525

Step 7   526

Computer Printouts of the Pearson Product-Moment Correlation   **527**

SPSS and Pearson Product-Moment Correlations   527

Interpreting SPSS Correlation Results   529

APA Write-Up   529

Discussion   530

Relationships Among CA, WTC, and Beliefs About Public Speaking **530**

APA Write-Up 531

Reading Large Correlation Tables **532**

Discussion of the Chesebro Article **534**

Article Purpose 534

Methodology 534

Results 534

Discussion of the Punyanunt Article **535**

Article Purpose 535

Methodology 535

Results 535

Research Outside the Walls of Academia **536**

Conclusion **537**

CHAPTER 19   Regression **539**

Case Study Introduction **541**

Regression Assumptions **542**

Step-by-Step Approach to a Linear Regression **543**

Step 1 543

Step 2 543

Step 3 544

Step 4 544

Step 5 544

Step 6 544

Computer Printouts of the Linear Regression **545**

SPSS and Simple Linear Regressions 545

APA Write-Up 549

Discussion 549

Relationships Between CA and Beliefs About Public Speaking **550**

APA Write-Up 551

Discussion 551

Understanding Multiple Linear Regressions **551**

APA Write-Up 554

Discussion 554

Discussion of the Wrench and Booth-Butterfield Article **555**

Article Purpose 556

Methodology 556

Results 556

Discussion of the Rocca and Vogl-Bauer Article   **557**

    Article Purpose   557

    Methodology   557

    Results   557

Research Outside the Walls of Academia   **558**

Conclusion   **559**

CHAPTER 20   Presenting Research   561

Writing a Discussion Section   **563**

    Summarize the Major Findings   564

    Interpret the Findings   564

    Discuss the Relationship Between Findings and Previous Studies   565

    Acknowledge Any Limitations   566

    Discuss Implications and Future Directions   566

Writing the Abstract   **567**

Presenting at Conferences   **567**

Divisions and Interest Groups   **569**

    Submitting Research for Conference Review   570

Types of Conference Presentations   **573**

    Paper Presentations   573

        Preparing Your Presentation   573

        Paper Respondents   576

    Poster Presentations   576

        Sample Poster   577

        Tips for Poster Presentations   579

    Scholar-to-Scholar Posters   581

    Panel Discussions   581

Publication   **582**

    Submission Process   582

    Review Process   585

Research Outside the Walls of Academia   **587**

    Writing for Business   587

        Write Short Reports   587

        Arrange Material for Emphasis   587

        Avoid Long, Complex Paragraphs and Sentences   587

        Avoid Jargon   588

        Use Active Voice and Concrete Words   588

        Use Pictures and Graphs   588

        Use Numbers Selectively   588

Writing for the General Public   588

Writing Statistical Stories   588

Data Visualization   591

Conclusion   **593**

APPENDIX A   Qualitative Research
(Available online: https://oup-arc.com/wrench)

APPENDIX B   Textbook Questionnaire
(Available online: https://oup-arc.com/wrench)

APPENDIX C   Free and Open-Source Statistical Software
(Available online: https://oup-arc.com/wrench)

APPENDIX D   Big Data
(Available online: https://oup-arc.com/wrench)

APPENDIX E   Advanced Statistical Procedures
(Available online: https://oup-arc.com/wrench)

Glossary   595

Index   607

Preface

REAL DATA. REAL STUDIES. REAL LIFE.

At the turn of the 20th century, noted science-fiction author H. G. Wells (1866–1946) once wrote, "The time may not be very remote when it will be understood that for complete initiation as an efficient citizen of one of the new great complex world-wide States that are now developing, it is as necessary to be able to compute, to think in averages and maxima and minima, as it is now to be able to read and write" (p. 204). So important was this prediction that President of the American Statistical Association, Samuel S. Wilks, paraphrased Wells's quotation in his 1951 national address to the association, "Statistical thinking will one day be as necessary for efficient citizenship as the ability to read and write" (p. 5). Both Wells and Wilks realized that understanding how statistics function within our world was no longer a luxury of scientists and mathematicians, but a necessary endeavor for all citizens. In the 21st century, however, increasing numbers of people sadly are numerically illiterate. John Allen Paulos (1988) first tackled the notion of numerical illiteracy, or innumeracy, by defining it as "an inability to deal comfortably with the fundamental notions of number and chance" (p. 3). Unfortunately, most people simply do not understand enough about the world of statistics and scientific research to make much sense of the statistics in their daily lives.

People are bombarded with statistics, and most are unable to accurately process the information to any usable degree. Milroy (2001) argued that with the proliferation of science and pseudo-science today, people must be able to engage in strategic "junk science judo." Yet most people are unaware of the extent to which their lives are controlled by quantitative research. Although the goal of this book is not to discuss nifty marketing tricks or medical research, the basics of quantitative research methods and reasoning are the same across fields that use social scientific research methods. And while this book does not attempt to correct all of the problems associated with innumeracy, it does engage communication students on two levels.

On the first level, this textbook hopes to teach readers the basics of the scientific process necessary in quantitative communication research. Although college students typically learned the scientific method in elementary school, most cannot accurately translate this understanding outside the physical sciences. In this text, we promote a strategic use of the scientific method when conducting quantitative research examining communication topics. Along the way, we hope that students begin to understand the steps necessary for conducting research in a manner that will be transferable to other parts of their lives. Scientific and statistical processes are the same whether they are utilized by communication researchers or by medical researchers. Therefore, one of our goals for this text is simply to educate readers about the scientific method and the most commonly used statistical tools. Although the examples used throughout this textbook focus on communication-related phenomena, we believe students can transfer this knowledge into other areas of science and statistics when faced with them.

On the second level, this textbook hopes to help students engage in real quantitative research projects of real importance. The four authors of this textbook have a history of working with both undergraduate and graduate students to develop, write, present, and publish quantitative research projects. We all believe that the only way for students to learn and grasp quantitative research methods is through real examples and hands-on work. In our vast experience teaching quantitative research methods, we have learned that students cannot transfer theoretical knowledge of research methods and statistics to actual projects and datasets unless they have actively engaged in the research process when learning. In other words, it is one thing to read about what a correlation is and how correlations work, but quite a different thing to find significant relationships in real datasets.

IMPROVEMENTS TO THE FOURTH EDITION

As with any new edition of the text, there are always a number of important improvements that are made to ensure that the quality of the book meets new demands and reflects the input from instructors who have used it in the past. The authors of this text have taught short courses at various national and regional conventions and received feedback from both students and instructors alike. The changes made to this book reflect this feedback along with our own insights after having regularly used the first three editions ourselves. Here are the important changes and additions we have made to this edition:

- Added more section headings to ease readability. We also focused more on the overall aesthetic look of the book as a factor of readability.
- Increased the number of illustrations within the book to add levity and to further illustrate concepts.
- Decreased the number of learning outcomes at the beginning of each chapter. Our goal here is to streamline the chapter learning outcomes to ensure that readers are more clearly able to ascertain what they should accomplish by reading the chapters.
- Starting in the second edition of the textbook, we made a real effort to demonstrate how the techniques discussed here could be used in the real world. We have expanded on these in the fourth edition. For example, we now have information on writing research in the organizational environment, writing research reports for the public, and data visualization.

- Updated the information on research ethics to include the 2017 update of the Common Rule.
- Updated the information on manuscript formatting, including references, footnotes, tables, and figures.
- Placed the chapters on Big Data and Advanced Research Methods on the textbook's website (https://oup-arc.com/wrench) along with the textbook survey, the chapter on qualitative research methods, and the discussion of free and open-source alternatives to Statistical Package for the Social Sciences (SPSS). We realize that not every professor will use these advanced chapters, but we still want to ensure that they are available to read.
- Added a new discussion on the use of computer simulations in experiments.
- Completely updated the book's website with even more features than ever before. Students will be able to access the research articles discussed in the textbook, the book's skeletal outline, and supplemental chapters. Plus, there will be video walkthroughs for various software packages including proprietary software packages like SPSS, Excel, and STATA and free/open source software like PSPP, JASP, and R.

KEY FEATURES OF THE BOOK

Students are often intimidated on the first day of a research methods class, so we wanted this book to be extremely practical for both students of quantitative research methods and their instructors. This book is built on decades of pedagogical theorizing and in-classroom teaching experience, and was written expressly to help alleviate the fear students may have by structuring a learning environment that clearly helps students succeed, and students who have learned quantitative research methods using the methods discussed in this textbook have gone on to have careers that utilize quantitative research both in the private sector and in academia. We strongly believe that this text is a great first step in understanding quantitative research methods utilized by modern communication researchers. For this reason, we have incorporated five unique factors within the book:

1. Actual Data Sample

One unique component to this text is an actual dataset that was collected by the authors of the project with its express purpose for use in this textbook. A series of research scales written by the authors of this book were used in the creation of a survey instrument:

Nominal variables (biological sex and political affiliation)

Ordinal variable (time spent each week online and year in school)

Interval variables (communication apprehension, willingness to communicate, ethnocentrism, humor assessment, nonverbal immediacy, sociocommunicative orientation—assertiveness and responsiveness, attitude about college, and belief that everyone should be required to take public speaking in college)

Ratio variable (age)

This dataset is available to book users in four different formats: SPSS, Excel, STATA, or text. By having three options available, a teacher can easily choose the format that he or she prefers. Furthermore, because data were collected from 654 actual people, students can manipulate data to receive real answers to research questions and hypotheses. Furthermore, the textbook's website also contains the example statistics discussed in the text in all three formats.

In essence, students will be able to conduct statistical tests on actual data and double-check that the findings we report in the book match the findings they are able to obtain using a statistical software package.

2. Actual Studies

The authors of this text made an agreement to republish a series of 10 articles from either *Communication Research Reports* or *Communication Quarterly*, two journals published by the Eastern Communication Association, for inclusion on the textbook's website. The articles were chosen because they are exemplars on how to conduct specific aspects of research methods and/or statistical analysis. When selecting the articles for inclusion on the textbook's website, we included those from an array of communication contexts (communication traits, instructional, listening, mediated, organizational, public relations, etc.). The articles chosen for this book are as follows:

SCALE DEVELOPMENT

McCroskey, J. C., Richmond, V. P., Johnson, A. D., & Smith, H. T. (2004). Organizational orientations theory and measurement: Development of measures and preliminary investigations. *Communication Quarterly, 52*, 1–14.

Thomas, C. E, Richmond, V. P., & McCroskey, J. C. (1994). The association between immediacy and sociocommunicative style. *Communication Research Reports, 11*, 107–115.

Wrench, J. S., & Richmond, V. P. (2004). Understanding the psychometric properties of the humor assessment instrument through an analysis of the relationships between teacher humor assessment and instructional communication variables in the college classroom. *Communication Research Reports, 21*, 92–103.

CHI-SQUARE

Brummans, B. H. J. M., & Miller, K. (2004). The effect of ambiguity on the implementation of a social change initiative. *Communication Research Reports, 21*, 1–10.

t TESTS

Weber, K., Fornash, B., Corrigan, M, & Neupauer, N. C. (2003). The effect of interest on recall: An experiment. *Communication Research Reports, 20,* 116–123.

ONE-WAY ANALYSIS OF VARIANCE (ANOVA)

Boiarsky, G., Long, M., & Thayer, G. (1999). Formal features in children's science television: Sound effects, visual pace, and topic shifts. *Communication Research Reports, 16,* 185–192.

CORRELATION

Chesebro, J. (1999). The relationship between listening styles and conversational sensitivity. *Communication Research Reports, 16,* 233–238.

Punyanunt, N. M. (2000). The effects of humor on perceptions of compliance-gaining in the college classroom. *Communication Research Reports, 176,* 30–38.

REGRESSION

Rocca, K. A., & Vogl-Bauer, S. (1999). Trait verbal aggression, sports fan identification, and perceptions of appropriate sports fan communication. *Communication Research Reports, 16,* 239–248.

Wrench, J. S., & Booth-Butterfield, M. (2003). Increasing patient satisfaction and compliance: An examination of physician humor orientation, compliance-gaining strategies, and perceived credibility. *Communication Quarterly, 51,* 482–503.

3. Hand Calculations and Statistical Package Summaries

This book takes students step by step through the statistical computation process. Although many books try to teach students the mathematical process for computing statistical tests, this text clearly spells out each step in the necessary sequence to come to an end result. In fact, in the classroom, this process has consistently been used, and students find the mathematical computations to be one of the easiest parts of learning quantitative research methods. We believe students must learn how to calculate the problems by hand because the physical process of calculating helps to solidify how the mathematical process works.

Besides providing the hand computations, we also provide information on how to conduct statistical tests with one of the most commonly used statistical packages: SPSS. We understand that most researchers do not calculate lengthy tests by hand, so demonstrating how the various statistical processes can be calculated using both programs helps the students conduct their own statistical analyses using the software packages. In addition to the instruction for SPSS, we also provide printouts of statistical results utilizing this software package. We understand that knowing how to use a software package is one thing, but that being able to read and interpret the statistical output is completely different. Although this edition only incorporates SPSS into the text itself, the corresponding website will contain video walk-throughs for the following additional packages: PSPP, R, JASP, and STATA.

4. Glossary

The book has an extensive glossary with commonly confused terms. We always tell our students that learning quantitative research methods is akin to learning a foreign language. For this reason, we have provided the students with a "language guide" to help them remember definitions.

5. Qualitative Research Chapter

Finally, we asked two prominent scholars in the field of qualitative and critical research, James W. Chesebro and Deborah J. Borisoff, to write a chapter for this book on qualitative research. Although the purpose of this text is to focus on quantitative research methods in communication, we strongly believe that students should at least be exposed to qualitative research methods so that they can more clearly differentiate between the two epistemological approaches. We believe that this chapter (located as Appendix A on the textbook's website) is a balanced and helpful introduction to the differences in epistemology and the tools utilized to draw research conclusions.

ACKNOWLEDGMENTS

Although the bulk of this text is based on our own experiences as both students and teachers of quantitative research methods, we thank the editorial teams at Roxbury Publishers and Oxford University Press for shepherding this project through its various phases. We also thank the reviewers who gave us such great insight along the way as we have written this text:

Cleo Joffrion Allen, Dillard University

Suzanne Atkin, Arizona State University

Diane M. Badzinski, Colorado Christian University

Daniel Bergan, Michigan State University

Jonathan Bowman, University of San Diego

Amanda Cote, University of Michigan

John Courtright, University of Delaware

Kristin Dybvig-Pawelko, Arizona State University

Douglas A. Ferguson, College of Charleston

Ann Bainbridge Frymier, Miami University

Mark Generous, Arizona State University

Michelle Givertz, California State University, Chico

Jo Anna Grant, California State University, San Bernardino

Rosanne Hartman, Canisius College

Marian L. Houser, Texas State University, San Marcos

Kumi Ishii, Western Kentucky University

Seung-A Annie Jin, Boston University

Antwan Jones, George Washington University

Doreen M. S. Jowi, Bloomsburg University of Pennsylvania

Jean Claude Kwitonda, Ohio University

Canchu Lin, L., Tiffin University

Yang Lin, University of Akron

Meina Liu, George Washington University

Yung-I Liu, California State University, East Bay

Joseph P. Mazer, Clemson University

Bree McEwan, Western Illinois University

Chris R. Morse, Bryant University

Heidi L. Muller, University of Northern Colorado

Kekeli Nuviadenu, Bethune–Cookman University

Youngrak Park, Columbus State University

Emily A. Paskewitz, University of Tennessee

Larry Powell, University of Alabama–Birmingham

David Schuelke, University of Minnesota

Lijiang Shen, University of Georgia

Joanna Showell, Bethune–Cookman University

Ross Singer, Southern Illinois University–Carbondale

Darren Stevenson, University of Michigan

Claire Sullivan, University of Maine

Tara Suwinyattichaiporn, Arizona State University

Adam Thrasher, University of Houston

Laura Umphrey, Northern Arizona University

Celeste Walls, Glendale Community College

Qi Wang, Villanova University

Katie Warber, Wittenberg University

Kirsten Weber, University of Georgia

Terry L. West, California State University, East Bay

Margaret A. Wills, Fairfield University

Xiaohe Xu, The University of Texas at San Antonio

Kenneth Yang, The University of Texas at El Paso

Shuo Yao, Radford University

Asta Zelenkauskaite, Drexel University

Aziza Zemrani, The University of Texas Rio Grande Valley

DEDICATION

Since the publication of the second edition of this book, we lost the single most published scholar in the field of communication and our coauthor, Dr. James C. McCroskey. This book has been a labor of love for all of us, but Jim's influence is clearly seen in every page of this text. In fact, trying to separate our memories of conducting communication research from our relationships with Jim is impossible. Each chapter brings forward different memories of conversations and research projects we conducted together. Without him, this book never would have been what it is today. And without him, the field of communication would not be what it is today. For these reasons, we dedicate this edition to our teacher, mentor, and friend.

Jason S. Wrench
Candice Thomas-Maddox
Virginia Peck Richmond

INSTRUCTOR ANCILLARIES

If you have not received a copy of the Instructor's Manual from your Oxford University Press representative, please ensure you get one. The instructor's manual has been completely overhauled for the fourth edition. Here are some of the important ancillary materials we have included to make your life easier as you prepare to teach this course:

1. Sample Syllabi

In the Instructor's Manual, you will find a variety of different types of courses contexts where this textbook has been previously used (e.g., undergraduate face-to-face class, undergraduate online class, and graduate face-to-face class). Furthermore, we offer multiple approaches a teacher could take with the course. Whether you take a strictly content-based approach to the class or a project-based approach to teaching research methods, the sample syllabi will definitely help you structure your course.

2. Chapter Outlines

On the textbook's website, every student has access to a skeletal outline of the different chapters' content. In the Instructor's Manual, we have not only the skeletal outlines, but also completely annotated versions to help you prepare your course notes. Many instructors tell us that all they need to do is grab the Instructor's Manual and take it with them to class for fully realized lectures.

3. PowerPoint-Based Slide Deck

Many instructors asked for a PowerPoint-based slide deck after the first edition of the textbook was released, so we added a comprehensive slide deck to the later editions. The comprehensive slide deck reflects the annotated chapter outlines within the Instructor's Manual directly.

4. In-Class Activities for Each Chapter

For each chapter, we provide a range of different activity ideas to make your class more engaging. Numerous worksheets and assignments that we have used in the past can be found in the Instructor's Manual. None of the activities or assignments discussed within the Instructor's Manual was created specifically for the Instructor's Manual. All of the activities and assignments have been utilized within our own classrooms.

5. Test Bank

The test bank has been completely updated and revised for the fourth edition of the Instructor's Manual. We provide a range of multiple-choice, true-or-false, and short-answer/essay questions for your course's examinations.

COMPANION WEBSITE

Please visit our companion website at http://www.oup-arc.com/wrench for a range of supplementary materials for both you and your students. The website has links to podcasts related to some of the chapters, sample American Psychological Association (APA) style papers, further discussion of statistical software (with video tutorials), and many other features.

LAST WORD

To Students:

Thank you for taking up the challenge of learning quantitative research methods for communication. For most of you, this is a daunting course and unlike any you have taken within a communication studies department before. Please realize that you can get through the course and succeed. We need a new generation of communication researchers coming through the pipeline for our field to grow and thrive. Furthermore, the methods and practice of conducting research that you learn in this book can be applied to any field of research that examines humans or phenomena statistically. Although different fields have their own avenues of interest and advanced statistical preferences, the basics you learn in this course could easily be applied to any social or physical science research undertaking.

To Instructors:

Thank you for choosing to use *Quantitative Research Methods for Communication: A Hands-On Approach*. If you would like help or clarification teaching communication research methods, please do not hesitate to reach out to any of the authors of this text. If one of us does not know the answer to a question, we will forward it to the others so that we can assist you best. Also, please feel free to give us your feedback. As we look toward revising the book in the future, instructor feedback is unbelievably helpful.

REFERENCES

Milroy, S. J. (2001). *Junk science judo: Self-defense against health scares and scams*. Washington, DC: Cato Institute.

Paulos, J. A. (1988). *Innumeracy: Mathematical illiteracy and its consequences*. New York, NY: Hill & Wang.

Wells, H. G. (1904). *Mankind in the making* (4th ed.). London, England: Chapman & Hall.

Wilks, S. S. (1951) Undergraduate statistical education. *American Statistical Association, 46*, 1–18.

QUANTITATIVE RESEARCH METHODS
for Communication

An Introduction to Communication Research

CHAPTER OBJECTIVES

1. Explain the difference between physical and social sciences.

2. Describe the history of social sciences and its relation to the field of communication.

3. Define the term *communication*.

4. Explain Claude Shannon and Warren Weaver's (1949) model of communication.

5. Understand the basic layout of this textbook.

Every day, people around the globe participate in an activity that helps shape our understanding of the world. This activity is research. Ever since you were a child in elementary school, you were taught all kinds of facts. But most students do not stop to think about where these "facts" come from in the first place. Whether it was learning that Newton created his theory of gravity after having an apple fall on his head or memorizing all of the elements in the periodic table, most of your academic endeavors have been built around knowledge that has not always existed. At some point in history, a scientist had to conduct a research study to find what we often take for granted as common knowledge today.

THE FOUR STAGES OF DATA LOSS
DEALING WITH ACCIDENTAL DELETION OF MONTHS OF HARD-EARNED DATA

STAGE 1: DENIAL

I DID NOT JUST ERASE ALL MY DATA. I SURELY MADE A BACKUP SOME-WHERE...

STAGE 2: ANGER

YOU STUPID PIECE OF CRAP! WHERE'S MY DATA!??

STAGE 3: DEPRESSION

WHY..? WHY ME??

STAGE 4: ACCEPTANCE

I'M NEVER GOING TO GRADUATE...

JORGE CHAM © 2003

www.phdcomics.com

▲ The Four Stages of Data Loss (Source: Piled Higher and Deeper by Jorge Cham—www.phdcomics.com)

Although most people are familiar with many basic facts about the **physical sciences**, or the study of the objective aspects of nature (biology, chemistry, physics, astronomy, etc.), as a result of K–12 schooling, people do not tend to be as aware of the research in the area called the social sciences. The **social sciences** consist of a group of fields that study how humans live and interact. These include many disciplines: anthropology, communication, cultural studies, economics, education, geography, history, linguistics, political sciences, psychology, sociology, social work, and so on. All of these fields have at their core a desire to understand how humans live and interact. Although each social scientific field may approach the study of human life and interaction differently, they all have the same basic origin in history. This chapter first presents a brief history examining the development of the social sciences and then discusses how the field of communication has become what it is today.

THE HISTORY OF THE SOCIAL SCIENCES

The earliest recorded scientists would be shocked to see the division that exists today between the physical sciences and the social sciences.

Ancient Greece

In ancient Greece, the physical sciences and philosophy were perceived as hand-maidens because one informed the other. Most of the ancient Greek philosophers wrote not only about science but also about rhetoric, poetry, drama, and other intrinsi-cally human-oriented topics.

For example, Hippocrates of Cos (c. 460 BCE) is most noted for the oath all physicians take that states physicians should first do no harm. Hippocrates was also the first researcher in history to classify his patients by various temperaments, which is now seen as the general origin of personality theory that social scientists study today. To Hippocrates, science was an extremely important part of understanding the world in both the physical sense and the humanistic sense; he wrote, "There are in fact, two things: science, and opinion; the former begets knowledge, the latter ignorance." Even later Greek thinkers such as Plato and Aristotle often wrote on both physical and social scientific topics and sometimes combined the two. Plato used geometric proofs (a physical science tool) to demonstrate his perspective on the intrinsic state of knowledge (a social scientific concept). Aristotle studied planetary motion with the same rigor and scientific processes with which he studied poetry and rhetoric. To the ancient Greeks, both physical nature and human social processes were avenues of research to be done scientifically.

▲ Hippocrates

Sir Isaac Newton

This lack of division between physical and social sciences stayed fairly intact until the publication of the three volumes of Sir Isaac Newton's *Philosophiae Naturalis Principia Mathematica* (*Mathematical Principles of Natural Philosophy*) in 1687. In essence, Newton sets forth in these three volumes the foundation of classical mechanics and his law of gravity. Newton's publication revolutionized scientific thought because he argued that the underlying rule of all physical nature was mathematics. Whereas physical scientists quickly latched onto and applied Newton's writings, only later did many scientists studying the social aspects of humans try to make their research more mathematically oriented as well.

▲ Sir Isaac Newton

Charles Darwin

This trend of physical sciences creating revolutions that remake how we understand science continued with the publication of Charles Darwin's **theory of natural selection**. Although mathematics clearly impacted physics and chemistry, natural selection revolutionized how we understood biology. Yet again, the physical sciences were light years ahead of social scientists in their understanding of nature, but eventually, the social scientists came to understand how Darwin's theory applied to the social sciences. In fact, Sigmund Freud (in Austria) and William James (in the United States) were the first social scientists to examine how natural selection applied to the social sciences.

Late 1800s to Early 1900s

During the late 1800s and early 1900s, the rise of quantitative or mathematical measurement in the physical sciences became the norm. Ernest Rutherford, the father of nuclear physics, once wrote that any knowledge that cannot be measured numerically is a poor sort of knowledge. Ultimately, during the early 1900s, a rift emerged between humanists, who believed in universal human qualities (rationality, common history, experience, and belief), and social scientists, who saw the need to objectively quantify human experience. In communication, we also saw this debate occurring within our own ranks.

James A. Winans and Everett Lee Hunt

Early in the 20th century, James A. Winans (1915) and Everett Lee Hunt (1915) led an interdisciplinary debate regarding the need for research in public speaking. Winans wanted scientific research to be conducted on three levels: speech pathology, speech psychology, and rhetorical history. Hunt, by contrast, believed the scientific approach was antithetical to the enthusiasm and inspiration needed for good public speakers. This divergence of ideology created the social science–versus–humanist debate in communication studies, which has continued for the greater part of the 20th and into the 21st century.

Social Sciences After World War I

Social scientific research started finding its own way after World War I as research in a variety of new avenues began to flourish. In 1918, William Isaac Thomas and Florian Znaniecki defined social psychology as "the study of attitudes." Along with the development of attitudinal research, Jowett and O'Donnell (1992) note,

> Other social sciences such as sociology and psychology were also stimulated by the need to pursue questions about human survival in an age in which social strain grew heavy with concerns about warfare, genocide, economic depression, and human relationships. These questions were about influence, leadership, decision making, and changes in people, institutions, and nations. Such questions were also related to the phenomena of propaganda, public opinion, attitude change, and communication. (p. 123)

▲ Charles Darwin

Overall, the period after World War I saw a dramatic increase in research in the social sciences. By the 1920s, marketing agencies were surveying consumer behavior, and politicians and media outlets realized that the new techniques being created by social scientists to research humans could examine political preferences. With the burgeoning need for social scientific research, Likert (1932), Guttman (1944), and Osgood (1952) developed three measures of attitudes that are still used by researchers today (these will be discussed in greater detail in Chapters 6 and 7).

Social Sciences During World War II

When World War II broke out in Europe, the US government turned to social scientists to understand propaganda, attitudes, and persuasion (Albarracín, Johnson, &

Zanna, 2006). The US government quickly realized that to maintain morale during wartime, the media was going to be extremely important. The creation of the US Office of War Information was one step in this effort (Lazarsfeld & Stanton, 1944). In 1941, Lazarsfeld published the first review of the discipline of communication based on his and others' research at the Bureau of Applied Social Research. Ultimately, Lazarsfeld determined that communication could be broken into four categories: (1) who, (2) said what, (3) to whom, and (4) with what effect. The US government was most interested in the last category as a way to fuel the war effort at home.

Carl Hovland and Post–World War II Research

At the conclusion of World War II, the shift in social scientific communication research took its next major step as a result of 30 researchers at Yale University led by Carl Hovland. The primary purpose of the research conducted by the Yale group was to analyze how attitude change occurred. Overall, the Yale group examined a wide range of differing variables shown to influence persuasion: source credibility, personality traits, argument ordering, explicit versus implicit conclusions, and fear appeals (Hovland, Janis, & Kelly, 1953). The legacy of the research conducted by Hovland and his colleagues ultimately led future researchers to examine other communication contexts.

Social Sciences in Communication Today

Today, the contexts for research in the field of communication are numerous. In fact, in 2004, Wickersham, Sherblom, and Richmond published a 20-year retrospective (1984–2004) of the types of empirical articles published in *Communication Research Reports* (*CRR*). Since its first publication, *CRR* has been devoted to short, concise, quantitative research articles. As a result of the nature of *CRR*, analyzing the concepts published in the journal allows researchers to see the overarching scope of the field of empirical communication research.

Figure 1.1 contains the results of the Wickersham et al. (2004) study. Overall, the top four concepts explored in *CRR* are general communication, relationships, perception,

Wilbur Schramm and David Berlo

Wilbur Schramm is credited with creating the modern conceptualization of the field of communication studies with the founding of the Institute for Communications Research at the University of Illinois. One of his students, David Berlo, is credited with the shift in focus to quantitative research methodologies within the field of communication while at Michigan State University.

Communication concept explored	No. of articles	% of total
General Communication	229	9.8
Relationships	116	4.9
Perception	90	3.8
Apprehension	68	2.9
Students	53	2.3
Self	45	1.9
Television	44	1.9
Behavior	37	1.6
Satisfaction	35	1.5
Culture	35	1.5
Social	34	1.5
Interpersonal	33	1.4
Organizations	32	1.4
Style	31	1.3
Teacher	31	1.3
Public	31	1.3
Gender	28	1.2
Development	28	1.2
Verbal	27	1.2
Anxiety	27	1.2
Roles	27	1.2
Aggression	26	1.1
Competence	26	1.1
Classroom	26	1.1
Motivation	26	1.1
Interaction	25	1.1
Influence	23	1.0
American	23	1.0
Immediacy	22	0.9
Sex	21	0.9
Messages	21	0.9
Group	20	0.9
Japan	20	0.9
Nonverbal	20	0.9

FIGURE 1.1
1984–2004 Articles Published in *Communication Research Reports*

and apprehension, which have been directly influenced by research in both attitudes and persuasion initiated during the early and mid-1900s. Along with an expansion in the type of research that qualifies as "communication research," our understanding of communication has also changed.

Since the publication of the previous edition of this book, the types of research being conducted in *CRR* have taken a modern turn. As you can see in Figures 1.2 and 1.3, the journal is publishing more new media and health research than it has in the past, which indicates how the field is changing and evolving. However, traditional research areas in communication like instructional, interpersonal, organizational, persuasion, political, and so on are still published as well. The size of a word in Figures 1.2 and 1.3 directly corresponds to the number of titles in which the word was found.

FIGURE 1.2
2005–2014
Communication
Research Reports Titles
Word Cloud

FIGURE 1.3
2014–2017
Communication
Research Reports Titles
Word Cloud

> ## Communication
> The process by which one person stimulates meaning in the mind(s) of another person (or persons) through verbal and nonverbal messages. (McCroskey, 2006, pp. 20–21)

THE NATURE OF COMMUNICATION

Although others may define communication from a different perspective than McCroskey (2006), we see **communication** as primarily meaning focused. And to comprehend McCroskey's definition fully, a few of its parts need some clarification.

The word "process" suggests that human communication is dynamic and changing, the notion that communication does not start, stop, or break. Berlo (1960) suggested that communication is like the river described by the Greek philosopher Heraclitus, who believed that it was impossible to step into the same river twice because the moment you take your foot out of the water, the river changes so much that it is no longer the same river. In life, humans are changing as we go through various events, and our communication with other people also naturally evolves over time. Therefore, humans never communicate in the same way twice. Even professional actors who recite the same lines over and over again never recite them in the same way.

The second part of McCroskey's definition of communication involves the phrase "stimulates meaning in the mind(s) of another person (or persons)." The basic goal of communication is to take a thought that you have inside your head and determine the appropriate method for getting that thought into the head of another person or the heads of a group of people. Through the processes of stimulating meaning, we develop, cultivate, share, expand, and reshape ideas. Rare is the occasion when we develop an idea on our own. The thoughts that lead to an idea result from our experiences of talking with others, reading various literatures, and observing and interacting with the world around us. Such ideas or combinations of ideas are the meaning stimulated through the verbal and nonverbal messages that are exchanged. But before we can discuss verbal and nonverbal messages, we must explain the basic model of communication.

Modeling Communication

Claude Shannon and Warren Weaver (1949) developed a model for describing the process of communication for the Bell Telephone Company. The Shannon and Weaver Model was simple because it explained how people use telephones. The telephone is designed with two basic parts: a source you talk into and a receiver in which you hear people on the other end. The full Shannon and Weaver Model is often referred to as the source–message–channel–receiver (SMCR) model.

SOURCE

The **source** is the person(s) who originates a message. This person(s) goes through a process called encoding to create a message. McCroskey and Wheeless (1976) defined **encoding** as "the process of creating messages that we believe represent the meaning to be communicated and are likely to stimulate similar meaning in the mind of a receiver" (p. 24). In other words, encoding involves translating ideas and information inside your head into messages that can be sent to a receiver(s). Encoding requires some degree of accuracy and precision for effective communication to take place, however, because if your receiver cannot understand what you are saying, communication will be ineffective. Inaccurate and imprecise encoding often leads to confusion. Therefore, it is important to select messages that have similar meanings for us and our receiver(s).

RECEIVER

Whereas the source sends messages, a **receiver** receives messages. And as receivers, we must not just receive messages but also assign meaning to them. The process we go through as receivers to assign meaning to messages is called **decoding**. The meaning we assign a given message depends to a great degree on previous messages we have received from either the source and/or our previous experiences. Often, the meaning(s) we assign specific messages may not be close to the meaning intended by the source. Remember when you first analyzed poetry in school and your teacher would tell you about the hidden meanings within a poem you simply did not see at all? Verbal and nonverbal communication and meaning can function the same way; people often completely miss the meaning of a message or assign a meaning to the message that was not intended. For communication to be effective, it is necessary for us, as receivers, to consider our background and experience compared with the background and experience of the source, which may require that we put ourselves in the other person's shoes. The converse of this is also true. As sources of messages, we must know who our receivers are. If we talk about media to a group of college freshmen, then using references to Lawrence Welk and Ed Sullivan might not be useful (if you do not know who either of those men are, you just proved our point).

MESSAGE

The next part of the SMCR model is the message. A **message** is any verbal or nonverbal stimulus that stimulates meaning in a receiver. As our definition of communication in this textbook is meaning focused, so is the basic model of communication. The message is simply what you want your receiver(s) to know, feel, and/or do when you are done communicating.

CHANNEL

The last part of the SMCR model of communication is the channel. A **channel** is the means by which a message is carried from one person to another. In communication, we typically talk about two primary channels: verbal and nonverbal.

By **verbal messages**, we mean **language**, which is a system of symbols or codes that represent certain ideas or meanings. The use of symbols and codes is regulated by a set of formal rules, which we call grammar and syntax. We transmit these messages either in spoken or in written form. According to Simons (2017), approximately 7,099 oral languages exist, but no single language is spoken or understood by a majority of humans (although Mandarin is spoken by more people in the world than any other language). Thus, even today, when people travel to various parts of the world, they often resort to communicating messages through nonverbal channels.

Nonverbal messages refer to any messages other than verbal ones. These messages include such things as tone of voice, eye movements, hand gestures, and facial expressions. All in all, nonverbal messages are important. Nonverbal researchers have estimated that between 65% and 93% of our understanding of a source's message is a result of how we decode the source's nonverbal communication. Humans look more to how a source communicates than to the language choices he or she uses to communicate; this does not mean that language is unimportant, only that meaning is a combination of both verbal and nonverbal messages.

Both verbal and nonverbal channels can be utilized when communicating messages. However, verbal and nonverbal channels are not the only channels available to communicators. A **mediated channel** is any channel that uses some kind of mediating device to help transmit information. Telephones, e-mail, newspapers, television, radio, and text messaging are all examples of technologies that help mediate communication between people. Whether two people are on opposite sides of the world using mediated channels to communicate or sitting side-by-side text messaging each other to avoid eavesdroppers, people in today's world are constantly communicating via mediated messages.

The first medium used to communicate messages was cave drawings, but these were neither efficient nor particularly effective channels for communicating anything but the most primitive of thoughts. In fact, some people try to make a case for prehistoric extraterrestrial contact based on the drawings found in caves. People can see pretty much anything they want in a cave drawing, so as an historical tool, they are not reliable. Such drawings slowly evolved into more complex picture systems as they took on more substantial forms, where specific pictures meant things, which then evolved into written language. If the history of human communication were represented by a typical 12-inch ruler, the history of writing would be included in less than the last quarter of an inch.

The most rapid improvement in mediated channels has occurred in the past 150 years. Ever since the first message was sent by Morse Code in 1844, mediated technology has been improving. From Morse Code to radios, to televisions, to cable televisions, to the Internet, to whatever comes next, mediated technology is evolving. For this reason, many people in the field of communication devote themselves to the study of mediated **communications**. In the field of communication, the letter "s" at the end of the word "communication" signifies mediated technologies. The field of mass communications studies how mediated technologies communicate messages to large numbers of people. However, most of the research within the field of communication does not examine mediated technologies, so the letter "s" must not be added to the word "communication" unless one is talking about communication occurring through mediated technologies.

Now that we have discussed both the history of social science research and the nature of communication, the rest of the chapter will briefly explain the organization of this volume.

UNDERSTANDING THE BOOK'S FORMAT

The authors of this book have more than 100 years combined experience conducting empirical research in the field of communication. Historically, the West Virginia University (WVU) Department of Communication Studies has mentored many of the top quantitative researchers in the field, although the department did not technically have its own doctorate program until the fall of 2006. Individuals who graduated from WVU with a doctorate received their degree in education (either curriculum and instruction or educational psychology), so all WVU graduates have extensive training in both communication and educational theory and practice. Overall, the approach that WVU takes to teach research methods has been successful; in 2003, WVU was listed as one of the top doctorate programs for graduates publishing research in the field (Hickson, Turner, & Bodon, 2003). Furthermore, WVU was the number-one program for faculty research publications. For this reason, our book takes the approach used at WVU to train many of the most prolific quantitative researchers in the field. All four of the authors of this text have WVU roots: two as faculty (James C. McCroskey and Virginia Peck Richmond) and two as program graduates (Candice Thomas-Maddox and Jason S. Wrench). In various analyses of the field, WVU graduates and faculty have made important contributions to the field of communication. Over a 30-year period, the instruction in quantitative research methods at WVU has been fine-tuned to enable both undergraduate and graduate researchers to understand the research process. This book is the culmination of years of teaching instruction in quantitative research methods by all of the authors.

Chapters 2 and 3 introduce you to the basic aspects of communication research. Chapter 2 explores empirical research and the scientific method, which is what this book is designed to teach you. If you are interested in nonquantitative research methods, Appendix A (see the textbook's website, https://oup-arc.com/wrench) includes a chapter written by James Chesebro and Deborah Borisoff that discusses qualitative and critical research methods. Chapter 3 discusses the ethical standards that modern researchers are required to follow both philosophically and legally.

Chapters 4 and 5 take you through the basic process necessary for conducting research. Chapter 4 examines how to use libraries and other sources for finding research previously conducted on a given topic. In addition to basic library skill discussions, Chapter 4 lays out how to format papers and cite sources using the sixth edition of the American Psychological Association's style manual. Chapter 5 then breaks down each section of a research study and gives tips and examples for writing these sections for your own research projects.

Chapters 6 through 8 examine the most fundamental parts of a research project. Chapter 6 explains what variables are, the different types of variables that exist in empirical sciences, and various communication variables. The communication variables discussed in this chapter will help you understand the majority of the examples used in this text. Furthermore, an actual research dataset was collected on the variables discussed in Chapter 6; you can find this dataset on the textbook's website. Chapters 7 and 8 explain how social scientists measure human behavior and perceptions and how to ensure these measurements are reliable and valid. Chapter 7 discusses how researchers measure communicative behaviors and perceptions. Chapter 8 details two important characteristics—reliability and validity—involved in the measurement process that must be clearly followed for research to be meaningful.

In Chapters 9 through 11 and Appendix D (see the textbook's website), we explore four common techniques for conducting communication research: survey, content analysis, experiment, and Big Data. Chapter 9 examines survey research. The methods discussed in this chapter date back to the techniques created during the 1930s and 1940s by the social scientists studying human attitudes. Chapter 10 explores the research method called content analysis, and Chapter 11 presents the nature of experiments and various methods researchers can employ to ensure that experiments are successful. Appendix D discusses the new and emerging field of Big Data and how it is impacting our understanding of human communication.

Chapters 12 and 13 explore some basic concepts related to research methods: sampling and hypothesis testing. Chapter 12 explains how to go about finding the appropriate research participants to ensure your research projects are successful and meaningful. Chapter 13 provides the basic explanation for how the statistical process is conducted. Although this chapter is the densest one in this text to read, the information it contains is important to understanding the next six chapters.

Chapter 14 starts our discussion of statistics by introducing you to descriptive statistics. Most people are somewhat familiar with the ideas of descriptive statistics, but here, we show how descriptive statistics are the basic building blocks for more advanced statistics.

Chapters 15 through 19 examine different statistical tools that can help you in answering actual questions about communication phenomena. The first segment in each chapter walks you through the step-by-step process necessary to compute statistical formulas by hand. This is the part of quantitative research methods that many students are nervous about when first learning. Trust us, if you follow our step-by-step instructions, you will have no problems whatsoever learning how to calculate these mathematical formulas. The first part of every chapter also presents a scenario for the type of statistical test that each chapter represents. These scenarios are designed to help you compute the statistical tests by hand. For this reason, the data used in these examples are fabricated to make the math as easy as possible. Although the first examples in each chapter may be interesting, they are not based on actual empirical data. In addition to calculating the problems by hand, you will be provided with statistical output using the Windows version of the IBM Statistical Package for the Social Sciences (SPSS), version 20.0, which is a useful tool used by quantitative communication researchers. Additionally, information will be provided on the utility of two open-source statistical software packages: PSPP and R. PSPP is a pared-down version of SPSS that is freely available. R, in contrast, is a statistical programming language and is best suited for those in graduate school. However, a graphic user interface called R-Commander enables R to function in a manner similar to that of SPSS. To learn more about these free statistical software packages, see Appendix C on the textbook's website.

The second segment in Chapters 15 through 19 consists of real data–driven research questions from the dataset collected for this textbook. In these examples, you will be presented first with a research scenario and then with the SPSS results, similar to the examples in the first part. The biggest difference between these examples and those in the first part of each chapter is that these examples are based on actual collected data, so these are real research findings. We could have used the examples in the second half of each chapter to compute the statistics by hand, but that process would have been much more complicated and not beneficial to your understanding of the mathematical processes needed to compute these statistics.

The third and final segment in Chapters 15 through 19 examines the articles on the textbook's website. To see how each of these statistical tests can be used by researchers to answer actual hypotheses and research questions, we recommend that you read the first two sections of every chapter first, then read the corresponding article on the textbook's website, and finally examine the analysis of the article we have provided for you in the chapter. By completing the readings in the way we recommend, you will be able to determine whether you truly understand the statistical concept and how it can be employed in research. If Chapters 15 through 19 aren't enough, we also have a chapter on Advanced Statistical Procedures in Appendix E online.

The final chapter in this book, Chapter 20, discusses the processes that researchers go through to present their findings to other people. This chapter examines how to design effective research posters for presentation at conferences and conventions, how to deliver papers at conferences and conventions, and how to submit your original research for possible publication.

RESEARCH OUTSIDE THE WALLS OF ACADEMIA

One area that surprises numerous communication students is the cross-transferability of the skills you learn in a quantitative research methods course to life outside of academia. A great deal of your life is governed by information derived through quantitative research. Everything from the medication you take, to the clothes you wear, to how you connect with friends exists because of quantitative research. Although this is not a book about medical research or market research, we do want you to be aware that numerous individuals are engaged in applied quantitative communication research. Periodically in this text, we will end a chapter by discussing key factors to consider when engaging in research outside the confines of higher education. Furthermore, we will discuss how people in the world outside of academia are using the same processes, tools, techniques, and statistics to answer a host of different problems outside of academia.

CONCLUSION

The authors of this textbook have a passion for conducting unique and interesting communication research. We sincerely hope that you will learn to share our passion as you journey with us through the text. In the next chapter, we will explain the process researchers go through when conducting scientific research in communication.

KEY TERMS

Channel p. 11

Communication p. 9

Communications p. 12

Decoding p. 10

Encoding p. 10

Language p. 11

Mediated channel p. 11

Message p. 10

Nonverbal messages p. 11

Physical sciences p. 2

Receiver p. 10

Social sciences p. 2

Source p. 10

Theory of natural selection p. 4

Verbal messages p. 11

REFERENCES

Albarraćin, D., Johnson, B. T., & Zanna, M. P. (Eds.). (2006). *The handbook of attitudes.* Mahwah, NJ: Erlbaum.

Berlo, D. K. (1960). *The process of communication.* New York, NY: Holt, Rinehart & Winston.

Guttman, L. (1944). A basis for scaling qualitative data. *American Sociological Review, 9,* 139–150.

Hickson, M. III, Turner, J., & Bodon, J. (2003). Research productivity in communication: An analysis, 1996–2001. *Communication Research Reports, 20*, 308–319.

Hovland, C. I., Janis, I. L., & Kelly, H. H. (1953). *Communication and persuasion: Psychological studies of opinion change.* New Haven, CT: Yale University Press.

Hunt, E. L. (1915). The scientific spirit in public speaking. *The Quarterly Journal of Public Speaking, 1*, 185–193.

Jowett, G. S., & O'Donnell, V. (1992). *Propaganda and persuasion* (2nd ed.). Newbury Park, CA: Sage.

Lazarsfeld, P. (1941). Remarks on administrative and critical communications research. *Studies in Philosophy and Social Science, 9*, 2–16.

Lazarsfeld, P., & Stanton, F. N. (1944). *Radio research, 1942–43.* New York, NY: Duell, Sloan, & Pearce.

Likert, R. (1932). A technique for the measurement of attitudes. *Archives of Psychology, 140*, 1–55.

McCroskey, J. C. (2006). *An introduction to rhetorical communication: A western rhetorical perspective* (9th ed.). Boston, MA: Allyn & Bacon.

McCroskey, J. C., & Wheeless, L. R. (1976). *An introduction to human communication.* Boston, MA: Allyn & Bacon.

Osgood, C. E. (1952). The nature and measurement of meaning. *Psychological Bulletin, 49*, 197–262.

Shannon, C. E., & Weaver, W. (1949). *The mathematical theory of communication.* Urbana, IL: University of Illinois Press.

Simons, G. (2017, February 21). *Welcome to the 20th edition* [Press release]. Retrieved from https://www.ethnologue.com/ethnoblog/gary-simons/welcome-20th-edition

Thomas, W. I., & Znaniecki, F. (1918). *The Polish peasant in Europe and America: Primary-group organization.* Chicago, IL: University of Chicago Press.

Wickersham, J. A., Sherblom, J. C., & Richmond, V. P. (2004). A twenty year retrospective on a research community: An analysis of scholarship published in *Communication Research Reports* (1984 to 2004). *Communication Research Reports, 21*, 437–444.

Winans, J. A. (1915). The need for research. *The Quarterly Journal of Public Speaking, 1*, 17–23.

FURTHER READING

Chesebro, J. W. (Ed.). (2010). *A century of transformation: Studies in honor of the 100th anniversary of the Eastern Communication Association.* New York, NY: Oxford University Press.

Salkind, N. J. (2012). *100 questions (and answers) about research methods.* Los Angeles, CA: Sage.

Wrench, J. S., McCroskey, J. C., & Richmond, V. P. (2008). *Human communication in everyday life: Explanations and applications.* Boston, MA: Allyn & Bacon.

2

Empirical Research

CHAPTER OBJECTIVES

1. Define the term *research*.

2. Describe the different epistemological approaches to communication scholarship.

3. Understand the basic processes involved in the modern scientific method.

4. Recognize and construct logical arguments.

5. Explain what empirical generalizations are and why they are important to the scientific processes.

Have you ever read a textbook and wondered where all the information came from? Have you ever wondered how your university professors became so smart? The simple—and the complicated—answer to both these questions is research. Now for many readers, when we say "research," you may think of the research you did in an English class where you looked at various books, articles, and Internet websites and then wrote a paper incorporating the information from those sources. Although this kind of research is important, it is not what we are referring to when we say "research."

Research, according to Merriam-Webster (n.d.), is the "studious inquiry or examination; especially: investigation or experimentation aimed at the discovery and interpretation of facts, revision of accepted theories or laws in the light of new facts, or practical application of such new or revised theories or laws." This definition implies that "research" uses the scientific method to answer questions. We will explain the "scientific method" and the scientific approach to conducting research later in this chapter, but first, let's quickly discuss the major epistemological approaches to research.

WAYS OF KNOWING

Epistemology

According to Moser (2002), epistemology is "the study of the nature of knowledge and justification: in particular, the study of (a) the defining components, (b) the substantive conditions or sources, and (c) the limits of knowledge and justification" (p. 3). Simply put, **epistemology** is a way of knowing. Of course, along with the idea of "knowing," we must admit there are various perspectives on the very notion of knowledge. For example, Klein (2002) argues that these foundations of "knowing" are controversial because of a range of different standpoints, and that there are three important considerations to consider when discussing knowledge.

HOW DOES ONE ANALYZE KNOWLEDGE AND JUSTIFICATION?

Or, how does someone use theory, data, and other forms of evidence to ascertain "knowledge"? Diverse epistemological perspectives will draw on different theoretical traditions. Furthermore, researchers often have varied approaches and ways of analysis to interrogate and find meaning within human communication.

WHAT SOURCES OF KNOWLEDGE DOES ONE USE?

Within the field of communication, three general branches are discussed: social scientific (also called positivism/postpositivism), qualitative (also called interpretive), and rhetorical (also called critical, postmodern, post-structuralist, etc.). We should mention that we divide the three branches through our vantage point as social scientists. If you asked post-structuralist scholars, their categorizing scheme would look different. Social scientific researchers rely predominantly on quantitative methodologies and believe human communication can be examined through both simple and complex statistical models. Interpretive researchers, in contrast, believe that to understand human communication, one must explore and appreciate how the individual(s) at the center of specific interactions or communicative acts understands his or her own communication. Last, critical scholars believe the central role of research is to examine the interplay between ideology and science.

Ideology refers to the common or partial knowledge that people have. Common or partial knowledge is problematic for two reasons. First, common knowledge serves the needs of specific people (generally those with the power and control within a group or culture). Second, common knowledge is incomplete because people do not understand where this common or partial knowledge originated from, so they assume that it must be factual, true, doctrine, and so on. Research, from the critical perspective, is the process a researcher uses to examine how power and domination create these forms of common knowledge and eventually shed light on how these forms of knowledge subjugate the people who have them.

Each of these three epistemological traditions is important within the field of communication. However, the epistemological traditions are not always suited for the same research questions. For instance, if you wanted to decide whether one group who views an advertisement responds differently toward a product than a second group, then the social scientific method is the best. If you want to know how people understand what it means to be members of a church from the perspective of the individual members of that church through the interactions that they have, then examining these perceptions interpretively would make the most sense. If you want to examine how crisis messages are steeped in traditions of privilege, power, and hegemony, then a rhetorical/critical tradition is probably the most appropriate. It is important to understand that epistemology is always the driving force behind the research questions someone asks and the methodological traditions someone uses.

WHAT IS THE IMPORTANCE AND USE OF SKEPTICISM?

Klein (2002) discusses skepticism and its importance to both knowledge and justification. Klein acknowledges three approaches to epistemological skepticism that align with the three theoretical traditions: (1) epistemist (acknowledging that knowledge of something is possible), (2) academic (arguing that knowledge of something is impossible), and (3) Pyrrhonian (withholding agreement from either the epistemist or the academic perspective). In essence, "knowledge" is often utilized with no acknowledgment of what the word means. Philosophically, uncertainty helps rein in the notions of what knowledge is and whether something can be known. If you ask people conducting research in the different epistemological traditions (social scientific, qualitative/interpretive, and rhetorical/critical), the answers you get about what is known—or even what is knowable—will vary greatly.

Epistemology and This Book

This book focuses on quantitative/scientific epistemology for research. However, beginning researchers, which this book presumes you are, should be exposed to all epistemological approaches to communication scholarship. After you have completed your initial study of quantitative research, you may stay with this approach (as all of us have done), or you may decide that you prefer one of the other epistemological traditions for research. If you decide that the qualitative/interpretive or critical approach fits you better, you can take a course in that approach to scholarship. Many communication programs require you to take courses in quantitative/scientific, qualitative/interpretive, and rhetorical/critical research methods to make sure that you have a broad exposure to how knowledge is created within the field. Many scholars, including the authors of this book, believe that all scholars (undergraduate students, graduate students, and academic professionals) should expose themselves to the three main approaches to communication scholarship because the only way to engage in academic discourse is to have a strong foundation in all three methodological approaches to research. Appendix A (see the textbook's website, https://oup-arc.com/wrench) broadly introduces you to the two epistemological traditions not focused on within this text.

Ordinary Versus Scientific Ways of Knowing

From the moment we are born, we start attempting to know the world around us. Admittedly, our attempts in infancy are minimal and do not get us far, but these attempts get larger and more complex throughout our lifetimes. Part of this knowledge involves our ability to understand our current situations and predict what will happen in the future. Over time, we realize that "future circumstances are somehow caused or conditioned by present ones" (Babbie, 2010, p. 4). Some of these realizations are easy: if you stick your finger in a light socket, your finger will hurt. Others are more complex: if you get a degree from a prestigious university, you will make more money compared to those individuals who do not go to prestigious universities. However, we also realize that these predictions are probabilistic, meaning they are not accurate 100% of the time. For every Ivy League graduate out there making huge amounts of money, there are others who are starving artists, authors, actors, musicians, and so on. We begin to realize we must narrow and fine-tune our predictions. For example, maybe getting an Ivy League education is only part of the picture. If you get a degree in business or economics from an Ivy League school, then maybe your long-term financial prospects are better than those of individuals with a degree in creative writing. According to Babbie (2010), "If you can understand why things are related to each other, why certain regular patterns occur, you can predict better than if you simply observe and remember those patterns. Thus, human inquiry aims at answering both 'what' and 'why' questions, and we pursue these goals by observing and figuring out" (p. 5).

ORDINARY SOURCES OF INFORMATION

Chances are you have never read a research report looking at the statistics of Ivy League graduates and incomes, so we often rely on ordinary sources of information. Babbie (2010) argues that two tools people often rely on to gain ordinary or common-sense knowledge are traditions and authorities.

First, traditions! Each of us is constrained by the culture in which we have grown up. Depending on the culture, you may learn things like when best to plant fruits and vegetables to ensure the most plentiful harvest. You also learn issues related to gender, sexuality, race/ethnicity, nationalism, and so on. Traditions are often dominant and dictate how people think, behave, and communicate with one another. However, traditions can also have a dark side and limit people. For example, in many parts of the world, tradition dictates that unmarried women should never interact with or communicate with men who are not their immediate family members.

Second, we often learn knowledge from some kind of authority figure. In any cultural group, authority figures' ideas on knowledge are deemed to be more valuable than those of others. Often, these values may have a factual basis in reality. If you are told by an astrophysicist that the earth rotates around the sun (as it does), that information would hopefully bear more weight than if a religious leader told you that the sun rotates around the earth (as was Catholic Church doctrine for many years).

PROBLEMS WITH ORDINARY KNOWLEDGE

Therein lies one of the biggest problems people face with issues of ordinary knowledge: which authority figure to believe. Should one rely on ordinary knowledge provided by a religious authority or a scientific authority regarding scientific information? Many authority figures will speak outside of their actual realm of real authority. Inquiry is hindered when someone listens to and believes the "common knowledge" of someone who is not an actual authority on a topic. For example, a huge national debate exists on the efficacy and outcomes of vaccines. On one side of the debate are the US Surgeon General, the medical establishment, and academic researchers from around the world. On the other side are a handful of celebrities and vocal parents fueling the "anti-vaxxer" debate. In a case like this, who do you listen to? One group of authority figures has studied the issue using science, and the other group has anecdotal evidence and opinions. Although the choice to align oneself with scientific authority figures makes the most sense, others are taught to distrust science. Many individuals may believe in larger scientific conspiracy theories (e.g., the world is flat, plane contrails contain chemical/biological agents created by the government, HIV was created by the CIA, etc.), so they will believe the celebrity authority figures.

Overall, tradition and authority figures both have positive and negative associations. On the positive side, both tradition and authority give us a grounding to understand our world. Admittedly, these understandings may not be true and must be adjusted as one grows older. For example, you may have been taught that women were second-class citizens without the full rights of men, only to realize that the subjugation of women in the name of religion is abhorrent. As such, people should always question common knowledge and why that common knowledge exists. Unfortunately, many traditions and authority figures teach that questioning their "knowledge" is a heresy one should avoid.

ORDINARY KNOWLEDGE VERSUS SCIENCE

What is the difference between ordinary knowledge and science? The knowledge that science arrives at is different from common knowledge because of the rigorous process used to gain that knowledge. Harris (2014) describes six specific differences between ordinary and scientific knowledge:

1. *Conceptualizing the topic.* Scientists carefully conceptualize their research studies while delineating clear boundaries for what is being studied and what is not.
2. *Reading the literature.* Scientists read a range of research studies on a single topic prior to engaging in a new study or scientific discourse to make sure their positions are backed by evidence and not opinion.

3. *Careful measurements.* Scientists try to create and then use precise measures of various phenomena while admitting any specific limitations that may exist in these measurement techniques.
4. *Collecting samples.* Scientists rely not on the opinions and anecdotes of the few but instead on larger, more carefully assembled samples that represent a specific phenomenon.
5. *Analyzing data and presenting results.* Scientists spend their entire careers learning how to analyze data and developing new methods for analyzing data in an effort to disseminate their results to both their academic peers and the general public.
6. *Ethics and politics.* Researchers must think through how to ethically collect and report data while minimizing any political and personal biases that may distort the research process.

When you compare these six processes to those that rely on tradition and authority, clear distinctions between what is knowledge and how one gains knowledge emerge. One of the biggest frustrations scientists run into is when they have mounds of evidence on a topic and someone feels that her or his opinion is equally valid to all of the data that have been painstakingly collected and analyzed. Opinions are not science. Unfortunately, we live in an age where opinions, if they are repeated often enough, are taken as "facts." For our purposes, we are interested in science rather than opinions related to how people behave, interact, and communicate.

One fairly recent phenomenon that is very disturbing for scientists is the inability of some people to agree on basic things—like facts. Facts are statements that can be proven true or false. Opinions, on the other hand, are statements that cannot be proven true or false. As the old saying goes, "Everyone is entitled to their own opinions; they are not entitled to their own facts." Unfortunately, some people are now trying to pass off their personal opinions, values, and beliefs as "alternative facts." Laine and Taichman (2017) have this to say on the issue:

> The scientific process demands an objective gathering and assessment of evidence to understand cause-and-effect relationships and to guide the subsequent design and evaluation of interventions when necessary. It aims to get at the truth, no matter what it might be. Unfortunately, social and political pressures can interfere with scientific advances when some dislike or fear what the truth might be. (p. 905)

As scientists (whether physical or social), our job is to promote truth and objectivity, not personal opinions, values, and beliefs. Laine and Taichman go on to note, "Good science cannot occur and its rewards cannot be reaped when we choose to pursue only the data and knowledge that seem to support our ideologies and denigrate the rest as 'fake'" (p. 905).

THE SCIENTIFIC APPROACH TO COMMUNICATION RESEARCH

The idea of a method for determining things scientifically is as old as the notion of **science** itself. The ancient Egyptians and Greeks both created systems for determining knowledge through a process that is loosely related to what we now know as the scientific method. Advances were made in the scientific method because of Muslim philosophers who believed experiments should test opposing theories. Our current understanding of the scientific method was first theorized by Sir Francis Bacon and René Descartes and then crystallized by Charles Sanders Peirce in 1878 in his article, "How to Make Our Ideas Clear."

Overall, the notion of a specific method for discovering scientific laws has been around for millennia. Whether you are a physical scientist (biologist, chemist, physicist, etc.) or a social scientist (psychologist, sociologist, communication researcher, etc.), the basic processes for conducting research stem from the scientific method. When you were in elementary school, you were probably introduced to the scientific method in much the same way we were. So, before we can go further in discussing the scientific approach to communication research, we must revisit the scientific method.

Scientific Method

The **scientific method** relates to the definition provided earlier from Merriam-Webster (n.d.) for the word "research." As Figure 2.1 illustrates, there are four primary steps to the scientific process as commonly discussed by scientists. Where one starts in the process is arbitrary, but it usually is most helpful if we start with the "theories" step and explain from that point forward.

Although most people have a general understanding of what the scientific method is, most do not know the history of this method. The scientific method was first used by a Muslim scientist, Hasan Ibn al-Haytham (965–1039 CE), who was born in Basra, Iraq, and died in Cairo, Egypt. Hasan Ibn al-Haytham can be described as a polymath, or an individual who studied a wide range of scholarly topics. He wrote about anatomy, astronomy, mathematics, medicine, philosophy, physics, psychology, and religion. However, it was his interest in the areas of optics, the branch of science that studies visible and invisible light, and vision that led to the creation of the scientific method. In the *Book of Optics*, Ibn al-Haytham describes a method for conducting experiments, which became the basis of modern science. His scientific method consisted of seven basic steps: (1) observation, (2) stating of the scientific problem, (3) formulating a hypothesis, (4) testing the hypothesis through experimentation, (5) analyzing the experimental results, (6) interpreting data and forming conclusions, and (7) publishing research. Although this method of conducting research may seem standard today, the practice was unheard of in his time.

FIGURE 2.1
Scientific Method

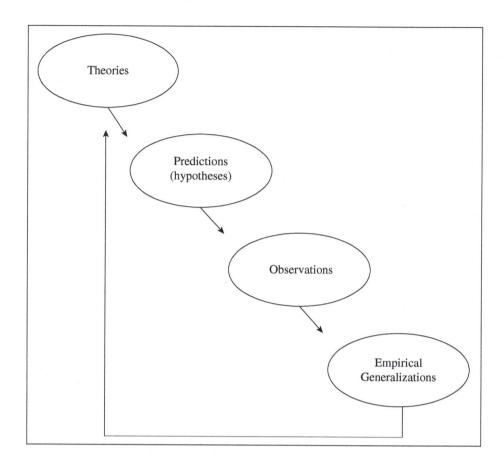

Over the next thousand years, many of our most famous scientists revisited and debated Ibn al-Haytham's method for conducting science (e.g., Galileo Galilei, Francis Bacon, René Descartes, Isaac Newton, Charles Sanders Peirce, David Hume, and Karl Popper). The version of the scientific method that is most used today stems from the work of Karl Popper (1934, 1968).

THEORIES

A **theory** is a proposed explanation for how a set of natural phenomena will occur that is capable of making predictions about the phenomena for the future and of being falsified through empirical observation (West & Turner, 2006). We will break down this definition and examine its major components.

DESCRIBE THE NATURAL PHENOMENON

A theory should be able to either explain or describe a natural phenomenon (an observable event). A number of different types of explanations are often used to explain various phenomena: appeal to authority, label the phenomenon, evoke empathy, define terms or give examples, and appeal to general empirical rules.

APPEAL TO AUTHORITY According to the sociologist Gwynn Nettler (1970), an explanation is an attempt to satisfy one's curiosity about an observable event. In one of our favorite movies, *The Gods Must Be Crazy*, a Bushman named Xi who lives in Botswana is presented a gift from "the gods." This so-called gift is actually a Coke bottle accidentally dropped by a pilot flying a plane above the tribe. Ultimately, the Bushmen become jealous of each other because there is only one Coke bottle; this causes the tribe to rename the bottle "the evil thing." The majority of the movie tells the story of Xi attempting to take the bottle to the end of the world and return "the evil thing" to the gods. In essence, the Bushmen faced a new and unexplainable event, the appearance of the bottle, and were forced to create an explanation for how the bottle appeared among their tribe after falling from the sky. The Bushmen's explanation for the observable event was that the gods had given them the bottle. This example is only one type of explanation that people give to observable events, and it is called an **appeal to authority** because the explanation centers on the gods being wise in their decision to give the Bushmen the bottle.

LABEL THE PHENOMENON The second way of explaining phenomena is to **label the phenomenon**. Humans use labeling with children to help explain why parents do things. A child might ask, "Why do we wash our hands?" In response, the parent explains the concept of bacteria and disease in a basic way that the child can understand. This is also seen with the Bushmen when the "gift from the gods" causes jealousy among the tribe members, who then label the Coke bottle an "evil thing."

EVOKE EMPATHY The third way to explain phenomena is to **evoke empathy**, or to show how a phenomenon has good, just, or moral reasons. For example, when explaining his reasoning to the American public for invading Iraq, President George W. Bush appealed to the American people, explaining that Iraq had weapons of mass destruction and that invading Iraq was the just and moral thing to do in order to prevent Saddam Hussein from being able to use those weapons.

DEFINE TERMS OR GIVE EXAMPLES The fourth way to explain a phenomenon is to define terms or give examples. For example, university professors often forget how large their vocabularies are and occasionally make the mistake of using a word on an examination that many students do not know. To give an **explanation** of what the word means, we will try to think of other words (synonyms) a student may be more familiar with to help her or him understand what the question is asking.

APPEAL TO GENERAL EMPIRICAL RULES The last way people can go about explaining phenomena is to **appeal to general empirical rules**. For example, when people experience stage fright, they often have sweaty palms. Sweaty palms occur during anxious periods because our body goes into a fight-or-flight mode, so blood is pumped to our extremities (arms and legs) at a fast rate, which causes the internal temperature to rise in our extremities in case we either have to fight what is causing the anxiety or have to run away fast. Although this physiological response to fear is useful when you come face to face with a man-eating bear in the wilderness, it is not useful when you have to give a public speech. In this example, we explained why sweaty palms occur by relating the physiological response to what we empirically know about how the body reacts to fear. Ultimately, appealing to general empirical rules as a method for explaining phenomena is important because it is the only way to explain the past and present, and help us to predict what could happen in the future, which is the second part of the definition of theory provided earlier.

PREDICT THE FUTURE

Our explanation of the behavior (fight or flight leads to sweaty palms) helps us to formulate predictions (when fearful, people's hands are more likely to sweat). When we talk about theories, our goal is to predict, explain, and control a phenomenon. If a theory is to be of any use, then the theory for why a behavior occurs should help direct us toward ways to control the phenomenon. For example, recent research has shown that certain psychiatric medications can decrease an individual's level of anxiety, even when he or she must give public speeches (Stein, Stein, Goodwin, Kumar, & Hunter, 2001; Van Ameringen et al., 2001; Van Ameringen, Mancini, Oakman, & Farvolden, 1999). Overall, we can predict that people who experience high levels of anxiety while giving a speech will have sweaty palms. We can explain why this occurs through the research conducted by scientists examining physiological responses to fear that result in a fight-or-flight state. Finally, based on new research conducted in psychopharmacology, we can now better control the physiological tendency to experience anxiety, thus preventing sweaty palms while giving a speech (Richmond, Wrench, & McCroskey, 2018).

FALSIFICATION

The last part of the definition of theory is often the hardest for nonscientists to completely understand. Karl Popper first argued in the 1930s that a theory must be falsifiable through empirical research (Popper, 1968). In essence, for a theory to truly be a theory, there must be a way to test it empirically. The word **empiricism** was originally coined by the Roman skeptic Sextus Empiricus regarding Greek physicians, who rejected beliefs in the divine nature of illness (i.e., you are sick because you made Zeus mad); instead, the physicians relied on the observation of phenomena as perceived in experience through the five senses (touch, smell, hearing, vision, and taste). In other words, empiricism is the belief that science is only acceptable insofar as the phenomenon in question can be "sensed" by average people. For example, people may not see atoms with their naked eyes, but they can see them using powerful microscopes.

Predictions/Hypotheses

The second step in the scientific method is the development of predictions about the relationship between phenomena that come in the form of hypotheses. A **hypothesis** is the conclusion that occurs at the end of a series of propositions. A **proposition** is a statement that either confirms or denies something. Although there are many types of propositions, the most important to researchers are conditional or hypothetical propositions, which comprise two primary parts: antecedent and consequent. An **antecedent** is an "if" statement, and a **consequent** is a "then" statement. For example, "If I was born in the United States (antecedent), then I am an American (consequent)." Or, "If this month is June (antecedent), then the next month is July (consequent)." In the world of propositions, the antecedent causes the consequent to be true if the antecedent is true. In both examples used here, the consequent is true if the antecedent is true. If someone is born in the United States, then he or she is an American. If the current month is June, the next month on the calendar must be July because we do not randomly shuffle the months just for the fun of it every year.

From hypothetical propositions, we can take the next step to forming arguments. An **argument** is a set of propositions in which one follows logically as a conclusion from the others. In the world of logic, logicians illustrate arguments through the **syllogism**. A basic syllogism has three propositions (two premises and one conclusion). The most famous syllogism was given by the philosopher Aristotle more than 2,000 years ago:

Major Premise:	All men are mortal.
Minor Premise:	Socrates is a man.
Conclusion:	Therefore, Socrates is mortal.

One of the problems with syllogisms, however, is that for the syllogism to be accurate, we must trust that the premises are true. So if our syllogism starts with false premises, then the conclusion can never be true. For example:

Major Premise:	All extraterrestrials are rich.
Minor Premise:	I am an extraterrestrial.
Conclusion:	Therefore, I am rich.

This syllogism, although correct in form, clearly is not true, and the conclusion cannot be trusted to tell us anything meaningful about the world around us. There is also a flip side to this problem—a completely invalid syllogism that is based on true statements. For example:

Major Premise:	All mammals are living.
Minor Premise:	All lizards are reptiles.
Conclusion:	Therefore, all lizards are living.

Although all three statements are true, the **major premise** and the **minor premise** do not go together at all. You are dealing with apples and oranges in the major and minor premises here. Therefore, the conclusion that one would draw based on these premises may be true, but the syllogism is considered invalid because of the breakdown in the logical process. Ultimately, a hypothesis is a valid conclusion arrived at by a series of hypothetical propositions.

The following is an example from a student research paper attempting to determine the major premise, the minor premise, and the conclusion. See whether you think this argument is logical.

Major Premise:	Lack of conflict discussion leads to insecurity in the workplace.
Minor Premise:	Cooperation among employees minimizes conflict.
Conclusion:	Cooperation aids individuals in the management of conflict, and conflict discussion leads to solution-oriented conflict-management strategies.

Let's examine this argument to see where the problem lies. The major premise clearly says that the less people talk about conflict, the more insecure they are. The minor premise states that employees who cooperate have less conflict. The conclusion then says two different things: (1) if employees cooperate with each other, then somehow the cooperation will aid in managing conflict, and (2) talking about conflicts helps people find a solution. The first conclusion simply does not make sense because it is not specific and we have no idea what "aids individuals in the management of conflict" means. This could indicate that people will have more conflict or less conflict—we cannot tell based on the information provided in the syllogism. The second conclusion introduces a new term not seen in either the major or the minor premise ("solution-oriented conflict management strategies"). If the term is not mentioned in any of the earlier propositions, it cannot magically appear in the conclusion of a logical argument. Finally, the major and minor premises have nothing to do with one another. The major premise discusses the lack of conflict, whereas the minor premise talks about minimizing conflict. Although the two ideas may sound similar, they are not the same, so you cannot put them together to form a logical argument.

Let's look at an example from a student paper that was published right after the first edition of this book came out (Wrench, Millhouse, & Sharp, 2007). The following argument has true major and minor premises and a true conclusion:

Major Premise:	Passengers on airplanes like flight attendants who use humor.
Minor Premise:	There is a positive relationship between liking someone and trusting them.
Conclusion:	Therefore, flight attendants who use humor will be more trusted by passengers.

In this example, we have a major premise (funny flight attendants are liked) that relates to the minor premise (liking and trust are related), which leads to the conclusion that funny flight attendants will be trusted. We can now hypothesize that flight attendants who are perceived as humorous will be more trusted than flight attendants who are not perceived as humorous. Note that both propositions are true because research examining flight attendant communication has generated empirical evidence to make those statements possible. When examining the major and minor premises that are used to create arguments in research, the propositions are based on actual empirical findings from previously conducted research. The premises are not made up because they help someone form an argument. If you do not have previous empirical research to support your argument's propositions, then the propositions cannot be used to form a logical conclusion.

Observations

The next step in the scientific method is referred to as observations. The **observations** part of the scientific method is where a researcher attempts to test the hypotheses created in the previous step. The most rigorous way to test a theory is to employ an experiment of some kind that directly allows a researcher to control a variable and then see the ramifications of this variable. For physical scientists, controlling a variable is easy—when one adds baking soda to vinegar, for example, we will always get the "volcanic" reaction we saw as a child in our earth sciences class. You could conduct this experiment hundreds of times, with varying brands of baking soda and vinegar, and always get the same reaction.

Unfortunately, the social sciences are not as neat and easy because people do not always react the same. You cannot always take one funny flight attendant and expect everyone to react to him or her in the same way, because many other characteristics of that flight attendant (e.g., biological sex, hair color, uniform, ethnicity, sexual attractiveness) could influence passengers' perceptions of the person. A certain amount of error is inherent in social scientific research because humans provide social scientists with too many possibilities. However, there are certain processes that social scientists can use to make sure they weed out as much uncertainty as possible when they are testing theories. We will discuss these issues in greater detail in Chapter 13; for now, we will test the hypothesis discussed above: "Flight attendants who use humor will be more trusted by passengers."

This hypothesis was actually created by a couple of undergraduate students who wanted to conduct research on the airline industry. There are a number of ways a researcher could go about observing this hypothesis. First, a researcher could fly hundreds of airlines to seek out funny and not-so-funny flight attendants. Clear criteria would have to be used to decide whether a flight attendant was funny. The researcher could then ask passengers whether they trust the flight attendants and keep a record of their responses. Unfortunately, flying many airlines and getting people's responses could be costly, so a researcher may opt to conduct an experiment instead. The researcher could have a video or audio tape of a flight attendant being funny or not so funny and then get participants' reactions to the flight attendant. In this case, the researcher manipulates whether the participants see the funny flight attendant or the not-so-funny flight attendant videos. After viewing one video or the other, the researcher could have the participants fill out a scale that measures their perceptions of the video flight attendant's trustworthiness. Although watching video tapes is not the most accurate way of observing this phenomenon, it is the most cost-efficient.

When observing a phenomenon, however, researchers must take great care that their observations are empirical, objective, and controlled.

EMPIRICAL OBSERVATIONS

We discussed the nature of empiricism earlier in this chapter, so we will not go into great detail here other than to say that empiricism, with regard to observations, basically means that scientists must make sure that what they are attempting to observe can actually be observed. In other words, if scientists cannot find a way to make observations about a specific phenomenon, then they cannot study that phenomenon, which in that case is beyond the domain of science.

Along with this notion is the idea that research must be able to empirically test a phenomenon. You may wonder how social scientists observe what is going on inside people's heads, and you would be right to question this because social scientists cannot read brain waves and translate them to actual thoughts. Social scientists have created specific ways to indirectly observe phenomena that cannot be easily observed through one of the five senses. I am sure that in your undergraduate career you have been asked to fill out a research scale or questionnaire. These scales and questionnaires are examples of indirect methods that social scientists have created to observe what is going on inside someone's head.

OBJECTIVE OBSERVATIONS

Scientists must be both empirical and **objective** when they are observing phenomena during research. By objective, we mean that a scientist must make sure that her or his personal emotions, predictions, and biases do not get in the way of the observation. For example, imagine a scientist interviewing students about their tendency to drink alcohol right before giving a speech in class. The more the student talks about her or his drinking behavior, the more the interviewer starts to scowl and give the student dirty looks. Do you think this student will be forthright and honest about her or his drinking behavior? Probably not. Scientists must ensure that they are as objective as possible when conducting research.

Another aspect of objectivity is reporting exactly what one finds in research, not just what one wants to find. Often, when researchers pose hypotheses and test them, the hypotheses will not be supported. Although there can be hundreds of reasons for why a hypothesis does not turn out the way a researcher expects it to, the researcher has an obligation to the scientific community to report those results and make them available for critique.

CONTROLLED OBSERVATIONS

Finally, when observing a phenomenon, a researcher must make sure that he or she takes every step possible to control the research process. By **control**, researchers are referring to the process where an individual both prevents personal biases from interfering with the research study and ensures that no other explanations are possible for what is seen in the study. We have already discussed the importance of preventing personal biases and will go into greater detail about how to do this in Chapter 13, so we will focus here on how to prevent other explanations for observations.

Empirical Generalizations

The final stage in the process of the scientific method is the creation of empirical generalizations. An **empirical generalization** is an attempt to describe a phenomenon based on what we know about it at the time. Of course, our empirical generalizations are based on what we observed in the previous step of the scientific method. For example, in an initial study looking at flight attendant humor, the students conducting the research had participants read flight attendant preflight briefings (where the flight attendants show you all the doors, explain what to do with the yellow mask when it falls from the ceiling, and what to do in case you crash). One preflight safety briefing was standard and covered all of the basics required by the Federal Aviation Administration; in the second briefing, the students added humor. Overall, the results of the study showed that people did not trust the flight attendant in the humorous script (Wrench et al., 2007). In fact, participants trusted the bland flight attendant more than the funny flight attendant. The hypothesis was not supported.

Unethical researchers might have just pretended this finding did not happen and not presented the results because the finding was contrary to previous research in humor. However, even results that go against common opinions on the subject are important for a number of reasons. First, this result could indicate that in situations where people feel their safety is involved, humor is not appreciated. The airline industry could be a context in which previous research in humor is not applicable. Second, the finding could be a result of the method used in the experiment. The student researchers relied on written scripts where they manipulated humor (one plain script vs. one funny script). The written humor may have been interpreted differently if the participants in the study had viewed an actor or actress performing the script instead of the participants reading the

Story of Clever Hans

A story that is often repeated as a warning when discussing explanations of observations is the story of Clever Hans. Clever Hans was an Arabian stallion (Figure 2.2) purchased in 1888 by Wilhelm Von Osten. Von Osten theorized that animals were intelligent beings and believed that with the proper education he could teach a horse to do simple arithmetic. By the end of Hans's education, he could answer many arithmetic questions, from simple square roots to telling the time. The answers given by Hans came in the form of him pounding the number with his hoof the correct number of times on the ground. The horse could even answer mathematical questions when Von Osten was not present. Many researchers observed Hans and believed that Von Osten had in fact educated the horse. Even the esteemed director of the Berlin Psychological Institute, Carl Stumpf, declared in 1904 that Von Osten had educated Hans.

One researcher, Oskar Pfungst, decided to empirically test Hans through a simple, controlled experiment. First, Pfungst would have Von Osten look at a flash card to see the answer and then test Hans. When Von Osten knew the answer to the question, Hans's answers were always correct. Then Pfungst had Von Osten show Hans the card without Von Osten knowing the answer, and Hans's answers became very random. Pfungst concluded that somehow Von Osten was giving

FIGURE 2.2
Story of Clever Hans
Source: Karl Krall, Denkende Tiere, S. 425

Hans the answers without even knowing it. At this point, Pfungst turned his attention to Von Osten as the teacher and observed his behavior. Pfungst started noticing that the teacher, whether Von Osten or another person, actually started changing her or his posture by standing up straighter as the horse neared the correct answer. When the teacher would stand fully erect, Hans knew he could stop pounding his hoof. Pfungst published his findings in 1907 in a book entitled *Clever Hans (the Horse of Mr. Von Osten)*. In the Clever Hans example, we see both what happens when a scientist is not objective in observing a phenomenon (how Von Osten actually nonverbally cued the horse's responses) and how another scientist, Pfungst, came into the situation and determined how to control for other possible explanations and got to the bottom of what was really going on with Clever Hans.

script themselves. Overall, there are limitations to this study, and any good study will be up front about its limitations. If we do not know the limitations to a study, people may attempt to overgeneralize the results—and start campaigns to pass laws banning flight attendant humor.

COMMON PROBLEMS WITH GENERALIZATIONS

Overall, when we try to generalize what we have learned in a study to the real world, we must be honest about how we are applying our research findings. There are three common problems that researchers face when generalizing results: hasty generalizations, ecological fallacies, and exception fallacies.

HASTY GENERALIZATIONS First, researchers should avoid **hasty generalizations**, or generalizing to something when not enough evidence is available to make the generalization. Scientists must avoid this problem in their own writing and in how others use their research. In the world of communication, for example, media scholars often investigate how the effects of violence in the media relate to violence in the real world. Although the media scholars will correctly attribute limits to their results, politicians often will inaccurately try to use media research in their attempts to get various media banned. However, scientists should not investigate a phenomenon thinking about the political ramifications of their findings.

One area in which there are ramifications to communication research is biological sex differences and communication. Empirical research generally shows that about 1% of a person's communicative behavior can be attributed to her or his biological sex (Canary & Hause, 1993); however, this finding contradicts what many people believe, which has largely been supported by pop psychologists such as John Gray (1992), who wrote the book *Men Are from Mars, Women Are from Venus*. Sadly, scientists who conflict with conventional wisdom often have problems in society, and those who buy into conventional wisdom see those scientists who try to thwart convention as "having an axe to grind." Remember, Pope John Paul II fully conceded in 1992 that the Catholic Church's teaching that the earth was stationary was wrong and Galileo's assertion during the 1600s was correct—the earth traveled around the sun. Overall, scientists rarely think about how their research will be used by nonscientists or how people who disagree with research will react. Unfortunately, research is often used in ways that was never intended, and people who disagree with research can be vocal.

ECOLOGICAL FALLACIES Second, researchers must be careful to avoid ecological fallacies, or making generalizations about an individual because he or she belongs to a specific group. For example, research has shown us that men are more aggressive than women. Does this mean that all men are aggressive? No. Does this mean that no women are aggressive? Obviously not. The ecological fallacy becomes problematic when we meet a male and immediately assume he will be aggressive because research has demonstrated that men are more aggressive than women. As we will discuss in numerous places within this book, quantitative sciences are often looking at and comparing averages of groups. In this case, men are more aggressive on average when compared to the average levels of aggression among women. However, there will always be a great deal of variety that happens within a single group. There are many highly aggressive women and many men who are not aggressive at all.

EXCEPTION FALLACIES Third, researchers want to avoid exception fallacies. An exception fallacy is almost a reverse ecological fallacy. Under this fallacy, people make generalizations about an entire group of people based on one person or a small handful of people. Imagine you hear that a purple person was recently involved in a home burglary, and you immediately think to yourself, *Those purple people are a bunch of thieves.* You may realize that this fallacy has nothing to do with purple people, but it is often the basis of inaccurate stereotypes. Just because one purple person steals does not mean that all purple people are thieves. However, these types of stereotypes—and the discrimination that results—often become deeply ingrained in our society.

GENERALIZATIONS HELP REFINE THEORY

Ultimately, the empirical generalizations made should lead to refinements in one's theory. As we learn more about theory, we must change our theory to take into account what we have learned about it through the empirical process. For example, whereas a general theory of humor shows that humor is positive in most communicative contexts, we may need to limit the scope of a general theory of humor as a result of our initial findings in the use of flight attendant humor. Maybe our theory needs a new clause that says humor is positive in communicative interactions except in situations where people feel their safety is involved. However, once you make adjustments to a theory, you must empirically test those adjustments, and thus the cycle of research continues.

RESEARCH OUTSIDE THE WALLS OF ACADEMIA

You may be surprised to find out that a great deal of your life happens because of people's pursuit of the scientific method. One area where quantitative researchers have made an impact in recent years is in how we purchase materials online. In their book *The Man Who Lied to His Laptop*, Clifford Nass and Corina Yen (2010) discuss how Nass's research team helped Dell Computers create an online persona that would "upsell" customers buying from the Dell website. Upselling happens when a customer service agent asks a customer whether he or she wants more of something or makes recommendations for other purchases. The classic upsell is McDonald's "Do you want fries with that?"

In their consulting for Dell, the research team started by selecting 250 male and female models and then weeded them out by circulating photographs to hundreds of people and through qualitative focus groups. Ultimately, the team settled on what Nass called the "perfect guy: he was attractive and seemed both friendly and intelligent" (Nass & Yen, 2010, p. 111). The web team videoed hours of the model in an attempt to "help" customers make smarter (i.e., more profitable) purchases.

Unfortunately, after the research team started testing their new-model-enhanced upselling on the website, upselling did not actually happen. According to Nass and Yen, "Everything was there: the agent [model] praised the customer, he had all the markers of honesty and sincerity, and his facial expressions perfectly matched the words he was saying" (p. 45). So what was the problem? Eventually, someone on Nass's team had a spark of recognition that the polo shirt the model was wearing had the Dell logo on it. Once they reshot the video without the logo, people interacting with the website saw the model as credible and were more likely to go along with the model's upselling attempts.

Everything about how this project was conducted happened in line with the scientific method. The project started with social scientific theories for how people communicate credibility, including making sure nonverbal behaviors match verbal utterances. The researchers made predictions that upselling would happen when the website went live. The research team then observed customers not finding the model credible or likeable. Once their original hypothesis did not pan out, the researchers looked for a generalizable explanation and then started again with a new theory—the Dell logo is causing problems. Once this was corrected, the team went back through the scientific method; this time, customers found the model likeable and credible and were persuaded to buy more.

Now that we have introduced you to the basic concepts involved in the scientific process of research, we can focus on the necessity of conducting research in an ethical and responsible manner in the next chapter.

CONCLUSION

Scientists begin a program of research with little more than a few questions and speculations. Scientists may speculate that something causes something else or that something is just related to something else. As the research program generates more data and results, these speculations may move toward becoming a real theory. If one does not have solid quantitative research results to support one's theory, all that is left is speculation.

Nevertheless, the line dividing speculation and theory is less than perfect. Generally, when researchers are just guessing about what is going on in the real world, they are using speculation and more often use research questions to guide their efforts. When a body of data and results allows a scientist to build a formal description of what is going on, he or she is developing a theory. Depending on the results obtained, the theory may be strongly supported, but it may not be. The theory may get partial support and need to be modified to be consistent with the results obtained, or the theory may fail to receive meaningful support from the research outcomes.

Many scientists work on both describing what goes on and explaining why these things occur. Some scientists focus on the descriptive phase of scholarship. These scientists often are described as employing inductive methods. Other scientists focus primarily on the explanation phase of scholarship. They are described as employing deductive methods. Although some people may want to argue which is more important, inductive research or deductive research, this is pretty much a "Which comes first, the chicken or the egg?" situation. Both are critical to the advance of science.

The term *theory* is used for many purposes and in many ways. Some theories are meaningless (chicken or egg?), and some theories are important (the theory that a certain medication will kill cancer). You can check yourself as to how valuable your theory is in your own mind. Would you bet real money that, if properly tested, your theory would be proven correct? And if so, how much? Five cents? Fifty dollars? Fifty thousand dollars? Five hundred thousand dollars? Five million dollars? Although this may seem like a silly game, it is not. Many scientists must convince granting agencies to provide the resources to conduct their research. Not only does the scientist have to believe her

or his theory is worth the financial risk, he or she must also be able to get others to believe it. People are not highly committed to their speculations or guesses. However, people are committed to theories they and others believe to be strong, solid theories supported by empirical research (anyone want to jump off a skyscraper and test the theory of gravity?).

Everybody is entitled to an opinion, and as noted by the number of bloggers on the Internet, in most circumstances most people have one. However, not everyone's opinion is equal in value to everyone else's opinion. The value of a scientist's opinion depends on the scientific support he or she has available. What are the data? What are the research results? How many replications are available? How much variance can the theory predict in realistic studies? Are there solid research results reported by credible scholars that suggest the theory is not right? Quantitative researchers depend on the results of data analyses for determining the validity of a theory, not on someone's opinion. Science makes a maximum effort to keep the emotions and beliefs of a researcher separate from the evaluation of a theory. In contrast, the emotions and values of the researcher are a critical part of the decision making in much of the qualitative research (see Appendix A on the textbook's website). The researcher's thoughts contribute directly to the results of the research. Although it often is not possible to keep the scientific researcher's thinking and/or believing 100% out of decisions about results in quantitative research, at least there is an extreme effort to do so.

KEY TERMS

Antecedent p. 27

Appeal to authority p. 25

Appeal to general empirical rules p. 26

Argument p. 27

Consequent p. 27

Control p. 31

Empirical generalization p. 31

Empiricism p. 26

Epistemology p. 18

Evoke empathy p. 25

Explanation p. 25

Hasty generalizations p. 33

Hypothesis p. 27

Label the phenomenon p. 25

Major premise p. 28

Minor premise p. 28

Objective p. 30

Observations p. 29

Proposition p. 27

Research p. 17

Science p. 23

Scientific method p. 23

Syllogism p. 27

Theory p. 24

REFERENCES

Babbie, E. (2010). *The practice of social research* (12th ed.). Belmont, CA: Wadsworth, Cengage.

Canary, D. J., & Hause, K. S. (1993). Is there any reason to research sex differences in communication? *Communication Quarterly, 41*, 129–144.

Harris, S. R. (2014). *How to critique journal articles in the social sciences.* Thousand Oaks, CA: Sage.

Gray, J. (1992). *Men are from Mars, women are from Venus: A practical guide for improving communication and getting what you want in your relationships.* New York, NY: HarperCollins.

Klein, P. (2002). Skepticism. In Paul K. Moser (Ed.), *The Oxford handbook of epistemology* (pp. 336–361). New York, NY: Oxford University Press.

Laine, C., & Taichman, D. B. (2017). Alternative facts have no place in science. *Annals of Internal Medicine, 166*, 905-906. doi:10.7326/M17-0878

Merriam-Webster (n.d.). *Research.* Retrieved from http://www.m-w.com/dictionary/research/

Moser, P. K. (2002). Introduction. In *The Oxford handbook of epistemology* (pp. 3–24). New York, NY: Oxford University Press.

Nass, C., & Yen, C. (2010). *The man who lied to his laptop: What machines teach us about human relationships.* New York, NY: Current.

Nettler, G. (1970). *Explanations.* New York, NY: McGraw-Hill.

Peirce, C. S. (1878). How to make our ideas clear. *Popular Science Monthly, 12*, 286–302.

Pfungst, O. (1911). *Clever Hans (the horse of Mr. Von Osten): A contribution to experimental animal and human psychology* (Trans. C. L. Rahn). New York, NY: Holt. (Originally published in German, 1907).

Popper, K. (1934). *Logik der Forschung* (Amplified English ed., 1959). Vienna: Springer.

Popper, K. R. (1968). *The logic of scientific discovery.* New York, NY: Harper & Row.

Richmond, V. P., Wrench, J. S., & McCroskey, J. C. (2018). Scared speechless: Communication apprehension, avoidance, and effectiveness (7th ed.). Dubuque, IA: Kendall-Hunt.

Stein, D. J., Stein, M. B., Goodwin, W., Kumar, R., & Hunter, B. (2001). The selective serotonin reuptake inhibitor paroxetine is effective in more generalized and in less generalized social anxiety disorder. *Psychopharmacology, 158,* 267–272.

Van Ameringen, M., Mancini, C., Oakman, J. M., & Farvolden, P. (1999). Selective serotonin reuptake inhibitors in the treatment of social phobia: The emerging gold standard. *CNS Drugs, 11,* 307–315.

Van Ameringen, M. A., Lane, R. M., Walker, J. R., Bowen, R. C., Chokka, P. R., Goldner, E. M., . . . Swinson, R. P. (2001). Sertraline treatment of generalized social phobia: A 20-week, double-blind, placebo-controlled study. *American Journal of Psychiatry, 158,* 275–281.

West, R., & Turner, L. H. (2006). *Introducing communication theory: Analysis and application* (3rd ed.). Boston, MA: McGraw-Hill.

Wrench, J. S., Millhouse, B., & Sharp, D. (2007). Laughing before takeoff: Humor, sex, and the pre-flight safety briefing. *Human Communication, 10,* 381–399.

Research Ethics

CHAPTER OBJECTIVES

1. Summarize eight actual research studies that have questionable ethical practices.

2. Explain the three principles for ethical research spelled out in the Belmont Report.

3. Explain the basic purposes for institutional review boards (IRBs).

4. Distinguish among anonymity, confidentiality, and privacy.

5. Explain the seven specific issues related to research ethics.

The word "ethics" evokes many images in different people. Typically, determining what is "ethical" falls along two tracks of thinking: theological or philosophical. Theologians will determine the rightness or wrongness of a behavior by searching specific religious texts, oral teachings, or traditions. Philosophers, by contrast, concern themselves primarily with the question, "What should a person do?" Whether a person uses a theological or a philosophical stance for determining the ethicality of a behavior, understanding ethics is important to almost any endeavor.

This chapter explains the current state of ethics in research and how it applies to the field of communication. To examine ethics in communication research, we first look at 10 different ethical scenarios. Then, we explore the meaning of the term *ethics* in more detail, examine the three-prong test for ethics established by the 1979 Belmont Report (persons, beneficence, and justice), explain the purpose and place of IRBs in research, and pose some basic ethical questions for communication researchers.

▲ **How IRBs Got Started**
Source: © Don Maybe www. researchcartons.com

ETHICAL SCENARIOS

What do you think of the ethicality of the following 10 research scenarios?

1. Researchers use rural African American men to study the course of an untreated disease. During the study, the men receive free examinations and medical care. However, the men do not receive information about the disease, are not informed that they are participating in research, and are not told that the research will not benefit them directly. Even after a known treatment for the disease is discovered, the participants are not informed of the new treatment, and the research continues for decades, which leads to the death of many study participants.

2. Researchers studying whether people will intervene when someone is about to experience harm decide to stage a crime. The researchers, with the consent of a shop owner, stage a burglary at a liquor store and then watch how bystanders react to the experiment.

3. A researcher wanting to understand the psychological processes involved in men who have sex with other men in public toilets poses as a voyeur or "watchqueen," an individual who stands watch and warns individuals engaging in public sex acts if someone is coming. After performing the job of watchqueen, the researcher writes the license plate numbers of the men. Next, the researcher traces the men's identities through the Department of Motor Vehicles under the guise of a market researcher. Once the researcher knows who the men are, he approaches them at their residences a year later and interviews them to learn more about them.

4. Researchers are interested in understanding how juries decide verdicts. To examine jury deliberations, the researchers get permission from a judge to record the deliberations (using audio means only) of six actual juries.

5. Researchers interested in watching how the roles of "guard" and "prisoner" influence subject reactions create a mock prison in the basement of a university building. Participants are assigned to the category of either "guard" or "prisoner," and they then live in that role for a two-week period in the mock prison.

6. A researcher interested in understanding how obedience to authority figures works devises an experiment under the guise of a teacher–learner scenario. In the

experiment, participants are told that they are going to deliver electrical shocks at increasing levels to a learner in another room when the learner does not correctly answer a question. The learner is a member of the research project, however, and the learner is never actually shocked. The goal of the project is to find out how long a participant will keep shocking the learner, even after the learner starts protesting, if the participant is encouraged by the researcher to continue with the shocks.

7. A researcher wants to determine whether media campaigns can discourage adolescents from drinking alcohol. To provide baseline measures of actual alcohol consumption, area adolescents are surveyed with the promise of confidentiality. Unknown to the adolescents, one of the strategies the researchers plan on using is publication of the data in the local newspaper. The strategy proves effective, with many parents clamping down on their adolescents' drinking behavior.

8. A researcher interested in understanding how undergraduates live at a university in the 21st century enrolls as a first-year college student. The researcher lives in the dorm after getting permission from her institutional review board (IRB). During the researcher's year as an undergraduate, she takes classes, makes friends, participates in intercollegiate sports, and joins various student organizations. The researcher also interviews undergraduate students living in her dorm or taking classes with her. She has her interview participants fill out a consent form, explaining that the researcher is conducting a study, which may be published, on perceptions of undergraduates. For the most part, however, the participants do not know that the researcher is actually a university professor and researcher.

9. Researchers interested in the effects that online reading has on moods purposefully manipulate what people see online. The team of researchers manipulates the reading material of 700,000 participants of a large social networking site, with none of the participants knowing the research is being conducted.

10. When a researcher does not get the results he wants, he starts to fabricate data. Over a 10-year period, he publishes a number of controversial studies in a variety of prominent journals around the world.

You may think to yourself that these research projects are ridiculous and no one would ever think of completing any of the listed projects. However, you would be wrong. All of these examples are actual research projects conducted during the 1900s and early 2000s. And all 10 of these studies are important to the history of ethics in research because each one has forced a reevaluation of how research ought to be conducted.

Tuskegee Syphilis Study

The first research scenario is commonly referred to as the Tuskegee Syphilis Study, which lasted from 1932 to 1972. In 1972, when it became clear that the US Public Health Services was involved in violating the basic human rights of the research participants, the American public was outraged, especially since penicillin, an effective treatment for syphilis, had been around and available since World War II. The researchers kept their research project going although adequate treatment options were available for the study participants. Ultimately, the US Senate held hearings on this study and other alleged health-care abuses, and Congress passed the National Research Act of 1974, established a policy for protecting human subjects with federal regulations, and created the National Commission for the Protection of Human Subjects of Biomedical and Behavioral Research. This commission went on to produce the Belmont Report, or the *Ethical Principles and Guidelines for the Protection of Human Subjects of Research* (https://www.hhs.gov/ohrp/regulations-and-policy/belmont-report/index.html).

Liquor Store Burglary Study

The second example, the staging of a liquor store burglary, was conducted by Bibb Latané and John Darley (1970). In this study, the two researchers staged a burglary to watch bystanders' reactions. One bystander responded by calling the police, who then showed up to the scene of the "crime" with guns drawn and ready to arrest the researchers. This research experiment could have ended badly for both the researchers and the bystanders.

Anonymous Sex Study

The third research example, conducted by Laud Humphreys (1975), examined what types of men engage in anonymous sex with other men in public restrooms. Humphreys's study was seen as both positive and negative by most researchers. Scholars believed Humphreys's ability to guard the actual identities of his research participants was to be applauded; however, his failure to get consent from his participants, his lying to the Department of Motor Vehicles to get his participants' home addresses, and his approaching the participants a year later in their home environments is indefensible. At the time Humphreys was conducting his research, however, homosexuality was still illegal in most states, with the penalty of jail time. Scholars look at Humphreys's research today and believe it could have caused his participants undue psychological, financial, and legal harm.

Wichita Jury Study

The fourth study mentioned is commonly referred to as the Wichita Jury Study of 1954. The researchers tape-recorded six jury deliberations in Wichita, Kansas, without the jurors' knowledge of their participation in the study. When this project came to light, the research was criticized by reporters and politicians around the country. This research project was seen as undermining the judicial system because, as Vaughan (1967) said, surveillance "threatens impartiality to the extent that it introduces any question of possible embarrassment, coercion, or other such considerations into the minds of actual jurors" (p. 72). Ultimately, the US Congress passed a law prohibiting the recording of jury deliberations.

Stanford Prison Study

The fifth example, the prison simulation study, was conducted by Philip Zimbardo, Craig Haney, Curtis Banks, and David Jaffe (1973) in a basement at Stanford University (http://www.prisonexp.org/). On the surface, this study may not appear controversial. However, the problems with this study lay not in what was being studied as much as in the problems that arose out of the methods used to study the phenomenon. When people were labeled "prisoners" or "guards," a cognitive shift occurred, and they confused who they were in real life with their new personas. Guards started to physically and psychologically abuse the prisoners. Prisoners either became rebellious and fought back against the guards or broke down and did the guards' wishes, even if those wishes were inhumane. The two-week experiment was closed after six days. Critics of this study believe the researchers did not do enough up front to guarantee the safety (both psychological and physical) of all the participants—guards and prisoners. This study is so widely known, a movie based on it, called *The Stanford Prison Experiment* and starring Billy Crudup as Dr. Philip Zimbardo, was released in July 2015.

Milgram Study

The sixth study, the Milgram study, was led by Stanley Milgram (1974), who wanted to understand how authority figures affected people's decisions to comply with requests or mandates. After World War II, many researchers started studying how Hitler had gotten many regular people to blindly follow orders and commit atrocities associated with the Holocaust. Although Milgram's study did not involve killing people, it did involve inflicting pain on another person. Participation in Milgram's study caused many people severe psychological discomfort because the participants believed they were inflicting pain on the learner in the other room. Of the 40 members of the general public paid to take part in the study, all complied with the order to administer shocks up to 300 volts (a marked, intense shock). As many as 26 participants responded obediently to the experimenter's urging to apply the maximum 450 volts. Videotapes of the Milgram Study show adult males crying while continuing to shock the learner in the other room. One participant was so overcome by stress, he had a convulsive seizure. Milgram and his colleagues had not thought about the long-term effects of the study on their participants' psyches.

Adolescent Alcohol Consumption Project

The seventh example, the adolescent alcohol consumption project, was a study conducted by Charles Atkin and reported by Garramone and Kennamer (1989). In this case, the question of ethics came in the form of the adolescents who felt deceived by the researcher. The adolescents had been open with the researcher about their alcohol consumption. When the researcher then published the results in the newspaper, many parents quickly clamped down on their children's behavior, and the adolescents felt their confidentiality had been violated. Atkin argued that the individual participant's confidentiality had not been violated but that the confidentiality of the group as a whole had been. However, the adolescents were taking part in illegal underage drinking, so the question could be posed, as Atkin did, "Does one have a *right* to do something illegal?" The publication of the research findings in the local paper enabled parents to prevent illegal adolescent behavior.

Professor Goes to School Undercover Study

The eighth example was a study published under the pseudonym Rebekah Nathan in 2005. The book was published under a pseudonym to protect the student participants who volunteered to be interviewed or who lived in the dorm or attended classes with the researcher. However, the researcher's real name, Cathy Small, was discovered long before her book hit the shelves. Although many researchers applauded Dr. Small's use of her anthropological background to study modern college students in their natural environment, in a way reminiscent of how Jane Goodall studied chimpanzees in their natural habitat, Small's methods have caused quite a stir in the academic community. Is it ethical to enter a college dorm under false pretenses and watch the students in their natural environment? Is it ethical to have students sign informed consent forms for participating in a research project when the participants do not know who the researcher is? The participants assumed that Small was a fellow undergraduate and that the chances of her research ever reaching print were unlikely, so were Small's participants really informed?

Facebook Newsfeed Manipulation Study

The ninth example hit home for many people in the summer of 2014, when it was found that Facebook had purposefully manipulated users' newsfeeds to see whether it affected their moods. Facebook manipulated the emotional level of newsfeeds to see whether users matched the emotional level of the newsfeeds they were reading. Basically, if someone read a happy newsfeed, would that person write more positive, upbeat posts her- or himself? Of course, the controversy was not that this study was conducted. The problem with this study was that none of the 700,000 people who were part of it knew they were being manipulated. Facebook's response was that they were well within their rights under the user agreements that all Facebook members agree to when joining and had done nothing unethical. Many people disagree with Facebook's stance on ethical research practices.

Facebook has not been the only social networking site to conduct research on its unknowing users. OkCupid, a dating website, admitted shortly after the Facebook study was revealed that it too had conducted research on its members. In the OkCupid study, the researchers wanted to see whether purposefully mismatching people effected love connections. OkCupid requires all users to complete a questionnaire and various questions to show compatibility between members (represented as a percentile score). OkCupid intentionally told people who received a low match (low percentage of compatibility) that they scored higher, and vice versa. People who use dating sites rely on these tools to meet dating partners and potential spouses, so they were disgruntled at having been lied to.

Dr. Diederik Stapel's Inconsistent Data

In the tenth ethical scenario, we have the interesting case of Dr. Diederik Stapel, a professor of psychology at Tilburg University. Three younger researchers who had been working with Dr. Stapel brought up ethical charges against the professor when they noticed inconsistencies within datasets, which led the researchers to think the data had been altered. Over the course of the investigation, researchers found cases of clear fraud in over 50 published research articles and 10 doctoral dissertations he shepherded. This case of academic fraud is the largest known incident to be caught.

All 10 of these studies are important to the history of ethics in research because each one has forced researchers to reevaluate how research ought to be conducted. This chapter explains the current state of ethics in research and how it applies to the field of communication. To examine ethics in communication research, we first explore the meaning of the term *ethics* in more detail, examine the three-prong test for ethics established by the 1979 Belmont Report (persons, beneficence, and justice), explain the purpose and place of IRBs in research, and pose some basic ethical questions for communication researchers.

DEFINING ETHICS

Although the study of ethical considerations dates back thousands of years, the modern analysis of **ethics** resides primarily in the understanding of two basic concepts: means and ends (McCroskey, Wrench, & Richmond, 2003; Wrench, McCroskey, & Richmond, 2008). **Means** are the tools or behaviors that one uses to achieve a desired outcome. Means can be either good or bad. **Ends** are those outcomes that one desires to achieve. Like means, ends can also be either good or bad. Figure 3.1 shows the four combinations of good and bad means and ends.

	ENDS	
	Good	*Bad*
MEANS *Good*	1. Ethical behavior	4. Subjective ethic
Bad	3. Machiavellian ethic	2. Unethical behavior

FIGURE 3.1
Ethical Matrix

Good Means–Good End: Ethical Behavior

The first quadrant of the ethical diagram in Figure 3.1 depicts what happens when someone has good means and a good end (**ethical behavior**). For example, a researcher wants to conduct a study to examine the influence that health campaign television advertisements have on positively changing health behaviors. The researcher brings in a group of participants and informs them of the project, obtains their consent, does not lie to them, and conducts the study in an ethical manner. The result of the study helps public health officials design appropriate mediated campaigns. In this example, the means and the ends are both positive. This would be considered ethical behavior or communication.

Bad Means–Bad End: Unethical Behavior

The second quadrant of the ethical diagram in Figure 3.1 depicts the exact opposite of the first quadrant, or what happens when someone has bad means and a bad end (**unethical behavior**). Some of the results seen in the Milgram study fall into this category. Researchers deceived their participants, and then one of the participants had a seizure because of the stress he was under during the experiment. Who knows how many of the participants had severe psychological trauma after the fact?

Bad Means–Good End: Machiavellian Ethic

The first two quadrants of Figure 3.1 are straightforward in their ethical understanding, but the other two quadrants in the ethical diagram are not as clear-cut. The third quadrant is an example of what happens when a person uses bad means to achieve a good end. This concept is referred to as the **Machiavellian ethic** because Niccolò Machiavelli believed that the ends justify the means. Machiavelli's greatest work, *The Prince*, written in 1513, created much controversy because he wrote that princes should retain absolute control of their lands and use any means necessary to carry out this end, including deceit. This notion was so outlandish that Pope Clement VIII described it as heretical.

This ethical perspective is still seen as outlandish and unethical by many today. As an example of how the Machiavelli ethic can be seen in a research situation, if a researcher overstates her or his findings (bad means) about the harmful nature of a drug to get people to stop doing it (good ends), is this researcher ethical? Some would consider this to be ethical behavior if it causes people to stop using a harmful substance, but others would say it is not ethical because the researcher had to lie to get the behavioral change.

Good Means–Bad End: Subjective Ethic

The fourth quadrant of the ethical diagram in Figure 3.1 examines what happens when a person uses good means that result in a bad end (**subjective ethic**). For example, a media researcher examines how to appropriately deliver communicated messages during a political campaign. A political candidate gets hold of the research and sees how he can use the study's findings to create manipulative messages that will get him elected. The researcher conducted the research in an ethical manner (the means), which led to the manipulation of the populace by a political candidate (the end). Is research ethical if it can later be used for harm? Many researchers who worked on the Manhattan Project, which created the atomic bomb, did not think about the loss of life and devastation their research would bring on the world.

THE BELMONT REPORT'S EFFECT ON RESEARCH ETHICS

Hopefully, by this point, you are starting to see that the world of research ethics is not completely clear-cut. Mostly, research is not innately ethical or unethical. Research can be methodologically sound or methodologically problematic, but determining whether a researcher is being ethical is complicated, and there are a number of opinions as to what constitutes ethical versus unethical research behavior. The US government has stepped in and provided a number of guidelines that researchers must follow by law.

In 1979, the National Commission for the Protection of Human Subjects of Biomedical and Behavioral Research completed the report entitled *Ethical Principles and Guidelines for the Protection of Human Subjects of Research*, which is commonly referred to as the **Belmont Report**. The Belmont Report devised three basic principles that all researchers using human subjects, regardless of research area, should be accountable for in their research. These three principles are informed consent, the principle of beneficence, and justice.

Informed Consent

This first part of the Belmont Report is commonly referred to as the ethical standard of "**informed consent**." Under this standard, *researchers should respect all possible research participants as autonomous individuals who have the capability of making decisions about their participation in a research project.* A researcher must make sure that her or his research participants are informed about their participation in the research process without coercion. Researchers should also make sure that possible participants are adequately informed about the purpose of the research, the voluntary nature of research, and the risks that may be associated with participation.

This ethical standard also has a second part that researchers must be aware of because not all possible participants have the ability to intellectually discern for themselves whether participation in a research endeavor is acceptable, so possible participants with "**diminished autonomy**" may need additional protections. You may wonder what types of people fall into the category of "diminished autonomy." The Belmont Report realized that children and adults who mentally cannot make informed decisions should not be allowed to volunteer for the research process. Under current standards, prisoners, fetuses, pregnant women, terminally ill individuals, students, employees, comatose patients, and persons under the age of 18 or who are legally given to the care of an adult because of severe developmental disorders or dementias fall into the diminished autonomy category as well. These populations are highly studied groups, so it's not that they cannot be studied, only that you must get informed consent from a legal guardian.

Principle of Beneficence

The second ethical principle spelled out in the Belmont Report is the need for researchers to *guarantee beneficence*. The **principle of beneficence** obligates researchers to make sure that during the research process they maximize possible benefits and minimize possible harms to the research participants themselves. One question asked of researchers when designing a research study is, "How will this study benefit the participants?" As a general response, the authors of this book think this question is extremely important, not only because ethically we should attempt to enhance our participants' lives while minimizing possible harms but also because good research should make people's lives better. Too often, researchers study small aspects of human communication that have no direct impact or bearing on real people's lives. For example, if research in the area of interpersonal relationships does not help people understand the interpersonal communication process better and lead to more successful interpersonal communication relationships, then what is the point of the research itself? You can peruse any discipline's journals and see many studies that make you wonder, "Why did they do that?!"

Ig Nobels & the *Annals of Improbable Research*

There is an association dedicated to ridiculous research that gives out the yearly Ig Nobel Prizes and publishes the interdisciplinary journal *Annals of Improbable Research*. Past Ig Nobel winners have fed Prozac to clams, examined the brain activity of locusts while watching *Star Wars*, noted the effect of country music on suicide, determined that when people concentrate they may miss the woman in the gorilla suit, and studied and classified belly button lint. To view the entire list of Ig Nobel winners dating back to 1991, you can visit the *Annals of Improbable Research* website at http://www.improb.com/. Please do not end up on the Ig Nobel list as a researcher. For all the humor this list provides, these research studies started as legitimate projects. To avoid creating a research project that is absurd, always ask yourself how your research could better the lives of your research participants.

Justice

The third and final Belmont Report ethical standard is that of **justice**. By justice, the authors of the report believed those who take the risks of research should receive the benefits from that research. As seen in the Tuskegee case, lower-income African American men were used as guinea pigs and received none of the benefits of the findings. Researchers today must make sure that risks and benefits are fairly distributed within society without bias. This is not to say that you cannot single out specific groups that you want to research, only that there must be a clear justification for this singling out and that the benefits will ultimately help that group. For example, maybe you want to examine differences in communication phenomena between patients and physicians when the patients and physicians are of different races. You may examine Hispanic patients' perceptions of Anglo/Caucasian (White) physicians. Although the risk of harm from this study would probably be minimal, every study contains some element of risk (either physical or psychological). The basic reasoning behind the notion of justice is that historically a lot of medical research was conducted on ethnically diverse groups or people on the lower rungs of the social hierarchy, but the benefits of the research only impacted those people at the top of the social hierarchy (primarily White males). Researchers must ask themselves whether some classes of people are overrepresented in their samples because of their availability, their compromised position, or their vulnerability. If the answer to these questions is "Yes," is there a clear justification for their inclusion, or were they selected inappropriately and will thus bear the brunt of the possible risks of the study? Mostly, this is not a problem that communication researchers have faced. Communication researchers have generally not conducted studies with risks beyond psychological discomfort. And although psychological discomfort can be serious, few studies in the field of communication would violate the justice principle of ethicality.

INSTITUTIONAL REVIEW BOARDS

By 1981, the US Department of Health and Human Services (HHS) and the US Food and Drug Administration approved a series of federal guidelines in Title 45, *Code of Federal Regulations*, Part 46 (45 CFR 46), which established the **Common Rule**. The Common Rule is a set of guidelines for the rights, welfare, and protection of research participants. In 2017, the HHS and its subsidiary, the Office of Human Research Protections (OHRP), released the first real update to the Common Rule. IRBs and researchers are still trying to make practical sense of some of the changes that have been made to the Common Rule. When applicable, we will highlight these changes throughout this section.

One of the most important aspects of the Common Rule was the requirement that any institution that receives federal funding and federal agencies themselves must establish an **Institutional Review Board** to review all research proposals for possible risks to research participants and to make sure that all research participants are informed of their rights as participants. To further understand the nature of IRBs, this section examines IRB basics, informed consent, and the IRB process.

IRB Basics

The IRB was established by 45 CFR 46 to make sure that past research atrocities like the Tuskegee experiment did not happen again on US soil. IRBs are charged with the task of ensuring that researchers take appropriate steps in protecting and informing research participants.

RESEARCH PARTICIPANT

According to the National Institutes of Health (NIH) (2002), a **research partici-pant** is "a living individual about whom a researcher obtains either: (1) data through intervention or interaction with the individual; or (2) identifiable private information" (p. 16). But what does this mean, exactly?

Data obtained through intervention are data that would occur in biomedical research situations. For example, one common medical publication is the case study. A medical case study is when a physician sees an interesting case and then writes an article for a medical journal detailing it. In this research instance, the information was obtained about the patient during a routine medical intervention, so for a physician to publish this information, he or she would need to obtain consent from either the patient or her or his legal guardian. Even if the physician does not use the person's name or photograph in the article, he or she is still obligated to obtain consent.

Data can also be acquired through interaction with the participant. If a communication researcher runs focus groups, investigates a culture, or hands out surveys, he or she is obtaining information about an individual through interaction, so the individual with whom the researcher is acting is a research participant.

Finally, a research participant is someone who could be identified through private information. For example, maybe you want to determine whether females and males differ in their likelihood of taking communication courses in high school, so you request to see high school transcripts for all incoming first-year students at your university. Although you may not think this is a big deal, when high school students apply for college and forward their transcripts to colleges, they are sending them to the college under the notion that the transcripts will be used to determine the applicants' eligibility for entrance to the university, not for a communication research project. High school transcripts are considered private information, and a researcher would have to obtain every first-year student's permission to use the transcripts for research purposes.

PAID PARTICIPATION

Another basic ethical dilemma that IRBs tackle is whether a participant should be paid for her or his participation. Researchers often offer some form of payment for an individual's participation in a research study. Whether the payment comes in the form of money or extra credit, payment is payment. There are no standard rules for how payments should work other than the notion that coercion of participants is wrong. For this reason, undergraduate students asked to participate in a research project are often offered extra credit for their participation. Since the extra credit points are above and beyond the points within the course itself, the "payment" is not coercion. Some IRBs will take "payment" a step further and require alternative extra credit opportunities for individuals who do not want to participate in the study itself. One common alternative activity is to have students read and abstract an article related to the study. If your IRB asks for an alternative exercise for individuals who do not want to participate, make sure the alternatives are equitable. For example, if it takes 10 minutes to fill out a survey, it should take 10 minutes to complete the alternative extra credit opportunity as well. Furthermore, some ethicists take it even further and actually argue that extra credit sways students to participate in a study, which theoretically will alter the results within a study because without the extra credit the students would not have participated.

ANONYMITY, PRIVACY, AND CONFIDENTIALITY

The last basic aspect of IRBs is the determination and understanding of anonymity, privacy, and confidentiality. Many researchers, when they are first starting research, often confuse the terms *anonymity*, *privacy*, and *confidentiality*. However, as far as an IRB is concerned, there are important distinctions among the three concepts.

ANONYMITY First, **anonymity** occurs when a researcher does not know who participated in a study or which results belong to which participants. For example, one of the authors of this text has done considerable work with online surveying. He sends out e-mails to various target groups requesting participation. Although this method of data gathering is problematic, it allows him to target groups that would otherwise be out of his reach. Individuals who then decide to participate fill out a survey on a website. Ultimately, the researcher has no way of knowing who filled out his survey, so the process is completely anonymous.

PRIVACY According to the NIH (2002), **privacy** is "defined in terms of having control over the extent, timing, and circumstances of sharing oneself (physically, behaviorally, or intellectually) with others" (p. 23). Research participants willingly give information about themselves to researchers with the understanding that the researcher will only share this information when necessary. For this process to work, researchers must make sure they keep the information learned from a research participant private.

Under the 1996 Health Insurance Portability and Accountability Act (HIPPA), privacy has entered a new stage of understanding. Under HIPPA, there are new classifications for what is **protected health information** (PHI), which is any individually identifiable health information (e.g., demographic data and biological specimens) that is transmitted or maintained by a covered entity (Bankert & Amdur, 2006). Although most communication researchers do not collect PHI, health communication researchers may analyze PHI data, so they should investigate HIPPA's effect on researchers in biomedical research to make sure they are in compliance with HIPPA statutes regarding research. For more on HIPPA responsibilities, talk to your campus's IRB.

We should also mention at this point that there are rules for research conducted in K–12 educational settings. Both the Family Educational Rights and Privacy Act (FERPA) and No Child Left Behind (NCLB) have other guidelines to which researchers conducting studies using K–12 participants also must adhere. We note these specific instances to further demonstrate the importance that the federal government has in overseeing social, behavioral, and educational research.

CONFIDENTIALITY Along with privacy, we must explore **confidentiality** because the two terms are interrelated. Confidentiality "pertains to the treatment of information an individual has disclosed in a relationship of trust and with the expectation that it will not, without permission, be divulged to others in ways that are inconsistent with the understanding of the original disclosure" (NIH, 2002, p. 24). Confidentiality is making sure you do not divulge any information about a participant that could lead to her or his identification. Some common ways of keeping confidentiality include removing signed consent forms from surveys, substituting codes for identifiers ("male" becomes "1" on a code sheet), properly disposing of computer data and other paper (generally with a shredder), limiting access to identifiable data (typically only to immediate investigators), and storing files in a secure space. It is also important to educate research assistants about confidentiality. Although most communication projects warrant little risk and confidentiality is not a huge problem, there are studies in communication that have examined more sensitive areas such as illegal, drug, and sexual behaviors that may require closer oversight by the IRB on a researcher's protection of her or his participants' confidentiality.

One area related to both privacy and confidentiality involves the European Union (EU) General Data Protection Regulation (GDPR). The EU GDPR is a new set of laws designed to protect an individual's personal data. These laws went into effect in Spring 2018, and many colleges and universities are still playing catch up to determine their own policies related to the GDPR as of the publication date of this book. The basic spirit of the GDPR is that people within the European Economic Area (EEA) should have the ability to control their private data. This law applies to individuals who live in the EEA or are visiting the EEA when data is collected about them. If the data is truly anonymous, then the GDPR does not apply. However, if a researcher is using confidential data, then the GDPR does apply and the researcher must follow the law or face a very steep penalty (currently 20 million Euros [$23,335,040] or 4% of the organization's financial year worldwide annual revenue). In this case, the organization would be the college or university that oversees the researcher collecting data. For our purposes in this text, we wanted to point out that research in foreign countries often varies with regard to these issues and the laws that govern them. If you are conducting any kind of research that involves non-US based participants, it's important to follow both the guidelines of the US and those of the foreign country. For more information, you should consult with your local IRB.

Communication Researchers and IRBs

The August 2005 issue of the *Journal of Applied Communication* focused on the process of communication researchers interacting with IRBs. Although the issue contained many horror stories, most criticisms were met with positive experiences as well. One interesting narrative (pp. 228–230) tells an experience of being subpoenaed by a district attorney. The researcher was investigating what types of evidence jurors used to render decisions and had conducted interviews with various jurors after the conclusion of a number of trials. After the interviews were finished, the researcher received a subpoena in which the defense attorney wanted to ask the researcher whether "the jurors had said anything to me about their verdict in the case that did not pertain to the facts presented at the trial" (p. 229). The researcher immediately called the university IRB because the participants had filled out a consent form guaranteeing confidentiality and the researcher did not know what to do. In the article, the researcher recalled the argument made on her/his behalf by a university attorney. The researcher "had a moral and contractual duty to not answer questions about what the jurors told me. The jurors would be put in jeopardy if I was forced to disclose the confidential information they provided" (p. 229). Although the judge in this case agreed with the defendant (the researcher), this is not always the case. Unfortunately, researchers are not granted a privileged status such as patient–physician, lawyer–client, or spouses when it comes to information. In essence, researchers can be compelled to disclose what was learned or be incarcerated for contempt of court. However, federal provisions under the Public Health Act can allow you to petition the Secretary of Health and Human Services for a Certificate of Confidentiality. A **Certificate of Confidentiality** enables a researcher engaged in "biomedical, behavioral, clinical, or other research (including research on mental health and on the use of and effect of alcohol and other psychoactive drugs) to protect the privacy of individuals who are the subjects of such research" (NIH, 2002, p. 25). If you are ever researching a highly sensitive topic that involves illegal activity, you will want to work closely with your IRB to see whether a Certificate of Confidentiality is possible.

You can also examine the Office of Human Research Protections website containing the International Compilation of Human Research Standards – https://www.hhs.gov/ohrp/international/compilation-human-research-standards/index.html

Informed Consent

Throughout this chapter, we have mentioned the need to inform participants about the nature of the research and any possible risks associated with that research. This section goes into further detail about the nature of informed consent and how to prepare a consent document for distribution during a research study.

Informed consent is a "person's voluntary agreement, based upon adequate knowledge and understanding of relevant information, to participate in research" (NIH, 2002, p. 64). In essence, a researcher must provide any potential participants with adequate information about the purpose of the study, how long the study will last, experimental procedures, alternatives, known risks, and any known benefits. The researcher must also explain to participants how they can ask questions about the research project and what their rights as research participants are. Figure 3.2 is an example of an informed consent document used by one of the authors of this text in a project examining how personalized coaching impacted weight loss.

The consent document in Figure 3.2 contains a great deal of information in a brief format. Let's examine the various parts of the document itself. The consent form is clearly broken down into different sections to make it easier for participants to follow the general idea of what is being presented. For example, note that the reasoning for the study is provided only in the section titled "Why Is This Study Being Done?" Confidentiality, on the other hand, is explained in the section titled "What About Confidentiality?" By keeping these sections short and titled, readers are more likely to understand what they are getting into when they agree to participate.

COMMON PARTS OF A CONSENT DOCUMENT

As we've discussed, consent documents are fairly standardized in modern research to ensure that participants know what they are getting themselves into. This section is going to explore the main parts of a consent document required under 45 CFR 46.

CONCISE SUMMARY The first part of a consent form is the concise summary of research. The concise summary is an addition to the consent process recommended with the 2017 changes to the Common Rule. According to the Common Rule, the concise summary should have five distinct parts: (1) a statement that this is a research project and participation is voluntary; (2) a summary of the research activity, including duration, procedures, and purpose; (3) an explanation of possible risks, (4) an explanation of possible benefits; and (5) a description of alternate procedures and/or treatments if they exist.

FIGURE 3.2
Informed Consent
Document—Signature
Required

Concise Summary

This is a research study to find out the impact a wellness coach has on weight loss and weight loss motivation. Participation in this study is completely voluntary.

Participants will undergo counseling with a certified wellness coach (30-minute sessions) two times per week for eight weeks for a total of 16 visits. After each coaching session, participants will be asked to complete a survey. Total study duration is about two months.

The greatest risks of this study include the possibility of injury during any physical activity recommended by the wellness coach and loss of confidentiality.

Although not guaranteed, it is possible that participants who engage with their wellness coaches and follow their instructions could benefit from their participation by losing weight.

If you are interested in learning more about this study, please continue to read below.

Study Title: Communicative Interactions Between Clients and Wellness Coaches

Name of Principal Investigator: Name of Researcher
Department: Communication Studies
Position: Associate Professor

Contact Name and Phone Number for Questions/Problems: Researcher's Name, (XXX) XXX-XXXX

This is a communication research study. This research study includes only participants who choose to take part. Please take your time to make your decision. If necessary, feel free to discuss your participation with any necessary friends and family. You are being asked to take part in this study because you are currently undergoing weight loss coaching.

WHY IS THIS STUDY BEING DONE?

I am conducting research to examine the impact that your wellness coach has had on weight loss and weight loss motivation. As a health communication researcher, I am interested in what you have to say about your wellness coach. I am specifically interested in the interpersonal relationship you have developed and continue to develop with your coach.

HOW MANY PEOPLE WILL TAKE PART IN THE STUDY?

About 200 people will take part in this study.

WHAT IS INVOLVED IN THE STUDY?

If you agree to participate in this study, you will be assigned a wellness coach who will work with you to achieve your weight loss goals for a period of eight weeks. You will meet with your wellness coach two times per week during the course of the study.

Each week, you will be asked to fill out a survey that contains basic demographic information (name, starting weight, weight loss goal, weight loss to date, current weight, and height).

After you have completed the survey, please return it to the locked box labeled "Research Surveys" in the waiting room. No one other than the principal investigator of this project has access to this locked box.

HOW LONG WILL I BE IN THE STUDY?

Completing the survey will take approximately 15 to 25 minutes.

This study is 100 percent voluntary, so you can stop participating at any time.

Continued

FIGURE 3.2
Continued

WHAT ARE THE RISKS OF THE STUDY?

The risks involved in this study are no more than those you would encounter in your everyday life.

Wellness coaches will be making recommendations about dietary and physical activity. There is always a certain amount of risk associated with starting and engaging in an exercise regimen. Always consult with your physician before starting an exercise program. For more information about risks, please feel free to contact the principal investor whose contact information is provided on this document.

ARE THERE BENEFITS TO TAKING PART IN THE STUDY?

If you agree to take part in this research, there may or may not be direct benefit to you. However, if you improve your diet and/or physical activity, weight loss could occur.

We hope the information learned from this research will benefit others who are attempting to lose weight by demonstrating the strategies and tactics that weight loss coaches can utilize to successfully encourage weight loss.

WHAT ABOUT CONFIDENTIALITY?

Efforts will be made to keep your personal information confidential. The survey attached contains no place for your name or other specific identifying information beyond those basic demographics at the top of the survey.

Furthermore, the researcher will not provide the wellness organization with a copy of your completed survey. The wellness organization will only have access to aggregated data analyses at the completion of the study.

However, we cannot guarantee absolute confidentiality. Your personal information may be disclosed if required by law.

WHAT ARE THE COSTS?

Taking part in this study may lead to added costs to you.
You will receive no payment for taking part in this study.

WHAT ARE MY RIGHTS AS A PARTICIPANT?

Taking part in this study is voluntary. Refusal to participate will involve no penalty or loss of benefits to which you are otherwise entitled. You may choose not to take part, may leave the study at any time, or not answer research questions that you consider inappropriate. Leaving the study will not result in any penalty or loss of benefits to which you are entitled. And participation will in no way affect the care and coaching you receive from the wellness organization.

We will tell you about new information that may affect your welfare or willingness to stay in this study.

WHOM DO I CALL IF I HAVE QUESTIONS OR PROBLEMS?

For questions about the study or a research-related injury, contact the researcher(s) at (XXX) XXX-XXXX or via e-mail at name@genericaccount.edu.

For questions about your rights as a research participant, contact the University's Name Institutional Review Board (which is a group of people who review the research to protect your rights) at (XXX) XXX-XXXX or via e-mail at irb@genericaccount.edu.

OTHER INFORMATION:

The Institutional Review Board at University's Name has determined that this research meets the criteria for human subjects according to Federal guidelines. You will get a copy of this form.

FIGURE 3.2
Continued

CONSENT:

I have read or have had read to me the preceding information describing the study. All my questions have been answered to my satisfaction, and this form is being signed voluntarily by me, indicating my desire to participate in this study. I am not waiving any of my legal rights by signing this form. I understand I will receive a copy of this consent form.

Printed Name of Participant	Signature	Date

Printed Name of Person Obtaining Consent	Signature	Date

Source: Based on the IRB Consent form created by the State University of New York at New Paltz

CONTACT INFORMATION, THE WORD "RESEARCH," AND GENERAL PURPOSE OF THE STUDY The researcher provides her or his contact information, followed by a short statement that indicates that he or she is asking the individual to participate in a *research* project. We added the emphasis in the previous sentence to the word "research" because most colleges and universities require that the topic sentence clearly state an individual is being approached about a research project. After this introductory material, there is a brief section where the researcher explains the general purpose of the study. The goal of this section is to help a participant determine whether he or she wants to participate and to explain the purpose of the study. Another aspect that helps someone decide whether he or she wants to participate involves the predicted number of participants. If a researcher plans on engaging only two or three participants, then guaranteeing confidentiality is almost impossible. In a large sample size—for example, 200 participants—guaranteeing confidentiality is much easier for a researcher.

STEPS INVOLVED IN THE STUDY The next section explains what is involved in the study itself. In this paragraph, the researcher explains the three steps involved in participation. First, the wellness coach will complete some basic demographic behavior. Second, the participant completes the survey. Lastly, the participant places the completed survey in the locked box in the wellness organization's lobby. For the purposes of a survey, a consent form is generally direct with regard to the procedure. However, if a research study is an experiment, a researcher would need to discuss all aspects related to the experimentation, including issues involving how participants are randomized into the different groups and any procedures to be conducted (more on this in Chapter 13).

LENGTH OF TIME IN THE STUDY In addition to the basic information about what is expected of a participant, a researcher must explain to the participant how long he or she will be involved in the study. Some studies involve completing a 15-minute survey, but others could involve years of participation (as is often seen in large clinical trials). The participant is informed that her or his participation is voluntary and that he or she may quit at any time during the study. This sentence is important because many participants believe that once they start they cannot stop, which simply is not the case. Legally, a person has the right to opt out of research at any point during a project. Researchers prefer for participants to stay through the entire project, of course, but researchers must respect an individual participant's wishes to stop participating in the study.

RISKS Next, the consent form discusses any aspects related to the "risks" of the study itself. A large sample survey collected anonymously poses "below minimal risk," or when the participant is exposed to no more risk than he or she confronts in her or his daily life. However, other studies can involve massive amounts of risk. One of the basic goals of an IRB member is to weigh the risks against the benefits, which is why the benefits to both the individual participant and society are presented. If a study poses below minimal risk, then there does not need to be a direct benefit to the individual participants. If a study does pose a risk, then the researcher must explain how being exposed to the risk is beneficial to both the participant and society.

CONFIDENTIALITY The next part of a consent document includes explaining to participants information about the confidentiality of the study. In this example, the researchers explain that the survey is anonymous and that the wellness organization will only see the analyzed results from the data, not the individual surveys. If you ever find yourself working for an organization conducting research, we strongly recommend that you make this process part of your understanding from the beginning. By not giving the organization the participants' completed surveys, you can make sure, as a researcher, that the organization cannot retaliate against a participant if the organization does not like her or his responses on the survey. The consent form further explains that participation—or lack of participation—will not affect an individual's standing with the organization the researcher was using to conduct the study. This line is common in research involving students and, in that case, would read something like, "Your participation in this study is completely voluntary, and will in no way affect your grade or athletic standing." This clause informs a participant that whether he or she participates in a research project, the participation will not negatively affect her or his grade or prevent her or him from participating in athletics.

COSTS OR PAYMENTS TO THE PARTICIPANT Next, the consent form articulates that there are no costs to the individual participating and that the individual is not getting paid for her or his participation in the study. If there is a cost, or if a participant is getting remunerated in some fashion, then the researcher must spell out how this process would work. For example, a study recently reviewed by one of this text's authors for IRB approval was broken into five phases. At each phase of participation, the participants were given an Amazon.com gift card with increasing values (Time 1, $5; Time 2, $10; . . ., Time 5, $25). The consent form clearly stated that if a participant dropped out of the study, he or she would be paid for their actual participation but not future participation.

PARTICIPANT RIGHTS The final section on a consent form reiterates the importance of the participants' rights, followed by a paragraph explaining how to contact both the researcher and the IRB if the participant has any questions. Researchers want participants to know what their rights are up front in order to make sure that participants do not feel coerced into participating in a study.

GETTING CONSENT The final section of the consent form is dedicated to the actual giving of consent by the participant. If the participant decides to participate, then he or she signs the consent statement at the bottom of the form, fills out the questionnaire, and returns the whole packet to the collection box. The actual consent box that a participant signs is loaded with legal terminology ensuring the participant understands the nature of the research, is volunteering to be a participant, understands that the university is not liable for any injury, is older than 18 years (or not a child), has the right to stop participating, and has been given the option of taking a copy of the consent form with her or him. In addition to getting a signature from the participant, the person who is obtaining consent (usually the researcher, but in this case the wellness coach) also signs the consent form.

DO CONSENT DOCUMENTS REALLY WORK?

This discussion of consent forms is based on the notion that a participant actively reads a consent form and understands the material provided within it. However, in a study conducted by McNutt et al. (2008), the researchers examin(ed) the extent to which participants read consent forms. The researchers timed the participants in a variety of different research studies. Additionally, McNutt et al. asked the individual obtaining consent to predict how accurately the participant read the consent form and interpreted its meaning. McNutt et al. found that the average participant spends about 30 seconds reading a consent form. However, the individual obtaining consent predicted that the participants read the consent form completely 38% to 74% of the time (depending on the sample). Most educated people cannot read and consider a consent form in 30 seconds, so there are ethical questions about how researchers obtain consent. Furthermore, we must always question the readability of consent forms. Depending on the participant population, highly technical consent forms may meet the requirements of an IRB, but may impede an individual's ability to decide whether he or she wants to participate in a research study. Ethical researchers must think through how they obtain consent in an effort to maximize the understandability of the study for their participants.

WAIVER OF CONSENT

Although Figure 3.2 is the most standard consent form one will see in research, another form is often used that does not require an individual to sign something for consent. Researchers can request permission from an IRB to *not* have a signed consent for one of two reasons:

1. A signed consent form would be the only record linking the participant and the research, which could result in potential harm resulting from breach of confidentiality. In this case, each participant will be asked whether he or she wants documentation linking her- or himself with research, and the participant's wishes will govern.
2. The research presents no more than minimal risk of harm to the participants and involves no procedures for which written consent is normally required outside of the research context.

In these cases, the following text is added as a paragraph to the consent form seen in Figure 3.2 instead of a signed statement:

> Returning this questionnaire certifies that you have read and understand this consent form and voluntarily agree to be a participant in the research described. Additionally, you agree that known risks for your participation have been explained to your satisfaction and you understand that no compensation is available from [your university's name] and its employees for any injury resulting from your participation in this research. Participation in this study also certifies that you are 18 years of age or older. Please understand that you may discontinue

participation at any time without penalty or loss of any benefits to which you may otherwise be entitled.

Note that the same basic information that was in the signed consent form is available in this statement. But in this version, the participant is not required to sign off on her or his understanding of the consent. Instead, active participation in the research endeavor is a sign of informed consent.

HANDLING DECEPTION DURING THE CONSENT PROCESS

There is one tricky ethical dilemma that must come under scrutiny in the informed consent process—deception. What if telling the participants about the nature of the research will skew their responses? For example, in the study conducted by Stanley Milgram discussed at the beginning of this chapter, he clearly did not inform his research participants that he was studying the effects of how authority figures impact people's decisions to comply with requests or mandates. Instead, he told his participants that they were taking part in a study designed to examine negative feedback (electrical shocks) on the learning process. Should deception be allowed?

Lying about the purpose of the study to receive a good study result is a clear example of the Machiavellian ethic discussed earlier in this chapter. And IRBs do not handle deception in a uniform manner at every college or university. If you are planning on using deception within your study, make sure you talk to your IRB before developing your IRB proposal (more on this in the next section) to learn what they will and will not allow. If you are planning on deceiving when obtaining informed consent, you will need to debrief your participants at the conclusion of their participation in your study. In the debrief, you will need to explain to your participants that they were deceived, what the purpose of your deception was, and what the nature of the project really is. You may think to yourself, *well, I won't actually lie to my participants; I just may not be as complete as I should be in explaining the nature of the project itself.* Under typical IRB guidelines, however, if your disclosure is incomplete, you will need to debrief your participants as well.

IRB Processes

This section explains the IRB process to which researchers who use human subjects must adhere. As mentioned earlier, the development of the IRB was set forth in 45 CFR 46 in 1981 as a result of the Belmont Report. Every university will have an Office of Research Compliance, Office of Funded Projects, Office of Institutional Research, or some other name where the university's IRB will be housed (we will be using the word "university" or "college," but this section also applies to IRBs in other locations like foundations, research firms, or governmental agencies). Federal regulations mandate that the IRB must have at least five members from various backgrounds. Membership on the IRB should be diverse and often will include both university personnel and members of the community (at least one nonuniversity member). If IRBs will be overseeing research involving protected groups (children, pregnant women, prisoners, or physically/mentally disabled persons), then at least one member of the IRB must have a specialization in working with these populations.

BASIC IRB FUNCTIONS

Each IRB oversees the human subject research conducted at that university. You will notice that we are using *human subject* here instead of *participant* because the federal guidelines use this term. At the most basic level, IRBs ensure that human subjects' rights are protected, and that informed consent occurs in all research. To do this, IRBs have several jobs they must complete.

REVIEW PROTOCOLS First, IRBs must review the full protocols for every planned research study and then decide whether the research protocol exposes participants to unreasonable risks. An IRB assigns a research protocol to a trained member of the IRB, who then evaluates the protocol and determines whether the benefits of the study outweigh the potential risks. This process can take weeks to complete, depending on the complexity of the case and the guidelines for IRB members established by a college or university.

REVIEW ONGOING HUMAN SUBJECTS PROJECTS Second, the IRB periodically reviews all research projects already underway to make sure that human protections are still in place. Research protocols that warrant a full-board review (more on this in a moment) must undergo, at a bare minimum, an annual review. One of the 2017 changes to the Common Rule is that many expedited studies will no longer need the annual review. Always double check with your institution's IRB to see if your study will need an annual review. Research projects that have higher levels of risk (commonly seen in biomedical studies) may undergo reviews even more often.

INVESTIGATE ADVERSE EVENTS Third, IRBs should examine adverse events (unexpected harms that result from a study), interim findings, and any recent literature in the project area that could force a change in the research protocol. Unfortunately, many types of research are dangerous and could cause unforeseen harm to an individual. If and when this happens during a study, a researcher is obligated to report the adverse event to the IRB, which will then investigate the research protocol to see whether changes must be made or if the project must be shut down completely. Some IRBs will also want to see your findings along the way. In short-term studies (those lasting less than five years), IRBs may just want to see the demographic makeup of your participants on a yearly basis. For longer studies (those longer than five years), IRBs may want more detailed updates along the way. IRBs should also be up to date on current trends in research that could force a change in a research protocol. Again, although not common in communication research, changes made as a result of new research are more common in biomedical research.

INVESTIGATE PROTOCOL VIOLATIONS The fourth responsibility of the IRB is to investigate suspected or alleged protocol violations, complaints expressed by research participants, or violations of institutional policies. In essence, an IRB must make sure that the researcher is doing what he or she said he or she was going to do. There are a range of different types of protocol violations that can occur. Some can be relatively minor missteps by researchers, like failing to inform the IRB if they collected more data than they had originally predicted. Other protocol violations could include using subjects not in the original protocol, bullying subjects into participation, not getting prior approval for studies, and so on. The IRB will investigate suspected protocol violations and then make a recommendation to the campus individual who oversees research. If the violation is serious enough, the IRB may be required by law to report the violation to the OHRP, a division of the HHS that oversees research in the US federal government.

ENSURE TRAINING IN RESEARCH ETHICS The last responsibility of the IRB is to make sure that federal guidelines dictating that all individuals conducting research undergo training are followed. Most colleges and universities today will require Collaborative Institutional Training Initiative (CITI) training before you can conduct a study (https://www.citiprogram.org/). CITI training is divided into modules that introduce researchers to the nature of ethics and includes much of the same content discussed in this chapter.

Advanced IRB Functions

Beyond their basic responsibilities, IRBs have the authority to engage in four different behaviors. First, university IRBs have the ability to approve, disapprove, or terminate all research activities at the university. Second, IRBs have the ability to require modifications to research protocols (both new and previously approved protocols). Third, IRBs have the ability to require researchers to divulge more information than that mandated in 45 CFR 46 if the IRB believes additional information will add to the protections of participants' rights and safety. Finally, IRBs have the ability to require or waive informed consent.

LEVELS OF IRB REVIEW

Before you get to the IRB stage of a research project, you will be required by your university to fill out an IRB protocol. Every university has the ability to create its own unique IRB protocol, which is adjusted to its specific needs. Some IRB protocols are one page in length, and others could be from 30 to 50 pages in length, depending on the nature of your project and the specific documentation your IRB wants to see. Once your IRB protocol is completed, you will generally be asked what kind of review your project should receive. There are three levels of review that IRBs have at their disposal: exempt, expedited, and full board.

EXEMPT REVIEW The term **exempt review** technically means you are exempted from undergoing an IRB review that adheres to the guidelines specified in 45 CFR 46. Having an exempt review does not mean that you do not have to submit your IRB protocol; only a trained IRB member or the IRB's designee can make determinations of exemption. However, some institutions will have different sets of IRB protocol documents for this level of review. Other institutions will only have one set of IRB protocol documents for all three levels of review. Again, be sure to check with your individual institution about the IRB process. This chapter is designed to introduce you to the generalities of ethics in research and the IRB process, not to be a definitive answer on how your university's IRB ought to run.

The exempt review can be granted to a research protocol if the project contains below-minimal-risk research and is exempted from federal regulations concerning IRB review and approval. In 45 CFR 46, the 2017 categories for research exemptions were created, as seen in Figure 3.3.

Much of the research that is conducted by communication researchers will be exempt under 45 CFR 46.104(d)(2)(iii). Specifically, much communication research will fall under the 45 CFR 46.104(d)(2)(iii) exemption because communication research relies heavily on survey procedures, interview procedures, and/or observation of public behavior. However, just because you think your research will fall under Category 2 for exempt research does not mean that your IRB will agree with you. Many researchers will think their research is exempt, only to have their research bumped up to the next level of review, the expedited review.

EXPEDITED REVIEW The **expedited review** (45 CFR 46.110) is designed for research projects that involve no more than minimal risk, do not include intentional deception, do not utilize vulnerable populations, and include appropriate consent procedures. Figure 3.4 contains the 15 categories for expedited review introduced in the 2017 revision of the Common Rule. Notice that most of the categories relate to biological specimens. For social scientists, the most commonly used expedited categories are 9, 10, 11, and 13.

FIGURE 3.3
Exempt Categories

The final rule exemptions subject to this limited IRB review requirement are:

Exempt Category 1: Research in Established or Commonly Accepted Educational Settings

Research conducted in established or commonly accepted educational settings that specifically involves normal educational practices that are not likely to adversely impact students' opportunity to learn required educational content or the assessment of educators who provide instruction. This includes most research on regular and special education instructional strategies, and research on the effectiveness of or the comparison among instructional techniques, curricula, or classroom management methods.

Exempt Category 2: Educational Tests, Surveys, Interviews, & Observations of Public Behavior

Research that only includes interactions involving educational tests (cognitive, diagnostic, aptitude, achievement), survey procedures, interview procedures, or observation of public behavior (including visual or auditory recording) if at least one of the following criteria is met:

(i) The information obtained is recorded by the investigator in such a manner that the identity of the human subjects cannot readily be ascertained, directly or through identifiers linked to the subjects;

(ii) Any disclosure of the human subjects' responses outside the research would not reasonably place the subjects at risk of criminal or civil liability or be damaging to the subjects' financial standing, employability, educational advancement, or reputation; or

(iii) The information obtained is recorded by the investigator in such a manner that the identity of the human subjects can readily be ascertained, directly or through identifiers linked to the subjects, and an IRB conducts a limited IRB review.

Exempt Category 3: Benign Behavioral Interventions in Conjunction with the Collection of Information from Adult Subjects

Research involving benign behavioral interventions in conjunction with the collection of information from an adult subject through verbal or written responses (including data entry) or audiovisual recording if the subject prospectively agrees to the intervention and information collection and at least one of the following criteria is met:

(i) The information obtained is recorded by the investigator in such a manner that the identity of the human subjects cannot readily be ascertained, directly or through identifiers linked to the subjects;

(ii) Any disclosure of the human subjects' responses outside the research would not reasonably place the subjects at risk of criminal or civil liability or be damaging to the subjects' financial standing, employability, educational advancement, or reputation; or

(iii) The information obtained is recorded by the investigator in such a manner that the identity of the human subjects can readily be ascertained, directly or through identifiers linked to the subjects, and an IRB conducts a limited IRB review.

For the purpose of this provision, benign behavioral interventions are brief in duration, harmless, painless, not physically invasive, not likely to have a significant adverse lasting impact on the subjects, and the investigator has no reason to think the subjects will find the interventions offensive or embarrassing. Provided all such criteria are met, examples of such benign behavioral interventions would include having the subjects play an online game, having them solve puzzles under various noise conditions, or having them decide how to allocate a nominal amount of received cash between themselves and someone else.

Continued

FIGURE 3.3
Continued

If the research involves deceiving the subjects regarding the nature or purposes of the research, this exemption is not applicable unless the subject authorizes the deception through a prospective agreement to participate in research in circumstances in which the subject is informed that he or she will be unaware of or misled regarding the nature or purposes of the research.

Exempt Category 4: Secondary Research for Which Consent Is Not Required
Secondary research uses of identifiable private information or identifiable biospecimens, if at least one of the following criteria is met:

(i) The identifiable private information or identifiable biospecimens are publicly available;

(ii) Information, which may include information about biospecimens, is recorded by the investigator in such a manner that the identity of the human subjects cannot readily be ascertained directly or through identifiers linked to the subjects, the investigator does not contact the subjects, and the investigator will not re-identify subjects;

(iii) The research involves only information collection and analysis involving the investigator's use of identifiable health information when that use is regulated under 45 CFR parts 160 and 164, subparts A and E, for the purposes of "health care operations" or "research" as those terms are defined at 45 CFR 164.501 or for "public health activities and purposes" as described under 45 CFR 164.512(b); or

(iv) The research is conducted by, or on behalf of, a Federal department or agency using government-generated or government-collected information obtained for non-research activities, if the research generates identifiable private information that is or will be maintained on information technology that is subject to and in compliance with applicable federal privacy standards found in the E-Government Act, Privacy Act, and the Paperwork Reduction Act.

Exempt Category 5: Research and Demonstration Projects that Are Conducted or Supported by a Federal Department or Agency

Research and demonstration projects that are conducted or supported by a Federal department or agency, or otherwise subject to the approval of department or agency heads (or the approval of the heads of bureaus or other subordinate agencies that have been delegated authority to conduct the research and demonstration projects), and that are designed to study, evaluate, improve, or otherwise examine public benefit or service programs, including procedures for obtaining benefits or services under those programs, possible changes in or alternatives to those programs or procedures, or possible changes in methods or levels of payment for benefits or services under those programs. Such projects include, but are not limited to, internal studies by Federal employees, and studies under contracts or consulting arrangements, cooperative agreements, or grants. Exempt projects also include waivers of otherwise mandatory requirements using authorities such as sections 1115 and 1115A of the Social Security Act, as amended. Each Federal department or agency conducting or supporting the research and demonstration projects must establish, on a publicly accessible Federal website or in such other manner as the department or agency head may determine, a list of the research and demonstration projects that the Federal department or agency conducts or supports under this provision. The research or demonstration project must be published on this list prior to commencing the research involving human subjects.

FIGURE 3.3
Continued

Exempt Category 6: Taste and Food Quality Evaluation and Consumer Acceptance Studies

Taste and food quality evaluation and consumer acceptance studies: If wholesome foods without additives are consumed, or if a food is consumed that contains a food ingredient at or below the level and for a use found to be safe, or agricultural chemical or environmental contaminant at or below the level found to be safe, by the Food and Drug Administration or approved by the Environmental Protection Agency or the Food Safety and Inspection Service of the U.S. Department of Agriculture.

Exempt Category 7: Storage or Maintenance for Secondary Use for Which Broad Consent Is Required

Storage or maintenance for secondary research for which broad consent is required: Storage or maintenance of identifiable private information or identifiable biospecimens for potential secondary research use if an IRB conducts a limited IRB review and makes the determinations required by §.111(a)(8).

Exempt Category 8: Secondary Research for Which Broad Consent Is Required

Secondary research for which broad consent is required: Research involving the use of identifiable private information or identifiable biospecimens for secondary research use, if the following criteria are met:

(i) Broad consent for the storage, maintenance, and secondary research use of the identifiable private information or identifiable biospecimens was obtained in accordance with §.116(a)(1) through (4), (a)(6), and (d);

(ii) Documentation of informed consent or waiver of documentation of consent was obtained in accordance with §.117;

(iii) An IRB conducts a limited IRB review and makes the determination required by §.111(a)(7) and makes the determination that the research to be conducted is within the scope of the broad consent referenced in paragraph (d)(8)(i) of this section; and 479

(iv) The investigator does not include returning individual research results to subjects as part of the study plan. This provision does not prevent an investigator from any legal requirements to return individual research results.

Source: https://www.federalregister.gov/documents/2017/01/19/2017-01058/federal-policy-for-the-protection-of-human-subjects

Do not think that just because you are collecting surveys your project is automatically exempt. Surveys that ask people highly sensitive information (illegal behavior, substance use, or sexual behavior) may be reviewed at this level depending on the specific guidelines of the college or university. The OHRP creates the guidelines for the HHS within the federal government as a baseline. Academic institutions have the right to interpret these guidelines differently, so do not think that just because a study was approved as exempt at one institution a similar study will be approved as exempt at a different institution. If the research is controversial, beyond a minimal risk, or involves confidentiality problems, the IRB chair will require that a research protocol be examined by the full IRB.

FIGURE 3.4
Expedited Categories

Health and Human Services Secretary's List of Expedited Research Categories:

1. Research involving the use of drugs and medical devices only when condition (a) or (b) is met.
   a. Research involving use of "over-the-counter" drugs, when used within their approved indications and dosages, and exempt from the IND requirements of 21 CFR 312.
   b. Research involving use of medical devices exempt from the IDE requirements of 21 CFR 812.1.

2. The collection of blood specimens for research purposes using techniques consistent with routine clinical practice to minimize pain and risk of infection and within the following limits:
   (a) from adults whose health will not be adversely affected by the blood draws who weigh at least 50 kg, the amounts collected should not exceed 550 ml in an 8-week period; or (b) from children and other adults whose health will not be adversely affected by the blood draws, the amounts collected should not exceed the lesser of 150 ml or 3 ml per kg in an 8-week period. Examples: Finger stick, heel stick, ear stick, venipuncture, collection of blood from an indwelling peripheral venous catheter (not including a PICC line) placed for research purposes, or collection of blood from an indwelling catheter already in place for clinical purposes.

3. Prospective collection of biological specimens, excluding blood, for research purposes by noninvasive means and not requiring sedation for research purposes. Examples: (a) tissues and fluids that the body produces continuously or sheds as a normal process (including hair, nails), which are collected in a non-disfiguring manner; (b) deciduous teeth at time of exfoliation; (c) excreta and external secretions (including sweat, urine, stool); (d) uncannulated saliva; (e) placenta removed at delivery; (f) amniotic fluid obtained at the time of rupture of the membrane prior to or during labor; (g) supra- and subgingival dental plaque and calculus, provided the collection procedure is not more invasive than routine prophylactic scaling of the teeth and the process is accomplished in accordance with accepted prophylactic techniques; (h) mucosal and skin cells collected by buccal scraping or mouth washings; (i) sputum collected after saline mist nebulization.

4. Prospective collection of biological specimens, excluding blood, for research purposes by minimally invasive means and not requiring sedation for research purposes. Examples: (a) tissues from non-facial, non-genital skin punch biopsy with allowable local anesthesia and limited to 2mm in diameter and not requiring sutures; (b) Specimens collected by swab (nasal, oral, urethral, vaginal, rectal); (c) teeth if routine patient care indicates a need for extraction.

5. Collection of additional information or biological specimens, excluding blood, for research purposes during procedures already being performed for clinical purposes, provided the additional collection does not introduce more than a minimal increase in risk, pain or discomfort over that imposed by the underlying procedure. When extension of general anesthesia is required, it must meet the criteria for minimal risk. Examples: (a) collection of additional bodily fluids and tissues (e.g., peritoneal fluid, bone marrow or cerebrospinal fluid); (b) tissue collected from pap smears; (c) collection of additional clinical information (e.g., vital signs, electroencephalography or echocardiography).

FIGURE 3.4
Continued

6. Collection of information for research purposes through noninvasive procedures and (interventions routinely employed in clinical practice and not requiring general anesthesia or sedation. Examples:
(a) physical sensors that are applied either to the surface of the body or used at a distance; (b) testing sensory acuity; (c) magnetic resonance imaging without use of contrast agent and using magnet and sequence parameters within accepted clinical use guidelines; (d) electrocardiography, electroencephalography, thermography, detection of naturally occurring radioactivity, electroretinography, ultrasound, diagnostic infrared imaging, Doppler blood flow, and transthoracic echocardiography; (e) measures of cognitive functioning; (f) exposure to ionizing radiation with a total effective dose not exceeding 0.1 mSv (the amount typically associated with a single chest x-ray) provided appropriate shielding techniques are employed.

7. Collection of information for research purposes through activities performed by persons in daily life in individuals and groups whose health will not be adversely affected by the activities. Examples:
(a) moderate exercise, muscular strength testing, body composition assessment, and flexibility testing; (b) measures of symptoms, mobility, range of motion, quality of life and activities of daily living in patient and non-patient populations by clinical or other trained personnel (e.g., nurses, physicians, social workers, physical and occupational therapists); (c) manipulations of diet and lifestyle; (d) measuring height, weight, circumference; (e) assessment of reading levels.

8. Activities at statistical and data coordinating centers or biospecimen repositories that are not responsible for the primary oversight of the primary data collection activities and are not involved in the primary collection of information or specimens, which may be ongoing at other sites.

9. Collection of information from voice, video, digital, or image recordings made for research purposes that are not exempt under §.104(d).

10. Research that only includes interaction involving
Interview procedures, or observation of public behavior (including visual and auditory recording) not eligible for exemption under §.104(d)(2) either because there are risks to subjects other than informational risks, or because the informational risks are not addressed as specified under §104(d)(2)(i) through (iii); (3) other data collection procedures (e.g., written or computer-assisted interactions or assessments) where the subject provides self-reports for the purposes of the research and/or may choose what data to provide; (4) non-invasive physical or behavioral tasks or manipulation of the subject's environment; and (5) observations of individual group behavior where the subject is a voluntary participant in the behavior and is aware that data are being collected.

11. Benign behavioral interventions that are not eligible for exemption under §.104(d)(3) because they
(a) involve children as subjects; (b) involve individuals with impaired decision-making capacity; (c) are conducted without the prospective agreement of the subject, including interventions involving deception; (d) are not brief in duration, or; (e) are not limited to verbal or written responses by the subject, data entry by the subject, or observation of the subject.

Continued

FIGURE 3.4
Continued

12. Creation and maintenance of subject databases to which subjects have provided prospective informed consent or informed consent has been waived by an IRB and does not qualify for exemption under §.104(d)(7). Examples: (a) collection of identifiable information for the purpose of establishing subject pools; (b) disease-specific patient registries; (c) screening protocols including interviews, questionnaires and minimally invasive physical assessments, when performed for research purposes, that could not be expedited under one of the categories listed above.

13. Secondary research uses of identifiable private information or identifiable biospecimens that are not exempt under §.104(d)(4) because (a) the identifiable private information or identifiable biospecimens are not publicly available; (b) information, which may include information about biospecimens, is recorded by the investigator in such a manner that the identity of human subjects can be readily ascertained directly or through identifiers linked to the subjects, or the investigator intends to contact the subjects or will re-identify subjects; (c) research use of identifiable health information not regulated under 45 CFR parts 160 and 164, subparts A and E.

14. Research involving the use of identifiable private information or identifiable biospecimens for secondary research use that is not exempt under §.104(d)(8) because the investigator includes returning individual research results to subjects as part of the study plan.

CONTINUING REVIEW OF PREVIOUSLY APPROVED RESEARCH

15. Research previously approved by the convened IRB and not otherwise eligible for expedited review under categories (1) through (13) above, where one of the following conditions apply:
a. the research remains active only for long-term follow-up of subjects; 5 or
b. no subjects have been enrolled at sites under the purview of the reviewing IRB and no additional risks have been identified; or
c. the IRB has determined and documented at a convened meeting that the research involves no greater than minimal risk (including, when applicable, a non-significant risk (NSR) determination was initially made by a convened IRB for research involving investigational medical devices), and no additional risks have been identified. In such cases, the exemption from further continuing review at §109(f)(1)(i) does not apply.

Source: https://www.hhs.gov/ohrp/regulations-and-policy/guidance/categories-of-research-expedited-review-procedure-1998/index.html

FULL-BOARD REVIEW A **full-board review** occurs when the chair of the IRB believes that a research protocol is beyond a minimal risk and that the complete IRB should make a decision as to whether a research protocol should be allowed. Nearly anything that falls outside the exemptions seen in Figure 3.3 can be cause for a full-board review, depending on the university. Typically, IRBs meet once a month at large universities and quarterly at small ones. Some IRBs only meet as needed, so they do not have a specific time frame for reviewing research protocols. If you suspect that your research

Research Note

As of right now (Fall 2018), a new revision to the Common Rule (45 CFR 46), the 2017 revision, is supposed to go into effect in January 2019 (after being delayed multiple times). Some of the categories in Figures 3.3 and 3.4 have changed from those that were in place prior to December 2017. However, some big questions remain about the implications and implementations of these changes. Once clearer guidance is given from OHRP, we will release an update on the textbook website (https:// oup-arc.com/wrench) explaining these changes. At this point, it's important to check with your own institution on how they are implementing the new changes. Furthermore, some of the changes to the Common Rule could impact state requirements for research.

study will not be exempt, it is often best to plan on a full-board review. If you get lucky and the IRB chair does not think you only need an expedited review, you will have already completed the work for that level of review.

SPECIFIC ETHICAL ISSUES FOR RESEARCH

To this point, this chapter has primarily examined research ethics from an institutional perspective. However, a number of major ethical issues affect the research situation: data accuracy, data sharing, duplicate data publication, post hoc hypothesis revision, participant identity protection, authorship credit, conflict of interest, and plagiarism.

Data Accuracy

The first ethical issue relates to the accuracy of your data. Historically, a number of researchers have falsified data in the sciences. **Data falsification** occurs any time one manipulates or alters the data to achieve the results wanted by the researcher. For example, perhaps a researcher predicted that men who view magazine advertisements of scantily clad women will have more negative views of women. To examine this research question, the researcher conducts a study and finds out that the hypothesis is not true. If the researcher then decides to change some participants' scores to slant the study in the direction he or she wants, then that researcher would be falsifying data, which is highly unethical.

One of the hardest things for researchers is when a hypothesis does not pan out. However, as scientists we cannot have an agenda for our research. For example, maybe the researcher in our example wanted the data to help further a feminist agenda against advertising. Even if the data do not support the hypothesis, the data should still be reported as such. Unfortunately, people both inside and outside of academia will often attach political agendas to scientific research. Although tempting, slanting our research results in a specific political direction is dishonest and unethical. As researchers, we must be honest and forthcoming with all of our results, not just the ones we like.

Data Sharing

Another reason to avoid falsifying data is because researchers are expected to engage in **data sharing** when other researchers ask to see the data. Because social scientists are expected to further our understanding of the human process, the only way that future scientists can build on our work is to have access to both the published analysis of our work and the actual data used for publication.

There are several reasons other researchers might be interested in seeing your actual data. First, other researchers may want to reexamine your results if a finding does not make sense. We all make mistakes, and often, researchers will make mistakes when reporting results. Although the review process that a research study goes through before publication should catch any glaring errors, this is not always the case. Second, there is an advanced statistical process called meta-analysis, which attempts to pool the results from numerous studies that examine a specific phenomenon to achieve a greater understanding. Although people conducting a meta-analysis can use published results much of the time, meta-analytic research is often much more useful when the original data are used.

We must also mention that there is one giant exception to sharing data: If releasing data will violate the participants' rights to anonymity and confidentiality because there is no way to **deidentify the data** (i.e., unlink the data to the participants), then the researcher has an ethical obligation to protect her or his participants.

Duplicate Data Publication

The next ethical issue that researchers must be aware of is the concept of **duplicate data publication**, or publishing the same set of data in two different research publications. In academia, publication is considered to be one of the three pillars of an academic's job (along with teaching and service). Although different colleges and universities will have varying degrees of publication requirements for untenured professors, most of these institutions today expect faculty to publish. For this reason, meeting a college or university's publication requirements is extremely important— and extremely competitive. However, some unethical researchers have published the same manuscript or the same data in more than one publication. In essence, these unethical researchers have double-dipped their chip in the salsa, and we all know that is just plain wrong. Along the same lines, other unethical researchers have presented the same paper at numerous conferences. Colleges and universities typically give researchers money to present research at academic conferences, so presenting the same paper at numerous conferences is seen as a way to cheat the college or university. Furthermore, if you are presenting the same paper at multiple conferences or publishing identical research in more than one journal, you are also preventing other researchers from presenting and publishing. Conferences and journals have finite space available, so if you double-dip, you prevent someone else from either presenting or publishing.

Post Hoc Hypothesis Revision

Another ethical area for communication researchers is related to data accuracy because this ethical dilemma involves the treatment of data in relation to proposed hypotheses. This ethical issue involves the revising of hypotheses once an individual receives her or his results, or **post hoc** (after the fact) **hypothesis revision**. Imagine a researcher predicts, based on previous research, that there will be a relationship between an organization's culture and the organization's webpage content. If the researcher then finds that the organization's webpage has nothing to do with the organization's culture, her or his proposed hypothesis would be wrong. Most people do not like being wrong, so it is tempting to just alter the hypothesis (i.e., say that an organization's culture and content on the organization's webpage would not be related to each other). When a researcher alters her or his hypotheses to fit the data, the scientific method is weakened, which leads to inaccurate research that cannot help foster future intellectual thought.

Participant Identity Protection

The next ethical consideration for communication researchers relates to information previously discussed in this chapter—protecting our participants' identities. Often, communication researchers will examine sensitive information from participants that could embarrass or harm them (either personally or professionally) if the information were made public. For this reason, communication researchers ensure that the information obtained from participants is protected. In large-scale quantitative projects, individual participant identity is easier to protect because it is impossible to ascertain one person's responses in a dataset that contains 200 participants. However, qualitative researchers often examine data from only a handful of people, so altering demographic information and changing participant names is often necessary to maintain confidentiality.

Authorship Credit

Authorship credit is basically the notion that ethical researchers give credit where credit is due. According to an article written by the ethics committee of the American Psychological Association (APA) (Ethics Committee, 1992), there are three basic aspects to the ethical standard for authorship credit.

First, authors should only take credit for research they have actually conducted or to which they have contributed. Historically, there have been cases where researchers have stolen another person's data and published those data as their own. At the same time, one should also note there is an ethical obligation to ensure that all parties who have actually contributed to the research get credit for their participation, which also relates to the second standard.

The second standard for authorship credit is to accurately give credit to all parties involved in the research process. Although this may seem to be common sense, a few unethical researchers have not given students credit for their contribution to research. Whether a contributor is an undergraduate, Master's, or doctoral student does not matter—all authors should get credit for their participation in research. Also involved in this ethical standard is the order in which researchers are listed.

When listing researchers for an article, authors should be listed in the order of their contribution, not alphabetically or by some other contrived listing format. You may be wondering why the order of authors matters. Academia (especially tenure and promotion committees) views the listing of authors seriously. Often, researchers will only get credit from their college or university if they are the principal or first author on an article. Ultimately, the order in which authors are listed is somewhat arbitrary, but researchers should be as objective as possible when listing authors to indicate the level of contribution of each one.

The final standard for determining authorship credit has to do with a specific type of article, one that stems from a student's Master's thesis or doctoral dissertation. According to the ethics committee, if an article contains multiple authors and is based on a thesis or dissertation, then the student should be listed as the first author.

Conflict of Interest

A **conflict of interest** occurs when financial or other personal considerations prevent a researcher from abiding by or can give the appearance of compromising scientific and ethical principles. For example, maybe you were asked by a pharmaceutical company to speak about patient health communication. If you then become involved with a research study that also involves that same pharmaceutical company, you would have competing interests that conflict: your financial incentives for the pharmaceutical company and your ability to complete ethical research. Although some people could still conduct ethical research when they have a conflict of interest, even the appearance of being in a compromising situation can be enough to discredit the researcher and her or his research.

Plagiarism

The last ethical area for communication researchers relates to the commonly discussed academic problem of **plagiarism**. Any time that a writer does not properly cite or give credit to any source of information, he or she is plagiarizing. Communication scholars "do not claim the words and ideas of another as their own; they give credit where credit is due" (APA, 2010, p. 15). Although the cited sentence in the previous sentence was taken from the APA's *Publication Manual*, the sentence is equally applicable for communication scholars. Note that although the sentence could equally apply to both psychologists and communication researchers, the authors of this text still cite the APA for the information because we did not write it originally ourselves. When people plagiarize, they steal other people's intellectual property and quite possibly infringe on copyright laws. In an article by Mahmood, Mahmood, Khan, and Malik (2010), the authors expanded on information from Plagiarism.org, examining the two types of plagiarism: source not cited and source cited.

SOURCE-NOT-CITED TYPES OF PLAGIARISM

Source-not-cited plagiarism involves using someone else's work and not attributing the information to a specific author or group of authors. There are five distinct types of source-not-cited plagiarism: the ghostwriter, the photocopier, the potluck writer, the disguiser, and the self stealer.

THE GHOSTWRITER The first type of plagiarism that some writers engage in is referred to as the ghostwriter because the "writer" has another person literally write the entire paper for her or him. There are many unethical websites from which writers can download prewritten papers for a fee. Other websites offer to put a student in contact with a ghostwriter who will write that student's entire paper, also for a fee. For obvious reasons, this practice is frowned on in higher education and can lead to a student being kicked out of school permanently if he or she is caught doing it.

THE PHOTOCOPIER The photocopier is a form of plagiarism in which the writer takes a chunk of material from a source and copies it word for word into her or his paper. If you are citing more than four words in a row, you must place those words in quotation marks and inform your readers where the original information is located.

THE POTLUCK WRITER According to Plagiarism.org ("Types of plagiarism," 2011), the potluck writer "tries to disguise the plagiarism by copying from several different sources, tweaking the sentences retaining most of the original phrasing" (para. 4). In this form of plagiarism, the writer mashes a bunch of sources together with a sentence from here and a sentence from there, all designed to look like the author's own original work.

THE DISGUISER The disguiser form of plagiarism occurs when a writer steals a sentence and then tries to rearrange or replace a few words within the sentence to disguise the fact that the sentence is not his or her own. Imagine that we have the following sentence: "A number of factors are responsible for the quality of research" (Mahmood et al., 2010, p. 193). Here is one way a disguiser would try to rearrange this sentence to "make it their own": "A number of *ideas* are *paramount* for *excellence* in research." Has switching out a few words really changed the basic idea in the first sentence? No! As such, this is a common form of plagiarism.

THE SELF STEALER The last plagiarizer is one who often does not even realize that plagiarism is occurring because he or she is just reusing her or his own writing. When a writer takes portions of previously used work (even if it is her or his own work), that work should be cited as such. Although you may have papers that overlap conceptually or even in the sources utilized, the writing should be unique for each individual paper.

SOURCE-CITED TYPES OF PLAGIARISM

Source-cited plagiarism involves partial attribution of information to a source, but the attribution is incomplete. There are five distinct types of source-cited plagiarism: the forgotten footnoter/referencer, the misinformer, the too-perfect paraphraser, the resourceful citer, and the perfect crime.

THE FORGOTTEN FOOTNOTER/REFERENCER The forgotten footnoter or forgotten referencer is a plagiarizer who may cite a source within her or his paper but forgets to include that source within her or his footnotes, works cited page, or reference page. Again, citing a source is a two-step process. We must (1) attribute information to a source within the paper and (2) provide information on how to locate that source in our footnotes, works cited, or references.

THE MISINFORMER The misinformer may either cite information within the text or even on a footnotes, works cited, or reference page, but the information is so vague that one cannot locate the source. For example, if you are writing a paper and you cite the information internally as "According to the *New York Times*" but this is all the information you provide, then you are misinforming your reader because the *New York Times* has been published since 1851. How is a reader supposed to know who wrote the information, when the information was written, or the context of the information? This is one of the main reasons we rely so heavily on style manuals to help us correctly cite information both within a paper and in our footnotes, works cited, or references. We will talk more about this in the next chapter.

THE TOO-PERFECT PARAPHRASER The too-perfect paraphraser is an individual who lifts a sentence and then attributes that sentence to the author but does not put the sentence within quotation marks. For example, the correct way to cite a direct quotation in APA style is like this: "A number of factors are responsible for the quality of research" (Mahmood et al., 2010, p. 193). If you just cited the sentence without the quotation marks—like this: A number of factors are responsible for the quality of research (Mahmood et al., 2010)—then you would not be correctly attributing the sentence to Mahmood et al. because it would look as if you had written that sentence yourselves.

THE RESOURCEFUL CITER According to Plagiarism.org ("Types of plagiarism," 2011), the resourceful citer is someone who "cites all sources, paraphrasing and using quotations appropriately. The catch? The paper contains almost no original work! It is sometimes difficult to spot this form of plagiarism because it looks like any other well-researched document" (para. 11). In this case, the writer sticks to the "letter of the law" on how to appropriately cite material within the paper and in her or his footnotes, works cited, or references; however, the writer does not have an original thought within the piece of writing.

THE PERFECT CRIME The perfect crime is a devious type of plagiarism. It occurs because the writer knows that the source of the information is problematic, so the writer purposefully alters information in her or his citation to disguise where the writing came from. For example, maybe you know that you are not allowed to cite material from Wikipedia. So instead of admitting that the information came from Wikipedia, you decide to cite one of the references at the bottom of the Wikipedia page.

In the next two chapters we will discuss how to conduct research and how to write research articles. We will emphasize how to correctly cite information using the style format created by the APA. For more on how to avoid plagiarism, we recommend Stern (2007) or Menager-Beeley and Paulos (2009). If you are not sure about your own plagiarism, you may want to consider using TurnItIn.com's website specifically geared toward students: Write Check (https://www.writecheck.com/).

RESEARCH OUTSIDE THE WALLS OF ACADEMIA

Ethical research in the world outside of academia is just as important as research conducted inside academia, but there are not the same federal protections for research participants. Regardless, we believe that thinking through research using the same basic model proposed originally by the Belmont Report is a good place to start. All of the ethical aspects discussed previously can be applied to conducting any kind of research in the world:

1. Ensure that participants know their participation is voluntary.
2. Do not recruit participants under the age of 18 without parental permission.

3. Do not plagiarize.
4. Do not falsify your results just to make your boss (or your boss's boss) happy.
5. Maintain the anonymity or confidentiality of participants.

And so on . . .

CONCLUSION

In this chapter, we have examined the ethics of conducting research in today's academic environment. We began by exploring some of the more ethically controversial research conducted. Then, we discussed the nature of ethics and what this meant for communication researchers. Next, we examined the legacy of the Tuskegee experiment and how it ushered in a new era of responsibility and oversight in research involving human subjects. Finally, we discussed specific ethical dilemmas that communication researchers often face.

Although the IRB process is not perfect, it is designed to prevent atrocities that have been seen in previous research. One of the biggest problems that critics of the IRB process have is that it is highly controlled by a biomedical model of research that does not apply well to social scientists (Dougherty & Kramer, 2005; Hamilton, 2005; Koerner, 2005). Maybe one day there will be separate evaluation processes for social scientific and biomedical research endeavors; however, until that happens, we must learn how to present our research protocols in as clear a way as possible for a variety of different audiences.

KEY TERMS

Anonymity p. 51

Authorship credit p. 73

Belmont Report p. 47

Certificate of Confidentiality p. 53

Common Rule p. 49

Confidentiality p. 52

Conflict of interest p. 74

Data falsification p. 71

Data sharing p. 72

Deidentify the data p. 72

Diminished autonomy p. 47

Duplicate data publication p. 72

Ends p. 45

Ethical behavior p. 46

Ethics p. 45

Exempt review p. 64

Expedited review p. 64

Full-board review p. 70

Informed consent p. 47

Institutional Review Board p. 50

Justice p. 49

Machiavellian ethic p. 46

Means p. 45

Plagiarism p. 74

Post hoc hypothesis revision p. 73

Principle of beneficence p. 48

Privacy p. 51

Protected health information p. 52

Research participant p. 50

Subjective ethic p. 46

Unethical behavior p. 46

REFERENCES

American Psychological Association. (2010). *Publication manual of the American Psychological Association* (6th ed.). Washington, DC: American Psychological Association.

Bankert, E. A., & Amdur, R. J. (2006). *Institutional review board: Management and function* (2nd ed.). Sudbury, MA: Jones & Bartlett.

Dougherty, D. S., & Kramer, M. W. (2005). A rationale for scholarly examination of institutional review boards: A case study. *Journal of Applied Communication Research, 33,* 183–188. doi:10.1080/0090 9880500149270

Ethics Committee. (1992). Ethical principles of psychologists and code of conduct. *American Psychologist, 47,* 1612–1628.

Garramone, G. M., & Kennamer, J. D. (1989). Ethical considerations in mass communications research. *Journal of Mass Media Ethics, 4,* 174–185.

Hamilton, A. (2005). The development and operation of IRBs: Medical regulations and social science. *Journal of Applied Communication Research, 33,* 189–203. doi:10.1080/00909880500149353

Humphreys, L. (1975). *Tearoom trade: Impersonal sex in public places.* Chicago, IL: Aldine.

Koerner, A. F. (2005). Communication scholars' communication and relationship with their IRBs. *Journal of Applied Communication Research, 33,* 231–241. doi:10.1080/00909880500149395

Latané, B., & Darley, J. M. (1970). *The unresponsive bystander: Why doesn't he help?* Englewood Cliffs, NJ: Prentice Hall.

Mahmood, S. T., Mahmood, A., Kahn, M. N., & Malik, A. B. (2010). Intellectual property rights: Conceptual awareness of research students about plagiarism. *International Journal of Academic Research, 2,* 193–198.

McCroskey, J. C., Wrench, J. S., & Richmond, V. P. (2003). *Principles of public speaking.* Indianapolis, IN: College Network.

McNutt, L. A., Waltermaurer, E., Bednarczyk, R. A., Carlson, B. E., Kotval, J., McCauley, J., . . . Ford, D. E. (2008). Are we misjudging how well informed consent forms are read? *Journal of Empirical Research on Human Research Ethics, 3*(1), 89–97.

Menager-Beeley, R., & Paulos, L. (2009). *Understanding plagiarism: A student guide to writing your own work.* Boston, MA: Houghton Mifflin Harcourt.

Milgram, S. (1974). *Obedience to authority: An experimental view.* New York, NY: Harper & Row.

Nathan, R. (2005). *My freshman year: What a professor learned by becoming a student.* Ithaca, NY: Cornell University Press.

National Institutes of Health. (2002). *Human participant protections education for research teams.* Washington, DC: US Department of Health and Human Services National Institutes of Health.

Stern, L. (2007). *What every student should know about . . . avoiding plagiarism.* Boston, MA: Allyn & Bacon.

Types of plagiarism. (2011). Retrieved from http://www.plagiarism.org

Wrench, J. S., McCroskey, J. C., & Richmond, V. P. (2008). *Human communication in everyday life: Explanations and applications.* Boston, MA: Allyn & Bacon.

Vaughan, T. R. (1967). Governmental intervention in social research: Political and ethical dimensions in the Wichita jury recordings. In G. Sjoberg (Ed.), *Ethics, politics, and social research* (pp. 50–77). Cambridge, MA: Schenkman.

Zimbardo, P. G., Haney, C., Banks, W. C., & Jaffe, D. (1973, April 8). The mind is a formidable jailer: A pirandellian prison. *New York Times Magazine, 122,* 38–60.

Searching for Previous Research and American Psychological Association Style

CHAPTER OBJECTIVES

1. Understand how researchers identify research topics.

2. Understand the different types of academic sources available, explain how to use them appropriately, and describe how to decide their worth.

3. Understand how to cite sources using the American Psychological Association (APA) style to create a reference page.

4. Describe how to internally (parenthetically) cite primary research within your own writing using APA style.

5. Understand how to format papers using APA style.

Formulating an idea for a research project can be intriguing, or it can be frustrating. If the researcher already has a question or idea in mind, the process can be relatively easy; in fact, it could almost be considered a "mystery" to be solved. However, some aspects of the process can be frustrating if the researcher lacks the knowledge or tools for finding answers.

Although the topics we discuss in this chapter can be applied to any social scientific field, we, as communication researchers, must always keep communication in our minds when thinking about research. This chapter provides an overview of the research process and assists in creating a road map for conducting a communication research project. After all, before starting out on a journey, it is a good idea to have a game plan for getting there! At the conclusion of this chapter, you will be able to identify a communication topic to research, understand the options available for examining and summarizing the communication research that already exists on your topic, and organize and cite sources of information to report your research.

Research takes time and should be approached in much the same way that a mystery would be analyzed on your favorite television crime drama. Before beginning the investigation, the "detective" (researcher) must establish a game plan. The investigator should have a good idea of the question to be answered, or he or she will spend many hours working to solve nothing at all. To understand the background of the question or mystery, evidence in the form of information and facts must be gathered. All of the evidence must be synthesized or organized to help you, the researcher/detective, establish a logical answer to the research/mystery.

This chapter discusses the five preliminary steps to beginning a research project: (1) identifying the question or topic to investigate; (2) clarifying the research question, and generating a list of key terms and concepts; (3) locating potential sources of background information on the topic; (4) organizing and evaluating information; and (5) citing sources of information using a standard format.

STEP 1: IDENTIFYING THE TOPIC

The first step in beginning the communication research project involves choosing a topic or question about communication to investigate. For some people, picking a communication topic can be one of the most daunting tasks. After all, the research project will consume a considerable amount of time, so researchers often put pressure on themselves to find the "perfect" topic. However, some researchers have indicated that choosing a topic has been the easiest part of their research process because they draw on and seek answers to events that have happened in their own lives. For example, maybe you will be reading a research article and a question will pop into your head, or maybe you will just be taking a shower one morning and think, *Hmmm, I wonder if anyone has researched that before?* Every researcher has a different process that he or she goes through when creating a research project, but there are some tips that can assist you in finding a topic to start your research journey.

Why Are You Doing the Research?

First, be sure that you understand why you are doing the research. Are you doing the research to get published or because you have to take a research methods class and are given an assignment to complete? Even before you begin thinking about a topic, clarify why you are conducting that research in the first place. Some questions to consider if conducting research for a college class may include the following:

- Is the focus on a specific communication context or phenomenon? For example, is the goal of the project to study communication in the health-care setting? Or is the goal of the project to examine a personality variable as it relates to communication?
- What types of sources are required? Should the search for sources focus exclusively on scholarly journals, or can sources from popular magazines and newspapers be included? Can websites be included as sources?
- Is there a particular number of resources that should be cited?
- What style format should be used? Is American Psychological Association (APA) format acceptable, or should the project adhere to Modern Language Association (MLA) guidelines or another format (*The Chicago Manual of Style*, international medical journal style, etc.)?

If you are not conducting research for a specific class, other questions must be considered as well:

- Are you conducting the research for an organization or for your own personal use?
- What do you plan to do with the research after it has been conducted (publish it, present it somewhere, etc.)?
- Will other people be interested in the research you are conducting?

What Interests You?

The second step to ensuring a successful research experience involves selecting a topic that interests you personally. You will experience greater motivation to spend time exploring sources and collecting data if the topic is one that you have an interest in studying. Since this book assumes that you plan to focus your research on a communication phenomenon, keep reminding yourself to concentrate on messages and meaning when identifying the research topic.

Research ideas can come from a variety of sources or experiences. Ideas can result from a conversation, other research articles, media examples, current events, or even a professor. If you experience difficulty in identifying a research topic, consider brainstorming with a group of friends or family members to generate a list of ideas. Browse through current magazines and newspapers to see whether there is a "hot" topic that has been the subject of attention. Examine a textbook or browse a subject-specific online database on a library website (e.g., Communication and Mass Media Complete in EBSCOhost) for ideas. Conduct a word or subject search using key terms that describe your interests.

As stated previously, an idea for research can result from a casual conversation. For example, the idea for a study conducted by Thomas, Booth-Butterfield, and Booth-Butterfield (1995) resulted from a lunch conversation between friends. During that conversation, the friends discussed what had happened the previous weekend. One of the women (Stacey) mentioned that she had visited her sister and her niece. Stacey had casually asked her sister, "So when is Joe [your husband] moving out?" The shocked expression on her niece's face—followed by the question "Why is Daddy moving out?"—led Stacey to realize that she had just disclosed to her niece that her parents were divorcing, and before they had had an opportunity to discuss it with her. Stacey's niece became upset and angry and accused her mother of lying to her. Stacey felt horrible! Would Stacey's niece continue to blame her sister for the divorce? As a result of hearing this story, Thomas et al. (1995) decided to investigate the impact of disclosure of the decision to divorce on a child's level of communication satisfaction with her or his parents. More specifically, the researchers wanted to see whether children reported more communication satisfaction with the parent who told them about the decision to divorce. Would the child of a divorce perceive the parent who revealed the decision to divorce as being more honest and the other parent as being more deceptive?

Three Possible Sources for Topics

To exhaust all options for identifying the topic for a project, consider a variety of sources for potential topics. Three possible sources include reflecting on personal experiences, reviewing the literature, and developing questions from existing theories.

PERSONAL EXPERIENCES

Let's build on the earlier example regarding the use of personal experiences. We discussed how the idea for a research study on divorce disclosure evolved from a personal conversation. In research methods classes that we have taught, students often use their own experiences to come up with ideas for research projects. One student researched the verbal aggressiveness of hockey parents because of watching them yelling at the teams, players, and officials during his son's hockey games. Another student researched interpersonal deception after watching several episodes of a reality television show *Big Brother*. Both of these topics resulted from personal experiences. Still another student focused on communication strategies used to inform employees of impending downsizing in a local organization after reading an article in her local newspaper. Potential research topics are everywhere!

REVIEWING THE LITERATURE

Another major way that researchers often find topics is by reading the literature within a specific communication context. For example, while reading an article on computer-mediated communication, maybe you realize that a lot of research has examined the use of chat rooms and instant messaging, but that no one has really looked at how cell phone text messaging affects communication. Most studies conducted probably stem from this type of initial noting of "gaps" in research. These gaps come in a variety of different forms:

1. Some researchers realize there is information missing in a specific context, like our example comparing computer instant messaging to cell phone text messaging. Although research on computer instant messaging has been around for a decade, cell phone text messaging is still a recent phenomenon, so it is clearly a new context to revisit older research findings.

2. Another type of gap deals with samples. For example, maybe when looking at research on the use of e-mail, you note that little research has been conducted on retired individuals. Retired people and college students may have different uses for e-mail, so examining a communication phenomenon in different samples is extremely important.

3. A certain type of research occurs when you note that information needs to be updated. Research in the area of computer-mediated communication dates back to the late 1980s and early 1990s. Although the research results of the late 1980s were interesting, do those results still hold true in the 21st century? As computer and Internet technology have rapidly advanced, do people still respond to computer-mediated communication in the same way they did in the late 1990s? Since people change with time, revisiting older studies in an updated fashion can be extremely important.

4. Still another type of research gap comes in the form of conceptual gaps, or when no one has studied a specific concept. While talking with other researchers or reading research literature, we often have "aha" moments when we realize that some aspect of human communication has not been studied at all. Of course, it is always important to double-check the literature to make sure that your "new" concept is actually something someone has not studied under a different term.

THEORETICALLY DRIVEN QUESTIONS

Another way that researchers find topics is from existing theories. If you remember our discussion of theories in Chapter 2, we discussed the notion that theories must be able to be proven false. Scientists will often examine a theory to make sure the theory stays true across a wide range of communication circumstances. Because theoretically driven research is common in communication, we will look at this area in more detail.

Berger and Calabrese (1975) created one of the most important theories of interpersonal communication, called uncertainty reduction theory (URT). At its basic level, URT posits that people will try to reduce uncertainty through our interactions with others in initial interactions. The goal of these initial interactions is to increase our ability to make *predictions* about another person in order to *explain* the outcomes of the interaction. One of the reasons why URT has had longevity in communication is because it is built on eight **axioms** (generally accepted principles or rules). Although we cannot go into detail here about the eight axioms of URT, we do recommend that you read either Berger and Calabrese (1975) or the summary of URT research by West and Turner (2006).

For our example, we will examine the eighth axiom from Berger and Calabrese (1975): shared communication networks reduce uncertainty, whereas lack of shared networks increases uncertainty. This axiom posits that the more people have shared communication networks (they find out they have friends in common, coworkers in common, etc.), the less uncertainty they will experience while interacting. However, the more different their communication networks are (they know none of the same people), the more uncertainty they will have while interacting. When completing theoretically driven research, researchers will look at a part of a theory and think, "How can I test this theory?" And in terms of the eighth axiom, maybe you want to examine parental uncertainty while interacting with their children's teachers. So, you set out to determine whether parents who have more communication network ties with teachers (e.g., they go to the same church, have friends in common, belong to the same social group) experience less uncertainty while interacting with their children's teachers than parents who share no common communication networks with their children's teachers. We have chosen to examine part of a theory, determined how to use the theory in a specific communication context, and can now set out to either provide more support for the theory or possibly provide information that contradicts the theory.

STEP 2: CLARIFYING THE RESEARCH QUESTION AND GENERATING KEY TERMS

Once a general topic has been identified, the next step is to develop and refine the topic to begin the search for existing information. There are three primary steps in this process: (1) state your topic in the form of a question (realize that this may result in more than one question depending on your topic), (2) identify key terms and concepts from the question(s), and (3) generate a list of key term synonyms that can be used to search for background information. (Steps 2 and 3 are often performed simultaneously, so we will discuss them together in the material that follows.)

Stating the Topic in the Form of a Research Question

The first step in refining your topic involves stating your research topic in the form of a question. We have included a worksheet (Figure 4.1) that can help you in working through the process of clarifying the research question and identifying potential sources. Note that the first step asks for the *initial* research question. We use the word "initial" because the research question may undergo multiple revisions as you examine existing sources of information. You may discover that the initial question is too broad or too narrow. Or, once you begin the search for information, you might find that your initial question has already been answered through previous research.

Suppose that you recently experienced the end of a romantic relationship. Based on this experience, you decide that the topic of your research project will be terminating relationships. Because this topic is broad, we must narrow the focus to help formulate a specific research question. Some things that you might want to consider in refining your topic and writing the initial research questions include the following:

- What type of relationship should be examined? Friendships? Romantic relationships? Family relationships?
- Is there a particular relational role that should be the focus of the study? The person who initiates the termination? The recipient?
- How is communication related to the topic? Should the focus be on strategies used to terminate relationships?

As you can see, there are several "mini-questions" that must be addressed before creating the initial research question. Suppose you decided that the focus of your study will be on the messages used by partners to communicate the end of a romantic relationship. The initial research question then could be phrased as "What communication strategies are used to terminate romantic relationships?" That is simple enough! But keep in mind that this research question may need to be revised as we continue through the remaining steps indicated on the Research Planning Worksheet (Figure 4.1).

Step 2 on the worksheet asks the researcher to identify what information is already known about the topic. Think about your own experiences and what you have studied in communication, psychology, family studies, history, biology, or any other class that you have taken. People in a wide variety of fields help communication scholars more fully understand communication phenomenon. What do you already know about communication strategies that are used to end romantic relationships? Probably the most obvious thing is that relational partners might avoid engaging in communication behaviors. You might even recall studying relationship dissolution in an interpersonal communication class. Maybe your own experience involved the use of deception. Brainstorm and think of anything that you already know about the topic. This information will be useful as you begin generating key concepts to describe your research topic.

FIGURE 4.1
Research Planning Worksheet

1. **What is your initial research question(s)?**

2. **What do you already know about this topic?** List any information you currently have about your topic

3. **What keywords can you use to assist you in conducting a library search?** Be sure to include synonyms for all terms identified!

4. **What resources should you examine to begin your review of literature?**

Electronic databases	Websites	Encyclopedias/ Handbooks

5. **Begin your search for information.** Be sure to complete a summary sheet for each source you think will be useful for your study!

6. **Review and evaluate the information.** What did you discover from your research?
What questions have been answered?
What questions remain unanswered?
Should any studies be replicated?
7. **Evaluate your sources.** Now that the initial research process is complete, revise your initial research question.

Identifying Key Terms and Synonymous Terms

Once the initial research question has been developed, the next steps involve identifying key words and concepts that can be used to describe the ideas included in your question as well as synonyms that can be used to search for background information.

Let's take a closer look at how Wrench and Booth-Butterfield (2003) generated the topic and research questions for their study examining physicians' use of humor and patient compliance and satisfaction. This project evolved as a result of their interest in humor, health communication, and compliance. Following are some initial questions that created the foundation for the study:

- Are patients more likely to listen to the advice of doctors who are humorous?
- Are patients more satisfied if their doctor uses humor?
- Do patients perceive doctors who use humor as being more credible?

By examining these questions more closely, key concepts and terms emerge to guide the search for information that has already been published on the topic. Create a list of the key terms included in your questions, but realize that these terms alone might not be sufficient to conduct your review of existing literature. Additional terms that are synonymous with the key terms should be included in the list of words that will be used to conduct the library search. Do not be afraid to list any and all words that could be used to describe your topic. Be sure to include both broad and narrow terms to describe each concept. Figure 4.2 includes sample questions and key terms that could be used to find sources for Wrench and Booth-Butterfield's study. The column on the far right lists synonyms for the key terms that were taken directly from potential research questions.

Questions	Key Terms from Questions	Related Terms	
Are patients more likely to listen to the directions of doctors who are humorous?	patient listen doctor	obey compliance requests message physician health	FIGURE 4.2 **Key and Related Search Terms**
Are patients more satisfied if their doctor uses humor?	patient satisfaction doctor humor	physician message health	
Do patients perceive doctors who use humor as being more credible?	patient doctor humor credibility	physician expertise	

As you generate lists of key terms to represent the research question, it may be useful to visually represent and organize your ideas by creating a concept map (also known as a web diagram). Doing so will create a picture of concepts that fit together and can assist in organizing ideas as you begin writing your review of literature (see Chapter 5). Think of the concept map as a "tree" for organizing ideas. The central concept of the research project serves as the tree trunk or the foundation for the project. The branches of the tree represent the concepts or ideas that the researcher wants to examine in relation to the central concept. Finally, the twigs are terms that are synonymous with those represented by the branches. A brainstorming map of Wrench and Booth-Butterfield's (2003) study might look like Figure 4.3. Because the concept of physician humor is central to the study, it is placed at the center of the diagram. Next, patient compliance, patient satisfaction, and expertise are included in the surrounding circles since the goal is to see how these concepts are linked to a doctor's use of humor.

It is important to continue generating terms that are synonymous with these key concepts and to include additional terms in the diagram. Suppose when searching for information in the library you discover that the words used in the search return only a few examples of books or articles that have examined the topic. At that point, it is helpful to have the list of related terms to aid in broadening the search. If a search for physician humor and credibility results in only three articles, the terms *doctor* and

FIGURE 4.3
Brainstorming Map

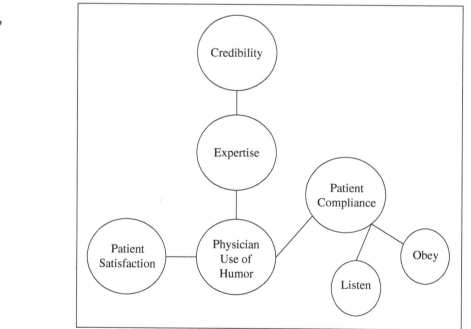

expertise could be included in a subsequent search to see whether more articles can be found. Remember to include communication, messages, and meaning as the central focus of your research.

STEP 3: LOCATING SOURCES OF INFORMATION

Once you have identified the initial research question and key concepts, the next task involves searching for information that has been published on the topic. In Chapter 1, we stated that a primary goal of research is to produce new knowledge that explains the "how" and "why" of communication. To build new knowledge, it is important to search for the information that already exists on a topic. After all, how useful would it be to keep answering the same research question over and over? Also, as mentioned earlier, you will note "gaps" or unanswered questions to help you refine your initial research question as you review existing articles on your topic.

Primary Versus Secondary Sources

You are likely to come across two basic types of sources while looking for previous literature: primary and secondary.

PRIMARY SOURCES

Hairston and Ruszkiewicz (1996) define **primary sources** as "materials on a topic upon which subsequent interpretations or studies are based, anything from first-hand documents such as poems, diaries, court records, and interviews to research results generated by experiments, surveys, ethnographies, and so on" (p. 547). Although the first part of this definition is not useful for our discussion, the second part specifically relates to research results generated by experiments and surveys. In other words, primary research reports the results of a study actually conducted by the author(s).

SECONDARY SOURCES

In contrast to primary sources, **secondary sources** are restatements or analyses of the primary research. For example, when you read an academic article, the first section is the review of literature. Within this review, the new article's author(s) summarizes preexisting research on a subject. This summarization of preexisting research is secondary because the new article's author did not conduct the research found in the literature review. Conversely, when the new article then explains what the author actually did in the study, the author is generating primary research because he or she is describing what was done in the current project. We want to make this distinction clear because many students fall into the trap of citing secondary sources from an author's literature review within the student's literature review without ever having read the original source being cited.

COMMON PROBLEMS WITH SECONDARY SOURCES Believe it or not, using secondary sources can actually be a form of plagiarism. One common problem that we have seen over the years arises when a student author finds a great citation or series of references that would be useful for her or his research. For example, imagine you are reading an article and find the following quotation: "More recently researchers have started becoming interested in the after-effects of detected deception in a variety of interpersonal relationships: coworkers (Aunne, Metts, & Ebesu Hubbard, 1998; Dunleavy, Chory, & Goodboy, 2007), customers (Jehn & Scott, 2008), friendships (Aunne et al., 1998), and romantic relational partners (Aunne et al., 1998; Jang, Smith, & Levine, 2002; McCornack & Levine, 1990)." You read this sentence and think that the information from Jehn and Scott (2008) and Dunleavy, Chory, and Goodboy (2007) will help build your argument. However, if you lift those citations (and corresponding references) from the article and place them into your own paper without ever reading those articles, you are plagiarizing. If you think those articles could be useful for your paper, you should always go back and read them yourself.

BACKTRACKING As a general rule, you should never cite a source you haven't read yourself. In fact, we often recommend that our students look in the reference sections of published articles as a launching point for finding more sources. We call this process **backtracking** because you are taking one article and then using that article's references to track down other published articles and books.

Again, we always recommend going back to the original source whenever possible because you may find something in the primary source that is more helpful to your research than what is discussed in the secondary source. Avoiding the use of secondary sources within your own writing does not mean that secondary sources are not useful, however. Often, if we read a secondary source written on a given topic at the beginning of the research process, we can greatly decrease the amount of time we must spend looking for literature because the secondary source can help us understand the breadth of information on a given topic. In essence, secondary sources are useful when starting the research process because they help you quickly grasp the general research subject area before you delve into the primary research.

TRANSLATIONS OF PRIMARY SOURCES There is one notable exception to the mentioned qualifications for use of secondary sources. If the primary source exists in a language that you do not read, then citing the secondary source's translation of the primary source is appropriate. Now that we have explained the differences between primary and secondary sources, we can look at the types of primary sources that exist.

Secondary Source Citation Example

Imagine you're writing a paper on the subject of homonegativity, or negative attitudes toward gay, lesbian, bisexual, transgendered, and transsexual individuals. One of the articles you see cited is Concha (2016). You search for Concha (2016) and find out that the paper is written entirely in Spanish. Well, unless you can read Spanish, you may not be able to cite the article directly because you cannot read it. When this happens, it can be appropriate to use a secondary source citation. Here's how that would look:

"Choncha's (2016) research (as cited by Author, Year) . . ."

The part where you see "(as cited by Author, Year)" is where you read the citation yourself. In this case, you will need to include the references for both articles in your references:

Concha, F. Q. (2016). *Una medida de la homonegatividad breve, unidimensional, e independiente de los afectos positivos y negativos: Evidencias de validez de la escala de Wrench en Chile* [A brief and mono-dimensional homonegativity measure, independent from positive and negative affects: Evidence of Wrench's scale validity in Chile]. *Salud & Sociedad, 7*(1), 10–28.

Types of Information Sources

Although it may be easy to turn on the computer and use a popular search engine such as Google or Yahoo! to compile a list of resources, scholarly research involves searching a variety of sources for relevant information. The best place to begin a quest for information is your campus library. Remember—librarians are our friends, so treat them well. Librarians enjoy being asked to assist students in locating sources of information if you do it nicely! Think of the librarian as a tour guide because there are literally thousands of sources and strategies that can be used to search for existing literature. In fact, some of our former students have said that they avoid the library because they suffer from "information overload"; there are so many sources of information that they are not sure where to begin the search. A librarian can help navigate the options available to make your search more efficient and effective.

Information about your research topic can come from a variety of sources. Of course, the sources you select for information will depend on the question you are trying to answer. The most common sources of information are books, magazines, scholarly journals, magazines, newspapers, encyclopedias, handbooks, and the World Wide Web. A summary of the different types of information sources is included in Figure 4.4.

The type of information needed will dictate the selection of the information source. Remember—research projects require you to conduct a review of existing scholarly literature on your topic. However, students often flock to popular magazines and websites for information on a topic. After all, they are familiar with various

Source Type	When to Use	Examples
Books	• To search for comprehensive coverage of a topic. • To locate historical information on the topic. • To find summaries of research conducted on the topic.	• McGhee, P. E. (1999). *Health, healing and the amuse system: Humor as survival training.* Dubuque, IA: Kendall Hunt. • Robinson, V. (1991). *Humor and health professions* (2nd ed.). Thorofare, NJ: Slack.
Magazines	• To examine information or opinions on topics related to popular culture. • To locate current, up-to-date information on a topic. • To review articles written in general "layman" terms.	• Patients pleased; doctors surprised. (1998, June). *Physician's Management, 38*(6), 12. • Laugh it off. (2005, June). *Prevention, 58*(6), 55.
Scholarly Journals	• To search for scholarly research articles. • To identify what research has already been conducted on a topic. • To review reference lists of existing research to assist in locating other potential sources.	• Wanzer, M., Booth-Butterfield, M., & Booth-Butterfield, S. (1995). The funny people: A source orientation to the communication of humor. *Communication Quarterly, 43*, 142–154. • Wolf, M. H., Putnam, S. M., James, S. A., & Stiles, W. B. (1978). The Medical Interview Satisfaction Scale: Development of a scale to measure patient perceptions of physician behavior. *Journal of Behavioral Medicine, 1*, 391–401.
Newspapers	• To identify the most current information on topic of interest. • To review editorial and commentaries on a topic of interest.	• Howlett, D. (2003, March 4). It hurts not to laugh. *USA Today*, p. D9.
Encyclopedias & Handbooks	• To locate comprehensive summaries or background information on a topic. • To identify key concepts, authors, or dates.	• Nature Encyclopedia of Life Sciences • Encyclopedia of Rhetoric • Handbook of Health Communication
World Wide Web	• To locate statistics and quick facts. • To identify opinions of others on a topic. • To connect to library resources.	• http://www.hnu.edu/ishs/ISHSbibs/MEDICINE.doc. Retrieved December 21, 2011. • http://www.doaj.org – Directory of Open Access Journals

FIGURE 4.4
Types of Information Sources

magazines, and these magazines are fairly easy to locate. Students express reluctance about reviewing scholarly sources. The language used in journal articles is sometimes foreign to beginning researchers, but there are shortcuts that can help you sift through scholarly articles to locate information you can understand. We recommend reviewing the abstract first, which will provide an overview of the article. Next, skim the review of the literature to see what key concepts the researchers examined in the project. Finally, look at the discussion section. What conclusions did the researcher make as a result of the study? As you progress through this book, we will provide you with more tools for interpreting and writing scholarly research, but for the time being, it is important to note the differences between magazines and scholarly journal articles so that you can understand what each has to offer when conducting your review of literature. A summary of their differences is provided in Figure 4.5.

	Scholarly	**Popular**
Author	Written by experts in a specific field. Institutional affiliation is typically included.	Written by staff members, freelance writers, or anonymous sources.
Audience	Readers familiar with discipline's terminology and research history. Typically professors, researchers, and students.	General audience
Documentation	Extensive citations to reference other research studies. Typically include a reference page.	Includes little or no documentation outside of quotes by "witnesses."
Writing style	Scholarly and formal	Informal, casual language designed to inform or entertain.
Review process	Peer-reviewed	Not peer-reviewed
Publication	Published less frequently (quarterly, annually)	Published frequently (weekly, monthly)
Appearance	Plain. Graphics typically include charts, tables, and graphs.	Appealing to the eye. Colorful with several pictures and advertisements.
Examples	*Communication Quarterly* *Journal of Applied Communication*	*Time* *Sports Illustrated* *US News and World Report*

FIGURE 4.5
Distinctions Between Scholarly Journals and Popular Magazines

Scholarly journals are easy to identify based on the title alone. Many of them contain the word "journal" in the title, or they may contain a reference to the frequency of publication (e.g., "Quarterly" or "Annual"). Another clue can be found by flipping through the pages of the publication. Although popular magazines are designed to grab the reader's attention with their glossy pages and use of color and photographs, the appearance of scholarly journals tends to be plain. You will rarely find photographs in these publications; rather, you will note the use of graphs, tables, and charts depicting the results of data analysis. Scholarly journals should always be at the top of your list of information sources to consult when conducting a research study. Figure 4.6 lists many of the major journals in which communication research is published. Although this list is long, it is in no way exhaustive. In fact, communication-related work is often published in a wide range of journals, so do not think that the list provided here is complete.

Locating Information Sources

Just as a variety of information sources exist to assist you in conducting a review of existing literature on a topic, a variety of search tools are available to assist you in locating the specific sources of information. Often, students comment that "I searched for books on the library home page, and there are no sources on my topic." Although

Academy of Management Journal
American Anthropologist
American Behavioral Scientist
American Journal of Psychology
American Journal of Sociology
American Political Science Review
American Psychologist
American Sociological Review
Archives of Psychology
Argumentation and Advocacy
Asian Journal of Communication
Atlantic Communication Journal
Audio-Visual Communication Review
Australian Journal of Communication
Basic and Applied Social Psychology
Behavioral Science
Behavior
British Journal of Psychology
British Journal of Social and Clinical Psychology
British Journal of Sociology
Business Communication Quarterly
Canadian Journal of Behavioral Science
Canadian Journal of Communication
Central States Speech Journal
Child Development
Chinese Journal of Communication
Columbia Journalism Review
Communication and Cognition
Communication and Critical/Cultural Studies
Communication and Research
Communication Book Notes Quarterly
Communication, Culture, and Critique[1]
Communication Education[2]
Communication Law and Policy
Communication Methods and Measures
Communication Monographs[2]
Communication Quarterly[4]
Communication Reports[6]
Communication Research
Communication Research Reports[4]
Communication Studies[3]
Communication Teacher[2]
Communication Theory[1]
Communication Yearbook
Critical Studies in Mass Communication[2]
Cyber Psychology
Current Directions in Psychological Science
Editor and Publisher
Electronic Journal of Communication
ETC: A Review of General Semantics

European Journal of Communication
European Journal of Social Psychology
Family Process
Family Relations
Gender and Communication
Group and Organization Management
Health Communication
Howard Journal of Communication
Human Communication
Human Communication Research[1]
Human Organization
Human Relationships
HUMOR
Intermedia
International Journal of Listening
International Journal of Psychology
Journal of Science Communication
International Journal of Strategic Communication
International Organization
International Political Science Review
International Social Science Journal
Journal of Abnormal and Social Psychology
Journal of Advertising Research
Journal of Advertising
Journal of Anthropological Research
Journal of Applied Behavior Analysis
Journal of Applied Communication Research[2]
Journal of Applied Psychology
Journal of Asian Pacific Communication
Journal of Black Studies
Journal of Broadcasting and Electronic Media
Journal of Business
Journal of Business Communication
Journal of Business and Technical Communication
Journal of Business Research
Journal of Clinical Psychology
Journal of Communication[1]
Journal of Communication and Religion
Journal of Computer Mediated Communication
Journal of Conflict Resolution
Journal of Consumer Research
Journal of Cross-Cultural Psychology
Journal of Educational Psychology
Journal of Experimental Psychology
Journal of Experimental Social Psychology
Journal of Family Communication
Journal of General Psychology
Journal of Health Communication
Journal of Homosexuality
Journal of Intercultural Communication Research

FIGURE 4.6
Partial List of Communication Journals

Continued

Journal of Intergroup Relations
Journal of International and Intercultural Communication[2]
Journal of International Communication
Journal of Marketing Research
Journal of Marriage and the Family
Journal of Media and Religion
Journal of Nonverbal Behavior
Journal of Personality and Social Psychology
Journal of Popular Culture
Journal of Popular Film and Television
Journal of Psychology
Journal of Social and Personal Relationships
Journal of Social Issues
Journal of Social Psychology
Journal of Speech and Hearing Research
Journal of Verbal Learning and Verbal Behavior
Journal of Written Communication
Journal of Public Relations Research
Journalism Educator
Journalism Monographs
Journalism & Mass Communications Quarterly
Language and Speech
Language and Society
Learning and Motivation
Management Communication Quarterly
Management Science
Mass Communication Review
Media, Culture, and Society
Memory and Cognition
Middle East Journal of Culture & Communication
Newspaper Research Journal
New Jersey Journal of Communication
Ohio Journal of Communication
Open Communication Journal
Organizational Behavior and Human Performance
Personality and Social Psychology Bulletin
Personal Relationships
Personnel Psychology
Philosophy and Rhetoric
Political Behavior
Political Communication
Political Communication Review

Political Science Quarterly
Politics and Society Popular Communication
Progress in Communication Science
Psychological Bulletin
Psychological Record
Psychological Reports
Psychological Review
Psychological Science
Psychological Science in the Public Interest
Psychology of Women Quarterly
Public Administration Review
Public Opinion Quarterly
Public Relations Journal
Public Relations Quarterly
Public Relations Review
Qualitative Research Reports in Communication[4]
Quarterly Journal of Speech[2]
Risk Analysis: An International Journal
Science Communication
Semiotica
Sex Roles: A Journal of Research
Signs: Journal of Women in Culture and Society
Small Group Research
Social Forces
Social Science Research
Sociological Inquiry
Sociological Methods and Research
Sociological Quarterly
Sociology: Journal of the British Sociological Association
Sociometry: Social Psychology Quarterly
Southern Communication Journal[5]
Studies in Communication
Television Quarterly
Text and Performance Quarterly[2]
The Review of Communication[2]
Vital Speeches of the Day
Washington Journalism Review
Western Journal of Communication[6]
Women's Studies
Women's Studies in Communication
Women's Studies International Quarterly
World Communication

[1] Journal Sponsored by the International Communication Association.
[2] Journal Sponsored by the National Communication Association.
[3] Central States Communication Association.
[4] Eastern Communication Association.
[5] Southern States Communication Association.
[6] Western States Communication Association.

this could be because the specific topic is unique or recent and there may not be any books dedicated to it, you, as a researcher, should not stop the quest for existing literature! Just as it is important to know which tools are most beneficial for fixing or building something, understanding which "tools" are the best to use in your search for sources is essential to a successful research project. A common mistake made by beginning researchers is that they experience "tunnel vision" when searching for sources. Remember the earlier example where we expanded the list of key terms to include in our search for information on physicians' use of humor? Just as we broadened our scope of concepts to explore, we must broaden our scope of resources or tools to use in the search for literature. Three excellent tools for beginning the search include handbooks and subject encyclopedias, electronic databases, and the World Wide Web. The fourth item on your Research Planning Worksheet (Figure 4.1) asks you to identify examples of each of these tools to assist you in beginning your search for information.

HANDBOOKS AND SUBJECT ENCYCLOPEDIAS

The first step in any research project should involve examining printed resources that provide comprehensive coverage of topics in a given subject area. Two excellent resources for locating general sources of information are handbooks and subject encyclopedias. Using your key concepts, a search of general reference resources can direct you to bibliographies and summaries of research that has been conducted on your topic. As you search these sources, take careful notes about any additional key terms and concepts used to describe your topic.

HANDBOOKS Handbooks provide a comprehensive summary of past research and often include commentaries or recommendations for future research directions. Handbooks are an excellent starting point for identifying the themes that have already been used to examine a topic. Although they provide a broad look at communication, the fact that many handbooks focus on specific contexts makes them useful for examining the historical foundations of a specific topic area. Examples of handbooks include the following:

- *ASTD Handbook for Workplace Learning Professionals*
- *Handbook of Attitudes*
- *Handbook of Closeness and Intimacy*
- *Handbook of Communication and Instruction*
- *Handbook of Communication and Social Interaction Skills*
- *Handbook of Communication Ethics*
- *Handbook of Communication Science*
- *Handbook of Conflict Communication*
- *Handbook of Family Communication*

- *Handbook of Gender and Communication*
- *Handbook of Group Communication Theory and Research*
- *Handbook of Health Communication*
- *Handbook of Intergroup Research*
- *Handbook of International and Intercultural Communication*
- *Handbook of Instructional Communication: Rhetorical and Relational Perspectives*
- *Handbook of Interpersonal Communication*
- *Handbook of Language and Intercultural Communication*
- *Handbook of Language and Social Interaction*
- *Handbook of Media Studies*
- *Handbook of Nonverbal Communication*
- *Handbook of Organizational Communication*
- *Handbook of Organizational Justice*
- *Handbook of Personality Development*
- *Handbook of Political Communication*
- *Handbook of Public Relations*
- *Handbook of Risk and Crisis Communication*
- *Handbook of Sexuality in Close Relationships*
- *Handbook of Visual Communication*
- *IABC Handbook of Organizational Communication*
- *Media Handbook*
- *Work and Family Handbook*

SUBJECT ENCYCLOPEDIAS Subject encyclopedias are different from the *Encyclopedia Britannica*, with which most of us are familiar. The *International Encyclopedia of Communication* was first published in 1989, with the most recent edition in 2008, and is the first communication subject encyclopedia of its kind. Bibliographies and articles covering a variety of communication contexts are included. The index of this source is particularly useful for building your list of key terms and concepts.

Other examples of subject encyclopedias include the following:

- *The Concise Encyclopedia of Communication*
- *The Encyclopedia of Deception*
- *The International Encyclopedia of Communication Online*
- *The International Encyclopedia of Communication Research Methods*
- *The International Encyclopedia of Communication Theory and Philosophy*
- *The International Encyclopedia of Digital Communication and Society*
- *The International Encyclopedia of Intercultural Communication*
- *The International Encyclopedia of Interpersonal Communication*

ELECTRONIC DATABASES

Considering the prevalence of computers in our lives, it should come as no surprise that the most efficient and comprehensive searches for sources are conducted using electronic databases. Your professors have probably shared stories of the "good old days" when they had to search for sources using tools called "card catalogs" and "periodical indexes." Listen to their stories (trust us, they are telling the truth), hug your computer, and be thankful that search strategies have come a long way! A task that used to take researchers many hours can now be accomplished in a fraction of the time. With our list of key concepts previously identified during Step 2 in hand, it is time to begin the journey.

FINDING DATABASES **Electronic databases** (also referred to as "computerized" or "online" databases) can be thought of as a virtual library index where you can search for articles and books. Have you ever looked in the index of a book to find a specific topic or concept? It is much easier to find the term *paralanguage* in a 300-page textbook, for example, with the assistance of the index, and electronic databases serve as an enormous index. They search through literally thousands of records in seconds to help you find books and articles containing the key words you use to search. There are hundreds of databases to choose from, so the most difficult task may be selecting the one that best suits your research needs. Most libraries list databases both alphabetically and according to subject or content area for ease of searching.

Figure 4.7 lists a wide variety of databases that are useful for locating resources specific to communication and related areas. Included in the column on the right is the format of information in the database as well as a general description of the types of articles included. An excellent starting point to search for articles on any communication topics is the Communication and Mass Media Complete database in EBSCOhost. This database contains abstracts, citations, and some full-text articles.

It is important to note that libraries may not be able to provide access to all the databases included in Figure 4.7. Many electronic databases also require a subscription to allow access, so your ability to search particular databases often is dependent on whether your library subscribes to them. Suppose that your research topic is on teachers' use of humor in the classroom. Although the Communication and Mass Media Complete database is an excellent starting point for locating articles that have focused specifically on communication, be sure to search the ERIC (Education Resource Information Center) database, which includes published articles by scholars in the field of education. If you do not know whether your library has access to a given database, ask your friendly research librarian for help.

Database	Type of Information
Academic Search Complete	• Full text articles and abstracts for more than 13,000 different publications. • Social sciences, humanities, education, language/linguistics, and ethnic studies.
Business Source Complete	• Full text articles and abstracts. • Management, economics, finance, and international business. • Cited references are provided for more than 1,300 journals.
Child Development and Adolescent Studies	• Full text articles and abstracts. • This is the go-to database for information on individuals under the age of 21. • Has over 350,000 citations.
Communication Abstracts	• Full text articles and abstracts. • Interpersonal, mass, organizational, and small group communication; journalism; and public relations. • Has over 244,000 references.
Communications and Mass Media Complete	• Full text articles and abstracts. • Access to bibliographic references, reviews, encyclopedias, and handbooks. • Communication Studies and Media Studies • The database includes indexing and abstracts for more than 770 journals and includes full text for over 450 journals.
Educational Research Complete	• Full text articles and abstracts. • Topics covered include all levels of education from early childhood to higher education, and all educational specialties, such as multilingual education, health education, and testing. • Provides indexing and abstracts for more than 2,100 journals, as well as full text for more than 1,200 journals, and includes full text for nearly 500 books and monographs.
ERIC	• Citations from journals and reports • Field of education and related areas. • Sponsored by the U.S. Department of Education • Has more than 1.3 million links with further links to over 300,000 papers and articles.
Family & Society Studies Worldwide	• Full text articles and abstracts. • Coverage spans from traditional academic journals to government publications and working papers. • Indexes articles from a wide range of social science disciplines: anthropology, sociology, psychology, demography, health sciences, education, economics, law, history and social work.
Gender Studies Database	• The database covers the full spectrum of gender-related scholarship inside and outside academia. • This database includes more than 921,000 records with coverage spanning from 1972 and earlier to the present.
LGBT Life	• Full text articles and abstracts • Includes text for more than 120 of the most important and historically significant lesbian, gay, bisexual, transgender/transsexual journals, magazines and regional newspapers. • Contains more than 150 full-text monographs and books.

FIGURE 4.7
Types of Databases

Continued

FIGURE 4.7
Continued

LexisNexis Academic	• Full text and abstracts • Popular, scholarly, trade, and professional periodicals.
Medline with Full Text	• Full text and abstracts • Medline is the number one database for health and medical related information • Provides full text for more than 1,470.
Newspaper Source	• Selected full text articles, indexes and abstracts • Over 180 regional U.S. newspapers, international newspapers, newswires, newspaper columns and other sources • Full text television & radio news transcripts are provided from CBS News, FOX News, NPR, etc.
Psychology and Behavioral Sciences Collection	• Full text and abstracts • This is the world's largest full text psychology database offering full text coverage for nearly 400 journals
PsychArticles	• Abstracts, citations and some full-text articles • Contains full-text articles from over 40 journals published by the American Psychological Association. • Contains other smaller journals from the field of psychology from other publishers.
Papers First	• Full text and abstracts • Papers presented at conferences worldwide, covering every congress, symposium, exposition, workshop and meeting
Proceedings First	• Tables of contents of papers • Papers presented at conferences worldwide.
Social Science Citation Index	• Abstracts and citations • Coverage from nearly 50 social science disciplines.
Vocational and Career Collection	• Full text and abstracts • This collection provides full text coverage for nearly 340 trade and industry-related periodicals.

DATABASE SEARCHES Once you have identified the database that best suits your research needs, the next step involves selecting the type of search you wish to conduct. A variety of fields or criteria can be used to search for articles. These include the following:

- **Subject search**—searches for key terms that the author has submitted to describe the article or book.
- **Keyword search**—searches for a specific keyword or a set of keywords that a researcher is attempting to find.
- **Title search**—searches for words included in the title of an article or book.
- **Author search**—searches for the author's name.

We recommend conducting a subject search first. For example, the key terms *humor* and *physician* could be used to conduct a subject search. But suppose that only a few results are returned from this search. Remember that the subject search only includes the key terms provided by the author of an article or a book as subject descriptors, and the terms you enter must match those that the author supplied exactly. Suppose that the author described an article using the term *doctor* instead of *physician*. If so, it is likely that your initial subject search would not retrieve this article.

After the subject search, attempt the search again by entering the same phrase into a keyword search. A keyword search looks for a term anywhere in the library record. Essentially, a keyword search tells the computer to look for any instances in which the words appear in the title or abstract rather than limiting the search to only those words that the author has supplied as subject descriptors.

What if your search of key terms results in only one or two articles? Or worse yet, suppose that the results include more than 500 articles. Two tools—Boolean logic and truncation symbols—are available to help you expand or narrow your search. Using these tools will increase your search flexibility and maximize your research effectiveness.

BOOLEAN LOGIC The first flexibility aspect available in keyword searches involves **Boolean logic**. Boolean operators can be used in situations such as these to help narrow or expand the search. Three of the most commonly used operator terms are AND, OR, and NOT. When searching for articles that focus specifically on the use of humor in health contexts, it is beneficial to use the Boolean operator AND to narrow the focus. Doing so will return only a list of articles that include both terms (*humor* and *physician*). Another example of the AND Boolean operator can be seen at the top of Figure 4.8. In that example, we are looking for instances that involve the words "humor" and "health" at the same time.

The Boolean operator NOT can also be used to limit a search. This operator will exclude terms from your search that might otherwise be included in the results. When searching for articles about communication apprehension, say, you might want to exclude any articles that include the term *shyness*. Using NOT will help limit the results to those that focus specifically on apprehension. An example of the NOT Boolean operator can be seen in the middle of Figure 4.8. In that example, we are looking for instances where the term *communication apprehension* exists but the term *shyness* is not also present.

In some cases, a researcher might discover that the topic must be expanded. To do so, the Boolean operator OR can be used to conduct a search of all articles that include

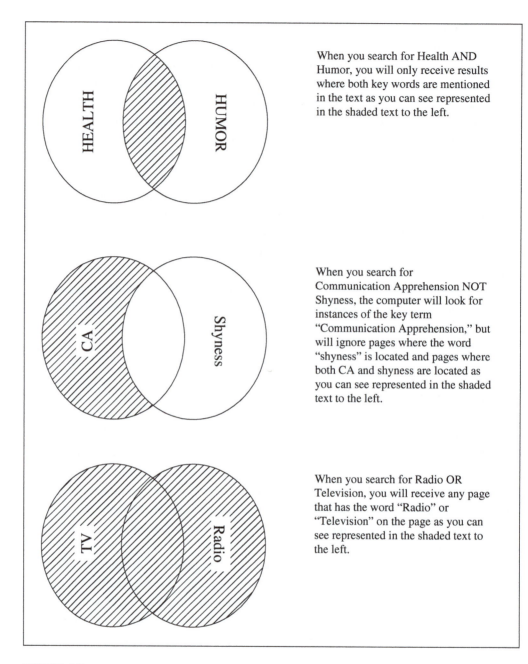

When you search for Health AND Humor, you will only receive results where both key words are mentioned in the text as you can see represented in the shaded text to the left.

When you search for Communication Apprehension NOT Shyness, the computer will look for instances of the key term "Communication Apprehension," but will ignore pages where the word "shyness" is located and pages where both CA and shyness are located as you can see represented in the shaded text to the left.

When you search for Radio OR Television, you will receive any page that has the word "Radio" or "Television" on the page as you can see represented in the shaded text to the left.

FIGURE 4.8
Boolean Operators

any of the search terms. Suppose that you were conducting a search for information about biased broadcast news coverage of the 2016 US presidential election and want to include all media types that people use as sources of information. The Boolean operator

OR could be used to tell the computer to search for any articles that contain at least one of the key terms included an example of the OR Boolean operator can be seen at the bottom of Figure 4.8. In that example, we are looking for instances where either the word "television" or the word "radio" is present.

TRUNCATION SYMBOLS The second flexibility aspect available in keyword searches involves **truncation symbols**. Have you ever searched for something only to discover that you forgot to explore some of your options or look in some places? Truncation symbols ensure that your search looks for every possible version of a word. Although the symbol used to truncate a word will differ from library to library, the one most commonly used is the asterisk (*). Suppose that you are searching for articles on the topic of children and divorce. In your list of key terms, you have identified "child" as a concept to explore. However, a search for the term *child* would overlook other versions of the word that might be used in subject fields. For example, this search would not pick up articles that use the words "children" or "child's." To ensure that your search grabs all versions of a word, include a truncation symbol with your key term. Entering "child*" would return a list of articles with any versions of the word "child."

THE WORLD WIDE WEB

Although electronic databases are the best tool for locating scholarly articles on a topic, the World Wide Web (WWW, or "the Web") can also assist in finding sources of information. When a topic has generated recent attention, it is essential that the researcher conduct a web search to obtain the most current information. After all, it

Search Engine	URL
General Search Engines	
Ask	http://www.ask.com/
Bing	http://www.bing.com/
Dogpile	http://www.dogpile.com/
Google	https://www.google.com
Yahoo	https://search.yahoo.com/
Specialty Search Engines	
Creative Commons	http://search.creativecommons.org/
Find Law	http://www.findlaw.com/
Library of Congress (multiple search engines)	http://www.loc.gov/
Medline Plus	http://www.nlm.nih.gov/medlineplus/
USA.gov	http://www.usa.gov/
Wolfram Alpha	http://www.wolframalpha.com/

FIGURE 4.9
Popular Web Search
Engines

can take anywhere from six months to two years for scholarly articles to be published. That means a significant period has elapsed before the article is listed in an electronic database. If you need to search for more current information, the Internet is the best tool for the job because it offers a multitude of research benefits. In addition to searching for current information, it can be used to locate scholarly articles that are housed in databases your campus library does not have available.

Some of the most commonly used search engines are listed in Figure 4.9. The first part of the list covers search engines that will yield general results across the WWW. The second part contains what are called specialty search engines that focus on more narrow topics of focus. For example, USA.gov is a great search engine to look across state and federal government websites for specific information.

Some professors may advise students against using the Web to search for information for a project. However, it is important to obtain clarification as to how they define "using the Web." Most often, instructors prefer that students refrain from citing only information from websites as sources for a research paper. But this does not mean that you should not use the Internet to assist you in locating research articles. After all, searches of electronic databases are conducted using the computer, and the articles are often retrieved in electronic format rather than going to the printed version of the journal or newspaper. You would not want to write a research paper on the topic of organizational culture and only cite information that you found through a Yahoo! search. However, you can locate scholarly articles on a topic using popular search engines if you take a few moments and search in the correct locations. (We will discuss special methods for citing sources that are retrieved electronically later in this chapter.)

Google Scholar

Did you know that Google has a section dedicated to searching for scholarly articles? Google Scholar is a database of scholarly research articles and texts that can be utilized to find academic, peer-reviewed information (http://scholar.google.com/). All you have to do to conduct a search is to type in a keyword or term into the search bar and click OK. For example, type in "communication apprehension" and you will find nearly 16,300 web sources (quite a bit more research since we initially ran this search for the first edition of this book in 2008—2,500). You will see that many of the initial results have J. C. McCroskey's name listed, which is a good sign because he is the originator of the term *communication apprehension*. Conducting a search in this fashion will return lists of articles and books that have been included in scholarly publications. Many of these articles can be downloaded in full-text format, whereas others will include online access.

Google Scholar is a great tool, but we do have some words of caution about using it. First, many of the citations listed in Google Scholar will take you to for-profit academic databases that will try to get you to pay money for access to the research article. From our experience using Google Scholar, most of those "for-pay" websites contain information you should have access to through your college or university's library. As such, you should never assume that you need to pay for information, or that you cannot get access to information because the link through Google Scholar takes you to a "for-pay" website.

Our second word of caution comes in the form of the type of manuscripts found on Google Scholar. Although many of the articles you can find through Google Scholar will be reproductions of physical articles (in the form of PDF documents), others may be preprints or .html files of research information. If an article is a scanned copy of the original article, you do not have to worry because it will look exactly the same as if you picked up the printed version in the library. However, when an article is a preprint copy, which should be clearly indicated on the first page, the article may look distinctly different than the final version. As such, you must follow the APA guidelines on citing a preprint publication. For articles found in .html, you must realize that there are not page numbers in a typical .html file, so you will need to cite information according to the paragraph number. We warn you about both of these problems because Google Scholar will present you with a variety of document types that will need to be cited differently according to APA style.

OTHER ONLINE RESEARCH DATABASES

Beyond various Internet search engines that can help you find scholarly information, a number of research organizations are also helping to catalog available scholarly journals that have full-text access online. One such open-access database is the Directory of Open Access Journals (DOAJ) (http://www.doaj.org/). The DOAJ's goal is to provide scholarly information to both scholars and the general public at no cost. The DOAJ had cataloged more than 7,000 full-text journals at the time the current edition of this textbook was written (again, this number has more than tripled since 2008, when the DOAJ cataloged around 2,000 journals), and it includes a number of publications from the list in Figure 4.6—for example, the *American Communication Journal*; *Conflict and Communication Online*; *Communication and Culture Online*; *Journal of Intercultural Communication*; *Journal of Literature, Culture, and Media Studies*; *Journal of Science Communication*; *Open Business Journal*; and *The Jury Expert*.

For information pertaining specifically to communication, the Communication Institute for Online Scholarship (CIOS) (http://www.cios.org/) is a not-for-profit service that has a searchable database of communication abstracts. Although some of the functions of CIOS are free to the public, others require a small annual fee. CIOS also houses the online publication *Electronic Journal of Communication* and a number of open-access communication books, including *Communication, Affect, and Learning in the Classroom* (3rd ed.) by Virginia Peck Richmond, Jason S. Wrench, and Joan Gorham. If you are going to be completing a lot of research, joining CIOS can be cost-effective. Furthermore, CIOS also features open-access books and journals on the website.

Working with Librarians

One invaluable resource that researchers have up their sleeves is the research librarian. Sadly, many people do not know the value of a librarian today. For some reason, there is a growing feeling among the general public that librarians are becoming antiquated because of the Internet and search engines. However, the reality is quite different. If anything, because of the sheer abundance of information at our disposal today, librarians are more important than ever before as they are trained in helping researchers weed out the rubbish and find the material most appropriate for their research. Although a librarian will not do the research for you, he or she can point you in directions that you never would have considered. Librarians at colleges and universities generally have a Master's degree, and sometimes even a doctorate, in library and information sciences, so librarians are a highly trained and specialized group of individuals. And in today's rapidly evolving information landscape, librarians keep on top of the newest trends in information delivery while ensuring that they understand how to utilize older models.

In a book that one of the authors of this text cowrote (Wrench, Goding, Johnson, & Attias, 2011), he sent an e-mail to research librarians across the country asking them about tips and strategies for students working with librarians. Sadly, there is little information available for students on working with research librarians. But after receiving responses from librarians around the country working at all shapes and sizes of academic institutions, 18 general recommendations for student researchers emerged:

1. Your librarian is just as knowledgeable about information resources and the research process as your professor is about his or her discipline. Collaborate with your librarian so that you can benefit from his or her knowledge.
2. Try to learn from the librarian so that you can increase your research skills. You will need these skills as you advance in your academic coursework, and you will rely on these skills when you are in the workplace.
3. When we are in our offices, we are not on reference desk duty. Whether an office door is open or closed, please knock first and wait to be invited in. With that said, if we are at the reference desk, we are there to help you. Please ask! You are not interrupting. Helping students does not bother us. It is our job and profession, and we like doing it.
4. I am here to teach you, not go to bat for you. Please do not expect me to write a note to your instructor because the materials (reference, reserve, or whatever) were not available.
5. Please, please, please do not interrupt me when I am working with another student. This happens regularly and we work on a first-come, first-served basis. Wait your turn.
6. If we help you find sources, please look at them, so we will be more likely to want to help you in the future.
7. Research is a process, not an event. If you have not allocated enough time for your project, the librarian cannot bail you out at the last minute.
8. Do not expect the librarian to do the work that you should be doing. It is your project and your grade. The librarian can lead you to the resources, but you must select the best sources for your particular project. This takes time and effort on your part.
9. Reference librarians are professional searchers who went to graduate school to learn how to do research. Reference librarians are here to help no matter how stupid a student thinks her or his question is.
10. Good research takes time and, although there are shortcuts, students should still expect to spend some time with a librarian and to trawl through the sources they find.

11. Students should also know that we ask questions like, "Where have you looked so far?" and "Have you had a library workshop before?" for a reason. It may sound like we are deferring the question, but what we are trying to do is gauge how much experience the student has with research and to avoid going over the same ground twice.

12. Students should approach a librarian sooner rather than later. If a student does not find what they need within 15 minutes or so, they must come find a librarian. Getting help early will save the student a lot of time and energy.

13. If you do not have a well-defined topic to research or if you do not know what information resources you are hoping to find, come to the reference desk with a copy of your class assignment. The librarian will be glad to help you to select a topic that is suitable for your assignment and to help you access the resources you need. Having at least a general topic in mind and knowing what the assignment entails (peer-reviewed only, three different types of sources, etc.) helps immensely.

14. Most academic librarians are willing to schedule in-depth research consultations with students. If you feel you will need more time and attention than you might normally receive at the reference desk or if you are shy about discussing your research interest in a public area, ask the librarian for an appointment.

15. Students should be as specific as possible in what they ask for, if they know their topic. Students who are struggling with identifying a narrow topic should seek help from either their professors or librarians. We cannot help you find sources if your topic is not clear.

16. Students must learn that many questions do not have ready-made or one-stop answers. Students must understand that an interface with a reference librarian is a dialog and part of a recursive, repetitive process. They must make time for this process and assume an active role in the exchange.

17. Students should understand that information can come in a variety of formats. If a student asks for a "book about" something without providing any other details about the information needed, that student could come away empty handed. Instead, students should get in the habit of asking for "information about" something first.

18. "Gee thanks!" every now and then will win every librarian's heart! (pp. 103–104)

Evaluating Web Sources

Let's revisit our earlier statement about professors discouraging students from using web sources for research projects. This is not because they fear a conspiracy against libraries. Typically, instructors will discourage the use of web sources because of the difficulty in evaluating the quality of information located on sites. There is no peer-review process for publishing information on the Internet. Anyone can post anything on the Web. A 14-year-old can create a website for a class project on media coverage of the recent election and include a personal commentary, for example. And if you fail to evaluate the credibility of the source, you could end up quoting a 14-year-old as an expert source for your persuasion research project. Four criteria should be used to examine the credibility and quality of web sources. These include accuracy, authority, currency, and objectivity.

ACCURACY

The accuracy of a site is evaluated by taking a closer look at its content. Is the information free of errors? If you notice spelling and writing errors on the site, this should be a signal that the author of the information has not taken care to proofread the material before publishing it. Look to see whether an editor for the site is listed. Unlike printed publications, web sources rarely go through any type of editorial process to check for errors.

AUTHORITY

To assess the authority of web sources, first look to see whether the page is "signed." Who is the author? What credentials are listed on the site? If the site is sponsored by a credible organization, this lends credibility to the information. But suppose the site does not include any information about the author or sponsoring organization. Clues about the authority of the source can sometimes be identified by examining the web address (or URL) for the site. For example, suppose you are conducting a research project on the topic of assessing the credibility of web resources. During your search, you locate a link to the following site: http://lib.nmsu.edu/instruction/eval.html/. By examining the web address more closely, you notice that the article is published by someone at New Mexico State University, as identified by the ".edu" extension in the URL. Because the information is from an academic institution, you can be fairly confident that it is a credible source. Other extensions that could signal credible sources include ".gov" (which are government sites) and ".org" (which are organization sites). Be careful of information found on ".com" sites because often these websites are used for advertising, not to provide unbiased information to the public.

CURRENCY

The currency of web sources can be determined by looking for dates that indicate when the site was created and when it was last updated. Dates will ensure that the information cited in a research paper is current. The dates of websites are typically included at the bottom of the page. Always check whether links to sites are still active. Do not include links to sites in your paper that are no longer in existence. Doing so indicates that you have not checked the currency of the information you are citing.

OBJECTIVITY

Last, but certainly not least, the objectivity of the site should be assessed. Look for links on the site to sections titled "About," "Philosophy," or "Background" to provide information about the goal or mission of the site. As you browse the website, ask yourself whether there is a hidden bias or purpose to including information on the page. If it appears that there is a bias, ask yourself how this biased information could be useful to your project if you decide to include it, or at least mention in your paper that the information may be biased because of the source.

The Wikipedia Problem

By this point in your academic career, you have undoubtedly come into contact with information from Wikipedia. Wikipedia is an open-source online encyclopedia that allows anyone to edit its entries. In essence, anyone can add information to Wikipedia that may or may not be factual. When we look at the four criteria for evaluating websites, Wikipedia only excels at one—currency. Yes, Wikipedia is great for current information and allows new information to be added constantly. However, it does have three huge problems: (1) entries in Wikipedia consistently contain inaccurate information, (2) there is a lack of clear authority of the authors of the entries, and (3) there is no way to ascertain the authors' objectivity. In other words, Wikipedia may be a good launching point for getting a basic understanding, but it should never be considered a useable source for academic research.

In essence, Wikipedia is a problematic secondary source of information. As we discussed earlier in this chapter, researchers should mainly use primary sources unless there is clear justification to use a secondary source. In an article for *The Chronicle of Higher Education*, Brock Read (2006) recalls an interview he had with Jimmy Wales, one of the cofounders of Wikipedia:

> *I get an e-mail every week from some college student who says, "Help me; I cited you and I got an F on my paper." I always say the same thing: "For God's sake, you're in college now!" People really need to be educated not just about whatever topic they're looking for, but about the meta-question of, "How do you decide what to trust?" (p. A36)*

In other words, even one of the cofounders of Wikipedia realizes that it should not be used for academic research purposes.

STEP 4: ORGANIZING AND EVALUATING INFORMATION

At this point in the research process, we must emphasize the importance of maintaining a working bibliography. After all, why spend hours conducting research on a topic if you do not have a game plan for organizing the sources and information you locate? The bibliography is simply a list of sources that you have located and examined in conducting the review of literature. Trust us—eventually you will need this information as you cite sources of information in your "Review of Literature" and "References." It is much easier to record the information now than to recreate the list later. Nothing is more frustrating than putting together a reference list only to discover missing information such as the year the source was published or the page numbers of an article.

Maybe you are not a fan of working with index cards, so try the sticky-note method instead. The sticky-note method requires you to print out all of the articles you plan on using within a research project. As you go through these articles, look for big ideas and mark them within the article, along with your immediate thoughts. Additionally, write down those ideas (along with the page numbers) on a sticky note. When you finish with an article,

Docear

One piece of software we recommend is called Docear; it is freely available and can be downloaded for multiple operating systems (http://www.docear.org/). Docear allows you to organize your thoughts electronically (and back them up to the Cloud). Unlike using either index cards or sticky notes, Docear assumes that you will be working completely electronically, so it works in conjunction with Adobe Acrobat Reader (http://get.adobe.com/reader/). Adobe Acrobat Reader allows you to read portable document formats, or PDFs. When you are reading PDFs, you save them to your hard drive, and you highlight the articles and even make notes electronically within the program. When you are done reading the articles, you can then import the PDF files (including all of your highlights and annotations) right into Docear. You also have the ability to highlight and annotate documents in Docear. Once you have all the research articles you think you will need, you can then start organizing your articles into a visual mind map. For people who like to think through things visually, Docear is a great tool. Go ahead, check it out! It is free, so you have nothing to lose and everything to gain.

place the sticky note directly on top of the article. By doing this, you will find your ideas (along with the relevant page numbers) within journal articles and books more effectively.

Effective library searches and organization strategies include the following steps:

- *Step 1:* Using your list of key terms, begin searching general reference materials. Review handbooks, subject encyclopedias, electronic databases, websites, or other reference sources.
- *Step 2:* As you locate potential sources of information, complete a source record card (see Figure 4.10) for each source. Be sure to include all required

SOURCE:	**Book**	**Journal**	**Text Journal**	**Webpage**	**Magazine**	**Newspaper**

Title:_____

Article Title (for journal, magazine or newspaper)

_____

Author(s) _____

Copyright Date OR if web site, date you used website_____

Publisher of book OR Sponsor of website_____

Place of Publication OR Web URL _____

NOTES:

_____
_____
_____
_____
_____

FIGURE 4.10
Source Record Card

information—this will save you the work of going back and looking for it later. The type of source will dictate the information that must be included in citations and references. Figure 4.11 provides a summary of the pieces of information needed to correctly cite sources.

- *Step 3:* Review the abstract as you locate each source. Next, review the discussion section if the article comes from a scholarly journal. If the source is a book, glance at the table of contents and the index. This will be useful in determining whether the source contains information that is relevant to your study.

- *Step 4:* Read through the bibliographies of the sources that you locate. You might discover that the author has cited articles that would be useful for your study!

Source	Citation Elements Needed
BOOK	• Author's Name (may be more than one) • Date of Publication/Copyright • Title • Publisher • City/State where published
PRINT JOURNAL ARTICLE	• Author's Name (may be more than one) • Publication Date • Title of Article • Title of Journal • Volume Number • Issue Number • Page numbers of article • Digital Object Identifiers (doi)
ELECTRONIC/FULL-TEXT VERSION OF A PRINT JOURNAL ARTICLE	• Same info as for Print Journals • Database name or access path • Date the article was accessed • NOTE: Some electronic versions of articles may not include page numbers
WEBPAGE	• Author's Name • Title or description of the page • URL • Date the page was accessed
MAGAZINE ARTICLE	• Author's Name • Publication Date • Title of Article • Title of Magazine • Volume Number • Issue Number • Page numbers of article
NEWSPAPER ARTICLE	• Author's Name (if available) • Publication Date (Month/Day/Year) • Title of Article • Title of Newspaper • Page Number
Interviews with People	• Interviewee's Name • Date of Interview

FIGURE 4.11
APA Information

STEP 5: CITING SOURCES OF INFORMATION USING THE APA FORMAT

Given the wide variety of communication contexts (e.g., rhetoric, interpersonal, media studies), scholars may adopt diverse writing styles when reporting on the research in their particular area. Consider the fact that each student in your own class has a unique writing style. If your professor did not provide any guidelines for how the paper should be written, sources that should be included, or page length, chances are that each paper written in your class would be vastly different in terms of format. The same is true for research that is published in academic journals. Guidelines exist to provide standards for how sources and references should be cited and how papers should be formatted.

Any researcher who is writing an article for publication is required to adhere to publication guidelines. Although a host of different style manuals exist (e.g., MLA, *The Chicago Manual of Style*), the preferred format for most communication journals is **APA style**. APA is a style of writing that was developed and is revised by the APA. Every detail of the format required for research papers is described in the *Publication Manual of the American Psychological Association* (APA, 2010). Most libraries keep a copy of this manual at the reference desk, and numerous online sites provide summaries for quick reference (http://www.apastyle.org/). To correctly adhere to format guidelines, it is important to understand what information must be referenced in a research paper and how sources of information should be cited. Figure 4.12 shows a checklist of APA format guidelines to refer to when preparing a research paper for submission to a conference or journal. Information about general formatting issues (e.g., margins, font size, and spacing) as well as details about the layout of subsequent pages and sections in the paper are included. It is important to note that this list is by no means comprehensive.

What Information Must Be Referenced?

As a general rule, all work done by other researchers that you wish to include in your own study must be referenced and cited. Any instance in which you include the exact words of another author must be quoted. Not giving proper credit to their work is considered plagiarism. Typically, any information you do not reference will be interpreted as general knowledge or your own work. Information that is general knowledge does not need to be referenced. For example, it is common knowledge that George H. W. Bush was a president of the United States, so it is unnecessary to cite a source for that particular fact.

A good strategy to use when writing your paper is to build your reference list as you work on the text of the paper. As you include a source in the paper, scroll down to a

Section of Paper	Citation Elements Needed
General Format of Paper	<ul><li>1 inch margins top, bottom, left & right</li><li>12 point font (Times Roman or Courier)</li><li>Double-space throughout paper</li><li>Align along left margin</li><li>Paragraph indentions 5 spaces</li><li>Page number located 1 inch from right edge of paper on first line of every page (including title page)</li><li>Running head on every page located five spaces to the left of the page number on every page</li><li>Use active voice</li></ul>
Page Order	<ul><li>Title</li><li>Abstract</li><li>Body of Paper</li><li>References</li><li>Appendices</li><li>Footnotes</li><li>Tables</li><li>Figures</li></ul>
Title Page	<ul><li>This is always page 1</li><li>Include Running Head, Paper Title, Author, Institutional Affiliation, and Author Note.</li><li>All text is double-spaced</li><li>The Words "Running head:" should be followed by the Running head in All Capital Letters.</li></ul>
Abstract	<ul><li>One paragraph summary of highlights of paper</li><li>Begins on page 2</li><li>120 words or less</li><li>Heading "Abstract" centered and bolded on first line below header</li><li>Body of abstract in block format, left justified</li><li>From this point forward, the words "Running head:" are no longer needed, but the running head itself should still be left justified with the page number right justified.</li></ul>
Body	<ul><li>Begins on page 3</li><li>Tile of paper centered on first line below header</li><li>Main headings (i.e., Methods, Results, Discussion) are centered using uppercase and lowercase letters</li><li>Subheadings are italicized and left justified using upper and lowercase letters</li></ul>
Reference Page	<ul><li>Begins on a separate page</li><li>Heading "References" is centered on first line after header</li><li>Names in alphabetical order of last name</li></ul>
Appendices	<ul><li>Begins on a separate page</li><li>Heading "Appendix" is centered on first line below header</li><li>For more than one appendix use "Appendix A" "Appendix B" and so forth</li></ul>
Tables	<ul><li>Begins on a separate page</li><li>Heading "Table 1" (or Table 2, etc.) is left justified on the fist line below the header.</li><li>Double-space after the title "Table x" and type the table title left justified</li></ul>

FIGURE 4.12
APA Style Checklist

reference page and list the source using APA format. This is where the information included on your source record cards (Figure 4.10) will come in handy. As a general rule, the reference page should begin on a separate page. The title "References" should be centered on the first line below the running head. All sources included in the references should be alphabetized by the first author's last name. Each reference includes four primary elements: (1) author(s) name, (2) year of publication, (3) title of book and or article, and (4) retrieval information. Figure 4.13 shows a sample of what many journal articles published in the field of communication look like on the title page. An example of a reference for a journal article would look like the one in Figure 4.14.

Figure 4.15 includes information for citing a variety of sources. If you have a source that is not included on this list, please consult your librarian, the APA style manual, or an online APA style guide. Finally, Figure 4.16 provides the various ways that articles should be cited within the text of a paper. Note that different types of author combinations will lead to different requirements for your in-text **citations**.

Citing Sources of Information

There are four general guidelines to consider when including citations. First, citations should be included for all sources of information that you have directly quoted in the paper. Second, citations should be included when summarizing or paraphrasing information from another source. Although you are not directly quoting the source, it is still

FIGURE 4.13
Sample Article

Journal of Generic Communication, Volume 9: 1–11, 2012
Copyright # Name of Publisher,
ISSN: 1081-07xx print/1087-04xx online
DOI: 10.1090/108107304902714xx

6th Edition of the APA Style Manual: New Trends & Changes

Jason S. Wrench

SUNY New Paltz

Candice Thomas-Maddox

Ohio University Lancaster

Year of publication appears in parentheses followed by a period.

Author's last name followed by a comma, then first initial followed by a period, and middle initial followed by a period. If there is more than one author, seperate the names with a comma followed by an ampersand (&) symbol.

The first word in the journal title is capitalized. All subsequent words begin with lower case letters (with the exception of formal names). If the title includes a colon, the first word after the colon is also capitalized.

Wrench, J. S., & Thomas-Maddox, C. (2010). 6th edition of the APA style manual: New trends & changes. *Journal of Generic Communication,* *9,* 3-11. doi: 10.1090/108107304902714XX

Journal titles are italicized. Each word in the title is capitalized. The title is followed by an italicized comma.

Next we have the volume number (notice it is still italicized). The volume number is followed by a comma (notice the comma is not italicized).

Next you have the page numbers for the article followed by a period.

Lastly, we have the digital object identifier (doi). The doi is written in lower case followed by a colon. The APA Style manual strongly recommends copying and pasting the doi from the PDF version of the journal article into your references to ensure that you do not make any mistakes. Just as an FYI, not all articles will have a doi.

FIGURE 4.14
APA Reference

FIGURE 4.15
Sample APA References

Research Article in a Journal—One Author, No doi

Wrench, J. S. (2010). Development and validity testing of the Risk Communicator Style Scale. *Human Communication, 13*, 233–257.

Research Article in a Journal—Two to Five Authors with a doi

Teven, J. J., Richmond, V. P., McCroskey, J. C., & McCroskey, L. L. (2010). Updating relationships between communication traits and communication competence. *Communication Research Reports, 27*, 263–270. doi:10.1080/08824096.2010.496331

Book – One Author

Kasssing, J. (2011). *Dissent in organizations.* Malden, MA: Polity Press.

Edited Book

Daly, J. A., McCroskey, J. C., Ayres, J., Hopf, T., Ayres Sonandré, D. M., & Wongprasert, T. K. (Eds.). (2009). *Avoiding communication: Shyness, reticence, and communication apprehension* (3rd ed.). Cresskill, NJ: Hampton Press.

Chapter in an Edited Book – One Author

Chory, R. M. (2010). Media entertainment and verbal aggression: Content, effects, and correlates. In T. A. Avtgis & A. S. Rancer (Eds.), *Arguments, aggression, and conflict: New directions in theory and research* (pp. 177–197). New York, NY: Routledge.

Chapter in an Edited Book – Two or More Authors

Bryant, E. M., Marmo, J., & Ramirez, A., Jr. (2011). A functional approach to social networking sites. In K. B. Wright & L. M. Webb (Eds.), *Computer mediated communication in personal relationships* (pp. 3–20). New York, NY: Peter Lang.

Continued

FIGURE 4.15
Continued

Newspaper Article	Richtel, M. (2011, December 18). Reframing the debate over using phones behind the wheel. *The New York Times*, p. A25.
Magazine Article	Spenner, P. (2010, December). Why you need a new-media "ringmaster". *Harvard Business Review, 88*(12), 78–79.
In press Version of an Article	Regazzi, J. J. (in press). Constrained? – An analysis of U.S. academic library shifts in spending, staffing and utilization, 1998–2008. *College and Research Libraries*. Retrieved from http://crl.acrl.org/content/early/2011/09/21/crl-260.full.pdf
Blog	Wrench, J. S. (2011, October 28). Stand Up, speak out: The practice and ethics of public speaking [Web log post]. Retrieved from http://www.jasonswrench.com/blog/blog1.php/stand-up-speak-out-the
Vlog	Wrench, J. S. (2009, May 15). Instructional communication [Video file]. Retrieved from http://www.learningjournal.com/Learning-Journal-Videos/instructional-communication.htm
Discussion Board	Wrench, J. S. (2009, May 21). NCA's i-tunes project [Online forum comment]. Retrieved from http://www.linkedin.com/groupAnswers?viewQuestionAndAnswers
E-mail List	Wrench, J. S.. (2009, June 19). Communicast [Electronic mailing list message]. Retrieved from http://lists.psu.edu/cgi-bin/wa?A2=ind0906&L=CRTNET&T=0&F=&S=&P=20514
Podcast	Wrench, J. S. (Producer). (2011, December 21). *Communication apprehension* [Audio podcast]. Retrieved from http://www.communicast.info/CA.mp3
Electronic-Only Book	Richmond, V. P., Wrench, J. S., & Gorham, J. (2009). *Communication, affect, and learning in the classroom* (3rd ed.). Retrieved from http://www.jasonswrench.com/affect
Electronic-Only Journal Article	Holton, A. E., & Lewis, S. C. (2011). Journalists, social media, and the use of humor on Twitter. *Electronic Journal of Communication, 21*(1&2), Retrieved from http://www.cios.org/www/ejcmain.htm
Electronic Version of a Printed Book	Wood, A. F., & Smith, M. J. (2004). *Online communication: Linking technology, identity & culture* (2nd ed.). Retrieved from http://books.google.com/books
Online Magazine	Lachlan, K.A. (2011, December). Using institutions of faith to communicate about crises and emergencies. *Communication Currents, 6*(6). Retrieved from http://www.communicationcurrents.com
Online Newspaper	Clifford, S. (2011, November 2). With an app, your next date could be just around the corner. *The New York Times*. Retrieved from http://www.nytimes.com
Entry in an Online Reference Work	Viswanth, K. (2008). Health communication. In W. Donsbach (Ed.), *The international encyclopedia of communication*. Retrieved from http://www.communicationencyclopedia.com. doi: 10.1111/b.9781405131995.2008.x
Entry in an Online Reference Work, No Author	Communication. (2009). In *Collins English dictionary* (10th ed.). Retrieved from http://dictionary.reference.com/browse/communication
E-Reader Device	Lutgen-Sandvik, P., & Davenport Sypher, B. (2009). *Destructive organizational communication: Processes, consequences, & constructive ways of organizing.* [Kindle version]. Retrieved from http://www.amazon.com

FIGURE 4.16
APA Parenthetical
Citations

Type of Citation	Citation Listed in the Text		Citation Set Apart from the Text	
	First Time	*Subsequent Times*	*First Time*	*Subsequent Times*
One work by one author	Wrench (2012)	Wrench (2012)	(Wrench, 2012)	(Wrench, 2012)
One work by two authors	Wrench and McCroskey (2012)	Wrench and McCroskey (2012)	(Wrench & McCroskey, 2012)	(Wrench & McCroskey, 2012)
One work by three to five authors	Wrench, Thomas-Maddox, Richmond, and McCroskey (2012)	Wrench et al. (2012)	(Wrench, Thomas-Maddox, Richmond, & McCroskey, 2012)	(Wrench et al., 2012)
One work by six or more authors	Wrench et al. (2012)	Wrench et al. (2012)	(Wrench et al., 2012)	(Wrench et al., 2012)
Groups (readily identified through abbreviation)	National Communication Association (NCA, 2012)	NCA (2012)	(National Communication Association [NCA], 2012)	(NCA, 2012)
Groups (no abbreviation)	Generic University (2012)	Generic University (2012)	(Generic University, 2012)	(Generic University, 2012)
Author (no date)	Wrench (n.d.)	Wrench (n.d.)	(Wrench, n.d.)	(Wrench, n.d.)
Author with manuscript in press	Wrench (in press)	Wrench (in press)	(Wrench, in press)	(Wrench, in press)

important to let your reader know where you located the original information. Third, citations should be used when you want to direct your reader's attention to relevant research or important facts or information. Finally, citations are not required for information that is common knowledge.

PARENTHETICAL CITATIONS

Parenthetical citations (also referred to as internal citations) are used when you are including information taken directly from another source. This enables the reader to identify where the information was obtained, and it lends credibility and authority to your research. Citing sources of information is often one of the most difficult aspects of research writing for some students because they are reluctant to use the words of others. We have all heard our instructors warning about the penalties for plagiarizing the work of others. But do not forget that the very nature of scholarly research *requires* you to use the work of others in order to build a rationale for your own work. After all, the foundation for research is built on the unanswered questions or weaknesses of previous studies.

Parenthetical citations include three primary elements of information: (1) the author's last name, (2) the date of publication, and (3) the page number(s) if a direct quote from the source is included in the text of your article. The format used to cite your sources depends on the goal of the reference. If your goal is to highlight a specific concept or idea, typically the parenthetical citation information would be included at the end of the sentence. Suppose your goal is to highlight the scholarship of a particular researcher. Then, the parenthetical citation should begin with the researcher's last name, followed by the year of the article you are citing in parentheses. When the goal is to follow a chronological order while citing information, the year of the source should appear first, followed by the author's name. Examples of how to cite information for these three goals are included in Figure 4.17.

QUOTATIONS AND PARAPHRASES

Quotations involve the use of another author's exact words in your study, and it is important to give credit where credit is due. After all, not citing a source is considered plagiarism. As a general rule, use direct quotations only if you have a good reason for doing so because including numerous quotations from sources causes the author's own voice and ideas to become "lost" in the project. Ensure proper credit is given to sources by using the author's exact words, including the quotations in quotation marks (unless you are citing a long source, in which case it should be included in an indented block), and indicating the page number where the quotation is published.

Use quotations to highlight strategically selected information. You have probably been told by teachers to provide as much evidence as possible in support of your thesis. But packing your paper with quotations will not necessarily strengthen your argument. The majority of your paper should still be your original ideas in your own words (after all, it is your paper). And quotations are only one type of evidence. Well-balanced

FIGURE 4.17
Internal Citations

Focus of Citation	Sample Citation
Conceptual/Idea	Physicians and other medical professionals personally use humor as a means of coping with the uncertainty that surrounds the medical profession (Bosk, 1996; Wanzer, Booth-Butterfield, & Booth-Butterfield, 1997).
Researcher	Fitzpatrick (1993) described patient satisfaction as an "emotional link to healthcare."
Chronology	In 1991, Booth-Butterfield and Booth-Butterfield identified the concept of humor orientation, otherwise referred to as HO.

papers may also make use of paraphrases, data, and statistics. The types of evidence you use will depend in part on the conventions of the discipline or the audience for which you are writing.

One of the biggest mistakes novice researchers make is including excessive direct quotations. Remember, the goal is to be original, so if more than 5% of your paper is directly quoted from other sources, you are not really being original. A good general rule of thumb is you should probably not have more than one direct quotation for a single section of a paper.

You should never have just a string of quotations in a paper. When you use quotations, you should (1) provide a clear context for the quotation, (2) attribute the quotation to its original source, (3) explain the significance of the quotation, and (4) provide the correct parenthetical citation. Note that none of these four steps involves just stringing a series of quotations together with no explanation or context.

Paraphrasing refers to including another author's ideas in your own words and involves summarizing or highlighting one or two important points from the author. Consider the following example:

ORIGINAL

"It is important to recognize that no single artifact, value, or assumption is, or can create, an organization's culture" (Keyton, 2005, p. 28).

PARAPHRASE

Keyton (2005) emphasizes that one cannot simply examine only one dimension of an organization and understand its current culture. Rather, a researcher

Using Direct Quotations

There is no great single rule for explaining when to use direct quotations. However, there are some pretty good questions to help you decide if that direct quotation is actually necessary:

1. Does the quotation contain exact wording needed for technical accuracy (e.g., definition, law, regulation, or theory)?

2. Does the quotation clearly show that a recognized authority supports your argument?

3. Does the quotation contain a contested or critical claim?

4. Does the quotation contain moving or historically important language?

5. Does the quotation include a term or expression coined or created by the author?

6. Does the quotation explain a difficult or complex concept in a concise manner?

must be willing to examine multiple facets of the organization to gain a comprehensive understanding of the history and factors that have led to the existing culture.

Remember that paraphrases should always include the author's name and the year of the publication from which the information was retrieved. Typically, paraphrases are not enclosed within quotation marks or indented. After all, these words represent your interpretation of the source's work and are not taken directly from the source article. Some find paraphrasing to be difficult at first. We recommend reviewing several examples of published work to increase your familiarity and comfort with the style used to cite information from other sources.

APA PAPER FORMATTING

The last part of this chapter discusses how to format your paper using APA style. Although the next chapter will discuss what goes in each section of a paper, there are a few formatting issues we must discuss first. In this section, we look at formatting issues related to the title page, abstract, first page, and reference page.

Creating a Title Page

The title page is the page that goes on top of your actual document when you are getting ready to either turn in your paper to your professor or send it off to a conference or journal for possible publication. A number of unique parts of an APA title page (in addition to the title itself) may be tricky if you are not used to working with APA style. Figure 4.18 shows what a title page should look like.

RUNNING HEADS

The first thing you may notice about an APA title page is that it has something called a running head. A running head is a series of words that is placed on every page, followed by a page number, so a reader knows that all of the pages with that running head on it belong to the same document. Often, people who review manuscripts for conferences or publications will read 20 to 50 manuscripts at a time, so the running head prevents pages from getting misplaced or attached to the wrong document. A good running head should be distinct and relate to the overarching topic of your paper. However, a running head can be no longer than 50 characters counting letters, characters, and spaces between words. You will notice that on the first line of the title page you type the words "Running head:" followed by your actual running head in all capital letters. By doing this, you enable your reader to quickly see what your running head is. You will also notice that your title page contains your running head in the upper left corner, down half an inch from the top of the page. Your running head is then flushed right about 1"

FIGURE 4.18
APA Title Page

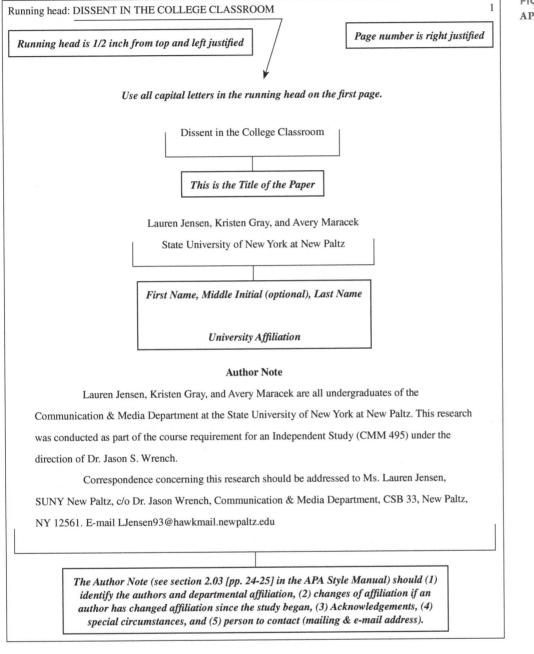

Running head: DISSENT IN THE COLLEGE CLASSROOM   1

Running head is 1/2 inch from top and left justified

Page number is right justified

Use all capital letters in the running head on the first page.

Dissent in the College Classroom

This is the Title of the Paper

Lauren Jensen, Kristen Gray, and Avery Maracek

State University of New York at New Paltz

First Name, Middle Initial (optional), Last Name

University Affiliation

Author Note

Lauren Jensen, Kristen Gray, and Avery Maracek are all undergraduates of the Communication & Media Department at the State University of New York at New Paltz. This research was conducted as part of the course requirement for an Independent Study (CMM 495) under the direction of Dr. Jason S. Wrench.

Correspondence concerning this research should be addressed to Ms. Lauren Jensen, SUNY New Paltz, c/o Dr. Jason Wrench, Communication & Media Department, CSB 33, New Paltz, NY 12561. E-mail LJensen93@hawkmail.newpaltz.edu

The Author Note (see section 2.03 [pp. 24-25] in the APA Style Manual) should (1) identify the authors and departmental affiliation, (2) changes of affiliation if an author has changed affiliation since the study began, (3) Acknowledgements, (4) special circumstances, and (5) person to contact (mailing & e-mail address).

from the edge of the page. Most computer programs have header programs built in to enable you to place your running head and page numbers automatically rather than attempting to do it by hand.

PAPER TITLES

Next on a title page, you will find the paper's title. A title should sell a reader on what the overarching topic of your paper will be so that the reader can see whether he or she wants to read further. APA recommends that your title be approximately 10 to 12 words, but this is only a guideline. Some titles are considerably longer, and some are shorter—it all depends on what you need so that your intended audience will realize your paper relates to a topic they are interested in reading about. Titles should also avoid using abbreviations, opting instead for spelling out technical acronyms. Titles are often used for cataloging research articles and papers, so ensuring that your title contains all of the appropriate key terms and words makes for a more efficient title.

AUTHOR NAME(S) AND AFFILIATION(S)

The next part of the title page consists of the author's name and university/professional affiliation or the authors' names and university/professional affiliations. Authors in academia are not listed alphabetically on a paper. Generally, author names are listed according to who contributed the most to a specific project. Although many articles have one author, other projects have listed as many as 900 authors. Most papers rarely have more than five authors, but some projects will have more people who have actually contributed to the success of the research project. The lead author on a project is the person who has contributed the most to the conceptualization and enactment of the research project itself and so is listed as the first author. Often, the first author then determines who shall be the second author, third author, and so on, listed on the title page. Besides the listing of the authors' names on a project, each author's university/organizational affiliation is also listed below her or his name.

Creating an Abstract

The second page in an APA style paper is an **abstract**. Although what goes into an abstract will be discussed in the next chapter, here we want to discuss the basic formatting of an abstract. Figure 4.19 contains an example abstract.

Abstracts should have one-inch margins all the way around (except for the running head, which is still half an inch from the top of the page). The word "Abstract" is centered on the first line, which should be one inch from the top of the page. The abstract should be double spaced and left justified, which means that there is not an indention or tab on the first line of written text.

FIGURE 4.19
APA Abstract
Formatting

DISSENT IN THE COLLEGE CLASSROOM   1

Notice the words "Running head:" are no longer shown.

Center the Word "Abstract"

Abstract

This study sought to evaluate two existing scales that measure dissent in the college classroom, one measuring dissent behaviors (articulated and latent), and the other measuring dissent motivators (expressive, rhetorical, and vengeful). Expressive and rhetoric motives seemed to be the most similar with articulated and latent dissent behaviors, with vengeful motives having no connection whatsoever. Additionally, teacher power was related to student dissent motives and behaviors with pro-social and anti-social types of power normally opposing with relationship to student dissent. As expected, rhetorical and articulate dissent had similar relationships with respect to teacher power, credibility, and learner empowerment. Learning loss was found to be positively related to both expressive and vengeful student dissent motives, and a negative relationship between learning loss and the rhetorical student dissent motive was uncovered. As expected, a negative relationship between both expressive and vengeful student dissent motives and affective learning was noted. However, a positive relationship between student affect for teacher (instructor evaluation) and the rhetorical student dissent motive was uncovered.

Keywords: student dissent, teacher power, teacher credibility, learner empowerment, student learning

Abstract text is completely left justified.

The keywords section is one of the new additions to the 6th edition of the APA Style Manual. The Keywords should include a short list of 4 to 6 terms that are highlighted within the basic body of the study. Notice the word "Keywords" is italicized followed by an italicized colon. The keywords themselves are not italicized and written in lower case letters unless a keyword is a proper noun.

Creating the First Page

The third page of your APA style paper is the first page of actual text and contains the text related to the actual paper you plan on writing. However, there are still a few important formatting issues that you should know about when creating your first page.

Figure 4.20 shows the first page of the paper by Jensen, Gray, and Maracek that we have been examining in the past few figures. You will see that the first few lines of the paper contain the same title that you have listed on the title page. The reason that your title is listed both here and on your title page is that often editors and conference reviewers never see your title page because academics use what is called blind review. Blind review is the process where an editor or conference program planner sends out papers anonymously to other scholars and has them evaluate the scholarly quality of the paper. Because editors and conference program planners want honest feedback about the quality of the paper, papers should have no identifying marks on them that would let a reviewer know who the author is. For this reason, title pages are taken off papers when they are sent out to reviewers, so it is important to have the title of your paper on the first page of the actual manuscript.

After the title on the first page of your written manuscript, you always indent new paragraphs using the tab function on your word processor. If you do not have a fancy word processor, one tab is approximately 10 spaces on your average key-board. Although this section gives you some basic information on how to format a paper, you should really buy a copy of the most recent version of the APA style manual because there are so many other formatting issues that we cannot go into in this textbook. Everything from politically correct language to formatting tables is covered in the APA style manual, so make sure you buy a copy if you have not already done so.

Creating the Reference Page

The aspect of APA formatting we will discuss in this section is how to format a **reference page** using APA style. Although you may have formatted works cited pages, a reference page is distinctly different. Figure 4.21 shows a brief reference page.

The first thing you will see on a reference page is the running head in the upper left corner, like it has been on every page of your manuscript. Next, you will have the word "References" centered one inch from the top of the page. Notice that the word "References" is not bolded because it is considered distinct from the other headings within your paper. From here, place all of your references for every source that is cited within your manuscript alphabetically by the first author on the source. The first line of the citation is left justified, but the rest of the citation is aligned to the right one tab (or 10 spaces), which is called a hanging indent. Also, note that the reference page is double spaced.

FIGURE 4.20
APA Style First
Page

Dissent in the College Classroom   1

Title is centered and double spaced on the first page of the actual paper.

Dissent in the College Classroom

First sentence of any new paragraph is indented 1 tab or roughly 1 inch.

Student dissent in the college classroom is a phenomenon that is vastly understudied. Only a few articles to date research this expression of disagreement or contrary opinions (Goodboy, 2011a, 2011b; Jensen. et al., 2011). Students dissent in a variety of ways, for a variety of reasons, a well-known fact to both instructors and students alike. This study has two main purposes to investigate the phenomenon of dissent in the college classroom. The first is to evaluate both the scales that attempt to measure student dissent. The two measures that have been created to measure dissent in the college classroom are the Student Dissent Scale (SDS) created by Jensen et al. (2011) and the Instructional Dissent Scale (IDS) created by Goodboy (2011a). This study compares the two scales to see where, and if, they differ in regards to students' expressions of dissent in the college classroom. The second general goal of this study is to gain further exploratory insight into student dissent. To gain this insight, this study also examines teacher power, teacher credibility, learner empowerment, student cognitive learning and student affective learning in regards to student, and instructional dissent.

Review of Literature   *First Level Heading (see page 62, sec 3.03 in the APA Style Manual)*

Classroom Dissent   *Second Level Heading*

There is so little research surrounding the area of student dissent, which is why the little exploratory and preliminary research there is based off of Organizational Dissent and the Organizational Dissent Scale (ODS) (Kassing, 1997, 1998). Organizational dissent is defined as "expressing disagreement or contradictory opinions about organizational practices, policies and operations" (Kassing, 1998, p. 183). Oftentimes when employees' dissent in their organization, it is because they feel apart from their organization (Kassing, 2011). Dissent "mandates a separation or distancing from the majority" (Kassing, 2011, p. 29). Although dissent requires disagreement and contradiction, it does not need to be destructive

There are many problems you can run into when creating a reference page, so we urge you to buy a copy of the APA style manual. Our brief help section here is simply not adequate to explain every citation you may face.

FIGURE 4.21
APA Reference
Page Formatting

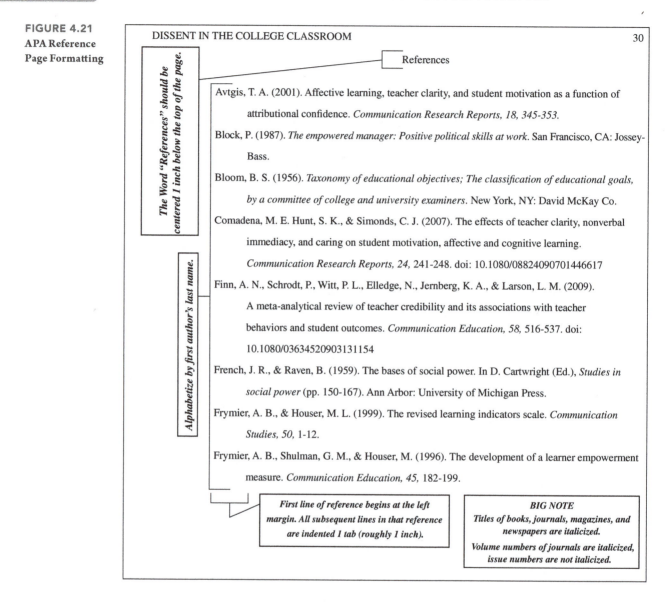

CONCLUSION

In this chapter, we have examined how to pick a topic, how to find research materials using a variety of different tools, and how to use basic APA style. In the next chapter, we will examine the various parts of a research paper, with special attention paid to how to write literature reviews, a rationale section (research questions and hypotheses), and a method section.

KEY TERMS

Abstract p. 124

APA style p. 114

Author search p. 102

Axioms p. 86

Backtracking p. 92

Boolean logic p. 103

Citations p. 116

Electronic databases p. 100

Keyword search p. 102

Paraphrasing p. 121

Parenthetical citations p. 119

Primary sources p. 91

Quotations p. 120

Reference page p. 126

Secondary sources p. 91

Subject search p. 102

Title search p. 102

Truncation symbols p. 105

REFERENCES

American Psychological Association. (2010). *Publication manual of the American Psychological Association* (6th ed.). Washington, DC: American Psychological Association.

Berger, C., & Calabrese, R. (1975). Some explorations in initial interaction and beyond: Toward a developmental theory of interpersonal communication. *Human Communication Research, 1,* 99–112.

Hairston, M., & Ruszkiewicz, J. J. (1996) *The Scott, Foresman handbook for writers* (4th ed.). New York, NY: HarperCollins.

Keyton, J. (2005). *Communication and organizational culture: A key to understanding work experiences.* Thousand Oaks, CA: Sage.

Read, B. (2006, October 27). Students flock to an easy-to-use reference, but professors warn that it's no sure thing. *Chronicle of Higher Education, 53*(10), A36.

Thomas, C., Booth-Butterfield, M., & Booth-Butterfield, S. (1995). Perceptions of deception, divorce disclosures, and communication satisfaction with parents. *Western Journal of Communication, 59,* 228–245.

West, R., & Turner, L. H. (2006). *Introducing communication theory: Analysis and application* (3rd ed.). Boston, MA: McGraw-Hill.

Wrench, J. S., & Booth-Butterfield, M. (2003). Increasing patient satisfaction and compliance: An examination of physician humor orientation, compliance-gaining strategies, and perceived credibility. *Communication Quarterly, 51,* 482–503.

Wrench, J. S., Goding, A., Johnson, D., & Attias, B. (2011). *Stand up, speak out: The practice and ethics of public speaking.* Irvington, NY: Flat World Knowledge.

FURTHER READING

American Psychological Association. (2010). *Concise rules of APA Style: The official pocket style guide from the American Psychological Association* (6th ed.). Washington, DC: American Psychological Association.

Anderson, C. E., Carrell, A. T., & Widdifield, J. L., Jr. (2007). *What every student should know about citing sources with APA documentation.* Boston, MA: Allyn & Bacon.

Frey, L., Botan, C., & Kreps, G. (2000). *Investigating communication: An introduction to research methods* (2nd ed.). Englewood Cliffs, NJ: Prentice Hall.

Girden, E. R., & Kabacoff, R. I. (2011). *Evaluating research articles: From start to finish* (3rd ed.). Los Angeles, CA: Sage.

Hocking, J. E., Stacks, D. W., & McDermott, S. T. (2003). *Communication research* (3rd ed.). Boston, MA: Allyn & Bacon.

Salkind, N. J. (2017). *Statistics for people who (think they) hate statistics* (6th ed.). Thousand Oaks, CA: Sage.

Singleton, R. A., Jr., & Straits, B. C. (2017). *Approach to social research* (6th ed.). New York, NY: Oxford University Press.

Research Structure and Literature Reviews

CHAPTER OBJECTIVES

1. Understand the basic information that one should include in a study abstract.

2. Explain how to write an introduction to a paper.

3. Apply the different methods for laying out a literature review.

4. Describe the different parts of a method section.

5. Explain the basic purposes for both results and discussion sections.

Organization is one of the most important processes in any endeavor we undertake. Many people try to jump right into the writing process without making sure all of the necessary tools, safeguards, and supplies are readily at hand. Have you ever tried to build something, only to realize halfway through your project that you do not have a tool you need? Have you ever known someone who bought a do-it-yourself building project-, only to finish that project and realize they have some leftover parts? Being organized helps people to see deficiencies and to prepare for future success. Whether you are building a bridge or writing an article for a communication journal, you must be organized in your thinking and organization to achieve success.

▲ That Thing You're Supposed to Be Writing
Source: Piled Higher and Deeper by Jorge Cham – www.phdcomics.com

Many authors do not organize their research articles in an effective manner, only to realize midway through the writing process that they are missing a key point. Other people finish writing a paper and then realize that it has serious gaps in logic. Being an organized writer means selecting and arranging the appropriate ideas and materials for the paper into a logical and discernible pattern. An organized writer has thought out her or his paper and created a clear pattern that readers can follow. Additionally, if a reader can understand a paper, the reader will recall the information more easily.

Although most of the information in this chapter is similar to what students receive in basic public speaking courses every year, there are some specific aspects to organizing a research paper that are unique. This chapter focuses on how to organize an article into a format that will ultimately help readers retain information. To examine organization, this chapter discusses the major parts of a research paper (abstract, literature review, methods, results, and discussion) in separate sections. The chapter also dissects portions of an article by Jason S. Wrench and Melanie Booth-Butterfield (2003) to aid in your understanding of the concepts discussed here. To read the entire article by Wrench and Booth-Butterfield, see the textbook's website (https://oup-arc.com/wrench).

Figure 5.1 illustrates the basic components of a traditional research article written in American Psychological Association (APA) style. The rest of this chapter walks through these different parts to help you understand the layout of a research paper.

THE ABSTRACT

You may have heard the old adage, "You never get a second chance to make a good first impression." This statement is undeniably true. No matter how hard we try, people will always remember the first time they met us. Although writing a research paper is not exactly like meeting someone, the paper's abstract is just as important as an introduction

FIGURE 5.1
Steps in a Research
Paper

is when meeting a person. For example, if you bore someone the first time you meet him or her, the two of you are not likely to become friends. Similarly, if you bore someone in your abstract, you will turn that person off to your paper immediately—and possibly even turn that person off to your topic in general. If you are an interesting person to talk to when you first meet someone, however, people will be drawn to you as a person. Likewise, if your paper has a good abstract, people will be drawn to you as an author and ultimately to your topic. An **abstract**, simply defined, is a short paragraph at the start of a scholarly paper that concisely and comprehensively explains the contents of the paper. In other words, an abstract is a snapshot of the overall paper.

According to the *Publication Manual of the American Psychological Association* (APA, 2010), an abstract should be accurate, self-contained, and concise/specific. Accurate means that an abstract should correctly reflect what occurs in the paper itself. If your paper is about public speaking and your abstract discusses football, your abstract is not reflecting what actually occurs in the paper. Self-contained indicates that the abstract should not need any specialized information for the reader to understand what it is communicating. To be self-contained, an abstract should clearly define any abbreviations and acronyms, spell out the names of tests and/or drugs, define any unique terms, and accurately cite any relevant research without directly quoting the source. Finally, concise/specific signals that a good abstract is not a complete retelling of your entire paper. Rather, it should give as much information as needed to help a potential reader understand what your paper is discussing. According to the APA manual, an abstract should not be more than 120 words in length. Although that may sound like a lot of words, it is not. An abstract should explain to your readers your basic purpose for writing the paper and any relevant results and conclusions. However, many research projects can have more than 10 or even 20 results or major conclusions, so it is usually best to limit your number of conclusions in the abstract to the five most important findings.

One note should be made about the abstract. Although we are discussing the abstract at this point in this text to present the parts of a paper, according to APA style, in the order in which they are read, an abstract is written after everything else is complete. You cannot write a meaningful abstract until you have finished writing the rest of the manuscript. Your abstract is like a quick snapshot of everything you did in your study.

Look at the abstract in Figure 5.2. Note how the abstract explains, in a brief manner, what is actually discussed in the rest of the paper. When researchers are conducting literature searches, they often will read only the abstract to see whether the article contains any useful information. Understanding the purpose of an abstract can also greatly reduce the time it takes to complete a full literature search.

This study examined the impact that patients' perceptions of a physician's humor orientation, credibility, and compliance-gaining strategies had on their satisfaction and compliance. Perceived physician humor orientation positively related to perceived physician credibility, physician compliance-gaining strategies, and patient satisfaction. Other positive relationships among perceived physician credibility, physician compliance-gaining strategies, and patient satisfaction emerged. Compliance did not relate significantly to physician humor orientation and perceived credibility. Aspects of patient satisfaction and physician use of compliance-gaining strategies affected compliance. Additionally, this study revealed minimal differences among data collection methods (undergraduate ($N = 44$), graduate ($N = 48$), general public ($N = 66$), and online participation ($N = 26$)).	General sentence explaining the overall purpose of the study. Goes into specific detail related to the various findings in this study. Lastly, the abstract mentions a secondary analysis examining the different data collection methods employed in this study.

Analysis	
Accurate	If you read the actual article completely, you will notice that the basic purpose discussed at the beginning of the abstract correctly explains what occurs throughout the study.
Self-contained	Although the abstract may be confusing if you do not know what the terminology means (e.g., perceived credibility, physician humor orientation), notice that no acronyms are used and tests were not specifically referred to by name. For example, instead of referring to a Physician's HO the authors specifically call it a physician's humor orientation.
Concise and specific	If you compare the results section with the results described above, you will notice that the results discussed above are the major results discussed in the article itself.

FIGURE 5.2
Article Abstract

THE INTRODUCTION

Now that we have discussed the first part of a paper, we can focus on the "traditional" **introduction** of a research paper. Overall, the introduction portion of a paper is extremely important. It focuses a reader's attention and helps that reader understand the scope and focus of a paper. This section uses a number of the articles from the textbook's website to illustrate various aspects of an introduction; an introduction by Wrench and Booth-Butterfield (2003) is shown in Figure 5.3.

A good introduction should have six basic components: an attention-getter, a link to the topic, a statement of the topic's significance, an espousal of credibility, a thesis statement, and a preview (McCroskey, Wrench, & Richmond, 2003).

Attention-Getter

The first part of an introduction is referred to as an attention-getter because this portion should be able to grab your reader's attention. After the abstract, the first words in your paper are probably the most important of your entire document. If you can grab your reader's attention in a unique or captivating way, your reader will continue to read what you have to say. There are a number of attention-getters that writers can use to successfully capture the reader's interest.

USING STATISTICS OR CLAIMS

One way to get the reader's attention is to alarm her or him with the use of a startling statistic or claim. People tend to respond to information that has a statistical assessment attached. Although statistics can be useful in demonstrating the extent to which there is a problem or the occurrence of a phenomenon, statistics can also be misleading and come back to haunt a writer. When using statistical information, knowing how the statistic was generated can add credence to your message. Consider the following statement: "According to a new study, 50 percent of the people exposed to a new drug will develop liver cancer (Hause & Botner, 2000)." If in this drug trial only two people had been exposed to the drug, repeating the results from this study as an attention-getter would be misleading.

Likewise, startling claims can be made to grab a reader's attention. "You have a greater chance of dying in your car on the way to the airport than you do once you have entered the terminal (Smith, 2000)" could be a startling claim to begin a paper on air safety. However, the same concerns that apply to startling statistics apply to startling claims as well. You must know the validity of the claim you are making.

When deciding whether a startling statistic or claim is a useful attention-getting device for a research paper, ask yourself three important questions. First, will this statistic or claim cause some readers to become interested in my research topic? If you start your research paper with a dull statistic or claim, readers are not likely to go beyond the introduction.

At the end of visits to a personal physician, the physician generally will prescribe some sort of medication, treatment, or lifestyle change to help patients recover from, or cope with, medical problems. Since physicians reportedly have high credibility as healers in our society, one might assume that patients would follow their physician's directions. Yet, nearly 50% of all patients do not follow the prescribed treatment from their physicians (Stone, 1979). This statistic has not changed much in the last twenty years (Bullman, 1996). Such data link to a number of negative outcomes, not only for noncompliant patients, but others in the community as well. People who do not comply may contribute to higher medical costs and insurance rates because they are often subject to re-treatment as a result of therapeutic failures, recurring, or lingering infections, which can ultimately lead to surgical interventions and hospitalizations that initially are not necessary (Baskin, 1998). Surprisingly, noncompliance rates are as high for individuals suffering from severe chronic pain as they are for those having symptomless diseases (Tamaroff, Festa, Adesman, & Waco, 1992; Turk & Rudy, 1991). One possible way to rectify this lack of compliance is through better patient–physician interactions (Fitzpatrick, 1991). Therefore, it is useful to examine variables that may indicate whether one will follow a physician's directions.	Notice in the first two sentences how the purpose of this article is foreshadowed.

An introductory discussion of the problem of patient noncompliance is initiated here.

Transition to thesis statement. |
| Our study concerned how a physician's perceived humor orientation, credibility, and communication competence relate to patients' levels of satisfaction and their compliance. We begin this report by examining scholarly literature concerning patient compliance, patient satisfaction, and medical humor. | Thesis statement.

Preview. |

Analysis	
Attention-getter	This attention-getter was a statement of fact. Most people expect to be told about a medication, treatment, or lifestyle change at the conclusion of a medical interview.
Transition to topic	"Since physicians reportedly have high credibility as healers in our society, one might assume that patients would follow their physician's directions."
Significance of topic	Discussion of how noncompliance affects cost of medical care for everyone.
Espousal of credibility	Consistent citation of both primary and secondary sources throughout the introduction paragraph.
Thesis	"Our study concerned how a physician's perceived humor orientation, credibility, and communication competence relate to patients' levels of satisfaction and their compliance."
Preview	"We begin this report by examining scholarly literature concerning patient compliance, patient satisfaction, and medical humor."

FIGURE 5.3
Article Introduction

Second, is the statistic or claim so outrageous that it could prevent someone from believing what I have to say? You must be careful to avoid offending the reader's logic with a statistic or claim. If an author wrote that "100 percent of Americans who travel in trains die," people would laugh at the author and think that he or she was nuts. If an author used this outlandish statement, it would not matter whether the author had a citation for her or his statistic; people would be highly skeptical and simply dismiss the paper based on this one simple fact. Lastly, is there a better way of grabbing the audience's attention? Always ask yourself this question when deciding on an attention-getting device. Often, our first idea for an attention-getting device is not ultimately the best device that we can use.

POSING A RHETORICAL QUESTION

A **rhetorical question** asks the reader to ponder the question internally, without audibly responding to it. Many research papers state the overall theme of the study right off the bat by posing a rhetorical question. For example, if an author was planning on studying communication apprehension across the life cycle (children, teenagers, young adults, and retirement age), he or she might ask, "Although the importance of communication apprehension to communication scholars is clear, how does communication apprehension affect people across the life cycle?" From this question, the author could discuss various articles that have examined communication apprehension in different populations or age groups.

USING AN ACKNOWLEDGED FACT

The next way to grab an audience's attention is to start with a widely acknowledged fact and build on it. To use an acknowledged fact as an introduction, the fact must be fairly universal so that any reader will have the ability to quickly understand and agree with what has been written. For example, in the article by Chesebro (1999), he began by saying the following:

> Most people have encountered different types of listeners. Some people seem quite responsive and notice even the slightest of our nonverbal cues. Others carefully scrutinize and analyze our messages. Some people can't wait until we just get to the point. Others look at their watches with the hope that we will recognize that they would rather be somewhere else. The way in which our interaction partners listen is important to us when we are the ones doing the talking. (p. 234)

In this attention-getter, Chesebro has identified common problems that everyone experiences and notices when communicating with other people.

USING A STORY OR ILLUSTRATION

An author can also grab a reader's attention by telling a story that relates to her or his topic. For example, if you are writing a paper about how test anxiety affects student performance in the classroom, you could start off by explaining how one student missed every test day because of apprehension, which ultimately caused that student to fail.

Another way to grab your audience's attention is to use an illustration. Whereas we use "stories" to refer to the telling of real or pseudo-real events that relate to your topic, **illustrations** are more general stories that can apply to a variety of different contexts. For example, one famous illustration is the story of the frog that agrees to transport a scorpion on its back across the river, on the condition that the scorpion will not sting him. During the trip, however, the scorpion stings the frog. While the scorpion and frog are drowning, the frog asks why the scorpion broke his promise, to which the scorpion responds, "I'm a scorpion; I sting things." This short illustration can apply to a number of contexts. You could use it to begin a paper on how humans have innate personalities that cannot be changed, on the problems of being too trusting, or on how organizations change. Ultimately, the usefulness of an illustration lies in an author's clear connection from the illustration to the topic at hand.

QUOTING OR ACKNOWLEDGING A SOURCE

The most common way of introducing a paper is to directly quote or acknowledge another source. As discussed in the previous chapter, directly quoting a source is when author A copies the exact text of author B's document and places it verbatim into author A's new work. For example, in the article by Brummans and Miller (2004), the authors start by quoting a chunk of text from Schumacher that reads:

> Ortega y Gasset once remarked that "life is fired at us point-blank." We cannot say: "Hold it! I am not quite ready. Wait until I have sorted things out." Decisions have to be taken that we are not ready for; aims have to be chosen that we cannot see clearly. (Schumacher, 1995, p. 15)

Following this quotation, Brummans and Miller then discuss how in the information age life moves quickly and our lives are earmarked by constant change.

The final way to grab an audience's attention is simply by acknowledging a source. As discussed in the previous chapter, acknowledging a source is when an author paraphrases specific information and then gives credit for that information to the scholars who are responsible for it. For example, in the article by Weber, Fornash, Corrigan, and Neupauer (2003), the authors started with "Much of the research conducted in the instructional realm has dealt with the effect of affective variables on cognitive learning (Wanzer & Frymier, 1999)." In this attention-getter, the authors did not directly quote from Wanzer and Frymier; they paraphrased what Wanzer and Frymier wrote in their study.

Link to the Topic

The next major part of the introduction is the link from the attention-getter to the actual topic of your paper. Some attention-getters are easy to link directly to your topic. For example, the attention-getter used by Chesebro (1999) discussed previously spends an entire paragraph explaining, in common terms, how he perceives the link between an individual's listening style and conversational sensitivity, which is the goal of his overall study. However, other attention-getters take more creativity to make a clear link to the topic. Of the examples listed in the previous subsection on attention-getting devices, the hardest one to link directly to a topic is usually an illustration (e.g., the scorpion and the frog) because an illustration is a metaphor for the topic itself and not all metaphors are clearly seen by people reading them.

Significance of the Topic

The third major step in the introduction of a paper is demonstrating why the topic is significant enough for your reader to care. If you are writing a paper about a communication phenomenon seen only by tribesmen in a remote part in South America, you are going to have a hard time demonstrating why academics in the United States should care about your topic. However, if you can demonstrate that this communication phenomenon is similar to something we do in the United States or contradicts something we think is a communication fact, then you can help others see why your topic is significant. One of the hardest facts to get new researchers to understand is that research for research's sake is not significant. Every researcher should be able to clearly answer the question "Why should we care?" or "So what?" in a couple of sentences.

Espousal of Credibility

The fourth major component of the introduction of a paper is the espousal of one's credibility to write a paper on the subject. Although in public speaking we talk about espousing one's credibility in terms of your personal qualifications for speaking on a subject, in writing papers credibility is less about explaining how one is credible and more about supporting one's assertions through the citation of empirical research. If you have not completely researched a concept, a trained reader will clearly see gaps in your literature that are extremely important. So within your introduction, you must start integrating literature appropriately, both to help build your case for significance and to demonstrate that you have examined previous research and are not just stating your opinions. Even the number-one researcher in the field of communication must demonstrate that a paper is thoroughly researched and supported by the literature. For example, look at the article by McCroskey, Richmond, Johnson, and Smith (2004) to see how McCroskey and his colleagues thoroughly cite previous research before starting the literature review.

Thesis

The fifth part of a good introduction is the thesis statement. A **thesis** is a short, declarative sentence that explains to a reader the purpose of the paper itself. If you are writing a paper on how cults use thought reform (brainwashing) to influence their victims, for example, your thesis may be "The process of thought reform, although often misunderstood, is not difficult when a person is unknowingly vulnerable to outside influences."

Preview

After the thesis, an author generally transitions into a brief preview of what will be examined in the literature review. In a **preview**, the author lists the specific subsections that he or she is planning on covering in the literature review of the paper. For example, to preview the thought reform paper, one could say, "To understand how thought reform occurs, an analysis of the history of thought reform research, common thought reform tactics, and how cults use these tactics will be examined in the literature review, followed by a series of hypotheses and research questions for the current study." In this case, each of the phrases mentioned in the preview would be a single distinct subsection written in the literature review.

LITERATURE REVIEW

One of the most important parts of a research paper, and often the largest, is the literature review section. A **literature review** is the selection of available documents (published and unpublished) on a given topic that contain information, opinions, data, and evidence written from a particular point of view that aid a reader's understanding of important concepts and research findings prior to examining the results in a new study. For most people, the literature review is the easiest section to write and the one they are most familiar with writing. A literature review is like a series of brief research papers about various related topics.

In an article by Rocca and Vogl-Bauer (1999) looking at sports fans' perceptions of appropriate fan communication, the researchers examined three major areas of literature. The authors first discussed some background on the popularity and known behavior of sports enthusiasts, then verbal aggression, and finally how individuals identify with various teams. By clearly explaining the research previously completed in the three subcategories, Rocca and Vogl-Bauer were able to help the reader gain a full understanding of the current state of research in each area and how these three separate areas could be studied together in the rationale for research questions section of their article.

Five Reasons for Literature Reviews

Literature reviews serve a very important function within the scope of a research study. Let's look at five basic reasons for literature reviews.

EXPLAINING VOCABULARY

One of the fundamental aspects of a literature review is that it is educational and definitional. A literature review must clearly explain all technical terms related to that research paper. In academia, we often create terms that have slightly different meanings than they do when used by the general public. For example, to communibiologists, the term *psychoticism* refers to the degree to which an individual believes that society's rules pertain to her or him. But if you ask people in the general public what psychoticism means, you will probably get definitions related to psychological disturbances, such as antisocial personality disorder, schizophrenia, or borderline personality disorder. Even scholars in different subfields of the same discipline can define the same term in slightly different ways, so it is always important to clearly specify what you mean by various terms in a literature review to ensure that everyone is on the same page. Also, having clear definitions helps a researcher to "operationalize" her or his, or when a researcher determines how to measure a specific variable, which will be discussed in detail in Chapter 7.

PLACING A STUDY IN HISTORICAL CONTEXT

Literature reviews place our current research into historical context, which helps readers synthesize existing research in a concise manner. One of the basic goals of the literature review is to provide enough historical and conceptual information about a research topic so that readers will be able to adequately judge the merits and usefulness of a new research study. For example, if you write a literature review section about the variable communication apprehension and only mention articles written in the past year, your readers will not have enough information to adequately judge your new study. This does not mean that you must include every article that has ever been written on the subject. In fact, after conducting a quick database search, the term *communication apprehension* has appeared in more than 400 journal article titles, and this does not even include journal articles that utilized communication apprehension within the study but did not include the term in the title. There is no way you can talk about each of these different articles in a literature review. In fact, around 15 different *books* take on the concept of communication apprehension alone. Ultimately, when creating the historical context for a new study, it is important to find the most important pieces of research directly related to your study. And if you find the best research sources, your reader should be able to understand where your new study fits into the history of research within a specific research area.

EXPLANATION AND RATIONALIZATION FOR VARIABLES

Literature reviews aid in the explanation and rationalization for why specific variables have been chosen as an object of study in a research project. In quantitative research, scholars are never just studying one variable like communication apprehension. Instead, scholars examine a variety of variables together in order to gain an understanding of how those variables relate to or differ from each other. For example, the articles that accompany this text examine a wide array of different variables:

Boiarsky, Long, and Thayer (1999)—children's television shows, content pacing, sound effects, and visual pacing

Brummans and Miller (2004)—organizational ambiguity and organizational effects

Chesebro (1999)—listening style and conversational sensitivity

Punyanunt (2000)—behavior alteration techniques, humor orientation, and humor effectiveness

McCroskey et al. (2004)—organizational orientations, job satisfaction, communication apprehension, nonverbal immediacy, sociocommunicative orientation, credibility, and human temperament

Rocca and Vogl-Bauer (1999)—verbal aggression, fan identification, and appropriate fan communicative messages

Thomas, Richmond, and McCroskey (1994)—nonverbal immediacy and sociocommunicative style

Weber et al. (2003)—cognitive learning, learner empowerment, and nonverbal immediacy

Wrench and Booth-Butterfield (2003)—humor orientation, credibility, compliance-gaining strategies, patient satisfaction, and patient compliance

As you can see from the short list of articles we present along with this text, a large variety of communication variables are studied in just these nine articles. More important, no one article utilizes the same combination of variables. Some studies include only a couple of variables, like Brummans and Miller (2004), who only study two variables. Other studies examine a large number of variables; for instance, McCroskey et al. (2004) studied seven different variables. Ultimately, it is the job of a literature review to demonstrate why a researcher is studying only two variables or seven variables in a specific project.

PREVIOUS FINDINGS AND RESEARCH NEEDED

Literature reviews help demonstrate what has been done in research and what still must be accomplished. We will never get to the point where there is no more research to be accomplished in the field of communication, and a literature review should demonstrate that you have examined the literature closely enough to know that there are still avenues to be explored. Although some studies replicate or reconduct previously completed studies, most research completed is new. Whether you are researching previously studied variables in a new context (political, educational, romantic relationships, physician–patient relationships, etc.) or variables that have never been examined together at all, literature reviews aid in explaining what has not yet been studied and why it should be studied at all.

ESTABLISHING YOUR ARGUMENT

Finally, literature reviews help establish the argument being tested in the study. In every study, there is some argument being made. And like giving a persuasive speech, a literature review ends with a persuasive argument for either a hypothesis or a research question. Although these hypotheses and research questions are discussed in more detail later in this chapter, we introduce the two concepts here. First, a **hypothesis** is defined as a statement about the relationship between independent and dependent variables, whereas a **research question** is an explicit question that researchers ask about variables of interest. Ultimately, whether one is able to form a hypothesis or research question is dependent on whether a researcher has the literature to support making a clear argument or hypothesis.

Now that we have examined the five main reasons academics write literature reviews, we can examine the two main parts of a literature review: previous research and study rationale.

Previous Research

The first major part of a literature review comprises an examination of pertinent previous research about the variables in your study. The previous research section of a literature review is what most people generally think of when they think about a literature review. This is the section where authors actually discuss previous research about the variables studied in the current research, and writing this section is the part of the research process with which most people are familiar. In fact, you have probably been writing traditional "research papers" since you were in junior high or middle school. And if you have completed your literature search in the way we discussed in the previous chapter, this section will be easy to write.

After you complete your literature search, you must determine how to organize the primary and secondary sources into a cohesive new product that clearly defines all key concepts, demonstrates the history of those concepts, and links those concepts together in your new research study to form your argument. When organizing the previous research section in a literature review, there are two aspects to consider (McCroskey et al., 2003). The first aspect to organizing the previous research section relates to the overall organization and style. Many people, when writing the previous research section of a literature review, will have one organizational pattern they start with and keep throughout the entire section. In essence, an author can pick one organizational pattern and then use that pattern to tell a story within the literature review. However, other people will break their previous research section of the literature review into different subsections or groupings and use similar or different organizational patterns for each subsection within the review.

CHRONOLOGICAL

The first pattern for arranging main ideas is **chronological order**, which places the main ideas in the order in which they appear in history—whether backward or forward. For example, if you were writing a literature review section that contains both communication apprehension and humor assessment, you would start off writing about communication apprehension, which has been around since the 1970s. And you would only write about communication apprehension until 2001, which was when the humor assessment was first published. Then, you would continue writing the literature review from 2001 to the most current research, incorporating information about both communication apprehension and humor assessment. You would cover 30 years of communication apprehension in your literature review before you integrated information about humor assessment. In this example of the chronological organizational pattern, the author uses one organizational pattern to create a single, constant story throughout the previous research section of the literature review.

If an author decided to chunk pieces of information within a previous research section of a literature review, however, he or she could also easily use the chronological organizational pattern. Considering the same example of communication apprehension and humor assessment as the variables being studied in a research project, in one subsection the author would explain the history of communication apprehension starting in the 1970s and continuing through the most recent research about it. This historical perspective on communication apprehension would then be followed by a subsection providing a historical telling of the origins of humor assessment. Although the history of humor assessment only dates back to 2001, a variety of research projects, both published and unpublished, have been written about the variable humor assessment, so a clear history of the concept does exist—even if it is much shorter.

CAUSE–AND–EFFECT

The **cause-and-effect order** explains what causes a specific situation and what the effect of that situation is. For example, if you are writing a study about a new miracle drug that can help individuals with high levels of communication apprehension, you could start the previous research section of your literature review by explaining how neurochemical processes may be a strong root cause of communication apprehension. After explaining the cause of communication apprehension, you could then explain the various effects of having elevated levels of communication apprehension (lower self-esteem, less likely to be called on by a teacher, more likely to be fired, fewer friends, lower grades in school, etc.). Ultimately, this organizational pattern helps you establish why your study should take place. In other words, you demonstrated what researchers think causes communication apprehension and what happens if you have high levels of it, so a new drug that can help lower people's levels of communication apprehension (or your new study) would be beneficial to highly communication apprehensive people.

If you are studying multiple variables within a study, the cause-and-effect organizational format can also be useful. If a researcher is examining racism and sexism, for example, he or she may decide to write two separate subsections on the causes and effects of both racism and sexism. If both the causes and the effects of racism and sexism are similar, the researcher can then assert that the two concepts should be highly related to one another, which could be the purpose of the study.

COMPARE–AND–CONTRAST

Another method for creating main points is the **compare-and-contrast order**. Comparing (showing how information is similar) and contrasting (showing how information is different) is a tool we have all used on many occasions to help us analyze chunks of information. If you want to arrange the whole previous research section of your literature review using a compare-and-contrast organizational pattern, you could compare and contrast two similar but different variables using existing literature. For example, in communication, researchers try to differentiate between argumentativeness (discussing ideas and issues in a debate) and aggressiveness (attacking the other person). However, these two terms are often confused with one another by both scholars and laypeople. So a literature review containing both communication variables could first show how the two variables are similar (compare) and then show how the variables are different (contrast).

Although this organizational pattern often consists of two main points (one subsection on comparing and one subsection on contrasting), an author can easily create an introduction point where basic information about the two variables is initially discussed. For example, you could spend a subsection of the previous research section of your literature review discussing what argumentativeness is and what aggression is. This would be followed by a subsection where you talk about the similarities of argumentativeness and aggression and finally a subsection where you examine how these two communication variables are different.

An author can also use the compare-and-contrast organizational pattern as an independent subsection. Maybe one of the major research variables you are studying in a project is sociocommunicative orientation. To discuss sociocommunicative orientation using compare and contrast, you could examine Richmond and McCroskey's (1990) concepts of sociocommunicative orientation (assertiveness and responsiveness) and compare and contrast them with Bem's (1974) concepts of masculinity and femininity. By the time your audience finishes reading this subsection of your literature review, they will have a general understanding of sociocommunicative orientation and how it is functionally different from Bem's concepts of masculinity and femininity.

PROBLEM–CAUSE–SOLUTION

Another format for creating distinct main points is the **problem–cause–solution order**. In this format, you discuss what a problem is, then what is causing the problem, and finally what the solution could be to correct the problem. Maybe a researcher wants to study whether a new training program helps people communicate better on a first date. The researcher can start her or his previous research section of the literature review by discussing the problems that many people face when dating (shyness, anxiety, not knowing what to say, etc.). These problems with first dates could then be followed by a discussion of what causes these problems to occur (lack of dating experience, bad previous dating experiences, poor communication skills, etc.). Finally, the researcher could explain how to solve the problems that occur with first dates. Ultimately, the researcher could run a study to see whether her or his "solution" to the first date problem actually works.

PSYCHOLOGICAL

The next way to organize your main ideas within a previous research section of a literature review is through a **psychological order** organizational pattern, or A leads to B and B leads to C. In most behavioral genetics research, researchers start with the premise that our genetics cause humans to have specific temperaments, and that these temperaments cause humans to behave in specific ways. Genetics (A) leads to temperament (B), and temperament (Bb) leads to human behavior (C)—or, again, A leads to B and B leads to C. When using the psychological organizational pattern, a researcher must clearly show how previous literature has established causal relationships. However, if a researcher need not explain causal relationships, this organizational pattern is probably not useful.

CATEGORICAL/TOPICAL

The last organizational pattern for arranging the previous research section of the literature review is using various categories or topics to lay out your main points. The **categorical/topical order** is the organizational pattern used most often by researchers. To use this organizational pattern, a researcher simply separates her or his main concepts or variables being explored in a study into separate subsections within the literature review. For example, if you are conducting a study and want to examine organizational orientations (upward mobile, ambivalent, and indifferent), sociocommunicative orientation (assertiveness and responsiveness), and workplace satisfaction, you could organize your previous research section into three main subsections, one for each variable.

You can also use this organizational pattern for your subsections if you have a section with clearly delineated parts. You could organize your section on organizational orientations into three subsections, or one for each orientation (upward mobile, ambivalent, and indifferent). You could organize sociocommunicative orientation into two subsections (assertiveness and responsiveness). Whereas the first two variables can easily be sectioned off into their own respective parts, workplace satisfaction would probably need to be organized using a different organizational pattern than those discussed previously. For this reason, there are three specific organizational patterns that can be used when organizing a subsection: general to specific, specific to general, and known to unknown.

GENERAL–TO–SPECIFIC The first subsection organizational pattern is **general-to-specific order**. Think of this organizational pattern as a funnel. The brim is wide at the top (general) and then gets narrow at the bottom (specific). This type of organizational pattern is useful when an author wants to start off writing about anything and everything in a topic and then narrow her or his way down to an aspect of that topic that relates to the current study. For example, if you are writing a subsection on communication apprehension for an article about workplace communication apprehension, you could start by explaining what communication apprehension is, follow that with some specific studies related to communication apprehension in general, and end with a discussion of any studies that have examined communication apprehension in the workplace.

SPECIFIC–TO–GENERAL The second subsection organizational pattern is **specific-to-general order**. You can also think of this organizational pattern in terms of a funnel, but this time, you must turn that funnel upside down to get the effect. The brim is narrow at the top (specific) and then gets wide at the bottom (general). Use this organizational pattern if you are trying to extrapolate some general ideas from specific information. Although it seems backward (and often is), this organizational pattern can be useful if you are trying to see the large picture instead of a more narrow one. Sticking with our previous example, if you were to use this organizational pattern, you could start your subsection on communication apprehension by talking about communication apprehension in the workplace, follow that with a discussion of some specific studies related to communication apprehension in general, and end with a general discussion of communication apprehension.

KNOWN–TO–UNKNOWN The last organizational pattern specifically for subsections of your previous research is **known-to-unknown order**. In this organizational pattern, an author discusses what we know about a specific topic or variable and then leads the reader to what we do not know. What we know is based on what has been studied in the previous research, and what we do not know is based on what seems to be a big hole in that literature. For example, maybe you are studying talkaholism, and you note when doing your literature search that talkaholism has never been studied in intimate relationships. When you organize your subsection of talkaholism, you would start off with all the information researchers have found about talkaholism and then lead into a discussion of the fact that research has never examined how talkaholism affects intimate relationships.

AN EXAMPLE LITERATURE REVIEW

Now that we have examined a number of different ways that researchers can organize previous research when writing a literature review, we switch our attention to the Wrench and Booth-Butterfield (2003) article to see how these researchers laid out their literature review. Figure 5.4 shows a subsection from their literature review examining "Humor in the Medical Context"—read this subsection now. You will note that this

Humor in the Medical Context

In a recent study in the *Journal of American Medical Association*, Levinson, Roter, Mullooly, Dull, and Frankel (1997) reported that physicians who used humor and laughed more during patient–physician interactions were less likely to engender malpractice suits. The use of humor as a variable in medical research has proved to be positive for both patients and their caregivers. Patients exposed to humorous messages have lower levels of stress-related hormones (Berk, 1989); increased immunoglobulin rates (Lambert & Lambert, 1995; McClelland & Cheriff, 1997); increased helper T-cells (Berk, 1993); lower levels of pain (Adams & McGuire, 1986; Cohen, 1990; Pasquali, 1991); lower blood pressure (Fry & Savin, 1982); and faster recovery rates from illnesses (McClelland & Cheriff, 1997). A patient's sense of humor and the degree to which he or she actively seeks humorous messages are predictive of her or his perceived health and morale (Simon, 1990). In a study conducted by Gaberson (1991), patients exposed to humorous messages had lower levels of anxiety before operations and higher post operation recovery rates. The inclusion of humorous messages in the patient–physician relationship can reduce fear while promoting trust (Robinson, 1991). Overall, humor in the medical environment appears to have an overwhelmingly positive effect and seems likely to increase positive perceptions of caregivers and subsequently compliance with their directions (James, 1995).

Physicians and other medical professionals personally use humor as a means of coping with the uncertainty that surrounds the medical profession (Bosk, 1996; Wanzer, Booth-Butterfield, & Booth-Butterfield, 1997). The use of humor appears to allow doctors and other medical personnel to ease tension (Ditlow, 1993). Medically speaking, the enactment of humor causes us to laugh, which physiologically increases endorphin levels, which, in turn, are associated with decreased anxiety levels (McGhee, 1996).

Despite the benefits of integrating humor into the medical office, humor should not be unskillfully used. Mulkay (1988) mentions that humor has the potential to create a language of domination and opposition rather than collaboration. Misinterpretation of humorous language could force the individuals interacting to see each other as foes instead of collaborators (Witkin, 1999). Hence communicators must be aware of potential negative effects of poorly enacted or misperceived humor, as well as the potential of positive outcomes. It may be diagnostic that highly humor-oriented individuals spend more time rehearsing jokes when compared to minimally humor-oriented individuals (Honeycutt & Brown, 1998). Hopefully, a portion of this rehersal time involves considering the possible positive and negative implications of enacted humor. Honeycutt and Brown (1998) suggest that people who use humor well probably have a contingency plan if the first one fails to have the desired impact or leads to a negative outcome.

Right off the bat you should notice that this is clearly categorical. The other major categories in this literature review are patient compliance, patient satisfaction, perceived credibility, and compliance-gaining strategies.

The first part of this subsection explains the biological benefits of humor.

The second part of this subsection examines the psychological benefits of humor in the medical environment.

Here we have a discussion of physician use of humor in the medical environment.

This section discusses problems and suggestions for using humor in the medical environment.

FIGURE 5.4
Literature Review Subsection

subsection of the literature review is categorical with regard to what is discussed in each paragraph. To see how this subsection fits into the overall scheme of the article, read the previous literature section from the article on the textbook's website.

STUDY RATIONALE

After you have developed the background information for your study in the previous research section of the literature review, you are ready to explain to your readers why you have performed the current study. The **rationale section** of the literature review is where you explain why and how you will perform your analysis of the variables you have described in your literature review (Figure 5.5). More important, the study rationale section of a literature review is where a researcher introduces her or his specific hypotheses and research questions.

Recently, communication researchers have begun examining humor from an enactment perspective to see how individuals differ in the production of humorous messages (Booth-Butterfield & Booth-Butterfield, 1991; Punyanunt, 1997, 2000; Wanzer, Booth-Butterfield, & Booth-Butterfield, 1995, 1996a, 1996b, in press; Wanzer & Frymier, 1999). Booth-Butterfield and Booth-Butterfield (1991) identified the concept of humor orientation (HO), or an individual's predisposition to enact humorous messages in interpersonal situations. Research has shown humor orientation to be a positive trait among nurses (Wanzer et al., 1996b, 1997), in supervisor–subordinate relationships (Rizzo, Wanzer, & Booth-Butterfield, 1999), and in teacher–student relationships (Punyanunt, 1997, 2000; Wanzer & Frymier, 1999). Although no research has directly examined the effects of humor orientation in physician–patient interactions, the link is readily made to satisfaction and compliance.	This paragraph functions as the quick version of a study rationale. You'll notice that the beginning part explains that humor has been studied in a variety of different types of interpersonal situations, but it has not been studied in physician–patient interactions.
Fitzpatrick (1993) described patient satisfaction as an "emotional link to healthcare." And since humor creates a positive emotional state (Wrench & McCroskey, 2000), those patients who find their physicians humorous presumably would also be more satisfied than those patients who do not find their physicians humorous. Hence:	Starting here the authors make the link between emotion, humor, and satisfaction to generate a clear hypothesis.
H1: Physicians with higher levels of perceived humor orientation will also have higher levels of patient satisfaction.	

Analysis

This hypothesis is a very clear series of two If statements followed by a Then statement:

If (a): Patient satisfaction is an emotional link to healthcare.
If (b): Physician humor creates a positive emotional state in their patients.
Then: Physician humor will cause patients to be satisfied.

FIGURE 5.5
Rationale Section

In Chapter 2, we discussed in great detail how researchers go about creating arguments using the findings of previous research. And in empirical research, we must be able to form clear arguments before we can pose a hypothesis. As mentioned in Chapter 2, a hypothesis is a tentative statement about the relationship between two or more variables. This tentative statement occurs at the end of a logical argument. Unfortunately, researchers often have questions they want to ask in research but find that a logical argument simply cannot be created to offer support for a hypothesis. When a researcher cannot create a hypothesis, he or she may ask a research question. The difference between a hypothesis and a research question is the ability to form an argument for the proposed relationship or difference. In a hypothesis, we use the previous research to make a prediction that is logical, whereas in a research question, the previous research cannot help us make a prediction and so we must simply ask a question. To aid in the clarification of the purpose of a study rationale, we will examine hypotheses and research questions separately.

METHOD SECTION

The **method section** helps readers understand who the participants were in a study and how the study was conducted. The purpose of the method section is twofold. First, it enables readers to see exactly what you did and either agree with or question your research strategies when they are attempting to determine the overall significance of your research. Second, the method section allows future researchers to replicate what you have done in a consistent manner. According to the APA (2010), the method section can be broken down into four basic areas: participants, apparatus, procedure, and instrumentation.

Participants

First, when writing a method section, you want to give as much detail about your participants as necessary. We call this the **participant subsection**. Although there are countless demographic questions you can ask participants, not everything is actually necessary. The two most common demographic questions asked are sex and age. When reporting sex, it is best to do a simple frequency report followed by a percentile for the total population—for example, 50 females (50%), 48 males (48%), and 2 (2%) participants who did not indicate their biological sex. Note that we did report missing data in this answer. When filling out surveys, people will often accidentally miss one of the questions or opt to not answer a specific question, and unlike our example just now, you should report these as missing data. When you are reporting a sample's mean age, it is important to also report the standard deviation. When writing articles using the APA style, report the sample age using the notation M (mean) and SD (standard deviation), both of which will be discussed in greater detail in Chapter 14. For example, when reporting the mean, you could write, "Overall, the sample consisted of 245 participants with a mean age of 23.45 (*SD* = 5.25)," or "The 245 participants represented a typical college age sample (*M* = 23.45, *SD* = 5.25)." Whether you choose the first or the second way does not matter; it is ultimately a matter of personal writing style.

Whether you need to report other demographic characteristics such as ethnicity, sexual orientation, hair color, social economic status, and so on will depend on the overall purpose of your study. If you are studying the impact of hair color on perceived physical attractiveness, then identifying your participants' hair colors could be extremely important. However, if you are studying the impact of verbal aggression on political campaigns, hair color is clearly not a useful demographic characteristic. Look at Figure 5.6 to see how Wrench and Booth-Butterfield (2003) described their participants. Note that the researchers actually had four different subsamples about which they reported demographic characteristics.

Apparatus

The second part of the method section is the **apparatus** subsection. In this subsection, researchers briefly describe any special equipment (apparatuses) or materials they used in the course of a specific study. According to the APA (2010), standard laboratory equipment furniture, stopwatches, screens, pencils, paper, scantrons, and so on need not be mentioned. However, if you are using magnetic resonance imaging or computed tomography scanning, then you must elaborate on the equipment. Some researchers go so far as to add ordering instructions in an appendix if the equipment is specialized. Also, if you build or have equipment built for you, it is often necessary to provide schematics or at least technical drawings of the equipment for your readers.

Procedure

In the **procedure** subsection, you describe the exact procedures that were used in your study in a step-by-step fashion. The last paragraph in Figure 5.6 is the procedure subsection. This paragraph explains to the reader that participants were asked to fill out a questionnaire while thinking about their primary-care physician. The paragraph is short and not overly technical. In some studies, this paragraph could be expanded to three or four pages, depending on how technical your procedures are. In the article by Boiarsky et al. (1999), the researchers go into great detail describing how the children's shows were selected for inclusion in the study, how the sample of episodes from each show was selected, and how the selected episodes were then coded for the study. A lot of technical information was necessary to share in case any future researchers decided to replicate this specific study.

Instrumentation

The last part of the method section is the **instrumentation** subsection or measurement subsection. The instrumentation or measurement section is where a researcher explains which research measures were used to measure the specific study variables.

Participants

To maximize external validity, participants for this study represented four groups. Some participants were diverse undergraduates enrolled in communication courses at a large Middle Atlantic public university. This portion included 25 (56.8%) males and 19 (43.2%) females and constituted 16.9% of the total sample. The second segment of participants consisted of graduate students in an applied master's degree program. Individuals in this program are all adult students who primarily focus on their occupations while taking courses throughout the year in educational cohorts. This portion of the sample consisted of 7 (14.6%) males and 41 (85.4%) females and was 18.4% of the total sample. The third group included individuals from the general public, shopping at a mid-Atlantic mall. Trained student interviewers conducted surveys in the mall. The mall was attractive because its patrons represent a diverse community, not just people associated with the university. This portion of the sample consisted of 76 (53%) males and 66 (46%) females and constituted 54.8% of the total sample.

The final portion of the sample was the product of fifty Internet postings in AOL chat rooms asking for volunteers. The postings occurred over a two-day period in order to reach a wide range of individuals. Individuals in the chat rooms were also asked to forward the call for participants to any friends and family members. Those who decided to participate in the study received information concerning the World Wide Web site where they could participate. This portion of the sample consisted of 6 (23%) males and 20 (77%) females, or 10% of the total sample.

The overall sample included 146 females (55.5%) and 114 (43.3%) males. Mean ages were: undergraduate students, $M = 22$; master's students, $M = 38.6$; general public, $M = 38.7$; and Online, $M = 37.3$. The overall mean age of 35.7. The ethnic breakdown was: 46 (17.5%) African Americans, 189 (71.9%) Anglos/Caucasian, 9 (3.4%) Middle Eastern, 15 (5.7%) Asian, 6 (2.3%) Hispanic/Latino, 10 (3.8%) Native American, and 1 (.4%) other. A final demographic category, highest level of education, showed the following statistics: 46 (17.5%) high school/ GED, 70 (26.6%) some college, 12 (4.6%) associate's degree, 79 (30%) college degree, 40 (15.2%) graduate/professional degree, and 15 (5.7%) postgraduate. Thus, the sample was quite diverse in background representing a wide variety of perspectives.

Procedure

Participants completed the Humor Orientation Scale, Compliance-Gaining Questionnaire, Perceived Credibility Scale, and Patient Satisfaction Scale, with their personal physician as the object of focus. If they did not have a personal physician, they were instructed to think of the most recent physician with whom they had interacted. Participants then indicated on a 0–100 scale the extent to which they had followed their physician's prescriptions and/or treatments after their last visit.

The first part of the method section clearly explains where the sample came from in this study. This study had four different population groups.

Here the number and percentages of females and males for each subsample is given.

The overall sample is discussed here including demographic characteristics (biological sex, age, ethnicity, and education level). Notice that the Standard Deviations for the mean ages were not given. Generally speaking, it is always best to report Standard Deviations with means.

The procedure section explains what the study participants actually did during their participation.

FIGURE 5.6
Method Section

For example, if you were running a study examining the time that it takes for a talka-holic's heart rate to slow down after giving a public speech, you would need to explain how you measured talkaholism and her or his heart rate. Did you randomly observe people in public and then choose people who you thought talked a lot to participate in your study, or did you give them a scale that measures a person's talkaholism and then select your sample? Did you use an electrocardiogram to measure heart rate, or did you just use fingers on the wrist or neck to measure heart rate? Ultimately, how we go about measuring things is extremely important.

Chapter 7 will go into detail regarding how we measure variables. For now, we can explain the basic components of what you must write down in this specific subsection by examining how to write up the measurement part for a scale. First, an author must explain what the scale is attempting to measure and who wrote the scale. For example, in the article by Rocca and Vogl-Bauer (1999), they wrote a measurement subsection for verbal aggression:

> The Verbal Aggression Scale (VAS) has been found to be both valid and reliable in assessing verbal aggression (Infante & Wigley, 1986; Rubin, Palmgreen, & Sypher, 1994). The VAS is a 20-item Likert-type scale with response categories ranging from (1) *almost never true* to (5) *almost always true*. This measure includes 10 positive worded and 10 negatively worded items. The reliability has been .80 or above in several studies (Infante & Wigley, 1986; Rubin et al., 1994). Obtained reliability for the Verbal Aggression Scale in this study was .81. The mean for the VAS was 50.73 out of a possible 100 (*SD* = 9.93). (pp. 242–243)

The first sentence explains that the VAS is a research measure that has been used in previous research and has been shown to be both reliable and valid. After reading the next two sentences, you can tell that the VAS has 20 items (10 positively worded and 10 negatively word) and uses a 5-point Likert scale ranging from *almost never true* to *almost always true*. The next two sentences examine the scale's reliability (reliability will be discussed in greater detail in Chapter 8). The first of the two reliability sentences explains the level of reliability that is typically seen with the VAS, and the second sentence reports the obtained reliability for the VAS in the researcher's study. In the last sentence, the researchers report the mean and standard deviation for the VAS as seen in the study. This paragraph is a quick way of reporting the necessary information a reader needs about any scale to be used in research. For another example of how to write up a scale in the measurement subsection, see Figure 5.7, in which Wrench and Booth-Butterfield (2003) included a subsection on the scale's validity, which will be discussed in greater detail in Chapter 8. Although it is always important to explain the validity of a scale, some journals and editors will require more information about a scale's validity than others. Our recommendation is to add as much validity information about a scale

Measurement
 	
    This study incorporated three measures of patient perceptions of their physician's communicative behavior (Humor Orientation, Physician Credibility, and Physician Compliance Gaining) and two others relating to perceptions of themselves (Satisfaction and Compliance).
 	
    Humor Orientation Scale. The Humor Orientation (HO) Scale is a 17-item, self-report measure that uses a 5-point Likert format ranging from 1 *strongly disagree* to 5 *strongly agree*. Booth-Butterfield and Booth-Butterfield (1991) developed the HO to permit an encompassing look at an individual's overall propensity to use humorous communicative messages in interpersonal situations. An adapted version of this instrument permitted examination of the perceived humor orientation of a physician in a format similar to that in studies by Wanzer and Frymier (1999) and Rizzo, Wanzer, and Booth-Butterfield (1999) involving teachers and supervisors. Previous research examining humorous communication in the classroom has shown that perceived humor enactment enhances teacher evaluations (Bryant, Cominsky, Crane, & Zillmann, 1980; Javidi, Downs, & Nussbaum, 1988); student learning (Gorham & Christophel, 1990); perceptions of teacher nonverbal immediacy (Gorham & Christophel, 1990); and affect in the classroom (Wanzer & Frymier, 1999), suggesting criterion validity for HO.
 	
    The Humor Orientation scale demonstrates predictive validity in that it has specifically been related to enhanced perceptions of social attractiveness (Wanzer et al., 1996a), greater skill in humorous presentation of information (Wanzer et al., 1995), and heightened perceptions of liking for supervisors (Rizzo et al., 1999), all of which would be expected outcomes for someone who enacts humor effectively. Scores for the HO can range from 17 to 85. For this sample, the HO had a Cronbach's alpha of .91 ($M = 52.74$, $SD = 10.47$).
	This sentence is a very general introduction to the measurement section listing the scales used in the entire study.
	
	Notice that the scale is named, format explained (Likert), author identified, and what the scale purports to measure is explained.
	
	The authors then explain that the scale is used in a variety of contexts and relate some of the previous findings associated with the scale.
	
	Authors explain validity of the scale.
	
	Authors explain overall scoring and then the scale's reliability.

FIGURE 5.7
Instrumentation or Measurement Subsection

as possible up front and then take it out later if it is deemed unnecessary or extraneous to the research project. It is always faster to take material out than to try to add material at a later point.

RESULTS SECTION

At this point, we will mention the **results section** only briefly because most of the last part of this book is devoted to running statistics and writing up the results. The results section is the part of a research article that untrained individuals pass over completely because it contains the bulk of the statistical information in the article. A general idea for a results section is that you will have one or two paragraphs for each hypothesis or research question unless one statistical device is able to analyze multiple hypotheses or research questions simultaneously. Either way, you should always explain in the first line of a paragraph what results are analyzed in that paragraph. It is often helpful to say up front, "In this paragraph, hypothesis three will be analyzed, which stated . . ." Being up front about what is in a paragraph keeps you focused while writing and makes your writing easier for others to read. Overall, the results section is not a place to write fancy treatises on life or research. The results section is simply that—a place to present the statistical results from the study you have conducted. Figure 5.8 presents an example of a portion of a results section from Wrench and Booth-Butterfield (2003).

The first hypothesis was that a physician's perceived humor orientation would relate to her or his patient's level of satisfaction. Testing this hypothesis occurred by means of a series of bivariate linear regression analyses involving three dimensions of the patient satisfaction variable (cognitive, affective, and behavioral), with physician's humor orientation as the dependent variable. The regression equation for the first analysis was as follows: *Cognitive Satisfaction = .26 Humor Orientation +* 21.22, F (1, 260) = 36.66, p < .0001. As hypothesized, the stronger the physicians' humor orientation, the more likely their patients were to report cognitive satisfaction. This equation suggests that accuracy in predicting the overall cognitive satisfaction would be moderate. The correlation between physician humor orientation and patient cognitive satisfaction was .35. Approximately 12% of the variance of cognitive satisfaction was accounted for by its linear relationship with physician humor orientation.	Notice how the first line of the results section explains what the first hypothesis was.
The resulting regression equation for the second analysis was as follows: *Affective Satisfaction = .30 Humor Orientation +* 18.19, F (1, 261) = 57.52 , p < .0001. As hypothesized, physicians with a more pronounced humor orientation tended to have patients who were more affectively satisfied. With this equation, accuracy in predicting affective satisfaction would be moderate. The correlation between physician humor orientation and patient affective satisfaction was .43. Approximately 18% of the variance of affective satisfaction was accounted for by its linear relationship with physician humor orientation.	To avoid making you more confused at this point, just trust us when we say that the rest of this section explains the statistical processes that were used to examine the first hypothesis in the Wrench and Booth-Butterfield (2003) study.
The regression equation for the last analysis relating to Hypothesis 1 was as follows: *Behavioral Satisfaction = .19 Humor Orientation +* 19.53, F (1, 261) = 31.38 , p < .0001. As physicians' humor orientation increased, patients were more behaviorally satisfied. The predictive accuracy of humor orientation for the behavioral satisfaction measure was moderate. The correlation between physician humor orientation and patient behavioral satisfaction was .33, which accounts for 11% of the variance of behavioral satisfaction from its linear relationship with physician humor orientation.	

FIGURE 5.8
Results Section

DISCUSSION SECTION

The **discussion section** of a research study is broken into three major parts: the results discussion, the limitations, and future directions for research.

Discussion of the Results

The first part of a discussion section provides a researcher space to explain her or his interpretation of the basic results found within a study, which is sometimes referred to as the discussion of the results. The purpose of the results discussion is to interpret results in light of the study outcomes and explain how readers can understand the study variables differently than they could at the onset of the study. The discussion section should be connected to the literature review by way of the hypotheses and research questions posed and the literature cited. However, a discussion section should not be a retelling of the arguments made when forming hypotheses in the rationale. Instead, a results discussion explains how a study has moved our knowledge of the study variables forward from where the arguments were made during the rationale.

One of the primary reasons for even having a discussion section is for an author to provide her or his reasoning for why the results turned out the way they did. Specifically, an author must give reasons for why hypotheses were either supported or not supported and for why research questions were able to detect relationships and differences. One important note is that your results did not prove or disprove anything. In academic writing, when discussing one's results, it is important to avoid language that makes it sound like you discovered or proved something; instead you can support or not support hypotheses based on your research. Make sure you always tackle the results that are directly related to your hypotheses and research questions first, and then discuss any interesting features in the results that are worthy of explanation. Furthermore, the discussion section is not the place to attempt to introduce new findings and results. Although you might occasionally include tables and figures that help explain a result you are discussing in this section, those tables and figures must not contain new results.

When interpreting your results, you should also find yourself comparing your results with those found in the past literature. It is extremely important to integrate sources from your literature review to help in the explanation of your results. Your literature review will help determine whether your results are in line with those of previous research or are breaking new ground. If your results are consistent with those of previous research, you may feel your task is complete. However, the ultimate challenge is not reiterating research, but demonstrating how your findings actually add to the ever-growing body of research on your subject. In Figure 5.9, Wrench and Booth-Butterfield (2003) analyze one part of their results. In the first paragraph, the authors establish how the whole section will be laid out, followed by a quick preview.

The primary goal of this study was to determine how physicians' humor orientation, credibility, and use of compliance-gaining strategies relate to patient satisfaction and compliance. The findings revealed significant relationships suggesting that better physician communication skills were associated with improved patient perceptions of physician credibility and patient satisfaction. The following paragraphs focus on the relationship that a physician's humor orientation has on patient satisfaction and physician credibility, the relationship between patient satisfaction and physician credibility, the relationship of compliance-gaining strategies with physician–patient interactions, and the post hoc analysis of the data sources used.	The first sentence re-explains the basic reason for this study.
	This sentence explains how the discussion section will be laid out (it's basically an easy-to-follow preview).
The first major area of emphasis was patients' perceptions of physician humor orientation and how these perceptions related to patient satisfaction and physician credibility. Results for the first hypothesis indicated that a physician's humor orientation accounted for a moderate portion of the variance in each of Wolf et al.'s (1978) three dimensions of patient satisfaction (cognitive, affective, and behavioral). These results indicate that a physician's enactment of humor as an interpersonal communication tool, in general, positively relates to a patient's level of satisfaction. Although a physician's humor orientation accounts for some of the variation in a patient's satisfaction, the low coefficients of determination indicate that it is not the primary variable determining what ultimately causes patient satisfaction. This finding is similar to the one that Fitzpatrick (1991) reported in looking at patient satisfaction and physician friendliness and previous research that has also linked humor orientation with friendliness (Wanzer, Booth-Butterfield, & Booth-Butterfield, 1996a).	This part explains actual findings that occurred in the results section related to physician humor orientation, patient satisfaction, and physician credibility.

Notice how the result is explained and previous research is integrated to aid in the reasoning for why this finding actually occurred in this study. |

FIGURE 5.9
Discussion Section

Writing your discussion section in this manner is primarily about organization and making it easy for readers to follow where you are going with your findings.

Limitations

The second part of the discussion section is the limitations subsection. When organizing a limitations subsection, it is important to include discussions of both design flaws and procedural problems. A design flaw is an oversight that does not come to the surface until the data have been collected. In cases where a flaw in the design of the experiment is the cause or possible cause of a peculiar data pattern, the design flaw must be brought to the attention of your readers. One of the most common design flaws is that much research, ours included, often relies on samples of college students, who may or may not be representative of the general public. Although a college student sample may not change many results in research studies, it is also possible that college students could be systematically different from the general public. For example, if you are conducting a study on the amount of alcohol being consumed in a given week, it is possible that college students could consume more or less alcohol than the general public. If you do not attempt to correct for this problem, you could end up with skewed results. Ultimately, when writing a discussion section it is important to admit when you have an actual or potential design flaw.

The second type of problem that you will want to discuss in your limitations is a procedural problem. A procedural problem is usually a mistake made by an experimenter (or experimenters), through either carelessness or ignorance, that resulted in the data being collected in a way not intended by the design of the experiment. For example, maybe you are conducting a study examining heart rates during impromptu speeches. If immediately prior to the study, you offer your participants cookies and coffee while they are waiting (sugar and caffeine are stimulants), your results may be altered because of the stimulants and not the impromptu speeches. If this kind of problem occurs, it is best to be forthright about it in your discussion section. In Figure 5.10, Wrench and Booth-Butterfield (2003) examine two possible limitations to their study.

Future Directions for Research

The last part of the discussion section is the future directions for research subsection. This subsection is a paragraph or series of paragraphs explaining your ideas for where future research should go as a result of your study. The goal of all new research is to

Limitations. No matter how rigorously a study is conducted, there are always limitations. Measurement issues are of concern. First, using a single perception-oriented answer to determine whether or not a patient would comply with her or his doctor's medication/treatment may not be the best way to measure compliance. Although this was the method devised by Dillard and Burgoon (1985) and also used by Burgoon et al. (1987), the results could be enhanced by taking into account more situational variables that conceivably affect compliance.	This limitation is a form of a design flaw.
The second major limitation in this study is the online sample used. Although individuals on AOL and in the general public samples were randomly selected to participate in the study, the completed sample was still admittedly self-selected. In addition, the small number of individuals who did participate in the online version was somewhat unsettling. New and more accurate attempts at getting online participants should be developed. At the same time, contrary to Sheehan and Hoy's (1999) fear that online samples are not generalizable to a larger and more diverse population, the lack of a meaningful significant difference between the online sample and those involving the other means of data collection does show the promise of online samples. As use of the Internet becomes more prevalent, concerns about skewed online samples should recede.	This limitation is a form of a procedural problem.

FIGURE 5.10
Limitations Subsection

gain knowledge. However, when we gain knowledge, new questions always surface, so good research should lead to both an increase in knowledge and new questions that can be posed for future studies. When creating your future research subsection, make sure you are specific about future developments. Do not write statements like "This needs more research," or "In the future, more research should be done." The purpose of this section is for you as a researcher to explain how you see future research in this area being conducted. Provide constructive and specific instructions to your readers about how they can further your study and answer some of the questions left unanswered. For example, maybe your research found an odd relationship or difference that should be replicated. Or maybe someone should examine your variables in a different communication context to see whether the same results appear. Any possible future avenues of research that come about as a result of your study should be discussed.

THE CONCLUSION

The final section of a paper is the conclusion. When reading a research article, it is common to find that the concluding section does not exist. Like a speech, however, a research paper must have a solid concluding device. The concluding section should briefly summarize the main finding(s) from your study and demonstrate that the main arguments made in your study are all clearly explained. Think of the concluding section as the dinner mint after eating a five-course meal. It should be brief, contain no new information, and neatly wrap up the paper. It is often helpful to end your paper by reexamining the attention-getter you used in the introduction of your paper, if appropriate. In Figure 5.11, Wrench and Booth-Butterfield (2003) demonstrate how a conclusion can be easily written.

Conclusion. This study clearly linked communication variables (humor orientation, credibility, and compliance gaining) to patient satisfaction and compliance. It also demonstrated why physicians need to think consciously about how they are using communication during patient–physician interactions. Although the results may seem to be intuitively obvious to communication researchers, further explanation of communication concepts in unique professional and social contexts helps to validate our theoretical conceptualizations of human communication in applied settings. Additionally, information concerning patient–physician communication has the potential for improving patient compliance, minimizing malpractice claims, and improving patient satisfaction.	Notice that the first sentence clearly summarizes the major results. The rest of this paragraph is explaining the benefits of research in the area of patient–physician communication.

FIGURE 5.11
Conclusion

REFERENCES AND END MATERIALS

Although the conclusion may be the final written part of a research paper, there is still a wealth of information that may appear after it. The first section after the conclusion, the references, is a required part of a paper formatted according to APA style. The second section, the end materials, is only necessary if you have corresponding end materials. Let's look at both of these sections briefly.

References

On a new page following the conclusion is where you will find the list of references one has cited within the paper. We discussed how to reference material in Chapter 4, so we will not go into a lot of detail here. However, we do have a quick checklist for you to think through when it comes to references:

1. Have you started your references list on a new page (not the same page where there is text from the conclusion)?
2. Does the word "References" (not "Works Cited" or "Bibliography") appear at the top of the page centered?
3. Are all of your references alphabetized by first author?
4. Are all of your references aligned to the left side of the page (not right-aligned or centered)?
5. Is each reference formatted so that the first line is a hanging indent and all subsequent lines are indented half an inch?
6. Are all of your references double spaced?
7. Do all of your in-text citations have references on the references page?
8. Do all of your references on the reference page have corresponding in-text citations?
9. Did you remember to include all relevant information within your references (including the doi for articles)?
10. Have you double- and tripled-checked the formatting of all of your references to ensure they are completed in APA style?

End Materials

In addition to your references, you also may have a range of other end materials associated with your paper. The three most common ones are footnotes, tables, and figures.

FOOTNOTES

Most research papers do not include footnotes. However, sometimes a footnote is appropriate. The APA manual has always steered away from using footnotes as a tool for citations, so that's not really what a footnote should be used for. Instead, the APA manual breaks footnotes down into two categories: content and copyright.

A content footnote includes information that is designed to "supplement or amplify substantive information in the text" (APA, 2010, p. 37). In other words, content notes primarily provide either supplemental information or a direction for more information. Either way, the goal is to be very short and to the point. An example of each would be as follows:

[1] The origin of the footnote can be traced back to Medieval scholars who often wrote comments in the margins of the page, but these were often hard to track and link to the text the margin notes referred to.

[2] To learn more about the history of footnotes, read Anthony Grafton's (1997) *The Footnote: A Curious History* or Chuck Zerby's (2006) *The Devil's Details: A History of Footnotes*.

The second type of footnote is a copyright permission footnote. A copyright permission footnote "acknowledges the source of lengthy quotations, scale and test items, and figures and tables that have been reprinted or adapted" (APA, 2010, p. 38). When it comes to text, scholars have what is called "fair use" with regards to copyrighted material. Basically, you are legally allowed to quote material from another source in your own work. However, there does come a point when the quoted material is very lengthy and ventures beyond fair use, so it's possible that you will need permission. The most common uses of copyright footnotes are for a figure or a table that has been created by someone else. In these cases, you need to provide the footnote to explain your permission to use the material. For example:

[1] From "Here's an Article That Has a Footnote" by J. D. Smith, 2019, *Journal of Footnotes, 1*, p. 13. Copyright 2019 by J. D. Smith. Reprinted with permission.

[2] From *Quantitative Research Methods for Communication: A Hands-On Approach* by J. S. Wrench, C. Thomas-Maddox, V. P. Richmond, and J. C. McCroskey (2016), New York, NY: Oxford University Press. Copyright 2016 by Oxford University Press. Reprinted with permission.

The first example is how you would demonstrate that you have permission to use information (whether text or a figure/table) from a journal. The second footnote is how it would look if someone used information from the third edition of this textbook.

Overall, footnotes are only occasionally used, so do not be surprised if you have no reason to include a footnote at all. However, if you do use a footnote, it's important to make sure that you use it correctly. For an example, check out page 51 in the APA (2010) style manual to see what a footnote would look like as part of a manuscript.

TABLES

Chapter 5 in the APA (2010) manual is all about displaying research results. The majority of that chapter explains how to format either tables or figures. The purpose of a table is to increase understanding by simplifying text. For example, look at Figure 1.1

in Chapter 1 of this textbook. Although called a "figure" in this text, this is really an example of a table. We could write a sentence for each line in the table (e.g., "The communication concept explored, general communication, appears in 229 articles for 9.8% of the total"), but this wouldn't be very easy to understand. Instead, we use tables to quickly present a lot of information in a format that is easily comprehended. When writing research, we often use tables to summarize results for readers. These tables may look scary to novices, but when you understand the content within them, reading tables definitely takes a lot less time than reading paragraphs.

FIGURES

Figures, on the other hand, are graphical representations of information. For example, in Figures 1.2 and 1.3 in this book, you'll see two different word clouds representing different time periods and how the content of *Communication Research Reports* has evolved. As the old adage goes, a picture is worth a thousand words. And pictures can often help explain complicated ideas that would be very difficult to understand if we relied on text alone. Again, Chapter 5 in the APA (2010) manual explores how to use figures in your own writing. In the end, however, most papers do not need figures, so do not be surprised if your own research doesn't have figures at all.

READING AND CRITIQUING ACADEMIC LITERATURE

Now that you have a general idea about the setup of quantitative research articles, let's discuss reading and critiquing academic literature. Academic articles are not always the easiest or fastest reads. Anyone who thinks that he or she can quickly scan an article and come away with a good conceptualization of what occurred within the study is going to have problems. As such, it is important to think through strategies to make your reading experience easier. For our purposes, here are 16 questions you should consider when reading an academic article:

1. Are there any key terms that are defined?
2. What did the authors state as the purpose of their study?
3. Do the authors have a clear summary of previous research?
4. Do the authors provide a clear critique of previous research?
5. Do the authors clearly identify a gap in the research? Do you note any gaps in the literature that the authors did not identify?
6. What is the rationale for the current study?
7. What are the explicit hypotheses and/or research questions in this study? If there are no explicit hypotheses and/or research questions given, what do you think they are?
8. What was the sample used in this study?

9. How was the sample recruited in this study? Are there any known flaws in this method?

10. Are the demographics of the sample generalizable?

11. What was measured in this study and how? Are there any flaws that you see in how the authors went about measuring?

12. What are the results in this study? What statistical methods were used to achieve these results? Do the statistical methods make sense in the context of this study?

13. Are there any results that seem to be missing?

14. Do the authors explain how the results are consistent with existing literature? Do the authors explain how the results are inconsistent with existing literature?

15. What limitations did the authors mention to their study? Do you note any additional limitations not discussed by the authors?

16. Do the authors discuss any future directions for this line of work? Do you see any additional lines of research that could stem from this study?

One common way of using these questions is to go through an article and answer them as you read. By answering these questions, you force yourself to really delve into the literature itself and see what is written.

PREPARING A FIRST DRAFT OF A LITERATURE REVIEW

So, you have been asked to write a literature review. We cannot attempt to discuss all of the ins and outs of writing a literature review in one section, but the "Further Reading" section at the end of this chapter includes a number of books that focus specifically on the topic. Here are 12 basic steps to help you write an effective literature review.

Step 1: Identify Your General Topic

Before you can do anything regarding a literature review, you must have a general topic. In Chapter 4, we discussed creating a topic, so we will not reiterate that here. What we will add is that searching for literature before you have a clear idea of what you are interested in studying will waste a lot of valuable time.

Step 2: Determine the Type of Study You Are Conducting

Once you have a general topic, it is important to think about what type of study you will be conducting. We will go into more detail later in this book about the four primary methods quantitative researchers use (e.g., survey, content analysis, experiments, and Big Data), so for now, we will just mention that it is important to have a general direction. One of the primary reasons this becomes important is because it can help you narrow down your literature search in some ways.

Step 3: Determine What Variables You Will Examine

In the next chapter, we will discuss the idea of variables in detail, but for now, we will say that a variable is anything that can change from person to person within the confines of an ordered structure. For example, you can have the variable biological sex, which has two basic categories: female and male. Students' GPAs are another type of variable because GPAs vary from person to person. Before you can really start searching for literature, it is important to know what you need to be looking for, so having a clear idea of what your variable will be is important.

Step 4: Search for Primary Sources

Once you have your topic and a list of the variables you plan on having in your study, start looking for articles and books related to those areas. Now, because we are talking about academic literature reviews here, it is important to remember that we are primarily looking for academic sources and not popular press materials (e.g., newspapers, magazines, and books in jargon-free language for a general audience with little or no technical knowledge on a given subject that are written by professional journalists whose publishers provide varying degrees of control over the accuracy or validity of the content).

Step 5: Obtain Full Text References

Part of searching for primary sources is obtaining the full text references you will be using within your literature review. It is important to keep yourself organized during this process. Whether you want to download all of the PDF files to your hard drive or you decide to print everything out, you must do this in a mindful manner. It is easy to forget where you found an article, so write down the full APA style reference to ensure you have the information you need when using the article later on in your literature review.

Step 6: Look for Other References in Obtained Materials

As discussed in the previous chapter, one way to locate relevant sources is through a process called backtracking. Backtracking is when you look at the references of articles you have found and then use those references to find new ones. When you start reading through your articles, look at other authors' literature reviews for possible relevant references. If you find one, grab the article and read it for yourself. However, never take a reference from an author's literature review and simply place it inside your own because it is unethical. As we always say, if you do not lay your own eyes on it, you should not be using it.

Step 7: Narrow Your List of References

All of the articles and books you find will not be useful. However, novice researchers often feel that any and every article they find should be used. Some do this because they do not want to spend the appropriate amount of time searching for relevant articles. Others simply have problems distinguishing between relevant and irrelevant information. If you fall into the first camp, keep searching for relevant research that will help you make the case for your study. If you fall into the second category, look through your articles and ask yourself, "Does this article help me build the case for my study?" If the article does not help you, it may not be necessary for your literature review.

Step 8: Organize References by Major Topics and Subtopics

Once you think you have the requisite set of references needed to adequately discuss the relevant literature, start organizing your references into major topics and subtopics. Say you are writing a literature review on the effectiveness of social media. You may have articles that define what social media is. You may have other articles that explain the history of social media. You may also have articles that discuss the effectiveness of social media in differing contexts (e.g., health, job searches, and relationships). At this point, start organizing these references into the relevant categories. A single article may cross over into multiple areas, however, so it is always important to make note of that.

Step 9: Look for Gaps in Your References

Once you start narrowing down your list of references into major topics and subtopics, see whether the areas within your study are equally balanced. Say you are conducting a study on two public relations campaigns. The goal of the study is to see whether fear appeals work with public relations. After reviewing the different sources you have found, you may note that you have many articles on fear appeals, fear appeals in health communication, fear appeals in advertising, and so on, but that you do not have any specifically looking at fear appeals and public relations.

Step 10: Find References to Fill Gaps

Once you have noted any specific gaps, you must plug the holes in your argument. It is possible that there is no relevant research on a specific topic, but this is rare. Start a specific search to fill the gap. You may need to consider using an array of synonyms to help you find relevant literature, but your literature review must be balanced.

At this point, we hope you are seeing that you really cannot research and write an effective literature review overnight. Often, the references you need may not be located on your college or university campus. Thankfully, colleges and universities participate in a program called interlibrary loans that allows you to get materials from other colleges and universities. Librarians are amazing at what they do, but you cannot expect them to find the one rare article you need at the last minute. The rarer something is, the longer it may take to find another library willing to loan the material.

Step 11: Create a Literature Review Outline

One of the biggest mistakes that novice literature review writers make is to forget everything they have learned about the basics of writing. Although social scientific writing is different in tone from the types of writing you learned in English classes, the basic writing process is still the basic writing process. One of the fundamental steps of any good piece of writing is a clear organizational structure. Whether you are writing the next great American novel or a quantitative research paper, you must have a clear organization before you start. As such, you will still have all of the basic parts of traditional writing: introduction, thesis statement, preview of main ideas, major body points, and conclusion. At the beginning of this chapter, we discussed multiple ways that you can organize your literature review. Ultimately, you must pick which outline format is going to work best for your literature review. Whatever format you choose, list your APA style citations within the outline to again ensure your different sections are balanced regarding the amount of research you are discussing.

Common Pitfalls in Literature Reviews

1. Not having a clear thesis statement in your introduction.
2. Not clearly previewing the body of your literature review.
3. Not including transition sentences between the major parts of your literature review.
4. No definitions for important key terms in the study.
5. Using dictionary definitions for key terms (stick to academic ones).
6. Writing about a single article across multiple paragraphs or pages.
7. Each paragraph discusses a separate research study with no links between the paragraphs (these are annotations, not a literature review).
8. Using flowery language to make the literature review longer.
9. Stating one's opinions on a topic and not sticking to the literature.
10. Not having enough research to adequately write a thorough literature review.
11. Discussing literature that is irrelevant to your topic.
12. Missing important or seminal articles or books related to the literature review.
13. Overreliance on direct quotations. Keep direct quotations to a minimum.
14. Using nonscholarly sources.
15. Only citing sources that support your argument when contradictory research is available.
16. Relying on literature that is out-of-date.
17. Using secondary source citations.
18. Citing sources within your literature review and not including the corresponding references.
19. Including references that do not have in-text citations.
20. Lack of a clear organizational structure.

Step 12: Write

Finally, begin writing your literature review. Some authors prefer starting with the introduction and going from there. Others prefer working on the different main points and then writing the introduction and conclusion once they have the full body of the literature review written. The method you choose is not as important as making sure you have all of the necessary parts.

RESEARCH OUTSIDE THE WALLS OF ACADEMIA

Although research outside of academia may not be presented in a traditional research paper, there are common conventions for writing about such research. Remember, research is only as good as the utility of that research in the hands of the people who need that information. We must ensure that we present our research in a format that is commonly suited for different contexts. Although an academic paper may be appropriate for a research conference or a peer-reviewed journal, O'Shea (1986) recommends breaking a professional research report into nine distinct sections:

1. *The executive summary.* An executive summary is a short, one-page (or less) explanation of the major findings from the study itself.
2. *Project background.* The project's background explains the reason(s) why the project was undertaken. You should include the project's original goals. You can also include any relevant literature that helps support the basic reasoning for the study or if there are concepts or terms with which a lay audience may be unfamiliar.
3. *Objectives and scope.* Explain the specific objectives of the research study. You should also clearly articulate the study's basic aim. Business people appreciate someone explaining how what was originally discussed was actually achieved.
4. *Methods.* The method section in a business report is identical to that in a more formal research study. One major difference, however, is that it is appropriate to include graphs and charts in a business report to more clearly explain one's participants.
5. *Analysis.* The analysis section should be as complete as it is in a traditional research paper. However, after conducting a statistical test, you should also provide a short explanation of what the test means and what the findings indicate. You should not try to extrapolate meaning from the findings at this point, but you do want to explain the purpose of the results and how to interpret the results for novices.
6. *Findings and conclusions.* Clearly articulate what the basic findings of the study were and what conclusions can be drawn from the study. Unlike a discussion section in a traditional research paper, the findings and conclusions section should be explicit, and it is not designed to enhance theory. Instead, the findings and conclusions should be clearly stated and relate back to the objectives of the original study.
7. *Recommendations.* In the recommendations section of a business report, the researcher explains what he or she thinks an organization should do based on the

results of the study. In academic research, we often avoid making specific recommendation statements, but in applied business research, such recommendations are expected.

8. *Expected benefits.* In addition to making recommendations, explain what benefits an organization can expect to gain if your recommendations are followed. These should be realistic benefits, so do not promise something you cannot actually deliver to your organization.

9. *Implementation guide.* The last part is where you explain to your business audience how they can implement your recommendations within their organization.

Note that the last three parts force you, as a researcher, to function as a consultant and not just someone conducting research.

CONCLUSION

This chapter has focused on the basic parts of a research paper: abstract, introduction, literature review, method section, results section, discussion section, and conclusion. Although this style of writing is clearly not a format that most people learn in their formative school years, the tricks and tools presented here will help as you attempt to write your own research papers. The best piece of advice we can give you from our years of writing research articles is to write, edit, rewrite, edit again, and keep on writing. Most research articles barely resemble their first drafts by the time they are published in a scholarly journal. Although the writing process is arduous and complex, the impact that you can have on the academic world and the rewards you get when you see your name in print are worth the process.

KEY TERMS

Abstract p. 133

Apparatus p. 151

Categorical/topical order p. 146

Cause-and-effect order p. 144

Chronological order p. 143

Compare-and-contrast order p. 145

Discussion section p. 156

General-to-specific order p. 146

Hypothesis p. 143

Illustrations p. 138

Instrumentation p. 151

Introduction p. 135

Known-to-unknown order p. 147

Literature review p. 140

Method section p. 150

Participant subsection p. 150

Preview p. 140

Problem–cause–solution order p. 145

Procedure p. 151

Psychological order p. 146

Rationale section p. 149

Research question p. 143

Results section p. 154

Rhetorical question p. 137

Specific-to-general order p. 147

Thesis p. 139

REFERENCES

American Psychological Association. (2010). *Publication manual of the American Psychological Association* (6th ed.). Washington, DC: American Psychological Association.

Bem, S. L. (1974). The measurement of psychological androgyny. *Journal of Consulting and Clinical Psychology, 47,* 155–162.

Boiarsky, G., Long, M., & Thayer, G. (1999). Formal features in children's science television: Sound effects, visual pace, and topic shifts. *Communication Research Reports, 16,* 185–192.

Brummans, B. H. J. M., & Miller, K. (2004). The effect of ambiguity on the implementation of a social change initiative. *Communication Research Reports, 21,* 1–10.

Chesebro, J. (1999). The relationship between listening styles and conversational sensitivity. *Communication Research Reports, 16,* 233–238.

McCroskey, J. C., Richmond, V. P., Johnson, A. D., & Smith, H. T. (2004). Organizational orientations theory and measurement: Development of measures and preliminary investigations. *Communication Quarterly, 52,* 1–14.

McCroskey, J. C., Wrench, J. S., & Richmond, V. P. (2003). *Principles of public speaking.* Indianapolis, IN: College Network.

O'Shea, T. J. (1986). Presentation of results. In S. W. Barcus & J. W. Wilkinson (Eds.), *Management consulting services* (pp. 235–252). New York, NY: McGraw–Hill.

Punyanunt, N. M. (2000). The effects of humor on perceptions of compliance-gaining in the college classroom. *Communication Research Reports, 176,* 30–38.

Richmond, V. P., & McCroskey, J. C. (1990). Reliability and separation of factors on the assertiveness-responsiveness measure. *Psychological Reports, 67,* 449–450.

Rocca, K. A., & Vogl-Bauer, S. (1999). Trait verbal aggression, sports fan identification, and perceptions of appropriate sports fan communication. *Communication Research Reports, 16,* 239–248.

Thomas, C. E, Richmond, V. P., & McCroskey, J. C. (1994). The association between immediacy and sociocommunicative style. *Communication Research Reports, 11,* 107–115.

Weber, K., Fornash, B., Corrigan, M, & Neupauer, N. C. (2003). The effect of interest on recall: An experiment. *Communication Research Reports, 20,* 116–123.

Wrench, J. S., & Booth-Butterfield, M. (2003). Increasing patient satisfaction and compliance: An examination of physician humor orientation, compliance-gaining strategies, and perceived credibility. *Communication Quarterly, 51,* 482–503.

FURTHER READING

Cooper, H. (1998). *Synthesizing research: A guide for literature reviews* (3rd ed.). Thousand Oaks, CA: Sage.

DeWine, S. (2001). *The consultant's craft: Improving organizational communication* (2nd ed.). Boston, MA: Bedford/St. Martin's.

Fink, A. (1998). Conducting research literature reviews: From paper to the Internet. Thousand Oaks, CA: Sage.

Girden, E. R., & Kabacoff, R. I. (2011). *Evaluating research articles: From start to finish* (3rd ed.). Los Angeles, CA: Sage.

Hart, C. (1998). *Doing a literature review: Releasing the social science research imagination.* Thousand Oaks, CA: Sage.

Pan, M. L. (2008). *Preparing literature reviews: Qualitative and quantitative approaches* (3rd ed.). Glendale, CA: Pyrczak.

Salkind, N. J. (2012). *100 questions (and answers) about research methods.* Los Angeles, CA: Sage.

6

Variables

CHAPTER OBJECTIVES

1. Explain the concept of a variable.

2. Differentiate between positive, negative, and neutral relationships.

3. Differentiate among the four levels of variables (nominal, ordinal, interval, and ratio).

4. Explain the four basic types of interval scales (Likert, semantic differential, Staple, and scalogram).

5. Apply information from this chapter to write an American Psychological Association (APA) style method section.

Ask a researcher how a particular research project was developed and you will likely hear a fascinating story. Sometimes the stories about how projects were conceptualized are almost as intriguing as the research itself. Recall our discussion in Chapter 4 of the methods for conceptualizing a research topic—some topics evolve from personal experiences, and others may result from current events or unanswered questions in earlier studies. Once the idea for a study has been identified, the real task is in creating a "recipe" for the research project. Just as a chef is responsible for identifying the food ingredients necessary for a gourmet dish, a researcher creates a list of research "ingredients" (more commonly referred to as variables) that will be used to conduct a study. This chapter identifies the research variables necessary for a successful project and discusses various methods of analysis.

HOW ARE RESEARCH PROJECTS DEVELOPED?

Ideas for a project can come from a variety of sources—a conversation, other research articles, or media examples. Once the conceptual idea has been identified, the next task involves writing a specific research question and identifying key terms or concepts. Remember the list of key concepts we discussed in Chapter 4 to aid you in conducting library research on the topic? This same list can be used to help you find potential variables to include in your study and to narrow your research topic. Specific questions that may be beneficial to ask when determining the overarching research question could include the following:

- How is communication related to the topic?
- What specific communication behaviors are involved?
- Are there other factors that might influence the behavior?

Answers to these and other questions involve identifying the specific "things" that should be examined in a study. Returning to our earlier analogy of the recipe, the answers to the questions often require a researcher to identify the research "ingredients" that will be included in the study to find answers.

VARIABLES

Variables are the ingredients of research projects. A **variable** can be defined as any entity that can take on a variety of different values. The manipulation, measurement, and control of variables is the primary mission of research.

In essence, a variable is a concept or construct that varies. Examples of variables include age, sex, or level of public speaking anxiety (or fear of public speaking). Each of these variables will take on a different value for different people at a given time. One participant in a study could be a 32-year-old female with low public speaking anxiety, and another could be a 19-year-old male with moderate public speaking anxiety. **Concrete variables** are stable or consistent. Examples might include characteristics such as biological sex or birth order (e.g., first born, middle child, or last born). **Abstract variables** are those that change or differ over time or across situations or contexts. Examples of abstract variables could include communication satisfaction or self-disclosure.

Researchers identify the specific variables or elements in order to compare differences between individuals and groups. For example, we might compare the level of parent–child communication satisfaction for first-born, middle-born, and last-born children. Birth order is a concrete variable that remains constant, and communication satisfaction is classified as an abstract variable. Differences could emerge when asking a participant to report on the level of communication satisfaction with one's mother versus one's father. Let's look at another example. Suppose you wanted to compare the self-disclosure of men and women. In this study, biological sex would be considered a concrete variable—it does not change. Self-disclosure would be classified as an abstract variable. An individual may engage in different patterns of disclosure with friends compared to family members. As you can see from these examples, the next task when determining the research question to guide the project involves identifying the types of units that will serve as the focus of the study.

UNITS OF ANALYSIS

Once a researcher has determined the specific communication behaviors to include in a study, the next step involves determining the unit of analysis for the project. Most communication research examines communication in one of four units of analysis: individuals, dyads, groups, and organizations.

Individuals

Communication studies examining individuals as the unit of analysis may focus on an individual's temperament, personality, or communication traits, or the research might focus on specific communication strategies or behaviors selected by a person. In their study of sports fans (located on http://www.oup.com/us/wrench/), Rocca and Vogl-Bauer (1999) selected the individual as the unit of analysis. Data were collected to identify an individual's level of verbal aggressiveness (attacking the self-concepts of people instead of the positions they espouse; e.g., "Only an idiot would think that," or "What kind of moron are you?") and its relationship to perceptions of the appropriate communication at sporting events. Verbal aggressiveness and perceptions of appropriate behavior use the individual as the unit of analysis.

Dyads

Research on dyads focuses on collecting information about two people involved in an interpersonal relationship. Barbato, Graham, and Perse (2003) asked 202 parent–child pairs to complete questionnaires assessing perceptions of the family communication climate and interpersonal communication motives for interacting with one another. Results of this study indicated that the communication climate had a significant influence on the motives selected for communicating in the dyad.

Groups

Sometimes the communication dynamics change when individuals are placed together in groups to carry out a goal. Kuhn and Poole (2000) focused on 11 groups in two major corporations as the unit of analysis in their examination of the effects of group conflict management styles on decision making. They found that groups that were more integrated in their conflict styles and addressed conflict openly were more

effective in decision making than groups that engaged in conflict avoidance or confron-
tational styles.

Organizations

If a researcher is interested in identifying how organizational members interact with one
another and the resulting impact on task completion, efficiency, satisfaction, or a host
of other variables, the organization becomes the unit of analysis. Coombs and Holladay
(2004) designed the Workplace Aggression Tolerance Questionnaire to identify perceptions about the appropriateness of workplace verbal aggression. Although at first glance
it may appear that the unit of analysis here is an individual's perceptions, the core of the
research focuses on appropriateness of behavior in the organizational context.

Generalizations and Inferences

Identifying the unit of analysis is essential to maintain focus during the research project
and to enable researchers to generalize results to similar units. However, it is important
to resist the temptation to make inferences about individuals based on their group membership. The concept of ecological fallacy is similar to stereotyping and occurs when
researchers assume that because a participant is a member of a specific group (e.g., a
culture), he or she possesses all the same communication characteristics as the group.
Similarly, assuming that one organization is similar to all others would lead to erroneous
conclusions. It is important to keep in mind that units of analysis have unique
characteristics—after all, this is what makes communication research an exciting venture!

ASPECTS OF VARIABLES

Once the researcher has identified the unit of analysis for a particular study, the next
step involves revisiting the list of variables that will be examined in order to identify
the specific aspects associated with each variable. Here, we examine two aspects of
variables—attributes and values—in more detail.

Variable Attributes

Variable attributes refer to the specific categories of a variable. For example, the
variable biological sex includes the attributes of male or female, whereas the variable
sociocommunicative orientation has the attributes of assertiveness, responsiveness,
and versatility. To ensure that you have included all relevant information for your own
research study, consider the various categories or attributes for each variable you will
be examining.

Variable Values

Whereas attributes identify the categories for variables, **variable values** refer to the
numerical designation assigned to each variable to allow statistical analysis. Some

variables, such as age, possess a numerical value on their own because the value of the variable already exists. Other variables may require a researcher to assign a number to represent each attribute of the variable. For example, if biological sex of the respondent is a variable being examined, numerical values must be assigned to designate male and female respondents. Values are arbitrarily assigned by the researcher. The number "1" can be used to represent males, and the number "2" can be used to represent females, or vice versa. As you assign values to each variable, it is important to write down this information because it will be important in the data-analysis phase.

Understanding Relationships and Differences
Beyond attributes and values, all variables in statistical research enable researchers to generally understand two basic phenomena: relationships and differences.

RELATIONSHIPS
Just as the concept of interpersonal relationships refers to the connection between two people, **relationships** as a research concept refer to the correspondences or connections between variables. The vast majority of communication studies are designed with the goal of identifying connections or relationships between variables. Beatty (1988) set out to examine the relationship between an individual's level of public speaking anxiety and one's level of conspicuousness (feeling like you are under a giant spotlight and everyone is watching) and between an individual's level of public speaking anxiety and one's level of perceived similarity with the audience. Relationships between variables typically fall into one of three categories: positive, negative, or neutral.

POSITIVE RELATIONSHIPS Positive relationships exist when an increase in one variable produces an increase in another variable, or a decrease in a variable corresponds to a decrease in another variable. Beatty found that an individual's level of public speaking anxiety was positively related to an individual's level of conspicuousness. Increases in one variable (an individual's level of conspicuousness) correspond to increases in the other (level of public speaking anxiety). The more conspicuous a person feels, the more anxious he or she will be while engaging in public speaking. The opposite is also true—the less conspicuous a person feels, the less anxious he or she will be while engaging in public speaking. This relationship is visually represented in Figure 6.1.

NEGATIVE RELATIONSHIPS Negative relationships exist when a decrease in one variable corresponds to an increase in another variable, or vice versa. Beatty (1988) found a negative relationship between public speaking anxiety and perceived similarity with one's audience. Increases in one variable (perceived similarity) correspond to decreases in the other variable (level of public speaking anxiety). The more a speaker

FIGURE 6.1
Positive Relationship

FIGURE 6.2
Negative Relationship

perceives an audience as being like her or him, the less anxious he or she will be while engaging in public speaking. However, the converse is also true. The more dissimilar a speaker perceives her or his audience to be, the more anxious he or she will be. This relationship is visually represented in Figure 6.2.

NEUTRAL RELATIONSHIPS Sometimes, a researcher may discover that the variables selected for a study are not related to one another. **Neutral relationships** refer to this lack of relationship, or when the change of one variable does not correspond with a change in another variable. Figure 6.3 provides a visual representation of two variables that have no relationship to one another: the amount of pizza one consumes and an individual's level of public speaking anxiety. As you can see, no pattern in the data is evident when the points are plotted on the diagram. Hence, changes in one variable do not produce consistent changes in the other variable being studied.

DIFFERENCES

Besides looking at relationships, statistics enables researchers to examine differences. A **difference** refers to the degree to which one person or a group of people are dissimilar from another person or group of people. In research, differences fall into one of two categories: differences in kind and differences of degree.

DIFFERENCES IN KIND **Differences in kind** occur when two or more groups do different things associated with their groups. For example, football players play football, and cheerleaders lead the crowd in cheers. These two groups (football players and cheerleaders) are fundamentally different and exhibit different behaviors. Although it may entertain some, we really do not want to see a 90-pound cheerleader being tackled by a 350-pound linebacker, nor would we want to see the 350-pound linebacker trying to stand on the top of a human pyramid. Although differences in

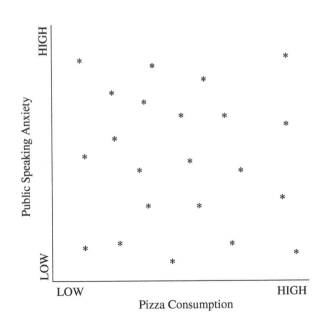

FIGURE 6.3
No Relationship

kind are interesting, they really do not relate to statistics except in that differences in kind create grouping variables (or nominal variables, which will be discussed soon).

DIFFERENCES OF DEGREE Rather than differences in kind, quantitative researchers are often interested in **differences of degree**, or when two groups have differing degrees of a variable they both display. For example, perhaps we wanted to determine whether females and males differed in their levels of verbal aggression. We may give each group a survey to fill out and then look at the averages of the two groups. Statistical difference tests would then allow a researcher to determine whether the two groups have different average scores for verbal aggression. Figure 6.4 shows two curves representing theoretical scores on a test of verbal aggression. The curve to the left represents female verbal aggression scores, and the curve to the right represents male verbal aggression scores. Although eyeballing the two curves may make it appear that males have higher verbal aggression scores, researchers cannot use the eyeballing technique, which is why we use difference tests to determine whether the two groups are really different.

STATISTICAL DIFFERENCES Unfortunately, difference tests only tell us half of the story. Let's pretend that the two curves seen in Figure 6.4 represent a difference between the male and female levels of verbal aggression. The curves can be "statistically different," but the difference between the female average score and the male average score could only be a matter of four or five points. Researchers are also interested in the size of the difference (effect size), not only the fact that a difference exists. For example, look at the two curves in Figure 6.5. In these two curves, the difference between the male and female verbal aggression average scores is much greater than that in the two curves seen in Figure 6.4.

FIGURE 6.4
Small Difference Between Means

Verbal Aggression

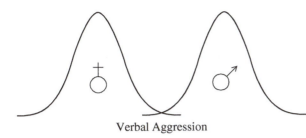

Verbal Aggression

FIGURE 6.5
**Large Difference
Between Means**

TYPES OF VARIABLES

To answer the research question or hypothesis, the next step in the process involves identifying the two types of variables chosen as the focal points of the study. Variables can be classified as independent, dependent, intervening, and antecedent.

Independent and Dependent Variables

Independent variables are the part of the research environment that are manipulated or changed. The **independent variable** is what we are studying with respect to how it impacts a dependent variable.

A **dependent variable**, by contrast, is not manipulated. These variables are recorded or measured, but they are not exposed to any type of alteration. Researchers look for any change in the dependent variable as a result of the manipulation of the independent variable. In essence, the goal of the research is to find out whether the dependent variable changes in response to the change or manipulation of the independent variable. Although the distinction between dependent and independent is easy when variables are used in an experimental situation, identifying these variables can be confusing in nonexperimental situations. Because of this, the term *criterion variable* is sometimes used to refer to the dependent variable.

So, how can you determine which variable is the independent variable and which is the dependent variable in a study? Consider the following hypothesis from Weber, Fornash, Corrigan, and Neupauer's (2003) study on the effect of student interest in a topic on recall of information:

> *H*: Lectures utilizing interest-based examples should result in participants with higher scores on subsequent tests of cognitive recall.

The independent variable in this hypothesis is lecture examples. Lectures were manipulated by showing students two different versions of videotapes: (1) lectures that incorporated current examples and (2) lectures using standard examples. Cognitive recall of information serves as the dependent variable. The researchers are trying to explain the difference in information recall as a result of the types of examples used in lectures.

Some studies examine variables that the researcher does not manipulate. Rather, the differences in a variable may occur naturally. Consider the following research question from a 1995 study examining communication satisfaction of children from divorced families (Thomas, Booth-Butterfield, & Booth-Butterfield, 1995):

H: Communication satisfaction with parents will be lower among children from divorced families than among children from intact families.

At first glance, it may be difficult to distinguish between the dependent and independent variables in this hypothesis, but recall the definitions for both concepts. The study is intended to examine the level of communication satisfaction of children from divorced and intact families. Thus, family status (divorced or intact) is the independent variable for the hypothesis. The goal is to determine whether differences in family status affect the dependent variable, or communication satisfaction.

Our third example is more difficult. Consider the following research question:

RQ: What is the relationship between parents who engage in verbally aggressive behavior at sporting events and a child's verbal aggressiveness?

According to this research question, we simply want to ascertain a possible relationship between the two variables. In other words, there is not a dependent variable and an independent variable in this example. However, if we proposed that a parent's level of verbally aggressive behavior at sporting events caused her or his child's level of verbal aggression, then we could say that the parents' level of verbal aggression is the independent variable and use that in an attempt to predict the child's level of verbal aggression.

Intervening Variables

If we only dealt with independent and dependent variables in research, our task would be fairly simple. But we know that nothing in life can ever be as easy as it looks. Sometimes there are additional variables whose presence may impact the relationship between the dependent and independent variables. **Intervening variables** are often included in a study to determine whether the effects of a change in the independent variable in turn cause a change in the dependent variable. If you wanted to examine the effect of teacher feedback on student motivation, it might be beneficial to consider the variable of self-esteem as a potential intervening variable. Positive feedback from a teacher may boost a student's level of self-esteem, which in turn may impact the level of motivation.

Antecedent Variables

Antecedent variables also have the potential to affect the relationship found between the independent and dependent variables. These variables answer the question "What happened before the data were collected?" and shed light on some differences that could emerge between the independent and dependent variables. For example, a study examining the impact of conflict (independent variable) on marital satisfaction (dependent variable) should take into consideration possible antecedent variables that might impact the results. If both partners had incompatible personalities before marriage, say, this could lead them to experience or view conflict in their relationship differently than those who are deemed to be compatible. Similarly, if a person comes from a family where parents often engaged in conflict, the impact of conflict on marital satisfaction may be a result of the predetermined expectations for conflict.

VARIABLE LEVELS

Another integral part of the research design process involves selecting variables to examine that will answer the proposed research question or hypothesis. Each variable selected for a study will be directly associated with identifying the particular statistical method appropriate for answering the research question. Variables can possess qualitative or quantitative characteristics. Variables with qualitative characteristics involve assigning items to groups or categories to describe the population. No quantitative value is implied with these variables. In contrast, quantitative variables are easily identified because they represent differences in quantity or amount.

A research variable can be classified into one of four levels. These levels, listed in order of precision in measuring variables, are nominal, ordinal, interval, and ratio.

Nominal Variables

Nominal variable data make up the variable level that is identified by its qualitative characteristics. To categorize nominal level data, simply name each characteristic using categories that are mutually exclusive. It is important to remember that a characteristic can only be represented by one category of a variable. No logical order is followed for creating the categorization, and values cannot be assigned quantitative values or rank ordered.

There are three primary rules for categorizing nominal level data. First, the categories used to classify the attributes must be mutually exclusive. Second, all categories used to represent the data must be equivalent. Remember the old adage "Don't compare apples to oranges!" The same principle applies in developing nominal categories. Finally, all categories used to classify nominal level data must be exhaustive.

Examples of nominal level data include political affiliation (a person can be a Democrat, Republican, other, or not registered) and sex (a participant is either a male or a female). As you can see from the categories created to describe each characteristic, a participant can only "fit" into one category. Thus, the categories established meet the first criteria of being mutually exclusive. Further, the categories used to represent the participants are exhaustive. As a variable, a person can only be a male or a female in terms of biological sex, and the categories of "other" and "not registered" are included to capture all participants who are not registered Republicans or Democrats.

Descriptive statistics and frequency distributions are the primary method of data analysis for nominal level data. For example, the dataset collected for this textbook and located on the website (http://www.oup-arc.com/wrench) can be used to examine the nominal variable biological sex. The nominal variable sex can be described in terms of percentages of males (49.98%) and females (50.02%) or in terms of frequencies representing the number of participants that fall into each category (males = 320, females = 321). Although a researcher would typically assign values to the categories of "male" and "female" for data entry purposes (perhaps a "1" to represent males and a "2" to represent females), it is important to note that these numbers have no relationship to the categories they represent. It would make no sense to try to compute a mean score for sex. Because the categories are mutually exclusive (a participant is either a male or a female), calculating a mean of 1.5 for sex would have no meaning. Instead, the mode (the number that occurs most frequently in the dataset) is the typical statistic used to describe nominal level data because it is meaningful to say that most participants were males. In this example, the mode would be 2 because we had more female participants. When a researcher wants to examine the differences between two nominal level variables, a chi-square test is the most appropriate method of statistical analysis (this statistic will be discussed in more detail in Chapter 15).

Ordinal Variables

Ordinal variables allow us to rank order attributes with regard to which has less versus which has more of a characteristic. Ordinal variables have both qualitative and quantitative characteristics. Ordinal variables are qualitative because people are placed into categories that are used to represent characteristics. However, these categories have real numerical associations, so the variables are also quantitative. Although there is a logical order to the creation of categories used to represent characteristics, it is important to note that the researcher is not able to make comparisons regarding the size of difference between categories.

Examples of ordinal level data include socioeconomic status (lower, middle, or upper class), education level (elementary, junior high, high school, or college), or letter grades (A, B, C, D, or F). It is evident that there is a distinct difference between each of the levels, and that there are quantitative differences between them, but we are unable to specify an amount or quantify the differences that exist. Suppose we know that the category of "middle class" is used to represent individuals with an income between $30,000 and $50,000, and that "upper class" is the category used to represent those earning more than $50,000 per year. The difference between middle and upper class could be one penny (the difference between $50,000.00 and $50,000.01) or millions of dollars.

There are three primary properties for categorizing ordinal variables. First, the categories must be mutually exclusive. That is, a participant can only "fit" into one of the categories. Second, the researcher must follow a logical ordering of the categories. Consider the ordinal variable of military rank. As a participant achieves status within the organization, a higher level of rank is awarded. Finally, each category must be balanced to represent the amount of a characteristic possessed by a participant.

To quantify ordinal level data for statistical analysis, numerical values are assigned to represent each category. However, the numbers used to represent each quality of the variable must increase such that higher numbers are used to represent high values. For example, a "1" could be assigned to represent the lower class, a "2" for the middle class, and a "3" for the upper class. It is important to remember that the intervals between the numbers used to represent each category are not necessarily representative of equal distances or quantities, nor does a zero point exist.

Interval Variables

Interval variables are quantitative and are classified in a logical order that represents equal distances between levels within each category. Examples of interval variables include levels of people's public speaking anxiety, levels of perceived similarity, and levels of perceived conspicuousness (to use the earlier example in this chapter when we discussed relationships).

Interval variables enable a researcher to rank order items and to compare the size of differences between each category. For example, McCroskey (1970) created the Personal Report of Public Speaking Anxiety (PRPSA) to measure an individual's level of public speaking anxiety, and scores on the scale range from 34 to 170, with higher scores indicating higher levels of anxiety when delivering a speech. We can say that a PRPSA score of 160 is higher than a PRPSA score of 80. However, we cannot state that an individual with a PRPSA score of 160 is twice as anxious as someone who has a PRPSA score of 80. This is because PRPSA does not have a zero as the scale's absolute starting point.

Four types of scales are used to measure interval level variables. These are the Likert, semantic differential, Staple, and scalogram scales.

LIKERT SCALE

In a **Likert scale**, participants are presented with a number of statements and then asked to respond to those statements based on a preexisting scale. Figure 6.6 shows an example of a short Likert scale called the Homonegativity Short Form, created by Wrench (2005). This scale has 10 scale items, all generally measuring an individual's perception of gay and lesbian people, and it is measured using a five-step system ranging from 1 (*strongly disagree*) to 5 (*strongly agree*). Each participant who fills out this scale only has five possible choices for each item on the scale: 1, 2, 3, 4, or 5. The scores

FIGURE 6.6
Likert Scale

> ## Homonegativity Short Form
>
> *Instructions:* Below are several descriptions of how you may feel. Please use the scale below to rate the degree to which each statement applies to you. Remember, we want you to be completely honest and we appreciate your cooperation.
>
> | Strongly Disagree | Disagree | Neutral | Agree | Strongly Agree |
> |:--:|:--:|:--:|:--:|:--:|
> | 1 | 2 | 3 | 4 | 5 |
>
> ____ 1. Gay and lesbian people make me nervous.
> ____ 2. Homosexuality is perfectly normal.
> ____ 3. I wouldn't want to have gay or lesbian friends.
> ____ 4. I would trust a gay or lesbian person.
> ____ 5. I fear homosexual persons will make sexual advances towards me.
> ____ 6. I would have no problem living with someone who is gay or lesbian.
> ____ 7. Homosexual behavior should be perfectly legal.
> ____ 8. I would have a serious problem if I saw two men or women kissing in public.
> ____ 9. I think that gay and lesbian people need civil rights protection.
> ____ 10. When I see a gay or lesbian person I think, "What a waste."
>
> SCORING: To compute your scores follow the instructions below:
>
> 1. How to Score:
>   Step One: Add scores for items 1, 3, 5, 8, & 10.
>   Step Two: Add scores for items 2, 4 6, 7, & 9.
>   Step Three: Add 30 to Step One.
>   Step Four: Subtract the score for Step Two from the score for Step Three.
>
> Source:
>
> Wrench, J. S. (2005). Development and validity testing of the homonegativity short form. *Journal of Intercultural Communication Research, 34*, 152–165.

for each individual item can be added together to achieve a composite score, which can then be used in various statistical analyses. McCroskey's (1970) PRPSA is another example of a Likert scale.

SEMANTIC DIFFERENTIAL SCALE

The second type of research scale commonly used to examine interval level measurements is the **semantic differential scale**. And we should note here that many researchers use the terms *semantic differential scale* and *bipolar scale* interchangeably. For our purposes, we will just use the term "semantic differential" going forward. The semantic differential scale consists of a series of adjectives that are oppositely worded (good/bad, happy/sad, eventful/uneventful, positive/negative, etc.). There then exists a

---

Work Motivation Scale

Instructions: The following scale is designed to examine how you currently feel about work. Only think about this one class when filling out the following scale. Numbers 1 and 7 indicate a very strong feeling. Numbers 2 and 6 indicate a strong feeling. Numbers 3 and 5 indicate a fairly weak feeling. Number 4 indicates you are undecided.

Unmotivated	1	2	3	4	5	6	7	Motivated
Excited	7	6	5	4	3	2	1	Bored
Interested	7	6	5	4	3	2	1	Uninterested
Involved	7	6	5	4	3	2	1	Uninvolved
Dreading it	1	2	3	4	5	6	7	Looking forward to it

Scoring:

To determine your level of work motivation, add your scores for each question together.

Source:

Richmond, V. P. (1990). Communication in the classroom: Power and motivation. *Communication Education, 39*, 181–184.

FIGURE 6.7
Semantic Differential/ Bipolar Scale

continuum of possible choices between the adjectives, and participants are asked to select the number that most represents their perception between the two adjectives.

For example, we may ask participants to rate the movie *Charlie and the Chocolate Factory* using the bipolar adjectives "good" and "bad," with a choice of 1 to 7 between the two words. Numbers 1 and 7 indicate a very strong feeling, 2 and 6 indicate a strong feeling, 3 and 5 indicate a fairly weak feeling, and 4 indicates you are undecided. If you thought the movie was good but not amazing, you might give the movie a rating of 2 or 3 because these are closest to the word "good," whereas if you thought it was the worst movie you had ever seen, you might rate the movie a 7 because that number is closest to the word "bad."

Figure 6.7 is another example of a semantic differential scale. In this example, we see the job motivation scale, which is a retooling of Richmond's (1990) student motivation scale. This scale asks people to respond to how they feel about work using five adjective pairs. When you add up the responses from all five adjective pairs, you can then use this number in a variety of statistical tests.

STAPLE SCALE

As an offshoot of the semantic differential scale, Jan Staple, codirector of the Netherlands Institute of Public Opinion, devised a different way to measure people's opinions (Crespi, 1961). The Staple scale is designed to measure individual attitudes toward a topic by providing participants with a set of adjectives and then having them rank those adjectives from –5 (words are not an accurate portrayal of something) to +5 (words are an accurate portrayal of something). Imagine we wanted to create a Staple scale for evaluating anxiety; it could look something like Figure 6.8. Items 3 and 4 (calm and relaxed) are functional opposites of items 1, 2, and 5 (anxious, nervous, and agitated), so they would have to be recoded to reflect the opposite score to achieve a composite score for this measure.

SCALOGRAM

The last scale that is used to create an interval variable is called the Guttman scale, or **scalogram**. Although scalograms are interesting, they are rarely actually employed in communication research. The goal of a scalogram is to ascertain an individual's belief about a given topic.

A perfect Guttman scale would consist of a set of unidimensional items that respondents rank in order from the least extreme to the most extreme position (Guttman, 1944). For example, maybe you want to determine how much homework is too much for high school students. You give them a list of 10 possible time frames ranging from 0 to 10 hours or more of homework. You then have your participants answer yes or no next to each time frame: "No Homework to 1 Hour" up to "10 Hours or More of Homework." The goal of a scalogram scale is that at some point along the way, you will hit a cutoff point beyond which people will not go. For example, maybe someone believes

FIGURE 6.8
Staple Scale

Staple Scale
Below are a series of adjectives that indicate how you may currently feel. For each adjective, circle the number that most closely corresponds to how you feel from –5 (this does not at all explain how I feel) to +5 (this is exactly how I feel).

+5	+5	+5	+5	+5
+4	+4	+4	+4	+4
+3	+3	+3	+3	+3
+2	+2	+2	+2	+2
+1	+1	+1	+1	+1
Anxious	Nervous	Calm	Relaxed	Agitated
–1	–1	–1	–1	–1
–2	–2	–2	–2	–2
–3	–3	–3	–3	–3
–4	–4	–4	–4	–4
–5	–5	–5	–5	–5

that "4 to 5 Hours of Homework" is legitimate, but that "5 to 6 Hours of Homework" is unreasonable. If someone marks that "5 to 6 Hours of Homework" is unreasonable, we would not expect her or him two questions later to state that "7 to 8 Hours of Homework" is okay. A scalogram scale attempts to determine where people cut themselves off in relation to a specific belief.

Figure 6.9 contains an example of a scalogram scale created to examine environmentalism. As this scale progresses, each statement becomes slightly more radicalized with regard to an individual's perception of environmentalism.

Ratio Variables

Ratio variables are like interval variables with one notable exception—ratio variables have an absolute zero starting point to represent the absence of the characteristic. Examples of ratio variables include income, exam scores, temperature (when measured by the Kelvin scale, which has an absolute zero), and speed. Whereas we could not

FIGURE 6.9
Scalogram

Environmentalism Scale		
Instructions: For each phrase circle whether you agree with that statement by circling YES or disagree with the statement by circling NO.		
1. I never throw trash on the ground because it hurts our environment.	YES (1)	NO
2. I think recycling is a noble endeavor.	YES (2)	NO
3. I always participate in recycling in my city.	YES (3)	NO
4. My friends and family know my commitment to the environment.	YES (4)	NO
5. I would send a letter to a company that willfully hurts the environment.	YES (5)	NO
6. I vote for politicians based on their environmental policies and voting behaviors.	YES (6)	NO
7. I would picket a company that is hurting the environment.	YES (7)	NO
8. I would organize a campaign against a corporation that is polluting the environment.	YES (8)	NO
9. I would participate in tree spiking to prevent companies from destroying our environment.	YES (9)	NO
10. Bombing a company that hurts the environment is completely justifiable.	YES (10)	NO
Scoring: To score this measure, add the numbers under each YES answer selected. Scores can run from 0 to 57. Higher scores indicate a more radical environmental stance.		

make statements regarding the size of any difference between categories of interval level data, we can make statements such as "An exam score of 50 is two times more than an exam score of 25."

Most statistical analysis procedures view interval and ratio characteristics in the same way, so the same statistical tests are used to describe and compare both types of variables. The *t* test (comparing two groups) and one-way analysis of variance (comparing two or more groups) are the appropriate difference tests when analyzing interval/ratio variables. We will discuss *t* tests in Chapter 16 and one-way analysis of variance in Chapter 17. To describe linear relationships between two or more interval variables, correlations (Chapter 18) or regression analyses (Chapter 19) are most appropriate.

Choosing the Right Test

Figure 6.10 summarizes the appropriate statistical tests to be used when analyzing each type of variable. For example, if a researcher wanted to test for differences on public speaking anxiety (an interval scale) between females and males (two groups), that researcher would need to conduct a *t* test. In this example, we started off with our interval scale and realized we had two groups that we were testing

(female and male), so the only choice of statistical test was the *t* test. But if we had two or more ordinal variables and wanted to test for a relationship, what test would we use? According to our chart, if we have two ordinal variables, the only test available for examining relationships is a correlation (specifically a Spearman rho correlation). Figure 6.10 will become *very* important later in this book.

Interval/Ratio	Differences	Two groups	*t*-Test
		More than two groups	ANOVA
	Relationships	Two variables	Correlation
		More than two variables	Regression
Ordinal	Differences	Two groups	Mann-Whitney or *t*-Test
		More than two groups	ANOVA
	Relationships		Correlation
Nominal	Differences		Chi-square
	Relationships		Percentage differences

FIGURE 6.10
Summary of Appropriate Statistical Tests for Variable Levels

COMMUNICATION VARIABLES

Earlier in this chapter, we introduced the major levels of variables that social science researchers are concerned with: nominal, ordinal, interval, and ratio. The authors of this book believe that the best way to really learn how to conduct quantitative research is to actually conduct quantitative research on real variables. With this in mind, we decided to put together a study using some common communication variables and then supply you, the reader, with the actual data gathered from real research participants.

In the spring of 2005, the authors of this book recruited 325 undergraduate students to participate in a research study, and in the fall of 2011, we recruited an additional 329 students, for a total of 654 participants. Not only will we discuss the data from these participants at various parts of the book, but you also have access to the datasets on the textbook's website (https://oup-arc.com/wrench). These datasets can be analyzed using your favorite statistical software package. The goal of this data collection was to provide the readers of this text an actual dataset that can be used to ask real research questions. The questionnaire distributed can be seen in Appendix B (see textbook's website) exactly as we distributed it to the participants. Since this dataset was meant to enable you to use real participant data to ask real research questions, we made sure that we had variables from each level (nominal, ordinal, interval, and ratio) in it. The rest of this chapter explains each of the variables we collected.

Nominal Variables

For the purposes of this book, we decided to include two nominal variables: biological sex and political affiliation.

BIOLOGICAL SEX

The first variable was a common nominal variable included in most research studies: biological sex. As a variable, biological sex has only two possible attributes (female and male). For a variable to be nominal, the categories must be equivalent (the categories of female and male are equivalent), mutually exclusive (you cannot be both female and male), and exhaustive (there is not a third or fourth biological sex).

POLITICAL AFFILIATION

The second nominal variable we included in this study was political affiliation. The concept of political affiliation is tricky, so ultimately, how participants respond when asked "What is your political affiliation?" will depend on the categories that a researcher provides her or his participants. We could have listed different political parties—Communist Party, Democratic Party, Green Party, Libertarian Party, Natural Law Party, Republican Party, and even "Independent" (no affiliation)—until we had listed every known political party in the United States, which would be a long list. Instead, we opted to use the two most prominent parties (Democratic and Republican) as categories and then add a third category ("Other") for anyone who belonged to a party outside the mainstream political process or who had no party affiliation. However, on further contemplation, we realized that those three categories were not completely exhaustive. Not everyone in this country belongs to a political party or sees her- or himself as an independent voter. In fact, many people are simply not registered to vote at all. For this reason, we decided that our fourth category should be "Not Registered to Vote." Everyone who filled out the survey should fall into one of the categories provided ("Democrat," "Republican," "Other," or "Not Registered to Vote"). Not only are the categories exhaustive, but someone who is not registered to vote is not someone who belongs to the Democratic Party because registering to vote is how people join political parties in our country. Furthermore, someone who is a Republican cannot also be an Other, so our categories are mutually exclusive as well. And all of the categories relate to political affiliation (even "Not Registered to Vote"), so our categories are equivalent.

Ordinal Variables

For the purposes of the study conducted for this textbook, we created two ordinal variables for analysis: university classification and time spent online.

UNIVERSITY CLASSIFICATION

The first ordinal variable we used in this study was university classification. We created a variable with five levels (first-year student, sophomore, junior, senior, and graduate student). You may be wondering why these are ordinal and not nominal. The reason they are ordinal is the same reason someone is labeled as upper class as opposed to middle class—there is no true indication of magnitude. In college, these categories are based on the number of hours taken and passed, not on the number of years someone has been in school. For example, one of the authors of this textbook was one hour shy of being a sophomore at the beginning of his second year in college, he was still classified as a freshman according to the university. On the flip side, how many of us have known people who are eighth- or ninth-year seniors?! In essence, the labels associated with university classifications represent a difference between the classification levels, but we do not get any indication of the size of this difference.

TIME SPENT ONLINE

The second ordinal variable that we selected to include in this book's dataset was the amount of time someone spent online. Specifically, we asked the study participants to disclose how much time they spend online during a given week. We then provided the participants a series of categorical answers: 0–½ hour, ½–1 hour, 1–2 hours, 2–5 hours, 5–10 hours, 10–15 hours, 15–20 hours, and 20+ hours. With each categorical level, we increase the size of the difference, but the exact size is not known. Someone who spends 80 hours a week online would fall into the 20+ hour group, as would someone who spends 21 hours a week online. In the same vein as university classification, the difference in how one classifies her- or himself can be a matter of minutes. Maybe someone spends an average of 9 hours and 45 minutes online each week, so he classifies himself as spending 5–10 hours online. However, another participant spends an average of 10 hours and 15 minutes online each week, so she classifies herself as spending 10–15 hours online. This gradient of 30 minutes cannot be taken into account when dealing with the categorical nature of this ordinal variable.

Interval Variables

Most interval variables studied by communication researchers measure traits, behaviors, beliefs, and attitudes. Luckily, the study that we compiled for this textbook measured all of those. In this section, we first examine what personality and communication traits are and then look at the various communication traits measured in this book using an interval scale. The interval variables included in the dataset for this text are communication apprehension, ethnocentrism, humor assessment, nonverbal immediacy, sociocommunicative orientation, willingness to communicate, beliefs and attitudes.

COMMON INTERVAL VARIABLE MEASURES

PERSONALITY AND COMMUNICATION Personality is the total psychological makeup of an individual, which is a reflection of her or his experiences, motivations, attitudes, beliefs, values, and behaviors, derived from the interaction of these elements with the environment external to the individual. Thus, personality can be defined as the sum of an individual's characteristics that make him or her unique (Hollander, 1976). If everyone had the same personality, we would all communicate the same way all the time in every situation. Thankfully, we do not all communicate the same way, and these differences in our communicative behaviors can be observed.

Ultimately, Hollander (1976) noted that personality consists of two basic dimensions that are important to communication researchers. These dimensions are external/internal and dynamic/consistent.

EXTERNAL/INTERNAL The first dimension of personality distinguishes the external level (observable characteristics of an individual) from the internal level (individual's attitudes, values, beliefs, interests, aspirations, and motivations). We often use an individual's external personality to determine her or his internal personality during interpersonal interactions. As humans, we expect people to behave according to the way they think and feel and therefore expect the external behavior to be a window into the internal reality. So, when we see someone shaking and turning red during a speech, we reach the conclusion that he or she is experiencing anxiety brought on by the speech itself.

In reality, however, the internal and external personalities are not always in sync with each other. We may feel that someone who is shaking and flushing during a speech has anxiety, but there could be many other reasons that the specific behavior is being exhibited. For example, the person might just be ill, which could cause the shaking and red flushing during the speech.

DYNAMIC/CONSISTENT The second feature of personality distinguishes its dynamic aspects (the degree to which a personality trait can change over time or during certain contexts or situations) from its consistent aspects (the degree to which a personality trait does not change over time or during certain contexts or situations). We have a continuum of personality traits ranging from consistent to dynamic. Many external and internal factors can cause personality traits to change. For example, getting married, moving to another country, experiencing a crisis, losing a job, and so on can change how a person looks at life (internal level) and how he or she behaves (external level). Many aspects of our individual personalities, however, do not alter over time. Elements of the internal level of personality least likely to undergo change are those that comprise the consistent aspect of personality (e.g., values). Another reason why some personality traits are resistant to change is human genetics. There is an increasing body of research examining how our genetic code affects various personality traits. Although this textbook is outside the purview of examining how genetics affects human behavior, we recommend reading Dean Hamer and Peter Copeland's (1998) *Living With Our Genes: Why They Matter More Than You Think* to examine how genetics influence various personality traits and Michael Beatty, James McCroskey, and Kristin Valencic's (2001) *The Biology of Communication: A Communibiological Perspective* to examine how genetics influence human communication specifically.

TRAITS AND COMMUNICATION

The perceptions we have about people based on their exhibited behaviors also affect how we view them. In our daily interactions with others, we constantly assume that because an individual is exhibiting a particular behavior, he or she is "that kind of person." We make these assumptions because we expect internal and external personality traits to be consistent. Imagine you watch that same flustered speaker over an entire semester. Every time he or she speaks, you see the same shaking and turning red. And after watching an individual shake and turn red every time he or she spoke, we would begin to see this anxiety as characteristic of her or his personality. As Hollander (1976) notes, it is only a short time until you begin to view this characteristic in others as a *trait*, or the way he or she "typically" behaves. There are four different ways that personality characteristics can be exhibited by specific individuals: traits, contexts, audience, and situational.

TRAITS In the psychology of personality, **trait behavior** (or "traits") refers to individual characteristics that are not found in all people, only in relatively few. Traits are an individual's predispositions for responding in a certain way to various situations. A given trait will exhibit itself in almost any situation responded to by the individual. For example, if our anxious speaker was later seen talking in a meeting and was turning red in that communicative situation as well, we might conclude that this individual's communicative anxiety is clearly trait based because it is seen across multiple contexts.

CONTEXTS The second way that personality characteristics can be demonstrated by individuals is within specific contexts. The basic contexts that communication scholars examine are interpersonal, group, meeting, public, and mediated. Contexts are specific modes where behavior can be different, which leads to contextual behavior. For example, maybe our anxious speaker gets anxious when having to give a public speech (public context) but experiences no anxiety while communicating interpersonally, in groups, in a meeting, or when talking online. Here, we can say that her or his speech anxiety is context based.

AUDIENCE The third way that personality characteristics surface depends on the audience with whom an individual is communicating, or **audience-specific behavior**. Different audiences have differing perspectives of how interactions should occur, so we tend to act differently based on the type of audience we are interacting with. Maybe our anxious speaker is fine while giving a speech to her or his Rotary Club but gets anxious in front of someone who is giving her or him a grade. Here, a teacher grading the student could cause the student to experience audience-based speech anxiety.

SITUATIONAL The final way in which personality characteristics surface depends on the situation, which can lead to **situational behavior**. Sometimes we communicate in a manner that is not normal for us because of the situation. We refer to this behavior as situational because it is not generally replicated. In the case of our nervous speaker, it is possible that this person has never before in her or his life experienced any kind of anxiety while giving a speech, but during this particular speech, she or he was overcome with anxiety. Sometimes, out of nowhere, we alter our normal communication patterns because of the situation, or our "odd" communicative behavior happens only within a specific situation.

A COMMUNICATION TRAIT CONTINUUM

Overall, personality differences manifest themselves as variations in communicative behavior. To take this concept one step further, we can examine the notion of a specific type of personality trait—a communication trait. A **communication trait** is a hypothetical construct that accounts for certain kinds of communication behaviors. Researchers in the field of communication have examined numerous

FIGURE 6.11
Communication Trait Continuum

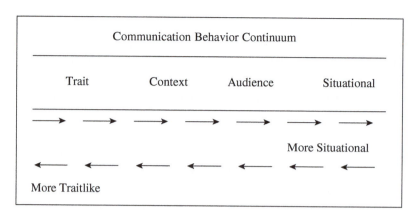

communicative patterns that are traitlike because in some people they are not alterable whereas in others they can be situationally based. For the remainder of this chapter, it is useful to think of all of the communication traits we examine as existing along a four-point continuum (see Figure 6.11). Starting at one extreme end of the continuum and moving to the other extreme, the four points are communication behavior (1) as a trait, (2) in a generalized context, (3) with a specific audience, and (4) within a specific situation.

Communication Apprehension

Communication apprehension (CA) is defined as the fear or anxiety associated with either real or anticipated communication with another person or persons. Before we discuss the nature of this first communicative trait, however, please fill out the Personal Report of Communication Apprehension–24 (PRCA-24) in Figure 6.12.

Let's break this definition down into its various parts. First, CA is about fear and anxiety. People exhibit fear and anxiety differently. Some people are generally fearful and anxious about almost everything, whereas others are more focused in their fear and anxiety. People who are said to be high CA (scores between 80 and 120 on the PRCA-24) will experience fear and anxiety in every context when having to communicate (actual or real communication). However, people with high CA do not stop having anxiety just because they do not have to engage in communication at that moment. In fact, people with high CA experience apprehension and anxiety even when they *think* about having to communicate with another person (anticipate communication). High-CA people often experience severe anxiety while practicing a public speech alone in their house, thinking about having to interact with someone interpersonally, or imagining having to talk in a group or meeting the next day. Research has shown that approximately one in five people, or 20% of the general population, suffers from high CA.

FIGURE 6.12
**Personal Report of
Communication
Apprehension–24**

DIRECTIONS: This instrument is composed of 24 statements concerning feelings about communicating with other people. Please indicate the degree to which each statement applies to you by marking whether you (1) strongly agree, (2) agree, (3) are undecided, (4) disagree, or (5) strongly disagree. Work quickly; record your first impression.

_____ 1. I dislike participating in group discussions.

_____ 2. Generally, I am comfortable while participating in group discussions.

_____ 3. I am tense and nervous while participating in group discussions.

_____ 4. I like to get involved in group discussions.

_____ 5. Engaging in a group discussion with new people makes me tense and nervous.

_____ 6. I am calm and relaxed while participating in group discussions.

_____ 7. Generally, I am nervous when I have to participate in a meeting.

_____ 8. Usually I am comfortable when I have to participate in a meeting.

_____ 9. I am very calm and relaxed when I am called upon to express an opinion at a meeting.

_____ 10. I am afraid to express myself at meetings.

_____ 11. Communicating at meetings usually makes me uncomfortable.

_____ 12. I am very relaxed when answering questions at a meeting.

_____ 13. While participating in a conversation with a new acquaintance, I feel very nervous.

_____ 14. I have no fear of speaking up in conversations.

_____ 15. Ordinarily I am very tense and nervous in conversations.

_____ 16. While conversing with a new acquaintance, I feel very relaxed.

_____ 17. Ordinarily I am very calm and relaxed in conversations.

_____ 18. I'm afraid to speak up in conversations.

_____ 19. I have no fear of giving a speech.

_____ 20. Certain parts of my body feel very tense and rigid while I am giving a speech.

_____ 21. I feel relaxed while giving a speech.

_____ 22. My thoughts become confused and jumbled when I am giving a speech.

_____ 23. I face the prospect of giving a speech with confidence.

_____ 24. While giving a speech, I get so nervous I forget facts I really know.

SCORING: To compute context subscores begin with a score of 18 for each context and follow the instructions below.

1. Group discussion—add scores for items 2, 4, & 6. Subtract scores for items 1, 3, & 5. Scores can range from 6 to 30.

2. Meetings—add scores for items 8, 9, & 12. Subtract scores for items 7, 10, & 11. Scores can range from 6 to 30.

3. Interpersonal—add scores for items 14, 16, & 17. Subtract scores for items 13, 15, & 18. Scores can range from 6 to 30.

4. Public speaking—add scores for items 19, 21, & 23. Subtract scores for items 20, 22, & 24. Scores can range from 6 to 30.

To compute the total score for the PRCA-24, add the four subscores. Total scores can range from 24 to 120. Scores above 80 = high CA; below 50 = low CA.

Source:

McCroskey, J. C. (1982). *An introduction to rhetorical communication* (4th ed). Englewood Cliffs, NJ: Prentice-Hall.

Scores on the PRCA-24 should be between 24 and 120. If your score is between 24 and 50, you are among those in our society who experience the least CA and whom we refer to as low-CA individuals. You are apt to be a higher talker and may actively seek out opportunities to interact with others. Few, if any, communication situations cause you to be fearful or anxious. If your score is somewhere between 50 and 60, you experience less CA than most people, but you are likely to feel some fear or anxiety about a few situations. If your score falls between 60 and 70, your level of CA is like that of most people. At this level, there are some communication situations that may cause you to feel anxious or tense, but in others, you will feel quite comfortable. If your score is between 70 and 80, you experience more CA than most people. Probably many communication situations cause you to be fearful and tense, but some still do not bother you. If your score falls between 80 and 120, you are among those who experience the most CA. You are likely a low talker, one who actively avoids many communication situations because you feel much anxiety and tension in those situations.

TRAIT CA

Although having high levels of CA (trait CA) will impact a person's social life, trait CA has been shown to impact other areas as well. Research has shown that high-CA individuals tend to have low self-esteem and are more prone to depression than low-CA individuals. High-CA individuals are also perceived as having low intelligence by peers, teachers, and supervisors, although there is no research to support any difference in IQ levels based on an individual's CA. Research has shown that people with high levels of CA are less likely to visit their physicians and, when they do go, are less likely to ask questions about medical treatment and medication. Overall, CA impacts every aspect of an individual's life. People with trait CA can be truly crippled in our society.

CONTEXTUAL CA

Other people are likely to have contextually based CA, or they experience apprehension in one of the communicative contexts (interpersonal, meeting, group, or public). For example, an individual may experience CA while interacting with someone on a one-on-one basis but have no problem standing up before an audience of 1,000 people and giving a speech. Yet other people experience CA based more on the audience with whom they must communicate. Almost everyone experiences CA at some point with a specific audience. Whether you are giving a presentation in front of your peers or your boss, for example, can impact the degree of anxiety you may feel.

SITUATIONAL CA

The last type of CA that can occur is referred to as situationally based CA. Sometimes the uniqueness of a specific situation may cause you to experience anxiety. One of the authors of this text has given countless public speeches. During one particular speech, however, our colleague looked down and noticed that his hand was visibly shaking. He had never before in his life had a shaking hand while giving a speech. His outward nervousness made him even more anxious, and before he knew it, he had no idea what he was saying because he was focusing on his own anxiety.

Ethnocentrism

We all know that people around the world believe the following: "The United States is the best country on the face of the planet. Without the United States, the world would be less artistic, less moral, and less intelligent. In fact, if everyone would be more like the United States, this world would be much better off." Yes, people from around the world say these exact sentences—they just plug in their own country of origin in place of "the United States." The Russians, Chinese, Australians, South Africans, Finns, Brazilians, Egyptians, Singaporeans, and Japanese all feel their country is the best and that if everyone would just behave like people in their country, the world would be much better off. Few things have been found to be truly **pancultural** (the same across all cultures), but this view that an individual's own culture is superior to all the rest is. The view that the customs and practices of one's own culture are superior to those of other cultures is known as **ethnocentrism**. People in all cultures are ethnocentric to varying degrees. Neuliep and McCroskey (1997) created an ethnocentrism scale to measure this phenomenon; before we discuss the nature of ethnocentrism, please fill out the ethnocentrism scale in Figure 6.13.

The term *ethnocentrism* comes from the combination of two Greek words: *ethnos* (nation) and *kentron* (center). In combination, *ethnos* and *kentron* suggest that an individual's nation is the center of the universe. When one holds ethnocentric views, as virtually everyone does, an individual's culture is used as the standard by which all other cultures are evaluated. In fact, any deviation from an individual's culture is most likely (but not always) seen as negative, which indicates the inferiority of the *other* culture and the people from that culture. Although ethnocentrism may sound innately bad, it is not inherently negative to have some level of ethnocentrism. In fact, ethnocentrism can be positive.

One way in which ethnocentrism is positive is that it gives the people in a culture an identity and helps make them more cohesive, which in turn helps promote positive and effective communication among members of the culture. For a short period after September 11, 2001, people in the United States truly functioned as Americans. During that time, Americans were welcoming of all other Americans, but wary of anyone who was not an American citizen. In New York City on 9/11, people saw everyone around them as New Yorkers despite the amazing cultural diversity that exists there. You may think to yourself that these are just examples of patriotism, and you would be right. Patriotism is innately ethnocentric. Wars are often fought in cultures because one culture views their way of life as something ultimately moral and worth fighting for.

Humor Assessment

Have you ever noticed that people who can get everyone around them laughing tend to have more friends and are invited to more parties? The ability to use humor effectively

FIGURE 6.13
Ethnocentrism Scale

Instructions: Below are items that relate to the cultures of different parts of the world. Work quickly and record your first reaction to each item. There are no right or wrong answers. Please indicate the degree to which you agree or disagree with each item using the following five-point scale:

Strongly Disagree	Disagree	Neutral	Agree	Strongly Agree
1	2	3	4	5

_____ 1. Most other cultures are backward compared to my culture.
_____ 2. My culture should be the role model for other cultures.
_____ 3. People from other cultures act strange when they come to my culture.
_____ 4. Lifestyles in other cultures are just as valid as those in my culture.
_____ 5. Other cultures should try to be more like my culture.
_____ 6. I am not interested in the values and customs of other cultures.
_____ 7. People in my culture could learn a lot from people in other cultures.
_____ 8. Most people from other cultures just don't know what's good for them.
_____ 9. I respect the values and customs of other cultures.
_____ 10. Other cultures are smart to look up to our culture.
_____ 11. Most people would be happier if they lived like people in my culture.
_____ 12. I have many friends from different cultures.
_____ 13. People in my culture have just about the best lifestyles of anywhere.
_____ 14. Lifestyles in other cultures are not as valid as those in my culture.
_____ 15. I am very interested in the values and customs of other cultures.
_____ 16. I apply my values when judging people who are different.
_____ 17. I see people who are similar to me as virtuous.
_____ 18. I do not cooperate with people who are different.
_____ 19. Most people in my culture just don't know what is good for them.
_____ 20. I do not trust people who are different.
_____ 21. I dislike interacting with people from different cultures.
_____ 22. I have little respect for the values and customs of other cultures.

SCORING: To compute your scores follow the instructions below:

1.   How to Score Drop questions 3, 6, 12, 15, 16, 17, 19

Step One: Add scores for items 1, 2, 5, 8, 10, 11, 13, 14, 18, 20, 21 & 22.
Step Two: Add scores for items 4, 7, & 9.
Step Three: Add 18 to Step 1.
Step Four: Subtract the score for Step two from the score for Step Three.

The result is your Ethnocentrism score. Higher scores = higher levels of ethnocentrism.

Interpretation:

Scores should be between 15 and 75. Most people score between 20 and 40. Scores over 32 are considered high.

Source:

Neuliep, J. W., & McCroskey, J. C. (1997). Development of a US and generalized ethnocentrism scale. *Communication Research Reports, 14,* 385–398.

is a trait that many people wish they could have, but only some people seem to have that extra spark that makes their humor usage appear flawless. In an attempt to measure the extent to which an individual uses humor during interpersonal interactions, Wrench and Richmond (2004) created the humor assessment instrument. Before we start discussing the nature of an individual's **humor assessment**, please fill out the humor assessment instrument in Figure 6.14.

FIGURE 6.14
Humor Assessment
Instrument

Directions: The following statements apply to how people communicate humor when relating to others. Indicate the degree to which each of these statements applies to you by filling in the number of your response in the blank before each item:

Strongly Disagree	Disagree	Neutral	Agree	Strongly Agree
1	2	3	4	5

_____ 1. I regularly communicate with others by joking with them.
_____ 2. People usually laugh when I make a humorous remark.
_____ 3. I am not funny or humorous.
_____ 4. I can be amusing or humorous without having to tell a joke.
_____ 5. Being humorous is a natural communication orientation for me.
_____ 6. I cannot relate an amusing idea well.
_____ 7. My friends would say that I am a humorous or funny person.
_____ 8. People don't seem to pay close attention when I am being funny.
_____ 9. Even funny ideas and stories seem dull when I tell them.
_____ 10. I can easily relate funny or humorous ideas to the class.
_____ 11. I would say that I am not a humorous person.
_____ 12. I cannot be funny, even when asked to do so.
_____ 13. I relate amusing stories, jokes, and funny things very well to others.
_____ 14. Of all the people I know, I am one of the "least" amusing or funny persons.
_____ 15. I use humor to communicate in a variety of situations.
_____ 16. On a regular basis, I do not communicate with others by being humorous or entertaining.

SCORING: To compute your scores follow the instructions below:

1. How to Score:
    Step One: Add scores for items 1, 2, 4, 5, 7, 10, 13, & 15.
    Step Two: Add scores for items 3, 6, 8, 9, 11, 12, 14 & 16.
    Step Three: Add 48 to Step One.
    Step Four: Subtract the score for Step Two from the score for Step Three.

Scores should be between 16 and 80. Scores over 63 are considered high.

Source:

Wrench, J. S., & Richmond, V. P. (2004). Understanding the psychometric properties of the Humor Assessment instrument through an analysis of the relationships between teacher humor assessment and instructional communication variables in the college classroom. *Communication Research Reports, 21,* 92–103.

Humor is a fascinating variable to study because of the dramatic effects that it can have on people's everyday lives. The ability to use humor as a tool for interpersonal communication has consistently been shown to be useful whether you are in a health-care setting, a classroom, or a boardroom. In research that has examined humor in health-care settings (Wrench & Booth-Butterfield, 2003; see textbook's website for this article), physicians who are more humorous are perceived by patients as being more credible. Patients are also more satisfied with physicians who are funny and are less likely to sue a physician who uses moderate levels of humor during a medical interview. In the area of educational research, teachers who are more humorous are also perceived as more trustworthy and credible by their students when compared to teachers who are not perceived as humorous. Students also like humorous teachers more than nonhumorous teachers, and they even like the content from humorous teachers more than that from nonhumorous teachers. In fact, teachers who are humorous in the classroom have students who learn more in the class. In the organizational setting, many businesses hire humor consultants to come in and "liven things up" around the office because a humorous work environment has been shown to increase productivity levels. Employees who perceive their superiors as being humorous experience higher levels of job satisfaction and are less likely to quit their job, which ultimately saves an organization lots of money.

When you examine the results from research on humor in different contexts, it points in one direction—humor is a good thing. Although what people find humorous is culturally based, the ability to enact it appears to be more biologically based. When we talk about a cultural basis for what we find humorous, think about the types of stand-up comedians you like versus the types your parents or grandparents would like. What people within a different culture or co-culture enjoy as humorous depends on what they are taught is funny. If you are taught that farting in public is rude and obnoxious, you will not find a "fart joke" funny, although other people will think the joke is hysterical.

Nonverbal Immediacy

Have you ever noticed that you are drawn to some people and not to others? One reason for this is an individual's level of nonverbal immediacy.

As a general concept, **immediacy** refers to the degree of perceived physical or psychological distance between people in a relationship. An immediate relationship is one in which the people in the relationship see themselves as close (both physically and mentally) to one another. When we talk about physical closeness, we are not talking about intimacy—just a perception that the other person is physically near you. Have you ever noticed how some people can make themselves look unapproachable just by the way they hold their bodies and look at you? Although these people may be in the same physical environment as you are, you probably will not perceive yourself as being close to these people. On the flip side, many people experience a certain feeling of closeness with a public speaker even though they are 100 yards away during the speech. All of us communicate a certain presence to other people. How we hold our bodies and look at people will determine whether we start, continue, or terminate interactions with others. Whom we desire to communicate with is communicated to that other person through both our verbal and our nonverbal messages. Thus, the verbal and nonverbal messages we send and receive in a relationship will define the level of immediacy that develops in that relationship.

As mentioned earlier, immediacy is created through both verbal and nonverbal messages. **Verbal immediacy** is created through comments such as "I see what you mean," "Tell me more," "That is a good point," and "I think so too." Contrast these comments with "Oh, shut up," "I do believe a village lost its idiot," "I thought of that years ago," and "Frankly, I don't care what you think." The first series of phrases helps increase the perceived physical and psychological closeness between two people, whereas the second series only increases the perception of distance. **Nonverbal immediacy**, by contrast, consists of communicative behaviors like leaning in toward the other person while talking to her or him, maintaining eye contact, smiling, nodding your head, not folding your arms in front of you while talking, and many others. Nonimmediate nonverbal behaviors would be the opposite of the immediate ones: leaning away from the other person while talking, avoiding eye contact, frowning or scowling, not moving your head at all (looking rigid), folding your arms in front of you, and so on. The Nonverbal Immediacy Scale (Figure 6.15) was designed to examine an individual's tendency to employ different nonverbally immediate behaviors while avoiding communicative behaviors that are not nonverbally immediate.

You may be wondering why nonverbal immediacy is so important that we need to research it as a variable. Nonverbal immediacy has been linked to a number of important communication outcomes. First, immediacy will usually lead to an increase in communication between participants and interactants. When someone feels that another person is either physically or psychologically close, he or she becomes more relaxed and open to communication. Second, immediacy will lead to increased attentiveness by the receiver. If we perceive that someone is immediate, we naturally focus attention on that person. So if you want someone to listen to what you are saying, employing nonverbally and verbally immediate behaviors is a trick that can be used to get and maintain that person's attention. Third, immediacy will increase the likelihood that listening will improve between the interactants. People are more open to listening to what another person is saying when they perceive that the person is immediate. Fourth, immediacy leads to increased liking between interactants. If you perceive that someone is physically and psychologically close, you are simply going to like that person more. Overall, these four outcomes lead to more effective communication.

FIGURE 6.15
Nonverbal Immediacy
Scale–Self-Report

DIRECTIONS: The following statements describe the ways some people behave while talking with or to others. Please indicate in the space at the left of each item the degree to which you believe the statement applies to (**fill in the target person's name or description).** Please use the following 5-point scale:

1 = Never; 2 = Rarely; 3 = Occasionally; 4 = Often; 5 = Very Often

_____ 1. I use my hands and arms to gesture while talking to people.
_____ 2. I touch others on the shoulder or arm while talking to them.
_____ 3. I use a monotone or dull voice while talking to people.
_____ 4. I look over or away from others while talking to them.
_____ 5. I move away from others when they touch me while talking.
_____ 6. I have a relaxed body position when talking to people.
_____ 7. I frown while talking to people.
_____ 8. I avoid eye contact while talking to people.
_____ 9. I have a tense body position while talking to people.
_____ 10. I sit close or stand close to people while talking with them.
_____ 11. My voice is monotonous or dull when talking to people.
_____ 12. I use a variety of vocal expressions when talking to people.
_____ 13. I gesture when talking to people.
_____ 14. I am animated when talking to people.
_____ 15. I have a bland facial expression when talking to people.
_____ 16. I move closer to people when talking to them.
_____ 17. I look directly at people while talking to them.
_____ 18. I am stiff when talking to people.
_____ 19. I have a lot of vocal variety when talking to people.
_____ 20. I avoid gesturing while talking to people.
_____ 21. I lean toward people when talking to them.
_____ 22. I maintain eye contact with people when talking to them.
_____ 23. I try not to sit or stand close to people when talking with them.
_____ 24. I lean away from people when talking to them.
_____ 25. I smile when talking to people.
_____ 26. I avoid touching people when talking to them.

SCORING: To compute your scores follow the instructions below:

Step One: Add scores for items 1, 2, 6, 10, 12, 13, 14, 16, 17, 19, 21, 22, & 25.
Step Two: Add scores for items 3, 4, 5, 7, 8, 9, 11, 15, 18, 20, 23, 24, & 26.
Step Three: Add 78 to Step One.
Step Four: Subtract the score for Step Two from the score for Step Three.

Scores should be between 26 and 30. Scores over 112 for females and over 104 for males are considered high.

Source:

Richmond, V. P., McCroskey, J. C., & Johnson, A. D. (2003). Development of the nonverbal immediacy scale (NIS): Measures of self- and other-perceived nonverbal immediacy. *Communication Quarterly, 51,* 504–517.

Sociocommunicative Orientation

Psychologist Sandra Bem (1974) researched the concepts of masculinity and femininity and created a scale she called the Bem Sex-Role Inventory (BSRI). The BSRI was originally constructed by having different groups of participants read a list of adjectives and then determining which characteristics on the list were seen as more desirable in the United States for one biological sex or the other. After participants rated these lists, Bem had females and males rank a list of characteristics. The participantes ranked 20 items to be desirable for a man to possess (masculine scale) and 20 different items to be more desirable for a woman to possess (feminine scale). A number of researchers examined the BSRI and realized that what Bem thought she was measuring really was not a scale of maleness and femaleness, but a scale of how people interact with each other.

For this reason, Richmond and McCroskey (1985) created a scale to measure how people communicate either assertively (Bem's masculinity) or responsively (Bem's femininity) and named it the Sociocommunicative Orientation Scale. (Figure 6.16 illustrates this scale; please fill it out.) In the Sociocommunicative Orientation Scale, two factors are measured: assertiveness and responsiveness.

ASSERTIVENESS

Assertiveness is the capacity to make requests; actively disagree; express positive or negative personal rights and feelings; initiate, maintain, or disengage from conversations; and stand up for oneself without attacking another. Bem's research originally suggested that these communicative behaviors were only enacted by males, but we all know many women who are equally adept at these assertive behaviors. Even so, despite many women employing assertive communication behaviors, many societies stereotype these behaviors as being appropriately male forms of communication.

RESPONSIVENESS

Conversely, **responsiveness** is the capacity to be sensitive to the communication of others, to be a good listener, to make others comfortable in communicating, and to recognize the needs and desires of others. Wording commonly used to describe a person who engages in responsive communication behaviors would include helpful, sympathetic, compassionate, sensitive to needs of others, sincere, gentle, warm, tender, friendly, understanding, and (of course) responsive to others. Although such terms do describe the stereotypical perception of how females communicate in the United States, in a broader sense they describe any person who is open to the communication of others and is empathetic with those others.

FIGURE 6.16
Sociocommunicative
Orientation Scale

DIRECTIONS: The questionnaire below lists 20 personality characteristics. Please indicate the degree to which you believe each of these characteristics applies to YOU, as you normally communicate with others, by marking whether you (5) strongly agree that it applies, (4) agree that it applies, (3) are undecided, (2) disagree that it applies, or (1) strongly disagree that it applies. There are no right or wrong answers. Work quickly; record your first impression.

_____ 1. Helpful
_____ 2. Defends own beliefs
_____ 3. Independent
_____ 4. Responsive to others
_____ 5. Forceful
_____ 6. Has strong personality
_____ 7. Sympathetic
_____ 8. Compassionate
_____ 9. Assertive
_____ 10. Sensitive to the needs of others
_____ 11. Dominant
_____ 12. Sincere
_____ 13. Gentle
_____ 14. Willing to take a stand
_____ 15. Warm
_____ 16. Tender
_____ 17. Friendly
_____ 18. Acts as a leader
_____ 19. Aggressive
_____ 20. Competitive

Items 2, 3, 5, 6, 9, 11, 14, 18, 19, & 20 measure assertiveness. Add the scores on these items to get your assertiveness score. Items 1, 4, 7, 8, 10, 12, 13, 15, 16, & 17 measure responsiveness. Add the scores on these items to get your responsiveness score.

Source:

Richmond, V. P., & McCroskey, J. C. (1990). Reliability and separation of factors on the assertiveness-responsiveness scale. *Psychological Reports, 67*, 449–450.

SOCIOCOMMUNICATIVE ORIENTATION AND STYLE

At this point, we should note that **sociocommunicative orientation**, which is a self-report scale, is only half of the puzzle when examining this variable. The scale seen in Figure 6.15 can easily be retooled to examine someone else's behavior in what is called the sociocommunicative style scale using the following instructions: "Please indicate the degree to which you believe each of these characteristics applies to the [place name here] by marking whether you (5) *strongly agree that it applies,*

(4) *agree that it applies*, (3) *are undecided*, (2) *disagree that it applies*, or (1) *strongly disagree that it applies.*"

A lot of research has examined how an individual's **sociocommunicative style** impacts people's perceptions of other behaviors. For example, research in instructional communication has found that highly assertive and responsive teachers are perceived as more nonverbally immediate, more trustworthy, and more humorous. In fact, teachers who are highly responsive have been shown to have students who learn more, are more satisfied with their teacher, and are more likely to talk to their teacher outside of class. Sociocommunicative style has also been examined in the health-care setting, where physician assertiveness and responsiveness were both shown to relate to patient perceptions of the physician's credibility. Patients who perceived their physicians as responsive were more satisfied and believed that they received good medical care compared to patients who did not perceive their physicians as responsive. These results were also seen in subordinate–supervisor relationships in organizations. Subordinates who perceived their supervisors as assertive and responsive also perceived their supervisors as credible. And subordinates who perceived their supervisors as assertive and responsive also reported higher levels of job satisfaction and motivation. Overall, sociocommunicative orientation/style has been shown to be an extremely important communication variable.

Willingness to Communicate

The next interval variable is willingness to communicate (WTC). Communication research has found that some people are more likely to initiate communicative interactions than others. Burgoon (1976) initiated this line of research by examining the construct she labeled as "unwillingness to communicate," which she described as a "chronic tendency to avoid and/or devalue oral communication" (p. 60). McCroskey and Richmond (1987) retooled the concept to examine an individual's general attitude toward communicating with other people. McCroskey (1992) wrote that "the construct is that of an orientation toward communication which we have referred to previously as a predisposition to avoid communication . . . a behavioral tendency regarding talking frequency" (p. 21). In essence, **willingness to communicate** can be defined as the tendency of an individual to engage in communication with other people. Please complete the WTC scale in Figure 6.17. (Be sure to read the directions on this scale, however, because it is not a Likert-type scale and can throw off some participants because it asks for percentages.)

As previously mentioned, WTC examines the extent to which an individual initiates or avoids communication. Look at your own scores for WTC. Do you have any areas in which you exhibit a low WTC? Maybe you have a high WTC in public speaking situations but a low WTC in meetings? Or a high WTC score in every context but a low

FIGURE 6.17
Willingness to Communicate

DIRECTIONS: Below are 20 situations in which a person might choose to communicate or not to communicate. Presume you have *completely free choice*. Determine the percentage of times you would *choose to initiate communication* in each type of situation. Indicate in the space at the left what percent of the time you would choose to communicate. Choose any numbers between 0 and 100.

_____ 1. Talk with a service station attendant.
_____ 2. Talk with a physician.
_____ 3. Present a talk to a group of strangers.
_____ 4. Talk with an acquaintance while standing in line.
_____ 5. Talk with a salesperson in a store.
_____ 6. Talk in a large meeting of friends.
_____ 7. Talk with a police officer.
_____ 8. Talk in a small group of strangers.
_____ 9. Talk with a friend while standing in line.
_____ 10. Talk with a waiter/waitress in a restaurant.
_____ 11. Talk in a large meeting of acquaintances.
_____ 12. Talk with a stranger while standing in line.
_____ 13. Talk with a secretary.
_____ 14. Present a talk to a group of friends.
_____ 15. Talk in a small group of acquaintances.
_____ 16. Talk with a garbage collector.
_____ 17. Talk in a large meeting of strangers.
_____ 18. Talk with a spouse (or girl/boyfriend).
_____ 19. Talk in a small group of friends.
_____ 20. Present a talk to a group of acquaintances.

SCORING: The WTC permits computation of one total score and seven subscores. The range for all scores is 0–100. Follow the procedures outlined below.

1. Group discussion—add scores for items 8, 15, & 19; divide sum by 3. Scores above 89 = high WTC, scores below 57 = low WTC in this context.
2. Meetings—add scores for items 6, 11, & 17; divide sum by 3. Scores above 80 = high WTC, scores below 39 = low WTC in this context.
3. Interpersonal—add scores for items 4, 9, & 12; divide sum by 3. Scores above 94 = high WTC, scores below 64 = low WTC in this context.
4. Public speaking—add scores for items 3, 14, & 20; divide sum by 3. Scores above 78 = high WTC, scores below 33 = low WTC in this context.
5. Stranger—add scores for items 3, 8, 12, & 17; divide sum by 4. Scores above 63 = high WTC, scores below 18 = low WTC with these receivers.
6. Acquaintance—add scores for items 4, 11, 15, & 20; divide sum by 4. Scores above 92 = high WTC, scores below 57 = low WTC with these receivers.
7. Friends—add scores for items 6, 9, 14, & 19; divide sum by 4. Scores above 99 = high WTC, scores below 71 = low WTC with these receivers.

Source:

McCroskey, J. C. (1992). Reliability and validity of the willingness to communicate scale. *Communication Quarterly, 40*, 16–25.
Richmond, V. P., Wrench, J. S., & McCroskey, J. C. (2013). *Communication apprehension, avoidance and effectiveness* (6th Ed.). Boston: Allyn & Bacon.

WTC with strangers? Your individual WTC is deeply rooted and has been shown to have a largely genetic basis.

Research has shown that an individual's level of CA is probably the best predictor of a person's level of WTC. If someone is high CA, then he or she is probably low WTC, and vice versa. WTC is generally thought of as a trait-based predisposition that determines the degree to which people communicate in a variety of contexts (interpersonal, meeting, group, and public). Whether a person will communicate with another in a given interpersonal example (e.g., student–teacher, parent–child, or subordinate–supervisor) is often affected by situational constraints within the encounter, such as the nature of the relationship of the interactants. Someone may be willing to talk to a teacher but less willing to talk to her or his supervisor. Although WTC depends on the situation, people usually exhibit regular WTC tendencies across situations, contexts, and audiences.

When people talk about WTC, they often mistake it for shyness, which is not the same thing. Shyness is the behavioral tendency to not initiate communication and/or respond to the initiatives of others. Shyness stems from a preference for noncommunication by the individual—a reduced WTC. But WTC may be considered an attitude toward initiating communication or, as some prefer, the person's intent or disposition toward the behavior of initiating communication. This notion of shyness is similar to CA, previously defined in this chapter as the fear or anxiety associated with either real or anticipated communication with another person or persons.

When one examines the interrelationships among CA, WTC, and shyness, the three constructs can appear similar. However, with regard to how communication researchers utilize the terms, they do not overlap in definition: CA is what a person feels (fear or anxiety), shyness is the degree to which one refrains from actual communication, and WTC is one's inclination to talk.

Although research has shown a number of possible causes (both nature and nurture) for an individual's WTC level, as a variable WTC is interesting in how it relates to other communication variables. Previous research in WTC has primarily occurred in classroom, health-care, and organizational settings. This research has found that students with low WTC scores participated less in the classroom than students with high scores. Students with high WTC scores have also been shown to be perceived as more communicatively competent by others than students with low WTC scores.

In essence, not every person you run into who is quiet has the same reasons for being quiet; however, the consequences of being perceived as quiet are similar. As we discussed earlier in this chapter, quiet people are generally perceived as less intelligent, lazy, and unfriendly, so they have a number of stereotypes to battle simply based on their degree of willingness to talk.

Beliefs and Attitudes
GENERALIZED BELIEF SCALE

Unlike the previous interval variables discussed in this section, the next two variables are different because they are designed to be utilized in a wide variety of contexts. The Generalized Belief Scale was created by McCroskey (1966) as a tool for examining the strength of an individual's belief on a given topic. A **belief** concerns our perception of reality about whether something is true or false. The scale in Figure 6.18 is designed to be a general scale that can be utilized in a number of different situations. The scale in Figure 6.18 could be used to measure a person's belief about abortion, euthanasia, capital punishment, or, as we have in this case, the belief that "everyone should be required to take public speaking in college."

GENERALIZED ATTITUDE MEASURE

Another scale that has the ability to measure different things every time it is employed is the Generalized Attitude Measure. Like the Generalized Belief Scale, this scale measures a range of different attitudes depending on what a researcher needs to analyze.

An **attitude** is defined as a predisposition to respond to people, ideas, or objects in an evaluative way. When we define an attitude as a predisposition, we are defining an attitude as an individual's tendency to do something. Here, it is a tendency to *evaluate* people,

FIGURE 6.18
Generalized
Belief Scale

Instructions: On the scales below, please indicate the degree to which you believe the following statement **"Everyone Should Be Required to Take Public Speaking in College."** Numbers "1" and "7" indicate a very strong feeling. Numbers "2" and "6" indicate a strong feeling. Numbers "3" and "5" indicate a fairly weak feeling. Number "4" indicates you are undecided or do not understand the adjective pairs themselves. There are no right or wrong answers. *Only circle one number per line.*

1.	Agree	7	6	5	4	3	2	1	Disagree
2.	False	1	2	3	4	5	6	7	True
3.	Incorrect	1	2	3	4	5	6	7	Correct
4.	Right	7	6	5	4	3	2	1	Wrong
5.	Yes	7	6	5	4	3	2	1	No

* To compute your score, simply add up the numbers you circled.

Sources:

McCroskey, J. C. (1966). *Experimental studies of the effects of ethos and evidence in persuasive communication.* Unpublished doctoral dissertation. Pennsylvania State University.

McCroskey, J. C., & Richmond, V. P. (1989). Bipolar scales. In P. Emmert & L. L. Barker (Eds.), *Measurement of communication behavior* (pp. 154–167). New York, NY: Longman.

ideas, or objects. The word "evaluative" in this definition means making judgments of good or bad, desirable or undesirable, likable or unlikable, and so on. There are countless attitudes that an individual could examine using the Generalized Attitude Measure. For example, you could use it to measure an individual's attitude about sex, broccoli, public speaking, or, as we have in this book, higher education. Figure 6.19 contains the Generalized Attitude Measure geared toward an individual's attitude about higher education.

BELIEFS VERSUS ATTITUDES

We believe that studying beliefs and attitudes is important for communication researchers. By using the word "believe," we imply that for us (not necessarily for everyone else) the study of beliefs and attitudes is a true, correct, appropriate set of variables to study. We "believe" in the studying of beliefs and attitudes by communication researchers. We also think that studying beliefs and attitudes is good, so we have a positive attitude toward it. Belief has to do with our perceptions of reality, whereas attitude has to do with our evaluation of that reality.

Ratio Variables

For the dataset collected for this book, we included one ratio variable. For a variable to be seen as ratio, the distance between attributes must have real quantitative meaning and an absolute zero. Age is the only variable that meets these criteria. We know for a

FIGURE 6.19
Generalized
Attitude Measure

Instructions: On the scales below, please indicate your feelings about **"Higher Education."** Numbers "1" and "7" indicate a very strong feeling. Numbers "2" and "6" indicate a strong feeling. Numbers "3" and "5" indicate a fairly weak feeling. Number "4" indicates you are undecided or do not understand the adjective pairs themselves. There are no right or wrong answers. *Only circle one number per line.*

1.	Good	7	6	5	4	3	2	1	Bad
2.	Wrong	1	2	3	4	5	6	7	Right
3.	Harmful	1	2	3	4	5	6	7	Beneficial
4.	Fair	7	6	5	4	3	2	1	Unfair
5.	Wise	7	6	5	4	3	2	1	Foolish
6.	Negative	1	2	3	4	5	6	7	Positive

* To compute your score, simply add up the numbers you circled.

Sources:

McCroskey, J. C. (1966). *Experimental studies of the effects of ethos and evidence in persuasive communication.* Unpublished doctoral dissertation. Pennsylvania State University.

McCroskey, J. C., & Richmond, V. P. (1989). Bipolar scales. In P. Emmert & L. L. Barker (Eds.), *Measurement of communication behavior* (pp. 154–167). New York, NY: Longman.

fact that someone who is 12 years old is exactly twice as old as someone who is 6 years old. You cannot say the same thing with interval variables. We could not say, for example, that someone with a CA score of 80 is twice as apprehensive as someone with a CA score of 40 because the ranges do not have real quantitative meaning. Age also has an absolute zero—of course, with humans, the absolute zero for age is birth.

WRITING UP SCALES USING APA STYLE

To this point, we have discussed the variables collected for this text's real-world dataset. However, being able to identify the different variables and the different measurement levels is only part of the picture when conducting a research project. Once a researcher has determined which variables should be examined in a study, he or she must clearly explain the variables in the method section of the research paper in a clear and concise fashion. This section walks you through how to more clearly write a method section than originally discussed in Chapter 5.

Participants

According to Chapter 5, the first part of a method section should report who the participants were. You must report basic demographic characteristics (sex and age) of the participants along with how you recruited them. All of the numbers we need for this section will be calculated in the next chapter, so for now, trust us that these numbers do come from somewhere and have a legitimate purpose. Here is an example of how this might appear in APA style:

> Participants for this study were undergraduate students taking both lower and upper division courses at a variety of colleges and universities. The sample can be broken into two main groups. First, in spring of 2005, 325 undergraduate students agreed to participate in this project. In the study sample, there were 139 (42.8%) females, 183 (56.3%) males, and 3 (0.9%) who did not respond to the biological sex question. The age of this sample ranged from 18 to 48 with a mean of 21.68 (*SD* = 3.69). Second, in fall of 2011, 329 undergraduate students agreed to participate in the continuance of this project. In the study sample, there were 182 (55.3%) females, 137 (41.6%) males, and 10 (3.0%) who did not respond to the biological sex question. The age of this sample ranged from 18 to 52 with a mean of 22.48 (*SD* = 5.90).
>
> Further demographic variables were also collected to examine school classification and political affiliation of the entire sample. Our sample contained 52 (8.0%) freshman, 107 (16.4%) sophomores, 231 (35.3%) juniors, 244 (37.3%) seniors, 4 (0.6%) other, and 16 (2.4%) who did not respond to the question. The recorded political affiliations of the study participants are as follows: 220 (33.6%) Democrats, 220 (33.6%) Republicans, 131 (20.0%) others, 64 (9.8%)

participants who are not registered to vote, and 19 (2.9%) who did not respond to the question.

Apparatus

Once you have explained who your sample is, you must explain the apparatus used in the research (if you used one, as discussed in Chapter 5). Because this study did not use an apparatus, we can move on and discuss the procedures.

Procedures

When discussing the procedures, you should be as brief as possible while giving all of the appropriate and necessary information about what you did. For example, here is how you could describe the procedures for this project:

> The study participants were approached during their communication class and asked to participate in the study. All participants were handed a copy of the survey instrument that contained a cover letter explaining the purpose of the study. Participants were asked to sign and detach the cover page if they consented to filling out the questionnaire. All students who participated received extra credit for their participation. An alternative extra credit assignment was available to students who did not opt to participate in the study.

In this example, we start by explaining that all students were approached during class and asked to participate in the study. We then specified that we obtained consent, which is required by law (see Chapter 3), from the students indicating their desire for participation. We also informed our potential participants that all students who took part in the project would be given extra credit, but we coerced no one into filling out the survey because we had an alternative extra credit assignment that students could choose to complete if they were uncomfortable with the study.

Instrumentation

Once you have finished with the first three parts of a method section, you must explain all of the measurement tools employed in your study. In this study, we have eight interval scales plus one ordinal scale that must be explained. To explain a scale, start by telling your audience who the creator of the scale was and what the scale is supposed to measure. Then, explain how the scale is formatted, including a discussion of type of scale (Likert, semantic differential, Staple, or scalogram), numerical scale used (5 steps, 7 steps, or 10 steps), range possible on the scale, range received on the scale, and how to interpret the scale results. For example:

> The Personal Report of Communication Apprehension-24 (PRCA-24) was created by McCroskey (1982) to measure an individual's level of fear or anxiety associated with either real or anticipated communication with another person

or persons. The scale consists of 24 Likert-type items ranging from 1 (*strongly agree*) to 5 (*strongly disagree*) with a range of scores from 24 to 120, which was seen in this study. Higher scores are designed to indicate higher levels of communication apprehension.

In this example, we wrote about the PRCA-24. The first sentence explains that McCroskey (1982) wrote the PRCA-24 to measure CA. The second sentence explains that the scale consists of 24 scale items that were written in a Likert-type format with five steps: 1 = *strongly agree*, 2 = *agree*, 3 = *neutral*, 4 = *disagree*, and 5 = *strongly disagree*. Note that you only have to give the first step and the last step because researchers who see those two will immediately understand how to interpret the scores. The second sentence also contains the range of possible scores available on the PRCA-24 and mentions that the range was found in the study. The last sentence then explains how the scores can be interpreted. Specifically, the higher someone's PRCA-24 score is, the higher her or his level of CA is. Figure 6.20 shows the complete list of variable write-ups using APA style.

FIGURE 6.20
APA Write-Ups for Scales

PRCA-24. The Personal Report of Communication Apprehension–24 was created by McCroskey (1982) to measure an individual's level of fear or anxiety associated with either real or anticipated communication with another person or persons. The scale consists of 24 Likert items ranging from (1) *strongly agree* to (5) *strongly disagree* with a range of scores from 24 to 120, which was seen in this study. Higher scores are designed to indicate higher levels of communication apprehension.

Ethnocentrism. The Ethnocentrism Scale was created by Neuliep and McCroskey (1997) to measure an individual's tendency to feel that her or his culture is the center of the universe. The revised version of the scale employed here (Neuliep & McCroskey, 2000; McCroskey, 2001) consists of 22 Likert items ranging from (1) *strongly disagree* to (5) *strongly agree*. Fifteen of the items are scored; the remaining items are used as distracters. This scale has a possible range of 15–75; however, the range seen in this study was 16–61. Higher scores are designed to indicate higher levels of ethnocentrism.

Humor Assessment. The Humor Assessment (HA) was created by Wrench and Richmond (2004) to measure an individual's use of humor as a communicative device in interpersonal relationships. The scale was originally published in Richmond, Wrench, and Gorham (2001) as a tool for teachers to assess their own use of humor in the classroom. The HA was then validated by Wrench and McCroskey (2001), who found that it functioned distinctly differently from M. Booth-Butterfield and S. Booth-Butterfield's (1991) Humor Orientation scale. The HA consists of 16 Likert type items ranging from (1) *strongly disagree* to (5) *strongly agree* with a range of scores from 16 to 80, which was seen in this study. Higher scores on the HA indicate a higher extent to which an individual uses humor while communicating interpersonally.

Nonverbal Immediacy Scale. The Nonverbal Immediacy Scale was created by Richmond, McCroskey, and Johnson (2003) to measure a receiver's perceived nonverbal immediacy between her- or himself and a source. The scale consists of 26 Likert-type items ranging from (1) *strongly disagree* to (5) *strongly agree*. This scale has a possible range of 26–130; however, the range seen in this study was 63–130. Higher scores are designed to indicate higher levels of nonverbally immediate behavior.

FIGURE 6.20
Continued

Sociocommunicative Orientation. The Sociocommunicative Orientation scale was created by Richmond and McCroskey (1985) as an instructional tool to examine the extent to which individuals use assertive or responsive communication. The instrument was first utilized in research by Thompson, Ishii, and Klopf (1990) and Ishii, Thompson, and Klopf (1990) to examine cultural differences in assertive and responsive communication. After the publication of these two articles, Richmond and McCroskey (1990) demonstrated the reliability and dimensionality of the measure itself. The sociocommunicative orientation scale consists of 10 items on each factor for a total of 20 items. Participants are asked to respond to short descriptive phrases that range from one to five words in length that indicate ways in which they may communicate. The measure asks a participant to respond in terms of how well the item applies to her or him using a Likert scale from (1) *strongly disagree that it applies* to (5) *strongly agree that it applies.* Each factor can range from 10 to 50. In the current study, assertiveness had a range from 19 to 50 and responsiveness had a range from 20 to 50. Higher scores on each factor are designed to represent either higher assertive or responsive communicative behaviors.

Willingness to Communicate. The Willingness to Communicate (WTC) scale was devised by McCroskey (1992) to measures a person's willingness to initiate communication with another person or persons. The scale consists of 20 items. Each of the items is designed to measure whether an individual would initiate communication in a specific situation or with a specific individual. Eight of the items are fillers and 12 are scored as part of the scale. Using a 101-point range from 0 (*never*) to 100 (*always*), participants are asked to indicate the percentage of time they would choose to communicate in each type of situation. Ultimately, the scores on the 12 items are added together to create a composite score, with higher scores indicating a higher willingness to communicate. Scores on the WTC scale can range from 0 to 100; however, scores in the current study ranged from 18.25 to 100. Higher scores on the WTC scale are designed to indicate stronger likelihoods to initiate communicative interactions.

Generalized Belief Scale. The Generalized Belief Scale was created by McCroskey (1966) and validated by McCroskey and Richmond (1996). The Generalized Belief Measure was created by McCroskey (1966) as a way to measure beliefs about specific concepts. By attaining an individual's general belief about a given topic, the researcher can measure the degree to which an individual believes in a given statement. The statement measured in this study was "Everyone Should Be Required to Take Public Speaking in College." The belief statement is then measured using a five-item semantic differential scale with seven steps. The Generalized Belief Scale has a range of 5 to 35, which was seen in this study. Higher scores on the Generalized Belief Scale indicate stronger beliefs.

Generalized Attitude Measure. The Generalized Attitude Measure was a scale originally created by McCroskey (1966) and later validated by McCroskey and Richmond (1989) as a tool for determining someone's overall attitude about a specific subject. The Generalized Attitude Measure is measured using a six-item semantic differential scale with seven steps. For the purposes of this study, the Generalized Attitude Measure was utilized to determine the attitude of participants about higher education. The Generalized Attitude Measure has a range of 6–42; however, a range of 19–42 was seen in this study. Higher scores on the Generalized Attitude Measure indicate more positive attitudes.

Time on the Internet. In addition to the above interval variables, one ordinal variable was also collected in this study to examine the amount of time an individual spends communicating using the Internet. In response to the question how much time they spend online during a given week, participants were given the following categories to select from: 0–½ hour, ½–1 hour, 1–2 hours, 2–5 hours, 5–10 hours, 10–15 hours, 15–20 hours, and 20+ hours. This is similar to the method used by Wrench, Fiore, and McCroskey (2005) to examine the same construct.

CONCLUSION

In this chapter, we have examined a wide variety of communication variables that were included in this book's accompanying dataset. The variables discussed in this chapter will be used many times throughout the rest of this book, so make sure you understand them: how they function in the world, how they are measured, and what they mean to communication researchers. In the next chapter, we will go further into how each of these scales was made by talking about the important issue of measurement.

KEY TERMS

Abstract variables p. 172

Antecedent variables p. 180

Assertiveness p. 203

Attitude p. 208

Audience-specific behavior p. 193

Belief p. 208

Communication apprehension p. 194

Communication trait p. 193

Concrete variables p. 172

Dependent variable p. 179

Difference p. 177

Differences in kind p. 177

Differences of degree p. 178

Ethnocentrism p. 197

Humor assessment p. 199

Immediacy p. 200

Independent variable p. 179

Interval variables p. 183

Intervening variables p. 180

Likert scale p. 183

Negative relationships p. 175

Neutral relationships p. 177

Nominal variable p. 181

Nonverbal immediacy p. 201

Ordinal variables p. 182

Pancultural p. 197

Personality p. 191

Positive relationships p. 175

Ratio variables p. 187

Relationships p. 175

Responsiveness p. 203

Scalogram p. 186

Semantic differential scale p. 184

Situational behavior p. 193

Sociocommunicative Orientation p. 204

Sociocommunicative style p. 205

Trait behavior p. 192

Variable p. 172

Variable attributes p. 174

Variable values p. 174

Verbal immediacy p. 201

Willingness to communicate p. 205

REFERENCES

Barbato, C. A., Graham, E. E., & Perse, E. M. (2003). Communicating in the family: An examination of the relationship of family communication climate and interpersonal communication motives. *Journal of Family Communication, 3*, 123–148.

Beatty, M. J. (1988). Situational and predispositional correlates of public speaking anxiety. *Communication Education, 37*, 28–39.

Beatty, M. J., McCroskey, J. C., & Valencic, K. M. (2001). *The biology of communication: A communibiological perspective.* Cresskill, NJ: Hampton Press.

Bem, S. L. (1974). The measurement of psychological androgyny. *Journal of Consulting and Clinical Psychology, 47,* 155–162.

Burgoon, J. K. (1976). The unwillingness-to-communicate scale: Development and validation. *Communication Monographs, 43,* 60–69.

Coombs, W. T., & Holladay, S. J. (2004). Understanding the aggressive workplace: Development of the workplace aggression tolerance questionnaire. *Communication Studies, 55,* 481–497.

Crespi, I. (1961). Use of a scaling technique in surveys. *Journal of Marketing, 25*(5), 69–72.

Guttman, L. (1944). A basis for scaling qualitative data. *American Sociological Review, 9,* 139–150.

Hamer, D. H., & Copeland, P. (1998). *Living with our genes: Why they matter more than you think.* New York, NY: Doubleday.

Hollander, E. P. (1976). *Principles and methods of social psychology* (3rd ed.). New York, NY: Oxford University Press.

Kuhn, T., & Poole, M. S. (2000). Do conflict management styles affect group decision making? *Human Communication Research, 26,* 558–591.

McCroskey, J. C. (1966). *Experimental studies of the effects of ethos and evidence in persuasive communication.* Unpublished doctoral dissertation, Pennsylvania State University.

McCroskey, J. C. (1970). Measures of communication-bound anxiety. *Speech Monographs, 37,* 269–277.

McCroskey, J. C. (1982). *An introduction to rhetorical communication* (4th ed.). Englewood Cliffs, NJ: Prentice Hall.

McCroskey, J. C. (1992). Reliability and validity of the willingness to communicate scale. *Communication Quarterly, 40,* 16–25.

McCroskey, J. C., & Richmond, V. P. (1987). Willingness to communicate. In J. C. McCroskey & J. A. Daly (Eds.), *Personality and interpersonal communication* (pp. 119–131). Newbury Park, CA: Sage.

Neuliep, J. W., & McCroskey, J. C. (1997). Development of a US and generalized ethnocentrism scale. *Communication Research Reports, 14,* 385–398.

Richmond, V. P. (1990). Communication in the classroom: Power and motivation. *Communication Education, 39,* 181–195.

Richmond, V. P., & McCroskey, J. C. (1985). *Communication: Apprehension, avoidance, and effectiveness.* Scottsdale, AZ: Gorsuch Scarisbrick.

Rocca, K. A., & Vogl-Bauer, S. (1999). Trait verbal aggression, sports fan identification, and perceptions of appropriate sports fan communication. *Communication Research Reports, 16,* 239–248.

Thomas, C., Booth-Butterfield, M., & Booth-Butterfield, S. (1995). Perceptions of deception, divorce disclosure, and communication satisfaction with parents. *Western Journal of Communication, 59,* 228–245.

Weber, K., Fornash, B., Corrigan, M., & Neupauer, N. (2003). The effect of interest on recall: An experiment. *Communication Research Reports, 20,* 116–123.

Wrench, J. S. (2005). Development and validity testing of the homonegativity short form. *Journal of Intercultural Communication Research, 34,* 152–165.

Wrench, J. S., & Booth-Butterfield, M. (2003). Increasing patient satisfaction and compliance: An examination of physician humor orientation, compliance-gaining strategies, and perceived credibility. *Communication Quarterly, 51,* 482–503.

Wrench, J. S., & Richmond, V. P. (2004). Understanding the psychometric properties of the humor assessment instrument through an analysis of the relationships between teacher humor assessment and instructional communication variables in the college classroom. *Communication Research Reports, 21,* 92–103.

7

Measurement

CHAPTER OBJECTIVES

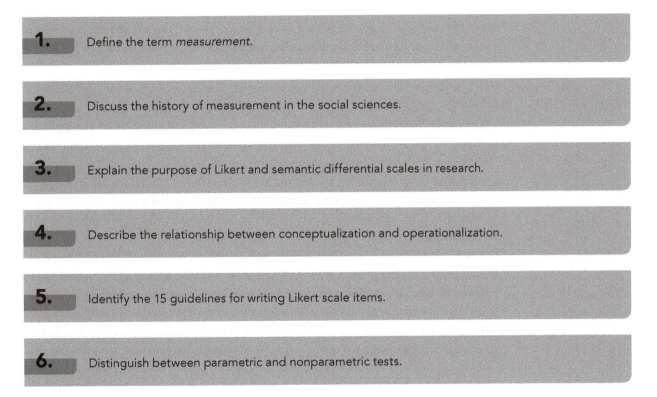

1. Define the term *measurement*.

2. Discuss the history of measurement in the social sciences.

3. Explain the purpose of Likert and semantic differential scales in research.

4. Describe the relationship between conceptualization and operationalization.

5. Identify the 15 guidelines for writing Likert scale items.

6. Distinguish between parametric and nonparametric tests.

When you hear the word "measurement," what comes to mind? Maybe you think of pulling out a ruler and seeing how long a line is, or pulling out a tape measure to measure the inseam of a pair of pants. In many ways, communication researchers define measurement in the same way as using a ruler or a tape measure.

DEFINING THE TERM

Measurement is the process of systematic observation and assignment of numbers to phenomena according to rules. The first part of this definition suggests that measurement is a process. The word "process" is defined as a set of progressive, interdependent steps. In other words, when we measure something, we must go through a series of steps. According to the definition, this series of steps helps us systematically observe a phenomenon and then assign numbers to that phenomenon.

Let's look at what we mean by "observe." To examine a phenomenon, we must have the ability to see or perceive that phenomenon. If we cannot see or perceive a phenomenon, there is no way for us as researchers to measure it. Once a researcher has a general idea of what the phenomenon is, he or she can then assign numbers to it based on some set of established rules. In essence, when we know what the phenomenon is, we can then determine a way to quantify it. However, we must be systematic in our quantification, so we must have some form of established rules.

Measuring a Line

Let's take the process of measuring a line as an example to walk us through this definition. First, we must define what the phenomenon is that we are attempting to measure. With a line, we are attempting to measure the length of something, or in mathematics speak, we are attempting to measure the greatest dimension of a plane or solid figure. In essence, length must have a beginning and an end. Once we know what the phenomenon is, we can try to determine how we will assign numbers to that phenomenon.

With length, many numerical categorizing systems have been created. In ancient Greece, one may have measured the line in *daktylos*, which was roughly equivalent to between 1.8 and 2.0 centimeters. Centimeters are part of a measurement system for distance called the metric system, which is the international system of units created by French scientists at the request of Louis XVI in the late eighteenth century. In fact, in most countries around the world, the metric system is the measure of choice for measuring distance. However, in the United States, we have our own system for measuring length called the US customary units, or English units. Whereas the metric system is based on millimeters, centimeters, meters, and kilometers, the US customary units are based on the inch, foot, yard, and mile. This is not to say that the metric system and US customary units are not related to each other, because 1 centimeter is equivalent to 0.3937 inch; however, each has its own specific rules for how measurement works. When we measure phenomena like distance, we do not combine the two systems of measurement because they have separate measurement rules. For example, we would not tell someone to drive six kilometers and five miles because your average driver would need a calculator to figure out how far that actually is.

Measurement Procedures and Rules

The two important considerations in all measurement are the procedures used in observation and the rules used in assignment of numbers. Suppose that we wanted to know how many cars passed through a certain intersection on any given day. We might ask several people who we know are often near that intersection how many cars they think travel the intersection in a given day. Person A might tell us he thinks about 300 or 400 cars pass through. Person B might say he figures between 100 and 200, and person C might suggest between 700 and 800 cars in a given day. We cannot say, however, that we have engaged in measurement. We have not "systematically" observed the passing cars at the intersection. Rather, our observation has been chaotic.

A better way to determine how many cars pass through an intersection would be to station a person at the intersection with a pencil and paper, and each time a car drove by, he or she would mark down a "1." If we followed this procedure, we would be engaged in the two essential activities involved in measurement: systematic observation and assignment of numbers to objects according to rules. For some purposes, such low-level measurement might be adequate—if, for example, we were interested in determining the probability that we could "hitch a ride" at that intersection. For many other purposes, such low-level measurement would be inadequate. For example, if we happen to be employed by the state highway department and wanted to estimate how long it would take for the road surface to wear out at that intersection, we would need to know how heavy the cars were.

NUMBERS AND THINGS

In measurements, numbers are assigned to represent "things." And if our measurement is to be of any value, it is important that the numbers and the things are *isomorphic*.

Isomorphism means identity or similarity of form. The question we are asking when concerned with whether our measurement is isomorphic with the thing being measured is "Are our rules for numerical assignment tied to reality?" Let us presume, for example, that we wish to estimate the level of anxiety felt by a public speaker. As the speaker is speaking before us, we may rate her or him on a scale from 1 to 5 (*low anxiety* to *high anxiety*) based on the distracting mannerisms she or he evidences in speaking. Such ratings would be isomorphic with anxiety if distracting mannerisms are positively related to anxiety, but if, as is actually the case, distracting mannerisms are more a product of habit and lack of experience in public speaking than a product of an internal state of anxiety, then our ratings are non-isomorphic. As such, the ratings are useless, and we have "measured" nothing.

In many cases, we are forced to assume that our assignment of numbers is isomorphic with reality. The reason that this problem is so important is that it is not legitimate to do anything with numbers that could not be done (if it were physically possible) with the thing that the number represents. Numbers do not know what we can do with them. But we know that we can add them, subtract them, multiply them, or divide them. Sometimes we are justified in engaging in all of these operations, and sometimes we are not.

REVIEW OF MEASUREMENT LEVELS

The mathematical operations that are legitimate for a given set of participant scores depend on the level of measurement that has been achieved. Recall from Chapter 6 that there are four levels of measurement: nominal, ordinal, interval, and ratio. Before we discuss different methods for creating scales, we reexamine these four levels to reinforce how important it is for you to understand them.

Nominal

Nominal measurement is a simple classification. When we assign a person a number because he or she is a member of a certain classroom, we are engaged in nominal measurement. The numbers are arbitrarily selected and meaningless in themselves. For example, if we wish to measure the sex of the students in a class, we may choose to classify men as "1" and women as "2." Therefore, each male in the class is labeled a "1" and each female in the class a "2." The selection of "1" and "2" is arbitrary. We could just as easily use "469" and "932." None of the normal mathematical operations may apply to the numbers assigned at this level of measurement. All that is permissible is to extend our measurement slightly and count the number of people who were assigned "1" or "2." Thus, we could determine that our classroom has 48 men and 40 women.

This is the lowest level of measurement, and it is seldom desired by the social scientist. In some cases, however, it is the only level of measurement that would be isomorphic. Continuing with the same example, to think of measuring sex more precisely than "female" or "male" is somewhat ludicrous. If we wish to talk about something such as the "degree of maleness" or "degree of femaleness," we are talking about something more than biological sex, so we would measure something other than biological sex. In human beings, biological sex is only measurable at the nominal level, and a more "precise" measure would be non-isomorphic and meaningless.

Ordinal

Ordinal or rank-order measurement assigns numbers to things in such a way as to show relationships among the things. Whereas nominal measurement shows the things that are different from one another, ordinal measurement shows the direction of the difference in some meaningful way. Typical relationships among things include more favorable, more difficult, more preferred, higher, and so on. In ordinal measurement, we may assign something at the lowest level a "1," the thing that is just above it we may assign a "2," and so forth. For example, in most institutions of higher education, seniors receive the nominal categorization of "4," juniors a "3," sophomores a "2," and freshmen a "1." How these numbers are assigned is arbitrary. We could just as easily assign seniors "940," juniors "623," sophomores "212," and freshmen "5."

Ordinal measurement only indicates the direction of the relationship between two things. If a sergeant wears three stripes, a corporal two stripes, and a private one stripe, this merely establishes a hierarchical relationship among the three military personnel. The sergeant could just as well wear seven stripes, the corporal two, and the private one. The relationship, as measured at the ordinal level, would still be exactly the same. Ordinal measurement, then, can tell us that the sergeant is more important (presuming that the number of stripes indicates importance) than the corporal and that the corporal is more important than the private. Ordinal measurement does not tell us how much more important the sergeant is than the corporal or the corporal is than the private. Even on the day a private is being promoted to corporal, he or she would still be classified as a private. People do not say that someone in the military is an almost corporal or has 1.9 stripes; he or she either has the rank of corporal or the rank of private—there is nothing in between. Ordinal measures allow us to see the hierarchical level between groups, but not to determine the degree to which people belong within these groups.

Interval

Interval measurement has all the characteristics of ordinal measurement and one crucial addition. Interval measurement identifies the distance between any two things that are measured. In this type of measurement, we assign numbers to things in such ways that the distance between things assigned "1" and "2" is equivalent to the distance between two things assigned "4" and "5." This assignment on the basis of equal intervals is essential to establish an isomorphic relationship between our use of numbers in measurement and the mathematical operations of many statistical tests.

The numbers that we use to indicate the distance of an interval are arbitrary. If the interval of distance is, for example, 36 inches, we may measure that interval by employing the numbers 36, 72, 108, and so on, or we may use the numbers "1" (i.e., 36), "2" (i.e., 36 + 36), "3" (i.e., 36 + 36 + 36), and so on. The important consideration is that the difference between levels be consistently noted in our numerical scheme. The same degree of difference may be alluded to as "1" unit, "2" units, or "200" units. The numbers, in themselves, have no meaning, but the relationships between the numbers do.

The most common example of interval measurement is the way we measure temperature (excluding the Kelvin scale). Typically, nonphysical scientists discuss temperature using both a centigrade and a Fahrenheit system. Both systems measure exactly the same thing—temperature—but the scaling systems they employ are different. For example, on the centigrade thermometer water freezes at 0 degrees, but on the Fahrenheit thermometer, water freezes at 32 degrees. The important thing on interval scales, such as measurement of temperature, is that they are internally consistent in their assignment of numbers. The difference between 80 degrees and 78 degrees is exactly equivalent to the difference between 20 degrees and 18 degrees. The two degrees of difference must mean the same thing at any point on the scale.

Interval measures (Likert scale, semantic differential scale, and scalogram) are probably the most common measures taken by social scientists. This is because most scales created for examining various variables are interval oriented.

Ratio

A ratio scale has all of the characteristics of an interval scale but in addition has a true zero point as its origin. As we noted when discussing the measurement of temperatures, zero could mean different things on the two different measures. In ratio measures, however, zero has an absolute value of its own. (One deviation from the prior discussion examining temperature is the Kelvin scale, which emphasizes that there is a point where atomic movement stops completely and it is called absolute zero, so the Kelvin temperature scale would be a ratio scale because it has an absolute zero.)

Two common ratio measures are the measures employed for distance. We may use the metric system or the common system of inches, feet, and yards. In each case, zero means no distance. Zero meters and zero inches are exactly equivalent; they indicate the absence of distance. On interval scales, it is not meaningful to compare the absolute numbers assigned in terms of their geometric relationships with each other. However, such comparisons are possible with ratio scales. For example, a person who scores 60 on an intelligence measure is not necessarily precisely half as intelligent as a person who scores 120, but a city that is 500 miles away is precisely twice as far away as a city that is 250 miles away.

A HISTORY OF MEASUREMENT

By this point, you may be wondering, *I know how to measure distance, but what does this have to do with measuring communication?* This is a good question. To help answer that question, we must first look at the history of measurement with regard to human behavior. As discussed in Chapter 1, the history of the social sciences depends on the scientific community's understanding of quantitative methods.

Charles Darwin and Francis Galton

Darwin, in his 1859 book *On the Origin of Species*, was the first to truly draw attention to variation, or the idea that certain traits and attributes are selected to be passed from one generation to the next whereas others are not. Ultimately, some traits and attributes thrive, and others die out.

Darwin's work on genetic variation spurred the drive to measure individual differences. The first person who set out to accomplish this task was Darwin's half-cousin

Francis Galton in his 1892 text *Hereditary Genius: An Inquiry into Its Laws and Consequences*. In *Hereditary Genius*, Galton wanted to apply Darwin's ideas to humans by showing "that a man's natural abilities are derived by inheritance, under exactly the same limitations as are the form and physical features of the whole organic world" (p. 1). Galton realized that he needed to develop a way to assess an individual male's genius, so Galton examined a man's fame in his career and then looked at how that man's male children fared in their careers. Ultimately, Galton demonstrated that individuals who were famous in their careers had children who were also famous in their careers. Based on this evidence, Galton noted "[Hereditary genius] has been advocated by a few writers in past as in modern times. But I may claim to be the first to treat the subject in a statistical manner, to arrive at numerical results, and to introduce the 'law of deviation from an average' into discussions of heredity" (p. vi).

Ultimately, this publication led to the proliferation of quantitative differential psychology, or the study of how individuals or groups differ. Galton became one of the foremost scientists of his day, and a large collection of his research articles, book chapters, pamphlets, and books can be accessed for free at http://www.galton.org. Galton also wrote extensively on the use of statistics in social scientific research.

James McKeen Cattell

Psychologist James McKeen Cattell was one of many people influenced by Galton's work. In fact, Cattell ultimately traveled to England to work with Galton and see how he was using statistics to understand humans. In 1890, Cattell was the first social scientist to develop measurements for nonphysical attributes. He began to measure simple mental processes like the time it took subjects to perform simple mental acts like naming objects in a sequence or colors (Baldwin, Cattell, & Jastrow, 1889; Cattell, 1890, 1895). While at the University of Pennsylvania, Cattell began to administer newly developed measures to students, which he ultimately labeled "mental tests." Ultimately, mental tests became labeled **mental measures**, or tools used for the measurement of mental functions like attitudes, beliefs, cognitive knowledge, perceived knowledge, and personality/behavioral traits. Basically, any achievement test, personality test, aptitude test, intelligence test, or career choice test qualifies as a mental measure (Salkind, 2017). More colloquially, mental measures are known as research scales, so in the next few chapters, we will use these terms interchangeably. By the time the 20th century rolled around, mental measurement began to pick up steam both in the United States and around the world.

Alfred Binet and the Rise of Intelligence Tests

In 1905, Alfred Binet, a French psychologist, was commissioned to create the first test to determine whether children were functioning at lower-than-normal levels. Binet, along with his doctoral student Theodore Simon, ultimately created the

Binet–Simon scale, which measured a child's adeptness at completing various age-appropriate tasks (Binet, 1905). This became the first known intelligence test of its kind. Binet's research was then furthered by a Stanford University professor, Lewis Terman (1916).

Intelligence testing quickly turned to academic achievement testing when in 1937 the Stanford Achievement Test (SAT) became required for entry into Ivy League schools. E. L. Thorndike is credited with creating the multiple-choice test, but its popularity and widespread use began in 1914 when the US Army asked Frederick J. Kelly to develop a way to measure recruits' abilities that could be quickly and easily scored by anyone, without need for specialized scoring knowledge (Sokal, 1987). Another test developed around the same time as the multiple-choice test was Arthur Gates's (1921) true-or-false test.

The first three decades of the 20th century radically changed how educational assessment was completed. These new advancements in educational testing led to more and more high school students taking the SAT and other college entrance examinations (the SAT is still the most prominent). The Educational Testing Service (ETS) was created in 1947 to oversee numerous tests, including the SAT, Graduate Record Exam (GRE), Test of English as a Foreign Language (TOEFL), and Praxis tests, to name a few.

Robert Woodworth and the Creation of Personality Tests

In addition to achievement tests, a new breed of measurements was also on the horizon as the United States entered World War I. Although the notion of personality had been around since the time of Hippocrates, measuring personality really was not feasible until the early 1900s. The first modern personality test was created in 1920 by Robert Woodworth, who had been commissioned by the American Psychological Association (APA), on behalf of the US military to create a measure of emotional stability that could be used to test new recruits. Woodworth eventually created the Woodworth Personal Data Sheet, which contained a series of 116 yes-or-no questions. Unfortunately, the test was developed too late in World War I to be used in the screening of new recruits, but it became the forerunner of future personality tests (Segal & Coolidge, 2003).

Another test developed around the same time was Pressey and Pressey's (1919) Cross-Out Test. This test had respondents cross out any words on a list that the respondent considered to be wrong, inappropriate, unpleasant, or worrisome. Pressey and Pressey believed that the resulting pattern of crossed-out and un-crossed-out words could be used to help categorize respondents' emotional states.

Emory S. Bogardus's Social Distance Scale

Beyond traditional personality testing, further methods for measuring attitudes became increasingly important during the early 1900s. And one of the most important figures in these early measurements was Emory S. Bogardus. A prominent sociologist, he created the Bogardus Social Distance Scale, which was the first scale to attempt to measure people's willingness to interact with different types of people by measuring degrees of tolerance or prejudice between social groups (Bogardus, 1925). The Bogardus scale is considered to be the oldest attitudinal research scale still in use today.

Likert Scales

In 1932, Rensis Likert published a monograph based on his dissertation in which he developed a new attitude-scaling technique, the **Likert scale**. The basic premise of the Likert scale was simplistic, but it revolutionized social scientific research. Likert started off presenting respondents with a declarative statement of some kind (e.g., "Cold pizza is a good breakfast") and then offered them a range of possible choices: *strongly disagree, disagree, neither agree nor disagree, agree,* or *strongly agree.* With only have five choices, the respondents must select one category. Because these categories have weighted distances, the answer on a single Likert item is considered to be ordinal because researchers cannot assume that respondents perceive the difference between the different levels evenly. However, if multiple Likert items are summed together, the summed total may be treated as interval data that actually measure a latent variable.

A **latent variable** or **hypothetical variable** is a variable that a researcher cannot directly observe, but that can be inferred from other variables that are observed and measured directly. For example, the statement "I dislike participating in group discussions" when measured using Likert's five steps (*strongly disagree, disagree, neither agree nor disagree, agree,* or *strongly agree*) is an ordinal variable. But when we combine this statement with the other 23 statements on the Personal Report of Communication Apprehension–24 (PRCA-24), we end up with an interval variable that measures the latent variable communication apprehension.

Although the five-step scale from 1 (*strongly disagree*) to 5 (*strongly agree*) is probably the most commonly used Likert scale in all measurement, those anchors (*strongly disagree/strongly agree*) are hardly the only types that exist. Figure 7.1 contains a wide range of Likert-type anchors ranging from simplistic to more complex. Each of these anchors has been utilized over the years by a variety of researchers to help measure various attitudes, beliefs, values, and personality traits. (A quick side note: according to APA style, you should always italicize the anchor name in your text.)

The first comprehensive discussion of Likert scales in communication research was in 1967 by Arnold, McCroskey, and Prichard, who wrote a short introductory essay to the use and creation of Likert scales in *Today's Speech.* Likert scales have become

1	2	3	4	5
Strongly disagree	Disagree	Neutral	Agree	Strongly Agree
Never	Rarely	Sometimes	Often	Always
Definitely not possible	Very unlikely	Don't know	Somewhat likely	Extremely likely
Not at all	To a little extent	To some extent	To a great extent	To a very great extent
Not concerned at all	Not really concerned	Somewhat concerned	Concerned	Very concerned
Definitely false	Possibly false	Don't know	Possibly true	Definitely true
None	Very mild	Mild	Moderate	Severe
Lacking or ineffective	Below average	Average	Above average	Excellent
Very unrealistic	Unrealistic	Not sure	Realistic	Very Realistic
NO	no	?	yes	YES
Poor	Fair	Good	Very good	Excellent
Not important	Somewhat important	Important	Very important	Extremely important
Substantially worse	Somewhat worse	About the same	Somewhat better	Substantially better
Very dissatisfied	Dissatisfied	Neither dissatisfied nor satisfied	Satisfied	Very satisfied
1–20%	21–40%	41–60%	61–80%	81–100%
Definitely did not use	Rarely used	Used moderately	Above average use	Great use
Absolutely do not agree	Do not agree	Neither agree nor disagree	Agree	Absolutely Agree
Not at all like me	Not really like me	Neither like me nor dislike me	Somewhat like me	Definitely like me

F	D	C	B	A
Not at all	Somewhat	Moderately	Quite	Extremely
No Chance	Very little chance	Not sure	Good chance	Certain to happen
Far below expected level	Below expected level	At expected level	Above expected level	Far above expected level
Extremely negative	Moderately negative	Neither positive nor negative	Moderately positive	Extremely positive
Have not	Have slightly	Have moderately	Have mostly	Have fully
Very bad	Rather bad	Neutral	Good	Very good
Never	Occasionally (once or twice altogether)	Regularly (once or twice a year)	Often (several times a year)	Very often (about weekly)
Not at all	Slightly	Moderately	Markedly	Extremely
Very much a loner	Moderately a loner	Average	Somewhat socially sought after	Very socially sought after
None	Slightly	No opinion	Moderately	Extensively
Definitely would not do this	Might not do this	Not sure whether I would do this	Might do this	Would definitely do this
I reject this	I am inclined to reject this	I neither reject nor accept this	I accept this as important	I accept this as of the greatest importance
Extremely Conservative	Conservative	Moderate: Middle of the road	Progressive	Extremely progressive
–	–	0	+	++
Infrequently	Fairly infrequently	No opinion	Fairly frequently	Frequently

FIGURE 7.1
Likert-Type Anchors

common in communication research. We will discuss creating Likert scales in much more detail later in this chapter.

Semantic Differential Scale

The next breakthrough in the area of attitudinal measurement came from Osgood (1952) and Osgood, Tannenbaum, and Suci (1957). A **semantic differential scale** asks respondents to rate their opinions on a linear scale between two endpoints that have opposite meanings (e.g., *good/bad*, *dirty/clean*, *slow/fast*, *weak/strong*, *light/heavy*, or *moral/immoral*). Between these two oppositely worded adjectives exists a series of steps. The most common number of steps in a semantic differential scale is seven, so instructions for a semantic differential test read like this: "Circle the number between the adjectives which best represents your beliefs. Numbers 1 and 7 indicate a very strong feeling. Numbers 2 and 6 indicate a strong feeling. Numbers 3 and 5 indicate a fairly weak feeling. Number 4 indicates you are undecided or do not understand the adjectives themselves." For example, maybe we want respondents to tell us whether they believe capital punishment is good or bad. We would place the adjectives "good" and "bad" on opposite sides of a continuum with seven steps like this:

Good   1   2   3   4   5   6   7   Bad

or

Good   __ __ __ __ __ __ __   Bad

Whether we actually have the physical numbers present in a semantic differential is not important as long as we, as the researchers, know that we have direct quantifiable distances between each step. Because these steps are weighted distances, the answer on a single semantic differential item is considered to be ordinal because researchers cannot assume that respondents perceive the difference between the steps evenly. However, if multiple semantic differential items are summed together, the summed total may be treated as interval data that actually measure a latent variable.

As discussed earlier, a latent variable is a variable that a researcher cannot directly observe but can infer from other variables that are measured directly. For example, respondents can be asked to rate their supervisor using the following bipolar adjectives:

Good   7   6   5   4   3   2   1   Bad

This single semantic differential item is ordinal; however, when we combine this item with the five other semantic differential items on McCroskey's (1966) Generalized Attitude Measure, we end up with an interval variable that measures the latent variable—attitude toward a specific target.

Heise (1970) had one major warning when constructing semantic differential scales: the adjectives must be relevant and understandable for respondents. For example, if you want to have respondents rate their interaction with someone, using the adjectives *sweet/sour* would not be as useful as the adjectives *helpful/unhelpful*. You should also avoid using jargon-loaded language that may be too specialized for nonscientists, such as *extroverted/introverted*; use more common adjectives like *talkative/quiet* instead.

The first real discussion of semantic differential scales in communication research was in 1966 by Arnold, McCroskey, and Prichard, who wrote a short introductory essay about the use and creation of semantic differential scales in *Today's Speech*. Since then, semantic differential scales have become common in communication research.

MEASURING COMMUNICATION

In 2004, James McCroskey, Virginia Richmond, Aaron Johnson, and Heather Smith wanted to create research instruments to help measure the concept of organizational orientations theory, which stated that different people view their relationships with their jobs in different ways (this article can be found on the textbook's website, https://oup-arc.com/wrench). Some people see work as a central focus of their life, whereas others see work as a means to an end—namely, their social life. Ultimately, organizational orientations theory proposes that how people see their relationships with their jobs will impact various job-related outcomes. Although this theory sounds reasonable and some early research seemed to support it, the question that McCroskey et al. found problematic was how to go about determining one's organizational orientation.

Also in 2004, Jason Wrench and Virginia Richmond were talking about yet another measurement-oriented problem. They noted that a scale previously developed by Melanie Booth-Butterfield and Steven Booth-Butterfield (1991) had a problem. This scale was called the Humor Orientation Scale, and it allegedly measured the degree to which an individual used humor as a communicative tool in interpersonal relationships. However, when one looked at the Humor Orientation Scale, the questions centered on an individual's ability to tell jokes or funny stories. Is humor only about jokes and funny stories? If so, then comic legends such as Mr. Bean and Charlie Chaplin would not even be considered humorous because they relied greatly on nonverbal forms of humor.

In both of these examples, researchers faced a problem in measurement. McCroskey et al. (2004) needed to determine how to measure an individual's organizational orientation, and Wrench and Richmond (2004) needed to determine how to measure a person's use of humor in interpersonal interactions without relying on jokes and storytelling as the only form of humor. Although both groups of authors could have had outside observers watch people over an extended period of time to determine either their organizational orientation or their tendency to use humor in communicative interactions, this process would have taken many hours of observation, which is unrealistic in most research circumstances. This is why research scales are often created—to enable a researcher to ask participants about their personality traits/states, beliefs and attitudes, and knowledge. Let's look at each of these three categories separately.

Personality Traits/States

We first visited the concepts of traits and states in Chapter 6, when we introduced the variables in the dataset that accompanies this textbook. To refresh your memory, we discuss these two concepts again briefly.

Trait behavior is behavior that is assumed to be consistent across contexts and specific situations within particular constructs. For example, an individual's level of communication apprehension (CA) is fairly trait oriented. People with high levels of CA are anxious about communication in any situation, in any communicative context, or with any audience. State behavior, by contrast, is behavior that varies from one situation to another within the same context. Some people tend to be more state oriented in their CA. People who are more moderate in their CA may only experience apprehension in one of the four major contexts (group, meeting, interpersonal, or public), or they may experience CA differently depending on the audience they are in front of at a given moment. Although the first case is clearly more trait CA and the second case is state CA, we are able to measure this personality trait using the PRCA-24 scale.

When researchers discuss personality traits or communication traits, they are discussing the measurement of hypothetical constructs that account for certain behaviors. The hypothetical construct must be clear; if it is not, there can be serious measurement issues (see Chapter 8). In the case of CA, the hypothetical construct is anxiety associated with either real or perceived communication. Research has shown that the hypothetical construct CA can help account for a wide variety of communicative behaviors, ranging from the tendency to sweat while giving a speech to the likelihood of being hired for a job or promoted within one's current employment situation.

Personality traits/states can also be classified in terms of psychological and behavioral traits/states. Behaviorally oriented trait/state research scales involve both perceptions of one's own behavior and other individual's perceptions of one's behavior. For example, it would be difficult to answer the PRCA-24 for another person because the questions are designed to measure an individuals' internal psychological state while communicating with other people. However, we could ask people to look for observable signs of anxiety while they are giving a speech (lack of eye contact, discoloration of the skin, fidgeting, hand shaking, voice quivers, etc.). For example, the Nonverbal

Immediacy Scale–Self Report measures an individual's perception of her or his own tendency to exhibit nonverbal behaviors that increase the feelings of immediacy in other people (e.g., I use my hands and arms to gesture when talking to people). However, the scale can be retooled to be an Other Report, and then an individual can report the tendency of another person's use of nonverbal behaviors that increase feelings of immediacy (e.g., my teacher uses her or his hands and arms to gesture while talking to people). In both cases, the intent of the scale is not changed, but the object of measurement is shifted from the first person (my behavior) to another person (someone else's behavior).

Beliefs and Attitudes

The second classification of things that can be measured by a research scale are beliefs and attitudes. As we discussed in Chapter 6, a **belief** is our perception of reality about whether something is true or false, whereas an **attitude** is a predisposition to respond to people, ideas, or objects in an evaluative way. In Chapter 6, we introduced two scales that can be employed to measure beliefs (Generalized Belief Scale) and attitudes (Generalized Attitude Measure). Although these two scales are easy to employ in order to measure any belief or attitude, other scales can also be created to measure a belief.

One type of scale designed to measure a set of beliefs is called a scalogram. The purpose of a scalogram is to create a series of beliefs about a single topic starting from very weak (e.g., I never throw trash on the ground because it hurts our environment) and moving to very strong (e.g., bombing a company that hurts the environment is completely justifiable). The environmentalism scale discussed in Chapter 6 measured different beliefs that people can have about environmentalism. With each new belief statement, a person answers either "yes" or "no." If the scalogram is accurate, a person who says "no" to the first question will say "no" to every item on the scale. If the person says "yes" to question 1 through 3 and then says "no" to question 4, then questions 5 through 10 should also be answered "no." In essence, a scalogram measures a series of beliefs and how strongly a person holds those beliefs. (Although the authors of this book all think recycling is a noble endeavor, not all of us actually recycle regularly.)

Knowledge

The history of measuring an individual's cognitive knowledge of a subject goes back to the earliest formation of schools. Even Socrates tested his students, but he measured his students' learning through their abilities to orally defend and explain themselves. There is even evidence of a basic form of testing of Chinese public officials by the emperor around 2200 BCE. In other words, the idea of testing has been around for 4,000 years. However, as mentioned, the first multiple-choice test did not appear until 1914, when Frederick J. Kelly was asked by the US Army to develop a way to measure recruit abilities (Sokal, 1987). Another test developed around the same time as the

Kelly multiple-choice test was the true-or-false test (Gates, 1921). Since this time, a variety of different types of measures of cognitive knowledge have been created, including fill-in-the-blank, word completion, matching, and many others.

As we've discussed here and earlier in the chapter, measuring knowledge is one of the earliest types of measurement social scientists attempted. Ultimately, two types of knowledge can be measured by a scale: cognitive knowledge and perceived knowledge.

COGNITIVE KNOWLEDGE

All of us are familiar with scales that attempt to measure knowledge. A multiple-choice or true-or-false test is a simple example of a scale that measures knowledge. Maybe you want to measure the effect that a teacher's choice of clothing has on retention of a lecture. The easiest way to determine retention of a lecture is to test participants about information that was in the lecture after the fact. And in education, we constantly survey students' acquisition of **cognitive knowledge** in a class. A good teacher will understand that a test basically lets us know two different things: (1) how well every student understands the material and (2) how well our teaching methods are working for student understanding as a whole. Some people in education believe that if all students fail a test, then the teacher has done a good job weeding out the bad students. However, the testing mechanism was not appropriate or the teaching strategies were not working. (Although it is outside the purview of the current text, we should mention that there is an entire field of educational psychometrics, or the creation and analysis of cognitive tests. Although many of us hate standardized tests, substantial time and politics goes into their creation. After students have taken a standardized test, psychometricians spend a lot of time analyzing the statistical properties of the test to make sure the test is effective and appropriate.)

PERCEIVED KNOWLEDGE

The second type of knowledge that can be measured is **perceived knowledge**. Although understanding what a person knows is important, it is also important to be able to measure what a person thinks he or she knows. The Risk Knowledge Index shown in Figure 7.2 was originally created by Wrench (2007) as a way to measure the degree to which an individual believed that he or she understood the risk associated with a specific hazard (something that could cause loss of life or limb). In Figure 7.2, the scale measures an individual's perception of her or his knowledge about the risks associated with bungee jumping. We could have determined a person's perception of her or his perceived knowing by asking, "How much do you know about the risks of bungee jumping from the range of 0 (*I know nothing about the risks*) to 9 (*I know about all of the risks involved*)?" However, a one-shot question can be problematic because it does not allow a statistical way to determine whether your sample's response to this question is random or consistent.

FIGURE 7.2
Risk Knowledge Index

Instructions: Below are several descriptions dealing with the extent to which you are aware of the risks involved in bungee jumping. Please use the scale below to rate the degree to which each statement applies to your perceptions about your knowledge of the risk(s):

Strongly Disagree	**Disagree**	**Neutral**	**Agree**	**Strongly Agree**
1	2	3	4	5

_____ 1. I know the risks involved.
_____ 2. I do not feel knowledgeable about the risks involved.
_____ 3. The risks involved are very clear to me.
_____ 4. I do not know the risks involved.
_____ 5. I do not comprehend the risks involved.
_____ 6. My knowledge of the risks involved is limited.
_____ 7. I completely understand the risks involved.
_____ 8. I feel knowledgeable about the risks involved.
_____ 9. I comprehend the risks involved.
_____ 10. The risks involved are not clear to me.

SCORING: To compute your scores follow the instructions below:

Step One: Add scores for items 1, 3, 7, 8, & 9.
Step Two: Add scores for items 2, 4, 5, 6, & 10.
Step Three: Add 30 to Step One.
Step Four: Subtract the score for Step Two from the score for Step Three.

Interpreting Your Score:

Scores on the Risk Knowledge Index should be between 10 and 50. Individuals with scores above 40 are considered to have a high perceived understanding of a risk, and individuals with scores below 40 are considered to have a low perceived understanding of a risk.

NOTE: The mean for risk knowledge tends to be fairly high.

Source:

Wrench, J. S. (2007). The influence of perceived risk knowledge on risk communication. *Communication Research Reports, 24*, 63–70.

THE PROCESS OF CREATING A NEW MEASURE

In the previous section, we examined the three primary variable types that can be analyzed through research scales (personality traits/states, beliefs and attitudes, and perceived and real knowledge). However, before one can measure anything at all, he or she must have a clear idea of what the variable is that he or she is attempting to measure.

The Germinal Idea

In the organizational orientations and humor assessment measure examples discussed in this chapter, both scales started with what we call a **germinal idea**. A germinal idea refers to the spark that causes an individual to realize that something new can be measured. We often get the ideas for new scales because we face real events in our lives that cause us to wonder about some communication phenomena, or maybe when we read what an author says and wonder, *Has anyone ever really studied this concept?* Recently, two of our coauthors were having a late-night discussion about organizational communication that led to the realization of a huge gap in the organizational communication measurement literature, which then led to the creation of nine new scales. Although a germinal idea can help you get the initial push to create a scale, it is the conceptualization of that germinal idea that allows you to start the measurement process.

Conceptualization

Conceptualization is defined as the development and clarification of concepts of your germinal idea. Conceptualization is basically when you take a germinal idea and determine what it is that you want to measure and whether you can realistically measure that phenomenon. One of the biggest problems many researchers have when creating research scales is that they attempt to measure too much. For example, maybe you wanted to create a scale to measure an individual's perception of health communication. What part of health communication are you interested in? Are you looking at communication between patients and physicians, patients and nurses, clients and therapists, or clients and pharmacists?

A scale should measure a single concept or a set of concepts that are closely related to each other. For example, Richmond and McCroskey's (1990) Sociocommunicative Orientation Scale measures the two related constructs of assertiveness and responsiveness. Realistically, each of those concepts could be measured separately by a single scale, but since the two concepts work together so closely, it makes sense to develop a single scale in which both concepts can be analyzed together. You would not want to create a scale that attempts to measure both assertiveness and conflict management, however, because these are two separate concepts. Although you could examine both concepts in a single research study, you would need to create two different scales: one for assertiveness and one for conflict management strategies.

Operationalization

Once you have determined the basic concept you are actually planning on measuring, you must operationalize your concept. **Operationalization** is the detailed description of the research operations or procedures necessary to assign units of analysis to the categories of a variable in order to represent conceptual properties. Operationalization applies to all forms of measurement, not just working with scales.

PUTTING PEOPLE INTO GROUPS

This first form of operationalization is referred to as manipulation into categories. For example, if you want to create a study where you will analyze the types of clothing that people have on and their likelihood of spending money in a department store, you would need to create an a priori (before the fact) coding scheme for how you will classify clothing choices. This way, if a woman comes in wearing a Gucci business suit and carrying a Prada handbag, she will not be classified into the same category as a male wearing cutoff shorts and a tank top. In other words, you operationalize that dress is some sort of nominal/categorical variable, and you purposefully classify people into different groups based on what they are wearing when they enter the store.

OBSERVING EXISTING RECORDS/ASKING PEOPLE

The second way that we can operationalize a concept is to estimate the category either by observing existing records or by asking people. The observation of existing records is how Boiarsky, Long, and Thayer (1999) operationalized their concept in their article about children's science television (included on the textbook's website). Boiarsky et al. examined a variety of mediated characteristics (sound effects per minute, cuts per minute, fades/dissolves per minute, wipes per minute, and topic shifts per minute) in a series of children's television shows (*Beakman's World*, *Bill Nye the Science Guy*, *Magic School Bus*, and *Newton's Apple*). Each of these shows was preexisting, so the researchers had to determine what it was they wanted to examine in the show and then operationalize how they would go about analyzing these mediated characteristics. By clearly spelling out their operationalization of coding procedures, future researchers can more accurately understand the findings of this study and replicate the research in the future, either in this genre or in a different genre of television. And using preexisting sources of information for the collection of data, as Boiarsky et al. did, can be beneficial when doing research. However, as already discussed, you must have a clear idea of what you are looking for before you can operationalize your measurement process.

INTERVIEWS AND SURVEYS

The last form of operationalization is asking for verbal/nonverbal reports of a phenomenon through either interviews or traditional survey techniques. For example, maybe you want to determine the effect of a new political attack advertisement on the public. What kinds of questions would you want to ask to determine "the effect"? Maybe you would want to ask questions about the target of the attack ad's credibility or the attractiveness of the target after viewing the ad.

Operationalization is in essence the procedures we go through to place someone in a variable category. When Wrench and Richmond (2004) were first writing a new scale for measuring interpersonal humor, the two fell into the same trap that the Booth-Butterfields had fallen into when developing the Humor Orientation scale in 1991. It was not until a colleague read the initial version of the scale and noted that they had also included a number of items about jokes and humorous storytelling that the two researchers realized the scale needed to avoid such language altogether if it was to truly be a general humor measure. This process where you narrow the focus of the scale and really try to get at the basic concept being measured is the operationalization of the concept.

CONSTRUCTING QUESTIONS

Now that we have discussed the initial steps necessary in conceptualizing and then operationalizing a scale, we can turn our attention to the actual construction of research scales. And writing research measures that will stand the test of time is not a task to underestimate. Too many people who are not familiar with the psychometric process of creating reliable and valid research measures think that creating a new scale is simply writing down a series of questions. Writing scale questions can be problematic, however, because even the slightest conjecture or ambiguity in an item can cause people to respond inaccurately to that item, which makes your scale's purpose and meaning highly suspect. Scale creation is not simply about writing a series of sentences and attaching several Likert scales to those sentences. The art and science of research measurement is complex and takes substantial time and effort to scientifically perform.

Once you have determined what you really want to measure (through the conceptualization and operationalization processes), you can begin to actually write a research scale. The following discussion is focused primarily on the creation of Likert-type scales because they are most often used by communication researchers. Although some concepts may not directly apply to semantic differential scale or scalogram, most of this discussion can be cross-applied to those scales. We will now examine 15 important guidelines for creating reliable and valid Likert-type research scales.

1. Start with Twice as Many Items as You Will Need

When you are first developing a scale, you must begin with nearly twice as many items as you think you will need in the long run. For example, if you want to have a 15-item scale to measure sibling communication satisfaction, you must start off with 30 items. Why? Some of your items will be problematic and eventually discarded from your scale as they either do not help the reliability of your scale or do not measure the actual construct you are attempting to measure (these will be discussed in Chapter 8).

Because you must write a considerable number of items for each scale you create, you will often find redundancy a necessity. One easy way to do this is to oppositely word each item you create later in the scale. For example, if you have a scale for which you are writing 20 items, you may want to have item 1 as "I like potatoes" and item 11 as "I do not like potatoes." In the long run, this will provide you with a healthy balance between positively worded and negatively worded items in your scale. The reason we have both positively and negatively worded items in a scale is to make sure that a person is not randomly answering the questions without reading them. If we have both of those questions being answered by a Likert scale ranging from 1 (*strongly disagree*) to 5 (*strongly agree*), we would expect that if someone answers "5" to question 1, he or she will answer "1" to question 11 since the two questions are oppositely worded. This concept will be discussed in greater detail in the next chapter.

2. Every Item Should Reflect the Construct

As a scale writer, ensure that every item that you write on a scale clearly (at least in your mind) reflects the construct you are attempting to measure. For example, you want to make sure that you do not have items on a scale that are supposed to be measuring physician use of storytelling to reflect patient apprehension while talking to her or his physician. Although both scales could be important, the concepts should be operationalized separately into two different scales.

3. Use Concise, Clearly Worded, Unambiguous Items

One problem that people have early on when creating scales is that they write survey items that are complex. Unfortunately, when working with the general public, the more simplistic a question is, the more likely you will get an accurate response from your survey participants. To avoid the pitfall of complicated language, always try to pilot test your scale with a group of people prior to mass distributing the scale in order to determine whether there are any problem areas in the wording itself. If you know the test pilot group well, you may even ask them why they responded to specific questions in ways that you feel are opposite to how they should have scored based on their other answers. This will enable you to determine whether any ambiguity has crept into your scale by accident.

4. Construct Relatively Short Items

As an extension of the previous concept, not only do you want to avoid ambiguity, but also you want to have items that are fairly short. The more text that an individual must read for a scale item, the more likely that he or she will become confused and end up responding in a manner that is disjointed, which will skew your results. Although we suggest that a single item on any given Likert scale should not exceed 20 words, the shorter you can make a scale item, the easier it will be for participants to read and respond to your scale.

5. Pay Attention to Terminology in the Item

Another important problem to look out for when writing a scale is any jargon or discipline-specific terminology in the scale. Recently, the authors of this book were writing a scale to measure an individual's perception of an interactant's verbal and nonverbal communication during a specific type of romantic interaction. On further thinking about some of the scale items, we realized that not everyone may completely understand what is meant by "verbal communication" and "nonverbal communication" because communication researchers have specific meanings associated with the two terms. Ultimately, the researchers opted to provide a concise definition of the two terms before the scale to aid in the understanding of these concepts by participants.

6. Avoid Emotionally Charged Items

Unless you are attempting to measure an individual's emotional state, avoid items that are emotionally loaded. An emotionally charged item is a scale item designed to assess an individual's emotional response instead of her or his belief, attitude, or behavior. Suppose that you want to create a scale for assessing a subordinate's perception of her or his supervisor's coaching and teaching on the job. You may have items like "My supervisor makes sure I understand what I'm doing" or "My supervisor makes sure I understand what I did wrong when I make a mistake." You would not want to have an item like "I hate it when my supervisor corrects my mistakes." Having items that cause people to respond to emotions in otherwise nonemotional scales can result in participants responding to the whole scale in an emotional state, which will skew your results.

7. Avoid Leading Items

Another trap you want to avoid when writing scale items involves leading items. A leading item is an item on a scale that clearly informs a person about the answer you are hoping to receive. For example, if you are creating a scale to measure the extent to which a teacher uses humor in a classroom, an item such as "Good students always think their teachers use humor in the classroom" would be extremely inappropriate. Instead, you would want general items (e.g., "My teacher uses humor in the classroom") that avoid leading anyone to believe that they should answer the scale item in a specific, socially desirable way.

8. Avoid Loaded Items

A loaded item is similar to a leading item, just generally in the opposite direction. For example, if you are creating a scale about verbal aggression, you would not want an item to say something like "Only an idiot cannot tell the difference between aggression and debate." Basically, if a person agrees with the statement, he or she is saying that many people in the world are idiots, and if a person disagrees with the statement, that person is setting up her- or himself to being labeled an idiot for not seeing the difference between aggression and debate.

9. Avoid Double Questions

One common problem in scale items occurs when an individual attempts to write an item with two actual questions involved—for example, "I believe that all students should go to college, and I believe that all students should get a master's degree." Although these two statements may both be true for some, they are not necessarily true for everyone. The best thing to do in this case would be to ask each one separately, as two different items on the scale. When reading items on a scale, always double-check to see whether a scale item is asking only one question.

10. Avoid Questions with False Premises

Often, people will attempt to write scale items based on premises that simply are not factual. For example, if you are attempting to measure the degree to which one believes in the current president, you may ask a question such as "Because people generally support the president, I believe the president is doing a good job." The premise of this item can be hotly contested since many people do not support the president (any president). If a question starts with a statement that is not factual, then the rest of the question will be ambiguous at best or unanswerable at worst.

11. Avoid Using the Words "Always" and "Never"

Using the words "always" and "never" often confuses people and can cause some participants to avoid answering an item at the extremes (like *strongly agree/strongly disagree* on a five-step Likert scale). If you had the item "I always communicate competently" on a scale, you could have problems because no one can honestly say they *always* communicate competently. On the flip side, if you substituted the word "never" for "always," you would run into the same problem because no one can honestly say that they *never* communicate competently either.

12. Avoid Double Negatives/Positives

As a whole, people find double negatives and double positives to be confusing. You would not want to have items like "Religious groups should not, not have to pay taxes." In this case, streamlining the question to "Religious groups should have to pay taxes" makes the statement more direct and easier to understand.

13. Avoid Hypothetical Questions

If you ask people to respond to a hypothetical question, then you will get a hypothetical (i.e., a made-up) answer. For example, if you create a scale on people's perceived interaction with extraterrestrial life forms, you will have people randomly answering your scale because interaction with extraterrestrials can only be speculated on. No real answers can be given (except by a few people in New Mexico). As a researcher, it is best to keep scales and what you are measuring as concrete as possible.

14. Avoid Ambiguous Pronoun References

When writing scales, do not include pronouns that make the participant unsure of what you are asking in a scale item. For example, if you included the item "I would rather it not happen to me" on a scale about euthanasia, people would be highly suspect of what "it" actually is in this scale item. Instead, you would want to be as concrete as possible and reword the scale item to read "I would rather not be euthanized" to avoid the ambiguous pronoun.

15. Consider Recall Issues for Certain Types of Items

The last major concept to keep in mind when writing a scale is the concept of recall. In essence, when we ask people to recall information about an attitude, belief, or behavior, we must know whether what we are asking someone to remember can actually be remembered. For example, we would not want to ask someone to recall the color of the tie a male physician was wearing three months earlier. We also need to think about whether the items on the scales we are creating force people to recall information that is unrealistic for them to remember at a later point. For example, if you are creating a scale on the posture that one uses while standing, the scale may be difficult for people to accurately fill out if the target of the participants' observations has not been seen in a while.

ONE MEASURE, MULTIPLE FACTORS

Before we continue, we must discuss one common area of confusion for people when it comes to measurement (and specific research measures). Often, a single research measure can actually measure multiple different (albeit related) concepts. Figure 7.3 contains a measure that was originally created by James McCroskey and Jason Teven (1999) to analyze a participant's perception of a specific target's credibility (in this case, the US president's credibility). Researchers dating back to Socrates have written and attempted to discuss what "credibility" is. And through a series of different research studies, McCroskey paired down his own measure of credibility (with the help of Teven) to consist of three distinct but closely related concepts. Here is what we want you to do before progressing further. In Figure 7.3, see whether you can find three sets of items that appear to be measuring a similar concept. Yes, there are only three concepts being measured by this scale, and each concept has six items, so see whether you can detect the six items that go along with each of the three subscales (or factors).

Instructions: Below are several oppositely worded adjective pairs that represent how you may feel about the United States President. Circle the number between the adjectives which best represents your beliefs. Numbers "1" and "7" indicate a very strong feeling. Numbers "2" and "6" indicate a strong feeling. Numbers "3" and "5" indicate a fairly weak feeling. Number "4" indicates you are undecided or do not understand the adjectives themselves. There are no right or wrong answers.

1.	Unintelligent	1	2	3	4	5	6	7	Intelligent
2.	Untrained	1	2	3	4	5	6	7	Trained
3.	Doesn't care about me	1	2	3	4	5	6	7	Cares about me
4.	Dishonest	1	2	3	4	5	6	7	Honest
5.	Doesn't have my interests at heart	1	2	3	4	5	6	7	Has my interests at heart
6.	Untrustworthy	1	2	3	4	5	6	7	Trustworthy
7.	Inexpert	1	2	3	4	5	6	7	Expert
8.	Self-centered	1	2	3	4	5	6	7	Not self-centered
9.	Not concerned with me	1	2	3	4	5	6	7	Concerned with me
10.	Dishonorable	1	2	3	4	5	6	7	Honorable
11.	Uninformed	1	2	3	4	5	6	7	Informed
12.	Immoral	1	2	3	4	5	6	7	Moral
13.	Incompetent	1	2	3	4	5	6	7	Competent
14.	Unethical	1	2	3	4	5	6	7	Ethical
15.	Insensitive	1	2	3	4	5	6	7	Sensitive
16.	Stupid	1	2	3	4	5	6	7	Bright
17.	Phony	1	2	3	4	5	6	7	Genuine
18.	Not understanding	1	2	3	4	5	6	7	Understanding

Source: McCroskey, J. C., & Teven, J. J. (1999). Goodwill: A reexamination of the construct and its measurement. *Communication Monographs, 66,* 90–103.

FIGURE 7.3
Source Credibility Measure

A **subscale** is a hypothetical subdivision of a mental measure. In the case of the Source Credibility Measure in Figure 7.3, there are three distinct hypothesized subscales. Each subscale measures a specific aspect of credibility. No one subscale encapsulates the whole concept of credibility, which is why all three subscales are necessary.

A factor, by contrast, is derived through a statistical test called a factor analysis. A **factor analysis** looks for patterns among your participants' responses to each scale question in order to determine whether participants respond in any discernable way. The goal of a factor analysis is to see whether any specific items tend to be answered in a consistent fashion by participants whereas other items are answered in a different, yet consistent, fashion by your participants. Think of the term *subscale* as the hypothesis and the term *factor* as the observance (through statistics) of the subscale. Often, researchers propose a subscale that is later not confirmed when they conduct a factor analysis, so the research measure must be tweaked to reflect the observed factor structure.

In the case of the Source Credibility Measure, research has shown that the three subscales are distinctly different factors. This means that research participants tend to answer six of the items in a similar fashion, another six items in a similar fashion, and the last six items in a similar fashion (these three groupings do not correspond to the numbers next to the individual items in Figure 7.2). Only after utilizing a factor analysis can a researcher be sure that hypothesized subscales are distinctly different factors. You can label anything a subscale, but only a factor analysis can statistically determine whether there are unique factors within a specific mental measure.

If you have not done so by this point, please see whether you can find the three distinct subscales/factors in the Source Credibility Measure (Figure 7.3). If you want to check your answers, the groupings of the three factors can be found at the end of the chapter. Also, see whether you can label the three distinct subscales/factors within the Source Credibility Measure.

Ultimately, it is important to remember that a single scale can measure multiple concepts in an effort to more fully understand the larger hypothetical construct. However, an ethical researcher should not say that a set of items has multiple subscales in a published research article unless he or she conducts a factor analysis to support the presence of subscales (more on this in the next chapter). Many pop-science measures have been created over the years purporting to measure a wide range of phenomena, and researchers should be leery of using these measures at face value because they often pretend to measure subscales when those subscales do not statistically exist. For more information on factor analyses, check out Appendix E on advanced statistical tests on the book website.

Finding Mental Measures

Surveys are prevalent in communication research. Thankfully, we do not have to spend all of our time creating new scales to conduct survey-based research. In fact, most studies do not attempt to reinvent the measurement wheel at all and instead rely on combining previously existing scales in new ways that have not been explored. Thousands of research scales already exist, so millions of variable combinations have yet to be explored.

The more time you spend conducting survey research, the larger your collection of interval scales will ultimately become. If you are just starting out in research, you may not know where to turn to find scales. Here are seven books that may be useful for finding communication scales:

Bucy, E. P., & Holbert, R. L. (Eds.). (2011). *Sourcebook for political communication research: Methods, measures, and analytical techniques.* New York, NY: Routledge.

Kim, D. K., & Dearing, J. W. (Eds.). (2016). *Health communication research measures.* New York, NY: Peter Lang.

Continued

Manusov, V. (Ed.). (2005). *The sourcebook of nonverbal measures: Going beyond words.* Mahwah, NJ: Erlbaum.

Rubin, R. B., Palmgreen, P., & Sypher, H. E. (Eds.). (2004). *Communication research measures: A sourcebook.* Mahwah, NJ: Erlbaum.

Rubin, R. B., Rubin, A. M., Graham, E. E., Perse, E. M., & Seibold, D. R. (2009). *Communication research measures II: A sourcebook.* New York, NY: Routledge.

Worthington, D. L., & Bodie, G. D. (Eds.). (2018). *The sourcebook of listening research: Methodology and measures.* Hoboken, NJ: Wiley.

Wrench, J. S., Jowi, D., & Goodboy, A. (2010). *The directory of communication related mental measures.* Washington, DC: National Communication Association.

These eight books may be useful for finding variables outside of the field of communication relating to communication phenomena:

Coviello, N., & Yli-Renko, H. (Eds.). (2016). *Handbook of measures for international entrepreneurship research: Multi-item scales crossing disciplines and contexts.* Northampton, MA: Edward Elgar.

Fisher, T. D., Davis, C. M., Yarber, W. L., & Davis, S. L. (Eds.). (2011). *Handbook of sexuality-related measures* (3rd ed.). New York, NY: Routledge.

Fields, D. L. (2002). *Taking measure of work: A guide to validated scales for organizational research and diagnosis.* Thousand Oaks, CA: Sage.

Gamst, G. C., Liang, C. T. H., & Der-Karabetian, A. (2011). *Handbook of multicultural measures.* Los Angeles, CA: Sage.

Goldman, B. A., & Mitchell, D. F. (2003). *Directory of unpublished experimental mental measures* (Vol. 8). Washington, DC: American Psychological Association. (See also Vols. 1–7.)

Hill, P. C., & Hood, R. W., Jr. (Eds.). (1999). *Measures of religiosity.* Birmingham, AL: Religious Education Press.

Robinson, J. P., Shaver, P. R., & Wrightsman, L. S. (Eds.). (1991). *Measures of personality and social psychological attitudes.* San Diego, CA: Academic Press.

Robinson, J. P., Shaver, P. R., & Wrightsman, L. S. (Eds.). (1993). *Measures of political attitudes.* San Diego, CA: Academic Press.

There are two online databases that also can be useful when searching for mental measures. By 1938, so many new mental measures were being developed that Oscar K. Buros decided to publish the first volume of the *Mental Measures Yearbook.* The *Mental Measures Yearbook* attempts to locate and provide descriptions of the test, one or two reviews of the test, and references for how to find the test. The Buros Center for Testing (http://www.unl.edu/buros/) is still an active research center for mental measures, and the 18th volume of the *Mental Measures Yearbook* is currently available (Spies, Carlson, & Geisinger, 2010). Your local library may have access to the *Mental Measures Yearbook* database through EBSCOhost. If you do not have access, the cost for a single copy is $15, but this is just the cost for the measure review and does not include a copy of the measure itself. The ETS (http://www.ets.org/) also has started compiling mental measures. If you are on ETS website, click the link that says "Tests and Products." You will be taken to the Tests and Products homepage. You will need to scroll down until you find the link to "ETS Test Collection." Click the link, and on the next page, you will see "Search Test Link Database," which is a database of more than 25,000 mental measures. In fact, a simple name search reveals more than 150 mental measures with the word "communication" in the title alone.

Directory of Communication Related Mental Measures

The *Directory of Communication Related Mental Measures* can now be accessed using an interactive wiki at http://communicationmeasures.com. The website categorizes measures into three broad categories: communication behaviors, communication traits and states, and communication contexts. An ongoing project, the site has already profiled more than 500 measures used by communication researchers, with new measures constantly being added. Some measures link to full-text versions of the measures on the Internet, but the reference for the article where the items were first published is provided for all measures.

MEASUREMENT AND STATISTICAL ANALYSIS

Because of the other chapters in this book, we will neither assume sophisticated knowledge of statistics nor attempt to explain statistical matters in any detail here. However, it is important that a student studying measurement have an elementary knowledge of statistics so that he or she may be better able to evaluate the measuring instruments he or she chooses or develops.

There are essentially two types of statistical tests: parametric and nonparametric. A **parameter** is a value of a population. For example, if we administered an intelligence test to all of the people in the world, we might then add all of their scores together, divide that total by the number of people, and obtain the "mean" or average score for all people on this measure of intelligence. This "mean" would be a parameter of the population. Because in most cases we are unable to apply any measure to all of the people to whom it might be applied, however, we are forced to use samples from a population. All statistical tests make certain assumptions, but **nonparametric** statistical tests make no assumptions about parameters of the population from which the research sample was drawn. **Parametric** tests, on the other hand, do make such assumptions. The important distinction between parametric and nonparametric statistical tests, for our purposes, is that parametric tests assume the level of measurement employed in obtaining the data was at least the interval level. Nonparametric tests make no such assumption. Parametric tests are normally considered more powerful—that is, they are precise and less subject to error than nonparametric tests. Thus, social scientists normally wish to employ parametric statistical procedures.

If we rigidly adhere to the characteristics required for the achievement of interval scales, many times we are forced to employ nonparametric statistical tests even though we might prefer to employ parametric ones. In some cases, this is a particularly difficult problem because some parametric analyses have no equivalent nonparametric approach—for example, factor analysis (see Appendix E at https://oup-arc.com/wrench for a brief explanation of factor analysis). Within the nominal, ordinal, interval, and ratio scaling category systems, most attitude measures fall in the ordinal or interval categories.

It is highly unlikely to affect general results whether one treats the data as ordinal or interval, but a much wider range of techniques is available with interval measures.

RESEARCH OUTSIDE THE WALLS OF ACADEMIA

Whether you are attempting to measure someone's trait level of CA or someone's level of customer satisfaction within your organization, measurement is a static process. Maybe you were asked to put together a short survey for your company about customer satisfaction for its latest website. Creating or finding good measures is an art and a science that should be taken seriously. Thankfully, there are a variety of useful sources that you can lean on for finding measures commonly used in the business world.

If your goal is to locate measures that relate to any aspect of marketing, we recommend looking at the books edited by Gordon Bruner (Bruner, 2009; Bruner, Hensel, & James, 2001). The 2001 book by Bruner et al. has full-text versions of 654 measures ranging from people's attitudes toward television advertising to communication about purchasing products between parents and adolescents. The 2009 book is similar in fashion to the 2001 book, but it is only available electronically through Bruner's website (http://www.marketingscales.com/). The 2009 book has 716 unique measures published within its pages. Overall, these two books are great sources for anyone interesting in surveying people about products and services.

If your goal is to measure communication within an organization, we recommend reading Cal Downs and Allyson Adrian's (2004) book *Assessing Organizational Communication: Strategic Communication Audits*. This book focuses specifically on the applied work that communication consultants can engage in within modern organizations. The book discusses numerous ways to conduct communication research within an organization and provides access to both proprietary and public domain measures that consultants can utilize.

CONCLUSION

In this chapter, we have discussed a number of extremely important factors involved in measurement. We started by defining the term, reviewing the purpose of measurement and the different levels of measurement (nominal, ordinal, interval, and ratio), and then examined the history of social scientific measurement that led to the creation of Likert scales and semantic differential scales. Next, we talked about how we measure phenomena in communication, concluding with a discussion of how to write Likert-type items effectively. Finally, we discussed where one can find mental measures and how mental measures are used in statistical research. However, our discussion of measurement is not over yet. In the next chapter, we will discuss two extremely important concepts related to measurement: reliability and validity.

KEY TERMS

Attitude p. 230

Belief p. 230

Cognitive knowledge p. 231

Conceptualization p. 233

Factor analysis p. 240

Germinal idea p. 233

Isomorphism p. 219

Latent/hypothetical variable p. 225

Likert scale p. 225

Measurement p. 218

Mental measures p. 223

Nonparametric p. 243

Operationalization p. 233

Parameter p. 243

Parametric p. 243

Perceived knowledge p. 231

Semantic differential scale p. 227

Subscale p. 240

Trait behavior p. 229

REFERENCES

Arnold, W. E., McCroskey, J. C., & Prichard, S. (1966). The semantic differential. *Today's Speech, 14*(4), 29–30.

Arnold, W. E., McCroskey, J. C., & Prichard, S. V. O. (1967). The Likert-type scale. *Today's Speech, 15*, 31–33.

Baldwin, J. M., Cattell, J. M., & Jastrow, J. (1889). Physical and mental tests. *Psychological Review, 5*, 172–179.

Binet, A. (1905). New methods for the diagnosis of the intellectual level of subnormals. *L'Année Psychologique, 12*, 191–244.

Bogardus, E. S. (1925). Measuring social distance. *Journal of Applied Sociology, 9*, 299–308.

Boiarsky, G., Long, M., & Thayer, G. (1999). Formal features in children's science television: Sound effects, visual pace, and topic shifts. *Communication Research Reports, 16*, 185–192.

Booth-Butterfield, M., & Booth-Butterfield, S. (1991). Individual differences in the communication of humorous messages. *Southern Communication Journal, 56*, 208–218.

Bruner, G. C., II. (2009). *Marketing scales handbook: A compilation of multi-item measures for consumer behavior and advertising* (Vol. V). Carbondale, IL: GCBII Productions.

Bruner, G. C., II, Hensel, P. J., & James, K. E. (2001). *Marketing scales handbook: A compilation of multi-item measures for consumer behavior and advertising* (Vol. IV). Chicago, IL: American Marketing Association and Thomson Southwestern.

Buros, O. K. (Ed.). (1938). *The 1938 mental measurements yearbook*. Lincoln, NE: University of Nebraska Press.

Cattell, J. M. (1890). Mental tests and measurements. *Mind, 15*, 373–381.

Cattell, J. M. (1895). Measurements of the accuracy of recollection. *Science, 2*, 761–766.

Darwin, C. (1859). *On the origin of species by means of natural selection*. London: Murray.

Downs, C. W., & Adrian, A. D. (2004). *Assessing organizational communication: Strategic communication audits*. New York, NY: Guilford Press.

Galton, F. (1869). *Heredity genius: An inquiry into its laws and consequences.* New York, NY: Macmillan. Retrieved from http://galton.org/books/hereditary-genius/

Gates, A. I. (1921). The true–false test as a measure of achievement in college courses. *Journal of Educational Psychology, 12,* 276–287.

Heise, D. R. (1970). The semantic differential and attitude research. In G. F. Summers (Ed.), *Attitude measurement* (pp. 235–253). Chicago, IL: Rand McNally.

Likert, R. (1932). A technique for the measurement of attitudes. *Archives of Psychology, 140,* 1–55.

McCroskey, J. C. (1966). *Experimental studies of the effects of ethos and evidence in persuasive communication.* Unpublished doctoral dissertation. Pennsylvania State University.

McCroskey, J. C., Richmond, V. P., Johnson, A. D., & Smith, H. T. (2004). Organizational orientations theory and measurement: Development of measures and preliminary investigations. *Communication Quarterly, 52,* 1–14.

McCroskey, J. C., & Teven, J. J. (1999). Goodwill: A reexamination of the construct and its measurement. *Communication Monographs, 66,* 90–103.

Osgood, C. E. (1952). The nature and measurement of meaning. *Psychological Bulletin, 49,* 197–237.

Osgood, C. E., Tannenbaum, P. H., & Suci, G. J. (1957). *The measurement of meaning.* Urbana, IL: University of Illinois Press.

Pressey, S. L., & Pressey, L. W. (1919). Cross-out test, with suggestions as to a group scale of the emotions. *Journal of Applied Psychology, 3,* 138–150.

Richmond, V. P., & McCroskey, J. C. (1990). Reliability and separation of factors on the assertiveness–responsiveness measure. *Psychological Reports, 67,* 449–450.

Salkind, N. J. (2017). *Tests & measurement for people who (think they) hate tests & measurement* (3rd ed.). Los Angeles, CA: Sage.

Segal, D. L., & Coolidge, F. L. (2003). Objective assessment of personality and psychopathology: An overview. In M. J. Hilsenroth, D. L. Segal, & M. Hersen (Eds.), *Comprehensive handbook of psychological assessment: Volume 2: Personality assessment* (pp. 3–13). New York, NY: Wiley.

Sokal, M. M. (Ed.). (1987). *Psychological testing and American society, 1890–1930.* New Brunswick, NJ: Rutgers University Press.

Spies, R. A., Carlson, J. F., Geisinger, K. F. (2010). *The eighteenth mental measurements yearbook.* Lincoln, NE: University of Nebraska Press.

Terman, L. M. (1916). *The measurement of intelligence.* Boston, MA: Houghton Mifflin.

Woodworth, R. S. (1920). *Personal data sheet.* Chicago, IL: Stoelting.

Wrench, J. S. (2007). The influence of perceived risk knowledge on risk communication. *Communication Research Reports, 24,* 1–8.

Wrench, J. S., & Richmond, V. P. (2004). Understanding the psychometric properties of the humor assessment instrument through an analysis of the relationships between teacher humor assessment and instructional communication variables in the college classroom. *Communication Research Reports, 21,* 92–103.

FURTHER READING

DeVellis, R. F. (2017). *Scale development: Theory and applications* (4th ed.). Los Angeles, CA: Sage.

Dillman, D. A., Smyth, J. D., & Christian, L. M. (2014). *Internet, phone, mail, and mixed-mode surveys: The tailored design method* (4th ed.). Hoboken, NJ: Wiley.

Fowler, F. J., Jr. (1993). *Survey research methods* (2nd ed.). Newbury Park, CA: Sage.

Linn, R. L., & Grolund, N. E. (2000). *Measurement and assessment in teaching* (8th ed.). Upper Saddle, NJ: Merrill.

Salkind, N. J. (2012). *100 questions (and answers) about research methods*. Los Angeles, CA: Sage.

Singleton, R. A., Jr., & Straits, B. C. (2017). *Approach to social research* (6th ed.). New York, NY: Oxford University Press.

Wrench, J. S., Jowi, D., & Goodboy, A. (2010). *The directory of communication related mental measures*. Washington, DC: National Communication Association.

SCORING THE SOURCE CREDIBILITY MEASURE

Competence Factor (1, 2, 7, 11, 13, and 16)
Caring/Goodwill Factor (3, 5, 8, 9, 15, and 18)
Trustworthiness Factor (4, 6, 10, 12, 14, and 17)

8

Reliability and Validity

CHAPTER OBJECTIVES

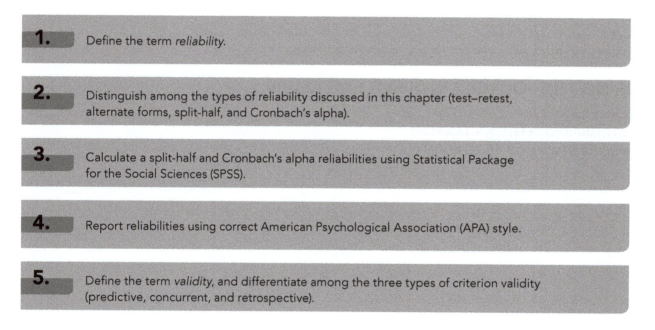

1. Define the term *reliability*.

2. Distinguish among the types of reliability discussed in this chapter (test–retest, alternate forms, split-half, and Cronbach's alpha).

3. Calculate a split-half and Cronbach's alpha reliabilities using Statistical Package for the Social Sciences (SPSS).

4. Report reliabilities using correct American Psychological Association (APA) style.

5. Define the term *validity*, and differentiate among the three types of criterion validity (predictive, concurrent, and retrospective).

This chapter explores two important characteristics in measurement: reliability and validity. We begin by discussing reliability.

RELIABILITY

When people think about the word "reliability," numerous synonyms come to mind: dependable, accurate, honest, trustworthy, consistent, and so on. Although the word is used in a specific manner by quantitative researchers, those adjectives still hold true. **Reliability** for this text is defined as the accuracy that a measure has in producing stable, consistent measurements.

The first part of this definition relates to the information we talked about in the previous chapter examining measurement, so reliability is about making sure our tools for measuring a phenomenon are accurate. And we are dealing with whether the measurement can find consistent results. One of the authors of this book has an unreliable cell phone—the clock on the cell phone is constantly changing. At one point in time, you will look down and the cell phone will say that it is 6:45, but five minutes later, you will look down and the phone will say 10:15. Obviously, this particular cell phone is not a reliable tool for telling the time because a clock should not indicate that three-and-a-half hours have passed in five minutes. Social scientists do not generally sit around watching clocks and watches to ascertain their reliability as tools for measuring time, however, so we must determine whether our tools for measurement are as reliable as a good clock.

In the social sciences, we often use research scales to conduct studies. Because research scales are a common form of measurement, social scientists must ensure that these scales are reliable measurements of the constructs they claim to measure. One of the first things a researcher must determine after collecting data is whether people have consistently filled out a research scale or completed the scale haphazardly. Imagine you just handed out the Generalized Attitude Scale about higher education to 300 people. How can you tell whether people randomly filled out the scale or actually put time and effort into their participation in a research project?

As stated earlier, the reliability of a measuring instrument is *whether a measure produces stable, consistent values.* If I give you the same measure under the same conditions multiple times, your score should not change significantly. A perfectly reliable instrument would produce the same score every time it is administered, even if it were administered an infinite number of times. In measuring human beings, however, it is impossible to measure an infinite number of times. Thus, we never know the precise reliability of our measures. Rather, we must estimate that reliability.

Scalar Reliability

Scalar reliability (the reliability of individual research scales) is the most common form of reliability assessed during quantitative research in communication. Almost every quantitative research study will use at least one research scale, and we must have a way to determine whether people are consistently filling out the scale. In Figure 8.1, we present a copy of the Generalized Attitude Measure used in this book.

In this scale, some adjective pairings are positively worded, and some are negatively worded. For example, in the first pairing (*good/bad*), the word "good" to the left receives a lower score (1) and the word "bad" to the right receives a higher score (7), whereas in the second pairing (*wrong/right*), the word "wrong" to the left receives the lower score (1) and the word "right" to the right receives the higher score (7). In this scale, is "good" equivalent to "wrong"? Not at all! When researchers create scales, we often do so with items that are oppositely worded to determine whether people are just randomly answering the scale.

Imagine you had a participant in your study who filled out the scale as shown in Figure 8.2. You will note that in this case someone just went through and circled almost

FIGURE 8.1
Generalized
Attitude Measure

Instructions: On the scales below, please indicate your feelings about **"Higher Education**." Numbers "1" and "7" indicate a very strong feeling. Numbers "2" and "6" indicate a strong feeling. Numbers "3" and "5" indicate a fairly week feeling. Number "4" indicates you are undecided or do not understand the adjective pairs themselves. There are no right or wrong answers. *Only circle one number per line.*

1.   Good   1 2 3 4 5 6 7   Bad

2.   Wrong   1 2 3 4 5 6 7   Right

3.   Harmful 1 2 3 4 5 6 7   Beneficial

4.   Fair   1 2 3 4 5 6 7   Unfair

5.   Wise   1 2 3 4 5 6 7   Foolish

6.   Negative 1 2 3 4 5 6 7 Positive

To compute your score:

Step One: Add the scores from items 2, 3, & 6.
Step Two: Add the scores from items 1, 4, & 5.
Step Three: Add 24 to Step One.
Step Four: Subtract Step Two from Step Three.

Scores should be between 6 and 42.

Sources:

McCroskey, J. C. (1966). *Experimental studies of the effects of ethos and evidence in persuasive communication.* Unpublished doctoral dissertation. Pennsylvania State University.

McCroskey, J. C., & Richmond, V. P. (1989). Bipolar scales. In P. Emmert & L. L. Barker (Eds.), *Measurement of Communication Behavior* (pp. 154–167). New York: Longman.

FIGURE 8.2
Generalized Attitude
Measure Scored
Inconsistently

1.   Good   1 2 3 4 ⑤ 6 7   Bad

2.   Wrong   1 2 3 4 5 6 ⑦ Right

3.   Harmful 1 2 3 4 5 6 ⑦ Beneficial

4.   Fair   1 2 3 4 5 6 ⑦ Unfair

5.   Wise   1 2 3 4 5 6 ⑦ Foolish

6.   Negative 1 2 3 4 5 6 ⑦ Positive

all 7's on the scale. This person perceives higher education to be bad, right, beneficial, unfair, foolish, and positive. Does this make sense to you? Well, do not worry—it makes little sense to us either. If a person consistently filled out the Generalized Attitude Measure, it might look like either option in Figure 8.3.

At the top of Figure 8.3, you have someone who has a strong, positive attitude toward higher education, with a score of 42. At the bottom of the figure, you have someone who has a moderately negative attitude, with a score of 36. Although this example was completed looking only at a semantic differential scale, the same principle holds true for a Likert scale as well. If you have two questions (e.g., "I like public speaking" and "I dislike public speaking") on a Likert scale with five steps running from 1 (*strongly disagree*) to 5 (*strongly agree*), a consistent participant may score the first question with a 5 and the second question with a 1. However, if a participant scored both questions as a 1, we have a problem with the participant's consistency.

In this section, we have talked about how an individual responds to a scale in this section, but when looking at the overall picture of reliability in a study, we examine a

FIGURE 8.3
Generalized Attitude
Measure Scored
Consistently

sample's responses to a scale collectively, not individual participant scores. And now that we have looked at some basic principles behind the concept of reliability, we turn our attention to a number of statistical tests that can be used to examine reliability. Specifically, we will discuss the test–retest, alternate forms, split-half, and Cronbach forms of reliability.

TEST–RETEST RELIABILITY

One of the most obvious methods for testing the reliability of an instrument is to measure the same thing on more than one occasion and see whether you get the same score, which is the essence of the **test–retest reliability** approach. If we presume that the thing we are measuring does not change, our measure should produce the exact same score the second time we use it as it did the first time. Test–retest reliability for attitude measures is estimated by administering the instrument to the same group of people on two occasions, separated by some given amount of time. The subjects' scores at "Time 1" and "Time 2" are then subjected to statistical analysis to obtain a correlation coefficient. This correlation coefficient is referred to as a reliability coefficient, or an estimate of the degree of association between the scores at Time 1 and Time 2. Good attitude-measuring instruments normally produce test–retest reliability coefficients of 0.70 or above, and many coefficients are 0.90 or above. If a researcher finds a test–retest reliability below 0.70, then her or his participants are not responding to the scale consistently. Conversely, test–retest reliability coefficients of about 0.90 indicate that people are filling out the scale at Time 1 and Time 2 in almost identical fashion.

ALTERNATE FORMS RELIABILITY

The logic and procedure for estimating **alternate forms reliability** are the same as that for test–retest reliability. In many cases, we can develop two attitude-measuring instruments to measure the same attitude and administer the first instrument at Time 1 and the second at Time 2. We may then obtain the reliability coefficient for the two forms.

Reliability coefficients for the alternate forms are normally somewhat lower than reliability coefficients developed through the test–retest procedure. This is because the test–retest procedure includes no variety in the items administered from Time 1 to Time 2. No matter how carefully alternate forms of the same test are developed, there is always some variability in the items from Time 1 to Time 2. Thus, slightly lower reliability estimates should be expected.

SPLIT-HALF RELIABILITY

In many instances, it is impossible or economically infeasible to administer instruments to the same people on two occasions. Therefore, we must be able to estimate the reliability of our measuring instrument with only one administration. The split-half reliability approach is similar to the test–retest and alternate forms procedures except that it uses only one measurement period. This avoids any time delay that could be accompanied by changes in the subjects, which would be reflected in lower reliability estimates.

The split-half reliability procedure involves computing two scores for each participant based on one administration of the test. One of the scores comes from one half of the test, and the other score comes from the other half. Several methods can be employed to divide the test in half to obtain the two scores. A common one is to have all the odd-numbered items compose one half of the test and the even-numbered items the other half. Alternatively, if we had 20 items in our test, we could take the first 10 items as one half of the test and the last 10 items as the other half. A somewhat less frequently employed method is to randomly select half of the items on the test to compose the first half and employ the rest to represent the second half.

The reliability coefficients that are produced by correlating the two scores of the two halves of the test must be corrected, however, before they are interpreted. This is because we have the reliability for only half of the test. For example, if we administered half of the items at Time 1 and the other half at Time 2, we would presume that we had a 10-item test at each time, but we have a 20-item test.

CRONBACH'S ALPHA RELIABILITY

The scalar reliability test most commonly used by social scientists is the single administration reliability, and the most consistently reported reliability test in the social sciences, including communication, is the **Cronbach alpha reliability** test (Cronbach, 1951). Because of Cronbach's alpha popularity, we will discuss how to determine and report a scale's Cronbach alpha in a research project.

For this analysis, we will use the Generalized Attitude Measure data gathered for this book. As we saw in Figure 8.1, the Generalized Attitude Measure has six oppositely worded items with a seven-step scale between the two adjectives. To determine the alpha reliability, all of the items must be recoded so that all of the positively worded items with low scores (*good*, *fair*, and *wise*) are scored with a 7 instead of a 1. For example, if a participant circled "2" on the first row (*Good*), that number would be reflected as "6." We do this recoding so that all the positive words (*good*, *right*, *beneficial*, *fair*, *wise*, and *positive*) receive high scores of "7" and all negative words (*bad*, *wrong*, *harmful*, *unfair*, *foolish*, and *negative*) receive low scores of "1." You cannot determine the alpha reliability of a scale until this recoding has occurred.

COMPUTER PRINTOUTS OF CRONBACH'S ALPHA Most researchers no longer compute statistics by hand. In fact, computing statistics by hand is dangerous because humans make errors easily when handling large quantities of data. To avoid simple computational mistakes, a variety of computer programs have aided in this process.

The statistical software package most commonly used by communication researchers is the Statistical Package for the Social Sciences (SPSS). If you look on the textbook's website (https://oup-arc.com/wrench), you will find the Book Datasets section. In this folder, you will find folders for SPSS datasets. If you do not have SPSS, you can use the SPSS dataset in JASP, PSPP, or R; the Excel file in Microsoft Excel; the STATA file in STATA; or the Notepad datasets to import the data into whatever program you prefer to use. In this book, we will only discuss how to read and interpret results from SPSS, but video recordings for those other software packages are available on the book's website. (To calculate your own alpha reliability, open the file called Textbook Data Set. The Textbook Data Set contains all of the scales recoded using the coding schemes discussed in Chapter 6.)

We should mention here that we specifically used SPSS 24.0 in the conducting of the statistical tests in this book. We mention this because earlier or later versions of the software may display more or less information in similar or different ways. Although the steps in conducting the tests will be the same for various versions of the software packages, often the display gets altered. For this reason, if you are using an earlier version (or later version) of either SPSS, you may want to consult the software guide that accompanied the software package. Mostly, these changes are minor, but for students new to dealing with statistical software packages the changes may be confusing.

SPSS AND CRONBACH'S ALPHA After opening SPSS, a window will pop up called SPSS for Windows. In this window, the Open an Existing Data Source button is preselected, so you can either scroll through a list of previously used data files or select More Files to find the data file you are attempting to open. Once you have selected either the correct data file or the More Files option, click OK. If you chose More Files before you clicked OK in the previous box, the Open File window will appear on your screen. At this point, you just need to search your computer's hard drive to find the data file you are attempting to use. If you do not know how to look for a file on your hard drive or textbook's website, you may want to pick up a simple MS Windows manual at your local bookstore.

If you are looking on the textbook's website, you will find a folder called Book Datasets. You can then select the SPSS Datasets folder. Once you are inside the SPSS Datasets folder, you will find a number of different SPSS files that are designed to be used with your textbook. The file marked Textbook Data Set is the file with the data that has already been recoded for your convenience, so the data can be easily manipulated in SPSS. To save the file to your hard drive, right click on the file hyperlink, choose "Save As," and then save the file to your hard drive in a desired location, or just run the dataset from the textbook's website. When you finally open the file you want to work with, your computer will import the data into the SPSS window.

If you encounter a problem opening the data file, go back to the beginning and repeat the steps or consult your computer's owner's manual for further instructions.

To determine Cronbach's alpha, click on the drop-down menu under the word "Analyze" (Figure 8.4). Then, scroll over the word "Scale." When you scroll over Scale, a menu will pop out to the left. Click on Reliability Analysis (Figure 8.5), and a window with that same name will open (Figure 8.6a). If you did not get this window, backtrack and try to find out what went wrong. In the Reliability Analysis window are three major scroll- or drop-down boxes. On the upper left, you will find a scrolling box with all the variables in the dataset, and on the right, you will see a scrolling box with nothing in it labeled Items. Underneath the box with all of your variables is a drop-down box with different types of reliability formats. The screen comes up with Cronbach's alpha reliability preselected for use (Figure 8.6b). To run Cronbach's alpha, simply highlight the scale items that you want to analyze. To run a Cronbach alpha reliability test for the attitude scale specifically, you must scroll down the list of variables until you find the ones listed as att1 to att6. Depending on which version of SPSS you are using, att1 may come up as "Attitude about Higher Education" in the variable list. To highlight more items than can be seen at one time, click the first item and hold the Shift

FIGURE 8.4
SPSS Textbook Data Set Image

| Analyze | Direct Marketing | Graphs | Utilities | Add-ons | Window | Help |

Reports	▶
Descriptive Statistics	▶
Tables	▶
Compare Means	▶
General Linear Model	▶
Generalized Linear Models	▶
Mixed Models	▶
Correlate	▶
Regression	▶
Loglinear	▶
Neural Networks	▶
Classify	▶
Dimension Reduction	▶
Scale	▶
Nonparametric Tests	▶
Forecasting	▶
Survival	▶
Multiple Response	▶
Missing Value Analysis...	
Multiple Imputation	▶
Complex Samples	▶
Quality Control	▶
ROC Curve...	
IBM SPSS Amos...	

prca4	prca5	prca6	prca7
4.00	2.00	3.00	3.00
2.00	4.00	5.00	5.00
3.00	4.00	3.00	4.00
2.00	4.00	2.00	1.00
2.00	3.00	3.00	3.00
5.00	5.00	5.00	5.00
2.00	2.00	1.00	2.00
3.00	2.00	2.00	2.00
3.00	2.00	2.00	2.00
5.00	5.00	5.00	5.00

Reliability Analysis...
Multidimensional Unfolding (PREFSCAL)...
Multidimensional Scaling (PROXSCAL)...
Multidimensional Scaling (ALSCAL)...

1.00	1.00	1.00	1.00
1.00	1.00	1.00	1.00
1.00	2.00	2.00	3.00
4.00	3.00	3.00	3.00
3.00	3.00	2.00	3.00
4.00	1.00	4.00	3.00
3.00	3.00		
3.00	4.00	3.00	4.00

FIGURE 8.5
Reliability
Analysis Menu

button on your keyboard. Then, scroll down to the last item and (still holding your Shift button) click the last item, which will allow you to highlight all six attitude items (Figure 8.6c). Now, simply send the six items to the Items box by clicking the arrow in between the two boxes. If this has been done correctly, you will now see all six attitude variables in the box on the right side of the screen (Figure 8.6d). At this point, you can do one of two things: click OK and get a simple printout of reliability (Figure 8.7), or click on the Statistics button at the bottom of the screen. We will click on the Statistics button.

When you click on the Statistics button in the Reliability Analysis window, the Reliability Analysis: Statistics window will appear (Figure 8.6e). Here, you will see many different types of tests that can be conducted. Most of these qualify as advanced statistical tests, so we will not explain what they mean in this book. However, in the upper left corner, you will find the "Descriptives for" box. These statistics give basic information about each item, the overall reliability of the scale, and the reliability of the scale if we deleted one item. Once you have selected these three options (Figure 8.6f), simply hit the Continue button. Once you have finished with the Reliability Analysis: Statistics window, you will be taken back to the Reliability Analysis window. You are now ready to run your Cronbach's alpha reliability test, so simply hit OK on the right side of the window. You will be given two different sets of information: the same reliability information that was given to you in Figure 8.7 plus the information you asked for about the descriptive statistics for the scale and the alpha reliability if the scale is deleted (Figure 8.8).

In Figure 8.7, you will find two boxes. The first is the Case Process Summary box, which tells you how many participants have scores for the Generalized Attitude Measure that were used in calculating Cronbach's alpha ($N = 625$). The second box is the box with the reported reliability, 0.909, and the number of scale items ($N = 6$) that were used in the calculation of the reliability.

In Figure 8.8, you are also presented with three boxes: Item Statistics, Item-Total Statistics, and Scale Statistics. The Item Statistics box presents you with the basic descriptive statistics (mean, standard deviation, and number of participants) for each individual scale item. The Item-Total Statistics box enables you to see what would happen to the overall scale if a single item was left out of the scale. The most important column in this box, for this discussion, is the last column (Cronbach's Alpha if Item Deleted), which lets us see whether our alpha reliability can be helped if we drop an item from the scale. For example, if we dropped the first item from the scale, which would be the *good/bad* item, the alpha reliability would drop to 0.895, which is below the overall scale reliability of 0.909. In the world of reliability, the higher the reliability (the closer

FIGURE 8.6A
Reliability Analysis Dialogue Box – Opened Window

FIGURE 8.6B
Reliability Analysis Dialogue Box – Arrow Pointing at Alpha

FIGURE 8.6C
Reliability Analysis Dialogue Box – Arrow Pointing
toward Arrow

FIGURE 8.6D
Reliability Analysis Dialogue Box – Statistics Button

FIGURE 8.6E
Reliability Analysis Dialogue Box – Reliability
Analysis Statistics Window

FIGURE 8.6F
Reliability Analysis Dialogue Box – Select Items,
Scale, and Scale if Item Deleted

FIGURE 8.7
SPSS Cronbach's
Alpha Reliability

Scale: ALL VARIABLES

Case Processing Summary		N	%
Cases	Valid	625	95.6
	Excluded[a]	29	4.4
	Total	654	100.0

[a] Listwise deletion based on all variables in the procedure.

Reliability Statistics	
Cronbach's Alpha	N of Items
.909	6

FIGURE 8.8
SPSS Cronbach's Alpha
Reliability–Other
Statistics

Item Statistics

	Mean	Std. Deviation	N
Attitude about "Higher Education"	6.2144	1.25401	625
att2	5.9952	1.29036	625
att3	6.1104	1.31155	625
att4	5.4128	1.51779	625
att5	5.9296	1.38496	625
att6	6.0672	1.27298	625

Item-Total Statistics

	Scale Mean if Item Deleted	Scale Variance if Item Deleted	Corrected Item-Total Correlation	Cronbach's Alpha if Item Deleted
Attitude about "Higher Education"	29.5152	32.494	.733	.895
att2	29.7344	31.625	.776	.889
att3	29.6192	31.428	.775	.889
att4	30.3168	31.611	.623	.914
att5	30.3408	30.606	.785	.887
att6	29.6624	31.224	.823	.883

Scale Statistics

Mean	Variance	Std. Deviation	N of Items
35.7296	44.547	6.67435	6

Interpreting Reliability

0.90 +	Excellent
0.80–0.90	Good
0.70–0.80	Respectable
0.65–0.70	Minimally acceptable
0.60–0.65	Undesirable
0.60	Unacceptable

your score is to 1), the more consistent your participants have been when filling out the scale. So, when examining Figure 8.8, are there any items that, if we dropped them from the scale, would increase our overall reliability? The answer is yes. If you look in the Cronbach's Alpha if Item Deleted column next to Item 4, you will see that the overall reliability of the scale would increase from 0.909 (overall reliability with six items) to 0.914 (with item 4 dropped from the scale). Overall, the slight bump up in reliability is not going to be that meaningful, so the item should be kept. Often, however, you will find that if you drop one item you will get a significant bump in your reliability (e.g., 0.65 to 0.89), so dropping an item from a scale can often be necessary.

APA Discussion

In American Psychological Association (APA) style, a write-up of the Generalized Attitude Measure, including information on its reliability, might be as follows:

> The Generalized Attitude Measure is a scale originally created by McCroskey (1966) and later validated by McCroskey (2006) as a tool for determining someone's overall attitude about a specific subject. The Generalized Attitude Measure is measured using a six-item, semantic differential scale with seven steps, which gives the scale a range from 6 to 42. For this study, the Generalized Attitude Measure was utilized to determine the attitude of participants about higher education. The scale is coded so that higher scores represent more positive attitudes about higher education. The alpha reliability found for the Generalized Attitude Measure in the current study was 0.91 (M = 35.73, SD = 6.67).

The first part of the APA write-up is a simple description of the scale itself. In this case, the scale was originally created by McCroskey in 1966 as part of his dissertation but then later validated and used in more research by McCroskey (2006). The second part of the APA write-up clearly explains what kind of scale is being used. In this case, the scale consists of six bipolar items with a seven-step scale between the adjectives (1, 2, 3, 4, 5, 6, 7). The next part of the write-up explains to the reader that higher scores represent more positive attitudes about higher education. This step is often skipped by researchers, which can end up leading to results that are extremely confusing to interpret. Finally, the scale's reliability is presented to the reader. Immediately after the reliability is presented, the mean (*M*) and standard deviation (*SD*) are presented as well. (Note that "*M*" and "*SD*" are italicized, but the equal signs and numbers are not.)

Alpha Reliabilities from This Book

Now that we have looked at the reporting of the attitude scale used in the creation of the dataset for this book, you might be wondering what all of the reliabilities are for the various scales. Figure 8.9 has all the alpha reliability information for every scale used in the creation of the dataset that accompanies this book, along with the means and standard deviations. Figure 8.10 presents the corresponding APA write-ups for each scale.

FIGURE 8.9
Reliabilities for Book Dataset Variables

Variable	Alpha Reliability	Mean	Standard Deviation
Communication Apprehension			
Group CA	.87	15.04	5.04
Meeting CA	.87	15.56	4.99
Interpersonal CA	.85	14.42	4.53
Public CA	.87	18.61	5.72
Total CA	.94	63.66	17.00
Ethnocentrism	.89	31.74	9.10
Humor Assessment	.91	63.24	9.53
Nonverbal Immediacy Scale – Self Report	.90	96.52	13.35
Sociocommunicative Orientation			
Assertiveness	.83	35.33	6.31
Responsiveness	.90	40.33	6.28
Willingness to Communicate			
Contexts			
Group WTC	.52	73.49	17.36
Meeting WTC	.68	65.34	21.60
Interpersonal WTC	.68	73.33	17.12
Public WTC	.48	65.01	20.91
Audience			
Stranger WTC	.85	45.76	25.63
Acquaintance WTC	.78	74.59	20.00
Friend WTC	.68	87.58	14.01
Overall WTC	.87	68.95	15.71
Belief That Every College Student Should Take Public Speaking	.96	23.38	9.20
Attitude Toward Higher Education	.91	35.73	6.67

FIGURE 8.10
APA Write-Ups
for Reliabilities

PRCA-24. The Personal Report of Communication Apprehension-24 was created by McCroskey (1982) to measure an individual's level of fear or anxiety associated with either real or anticipated communication with another person or persons. The scale consists of 24 Likert items ranging from (1) *strongly agree* to (5) *strongly disagree*. This scale has a range from 24 to 120 with higher scores indicating stronger levels of anxiety associated with communication. The alpha reliability found for the PRCA-24 in the current study was .94 ($M = 63.66$, $SD = 17.00$).

Ethnocentrism. The Ethnocentrism Scale was created by Neuliep and McCroskey (1997) to measure an individual's tendency to feel that her or his culture is the center of the universe. The revised version of the scale employed here (Neuliep & McCroskey, 2000; McCroskey, 2001) consists of 22 Likert items ranging from (1) *strongly disagree* to (5) *strongly agree*. Fifteen of the items are scored; the remaining items are used as distracters. This scale has a range from 15 to 75 with higher scores indicating stronger ethnocentric attitudes. The alpha reliability found for the Ethnocentrism scale in the current study was .89 ($M = 31.74$, $SD = 9.10$).

Humor Assessment. The Humor Assessment instrument was created by Wrench and Richmond (2004) to measure an individual's use of humor as a communicative device in interpersonal relationships. The scale was originally published in Richmond, Wrench, & Gorham (2001) as a tool for teachers to assess their own use of humor in the classroom. The HA was then validated by Wrench and McCroskey (2001), who found that it functioned distinctly differently from M. Booth-Butterfield and S. Booth-Butterfield's (1991) Humor Orientation scale. The HA consists of 16 Likert-type items ranging from (1) *strongly disagree* to (5) *strongly agree*. This scale has a range from 16 to 80 with higher scores indicating higher usage of humor as a communicative tactic. The alpha reliability found for the HA in the current study was .91 ($M = 63.25$, $SD = 9.53$).

Nonverbal Immediacy Scale. The Nonverbal Immediacy Scale was created by Richmond, McCroskey, & Johnson (2003) to measure a receiver's perceived nonverbal immediacy between her or himself and a source. The scale consists of 26 Likert type items ranging from (1) *strongly disagree* to (5) *strongly agree*. This scale has a range from 26 to 130 with higher scores indicating stronger degrees of nonverbal immediacy. The alpha reliability found for the Nonverbal Immediacy Scale in the current study was .90 ($M = 96.52$, $SD = 13.35$).

Sociocommunicative orientation. The Sociocommunicative Orientation scale was created by Richmond and McCroskey (1985) as an instructional tool to examine the extent to which individuals use assertive or responsive communication. The instrument was first utilized in research by Thompson, Ishii, and Klopf (1990) and Ishii, Thompson, and Klopf (1990) to examine cultural differences in assertive and responsive communication. After the publication of these two articles, Richmond and McCroskey (1990) demonstrated the reliability and dimensionality of the measure itself. The sociocommunicative orientation scale consists of 10 items on each factor for a total of 20 items. Participants are asked to respond to short descriptive phrases that range from one to five words in length that indicate ways in which they may communicate. The measure asks a participant to respond in terms of how well the item applies to her or him using a Likert scale from (1) *strongly disagree that it applies* to (5) *strongly agree that it applies*. Each subscale has a range from 10 to 50. The alpha reliability found for assertiveness in the current study was .83 ($M = 35.33$, $SD = 6.31$),

Continued

FIGURE 8.10
Continued

and the alpha reliability for responsiveness was .90 ($M = 40.33$, $SD = 6.28$). Higher scores for each subscale represent higher levels of that concept.

Willingness to Communicate. The Willingness to Communicate instrument was devised by McCroskey (1992) to measures a person's willingness to initiate communication with another person or persons. The scale consists of 20 items. Each of the items is designed to measure whether an individual would initiate communication in a specific situation or with a specific individual. Eight of the items are fillers and twelve are scored as part of the scale. Using a 101 point range from 0 (never) to 100 (always), participants are asked to indicate the percentage of time they would choose to communicate in each type of situation. Ultimately, the scores on the twelve items are added together to create a composite score with higher scores indicating a higher willingness to communicate. The alpha reliability found for Willingness to Communicate Scale in the current study was .91 ($M = 68.95$, $SD = 15.71$).

Generalized Belief Scale. The Generalized Belief Scale was created by McCroskey (1966) and validated by McCroskey & Richmond (1996). The Generalized Belief Measure was created by McCroskey (1966) as a way to measure beliefs about specific concepts. By attaining an individual's general belief about a given topic, the researcher can measure the degree to which an individual believes in a given statement. The statement measured in this study was "Everyone Should be Required to take Public Speaking in College." The belief statement is then measured using a five-item semantic differential scale with seven steps, which gives the scale a range from 5 to 35. The scale is coded so that higher scores represent stronger beliefs. The alpha reliability found for Generalized Belief Scale in the current study was .96 ($M = 23.38$, $SD = 9.20$).

Generalized Attitude Measure. The Generalized Attitude Measure was a scale originally created by McCroskey (1966) and later validated by McCroskey and Richmond (1989) as a tool for determining someone's overall attitude about a specific subject. The Generalized Attitude Measure is measured using a six item semantic differential scale with seven steps, which gives the scale a range from 6 to 42. For the purposes of this study, the Generalized Attitude Measure was utilized to determine the attitude of participants about higher education. The scale is coded so that higher scores represent more positive attitudes about higher education. The alpha reliability found for Generalized Attitude Scale in the current study was .91 ($M = 35.73$, $SD = 6.67$).

Alpha Reliabilities in the Real World

To help you further understand how research actually happens, the textbook's website has a number of different research articles on it that were originally published in *Communication Research Reports* and *Communication Quarterly*. Figure 8.11 contains the alpha reliabilities for every scale used in any of the articles on the textbook's website.

You will note that not all of the reported reliabilities are either good (0.80–0.90) or excellent (0.90+). In fact, if you look at the Chesebro (1999) article reliability results, the listening style scale clearly has a reliability problem. On this scale, the content factor is below 0.60, so it is unacceptable; people and action are between 0.60 and 0.65, so they are undesirable; and time is 0.66, which is minimally acceptable. In essence, people are not consistent when filling out this scale, so the scale clearly has some problems and is not reliable.

Improving Reliability of Measurement

We measure things because we want to know what they "are." And reliability is crucial to our measurement. If we measure something on several occasions and get nowhere near the same score, there are only two conclusions that we may draw: either the thing

Scale tested	Alpha reliabilities
McCroskey, Richmond, Johnson, & Smith (2004)	
Study #1 (Organizational Orientations Scale)	
Ambivalent	.91
Indifferent	.79
Upward Mobile	.66
Study #2 (Initial Validation)	
Job Satisfaction	.97
Personal Report of Communication Apprehension–24	.95
Self Report of Immediacy Behaviors	.84
Assertiveness	.86
Responsiveness	.88
Study #3 (Measurement Improvement)	
Upward Mobile	.84
Ambivalent	.89
Indifferent	.79
Study #4 (Etiology and Outcomes)	
Organizational Orientations	
Upward Mobile	.85
Ambivalent	.88
Indifferent	.80
Job Satisfaction	.96
Source Credibility	
Competence	.89
Caring/Goodwill	.94
Trustworthiness	.93
Eysenck's Big Three	
Extraversion	.78
Neuroticism	.82
Psychoticism	.65
Thomas, Richmond, & McCroskey (1994)	
Perceived Nonverbal Immediacy Behavior Scale	.83
Assertiveness	.90
Responsiveness	.91

FIGURE 8.11
Article Alpha
Reliabilities

Continued

FIGURE 8.11
Continued

Scale tested	Alpha reliabilities
Wrench & Richmond (2004)	
Humor Assessment	.95
Student Affective Learning	
Teacher Evaluation	.87
Affective Learning	.81
Nonverbal Immediacy Measure	.81
Student Motivation	.89
Teacher Credibility	
Competence	.80
Trustworthiness	.86
Caring/Goodwill	.86
Weber, Fornash, Corrigan, & Neupauer (2003)	
7-Item Multiple Choice Quiz	.73
Learner Empowerment Scale	
Impact	.71
Competence	.85
Meaningfulness	.85
Nonverbal Immediacy Scale	Not reported
Cheseboro (1999)	
Listening Style	
People	.61
Action	.61
Time	.66
Content	.54
Conversational Sensitivity	.85
Punyanunt (2000)	
Behavior Alteration Techniques	.92
Effectiveness of Humor	.94
Uses of Humor	.95
Wrench & Booth-Butterfield (2003)	
Humor Orientation	.91
Source Credibility	
Competence	.86
Trustworthiness	.90
Caring/Goodwill	.88
Compliance Gaining Questionnaire	
Expectancies/Consequences	.69
Relationship/Identification	.82
Values/Obligations	.74
Patient Satisfaction	
Cognitive	.89
Affective	.92
Behavioral	.85
Rocca & Vogl-Bauer (1999)	
Verbal Aggression Scale	.81
Sports Spectator Identification Scale	.93
Sports Identification Behavior Scale	
Fan Display	.78
Verbal Response	.93
Violent Response	.85

we are measuring is constantly changing or our measuring instrument is worthless. Presuming that we are attempting to measure a reasonably stable characteristic, the latter conclusion is probably the more appropriate.

Because there are excellent methods of estimating the reliability of our measuring instruments, and because there are ways of improving instruments that lack reliability, there is no excuse for the social scientist to employ measures that lack adequate reliability. Let's consider a few of the ways in which reliability may be increased:

1. *Item construction.* Nothing contributes more to unreliability in a measuring instrument than bad items. If an item is ambiguous, it will produce variable responses both among people and with the same person on different occasions. We suggest that the best way to improve reliability is to improve your items using the suggestions for scale item writing from the previous chapter.

2. *Length of the instrument.* Reliability is directly associated with the number of items included in the measuring instrument. Other things being equal, a 20-item test will be more reliable than a 10-item test. If everything possible has been done to improve the quality of individual items and the reliability is still somewhat below the level desired, creating more items of the same type should increase the reliability of the instrument. Obviously, limitations normally are imposed on the length that an instrument may be. Extreme increases in the length of the instrument may actually increase unreliability because subjects may become fatigued and merely record responses at random.

3. *Administration of the test.* Measures should always be administered under standard, well-controlled conditions. If the instructions that are given to the subjects are ambiguous, the subjects may interpret how they are supposed to respond differently and thus contribute to unreliability. Similarly, if the psychological conditions surrounding the subjects differ, this may influence the way the subjects respond. For example, one group of subjects may be in a friendly environment and do their best to record accurate responses, whereas another group may take a dislike to the person administering the instrument and give random responses. In such cases, the reliability of the instrument will be estimated at much below what the actual reliability of the instrument could be.

VALIDITY

In the first part of this chapter, we introduced the concept of reliability; in the latter part of this chapter, we will discuss another extremely important concept in measurement, validity.

Validity is the degree to which the instrument measures what it is intended to measure. For example, would you look at a clock and say, "It's 50 degrees outside"? Of course not, because a clock measures time, not temperature. If you want to know how hot it is outside, you look at a thermometer. And in social scientific research, we must be equally concerned with whether our measuring instruments actually measure what they are intended to measure. Let's look at a Likert-type item (1 = *strongly disagree* to 5 = *strongly agree*): "Children should be seen and not heard." Would you expect to see this item on a scale intended to measure happiness? Of course not. However, this item could be on a scale designed to measure people's traditional views of children.

When researchers talk about a scale's validity, we are discussing whether a created scale actually measures what we say we are measuring. Now that we have explained the general concept of validity, let's look at some examples of validity issues in communication research. First, a communication researcher is in the process of creating a new measure to examine individuals who experience apprehension during social settings. Because she wants to assess the efficacy of

Reliability and Validity

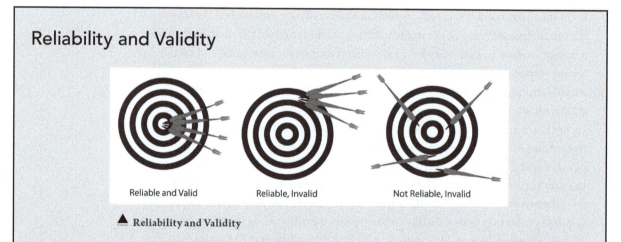

Reliable and Valid   Reliable, Invalid   Not Reliable, Invalid

▲ **Reliability and Validity**

The terms "reliability" and "validity" can be a bit confusing. To gain some clarity on this, think of an archery tournament. Let's say that hitting the bullseye is the equivalent of accurately measuring a hypothetical concept. If the archer is reliable, then all four arrows will clump together. If the archer is valid, then the archer will hit the bullseye. In the first image above, the archer's arrows all hit the same place on the target (reliable), and all the archer's arrows are right in the bullseye (valid). In the second image, the archer shoots four arrows, and they all clump together on the outside ring of the bullseye target. The archer still reliably shot her arrows but did not hit the bullseye. So this second archer was reliable, but not valid. Lastly, the archer shoots another four arrows, and they are all over the target. Here, the archer is neither reliable nor valid.

helping people who experience this form of communication apprehension (CA), she creates a physiological tool that can measure blood pressure, heart rate, and galvanic skin responses. She then takes to a bar and grill some participants whom she knows experience CA and some people who do not. If her new device is valid, the participants who are most afraid of communicating in social settings should register the highest ratings (increased blood pressure, heart rates, and galvanic skin responses) on her new device.

Another researcher is in the process of creating a new test for measuring non-verbal responses during greetings. Rather than creating a survey and asking participants how they interact with people when greeting them, he develops an observational checklist for measuring greeting behaviors. He believes that greeting behaviors will be distinctly more intimate depending on the length of time that people have known each other. He then trains a few coders to use the checklist and brings pairs of people (strangers, acquaintances, friends, family members, and romantic partners) into a lab. After separating the pairs for an hour, he brings the two people back together in a room with a one-way mirror, and the coders watch how the two people interact when they see each other again using the newly design observational checklist.

A third research team, Sandy and William, are in the process of trying to create a new scale to examine different forms of communicative humor in the classroom. Based on research by Wanzer and Frymier (1999), Sandy and William know that students perceive humor as either appropriate or inappropriate. Wanzer and Frymier designated appropriate classroom humor as content-related humor, humor not related to content, impersonation, nonverbal behaviors, disparaging humor, humorous props, sarcasm, and unintentional humor; inappropriate classroom humor was designated as humor that makes fun of a student, humor-based stereotypes, failed humor, sexual humor, irrelevant humor, sarcasm, swearing, joking about serious issues, personal humor (inside jokes), and sick humor. Sandy and William use this typology of humor behaviors from Wanzer and Frymier to create a new scale in order to measure appropriate and inappropriate classroom humor. Then, distribute the scales to a large group of undergraduates, asking them to rate a professor in whose classroom the students had been that day or the day before.

The question that you may be asking by this point is "How good will these new measures be?" Are they accurate measures for examining anxiety, nonverbal greetings, and classroom humor? What if the anxiety measure ends up measuring sexual attraction or drinking behavior, which a bar setting has in abundance? Maybe the greeting checklist is incomplete and only has a handful of behaviors on it, like handshaking, hugging, and kissing, which are predominant greeting patterns in the United States, but does not include greeting patterns between people from other cultures. Maybe the new classroom humor scale ends up measuring quantity of humor used and not appropriate versus inappropriate humor in the classroom setting. How can we determine whether a new measure employed in research is actually measuring what it alleges to be measuring? Social scientists have been examining these types of questions for years and have devised a number of strategies for combating these problems. And these questions all concern what researchers call a measure's validity.

As important as reliability is to measurement, validity is just as important. Again, validity may be defined simply as the degree to which the measuring instrument measures what it is intended to measure. If we wish to measure the number of apples produced in a county, it will do us no good whatsoever to count the number of oranges produced in that county. Similarly, if we want to know a person's attitude toward rap music, it will probably do us little good to ask him questions about his relationship with his mother.

There are three primary approaches to validity: face or content validity, criterion validity, and construct validity. Let's consider each one of these in turn.

Face or Content Validity

Face or content validity does not involve correlation coefficients. Rather, it is a subjective type of validity criterion. The researcher, or someone he or she employs for the task, examines the content of the measuring instrument to see whether on its "face" it appears related to what the researcher wishes to measure. Whether the items on the measure are reasonably representative of the universe of possible items that could be included is also examined.

Unfortunately, because of its inherently subjective nature, face or content validity is the validity approach most commonly employed by researchers. In some circumstances this is not as serious a drawback as in others. As long as the measure is susceptible to influence as a result of the message manipulations, the instrument is "valid" for the researcher's purposes. However, when the social scientist is concerned with predicting behaviors, there is no true test of validity except how well it predicts those behaviors.

Criterion Validity

Criterion validity is concerned with how accurately a new measure can predict a well-accepted criterion or previously validated concept. For example, if we wanted to test a newly developed anxiety tool, we could have people fill out the Personal Report of Communication Apprehension–24 (PRCA-24) and then give a speech. People who register the highest on our new anxiety tool should also have higher scores on the PRCA-24. To determine whether the anxiety tool corresponds with scores on the PRCA-24, we calculate the correlation between the two measures, and the end result would be a correlation coefficient. This coefficient estimates the degree to which a measuring instrument will predict a value on some outside criterion. That criterion might be the behavior of the person whose attitude was measured, or it might be some other measure of attitude. If our theory suggests that a high attitude score should be accompanied by a given behavior, a moderate score less associated with that behavior, and a low score not associated with that behavior, then we can determine a correlation coefficient between the attitude score obtained by subjects on our instrument and their subsequent behaviors. That correlation coefficient is referred to as a validity coefficient, and if it is reasonably high, we may suggest that our measure is a valid one. By contrast, if there is no or low correlation, then we have an indication that our instrument is invalid for making this kind of prediction.

Few attitude-measuring instruments are actually submitted to the test of predictive validity. This is because, in most cases, we are not interested in predicting a specific behavior. If the scores are highly correlated, we have an indication that one is, to the degree of the correlation, as valid as the other.

There are three subtypes of criterion validity that we should discuss briefly: predictive or prospective, concurrent, and retrospective.

PREDICTIVE OR PROSPECTIVE VALIDITY

Predictive or prospective validity is a subset of criterion validity that concerns whether a person's score on a new measure can be used to predict future scores on another measure. For example, maybe we have 10 teachers, all teaching the same class and using the same textbook, syllabus, and tests. We measure students' perceptions of teachers' use of appropriate and inappropriate humor utilizing our new measure. Previous research has shown that the use of humor in the classroom can lead to higher levels of learning. If our new tool is truly measuring the use of appropriate and inappropriate humor in the classroom, we could predict that teachers who use the most appropriate humor and the least amounts of inappropriate humor should have students who perform better on the final examination. We are using our newly created scale to predict scores on a future scale.

CONCURRENT VALIDITY

An alternative to predictive validity is to examine a measure's concurrent validity. In **concurrent validity**, a researcher obtains the score for the new measure and the score for the criterion measure at the same point, and then he or she determines how strongly the two scores correlate. For example, if we are testing our new apprehension-measuring tool, we could have people fill out the State Communication Apprehension Measure, a previously validated scale for examining state levels of communication apprehension, while wearing the new apprehension-measuring tool in a social setting. If our new apprehension-measuring tool is an accurate measure, it should strongly relate to an individual's score on the State Communication Apprehension Measure.

RETROSPECTIVE VALIDITY

The last way to examine criterion validity is to examine a newly developed scale's **retrospective or postdictive validity**. Retrospective validity occurs when a researcher has previously measured the criterion and then attempts to relate it to a newly developed measure at a later point. Maybe a researcher wants to determine whether a person's level of CA as a child correlates with her or his level of CA as an adult, so the researcher looks through old report cards for incidents of "doesn't talk," "is very shy," or "is very quiet" in the report card notes. The researcher then quantifies these messages to correlate them with an adult measure of CA.

Construct Validity

An important property of all hypothetical constructs is that they are a result of theoretical development. Chapter 7 discussed the development of theoretical constructs, and **construct validity** therefore is a validity test of the theoretical construct itself. There are three common ways of measuring construct validity: relying on theory, measuring known groups, and factorial validity.

RELYING ON THEORY

If we theorize, for example, that people with highly intense attitudes are less subject to influence by a persuader than are people with moderately intense attitudes, we must develop an attitude measure that taps the intensity dimension. We may then conduct an experiment in which we administer a persuasive treatment to subjects with an intense attitude and to subjects with only a moderately intense attitude. If the predicted difference in the amount of attitude change is observed on our measure, we not only have confirmed our theory, but also have an indication that our measuring instrument validly taps the intensity dimension. The difficulty with this approach to validity is that if our predicted effects are not obtained, we do not know whether it is because of our faulty theory or because our instrument is invalid.

MEASURING KNOWN GROUPS

Another approach to construct validity that is less susceptible to the confounding with theory is the measurement of known groups. If we are trying to develop an instrument to measure ethnic intolerance, we may administer that measure to members of the Ku Klux Klan (a group known for intolerance) and members of B'nai B'rith (a Jewish organization that fights anti-Semitism, racism, and bigotry while striving for human rights and peace throughout the world). If our measure is reasonably valid, we should observe large differences in the scores between these two groups, unless the former group was much more tolerant or the latter group much less tolerant than is customarily presumed.

FACTORIAL VALIDITY

A third approach to construct validity that deserves a category to itself is factorial validity, which is based on the statistical technique known as factor analysis. Factor analysis is a highly sophisticated statistical technique for examining a series of items to see which items correlate well with one another but are not highly correlated with other items or groups of items. Simply put, factor analysis can tell us how many groups of items, or factors, there are in our instrument.

This approach to validity was employed by McCroskey (1966) in the development of measuring instruments to tap source credibility (as discussed in Chapter 7 in the section called "One Measure, Multiple Factors."). At the outset, McCroskey presumed that this attitude was like other attitudes—that is, unidimensional. He therefore developed a set of items to measure this attitude. However, when he subjected these items to factor analysis, he found that there were two dimensions to this attitude rather than one. More simply put, he thought he was measuring "apples," but he found he was measuring "Granny Smith apples" and "Red Delicious apples." In essence, there were two parts (competence and trustworthiness) that created participants' perceptions of credibility, just like Granny Smith and Red Delicious are two different types of apples. As a result, he was forced to develop two separate measures in order to measure these two new constructs.

The only serious problem with the approach to validity through factor analysis is that it is a strictly negative approach. That is, factor analysis can tell someone that she is not measuring her construct, but cannot tell her that she is at least independent of other considerations.

Which Approach to Use?

Many social scientists are concerned with which approach to validity they should employ in the development of measuring instruments. The answer to this is simple. Do not choose among the approaches to validity. Rather, we should employ all of the approaches to validity that can be employed in the given case. If any one of the approaches indicates that the instrument is invalid, this is sufficient ground for substantial revision in the instrument that has been developed.

Nonverbal Immediacy Reliability and Validity

Richmond, McCroskey, and Johnson (2003) worked with the Nonverbal Immediacy Scale to improve its reliability and validity. Since nonverbal immediacy as a concept and measure had been around for over 30 years, Richmond et al. determined that the 14-item scale did not have high enough reliability and validity to continue using it. Thus, Richmond et al. revised the original measure from 30 years ago and then conducted the 2003 study finding that the reliability and validity of the Nonverbal Immediacy Scale was substantially improved. This is an example of how even older measures that are commonly used can be reexamined and updated to ensure and/or strenthen a measure's reliability and/or validity.

Validity Threats

A number of problems can occur when one is attempting to determine whether a newly developed measure is valid. In this section, we examine seven categories of threats to a newly developed measure's validity.

INADEQUATE PREOPERATIONAL EXPLICATION OF CONCEPTS

The first threat to a new measure's validity occurs when an individual really has not determined what a scale was supposed to measure in the first place. For example, if a researcher wants to create a scale about humor but includes questions about CA, the scale is going to have validity problems. Would you use a wristwatch to tell you how hot it is outside? Too often, researchers write countless numbers of scale items and then throw them against a statistical wall to see what sticks, which is not a good practice when writing a research scale. The more concrete your purpose is for creating a scale from the onset, the more valid your scale can be in the long run.

MONO-OPERATION BIAS

Another problem affecting the validity of a newly developed measure can occur when you only administer the measure once, which is known as the **mono-operation bias**. If you only measure something once, it is hard to determine whether you are truly measuring the variable you intend to or just a portion of the variable. It is also possible that some form of error will prevent you from accurately testing a newly developed measure's validity the first time you use it, so multiple administrations enable you to get a much clearer picture of your scale's overall validity.

INTERACTION OF DIFFERENT TREATMENTS

In research, we often want to determine whether a newly developed treatment for something is effective. For example, maybe we create a new way to reduce students' levels of public speaking anxiety. But to determine whether our treatment is effective, we must know whether the measure we are using for public speaking anxiety is valid. Unfortunately, intervening variables (see Chapter 6) could prevent you from accurately measuring the effectiveness of your treatment. For example, maybe one of your participants has hired a speech coach, and the individual attention has helped the participant lower her or his level of public speaking anxiety with no change occurring from your treatment. It is also possible that a participant could have a horrible public speaking experience that causes her or his public speaking anxiety to rise despite your treatment. In essence, this threat to validity is whether the results you see are real or whether they are the result of multiple treatments by yourself and others.

INTERACTION OF TESTING AND TREATMENT

Often, the combined effect of being measured multiple times along with receiving a treatment can cause someone to be more aware of the measurement process and alter her or his scores as a result of this awareness and not the treatment itself. When participants are aware of what is going on in an experiment, they can be more sensitive and/or receptive to future measures of a particular variable.

RESTRICTED GENERALIZABILITY ACROSS CONSTRUCTS

Another threat to the validity of a newly developed measure is how restricted that measure is across differing constructs. In the example given at the beginning of this chapter about the newly developed scale for examining appropriate and inappropriate humor in the classroom, is this measure generalizable to elementary school teachers, junior high/middle school teachers, high school teachers, and college professors, or is this tool only useful in the college classroom? It is possible that Wanzer and Frymier's (1999) appropriate and inappropriate categories of humor are only true in the college setting. If so, then the scale could not be applied to lower levels of education, and the results from the newly developed scale found in college classrooms could not be cross-applied to elementary, junior high/middle school, and high school classrooms.

CONFOUNDING CONSTRUCTS AND LEVELS OF CONSTRUCTS

Another problem that can affect the validity of a measure is whether you are measuring a single construct, multiple constructs, or multiple levels of one construct in a given measure. One of the biggest problems with newly developed measures is that they often are measuring more than one construct at a time or multiple levels of the same construct. For example, in the PRCA-24, the overall construct of CA has been found to have four basic subconstructs (or subscales) within it: meeting, group, interpersonal, and public. Statisticians often call subconstructs factors, as discussed earlier in this chapter. Unfortunately, a researcher often does not know which subconstructs or even multiple constructs exist in a set of scale items until he or she has collected the appropriate data to examine the validity of the scale.

SOCIAL THREATS TO VALIDITY

In addition to the threats already mentioned, four social threats also can affect a measure's validity. These are hypothesis guessing, evaluation apprehension, experimenter expectancies and social desirability bias.

The first social validity threat is hypothesis guessing. Participants will guess what a researcher is attempting to measure and then respond to a measure accordingly. When a person guesses your hypothesis (either correctly or incorrectly), it can skew how he or she responds to your survey.

A second social validity threat is evaluation apprehension. Many people experience anxiety when they know they are being evaluated, which can cause them to give responses that they might not have normally.

A third social threat involves experimenter expectancies. Experimenters may unknowingly influence a participant's scores when the experimenter encourages the participant to respond in a specific manner. Experimenters should be trained to avoid influencing a participant's answers and behaviors as much as possible in order to prevent this validity threat.

Finally, social desirability bias can be a threat to a measure's validity. **Social desirability bias** is the term used by researchers for when a participant changes how he or she scores on a measure in order to be perceived in a "better light" than her or his actual scores would reveal. For example, maybe you are asking your participants how often they drink alcohol, and a participant who normally drinks a case a day says that he or she only drinks a couple of beers a week for fear of being perceived as an alcoholic. Although social desirability bias cannot be completely avoided, explaining that responses are confidential or ensuring anonymity should lessen social threats to a measure's validity.

PROBLEMS WITH MEASUREMENT

Now that we have examined some threats to a measurement's validity, let's look at some general problems with measurement as a whole. The two most commonly discussed problems of measurement are reliability and validity, but these are actually parts of one problem. Researchers are only concerned with reliability because of its implications for validity. A measure can be perfectly reliable yet have absolute zero validity for the purpose for which a researcher created it. By contrast, a measure cannot be valid unless it is also reliable.

Coefficients

This idea may be better understood if we think in terms of reliability and validity coefficients for a moment. Presume we have two separate measures and are concerned with the ability of one measure to predict scores on the other measure. Through our research, we obtain a Cronbach alpha reliability coefficient for the first measure of 0.65 (minimally acceptable) and a Cronbach alpha reliability coefficient for the second measure of 0.30 (unacceptable). To obtain the maximum possible validity coefficient for the predictability of one of these measures for the other, we can multiply the two reliability coefficients by each other ($0.30 \times 0.65 = 0.195$). This does not give us the actual validity coefficient; rather, it indicates the *absolute maximum* validity coefficient that we could obtain. Thus, if either of our measures is unreliable, we will have little or no validity.

In the example we have just considered, one measure is minimally acceptable (0.65) and the other is simply unacceptable (0.30). Even if we increase the reliability of our most reliable instrument to the point of perfection, the highest validity coefficient we could obtain would be 0.30. Thus, we should not be overly concerned about the lack of high validity coefficients between our attitude measures and overt behaviors in the real world. This probably does not indicate that our attitude measure in itself is invalid. Rather, the validity is influenced by the extremely unreliable methods we have developed to measure behaviors in the real world.

Measures tend to have two major problems accompanying them: the difficulty in obtaining agreement among observers and the low level of potential measurement, seldom even ordinal, of such behaviors. Thus, even with a perfectly valid measure, we are unlikely to get a high validity coefficient because of the unreliability of our criterion measure. We must be extremely concerned with reliability and the less precise estimates of validity, such as content and construct validity, rather than with predictive validity. For example, it may be that attitudes toward federal finance of education and federal control of education are related to federal assistance to local schools. These two attitudes may not simply add together to produce our behaviors—more likely, they interact. Thus, to predict that particular behavior, we must be able to measure these two attitudes separately. The two procedures most commonly employed to determine whether a measure is tapping more than one variable are factor analysis, as previously discussed, and "scalogram analysis," as described by Guttman (1945).

Basic Measurement Problems

Let's further our explanation of validity problems by looking at three very specific issues that can impact the validity of a measure negatively: faking, response set, and bad measurement items.

FAKING

Faking responses refers to any circumstance in which a respondent to our instrument deliberately attempts to alter the results in some specific way. Whenever faking is present, the validity of our instrument is not.

Faking is actually a broad title for several types of problems: acquiescence, social desirability, and the screw-you effect. These faking behaviors have implications for reliability, but their main impact is on validity. Whenever faking is present, validity is not.

ACQUIESCENCE One type of faking can be referred to as **acquiescence**. The acquiescent individual wishes to cooperate with the investigator and give the researcher what she or he wants. Thus, the respondent tries to determine the kind of response the investigator wishes and then produce it. Another type of acquiescence that is somewhat different is produced by a personality type that says "yes" to anything.

SOCIAL DESIRABILITY A second type of faking is produced by the influence of perception of social desirability. Often, a respondent will not indicate his or her true beliefs, but will indicate beliefs that he or she thinks society accepts. This is particularly a problem when we are attempting to measure socially sensitive attitudes, such as those toward racial intolerance and morality. For example, a woman may indicate that she strongly disapproves of premarital intercourse because society opposes it. Her private behavior, however, may be contrary to this response. This type of faking can be overcome to a considerable extent by ensuring the participant that her or his responses will be anonymous.

SCREW-YOU EFFECT A third type of faking has been referred to by researchers using several colorful terms. For the sake of propriety, we shall refer to it as the "nuts-to-you" response, or as Joseph Masling (1966) described it, the **"screw-you"** effect. This is almost the exact opposite of acquiescence. Rather than attempting to give the researcher what he wants, the individual engaging in "nuts-to-you" behavior may attempt either to give the investigator the exact opposite of what he or she wants or to give a completely random response.

RESPONSE SET

Another problem that affects measurement, unless carefully avoided, is a response set. A **response set** is any tendency that causes a person to give different responses to test items than he or she would if the item had been presented in a different form. Although severely reducing the validity of any instrument, a response set may actually increase the obtained reliability estimate for the instrument. A response set is more often observed when all of the items in an instrument are worked in much the same way. For example, if all of the items are worded positively or negatively, then response set is likely to be present. In such cases, if the subject indicates the fifth response to the first question, he or she is likely to continue to make the fifth response to the rest of the questions. This problem may be overcome by including an equal or nearly equal number of positively and negatively worded items and then arranging the items in random order.

BAD MEASUREMENT ITEMS

The final major problem that affects measurement is also the worst. This is the problem of bad items on the measure. In the development of any measure, some bad items almost certainly will be included, but there is no excuse for them continuing to be included. A technique known as item analysis can be employed to help identify bad items in a group of items. Simply put, item analysis produces a correlation between an individual item and a total score across all items. A bad item will have a negative or a low positive correlation, whereas a good item will tend to have a high positive correlation. The solution to the problem of bad items is simple—identify them, throw them out, and develop good items to replace them.

Within the notable exception of the semantic differential scale as developed by Osgood (1957), almost all techniques developed for attitude measurement employ the use of declarative statements or questions as items. The most important part of attitude scale construction is creating items reflecting both a balanced and a representative set of opinions about the issue at hand. The question of which scaling technique to use is of secondary importance despite the emphasis that differences in these techniques have received in the professional literature over the years. Using essentially the same set of items, researchers have found that the various techniques place individuals at the same locations on attitude scales relative to each other. That is, one can gain little statistically from reliability or validity beyond what is already inherent in item content. A number of elements must be taken into consideration when developing items to reduce sources of spurious response, and these will be considered in another chapter.

RESEARCH OUTSIDE THE WALLS OF ACADEMIA

Many researchers working outside the walls of academia simply forget to think through issues related to measurement reliability and/or validity. We realize that reliability is difficult to calculate and that validity is a complicated subject, but measures that are neither reliable nor valid will lead people to conclusions that simply are not true. If your goal is to conduct research that is useful for an organization, then that research should conform to the basic practices of good measurement.

Imagine you have been asked to conduct a survey of people who call a medical insurance company's help line. After a phone call ends with a customer service representative, customers are redirected to your survey. If you utilize just one Likert question—"What was your level of satisfaction with the customer representative?" (1 = *satisfied*; 5 = *not satisfied*)—you will not be able to tell whether the information being provided is actually a measure of someone's attitude at all because only one item is ordinal data and not useful for inferential purposes. As such, you would need to develop a measure that has enough items on it to help you get a more holistic score of satisfaction to ensure that the new measure is reliable. Next, you would have to figure out whether the measure is valid using the strategies discussed earlier in this chapter.

CONCLUSION

This chapter has focused on how we can be sure that people answer our research scales consistently and how to make sure we are measuring what we say we are measuring. Reliability and validity are extremely important for researchers because if your measures are not reliable and valid, your results are not meaningful. Now that we have discussed the measurement process, reliability, and validity, we will examine how research is conducted using three research techniques—survey, content analysis, and experimental—in the next three chapters.

KEY TERMS

Acquiescence p. 276

Alternate forms reliability p. 252

Concurrent validity p. 269

Construct validity p. 270

Criterion validity p. 268

Cronbach alpha reliability p. 253

Face/content validity p. 268

Faking responses p. 275

Mono-operation bias p. 272

Predictive/prospective validity p. 269

Reliability p. 248

Response set p. 276

Retrospective/postdictive validity p. 270

Screw-you effect p. 276

Social desirability bias p. 274

Split-half reliability p. 252

Test–retest reliability p. 252

Validity p. 266

REFERENCES

Chesebro, J. (1999). The relationship between listening styles and conversational sensitivity. *Communication Research Reports, 16*, 233–238.

Cronbach, L. J. (1951). Coefficient alpha and the internal structure of tests. *Psychometrika, 16*, 297–333.

Guttman, L. (1945). A basis for analyzing test–retest reliability. *Psychometrika, 10*, 255–282.

Masling, J. (1966). Role related behavior of the subject and psychologist and its effects upon psychological data. In D. Levine (Ed.), *Symposium on motivation* (pp. 67–103). Lincoln, NE: University of Nebraska Press.

McCroskey, J. C. (1966). *Experimental studies of the effects of ethos and evidence in persuasive communication.* Unpublished doctoral dissertation. University Park: Pennsylvania State University.

McCroskey, J. C. (2006). Reliability and validity of the Generalized Attitude Measure and Generalized Belief Measure. *Communication Quarterly, 54*, 265–274.

Osgood, C. E. (1957). *The measurement of meaning.* Urbana, IL: University of Illinois Press.

Richmond, V. P., McCroskey, J. C., & Johnson, A. D. (2003). Development of the nonverbal immediacy scale (NIS): Measures of self- and other-perceived nonverbal immediacy. *Communication Quarterly, 51*, 504–517.

Wanzer, M. B., & Frymier, A. B. (1999, April). *Being funny in the classroom: Appropriate and inappropriate humor behaviors.* Paper presented at the Eastern Communication Association's Convention, Charleston, WV.

FURTHER READING

DeVellis, R. F. (2017). *Scale development: Theory and applications* (4th ed.). Los Angeles, CA: Sage.

Dillman, D. A., Smyth, J. D., & Christian, L. M. (2014). *Internet, phone, mail, and mixed-mode surveys: The tailored design method* (4th ed.). Hoboken, NJ: Wiley.

Fowler, F. J., Jr. (1993). *Survey research methods* (2nd ed.) (Applied Social Research Methods Series, Vol. 1). Newbury Park, CA: Sage.

Green, S. B., & Salkind, N. J. (2017). *Using SPSS for Windows and Macintosh: Analyzing and understanding data* (8th ed.). New York, NY: Pearson.

Grimm, L. G., & Yarnold, P. R. (Eds.). (2000). *Reading and understanding more multivariate statistics.* Washington, DC: American Psychological Association.

Singleton, R. A., Jr., & Straits, B. C. (2017). *Approach to social research* (6th ed.). New York, NY: Oxford University Press.

Tabachnick, B. G., & Fidell, L. S. (2013). *Using multivariate statistics* (6th ed.). Boston, MA: Pearson.

9

Survey Research

CHAPTER OBJECTIVES

1. Distinguish among surveys, questionnaires, and interview schedules.

2. Describe Fink's (2006) five steps for conducting a survey.

3. Distinguish among cross-sectional, longitudinal, and accelerated longitudinal survey designs.

4. Distinguish between unit and item nonresponses, and discuss how they affect surveys.

5. Understand the five different ways a researcher can translate a survey from one language to another.

Chances are, by this point in your academic career, you will have participated in some form of survey research. Whether filling out a questionnaire in class or being interviewed about our political opinions by a pollster, we are constantly completing surveys. You cannot even register a recently purchased product these days without filling out a questionnaire. Since the moment James Cattell (1890) started discussing the notion of mental measures and using them to examine college students, the art and science of surveying has become a mainstay of our cultural reality.

SURVEYS, QUESTIONNAIRES, AND INTERVIEW SCHEDULES

Before we can really discuss what a survey is, we first must distinguish among three terms that often prove confusing for people: *survey, questionnaire,* and *interview schedule.*

280

Survey

A **survey** is a social scientific method for gathering quantifiable information about a specific group of people by asking the group members questions about their individual attitudes, values, beliefs, behaviors, knowledge, and perceptions. There are two basic types of survey a researcher may conduct: descriptive and analytical or explanatory.

DESCRIPTIVE SURVEY

First, a researcher may conduct a **descriptive survey**, which is designed to find out how common a phenomenon is within a given group of people. For example, a researcher investigating how widespread communication apprehension (CA) is across the United States would be an example of using a survey to examine a specific phenomenon (CA) within a given group of people (people living in the United States).

"IF AT FIRST YOU DON'T GET THE SURVEY RESULTS YOU WANT ON YOUR FIRST SURVEY, GET MAD AND TEAR IT UP."

ANALYTICAL OR EXPLANATORY SURVEY

The second type of survey is an **analytical or explanatory survey**. The purpose of analytical surveys is "to explain why people think or act as they do by identifying likely causal influences on their attitudes and behavior" (Buckingham & Saunders, 2004, p. 13).

▲ **Survey Results**
Source: T-[Theresa] McCracken

Questionnaire

A **questionnaire** is a form containing a series of questions and mental measures that is given to a group of people in an attempt to gain statistical information about the group as part of a survey. A questionnaire is a tool that a researcher who is conducting a survey uses to get data from the group of interest.

Interview Schedule

The third term we use when discussing surveys in this chapter is an interview schedule. An **interview schedule** is the list of survey questions that an interviewer reads an interviewee when conducting an oral survey. Although some researchers will discuss interview schedules as questionnaires, we prefer to differentiate between paper-and-pencil methods (questionnaire) and oral interviewing (interview schedule).

WHEN TO USE A SURVEY

People utilize surveys for a number of different projects, but you should never just jump into a survey project without knowing why you are conducting the survey in the first place. Buckingham and Saunders (2004) believe there are four questions a researcher must ask before conducting a survey.

Do You Know What You Want to Ask?

Does a researcher know what he or she wants to ask? Because of the physical need to generate a questionnaire or list of interview questions before a survey can occur, a researcher must know what he or she wants to study. Whether the researcher wants to conduct a descriptive survey or an analytical survey, he or she must have some kind of a priori (before the fact) notion of what is being studied. Qualitative and rhetorical researchers have the ability to conduct exploratory research, where they go in and organically observe a phenomenon with no preconceived notions, but quantitative researchers simply do not have this luxury because of the nature of quantitative information.

Do You Really Need to Collect New Data?

Researchers must ask themselves whether they really need to collect new data on a specific phenomenon. In certain types of research, performing a survey would be meaningless, if not impossible. For example, we cannot conduct a survey of Irish American immigrants during the potato famine because they are all dead, and for some reason, dead people dislike filling out questionnaires. If the lives of immigrants during the potato famine is your research topic, conducting a survey is not going to help you. (There are research methods to study the lives of Irish immigrants during the potato famine, but they are beyond the scope of this book.)

A second reason why a researcher may not need to conduct a survey occurs when an observational method is available that does not interfere with how people live their daily lives. For example, one common type of research, often conducted without your knowledge, pertains to shopping behavior. Retail stores sometimes hire consulting firms to study shopping behaviors within a store for the purpose of determining the best way to lay out that store in order to maximize profits. Although some scholars say this research is unethical because it invades your privacy, others consider it to be perfectly ethical because the researcher is unobtrusively watching a shopper's behavior without direct contact or interference.

A third reason why a researcher may not need to collect data is if existing data are available. Many organizations are devoted to the collection and dissemination of information about people. In these cases, it is not that a survey was never conducted—it is that the survey was conducted by a third party for the purpose of disseminating the data to other researchers. The *Journal of Statistics Education* (http://www.amstat.org/publications/jse/)

has numerous datasets that people can use to learn statistics, and many of them are based on actual collected survey data. The dataset provided with this textbook is another example of a preexisting dataset that can be used for analysis. Furthermore, check out organizations such as the Centers for Disease Control and Prevention (http://www.cdc.gov/) and USA.gov (http://www.usa.gov/) to find a wide variety of datasets at your fingertips.

Do Your Participants Know Anything, and Will They Tell You If They Do?

Researchers must ask themselves not just how much their group of interest will know about what the researchers are interested in analyzing, but also whether the group members will even tell the researcher. Let's break this one down into some simple chunks.

As a researcher, you must ask yourself whether your future participants will even know about the topic you are studying. For example, if you want to examine the lasting impact of memorable messages after the *Challenger* explosion, using a group of college freshmen probably would not be useful since your typical freshman was born after the accident in 1986. The types of questions you are interested in may also be problematic. Say you are interested in the media's effect on perceptions of terrorism, so you ask a group of participants how many news stories about terrorism they remember seeing the week after the 9/11 attacks. If you are like us, we could not even tell you how many news stories on terrorism we saw in the last week, let alone more than a decade ago. Asking people questions about events that have happened in the past is always problematic. However, the closer you can get to the event in question, the stronger your data will actually be.

The flip side of this issue deals with whether participants are willing to tell you information about themselves. There are some issues that frankly make people antsy, and they often will not want to discuss these topics openly. There are three basic reasons people may have for not wanting to disclose information. First, some people may simply be embarrassed by certain information. For example, researchers who study issues involving sexual communication often find that people are embarrassed by some questions asked on a questionnaire or during an interview. For some people, filling out a questionnaire about human sexuality is as close to openly discussing sexuality as they will ever get, so this could really make them feel embarrassed, which could lead to socially desirable responding. **Socially desirable responding** occurs when a participant fills out a questionnaire or responds to interview questions in a way that the participant thinks makes her or him look better.

The second reason some people may be hesitant to disclose information is shame. In research that has looked at people who are victims of violent crimes, especially sex crimes, many victims feel shame for having been violated. When people experience deep shame, they are much less likely to open up about the topic that is causing the shame.

The third reason some people may be hesitant to disclose information during a survey is because they fear some kind of retribution for their answers. For example, if a manager hands out a survey to subordinates on her or his managerial skills and then has those subordinates turn the survey back into her- or himself, participants will hesitate to say anything negative for fear that the manager will hold their responses against them. Other people are simply hesitant to disclose information for fear that their disclosure will get them into legal trouble. Many researchers study illegal behaviors, and many people will either not participate in a study or lie during a study about illegal behaviors for fear that their answers will put them in jail.

We are not suggesting that you should never use surveys with people who might be embarrassed, shamed, or fearful. In fact, researchers have used survey methods with all kinds of people who experience embarrassment, shame, and fear as a result of the information discussed during a survey. However, it is extremely important that you ensure confidentiality and anonymity. The more certain people feel that their answers will not be used against them or even be traced back to them, the more honest they will be while filling out a questionnaire or answering a series of interview questions.

Does Your Goal Have Generalizability?

The last question a researcher should ask her- or himself is whether the goal of the study is **generalizability**. When discussing generalizability, there are two important terms to understand: populations and samples. A population is an entire set of objects, observations, or scores that have some characteristic in common. With survey research, a population is everyone who has a specific characteristic in common that a researcher is attempting to study. For example, if you want to examine television-viewing patterns among college females, your population consists of every female who is in college. A sample, by contrast, is a subset of the larger population. Instead of attempting to survey the entire female population on television-viewing patterns, you decide to survey 300 females at a local university. When researchers discuss the concept of generalizability, we are basically questioning whether the results of a sample (the 300 female students at a local college) mirror the results that would be found in the larger population (all college females). To make sure that your end results are generalizable—that is, your sample can be said to reflect the population correctly—you should randomly (i.e., every unit of analysis that exists within your population has an equal chance for inclusion in your sample) select your sample. We will discuss random sampling in more detail in Chapter 12.

HOW TO CONDUCT SURVEY RESEARCH

Many young scholars will find a series of random scales and throw them together to create a survey research project; this is not only ineffective for hypothesis testing, but also a waste of time. Randomly putting together a survey is like throwing a vat of spaghetti against a wall—something will stick, but you are left with a mess. If you create a large dataset for no other purpose than seeing what relationships and differences might exist, you will most definitely find statistical relationships and differences by chance. And your results may not mean anything.

Being haphazard in one's approach to research is not science. The authors of this textbook have stated from the beginning that you should start with an overarching research question and then determine the most appropriate ways to go about measuring that communication phenomenon. Overall, use previously existing research scales wisely. The temptation to throw a handful of research scales together is great, but the end result is generally substandard research that is not publishable. To make sure that you design a good study, you might use Fink's (2006) five steps for conducting a survey.

Step 1: Picking your Questions

First, there is no single way to go about picking the types of questions to include in a research survey. We wish that we could tell you there is a magic bullet, but there simply is not. The types of questions you will need to ask will be dictated by the hypotheses and research questions that you want to examine in your study. As Converse and Presser (1986) wrote, "Every questionnaire must, finally, be handcrafted. It is not only that questionnaire writing must be 'artful'; each questionnaire is also unique, an original. A designer must cut and try, see how it looks and sounds, see how people react to it, and then cut again, and try again" (p. 48). Although Converse and Presser were talking specifically about questionnaire development, the same is also true for developing an interview schedule. In this section, we consider a number of commonly used question formats seen on questionnaires by examining the types of variable levels.

NOMINAL LEVEL QUESTIONS

Many questionnaires will have a series of nominal level questions, which ask about things like biological sex, ethnicity, religious affiliation, political party, and so on. These questions are great for determining descriptive statistics of your research sample. When deciding which questions to include on your questionnaire, you must ask yourself which questions are related to the current study. If you are not planning on examining your participants' political affiliations, then you do not need to include that variable on the questionnaire. You may also find yourself at some point needing to ask a series of yes-or-no questions. Often, having a "don't know" category is also useful. You may want to ask your participants, "Have you ever lived in a country other than the United States?" In this case, you probably do not need the "don't know" category because some people will check off "don't know" just to say "screw you." Ultimately, when dealing with nominal level variables on a questionnaire, ensure that you follow the guidelines for creating nominal variables discussed in Chapter 6.

One difficult question to answer is where to place nominal level variables in the overall flow of a questionnaire. We recommend keeping participant demographics until the end. In longer surveys, you may end up with participant fatigue, but participants can generally recall their own demographic information without much cognitive expenditure. As for other types of nominal level questions, place the questions where they will be the most beneficial for your participants. For example, if you are having participants fill out a questionnaire examining their supervisor's communicative behavior, start by getting participants thinking about their supervisor before you jump into any mental measures related to him or her. To do this, place any nominal level demographic variables related to the supervisor before the more complex measures. When participants have to tell you their supervisor's biological sex up front, it forces them to start thinking about that specific supervisor, which will help the participant keep that supervisor in mind as he or she responds to the rest of the survey.

Demographic questions, however, must be thought of in terms of ethics as well. In an often-cited working paper by Lynn Sweeney in 2000, the Carnegie Mellon University researcher demonstrated that with just three pieces of information (zip code, biological sex, and birthdate), you could correctly identify 87% of people living in the United States. For obvious reasons, knowing that people can easily be identified with just three nominal demographic questions raises serious ethical considerations related to anonymity, confidentiality, and privacy. Do not be surprised if an institutional review board (IRB) member questions the utility of specific nominal questions because they may make it too easy to identify participants in a supposedly "anonymous" sample. In other words, it is not ethically sound to collect data about extra nominal variables just out of curiosity. All the data you collect should help you answer your research questions and/or hypotheses.

ORDINAL LEVEL QUESTIONS

Like nominal level variables numerous ordinal level variables also are commonly used in research (year in school, social economic status group, level of education, etc.). Any time someone uses a single Likert-type question or semantic differential question, it functions as an ordinal level question as well. One example of an ordinal variable discussed by Hildebrand, Laing, and Rosenthal (1977) related to political ideology is *left*, *left-center*, *center*, *right-center*, and *right*. Although these categories may not be measurable using a ruler, we can say that the categories clearly differ from each other qualitatively and quantitatively.

When it comes to using ordinal level variables on a survey, the biggest question concerns what statistical tests you plan on conducting. Although it is possible to use ordinal data in both relationship and difference tests, the results are based on one-shot questions, which leads to serious issues concerning reliability and validity. An ordinal question may be useful for determining someone's socioeconomic status (lower, middle, upper), for example, but an ordinal question would not be useful for measuring someone's level of CA.

INTERVAL LEVEL QUESTIONS

A great deal of communication research involves interval level variables. In fact, these are the most common type of question seen on questionnaires. All of the mental measures discussed in Chapter 7 are interval level variables, as are all of your Likert and semantic differential scales.

One of the biggest questions involving interval level variables is where to place them in your overall questionnaire. Especially if you have multiple interval variables, how should you order the mental measures so that you have a sequence which flows from one scale to the next and does not end up confusing your participants? Although there are no steadfast rules on this, you may want to consider some general guidelines.

GROUP ITEMS WITH LIKE ANCHORS TOGETHER An anchor is the technical term used for the words that you give people on a questionnaire and then ask them to pick one (e.g., *disagree, neither agree nor disagree, agree; ineffective, neutral, effective; unsatisfied, neutral, satisfied*). Many types of anchors exist in mental measures, so group measures that have similar anchors together to avoid confusion. You may also want to indicate in your instructions that you are using multiple anchoring systems so that your participants do not think the new anchor is a typo.

DO NOT START A STUDY WITH THE MOST CONTROVERSIAL QUESTIONS Wrench, Corrigan, McCroskey, and Punyanunt-Carter (2006) conducted a study examining numerous variables, including religious fundamentalism, ethnocentrism, intercultural CA, tolerance for religious disagreements, and homonegativity. In the initial version of the questionnaire, the homonegativity scale, which measures negative perceptions people have about bisexual, gay, and lesbian people, was one of the first scales. However, the researchers started discussing whether having that scale at the start might end up biasing the way the participants would respond to the other questions. People tend to assume that the first scale on a questionnaire reflects what the study is about as a whole. In public speaking, we talk about the concept of primacy—people remember the information at the beginning of a speech. People also tend to remember what the first set of scale items were asking, which can slant how they respond to the rest of the study.

KEEP LIKE QUESTIONS TOGETHER When we say "like questions," we mean questions asking about the same target (as in a teacher or a supervisor). When conducting survey research, you may have questions that the participant is supposed to respond to about her- or himself (e.g., participant's level of CA, ethnocentrism, or sense of humor) and questions that the participant is supposed to respond to about a specific target (e.g., supervisor's nonverbal immediacy, teacher's use of humor, or physician's credibility). Our recommendation is to keep questions about the participant together and questions about the target together in order to avoid confusion. If your survey jumps back and forth between the two, you may end up with some participants responding about themselves when they should be responding about the target, and vice versa.

KEEP LIKE CONTEXTS TOGETHER Often when conducting a survey, we may be interested in comparing more than one communicative context. Maybe you want to compare participants' reported use of compliance-gaining strategies with both Internet and face-to-face friends. In this example, you would have survey questions relating to both the Internet communicative context and the face-to-face communicative context on your questionnaire. To ensure that your participants are not confusing the two contexts, keep them separate on your survey.

PLACE SENSITIVE QUESTIONS TOWARD THE END OF A SURVEY If you start by asking for a participant's deepest, darkest secret, the chances that they will either start lying or start answering in a socially desirable manner increase. Keeping the initial questions more benign allows the participant to become more comfortable with the questions. If your participants are comfortable with the earlier questions, they will be much more willing to divulge more private and personal information later in the survey.

RATIO LEVEL QUESTIONS

Overall, there are few questions a researcher will ask using ratio level questions. The most common question of this type asked on a survey is a participant's age. However, other types of ratio questions may be asked during a survey that involve a number range starting with a possible zero. How many visits to your doctor have you made this year? How many times a week do you eat breakfast? How many different sexual partners have you had in the past month? How many children do you have? All of these questions start with a possible zero and then escalate in an actual numerical fashion.

Another common form of ratio level question that appears on surveys is cognitive-based questions. When designing tests to measure an individual's cognitive understanding of something, we rely on a number of different measurement mechanisms: matching, multiple choice, and true or false. These start with an absolute zero score (the participant got none of the answers correct), and then we can mathematically compare participants' scores as they go up from zero.

OPEN-ENDED QUESTIONS

The final type of question commonly asked during a survey is an open-ended question. Open-ended questions are designed to allow respondents to further explore a concept. Instead of limiting the possible number of choices like we do with nominal, ordinal, interval, and ratio level questions, the answers given during open-ended questions are realistically limitless. For example, an open-ended question might ask, "How do you think you can improve your interpersonal communication with your spouse?" This question could receive one-sentence-long answers or pages of information. Open-ended questions can be useful because they often present you with information that you did not expect to receive from your respondents. (You may be wondering how an open-ended question can be quantitative, and you are right to ask this question because the responses are not innately quantitative. However, there are quantitative tools at our disposal that can be used to analyze open-ended questions; we will discuss the most common one, content analysis, in the next chapter.)

As for placing open-ended questions on an actual questionnaire, the biggest consideration is providing enough space for your respondents to answer. People's handwriting will differ in size, so allow the participants enough room to adequately answer a question. We generally recommend at least half of a page for an open-ended answer. The more complex your question is, however, the more space your respondents may need to answer it.

Step 2: Creating Clear Instructions

Murphy's Law: If people can find a unique and creative way for screwing something up, they will. Over the years, all of the authors of this text have received a wide range of unique answers on questionnaires. We have also learned that if our instructions are clear, we can avoid some of the ambiguity people may have while filling out a questionnaire or responding during an interview. One of the easiest ways to avoid ambiguity during the first part of an interview questionnaire is to offer your participants dummy questions and then walk them through how to correctly answer those questions.

Figure 9.1 presents examples from an actual study that included dummy questions to walk participants through how to fill out the scales correctly. In our experience, college students tend to know how to fill out research surveys correctly, but the general public is more likely to need extra help, probably because they do not fill out as many questionnaires. When looking at your instructions, ask yourself a simple question: "Will these instructions make sense to my intended participants?" If you want to survey people in a nursing home, for example, you may want to show your instructions to someone who is elderly and get their feedback before moving on to pilot testing the questionnaire.

Step 3: Study Design

When designing a survey research study, we typically talk about two types of designs: cross-sectional and longitudinal (Fowler, 1993).

FIGURE 9.1
Sample Questionnaire
Questions

Weight Locus of Control

Directions: The following questions are concerned with how you perceive yourself across a variety of issues. For each statement, place an "X" in the box that corresponds with your perception of the item based on the following scale: SD = Strongly Disagree, D = Disagree, N = Neutral, A = Agree, and SA = Strongly Agree.

For example, if given the sentence "I like peanut butter," if you only agree with the statement, but do not strongly agree with the statement, you would place an "X" in the column marked "A" for Agree (See example below).

		SD	D	N	A	SA
Ex.	I like peanut butter.				X	
1.	Being the ideal weight is a matter of luck.					

Generalized Attitude Measure

Directions: On the scales below, please indicate your feelings about **"Restaurant X."** Circle the number between the adjectives which best represents your feelings about **"Restaurant X."** Numbers "1" and "7" indicate a very strong feeling. Numbers "2" and "6" indicate a strong feeling. Numbers "3" and "5" indicate a fairly weak feeling. Number "4" indicates you are undecided or do not understand the adjectives themselves. There are no right or wrong answers. Circle only ONE number per row.

For example, if you were given a pair of adjectives (cheap and expensive) and you felt the program was reasonably priced, you might circle 1 or 2.

Ex.   Cheap   (1)   2   3   4   5   6   7   Expensive
1.   Good   1   2   3   4   5   6   7   Bad

CROSS-SECTIONAL SURVEY DESIGN

A **cross-sectional survey design** is used when a researcher wants to get information from a group of participants at a given point in time. Maybe you want to conduct a study like Rocca and Vogl-Bauer (1999), who examined sports team identification and verbal aggression. In their study, the researchers asked a series of participants to fill out a scale containing items for sports team identification, verbal aggression, and sports spectator identification. Rocca and Vogl-Bauer simply wanted to get people's perceptions at the time they filled out the scale. When using a cross-sectional survey design, you can examine things like relationships between variables and differences between groups that exist within the research sample, but you cannot study changes that occur over time.

LONGITUDINAL SURVEY DESIGN

To examine how people change over time, one must employ a **longitudinal survey design**. Although a longitudinal design cannot be used to make causal conclusions about relationships and differences, it can allow you to make statements about variable order. The three types of longitudinal survey design are the trend survey, the panel survey, and the accelerated longitudinal survey.

TREND SURVEY DESIGN A **trend survey design** examines different samples of people at different points in time. For example, many researchers collected research data within the week before the 9/11 terrorist attacks in the United States. These same researchers could then collect data immediately after 9/11 using completely different samples to see whether changes had occurred within that short time period. If a change is found, however, it is possible that preexisting differences between the two groups caused the change to occur. There is no way to be certain of this in a trend survey design.

PANEL SURVEY DESIGN A **panel survey design** is when a researcher recruits a series of participants who agree to be surveyed periodically over a given period of time. Some researchers have used this type of design to examine marital conflict. Researchers recruit participants when they get married and agree to pay the participants a certain amount of money if they will agree to be surveyed every six months. Then, every six months, the researchers survey the couple about how they are handling conflict and the types of conflicts they are having. By surveying a panel over and over again like this, researchers can see how marital conflict strategies and themes change over time.

ACCELERATED LONGITUDINAL SURVEY DESIGN The last design is a combination of the previous two types and is called an **accelerated longitudinal survey design**. An accelerated longitudinal survey design is employed when a researcher wants to see how things change over a long period of time during a short period of time. We know this sounds odd, so we will use an illustration for clarification.

Suppose a researcher wants to see how perceptions of situation comedies on television change over the course of one's adult life until retirement. In other words, the researcher wants to see how people's perceptions change from age 18 to age 65. To complete this study using a traditional longitudinal study would take a researcher 47 years—or most of his or her career. For this reason, this type of study is not realistic. Instead, the researcher recruits people in five-year intervals starting at age 20. With this method, the researcher recruits 20-year-olds, 25-year-olds, 30-year-olds . . . all the way to 60-year-olds. The researcher then tracks these groups for five years. The idea is that we are seeing changes over this period from participants who started the project at age 20 and ended at age 25 to participants who started when they were age 60 and ended at age 65. This type of design allows researchers to track how time affects the individual age groups over time, as well as how the differing age groups change.

Step 4: Data Processing and Analysis

One area that is problematic for new researchers involves making sure the hypotheses and research questions can be answered by the information on the questionnaire. After you are done collecting data is not the time to realize that you should have asked another question(s). Before you ever set out to distribute your survey, make sure that you can statistically answer your hypotheses and research questions based on the questions you actually have on your questionnaire. For example, last year one of the authors of this text had a group of students conducting a project in organizational communication. At the end of the project, the students realized they had actually measured employee motivation and not employee satisfaction. One of the students said, "Well, if they're motivated, they're satisfied, right?" Nope! Although research has shown the two variables to be positively related, they are not synonymous. If a researcher does not measure employee satisfaction specifically, he or she cannot answer hypotheses or research questions about it.

You must know exactly how you plan on analyzing your data when you are finished with the study itself. In Chapter 6, Figure 6.10 contains a chart that helps you determine which tests are most appropriate to conduct. For example, if you have two interval level variables (e.g., CA and ethnocentrism) and you want to find the relationship between them, you would use a correlation to test for a statistical relationship. If you had one nominal variable (e.g., female and male), and you wanted to test for a possible difference between these two categories on an interval level variable (willingness to communicate [WTC]), the appropriate test would be an independent samples *t* test. The last part of this book will go into more detail examining each of these different types of tests.

Step 5: Pilot Testing

The only way a researcher can ever really know how respondents will provide answers to a survey is give it to people and find out directly. You may think your instructions were crystal clear and your survey questions all made sense, but once you give your survey to real people, that can all change quickly. In the study mentioned earlier in this chapter conducted by Wrench et al. (2006) examining religion, the researchers had listed "Protestant" as one of the possible religious affiliation categories (nominal variable). Protestants are any Christian groups who are not Roman Catholic, Eastern Orthodox, or Anglican. Baptists, Methodists, Disciples of Christ, and so on are all Protestants. However, the researchers ended up with more people selecting "Other" and defining themselves by their individual denominational names instead of as Protestant. Many respondents simply did not know that they were Protestants, so they answered the best way they could. In fact, in a more recent dataset, 54.5% of the sample didn't correctly identify themselves as Protestants. Thankfully, changing the respondents' answers to Protestant in both cases was easy because they provided their more specific Protestant labels (e.g., Baptist or Methodist), but this could have been a bigger problem.

One way to prevent problems like this from occurring is to administer a pilot study. According to Buckingham and Saunders (2004), a **pilot study** is a "small-scale test-run for a planned piece of empirical research" (p. 294). We use pilot studies to make sure our instructions are easy to follow and our survey questions make sense to potential respondents. The following are some basic guidelines for pilot testing a survey. These guidelines are applicable whether you are piloting a questionnaire or an interview schedule (the series of questions an interviewer asks during an interview).

USE ACTUAL SURVEY POPULATION MEMBERS

When pilot testing a survey, you want to use the people you actually plan on surveying. For example, if you will be surveying people in a retirement village, you do not want to pilot test your survey instrument on college students because they simply will not respond the same way.

ANTICIPATE SURVEY CONTEXT

Attempt to pilot the survey using the same conditions that people actually responding to the survey items will experience. For example, if you will be surveying people using an interview schedule over the phone, you would not want to pilot test your survey using college students sitting in a lecture hall. Although you may not anticipate every possible survey context (e.g., a person filling out a questionnaire in her or his car), at least try to approximate the general conditions under which most of your respondents will be participating.

TEST PARTS OF THE SURVEY

Another idea that can be helpful when developing a survey is to pilot test parts of your survey instead of the whole thing. Often, you have used parts of a survey in the past with the same population, so you do not need to retest those sections of the survey instrument. Instead, you may want to test a newly developed section to make sure that respondents understand the new instructions or questions.

DETERMINING A PILOT SAMPLE SIZE

Is there a magical number one should attempt to have in a pilot study? Not really. However, we do recommend that you pilot test your questionnaire or interview schedule using at least 5% to 10% of your target sample size. So, if you are planning on surveying 200 participants, pilot your questionnaire or interview schedule with at least 10 to 20 people. The larger your pilot test is, the more likely you will find potential problems with your questionnaire or interview schedule.

ASK QUESTIONS AFTER SOMEONE COMPLETES THE SURVEY

One common practice during the pilot phase of survey testing is to interview the respondents about their experience after they have completed the survey. Ask the respondents whether they found any instructions confusing, if the questions were clear, did they guess on any items, was the survey too long, and if they could physically read the survey (especially important when working with elderly populations). The more you know about how your participants felt while taking the survey, the more appropriate your revisions will be before disseminating your survey to the target sample.

DISSEMINATING YOUR SURVEYS

Once you have pilot tested your survey, you are ready to hand out your survey to potential participants. In this section, we discuss the dissemination of a research survey or questionnaire.

Although many different people use all five terms (*scale, measure, research instrument, survey*, and *questionnaire*) interchangeably, for the purpose of this book we are delineating a difference between scales/measures/research instruments and surveys/questionnaires. The first group is a single set of items designed to measure a specific variable. Surveys and questionnaires, by contrast, are a series of scales/measures/research instruments put together in an attempt to examine how variables relate to or differ from each other. More specifically, a survey or questionnaire is when you place a variety of scales together to examine statistical relationships and differences. For example, maybe you want to put together a survey to examine the variables sociocommunicative orientation, WTC, and humor assessment. To examine these three variables, you put the three scales together in one small packet and have each participant fill out all three scales. You may even include some basic demographic information like biological sex, ethnicity, sexual orientation, and so on.

Once you have created a survey/questionnaire, you then need to determine the best way to get your survey into the hands of your target population. There are two primary ways that people can go about disseminating a survey: surveying and self-administration.

Surveying Techniques
FACE-TO-FACE SURVEYING
Face-to-face (FtF) surveying occurs when a researcher asks a participant a set of questions. There are clear advantages and disadvantages to FtF surveying.

The first advantage is that you tend to get a high response rate. People have a tendency not to say "no, I don't want to participate" when they are looking at you. FtF surveys also tend to be beneficial for long surveys where fatigue might be a problem because the researcher can encourage the participant to continue answering questions at a point where they would stop answering them in other formats. The researcher can also answer questions about the survey items if a participant is having problems understanding a question, which can be important when a participant's language skills are not high. FtF surveying is also the best format in which to ask open-ended questions. In the first part of this chapter we focused on asking closed-ended questions, or questions that have a clearly defined set of possible choices. In a Likert scale with a range from 1 (*strongly disagree*) to 5 (*strongly agree*), the person is not given the option of 9. There is a clearly defined set of permissible answers. However, open-ended questions allow a wide variety of different answers. For example, maybe you want to know how someone perceives the federal government's propaganda about a new piece of legislation, so you ask, "How would you characterize the information you are receiving from Washington, DC, about this piece of legislation?" This enables the participant to express her or his thoughts in an open fashion. Although these open-ended responses can be coded and quantified, open-ended questions typically fall under the heading of qualitative rather than quantitative.

Unfortunately, however, there are also some clear disadvantages to the use of FtF surveys. First, the cost of FtF surveying is high. You need teams of trained researchers who orally survey people in the sample you are intending to examine. These teams of trained researchers cost a lot of money, not including the expenses of travel, food, and hotels that may be incurred. Another disadvantage is that the researcher can inadvertently affect how a participant responds to the questions. A simple sidewise glance from a researcher that says "I can't believe you answered that way" can cause the participant to start censoring her- or himself and start responding in ways that the participant thinks the researcher wants to hear. Another problem caused by FtF surveying involves slight changes in how the questions are asked regarding the actual text of the question; how a question is asked can change how people respond to questions either randomly or systematically. Even the biological sex or ethnicity of a researcher can affect how some people will respond. Although it is impossible to negate the effect that a researcher can have on a participant, training researchers to deliver questions in a systematic fashion and not outwardly respond to the answers they are given can help to minimize researcher effects.

One of the most famous social scientists to use FtF surveys as his primary form of research was a university professor at Indiana University named Alfred Kinsey. Kinsey initiated a line of research in the 1940s examining human sexuality in both females and males (Kinsey, Pomeroy, & Martin, 1948; Kinsey, Pomeroy, Martin, & Gebhard, 1953). Before Kinsey's studies, little research had been conducted on human sexuality in the United States. But Kinsey and a group of highly trained researchers set out to survey a wide variety of different people around the country about their sexual histories. Kinsey realized early on that FtF surveying enabled people to be more honest and forthright about their current and past sexual behaviors. Based on their research, Kinsey and his team revolutionized the discussion of sexuality in the United States and around the world.

TELEPHONE SURVEYING

The second way to disseminate a survey to a specific population is through the use of telephone surveying. Telephone surveys are similar to FtF surveys in that a researcher can clarify questions that participants have about the survey and can ask more probing, open-ended questions. Telephone surveys are also considerably cheaper and quicker than FtF surveys. A researcher no longer needs to send someone to physically survey a person, so telephone surveys cut down on travel, lodging, and meal expenses, which drastically reduces your overall research budget. In fact, telephone surveys enable researchers to include responses from geographically remote locations that they could not afford to visit, which makes a sample more representative of the total population.

Although there are some clear advantages to telephone surveys, there are some major drawbacks as well. A telephone survey cannot be as long as an FtF survey. In fact, a telephone survey that lasts 15 minutes is too long. Researchers using telephone surveys are also more likely to have people tell them that they are not interested in participating or to be hung up on altogether, which can randomly or systematically skew a sample. Participants also tend to trust researchers conducting telephone surveys less than they trust researchers conducting FtF surveys because there is always the perception in the back of the participant's mind that the researcher on the telephone is trying to sell something. And unfortunately for academic researchers, there are less than scrupulous people out in the world who do attempt to disguise product sales as telephone research, which confuses the public and makes them even less trusting of legitimate research endeavors as a whole. As with FtF surveys, telephone surveys also run the risk of inadvertently affecting the responses received from a participant, so again, training is extremely important to prevent this from occurring.

One major limitation with phone surveys is that not everyone has a phone, so a group of people who could be a part of our research sample is not reached. When we exclude people who do not have or have less access to a phone, we bias our sample in the direction of people with phone access. Although the bias caused by the lack of phone service is generally not important, for some research projects this could be problematic. If you wanted to determine people's perceptions of the phone as a communicative tool, you would get a slanted population if you surveyed only people you can reach by phone because these people already clearly use the tool for communication purposes.

Self-Administration

The other way to get your survey into the hands of your targeted research sample is through self-administration. Self-administration is when an individual receives and then fills out the survey without the help of an interviewer. There are three basic ways to distribute a self-administered survey: mass administration, mailed administration, and Internet administration.

MASS ADMINISTRATION

Mass administrations are useful when you have a large group of possible participants in a single location. For example, if you want to examine religious communication, maybe you would hand out surveys in a large church and have a collection box where people can place the surveys when they are done filling them out. One group that is consistently used in mass administration surveys is college students because they are conveniently available and their participation does not cost much money since students are most commonly paid in the form of class credit or extra credit.

MAILED ADMINISTRATION

Mailed administration is when you mail an individual a survey to fill out and that individual sends the completed survey back to you. Say that you wanted to survey all of the members of your state government on their use of persuasion during political campaigns. You could get a list of addresses for every elected state official and send them your survey, and when they are done filling it out, they could send it back to you. Mailing surveys is extremely expensive, however, and the people you have asked to participate often will not send the survey back.

Some techniques have been shown to help increase the number of participants you can acquire during mail-administered surveys. First, send a postcard to your potential participants letting them know that a survey is coming and why you are conducting your survey. This postcard hopefully will encourage people to participate, or at least be on the lookout for the survey packet itself. Second, send the survey packet with a self-addressed stamped envelope. You may even provide some kind of compensation in the envelope to provide an incentive to the participant. One coauthor of this book remembers receiving a $1 bill with a survey he received in the mail. Even that $1 made our coauthor feel somewhat obligated to participate, so he did. Finally, if you have not received a survey packet back from a particular participant, follow up with a second postcard reminding the individual to participate. Some scholars will even send another copy of the survey packet to the potential participant through certified mail to make sure that he or she is actually receiving the survey. However, the more mailings you send as a researcher, the more costly mail surveys will become.

INTERNET ADMINISTRATION

The Internet-administered survey is the newest form of research and can be used as a replacement for mass-administered and mailed surveys or as a unique form unto itself (Best & Krueger, 2004; Dillman, Smyth, & Christian, 2014). As a way to replace traditional pen-and-paper surveys, many researchers opt to put surveys online because it saves many trees on an annual basis. Instead of having church members, for example, fill out a survey and turn it in, you ask them to go to a website and fill out the survey there. Or, instead of mailing your survey to the members of your state government, you send an e-mail asking them to fill out the survey online instead.

The Internet can also be used to gain access to populations you may not reach using traditional means. For example, maybe you want to research the impact that image fixation has on female Buddhists. In the United States, finding a large enough sample of female Buddhists may be difficult, but this task could be considerably easier online. All you would have to do is find a series of Buddhist websites and ask whether they would post your call for research. Many groups will agree to help a researcher if they can sense that what is being studied is not derogatory toward their group and could possibly benefit their group in the long run.

ADVANTAGES AND DISADVANTAGES OF SELF-ADMINISTRATION

Like other forms of surveying, self-administration has basic advantages and disadvantages. First, self-administration is by far the cheapest form of surveying. With the exclusion of mail surveys, which can cost a few thousand dollars because of postage, most self-administered surveys do not cost more than a few hundred dollars in photocopying expenses or software and website development. One nice thing about Internet surveys is that once a website has been developed and the software purchased, you can run countless numbers of surveys at one time with no additional expense. Another advantage of self-administered surveys is that you can reach a large cross-section of people in a short period of time. With a solid research strategy, you can quickly gain 200 participants using a self-administered technique. You also do not have to worry about an interviewer affecting your sample inadvertently.

The authors of this book first started online surveying in 1999, and it was much easier to get people to participate because online surveys and research were new. Now, however, hundreds of thousands of surveys are constantly being conducted, so making your survey stick out is easier said than done. A series of studies conducted online under the direction of one of our coauthors showed the challenges and promises of online surveying. In one study, the students tried posting the survey link on Facebook and other social networking sites thinking the topic of the survey would encourage people to participate. Unfortunately, this strategy was wildly misguided. After attempting to collect data for a month, the survey had a grand total of 30 participants, so the study was a bust. In a different study, the researchers examined librarian interactions with their supervisors. One of the student researchers was a medical librarian and had numerous contacts within the librarian community. Using her own network, she sent out requests to participate in the project and ended up with almost 500 responses in a short period. These two cases demonstrate that knowledge of a specific population and access to a sample from that population are two important factors when conducting online surveys. If you think the participants will just flock to your online survey on their own, you will be disappointed.

There are other clear disadvantages. First, participants do not have the ability to seek clarification when they do not understand a question on your survey. In fact, you may end up with serious problems at the end of a study because you did not see an inherent flaw in the design that could have been discovered and corrected using FtF surveying. Second, you also do not have the ability to check whether people are randomly answering your survey until the survey itself is entered into a dataset and your reliability drops. Third, people may not take the survey as seriously if they are filling it out alone as they do when being asked the questions with the interviewer sitting in front of them or on the telephone. This problem is often seen in some of the questionnaire responses given by college students. Some patterns of response also clearly fall into the "screw-you" category. For example, if you are using a five-point Likert scale and you receive a survey that reads "123451234512345" or "12345432123454321," you can be guaranteed that the person just randomly filled out the survey because he or she obviously did not care. When we come across a survey where the respondent randomly filled in responses like this, we consider that survey to be a unit nonresponse (discussed later) and eliminate the survey from the dataset.

In the past few years, a number of different companies have emerged to help people (from business owners to academic researchers) conduct surveys. Some of the more common survey companies are Lime Survey (http://www.limesurvey.org/), Survey Monkey (http://www.surveymonkey.com/), and Zoomerang (http://www.zoomerang.com/). All three of these companies enable you to administer a short survey for free, but longer surveys (like those seen in academic research) will cost a fee. Lime Survey also has an open-source option that you can host on your own website if you have access to your school's web server or can work with your school's information technology department to launch the application. A nice thing about these online survey programs is that they come with a variety of survey item templates, including those for Likert, semantic differential, multiple-choice, open-ended, and other survey question formats. However, there are growing concerns in the research ethics community about the security and confidentiality of some of these services. Before investing time and money on one of these services, you should ask your local IRB about their thoughts and procedures for online surveying.

PROBLEM AREAS ASSOCIATED WITH SURVEY RESEARCH

As a whole, there are always disadvantages one must be aware of when conducting any specific type of research. This section discusses a series of situations that can be problematic for researchers.

Response Rate

One of the biggest questions a researcher must worry about when conducting research is her or his response rate. A researcher's **response rate** is the percentage of surveys returned compared to the percentage of surveys distributed. For example, if you initially hand out 100 surveys and 95 are returned, your response rate is 95%. However, in the real world of research, response rates of under 50% are not unheard of. One of the authors of this book completed a two-part study examining parent–adolescent conflict. When the first part of the study was completed, the researcher had approximately 200 participants. The second part of the study was to be completed 6 months later, and all of the participants in the first part had agreed to participate in the second.

Unfortunately, the researcher only received 26 surveys back during the second stage, which is a response rate of only 13%. Ultimately, this entire project had to be scrapped because of the low response rate from the participants. This study fell victim to the problem of **nonresponse**. According to Dillman, Eltinge, Groves, and Little (2002), "Nonresponse occurs when a sampled unit does not respond to the request to be surveyed or to particular survey questions" (p. 3). Based on this definition, we can see that there are two types of nonresponse problems that can affect a researcher's survey: unit nonresponse and item nonresponse.

UNIT NONRESPONSE

Continuing with our example that yielded a 13% response rate, we can say that the other 87% of the sample falls into the category of unit nonresponse. **Unit nonresponse** is defined as the "failure to obtain any survey measurements on a sample unit" (Dillman et al., 2002, p. 6). There are three reasons why people do not participate. First, some participants may not receive the invitation to do so. For example, if you use the National Communication Association's database of members, some people will have moved and not updated their information. If you randomly select any of these people to participate in a study, they may never receive the invitation. Second, some people simply refuse to respond. These people actually receive the request and ignore it. Finally, some people are either physically or mentally unable to respond. Maybe you send out an e-mail survey, and one of the people you asked to participate is ill in the hospital. He or she may even get the e-mail request but not be in a physical or mental position to respond.

Now that we have examined why people do not participate, you may be wondering why someone agrees to participate in a study. Dillman et al. (2002) argue that there are three basic reasons why people will agree to participate in a research survey (this information is also true for getting people to participate in any type of research). First, participants will weigh the potential costs and rewards of participating in the survey. If respondents sees participation as a waste of time, they will be unlikely to participate unless the researcher can adequately entice them to participate. Although some people believe participating in research is part of her or his "civic duty," most people feel the need to be compensated in some way for their participation. This "compensation" can come in many different forms, from monetary incentives to personalized letters asking for cooperation. If a person feels that the researcher is at least attempting to provide some benefit for participation, then he or she is much more likely to participate. This is the real reason why researchers offer college students extra credit to participate in research projects.

Second, the more interesting the topic of research is to the participant, the more likely that he or she will want to participate in your study. For example, if potential participants are not interested in politics, they will not be likely to participate in a survey examining political communication. This is especially true in self-administered surveys because respondents can preview the types of questions asked on the survey prior to actually filling it out. For this reason, the more mundane a research study is, the more likely the researcher will need to provide adequate compensation to get participants. However, if you land on a really "sexy" topic, people will be likely to participate without expecting compensation. Unfortunately, as a researcher, you often do not know whether your topic is going to be seen as salient to people until after you begin collecting your data.

Finally, many participants are influenced to participate in a research project based on their earlier participation in research. This is true for both new projects and continuing projects. For example, a person who feels that he or she was treated poorly by a researcher in the past will be unlikely to participate in future research studies when asked. Also, if a participant feels that he or she is being mistreated during a research project, that person may decide to leave the study. For these reasons, researchers must try to make the survey experience interesting and harmless.

ITEM NONRESPONSE

Item nonresponse occurs when an individual participant fails to answer individual or groups of questions on a survey. According to Dillman et al. (2002), there are seven causes of item nonresponse: survey mode, interviewer training, question topics, question structure, question difficulty, institutional requirements and policies, and respondent attributes.

SURVEY MODE The first reason participants may not respond to specific items on a survey deals with the nature of surveying. In a self-administered survey, individual participants are responsible for reading and responding to all of the questions. One of the simplest reasons some people do not respond to an item is that their eyes visually skip an item, whereas during an interview, an interviewer is responsible for making sure the participant responds to every survey question (though an interviewer could accidentally skip a question as well). In fact, if a participant is hesitant to respond to a question, the interviewer can even encourage the interviewee to answer, which is not possible during a self-administered survey.

INTERVIEWER TRAINING The second reason participants may not respond relates specifically to surveys that rely on interviewers. The interviewer can either help foster answers or actually cause participants to not answer survey questions. If an interviewer can develop a positive, friendly relationship with a participant, that interviewer is more likely to get the participant to answer the survey questions. If, however, the interviewer is either unfriendly or bland, the interviewee will be more likely to not answer questions. Also, interviewers have the ability to coax answers out of participants who may not otherwise answer a specific question.

QUESTION TOPICS The third reason participants may not respond to survey questions relates to the topics of the questions themselves. As discussed earlier in this chapter, many topics make people feel embarrassed, shamed, or fearful. When topics evoke these emotional responses, people may feel the questions are psychologically or physically threatening and avoid answering them altogether.

QUESTION STRUCTURE The fourth reason people may not respond to survey questions involves the actual structure of the survey questions. Certain types of questions are more likely to be answered than other types. For example, in self-administered surveys, open-ended questions are considerably more likely to be left unanswered compared to closed-ended questions such as Likert and semantic differential scales. Also, if you have questions that do not pertain to specific participants, those respondents may skip those questions along with more relevant questions at the same time. If you have properly pilot tested a survey, however, question structure is much less likely to be a cause of nonresponse.

QUESTION DIFFICULTY The fifth reason some people may not answer questions involves the difficulty of the question itself. Sometimes questions are either too difficult or too confusing for participants. If you follow the general requirements for writing Likert scales in Chapter 7, you will be less likely to run into this problem. Other questions may ask participants to recall information they simply cannot remember. For instance, if you ask a participant the number of times he or she communicated with a family member in the past month, this may be impossible for some people to recall, so they leave the item blank. Again, however, if you properly pilot test a study, this problem should take care of itself prior to administering your survey to your entire sample.

INSTITUTIONAL REQUIREMENTS AND POLICIES The sixth reason some people may not answer questions relates to institutional requirements and policies. Some participants will not respond to items because they are not legally allowed to answer all of the questions. IRBs will generally require researchers to include statements indicating that participants do not have to answer all the questions on the questionnaire and that participants may stop participation at any time. Other participants may not answer specific questions because they consider the information private or proprietary. An example of information that may be considered private is someone's salary, whereas information that is proprietary is information over which an individual or group exercises private ownership. For example, if you are surveying organizational members about organizational coaching practices, some may see you as trying to steal their organization's information, so they will refuse to answer questions. The easiest way to alleviate this problem is to reassure the participants that all information is confidential or anonymous and will not be seen by anyone outside the research team.

RESPONDENT ATTRIBUTES The last reason some people do not respond to surveys is more of a personal issue than one that the researcher can control. Dillman et al. (2002) note that "older people and those with less education are less likely to provide answers in many surveys" (p. 14). Mason, Lesser, and Traugott (2002) also found that people who are reluctant participants in the first place are much more likely to not respond to individual items during the study. This is yet another reason to make sure that you attempt to get participants to see their participation as beneficial.

EFFECTS OF NONRESPONSE

Every survey will have some level of nonresponse associated with it. However, the question is whether this nonresponse actually alters the results of your survey in some meaningful way. Ultimately, a researcher must ask, "Are those who are not responding distinctly different in some manner from those who are responding?" Fowler (1993) noted that in mail research "people who have a particular interest in the subject matter or the research itself are more likely to return mail questionnaires than those who are less interested" (p. 41). If a mail survey has a low response rate, then as a researcher, you must question the generalizability of your results to the whole population.

Low response rates can also cause a specific type of error in your study called nonresponse bias. In essence, **nonresponse bias** means that the people who did not participate are different enough from the people who did participate that it skews your results. Although we know that nonresponse bias is extremely detrimental to a study, we do not know how much of a bias there is. When you cannot get individuals to participate in the first place, it is hard to find out why they did not respond later. We often have no way of quantifying the actual bias within a dataset because of nonresponse.

Improving Response Rates

There is no way to prevent nonresponse in survey research. Some people, for whatever reason, simply will either not participate or not answer specific questions in a research study. However, here are some suggestions to help you minimize this problem.

1. *Make the survey easy to fill out.* The more confusing a survey is for a participant, the more likely that participant is going to quit. Make sure that your font is large enough to be read by an average audience and that your directions are clear. We even suggest adding sample questions that clearly illustrate how items in your study should be answered. For example, if you have a Likert scale, add a fake item, and explain how that item could be answered. In our experience, the survey format that is often the most confusing is the bipolar adjectives format. Too many people believe they need to select a step on the scale for each adjective. For example, if your adjectives are "Yes 1, 2, 3, 4, 5, 6, 7 No," many people will circle 2 for "yes" and 6 for "no." It does not matter whether you boldface, italicize, or underline the phrase "circle only one number per adjective pair"; people will still make mistakes filling out your survey. Having a sample question, however, has been shown to alleviate some of the more common mistakes.

2. *Keep it short.* Short surveys will always result in more participants, but longer surveys give you more information to analyze. Although there is no magic formula, we recommend that a pen-and-paper survey be no longer than three to four pages in length. It does not matter whether your survey is single or double sided. People tend to view four single-sided pages and four double-sided pages as being equal in length because they are still four pages. You should also vary the types of questions you have on a survey. Too often, people will have page after page of Likert-type items, which can cause people to become bored and tired and not complete the study.

3. *Include a self-addressed stamped envelope (SASE).* This particular hint is primarily for mail-administered surveys. If you do not include an SASE and put postage on the envelope, people will likely not return your survey. After all, people believe that they are doing you a favor by filling out your survey, so the least you can do is make the experience of filling out and returning it as easy as possible.

4. *Include a good cover letter.* The cover letter should explain to potential participants who you are and why you are conducting the research along with any legal notifications related to compliance as established by both the federal government and your university. Although the first goal of the cover letter is to convince people to participate in your project, the letter is also a legal notification of their rights as a participant. Some universities have simple guidelines for what must be in a cover letter, and other universities have specific guidelines. If you have any questions about what your university wants to see in a cover letter, contact your IRB.

5. *Use multiple administration techniques.* The concept of multiple administration techniques can be broken down into two categories: (1) options of survey method and (2) multiple contacts. The first multiple administration technique is to allow participants the option to fill out a survey by pen and paper or by Internet. When you allow people this option, those who may not be likely to fill out the pen-and-paper survey may go online and fill it out there. The second aspect of the multiple administration technique is to use the multiple contact method. In essence, you contact a potential participant about your study through a quick e-mail or postcard to let them know you will be sending a survey. Next, you send your survey. Two or three weeks later, you send a follow-up letter or e-mail either thanking the person for participating or reminding the person that you still need his or her participation. As mentioned earlier, some scholars even suggest sending a final survey through certified mail, but this can get expensive in the long run.

TRANSLATING SURVEYS INTO OTHER LANGUAGES

One area in which researchers conducting surveys may have substantial trouble occurs when they use samples from multiple intercultural groups. Often, researchers want to conduct surveys of people who do not speak English as their native language or even at all. Researchers have had to devise a range of different techniques for translating surveys into other languages.

Issues of Equivalence

Translating a survey into another language is easier said than done and involves three key equivalence issues: semantic, conceptual, and normative (Behling & Law, 2000; Gudykunst, 2002).

SEMANTIC EQUIVALENCE

The first major issue involved in translating surveys into other languages involves issues of **semantic equivalence**. Semantics is the study of meaning, and the simple fact is that languages are semantically different from each other. So when we say that there is a problem with semantics, we are describing a problem where a word in one language may not have an equivalent word with the same meaning in a different language. Words that exist in English may have no direct translation in Mandarin, for example. This will cause problems if you try to translate a survey from one language to another.

CONCEPTUAL EQUIVALENCE

When we create mental measures that are designed to measure one specific construct in one culture, the construct often will not hold true in another culture, which is referred to as **conceptual equivalence**. Does the basic concept a researcher is attempting to study in one culture even exist within another culture? In some cultures, for example, the notion that a child would be allowed to speak her or his mind to elders is absurd. So if you have a mental measure that examines openness of ideas shared within the family, the basic concept will not translate to some other cultures. Just because we can study a concept in the United States does not mean that the concept is able to be studied within other cultures. Zhang (2005a, 2005b, 2006) has examined the notion of nonverbal immediacy and how US students and Chinese students perceive it differently. In this case we have a concept that has been regularly studied within the United States that Zhang has shown does not translate for Chinese students. Zhang (2006) has created a new mental measure specifically designed to measure Chinese students' perceptions of teacher nonverbal immediacy.

NORMATIVE EQUIVALENCE

Every cultural group has its own set of norms or social conventions. These norms do not translate from one culture to the next, however, because they are culturally dependent. In turn, survey questions are often culturally specific. Behling and Law (2000) note that this issue of **normative equivalence** includes three behaviors that can impact the translating of research instruments: willingness to discuss certain topics, manner in which ideas are expressed, and treatment of strangers.

WILLINGNESS TO DISCUSS CERTAIN TOPICS The first behavior that can impact the translating of research instruments is whether people in a specific culture are open to discussing certain topics. Different cultures have different norms for discussing specific topics. Although the US culture has no problem gossiping about the sex lives of our political figures, other cultures are less likely to discuss sexuality as a general concept (Frayser, 2002). If you are conducting a survey on sexual communication in another culture, you may find that your nonresponse rate escalates because your participants do not like openly discussing the subject.

MANNER IN WHICH IDEAS ARE EXPRESSED The second behavior that can affect the translating of research instruments deals with how participants may respond to questions. In some cultures, people are less likely to engage in self-aggrandizement, or to make themselves appear better or greater than they really are. For instance, if you are conducting a study on WTC, you may find cultural differences. Barraclough, Christophel, and McCroskey (1988) found that American students reported higher levels of WTC and higher levels of self-perceived communication competence compared to Australian students. When results like this are found, we could be seeing actual differences between cultures or just differences in how people in different cultures rate themselves on mental measures.

Lonner and Ibrahim (1996) note that it is common for people in different cultures to respond to mental measures differently. In essence, Lonner and Ibrahim believe that people in different cultures have different positional response styles; that is, people within cultures respond to scales in similar patterns that are representative of cultural test taking and not the differences on the measures themselves. People may be more or less likely to use the extremes on mental measures, or they are more likely to go for the neutral option on mental measures, based on their culture rather than their actual perceptions of their own attitudes, behaviors, beliefs, cognitive knowledge, personality traits, and values.

TREATMENT OF STRANGERS The final behavior that can impact the translating of research instruments deals with different cultures' handling of strangers. As noted by Behling and Law (2000), "Reactions to strangers—particularly to strangers asking questions—also vary from society to society" (p. 6). Different people in different cultures therefore will have widely different reactions to people attempting to conduct research. Some people may give answers that they perceive the researcher wants. Or the respondent may simply go along with the survey out of politeness, but not give the researcher any useful information. We always recommend having at least one person on your research team who is from the target culture. If you are going to conduct research in Zimbabwe, for example, you should have at least one researcher on your project who is from Zimbabwe to prevent the issue of being a stranger conducting research in another culture.

Methods of Translation

Now that we understand some of the problems researchers face when translating surveys from one language to another, we must discuss how researchers can successfully complete a survey translation. Behling and Law (2000) expanded on Guthery and Lowe's (1992) original ideas for translating surveys and came up with five unique methods researchers can use for translating surveys.

SIMPLE DIRECT TRANSLATION

The first method that a researcher can use for translating scales from one language to another is the **simple direct translation**. In this method, a researcher recruits a bilingual individual who takes the original survey and then translates this survey from the primary language to the secondary language. However, there are some problems with this method. First, when conducting a simple direct translation, the translator is only paying attention to semantic issues of translation. In essence, the translator is making sure that the survey can be read and understood by people in the secondary language, but he or she does not pay attention to conceptual or normative issues. Furthermore, the translator is not really being double checked. We already know that people make mistakes, so relying on one person to conduct a translation automatically opens your research project to translation errors.

MODIFIED DIRECT TRANSLATION

The second method a researcher can use for translating scales from one language to another is the **modified direct translation**. In this method, a translator performs the same translation that he or she would do in the simple direct translation. After the translation process is completed, however, the translation is given to a panel of experts who know the primary and secondary languages, and the group decides whether the individual item translations are appropriate. Although this sounds better than a simple direct translation, the method is also open to a number of problems. First, the panel may be no more knowledgeable about translating information from one language to another than the original translator is. Second, this method is time-consuming and does not provide the researcher any information that he or she could not get from the original translation about the quality. If anything, the translation may end up making less sense after a group of people try to translate the survey.

TRANSLATION/BACKTRANSLATION

The third method a researcher can use for translating scales from one language to another is the **translation/backtranslation** process. In this method, a researcher has a translator complete the same steps that he or she would complete in the simple direct translation. Then, after this initial work is complete, the researcher provides the translation to another bilingual individual who has not seen the original survey, and the second translator attempts to translate the work back into the first language. If the original survey and the retranslated survey are similar, then the translation is semantically successful. If, however, the two translations are different, the original and secondary translator can discuss possible problematic areas, and a new translation can be completed. Although this provides great semantic verifiability, the researcher cannot be sure that the translator is actually paying attention to conceptual or normative issues. Furthermore, utilizing two translators can be quite expensive if they must be hired for the study.

PARALLEL BLIND TECHNIQUE

The fourth method that a researcher can employ for translating scales from one language to another is the **parallel blind technique**. In this method, a researcher has two independent translators translate the survey as in the simple direct translation. After both researchers complete their independent translations, the two translators then compare their translations and agree on a third translation that is given to the researcher. Ultimately, the researcher must trust her or his translators in this technique. However, the researcher cannot be sure that the translators are actually paying attention to conceptual or normative issues. And again, two translators can be expensive, but on the plus side, this method is fast.

RANDOM PROBE

The fifth method that a researcher can use for translating scales from one language to another is the **random probe translation**. In this method, the researcher has a translator complete the same steps as in the simple direct translation. After the researcher has the translation in hand, he or she then pilot tests the translation with a group of bilingual participants. After the participants complete the survey, the researcher asks a series of open-ended questions examining why the participants answered questions in a specific manner. The goal of this process is to ascertain whether the participants understand the questions in a manner that is similar to the researcher's own understanding of the mental measure. This method can actually help a researcher test for conceptual and normative issues during the open-ended interview portion of the pilot test. Behling and Law (2000) suggest using this approach in combination with the modified direct translation, translation/backtranslation, or the parallel blind technique to ensure that the survey's translation is equivalent on all three levels (semantic, conceptual, and normative).

USING THE RESEARCH PROJECT WORKSHEET

The last part of this chapter contains what we call the Designing a Research Project Worksheet (Figure 9.2). This worksheet was originally designed by Dr. Jason Wrench (one of the text's coauthors) while he was working for a medical school and teaching biostatistics. This worksheet is useful when planning your own research projects or

FIGURE 9.2
Designing a Research
Project Worksheet

Question (In a single sentence, what would you like to know when your project is done?)

Design
(Check one):   ( ) Survey   ( ) Content   ( ) Data Mining   ( ) Randomized   ( ) Nonrandom
                              Analysis   Study   Study

If a self-administered survey, how?	( ) Mass Administered	( ) Mail	( ) Web Based	
If an interview-based survey, how?	( ) Phone	( ) In Person		
If a content analysis, what type?	( ) Mediated	( ) Interactional	( ) Microlevel	( ) Macrolevel
If using preexisting data?	( ) Personally Collected	( ) Governmental Agency	( ) Other Records	( ) Other
Type of randomization?	( ) Nonblind	( ) Single Blind	( ) Double Blind	
Type of nonrandomized study?	( ) Case-Control	( ) Cohort		

Type of Experimental Design:

Quasi-Experimental Design			
( ) Pretest–Posttest	( ) Time Series	( ) Multiple Time Series	( ) Switching Replications
True Experimental Design			
( ) Pretest–Posttest	( ) Two-Group Posttest Only	( ) Randomized Switching Replications	( ) Solomon Four-Group

Setting (Where will the survey/study be conducted?)

Participants
1. Do your participants need to possess any specific characteristics (high levels of communication apprehension, users of instant messaging, relational partner, age grouping, biological sex, etc.)? ( ) YES ( ) NO
   If Yes, explain:

2. How are you going to select/acquire participants?

Continued

FIGURE 9.2
Continued

3. Do you need a letter of consent for participation? (NOTE: All survey and experimentally based studies must have a letter of consent.) ( ) YES ( ) NO
    If No, explain why not:

Variables (What are your IVs/DVs, how are they measured, and what level of measurement are they?)
1. Independent Variables (label as nominal, ordinal, interval, or ratio):

2. Dependent Variables (label as nominal, ordinal, interval, or ratio):

Hypotheses/Research Questions

Statistical Testing (Using the above Hypos/RQs, what statistical tests will you use to answer each question?)

Tentative Study Title:

Principal Researcher(s):

when analyzing someone else's study, and it contains components from this chapter and the next two chapters (on content analysis and experimental design). The rest of this chapter is going to walk you through a sample survey research project and demonstrate how you could fill out the Designing a Research Project Worksheet. You can find an MS Word document file containing this worksheet on the textbook's website (https://oup-arc.com/wrench) in the "Workbook" folder.

Question

The first section of the Designing a Research Project Worksheet asks a researcher to explain in a single sentence what he or she would like to know when the project is done. Researchers must have the ability to concisely explain the purpose of a research project, so forcing yourself to explain the purpose in one sentence will help keep you focused as you design your project.

For our example study, we will look for a possible difference between females and males in their levels of CA and WTC and for a relationship between CA and WTC. Therefore, our one-sentence question could be "Do females and males differ in their level of CA and WTC, and is there a relationship between CA and WTC?" This sentence is short, sweet, and to the point.

Design

The second section of the Designing a Research Project Worksheet is concerned with the basic study design. This section has components for surveys, content analysis, and experimental designs. Depending on which type of study you plan on conducting, you should focus on those design aspects.

For our example study, we are planning on conducting a survey, so we would place an "X" next to Survey. Once you have determined that you are conducting a survey, you must decide whether this survey will be self-administered (mass, mail, or Web) or interview based (phone or in person). For our study, we will use a mass-administered survey, so put an "X" next to Mass Administered. This is the last thing we must check in the Design section since the rest of the section is either for content analysis studies or experimental studies.

As you'll learn later in Chapter 11, there are a number of different ways a researcher can conduct experiments. Whether someone is conducting a survey or an experiment, both of them are ultimately issues of design. If you are conducting an experiment, we have a separate section called "Type of Experimental Design" on the worksheet to help you think through this process as well.

Setting

The third section of the Designing a Research Project Worksheet is concerned with the physical location you plan to use for your study. Although this section is not useful for a content analysis study, it is extremely important when conducting both survey research and experiments.

For our example study, we will pretend that we have gotten permission to hand out questionnaires at a local business club. So for our setting, we may include information like where the club meets, what time the meeting is, and the appropriate dress. When thinking about the setting, you must think about the context of the setting (a business club) and any ways in which this context will affect how you should present yourself as a researcher. If you are studying a sports team, for example, you may present yourself in a different manner than you would at a business club. Your goal for this section is to be as detailed as possible. Here is an example of what you might end up writing: "We will be handing out questionnaires at the local American Business Club meeting, which meets in Civic Center room 3-A on Mondays at noon. The researchers should be in professional dress since most of the potential participants are at the meeting during their lunch hour."

Participants

The fourth section of the Designing a Research Project Worksheet is concerned with the actual participants you plan to recruit during your study. Typically, there are three basic items you should know when thinking about potential participants: specific characteristics, how to recruit, and how to gain consent.

SPECIFIC CHARACTERISTICS

The first question you must ask yourself as a researcher is whether participants should have any specific characteristics for recruitment into a study. For example, if you are conducting a survey of physicians, one of the characteristics your participants must possess is an MD or DO. For our example study, we really have no specific characteristics in mind, so place an "X" next to the word NO.

RECRUITMENT

The second question to ask yourself is how you are going to get your participants. Throughout this chapter, we have discussed many ways you can recruit participants, whether in the college classroom, by random phone surveying, or by asking people at a business club meeting. The clearer your recruitment plan is up front, the easier it will be to actually recruit participants later on in your study. Also, if you have a unique group you want to study, you will have more time to determine how to best target those participants.

CONSENT

The third question you must think about is whether you will need to attach a cover letter explaining consent. You should also decide whether the consent form needs to be signed. Of course, these are decisions that you cannot ultimately make yourself because you must get approval from the IRB to conduct any survey research study.

Variables

The fifth section of the Designing a Research Project Worksheet concerns the variables you plan to study. Both independent and dependent variables are involved

INDEPENDENT VARIABLES

List all of your independent variables. In addition, label each of these variables as nominal, ordinal, interval, or ratio. In our study, the only truly independent variable is biological sex.

DEPENDENT VARIABLES

List all of your study-dependent variables, and again, label each of these variables as nominal, ordinal, interval, or ratio. For our study, we have two dependent variables: CA and WTC. If you are testing for relationships, you can list the variables where most appropriate for your study. This will be discussed further in Chapter 19 when we talk about regressions.

Hypotheses/Research Questions

In the next section, list any hypotheses and research questions. These should relate directly to your independent and dependent variables. Remember, if you do not list a variable on your independent or dependent variable list, you cannot have a hypothesis or research question that involves that variable. If you find you want to measure a variable not listed as an independent or dependent variable, you should add that variable to your study.

For our sample study, we list three variables (biological sex, CA, and WTC). Therefore, we could not have a hypothesis that predicts people who have been in their jobs longer will have lower levels of CA because we are not measuring how long someone has been in her or his job.

Statistical Testing

Once you know what your hypotheses and research questions are, you can decide which statistical tests will be the most appropriate to conduct. Although we will discuss how to determine which statistical tests to use in Chapters 13 through 19, you can always go back and use the chart in Chapter 6 (Figure 6.10).

For our current study, we are examining a difference between two groups (female and male participants) on one interval variable (CA/WTC), so we would use a t test to analyze this hypothesis. Our second hypothesis tests for a relationship between two interval/ratio level variables, so we would use a correlation to analyze this hypothesis.

Tentative Study Title

Every study must be called something. Although the title you create at this stage in your research project will probably not be the title at the end of your project, you should give your study a title just so you have something to call it while you're working. There is no clear-cut way to title a study. The only real rule is that your title must relate to your study itself. Our example study might be titled "Sex Differences and Communication Apprehension and Willingness to Communicate."

Principal Researcher(s)

Finally, list of all those involved in your project. Make sure that you list all of the principal investigators and your advisor, if you have one, for the study. If you need to remember the appropriate method for listing authors, reread the section in Chapter 3 on ethics related to authorship.

A completed version of the Designing a Research Project Worksheet can be seen in Figure 9.3.

FIGURE 9.3
Completed Project
Worksheet

Question (In a single sentence, what would you like to know when your project is done?)

Do females and males differ in their level of CA & WTC, and is there a relationship between CA and WTC?

Design (Check one): (X) Survey ( ) Content Analysis ( ) Data Mining ( ) Randomized Study ( ) Nonrandom Study

If a self-administered survey, how?	(X) Mass Administered	( ) Mail	( ) Web Based	
If an interview based survey, how?	( ) Phone	( ) In Person		
If a content analysis, what type?	( ) Mediated	( ) Interactional	( ) Microlevel	( ) Macrolevel
If using preexisting data?	( ) Personally Collected	( ) Governmental Agency	( ) Other Records	( ) Other
Type of randomization?	( ) Nonblind	( ) Single Blind	( ) Double Blind	
Type of nonrandomized study?	( ) Case-Control	( ) Cohort		

Type of Experimental Design:

Quasi-Experimental Design			
( ) Pretest–Posttest	( ) Time Series	( ) Multiple Time Series	( ) Switching Replications
True Experimental Design			
( ) Pretest–Posttest	( ) Two-Group Posttest Only	( ) Randomized Switching Replications	( ) Solomon Four-Group

Setting (Where will the survey/study be conducted?)

We will be handing out questionnaires at the local American Business Club meeting, which meets in Civic Center room 3-A on Mondays at noon. The researchers should be in professional dress since most of the potential participants are at the meeting during their lunch hour.

Participants

1. Do your participants need to possess any specific characteristics (high levels of communication apprehension, users of instant messaging, relational partner, age grouping, biological sex, etc.)? ( ) YES (X) NO

    If Yes, explain:

FIGURE 9.3
Continued

2. How are you going to select/acquire participants?

Participants will be recruited during the American Business Club meeting. Participants will be handed a questionnaire as they arrive to the luncheon and asked to turn the questionnaires back in to one of the researchers at the end of the luncheon.

3. Do you need a letter of consent for participation? (NOTE: All survey and experimentally based studies must have a letter of consent.) (X) YES ( ) NO
   If No, explain why not:

Variables (What are your IVs/DVs, how are they measured, and what level of measurement are they?)

4. Independent Variables (label as nominal, ordinal, interval, or ratio):
   Biological Sex (Nominal Variable)

5. Dependent Variables (label as nominal, ordinal, interval, or ratio):
   Communication Apprehension (Interval Variable)
   Willingness to Communicate (Interval Variable)

Hypotheses/Research Questions
   H1: There will be a difference between men and women in their levels of communication apprehension.
   H2: There will be a difference between men and women in their willingness to communicate.
   H3: There will be a negative relationship between communication apprehension and willingness to communicate.

Statistical Testing (Using the above Hypos/RQs, what statistical tests will you use to answer each question?)
   H1: There will be a difference between men and women in their levels of communication apprehension.
        A t-test will be conducted using biological sex as the independent variable and communication apprehension as the dependent variable.
   H2: There will be a difference between men and women in their willingness to communicate.
        A t-test will be conducted using biological sex as the independent variable and willingness to communicate as the dependent variable.
   H3: There will be a negative relationship between communication apprehension and willingness to communicate.

        A correlation will be conducted between communication apprehension and willingness to communicate.

Tentative Study Title:
   Sex Differences and Communication Apprehension and Willingness to Communicate

Principal Researcher(s):
Jason S. Wrench, Candice Thomas-Maddox, Virginia Peck Richmond, & James C. McCroskey

RESEARCH OUTSIDE OF THE WALLS OF ACADEMIA

As a quick caveat to conducting surveys in nonacademic settings, researchers should carefully attend to the length of survey they want to administer. We know that people are more likely to answer a lengthy survey if the study is being conducted for academic or intellectual pursuits, but people are less likely to answer a lengthy survey for an organization (unless they are highly involved with that organization). As such, we recommend keeping surveys in nonacademic settings to the bare essentials. Ultimately, the shorter your survey is, the more likely participants will respond and complete the whole survey.

If you are conducting a survey (or any type of study for that matter) in someone's place of work, you must take extra precautions to guarantee that person's confidentiality or anonymity. Imagine you are conducting a survey on someone's satisfaction with communication in her or his division. If a participant's manager reads that participant's survey, he or she could be in jeopardy of retaliation if the manager does not like the responses. For this reason, especially on surveys that involve controversial matters in the workplace, researchers must have a strict policy in place for how surveys will be handled and who has access to the raw data. As a consultant, it is important to ensure that who will have access to what kind of data is clearly spelled out in a contract or proposal before beginning the study.

CONCLUSION

This chapter has examined some of the basic concepts related to survey research. We started this chapter by examining the steps to conduct a survey. Next, we looked at various ways that researchers are able to disseminate their surveys (face-to-face, telephone, and self-administration). We then examined some common problem areas that negatively impact survey research. Lastly, we talked about issues related to translating surveys from one language into another along with some of the best practices for performing these translations. In the next chapter, we will discuss a second research method technique called content analysis.

KEY TERMS

Accelerated longitudinal survey design p. 291

Analytical/explanatory survey p. 281

Conceptual equivalence p. 305

Cross-sectional survey design p. 290

Descriptive survey p. 281

Generalizability p. 284

Interview schedule p. 281

Item nonresponse p. 301

Longitudinal survey design p. 290

Modified direct translation p. 307

Nonresponse p. 300

Nonresponse bias p. 303

Normative equivalence p. 305

Panel survey design p. 291

Parallel blind technique p. 308

Pilot study p. 293

Questionnaire p. 281

Random probe translation p. 308

Response rate p. 299

Semantic equivalence p. 305

Simple direct translation p. 307

Socially desirable responding p. 283

Survey p. 281

Translation/backtranslation p. 307

Trend survey design p. 291

Unit nonresponse p. 300

REFERENCES

Barraclough, R. A., Christophel, D. M., & McCroskey, J. C. (1988). Willingness to communicate: A cross-cultural investigation. *Communication Research Reports, 5*(2), 187–192.

Behling, O., & Law, K. S. (2000). *Translating questionnaires and other research instruments: Problems and solutions.* Thousand Oaks, CA: Sage.

Best, S. J., & Krueger, B. S. (2004). *Internet data collection.* Thousand Oaks, CA: Sage.

Buckingham, A., & Saunders, P. (2004). *The survey methods workbook: From design to analysis.* Malden, MA: Polity Press.

Cattell, J. M. (1890). Mental tests and measurements. *Mind, 15,* 373–381.

Converse, J. M., & Presser, S. (1986). *Survey questions: Handcrafting the standardized questionnaire.* Thousand Oaks, CA: Sage.

Dillman, D. A., Eltinge, J. L., Groves, R. M., & Little, R. J. A. (2002). Survey nonresponse in design, data collection, and analysis. In R. M. Groves, D. A. Dillman, J. L. Eltinge, & R. J. A. Little (Eds.), *Survey nonresponse* (pp. 3–26). New York, NY: Wiley.

Dillman, D. A., Smyth, J. D., & Christian, L. M. (2014). *Internet, phone, mail, and mixed-mode surveys: The tailored design method* (4th ed.). Hoboken, NJ: Wiley.

Fink, A. (2006). *How to conduct surveys: A step-by-step guide* (3rd ed.). Thousand Oaks, CA: Sage.

Fowler, F. J., Jr. (1993). *Survey research methods* (2nd ed.). Newbury Park, CA: Sage.

Frayser, S. G. (2002). Discovering the value of cross-cultural research on human sexuality. In M. W. Wiederman & B. E. Whitley, Jr. (Eds.), *Handbook for conducting research on human sexuality* (pp. 425–453). Mahwah, NJ: Erlbaum.

Gudykunst, W. B. (2002). Issues in cross-cultural communication research. In W. B. Gudykunst & B. Mody (Eds.), *Handbook of international and intercultural communication* (2nd ed., pp. 165–177). Thousand Oaks, CA: Sage.

Guthery, D., & Lowe, B. A. (1992). Translation problems in international marketing research. *Journal of Language and International Business, 4,* 1–14.

Hildebrand, D. K., Laing, J. D., & Rosenthal, H. (1977). *Analysis of ordinal data.* Newbury Park, CA: Sage.

Kinsey, A. C., Pomeroy, W. B., & Martin, C. E. (1948). *Sexual behavior in the human male.* Philadelphia, PA: Saunders.

Kinsey, A. C., Pomeroy, W. B., Martin, C. E., & Gebhard, P. H. (1953). *Sexual behavior in the human female.* Philadelphia, PA: Saunders.

Lonner, W. J., & Ibrahim, F. A. (1996). Appraisal and assessment in cross-cultural counseling. In P. B. Pedersen, J. G., Draguns, W. J. Lonner, & J. E. Trimble (Eds.), *Counseling across cultures* (4th ed., pp. 292–322). Newbury Park, CA: Sage.

Mason, R., Lesser, V., & Traugott, M. W. (2002). Effect of item nonresponse on nonresponse error and inference. In R. M. Groves, D. A. Dillman, J. L. Eltinge, & R. J. A. Little (Eds.), *Survey nonresponse* (pp. 149–161). New York, NY: Wiley.

Rocca, K. A., & Vogl-Bauer, S. (1999). Trait verbal aggression, sports fan identification, and perceptions of appropriate sports fan communication. *Communication Research Reports, 16,* 239–248.

Sweeney, L. (2000). *Simple demographics often identify people uniquely.* Data Privacy Working Paper 3. Pittsburgh, PA: Carnegie Mellon University.

Wrench, J. S., Corrigan, M. W., McCroskey, J. C., & Punyanunt-Carter N. M. (2006). Religious fundamentalism and intercultural communication: The relationships among ethnocentrism, intercultural communication apprehension, religious fundamentalism, homonegativity, and tolerance for religious disagreements. *Journal of Intercultural Communication Research, 35,* 23–44. doi:10.1080/1745740600739198.

Zhang, Q. (2005a). Immediacy, humor, power distance, and classroom communication apprehension in Chinese college classrooms. *Communication Quarterly, 53,* 109–124. doi:10.1080/01463370500056150.

Zhang, Q. (2005b). Teacher immediacy and classroom communication apprehension: A cross-cultural investigation. *Journal of Intercultural Communication Research, 34,* 50–64.

Zhang, Q. (2006). Constructing and validating a Teacher Immediacy Scale: A Chinese perspective. *Communication Education, 55,* 218–241. doi:10.1080/03634520600566231.

FURTHER READING

Groves, R. M. (2004). *Survey errors and survey costs.* Hoboken, NJ: Wiley.

Lee, E. S., & Forthofer, R., N. (2006). *Analyzing complex survey data* (2nd ed.). Thousand Oaks, CA: Sage.

Patten, M. L. (2001). *Questionnaire research: A practical guide* (2nd ed.). Los Angeles, CA: Pyrczak.

Punch, K. F. (2003). *Survey research: The basics.* Thousand Oaks, CA: Sage.

Rea, L. M., & Parker, R. A. (2005). *Designing and conducting survey research: A comprehensive guide* (3rd ed.). San Francisco, CA: Jossey–Bass.

Singleton, R. A., Jr., & Straits, B. C. (2017). *Approach to social research* (6th ed.). New York, NY: Oxford University Press.

10

Content Analysis

CHAPTER OBJECTIVES

1. Explain the basic principles underlying content analysis.

2. Implement the basic steps necessary to conduct a content analysis.

3. Define the term *coding*, and explain how one creates a codebook and coding form.

4. Define the term *intercoder reliability*, and calculate it using Cohen's kappa.

5. Identify four problems that a researcher may encounter with coders (coder misinterpretations, coder inattention, coder fatigue, and recording errors).

In Chapter 9, we discussed how communication researchers go about studying a communicative phenomenon (surveying). In this chapter and the next, we focus on two other methods that communication researchers can use to learn about human communication: content analysis and experimental research. Before delving into how communication researchers use content analysis, however, we first need to explain what content analysis is and how it can apply to a variety of communicative contexts.

DEFINING THE TERM

According to Neuendorf (2002), **content analysis** is a "summarizing, quantitative analysis of messages that relies on the scientific method (including attention to objectivity–intersubjectivity, a priori design, reliability, validity, generalizability, replicability, and hypothesis testing) and is not limited as to the types of variables that may be measured or the context in which the messages are created or presented" (p. 10). This definition has a number of important parts to understand.

First, content analysis attempts to quantitatively summarize different messages. These messages may be verbal (e.g., types of jokes told by comedians), nonverbal (e.g., incidence of facial expressions during conversations), or mediated (e.g., portrayal of global warming in magazines). In each of these three cases, a researcher using content analysis would attempt to understand how various messages function.

Second, Neuendorf's (2002) definition of content analysis is dependent on the scientific method. Although we will not rehash our discussion of the scientific method here (see Chapter 2 to refresh your memory), we do want to emphasize that the empirical use of content analysis should conform to the traditional norms of scientific research. Investigators should not randomly opt to use content analysis, but should have specific reasons for believing that content analysis is the most appropriate method to examine communicative phenomena.

Finally, Neuendorf (2002) notes that content analysis can apply to a wide range of differing communicative contexts: "Content analysis may be conducted on written text, transcribed speech, verbal interactions, visual images, characterizations, nonverbal behaviors, sound events, or any other type of message" (p. 24). Neuendorf acknowledges that the notion of content analysis started by specifically examining textual works. One of the earliest examples of a content analysis occurred during the 1770s in Sweden, where a hymnal entitled *Songs of Zion* was published and republished in multiple editions. At first, the Swedish authorities granted permission to publish the volume of songs, but then fear that the songs contained unorthodox (i.e., not approved by the Swedish Church) teachings arose. A well-read orthodox clergyman named Johan Kumblaeus attempted to solve the debate through a simple textual analysis of the hymnal itself. Kumblaeus counted various orthodox themes in the hymnal, compared them to the number of unorthodox themes, and "concluded on the basis of his analysis that the exclusion of certain Christian themes and emphasis on certain others tended to create new conceptions which threatened the doctrine of the established church" (Dovring, 1954–1955, p. 392). Overall, Kumblaeus quantitatively examined the text and determined that the hymnal was indeed a clear source of unorthodox teachings. But not only did Kumblaeus complete a quantitative analysis of the themes within the text, he also further suggested that these themes indicated the editor of the volume had an underlying motivation to spread unorthodox teachings in the hopes of converting more followers. This example illustrates how content analysis can be used to show how sources of messages construct messages and have motivations underlying the messages that are sent and how a source's message should influence a specific receiver.

In modern scholarship, content analysis has been used to examine a wide range of different communication phenomena. In the context of mass-mediated messages, content analysis has been used to examine types of merchandise sold by Evangelical

Christians (Hirdes, Woods, & Badzinski, 2009), portrayals of Muslims in American media (Cagle, Cox, Luoma, & Zaphiris, 2011), race and gender in the coverage of missing children (Min & Feaster, 2010), nonprofits' use of Facebook (Waters & Lo, 2012), self-help discussion boards on the Internet (Asbary & Powell, 2013), portrayals of stalking in films (Schultz, Moore, & Spitzberg, 2014), portrayals of science and sharks during Discovery Channel's Shark Week (Evans, 2015), portrayals of female video characters (Lynch, Tompkins, van Driel, & Fritz, 2016), romantic ideals in Disney princess movies (Hefner, Firchau, Norton, & Shevel, 2017), and depictions of body types in prime-time television (Mastro & Figueroa-Caballero, 2018). This list of content analyses in mass-mediated communication represents only a small selection of studies published between 2009 and 2018, but it gives a general portrayal of the types of studies being conducted in this area. Overall, media researchers have historically been the primary group to use content analysis methods (Riffe, Lacy, & Fico, 2005), but they are not the only communication researchers to do so.

Some communication scholars also conduct research that falls under the content analysis umbrella related to nonmediated messages. Some nonmediated messages have asked participants to write out how they perceived interactions would go: parent–adolescent conflict (Comstock & Buller, 1991), young adults' views of intergenerational communication (Harwood, 1998), and heterosexuals' perceptions of interactions with gay, lesbian, and bisexual people (Hajek & Giles, 2005, 2006). Other studies have attempted to code actual human interaction: communication strategies between patients and physicians (Roter, Lipkin, & Dorsgaard, 1991), gesturing (Feyereisen & Havard, 1999), dominance and control between husbands and wives (Ayres & Miura, 1980; Courtright, Millar, & Rogers-Millar, 1979), facial expressions (Ekman & Rosenberg, 2005), self-disclosure (Shaffer, Pegalis, & Cornell, 1991), and speech rate (Feyereisen & Havard, 1999). When we use the word "code" in content analysis, we simply mean to group one's findings in a consistent way. For example, maybe you are conducting a study on the incidence of biological sex in speakers at political conventions. For every person who speaks at the Democratic and Republican national conventions, you code the speaker as being either female or male. Overall, content analysis can be used in a variety of unique and interesting ways.

CONDUCTING A CONTENT ANALYSIS

Now that we have explained what content analysis is and how the technique can be used in a variety of different research studies, we focus our attention on the process one goes through when completing a content analysis. Here, we will pretend that we want to conduct a study examining the level of physical attraction of lead characters in situation comedies during prime-time television. According to Neuendorf (2002), there are nine steps that must be completed in order to correctly conduct a content analysis:

(1) theory and rationale, (2) conceptualization, (3) operationalization, (4) coding schemes, (5) sampling, (6) training and pilot reliability, (7) final coding, (8) final reliability, and (9) tabulation and reporting. To help us understand the content analysis process, we will examine each of these areas individually.

Theory and Rationale

Like previous research discussed in this book, research in content analysis should be conducted using the scientific method. Additionally, a good content analysis should be theoretically based. The only way to make sure that you can create a strong rationale for your study is to do the necessary library legwork.

In Chapters 2 and 5, we discussed how to create a rationale for hypotheses and research questions, and this discussion cross-applies when conducting a content analysis as well. If you conduct a content analysis, your hypotheses and research questions must stem from the work previously conducted by other researchers.

For our example of the attractiveness of sitcom actors, there is a wealth of available information about body shapes, facial characteristics, and even clothing choices. There is nothing lacking that might help you formulate theoretically based hypotheses and research questions about this topic.

Conceptualization

In Chapter 7, we defined **conceptualization** as the development and clarification of concepts of your germinal idea (the spark that causes an individual to realize that something new can be researched or measured). This definition is relevant to our discussion of content analysis.

When we conceptualize something, we must decide what variables we want to study and how we can define those variables combining all the necessary characteristics or particulars. There are many ways a researcher can go about defining a specific concept, so you must ensure that your definition is clear from the beginning. The more ambiguous your attempt to define your research variables, the more likely you will finish conducting a study only to realize that you have ended up with nothing to show for your work.

For our example study (attractiveness of sitcom actors), one of the primary concepts a researcher must define is "attractiveness." Should a researcher rate individual actors on a scale of 0 (Someone hit every branch on the ugly tree) to 100 (Oh wow, baby!!!!), which would be a ratio variable? Or should a researcher create more of an ordinal variable where people are separated into three categories: *unattractive*, *average*, and *very attractive*? Whichever conceptualization a researcher decides to utilize, he or she must be clear about how an actor is categorized. Additionally, in a study examining the attractiveness of television personalities, one must realize that all sitcom stars are fairly attractive by society's standards. Let's face the fact: television networks are not going to hire Quasimodo to star in the fall line-up anytime soon.

For this reason, your conceptualization of attractiveness may be a little skewed because of the context itself. In essence, you must determine what "attractiveness" means in the context of television sitcoms. More traditional ways of defining attractiveness cannot be used in this study because everyone would fall into the upper end of attraction. So a conceptualization of attractiveness of sitcom actors must take into account that everyone is attractive, but some actors are more attractive than others.

Operationalization

In Chapter 7, we defined **operationalization** as the detailed description of the research operations or procedures necessary to assign units of analysis to the categories of a variable to represent conceptual properties. When we operationalize a variable in a content analysis, many different questions must be asked.

First, a content analyst must determine whether her or his operationalization is consistent with his or her conceptualization of the variable itself. If a researcher's operationalization and conceptualization differ, then he or she will have problems with internal validity (e.g., categories are exhaustive, categories are mutually exclusive, measured with the highest level possible).

Second, researchers must determine their unit of analysis or the major phenomenon that is being analyzed within a study. In a content analysis, the **unit of analysis** is generally the specific message(s) that a content analyst is coding. There are many different typical units of analysis that a content analyst may opt to use. Keyton (2006) notes that words or phrases; complete thoughts or sentences; themes or a single assertion about some subject; paragraphs in text; message sources (both real and actors); communication acts, behaviors, or processes; advertisements; and television programs, films, or scenes have all been used in mediated research as units of analysis (p. 237). For studies that are more focused on interactional analysis, it is possible that a variety of units of analysis are also going to be utilized: nonverbal behaviors, turns in a conversation, an entire interaction sequence. When determining the appropriate unit of analysis, you must think about how your operationalization determines which unit of analysis is the most appropriate for your specific hypotheses and research questions. For example, maybe you are coding videos of marital conflicts. Do you code each sentence of the conflict, or do you code each spouse's turn during a conflict? Ultimately, if you want to look at micro-level functions of conflicts (i.e., how people interact on a moment-to-moment basis during a conflict), coding each sentence or turn may be useful. However, if you want to code macro-level themes (i.e., more overarching themes about conflict in general, not specific behaviors), coding each conflict interaction as one unit of analysis may be useful.

Thus you need to determine which level of measurement (nominal, ordinal, interval, or ratio) is the most appropriate for your conceptualization. Whichever level of measurement you decide to use, you must be clear about how the rating process occurs. For example, maybe you will define "unattractive" as someone who is overweight, is sporting out-of-date or plain clothing, and/or looks messy or dirty. Although we are not suggesting that people who are overweight are unattractive, we do argue that the lack of portrayals of overweight people in Hollywood indicates this perception exists among entertainment executives. You may define someone who is "average" as someone who is physically in shape and healthy looking, wears normal clothing, and is clean and kempt. You may then define someone who is "very attractive" as someone who has clear muscular definition, wears high-end fashions, and is meticulously groomed (i.e., not a hair out of place, eyebrows perfectly plucked, and cuticles cut). Once you have a working operationalization of your variable (attractiveness), you can move on to the next stage of a content analysis—creating coding schemes.

Coding Schemes

Previously in this chapter, we defined **coding** as the process a researcher goes through to group one's variable of interest consistently. Your coding scheme should stem directly from your operationalization. As a researcher, you will need to create two products to help you with your content analysis: a codebook and a coding form. A **codebook** is a book that a researcher creates to explain the operationalization in a clear and succinct way. The codebook should be so clear that even a stranger could pick it up and code the phenomenon of interest. A **coding form** is a form that contains all of the information in the codebook in a simple check-off sheet to make it easier for coders to code information quickly. In the long run, coding forms also make entering data into a statistical software program much faster.

For our example of sitcom attractiveness, Figure 10.1 represents what our codebook might look like. Our codebook has the operationalization discussed in the previous step to help coders understand exactly what we are looking for in our coding of sitcom actors' attractiveness. The codebook also asks for the show's identification number (we will discuss this in more detail during the next step) and for the coder's ID. When conducting a content analysis, it is always important to have multiple coders looking at a set of data. Multiple coders will help you decide whether your codebook is useful when coding the communicative phenomenon of interest. Often, the coders will read your codebook and have wildly different perceptions of the communicative phenomenon because your codebook is not clear, so you may need to spell some things out more clearly and revise the codebook, which is why we have a training stage in content analysis (more on this in a moment).

The blank coding form (Figure 10.2a) quickly summarizes the information in the codebook. In this case, we have spots for the Show ID, Coder ID, Character Name, and the coding of attractiveness (unattractive, average, and very attractive). Each coding form will look different depending on the codebook used in a given study. Some content analysis codebooks could contain 15 to 20 pages of information being coded, so the corresponding coding forms could be 5 to 8 pages in length as well. Because our example study is simple, the coding form is short.

FIGURE 10.1
Codebook

Sitcom Attractiveness Study

Unit of Data Collection: Each individual who is the lead in a situation comedy.

Show ID: Fill in the show's ID number, as indicated on the television show list provided.

Coder ID: Each coder has received an individual number, please write this number on every sheet.

Character Name: Please provide the name of the character you listed as the lead in each television show.

Character Attractiveness: Please rate each character's physical attractiveness using the following rating scheme:

1. <u>Unattractive:</u> Someone who is overweight, sporting out-of-date or plain clothing, or looks messy or dirty.
2. <u>Average</u>: Someone who is physically in-shape and healthy looking, wears normal clothing, and is clean and kempt.
3. <u>Very Attractive</u>: Someone who has clear muscular definition, wears high-end fashions, and is meticulously groomed (i.e., not a hair is out of place, eyebrow not teased, or cuticle uncut).

FIGURE 10.2
Coding Form

a) Coding form

Sitcom Attractiveness Study			
Show ID: _____	Coder: _____		
Character Name	Attraction Level		
	Unattractive	Average	Very Attractive

b) Coder 1

Sitcom Attractiveness Study			
Show ID: _____3_____	Coder:_____1_____		
Character Name	Attraction Level		
	Unattractive	Average	Very Attractive
Neil Patrick Harris			X

c) Coder 2

Sitcom Attractiveness Study			
Show ID: _____3_____	Coder: _____2_____		
Character Name	Attraction Level		
	Unattractive	Average	Very Attractive
Neil Patrick Harris		X	

In Figures 10.2b and 10.2c, we see two completed coding forms. In both cases, the coders indicate the Show ID (in this case "3" for *How I Met Your Mother*), their individual coder numbers, the lead actor (Neil Patrick Harris), and their rating of the lead actor's level of attractiveness.

Sampling

One of the hardest tasks for content analysts is determining the sample necessary to conduct a study. Although we will discuss the nature of sampling in much greater detail in Chapter 12, we want to discuss some pertinent sampling issues related to content analysis here.

When discussing sampling, there are two important terms to understand: populations and samples. A population is an entire set of objects, observations, or scores that have some characteristic in common. In our example study, the population would include every sitcom on television. A sample is a subset of the larger population. For example, maybe there are 20 sitcoms on television (whole population) and you want to only analyze half of these, so you would need to take a sample of 10 sitcoms for your study.

Although there are numerous methods for sampling, no one way is the best. However, to ensure that your end results are generalizable—that is, your sample can be said to reflect your population correctly—you should randomly (i.e., every unit of analysis that exists within your population has an equal chance for inclusion in your sample) select your sample. We will discuss random sampling in much more detail in Chapter 12.

Training and Pilot Reliability

Researchers use **coders** for a wide variety of reasons, but primarily because it helps maintain objectivity within the study. As researchers, we often spend many hours working on a study before we can begin to code our data. We may get to the point where we have spent so much time working on the project that we lose sight of some of the more simple aspects of it. We may be so focused on looking at the forest (i.e., our overall study) that we completely miss the trees (i.e., our individual pieces of data). Researchers use coders to look at the data for them. If you have completed the previous step (codebook and coding form) accurately, then training your coders should be easy. However, just because we train our coders to examine individual pieces of data does not mean that our data will be correctly coded, so the training process should always include some specific steps: introduction to the codebook and the coding form, sample coding, coding of initial data, initial reliability, and retraining.

INTRODUCTION TO THE CODEBOOK AND THE CODING FORM

The first part of coder training is to introduce your coders to the codebook and the coding form. You should make sure that you go through the codebook, explaining how each part of the codebook should be used on the coding form. This process should be comprehensive because you want to make sure that your coders will use the codebook accurately.

SAMPLE CODING

Once you have completed your codebook and coding form instruction, it is time to let your coders practice. We recommend having a number of sample pieces of data prepared before the coding session that can allow your coders to practice using the coding form. For example, in our sitcom study, maybe you will bring in snippets from dramatic shows instead of sitcoms and have the coders rate the dramatic actors' levels of attractiveness. Once your coders have completed the sample coding, it is time to go over their work and determine whether everyone is coding the data the same way. For example, if someone codes *White Collar's* Matt Bomer as "very attractive" and someone codes him as "unattractive," you must discuss which one you (as the researcher) would classify him as according to the information in the codebook. These practice sessions are important because it allows the researcher to see where any misunderstandings in the coding process are occurring and to correct them.

CODING OF INITIAL DATA

Once everyone has coded the practice data, it is time to let your coders work on some real data. However, do not let them code all of the data initially. You should tell your coders to code a specific number of pieces of data and then make sure that they are coding the same pieces. Depending on how large your sample is, you may need to have your coders code either a few hundred pieces of data initially or as few as 10.

INITIAL RELIABILITY

Once your coders have coded some initial pieces of data, you must decide whether they are coding the data reliably. In Chapter 8, we focused on the concept of reliability and on determining whether participants fill out a survey in a consistent fashion, but reliability is equally important in determining whether coders are consistent. In content analysis, we must determine whether multiple coders are actually perceiving the data in the same way, or what researchers call **intercoder reliability**.

In our example, your two research assistants are asked to rate the same sitcom actors as being unattractive, average, or very attractive. Neil Patrick Harris could be rated by one coder as "very attractive" (as shown in Figure 10.2b) and by the other coder as

Here are our results from the study. U = Unattractive, A = Average, and V = Very Attractive.

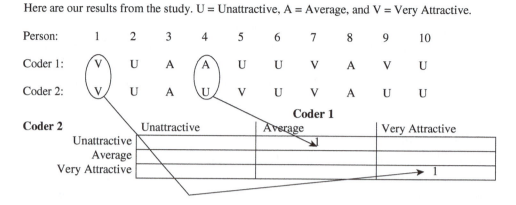

Person: 1   2   3   4   5   6   7   8   9   10

Coder 1:   V   U   A   A   U   U   V   A   V   U

Coder 2:   V   U   A   U   V   U   V   A   U   U

Coder 2	Coder 1		
	Unattractive	Average	Very Attractive
Unattractive			
Average			
Very Attractive			1

FIGURE 10.3
Coding Example

"average" (as shown in Figure 10.2c). How do you decide whether the two coders are using the same coding system to code attractiveness? If the first coder only finds redheads attractive and the second coder does not find redheads attractive, then you will end up with vastly different perspectives on attraction.

So, you ask your two coders to code 10 sitcom actors using the coding form. In Figure 10.3, you can see that your coders coded each of the 10 sitcom actors people as either "V" for very attractive, "A" for average, or "U" for unattractive. The first sitcom actor was coded as "V," very attractive, by Coder 1 and by Coder 2, so you have agreement. If both coders find someone very attractive, then we can count that as one match on our tally board (seen in Figure 10.3, in the 3 × 3 matrix).

Unfortunately, our coders did not always agree with each other. In fact, the fourth sitcom actor was rated as "A" by Coder 1 and as "U" by Coder 2. In this case, you must mark that as a miss in the appropriate box in Figure 10.3. To do this, go to Coder 1 (the columns) and find the "A" column, then go to Coder 2 (the rows) and find the "U" row, and where the two intersect, you count that as one occurrence. Ultimately, you will have placed all 10 of the matches or mismatches in the appropriate places on the 3 × 3 grid, which can be seen in Figure 10.4.

Once you have all of the matches and mismatches in place, you are ready to calculate the intercoder reliability. This calculation involves several steps.

STEP 1 Start by adding the columns separately. In the first column (Coder 1 "Unattractive"), Coder 1 agreed with Coder 2 three times about people who were "unattractive," Coder 1 found no one "unattractive" that Coder 2 found "average," and Coder 1 found one person "unattractive" that Coder 2 found "very attractive." In other words, 3 + 0 + 1 = 4 is the column total. You can then repeat this process for all of the

FIGURE 10.4
Coder Matches and
Mismatches

Coder 1

Coder 2	Unattractive	Average	Very Attractive
Unattractive	3	1	1
Average	0	2	0
Very Attractive	1	0	2

FIGURE 10.5
Coder Totals

Coder 1

Coder 2	Unattractive	Average	Very Attractive	SUMS
Unattractive	3	1	1	5
Average	0	2	0	2
Very Attractive	1	0	2	3
SUMS	4	3	3	TOTAL 10

columns and then for the rows as well. After you have done the simple addition, you should have a chart that looks like Figure 10.5.

STEP 2 Next, you must compute the total number of times that your two coders agreed. In other words, calculate the total of the numbers down the center diagonal (3, 2, 2), which is the Σa in the formula seen in Step 3 below.

Based on this, the percent of agreement would be 7/10, or 70%. If you only use the percentile agreement, then you are using an inflated agreement because it does not take into account the possibility that some of those agreements occurred by chance. To find out what is occurring by chance, you must use the formula in Figure 10.6.

This formula is easy to compute. First, multiply the row total by the column total. For the first column total (5) and first row total (4), simply multiply the totals by each other (5 × 4 = 20), and then divide that number by the overall total, or N(10), so 20/10 = 2. This process can then be repeated for the second column total (3) and second row total (2), so (3 × 2)/10 = 0.6. Repeat the process for the third column total (3) and third row total (3), so (3 × 3)/10 = 0.9. Finally, add the three values together to get the "sum of expected frequencies" (Σef) value, so $\Sigma ef = 2 + 0.6 + 0.9 = 3.5$.

STEP 3 Once you have obtained your sum of expected frequencies value, you can simply plug everything into the formula shown in Figure 10.7.

FIGURE 10.6
Expected Frequency
Formula

$$\text{Expected Frequency } (ef) = \frac{\text{Row Total} \times \text{Column Total}}{\text{Overall Total}}$$

FIGURE 10.7
Cohen's Kappa (κ)
Formula

$$\text{Cohen's Kappa } (K) = \frac{\Sigma a - \Sigma ef}{N - \Sigma ef}$$

Earlier in this section we calculated the sum of a (Σa) as being 7 and the sum of expected frequencies (Σef) as 4.1, and we know that the number of participants observed (N) in this study is 10. At this point, we have all of the parts we need to complete the formula:

$$\kappa = \frac{\Sigma a - \Sigma ef}{N - \Sigma ef}$$

$$\kappa = \frac{7 - 3.5}{10 - 3.5}$$

$$\kappa = \frac{3.5}{6.5}$$

$$\kappa = 0.5384615385 \text{ or } 0.54$$

So, for this study, the consistency to which the two coders rated the attractiveness of situation comedy actors was 0.54. According to Cohen (1960, 1968) if **Cohen's kappa** (κ) is 0.70 or greater, the intercoder reliability is satisfactory, and if κ is less than 0.70, the intercoder reliability is not satisfactory. In this example, Cohen's kappa = 0.54, so the intercoder reliability is not considered satisfactory.

APA WRITE-UP Here is how you would write up this result using American Psychological Association (APA) style:

> Two coders were asked to rate a series of television situation comedy lead actors using the categories not attractive, average, and very attractive. A total of 10 observations were made. To determine whether our two coders were assessing attraction uniformly, Cohen's kappa was calculated, κ = 0.54, which is not considered satisfactory.

REASONS FOR AN UNSATISFACTORY COHEN'S KAPPA If you get an initial Cohen's kappa that is unsatisfactory, a number of problems could be causing this to occur. First, your codebook could be flawed at either the conceptual or the operational level. If this is the case, you should rethink how you are conceptualizing and/or operationalizing your variables in the study. Second, your codebook could be confusing your coders, which could cause them to miscode specific communicative behaviors. If this is the case, you may need to revise the codebook to make it clearer for your coders. Third, one of your coders could not be following the codebook or could be misusing the coding form. If your low intercoder reliability results from either the second or the third problem, retraining is probably necessary.

RETRAINING

Once you have determined where the coding problem is occurring (if you have a low intercoder reliability), you must retrain your coders to correct any mistakes. During the retraining, you should go through all of the data that have been coded and discuss why the coders coded the data the way they have. Ask Coder 1 why he finds Neil Patrick Harris "very attractive," and then ask Coder 2 why she finds Neil Patrick Harris only "average." Often during the retraining phase, you will realize that there could be legitimate reasons why your coders disagree. If you end up in a situation where your coders disagree about a coding, you may need to utilize a third coder to break the tie. Many times, the researcher functions as the third coder. If one of your coders is simply refusing to follow the codebook, however, consider removing that coder from the project. Once you have everyone back on the same track, it is time to let your coders finish coding all of the data.

Final Coding

The final coding of the data should be overseen closely by the researcher to make sure the most accurate results are obtained. Neuendorf (2002) warns that four problems may surface during coding: coder misinterpretations, coder inattention, coder fatigue, and recording errors.

First, despite all of your training and the exactness of your codebook, it is always possible that a *coder may misinterpret a piece of data*. Although you do not want to influence a coder's decision about her or his coding, you may want to have them recheck the data to see whether they coded it accurately, but without telling the coder where you think the problem lies.

Second, a *coder may simply wander off mentally while coding*, which can cause errors in her or his coding. We all have moments when our minds drift for a second. When coding long, detailed conversations, a coder may miss something because he or she simply stops paying attention.

Third, *a coder gets so tired from coding that the coder starts to simply lose track of what he or she is doing*. You may walk into the room where your coders are hard at work, for example, and see one of them coding the same piece of data for the third time. Coders often wish to finish the coding more than they desire to do the coding correctly. As the researcher, you may have to tell your coder to stop coding for the day, or at least take a break and get some caffeine.

Finally, all *coders will make mistakes when coding*. The mistake could be as simple as placing their coder number in the spot where the episode number should be. Other coders may skip a question on the coding form, which throws off all of their codes by one question. As the researcher in charge, your job is to make sure that the coding is as consistent as possible.

Final Reliability

Once your coders have coded all the data in your study, it is time to find the final intercoder reliability. To find the intercoder reliability, follow the steps utilized for Cohen's kappa discussed earlier in this chapter. Cohen's kappa is useful if you have two coders with no missing data. Often, however, researchers will opt to use more than two coders, so they would want to use Krippendorff's alpha (Hayes & Krippendorff, 2007).

The textbook's website (https://oup-arc.com/wrench) has two articles that used forms of content analysis (Boiarsky, Long, & Thayer, 1999; Brummans & Miller, 2004). Although only two articles on book's website relied on coding observations, both of these reported Cohen's kappa to demonstrate that the people who were coding behaviors were coding these behaviors consistently. Figure 10.8 reports the Cohen's kappa values from these articles.

You will note that all the reported Cohen's kappa values fall into the satisfactory range, so you can say that the coders in both studies consistently coded the same observations. You will also note that Boiarsky et al. (1999) reported Pearson correlations for sound effects and visual pacing, since those were not categorical observations but the number of times that those occurred. We will discuss how to interpret correlations in detail in Chapter 18.

Tabulation and Reporting

Once a researcher has completed the basic reliability analysis, he or she is ready to summarize the information and place it into a statistical program such as the Statistical Package for the Social Sciences (SPSS). There are many ways that information can be presented, and the choice will depend largely on the types of variables that you have collected. The last part of this book includes information on how to properly analyze statistical information. These different statistical techniques can be used to examine the data collected in a content analysis. To see how various types of content analyses analyze data, look at the various examples discussed in the early part of this book.

FIGURE 10.8
Cohen's Kappa (κ) in Articles

Coding Tested	Reliability
Brummans & Miller (2004)	
Independent Variable (High vs. Low Ambiguity)	Cohen's Kappa = 0.86
Dependent Variable (Effects of Ambiguity on Initiative Success)	Cohen's Kappa = 0.70
Boiarsky, Long, & Thayer (1999)	
Content Pacing (Existence of a topic shift)	Cohen's Kappa = 0.77–0.87
Sound Effects (Counted number of effects)	Pearson Correlation = 0.83 − 0.97
Visual Pacing (Counted number of cuts, wipes, and fades/dissolves)	Pearson Correlation = 0.85 − 1.0

CONCLUSION

Overall, content analysis is one of the unique and interesting methodologies that communication scholars have developed. Whether you are using content analysis to answer questions related to mass communications or human communication, the technique can be revealing about how communication occurs. In the next chapter, we will look at the third type of quantitative study design, the experiment.

KEY TERMS

Codebook p. 324

Coders p. 326

Coding p. 324

Coding form p. 324

Cohen's kappa (κ) p. 330

Conceptualization p. 322

Content analysis p. 319

Intercoder reliability p. 327

Operationalization p. 323

Unit of analysis p. 323

REFERENCES

Amsbary, J. H., & Powell, L. (2013). Content analysis of self-help internet discussion boards: What they do, what they don't do. *Human Communication, 16*, 49-57.

Ayres, J., & Miura, S. Y. (1981). Construct and predictive validity of instruments for coding relational control communication. *The Western Journal of Speech Communication, 45*, 159–171.

Boiarsky, G., Long, M., & Thayer, G. (1999). Formal features in children's science television: Sound effects, visual pace, and topic shifts. *Communication Research Reports, 16*, 185–192.

Brummans, B. H. J. M., & Miller, K. (2004). The effect of ambiguity on the implementation of a social change initiative. *Communication Research Reports, 21*, 1–10.

Cagle, A., Cox, L., Luoma, K., & Zaphiris, A. (2011). Content analysis of the portrayal of Muslims in American media. *Human Communication, 14*, 1–16.

Cohen, J. (1960). A coefficient of agreement for nominal scales. *Educational and Psychological Measurement, 20*, 37–46.

Cohen, J. (1968). Weighted kappa: Nominal scale agreement with provision for scaled disagreement of partial credit. *Psychological Bulletin, 70*, 213–220.

Comstock, J. M., & Buller, D. B. (1991). Conflict strategies adolescents use with their parents: Testing the cognitive communicator characteristics model. *Journal of Language and Social Psychology, 10*, 47–59.

Courtright, J. A., Millar, F. E., & Rogers-Millar, E. (1979). Domineeringness and dominance: Replication and expansion. *Communication Monographs, 46*, 179–192.

Dovring, K. (1954–1955). Quantitative semantics in 18th century Sweden. *Public Opinion Quarterly, 18*, 389–394.

Ekman, P., & Rosenberg, E. L. (Eds.). (2005). *What the face reveals: Basic and applied studies of spontaneous expression using the Facial Action Coding System (FACS)* (2nd ed.). New York, NY: Oxford University Press.

Evans, S. (2015). Shark Week and the rise of infotainment in science documentaries. *Communication Research Reports, 32,* 265-271. doi:10.1080/08824096.2015.1052903

Feyereisen, P., & Havard, I. (1999). Mental imagery and production of gestures while speaking in younger and older adults. *Journal of Nonverbal Behavior, 23,* 153–171.

Hajek, C., & Giles, H. (2005). Intergroup communication schemas: Cognitive representations of talk with gay men. *Language and Communication, 25,* 161–181. doi:10.1016/j.langcom.2005.01.002

Hajek, C., & Giles, H. (2006). On communicating pride, crying in movies, and recruiting innocent bystanders: The effect of sex on communication schemas activated with gay and heterosexual targets. *Communication Research Reports, 23,* 77–84. doi:10.1080/08824090600668873

Harwood, J. (1998). Young adults' cognitive representations of intergenerational conversations. *Journal of Applied Communication Research, 26,* 13–31.

Hayes, A. F., & Krippendorff, K. (2007). Answering the call for a standard reliability measure for coding data. *Communication Methods and Measures, 1,* 77–89.

Hefner, V., Firchau, R., Norton, K., & Shevel, G. (2017). Happily ever after? A content analysis of romantic ideals in Disney princess films. *Communication Studies, 68,* 511-532. doi:10.1080/10510974.2017.1365092

Hirdes, W., Woods, R., & Badzinski, D. M. (2009). A content analysis of Jesus merchandise. *Journal of Media & Religion, 8,* 141–157. doi:10.1080/15348420903091030

Keyton, J. (2006). *Communication research: Asking questions, finding answers* (2nd ed.). Boston, MA: McGraw–Hill.

Lynch, T., Tompkins, J. E., van Driel, I. I., & Fritz, N. (2016). Sexy, strong, and secondary: A content analysis of female characters in video games across 31 years. *Journal of Communication, 66,* 564-584. doi:10.1111/jcom.12237

Mastro, D., & Figueroa-Caballero, A. (2018). Measuring extremes: A quantitative content analysis of prime time TV depictions of body type. *Journal of Broadcasting & Electronic Media, 62,* 320-336. doi:10.1080/08838151.2018.1451853

Min, S., & Feaster, J. C. (2010). Missing children in national news coverage: Racial and gender representations of missing children cases. *Communication Research Reports, 27,* 207-216. doi:10.1080/08824091003776289

Neuendorf, K. A. (2002). *The content analysis guidebook.* Thousand Oaks, CA: Sage.

Riffe, D., Lacy, S., & Fico, F.G. (2005). *Analyzing media messages: Using quantitative content analysis in research* (2nd ed.). Mahwah, NJ: Erlbaum.

Roter, D., Lipkin, M. Jr., & Dorsgaard, A. (1991). Sex differences in patients' and physicians' communication during primary care medical visits. *Medical Care, 29,* 1083–1093.

Schultz, A. S., Moore, J., & Spitzberg, B. H. (2014). Once upon a midnight stalker: A content analysis of stalking in films. *Western Journal of Communication, 78*, 612-635. doi:10.1080/10570314.2013.809475

Shaffer, D. R., Pegalis, L., & Connell, D. P. (1991). Interactive effects of social context and sex role identity on female self-disclosure during the acquaintance process. *Sex Roles, 24*, 1–19.

Waters, R. D., & Lo, K. D. (2012). Exploring the impact of culture in the social media sphere: A content analysis of nonprofit organizations' use of Facebook. *Journal of Intercultural Communication Research, 41*, 297-319. doi:10.1080/17475759.2012.728772

11

Experimental Design

CHAPTER OBJECTIVES

1. Explain the basic parts of an experiment (random assignment, manipulation of the independent variable, measurement of the dependent variable, and control).

2. List and explain the four issues researchers must be aware of when attempting to control an experiment (threshold effects, experimenter effects, Hawthorne effect, and intervening variables).

3. Differentiate among the three types of confounding variables (suppressor, reinforcer, and lurker).

4. Describe six external threats to validity associated with experiments (historical flaw, maturation, testing flaw, regression to the mean, selection threat, and attrition).

5. Recognize and explain preexperimental and true experimental designs.

Whether adding two chemicals together to see what would happen or attempting to make a trash bag float using straws, tape, and birthday candles, we have all conducted experiments in our physical science classes in grade school, but most people are not as familiar with the purpose of experiments. The general reason scientists perform experiments is to establish **time order**, or the idea that researchers can establish an exact order to when things occur—Time 1 (T_1) occurred and then Time 2 (T_2) occurred. For example, in a chemistry class, you must first combine baking soda and vinegar together (T_1) to get the "volcanic reaction" (T_2) we all remember as children. If you set the box of baking soda and the bottle of vinegar on the counter side by side without combining the two, you will never get the volcanic reaction. Although the social sciences may not be as exact as the physical sciences, social scientists also use experiments in research, so this chapter examines how communication researchers can use experiments.

▲ Alice Is Still
Wondering
Source: © Don Mayne www.
researchcartoons.com

Time order for experimental research is akin to the age-old question, "Which came first, the chicken or the egg?" Imagine you are a researcher who took on this question. If at the end of your study you have a chicken and you have an egg, would you know which came first? Nope! If, however, you can show scientifically that it is a necessity for an egg to exist prior to a chicken's existence, then you can establish the "time order" of events—first egg, then chicken.

Communication researchers may not be interested in chickens and eggs, but we are interested in whether specific phenomena must occur prior to exhibited communication behaviors. For example, imagine that you want to find out whether children playing violent video games will exhibit increased antisocial behavior. Specifically, you want to find a time order between playing violent video games (first instance of time) and its effect on antisocial behaviors (second instance of time). Although you could ask for self-reports of video game playing and antisocial behavior, these reports may not be completely accurate and could only show a relationship between the two variables, not a time order between them.

Techniques beyond surveying (which was discussed in Chapter 9) have helped researchers answer causal relationship questions. In this chapter, we examine what experiments are and why we do them, and we explore a series of common experimental designs.

WHAT ARE EXPERIMENTS AND WHY DO WE DO THEM?

An **experiment** occurs when a researcher purposefully manipulates one or more variables in the hope of seeing how this manipulation affects other variables of interest. In the physical sciences, manipulating a variable is easy. If you want to see the effects of liquid nitrogen on a blown-up balloon, simply submerge the inflated balloon in liquid nitrogen and watch what happens. Although some communication experiments can be designed in this fashion (e.g., placing doughnuts in a room full of people and watching what happens), most require considerably more complicated methods. This section explores three important aspects of experiments: rationale, aspects of experimental designs, and experimental process.

Rationale for Experimental Research

Researchers use experiments for a variety of reasons. Although establishing causal relationships is the primary reason for conducting experiments, researchers often conduct them for other reasons as well. Let's look at four basic reasons researchers conduct experiments: determining causal relationships, ruling out alternative explanations, determining the incidence of intervening and antecedent variables, and determining cause or chance.

DETERMINING CAUSAL RELATIONSHIPS

A researcher will conduct an experiment because it allows her or him to establish whether an independent variable causes a change in the dependent variable. In survey-based research, investigators essentially examine differences and relationships that individuals perceive, whereas in experimental research, they can examine differences and relationships that they manipulate. This process of examining how independent variables affect dependent variables is called time order. As discussed earlier, time order is the idea that researchers can establish an exact order as to when things occur. For example, to determine whether playing violent video games leads to antisocial behavior, a researcher could use two groups. The control group plays a video game that does not contain violence, but in the experimental group, the researcher has the participants play a video game that contains notable amounts of violence. If the control group's antisocial behavior does not change from a pre- to a posttest but the experimental group's antisocial behavior increases, then we can ascertain that a time order occurred (first test of antisocial behavior, playing a violent video game, and then second test of antisocial behavior).

RULING OUT ALTERNATIVE EXPLANATIONS

Experiments also allow researchers to rule out alternative explanations for their research findings. By having a baseline score (or pretest), the researchers in our video game study are able to know whether playing the violent video game led to violence. The antisocial behavior seen after playing the video game could actually occur for a number of reasons, but without an initial score of antisocial behavior, those other potential reasons cannot be ruled out. If the children placed in the nonviolent video game condition have already been exposed to many violent video game images, the results of antisocial behavior between those playing violent versus nonviolent video games may not be different at all. Furthermore, exposure to other violent media could also cause a difference in antisocial behavior. All in all, experiments enable researchers to **control** what occurs within the testing situation in a way that allows them to either prevent or rule out other explanations for changes seen.

DETERMINING THE INFLUENCE OF INTERVENING AND ANTECEDENT VARIABLES

Another reason for performing experiments is to determine whether intervening and antecedent variables are influencing the results. Since life is often complex, and understanding life requires complex questions and answers, experiments allow researchers to attempt to find underlying antecedent and intervening variables.

Antecedent variables are variables that occur prior to the experiment that may impact the way an independent variable or dependent variable functions. For example, maybe you want to determine whether the type of school a student went to in college affects her or his earning potential after college. Although this may seem straightforward, an individual's socioeconomic status could impact both her or his choice in colleges and her or his earning potential after college. Thus, socioeconomic status is a third variable that exists outside the simple linear model of how college affects earning potential. If a researcher thinks socioeconomic status may affect choices of colleges and earning potentials, then he or she could control for socioeconomic status to see how much impact the variable has.

As mentioned previously, an intervening variable occurs between an independent variable and a dependent variable. We will discuss intervening variables in more detail later in this chapter.

DETERMINING CAUSE OR CHANCE

The last reason we conduct experiments is to determine whether phenomena happen for some underlying reason or by chance. When researchers rely solely on survey research, they often will find relationships between variables do not mean much. For example, maybe a researcher found a relationship between a physician's use of touch and a patient's perception of that physician's physical attractiveness. For example, maybe a patient finds a physician more physically attractive if the physician touches them (in a professional, non-intimate way). When another researcher reads these results, he or she may be puzzled as to why such a relationship exists. To determine whether this relationship truly exists or simply occurred by chance, the researcher may perform an experiment to determine causal relationships. The researcher could train a series of physicians to randomly use touch with some patients (condition 1) and not use touch with other patients (condition 2). The researcher could have participants rate the physicians' physical attractiveness and test whether physicians' use of touch during medical interviews increases patients' perceptions of the physician's physical attractiveness.

ASPECTS OF EXPERIMENTAL DESIGN

When looking at experimental designs, we see a number of aspects that a researcher must constantly attend to while doing research: random assignment, manipulation of the independent variable, measurement of the dependent variable, and control of the experiment.

Random Assignment

Imagine that we want to determine whether an individual's use of verbal aggression affects an interaction partner's perception of the verbally aggressive person's likability. We may train a group of people called confederates (individuals who pretend to be researchers or research participants but are really part of the experimental manipulation) to use or not use specific verbal aggression strategies, and then have those confederates interact with the study participants in one-on-one interactions to see whether the participant perceives highly verbally aggressive people differently than people who are not verbally aggressive. If we let people choose whether they want to interact with a highly verbally aggressive person versus a low verbally aggressive person, however, we may see some outcomes that are not real. Maybe participants who are verbally aggressive themselves enjoy other verbally aggressive people, so they would flock to the highly verbally aggressive interactants and purposefully rate these people as highly likeable. And participants who are not verbally aggressive may avoid the verbally aggressive condition completely. Therefore, randomly placing participants into experimental conditions becomes extremely important for research to enable an accurate time order of experimental events.

Random assignment comprises the procedures experimenters use for placing participants into a research condition that ensures every participant in the sample has an equal chance to be in a given research condition. For example, in this case, everyone in our sample would have an equal chance of interacting with a highly verbally aggressive partner or a minimally verbally aggressive partner. The experimenter's job is to make sure that this randomization occurs.

So, how does one randomly assign people into experimental conditions? There are a number of ways. Maybe for each participant you flip a coin—participants who land on heads interact with the verbally aggressive individual, and participants who land on tails interact with the nonverbally aggressive individual. Maybe you have participants draw a condition out of a hat. You have equal numbers of pieces of paper in a hat labeled "A" for the verbally aggressive condition and "B" for the nonverbally aggressive condition. If a person draws the letter "B," he or she is taken to the room where a nonverbally aggressive interactant is waiting. Or maybe you use a random number generator or a random number table. Figure 11.1 was created using a random number generator located at http://www.random.org/.

FIGURE 11.1
Random Number Table

156	675	878	553	748	187	979	592
443	930	530	144	612	638	365	615
523	180	420	666	633	808	839	688
451	487	355	478	604	877	144	810
231	108	790	870	788	805	167	356
607	673	294	674	718	590	892	805
159	326	996	778	216	801	521	598
915	355	275	590	703	315	729	886
221	558	220	223	442	400	993	434
218	780	463	153	399	337	790	619
597	732	240	793	764	807	954	845
773	939	452	524	304	466	291	522
652	256	655	250	574	892	347	835
977	155	481	867	946	533	605	998
865	950	104	605	418	251	439	479
577	107	187	761	410	607	521	481
417	622	607	583	242	995	363	891
510	992	583	246	804	998	134	942
536	437	126	679	619	865	184	315
347	417	879	336	628	375	734	845
499	629	470	452	804	840	814	361
142	486	621	947	128	137	231	478
844	745	872	866	725	297	945	494
543	988	471	207	857	746	694	636
722	978	611	283	907	233	769	442
238	633	576	305	947	105	439	420
505	387	572	733	419	793	170	938
596	302	436	307	674	764	411	940
435	911	107	756	596	211	782	383
612	423	877	240	995	263	586	710
686	811	164	154	924	999	784	539
713	184	310	935	562	328	309	917
303	873	700	393	672	170	490	538
439	301	662	684	898	742	699	149
912	462	111	334	546	271	545	682
706	308	792	134	461	985	330	576
326	797	652	678	743	565	277	354

One way to use a random number generator is to create a single column of random numbers and place the estimated number of participants needed in each experimental condition next to the same number of random numbers. For example, if you needed 20 participants in the first condition (verbally aggressive interactant) and 20 participants in the second condition (nonverbally aggressive interactant), then you would place "VA" (verbally aggressive) next to the first 20 random numbers and "NVA" (nonverbally aggressive) next to the second 20 random numbers (Figure 11.2).

If I then took the random numbers and ordered them numerically, I would effectively randomize the order in which we assign people into one of the two conditions. In our example, the first participant in the study is placed in the nonverbally aggressive condition (as seen in Figure 11.3), and then the next five are randomly assigned to the verbally aggressive condition. This trend continues until we have placed 40 participants into one of the two conditions.

Manipulation of the Independent Variable

The second major part of experimental design is the **manipulation of the independent variable**. Before defining what we mean by this, let's look at an example.

FIGURE 11.2
Random Numbers Applied to Participant List

1	156	VA	21	499	NVA
2	443	VA	22	142	NVA
3	523	VA	23	844	NVA
4	451	VA	24	543	NVA
5	231	VA	25	722	NVA
6	607	VA	26	238	NVA
7	159	VA	27	505	NVA
8	915	VA	28	596	NVA
9	221	VA	29	435	NVA
10	218	VA	30	612	NVA
11	597	VA	31	686	NVA
12	773	VA	32	713	NVA
13	652	VA	33	303	NVA
14	977	VA	34	439	NVA
15	865	VA	35	912	NVA
16	577	VA	36	706	NVA
17	417	VA	37	326	NVA
18	510	VA	38	984	NVA
19	536	VA	39	675	NVA
20	347	VA	40	930	NVA

1	142	NVA		21	543	NVA
2	156	VA		22	577	VA
3	159	VA		23	596	NVA
4	218	VA		24	597	VA
5	221	VA		25	607	VA
6	231	VA		26	612	NVA
7	238	NVA		27	652	VA
8	303	NVA		28	675	NVA
9	326	NVA		29	686	NVA
10	347	VA		30	706	NVA
11	417	VA		31	713	NVA
12	435	NVA		32	722	NVA
13	439	NVA		33	773	VA
14	443	VA		34	844	NVA
15	451	VA		35	865	VA
16	499	NVA		36	912	NVA
17	505	NVA		37	915	VA
18	510	VA		38	930	NVA
19	523	VA		39	977	VA
20	536	VA		40	984	NVA

FIGURE 11.3
Randomized
Conditions

EXAMPLE OF MANIPULATING THE INDEPENDENT VARIABLE

In Chapter 2, we discussed an experiment conducted by Wrench, Millhouse, and Sharp (2007). In that study, the researchers wanted to see whether including humor in preflight safety briefings influenced how people saw the flight attendants. To determine whether humor influenced people's perceptions of flight attendants, the researchers created two preflight safety briefing scripts—one with humor and one without humor. In the experiment itself, participants were exposed to one script or the other and then asked about their perceptions of the flight attendant. In this study, Time 1 occurs when the participants are exposed to the preflight safety briefing (humorous vs. standard), and Time 2 occurs as the participants respond to a series of survey questions about the flight attendants.

Experimental designs involve manipulating an independent variable and seeing how that manipulation affects a dependent variable. By "manipulating," we mean that a researcher purposefully alters or changes the independent variable to see whether this alteration affects the dependent variable. In our example, the researchers "altered" a standard preflight safety briefing to include humor. By creating one preflight safety briefing with humor and one without humor (manipulation of the independent variable), the researchers could see whether including humor affected people's perceptions of their flight attendants (dependent variable). The goal of this experiment was to test for differences between the two experimental conditions (humorous preflight safety briefing and standard preflight safety briefing).

WAYS TO MANIPULATE AN INDEPENDENT VARIABLE

Now that we have introduced you to the basic components of independent variable manipulation, we look at a number of ways that communication researchers can manipulate an independent variable. These include providing a stimulus, written materials, audio or video recordings, computer simulations, confederates, and hypothetical scenarios and role-playing activities.

PROVIDING A STIMULUS First, researchers can provide some participants a specific stimulus or phenomenon (**experimental group**) and not give that same stimulus or phenomenon to the other participants (**control group**). In a study conducted by Tamborini, Eastin, Skalski, Lachlan, Fediuk, and Brady (2004), the researchers wanted to examine the effect that video games had on hostile thoughts. At the beginning of the semester, participants completed a self-report questionnaire designed to measure prior video game use and hostile thoughts. Participants were then randomly assigned to one of four conditions: (1) playing a violent virtual reality video game, (2) playing a standard violent video game, (3) observing a violent video game, and (4) observing a nonviolent video game. Ultimately, people in the first three conditions all experienced elevated hostile thoughts after engaging with or watching violent video games, but those in the fourth condition, where a nonviolent video game was observed, did not.

WRITTEN MATERIALS Second, researchers can rely on written materials to manipulate people. For example, Stewart (1994) wanted to examine whether an individual's expressed religious identity would add credibility to that individual as a speaker. To examine this research question, Stewart used written texts to introduce participants to a potential speaker. In one of the texts, Stewart mentioned that the speaker was "a regular churchgoer, is very active in church functions, and often publicly expresses his belief that prayer is important in achieving one's professional goals," whereas in the second introduction, no mention of religion was made. Stewart ultimately found that participants perceived the potential speaker whose introduction contained religious content as more credible.

AUDIO OR VIDEO RECORDINGS A third way of manipulating an independent variable in communication research is similar to the written method, but instead of using text, you record (using either audio or video) the manipulation. In the article by Weber, Fornash, Corrigan, and Neupauer (2003), which is on the textbook's website (https://oup-arc.com/wrench), the researchers recorded two public relations lectures. In the first lecture (the control), the researchers used examples that are traditionally found in public relations textbooks. In the second lecture (the experimental condition), the researchers used more modern examples of public relations that are not typically found in textbooks. The study determined that the use of more modern, updated examples helps students score higher on a quiz.

COMPUTER SIMULATIONS Computers have become increasingly used as a way to manipulate independent variables. In fact, some high-end survey software (e.g., Qualtrics and SurveyMonkey) now even allow researchers to randomly put participants into different manipulations. For example, imagine you wanted to test student perceptions of teacher credibility based on the color of the shirt a teacher wore. Computers allow researchers to use computerized avatars for this task, and even to change the color of the shirt for different manipulation conditions. In a study conducted by Pertaub, Slater, and Barker (2002), the researchers used virtual reality to test speakers' reactions to one of three different virtual audiences: neutral, positive (friendly and excited), and negative (hostile and bored).

CONFEDERATES Another prominent way of manipulating an independent variable is the use of confederates. A **confederate** is an individual who, without the participants' knowledge, is actually part of the experiment being conducted. An example of confederate use was found in a study conducted by Guéguen and De Gail (2003). These researchers had eight confederates (four females and four males) randomly walk by 800 customers in a supermarket (400 females and 400 males) and randomly smile or not smile at the person. Immediately after this interaction, a second confederate (who was blind to whether or not smiling had occurred) holding a portfolio and package of computer disks would "accidentally" drop the disks. Ultimately, the study wanted to determine whether the smiling of the first confederate would lead the participant to help the second confederate. Overall, this study found that smiling led to an increase in helping behavior.

HYPOTHETICAL SCENARIOS AND ROLE-PLAYING ACTIVITIES The last major way in which communication researchers manipulate independent variables is through hypothetical scenarios and role-playing activities. In this type of manipulation, researchers give the participants a scenario, and the participants are then asked to role-play a situation as if they were taking part in the fictionalized scenario. In a study by Wiener and Doescher (1994), the researchers wanted to determine the effect that expectation would have on willingness to comply with a request. The researchers placed 84 undergraduates into one of two conditions—high expectation or low expectation. The scenario given to the participants was the need to put an energy-regulating device on their apartment air-conditioning unit. In the high-expectation group, the participants were told that 70% of the people within their state had already indicated a willingness to add the energy-regulating device to their air conditioning units; the low-expectation group was told that only 15% would add the device. The participants were then asked whether they would be willing to add the device to their air conditioners. Of the participants in the high-expectation condition, 84% said they would add the device, compared to only 59% of the participants in the low-expectation group.

FACTORIAL EXPERIMENTAL DESIGNS

Typically, when people consider independent variable manipulation, it is easy to think of putting people into either an experimental condition or a control condition. However, as we have seen, a wide variety of different experimental forms are possible. Some experiments have more than two levels (control vs. experimental), and others manipulate more than one independent variable. When an individual attempts to manipulate more than one independent variable, he or she is using a **factorial experiment design**.

In the study by Guéguen and De Gail (2003), the researchers examined one dependent variable, smiling versus nonsmiling, but they also examined the impact of the biological sex of the confederate who smiled and the biological sex of the confederate who held the portfolio and disks. In this case, we have what is called a 2 × 2 × 2 factorial experimental design. Each variable in this study (smiling, biological sex of confederate who smiles, and biological sex of confederate who drops materials) is represented by one of the 2's in the factorial design. The numeral 2 is used because each variable only has two levels (smiling vs. not smiling, female vs. male for confederate 1, and female vs. male for confederate 2). If we broadened this study to examine the impact that a third characteristic, frowning, has on the study, then the study would become a 3 × 2 × 2 factorial experimental design because the smiling variable would be manipulated three different ways (frowning, smiling, and nonemotion). If this had been the case, our experimental design would look like Figure 11.4. In essence, we end up with 12 experimental conditions being compared to each other.

The more independent variables a researcher utilizes, the more participants he or she must have in a study. For statistical purposes, each experimental condition should have no fewer than 10 participants, but it is safer to have closer to 50 participants in each condition. The more factors (independent variables) a researcher wants to examine, the more complicated the design will become, and the more participants a researcher will ultimately need to complete the experiment. For example, if we decide to add yet another independent variable (participant's biological sex) to our study shown in Figure 11.4, we now have 24 experimental conditions in this example (3 × 2 × 2 × 2). For this reason, most experiments are greatly limited in the number of independent variables studied because it is not always realistic to recruit enormous samples for research.

	Female Confederate Smiling Condition		Male Confederate Smiling Condition	
	Female Confederate Dropping Condition	Male Confederate Dropping Condition	Female Confederate Dropping Condition	Male Confederate Dropping Condition
Smile at Participant				
Frown at Participant				
Show no Emotion Toward Participant				

FIGURE 11.4
Factorial Design

Measurement of the Dependent Variable

The third major part of experimental design is the measurement of the dependent variable. Often, the dependent variable can easily be measured by having a participant fill out a research scale. In the study of the impact of violent video games on antisocial behavior, for example, after a participant is exposed to the video game we could have the participant fill out a research measure examining levels of desire to engage in antisocial behavior. In the study of the impact of verbal aggression on likability, after a participant interacted with the verbally aggressive or the nonverbally aggressive person the researchers could have the participant fill out a scale measuring their interactant's likability. By doing this, researchers can measure the extent to which participants like both verbally aggressive and nonverbally aggressive people. In both of these studies, the dependent variable can be measured by having the participants fill out a pen-and-paper scale.

There are other, more observational ways to measure dependent variables, however. In the first example, after exposing a group of children to both violent and nonviolent video games, we could place all of them in a room together and watch for antisocial interaction behaviors. If the participants exposed to the violent video games are more likely to initiate antisocial behavioral patterns than those participants exposed to the nonviolent video games, we would establish a time order between exposure and outcome. If you wanted to measure likability of verbally aggressive versus nonverbally aggressive interactants, you could watch the participants' nonverbal communicative behavior during the interaction. Participants who are attracted to their interaction partners will exhibit more nonverbally immediate behaviors than those participants who are not attracted to their interaction partners. Ultimately, when determining how to measure a dependent variable, a researcher must ask her- or himself what the basic purpose of the study is and what would be the most efficient way to determine whether the independent variable manipulation is causing a change in the dependent variable.

One important concept must be discussed with reference to measuring dependent variables. If a dependent variable is to change because of time order, the manipulation of the independent variable must be substantial enough to cause a change. For example, some people may argue that video games such as *Frogger* and *Pac-Man* are violent. However, will exposing children to *Frogger* and *Pac-Man* lead to increases in antisocial behavior? Probably not. If exposing children to *Frogger* and *Pac-Man* are not adequate independent variable manipulations to cause a change in the dependent variable, exposing children to more obviously violent games, such as *Doom*, *Grand Theft Auto*, *Call of Duty*, and *Mortal Combat*, may be necessary to see changes in the dependent variable. Ultimately, if the manipulation of the independent variable is not substantial, the experiment will fail to see changes in the dependent variable that may exist.

Control of the Experiment

One of the most difficult aspects of conducting experiments is attempting to make sure that what a researcher is examining with an experiment is actually being examined. For example, what if you are trying to manipulate the types of conflicts a married couple engages in only to find out that you are actually manipulating the compliance-gaining strategies a couple uses instead? For this reason, researchers must be careful to avoid influencing an experiment in a way that is not being measured in the experiment itself. Researchers must be aware of a number of different issues that can affect the outcome of an experiment: threshold effects, experimenter effects, the Hawthorne effect, and extraneous variables.

THRESHOLD EFFECTS

The first issue that researchers must be keenly aware of is the possibility of threshold effects. A **threshold effect** occurs when changes in a specific dependent variable are only seen after an independent variable reaches a certain level. For example, maybe a person only decreases her or his perception of an interactant's likability when the interactant becomes absurdly verbally aggressive, so low levels of verbal aggression do not impact the interactant's likability. Maybe high levels of antianxiety medication decrease an individual's level of communication apprehension (CA) but low dosages change nothing. In both of these examples, there is a threshold or minimum level that the independent variable must meet before it will affect the dependent variable.

EXPERIMENTER EFFECTS

The second, and often the most problematic, issue that can affect the outcome of an experiment is experimenter effects. **Experimenter effects** are effects caused unknowingly by the experimenter on the participants. Experimenters often will accidentally influence research results without even knowing that they are doing so. For example, in a study examining placebo versus an antianxiety medication, it is possible that a researcher actually informs the participants slightly differently. Not that the experimenter is purposefully trying to slant the results in one way or the other, but people often unconsciously change their behavior in ways that can affect the results of an experiment. To control for this, a technique has been developed by researchers called the double-blind study, in which neither the researcher nor the participant knows whether the participant is receiving the actual manipulation (antianxiety medication) or the fake manipulation (placebo).

THE HAWTHORNE EFFECT

The third problematic area that researchers must be aware of is called the Hawthorne effect. The **Hawthorne effect** gets its name from a series of experiments conducted at the Hawthorne Works of Western Electric Company in Chicago from 1924 to 1932. In this set of studies, the researchers initially determined whether the level of lighting in an electric company affected the productivity level of the employees. In the original study, the researchers manipulated the lighting in the electric company (independent variable) to see whether it influenced worker output (dependent variable). Ultimately, the researchers were astonished when they determined that their manipulation of the lighting did nothing to affect productivity because worker output increased in all of the lighting conditions. When the experiment was complete, however, the researchers realized that the lighting had not changed the worker output, but that the researchers hovering over the workers and watching what they were doing had increased the worker output.

This same problem can exist in other experiments as well, so researchers have adopted a number of safeguards to help prevent the Hawthorne effect from occurring in an experiment. First, researchers will often try to observe participants through video monitoring systems or one-way mirrors so that the participants do not know when they are being watched. Researchers will also deceive participants about the actual nature of the study being conducted. Whereas deception involves ethical issues that clearly must be addressed (as discussed in Chapter 3), deception can be useful when employed in a fashion to help a researcher attain clear and consistent results. Other researchers will include blank or dummy experiments to throw a participant off the actual nature of the study. In the verbal aggression study, maybe the researcher will have the participants fill out a wide range of scales about the personality of the confederate interactant. Although this researcher is attempting to look at likability, he or she may also ask questions about the use of humor, immediacy, and so on.

EXTRANEOUS VARIABLES

The last problem that must be overcome when conducting experiments is to be aware that other variables may influence the outcome of your experiment. In any experiment, there can be a series of what are called **extraneous variables**—that is, variables not being measured in your study but affecting your results. There are two major categories of extraneous variable: intervening and confounding.

INTERVENING VARIABLES An **intervening variable**, often called mediating or latent variables, is a variable that intervenes between the independent variable and the dependent variable. For example, if you want to determine the effects of drinking in college on grades, it is possible that the two variables (independent and dependent) are not going to tell you the complete picture. Although there may in fact be a negative relationship between alcohol consumption in college and grades, it is also possible that what is really being seen is that alcohol consumption is a measure of partying at school, which means that a person is spending less time going to class and studying. And as a result of spending less time in class and studying, the participants' grades may then start to suffer. In other words, alcohol consumption does not necessarily cause grades to slip in college, but it may create the circumstances (not going to class and not studying) that lead to slipping grades. In this example, the variables identified as not going to class and not studying are examples of intervening variables.

CONFOUNDING VARIABLES A **confounding variable is a** variable that obscures the effects of your independent variable. Three types of confounding variables often occur in research: suppressor, reinforcer, and lurker.

Suppressor variables are variables that suppress or reduce the effect of the independent variable on the dependent variable. For example, research has shown us that introverts are more likely to have higher CA scores than extroverted people. One cause of this could be that introverts are less likely to communicate innately, so they do not end up gaining as much experience communicating with other people. This lack of experience could be a factor in causing introverts to be anxious when interacting with people. Thus, the variable "lack of experience" could be seen as a suppressor variable.

Reinforcer variables are variables that enhance the effect of the independent variable on the dependent variable. For example, research has shown that extroverted people are more communicatively competent. Does this mean that extroverts are born with more information on how to communicate in a competent way than introverts? Probably not. However, extroverted people probably do have more experience interacting with other people, so they have more opportunities to develop competent communicative behaviors. In this case, experience is a reinforcer variable.

Lurker variables are variables that explain both the independent variable and the dependent variable. For example, maybe a study finds that there is a relationship between CA and the number of friends a person has. However, it is possible that a third variable, introversion, is actually causing the other two variables to occur in the first place. In this example, introversion is a lurker variable because it is not a variable being directly studied but is ultimately responsible for the scores of both the independent variable (CA) and the dependent variable (number of friends).

CONDUCTING AN EXPERIMENT

Now that we have examined the key components of and the rationale for experiments, we can focus on the basic process of performing an experiment. The basic process that all researchers go through when conducting an experiment is as follows: introduce the experiment to the participant and obtain consent, randomly assign the participants to different conditions, manipulate the independent variable, measure the dependent variable, and debrief the participants when the experiment is completed.

Introduce the Experiment and Obtain Consent

The first part of any actual experiment involves explaining to a participant what the experiment will entail. Although researchers may use deception to prevent the participants from knowing what the researcher is examining, some cover story will be told to those participating. One reason researchers use deception when explaining what an experiment is examining is to prevent what Joseph Masling (1966) calls the "screw-you" effect. When participants know what a researcher is looking for, many participants will try to answer questions contrary to how they really feel in order to throw off the experiment. We will talk more about the ethical issues of deception in Chapter 12.

The initial part of an experiment also involves obtaining consent. In the United States, the federal government has mandated that anyone who participates in a research experiment should give her or his consent. If someone cannot give consent (e.g., children or mentally impaired individuals), a legal guardian is needed to give consent. Obtaining consent entails explaining any actual risks involved in a study. For the most part, communication research does not involve physical risks, but many researchers examine sensitive topics that could cause people psychological distress. To allow a situation that would make them feel uncomfortable, participants must be informed of their legal rights (e.g., ability to leave the experiment at any time) and the risks involved with the study. As discussed in Chapter 3, every university has an institutional review board that researchers must comply with to carry out research of any kind (both experimental and nonexperimental).

Random Assignment of Participants

The second part to conducting an experiment is to randomly assign participants to a treatment group. Earlier in this chapter, we discussed in much greater detail a number of ways to randomly assign people to different treatment groups. Once the participants are in a group, any pretesting of the dependent variable that is necessary for the experiment will be conducted.

Manipulate the Independent Variable

Once participants have been placed into the different conditions of an experiment, a researcher will manipulate the independent variable. All of the experimental examples discussed in this chapter thus far have involved manipulating an independent variable.

Whether studying interactions with verbally aggressive or nonverbally aggressive persons or the effects of playing a violent video game, a researcher will attempt to alter the independent variable in a way that could cause a change in the dependent variable.

One way to make sure that the participants are actually seeing the manipulation of the dependent variable is to perform a manipulation check. A **manipulation check** is a procedure where a researcher inserts a quantitative measurement into a study to determine whether different conditions portray the independent variable differently. For example, in a study that had participants interacting with confederates who did or did not verbally communicate aggressively, a researcher could have had the participants fill out the Verbal Aggression Scale on the confederates. If the researcher found that the participants did not perceive the verbal aggression and nonverbal aggression interactants differently regarding the verbal aggression levels, then the results of the study would be flawed. If, however, the participants rated the verbally aggressive confederate as being more verbally aggressive than the nonverbally aggressive confederate, then manipulation of verbal aggression was good.

For example, in the Wrench et al. (2007) study examining humorous versus standard preflight safety briefings, the researchers created the two scripts, but how did they know people perceived the humorous script as actually humorous? The three authors of the study could all have had the same sense of humor, which could differ from their participants' senses of humor. To make sure that the participants perceived the humorous script as funny and the standard script as not funny, the researchers asked a single question that participants answered at the end of the survey: "On a scale of "0" (*not humorous*) to "9" (*very humorous*), indicate how humorous you found the flight attendant's preflight briefing." By including this question, the researchers could then determine whether the two groups actually viewed the humorousness of the script differently. By checking to see whether the manipulation occurred, researchers are able to know whether the results they receive are actually a result of their manipulation of the independent variable (in this case, the preflight safety briefing).

Measure the Dependent Variable

Once you have manipulated the independent variable, the next step in performing an experiment is to measure the dependent variable. As mentioned previously, there are a number of ways to measure a dependent variable, and a researcher must be careful that the measure used for the dependent variable is both reliable and valid (as discussed in Chapter 8).

Debrief the Participants

The last part of an experiment occurs after a dependent variable has been measured for the last time. In the **debriefing** part of an experiment, a researcher first corrects any deception that was used at the beginning of an experiment. Researchers realize that it is unethical to let a research participant complete a study and not know what was done to them. In addition to correcting any deception, the researcher should also reaffirm the value of the study and the participants' addition to the research process. Finally, a researcher may ask a couple of pointed questions to determine whether a participant knowingly changed her or his results based on what he or she thought the experiment was testing. After a participant has been debriefed, participants are usually open to admitting that they may have slanted their answers in a particular direction because they thought it was what the researcher actually wanted to know ("demand characteristics"). Another problem that can also be noted during an experimental debriefing is whether a participant was more anxious than usual because he or she knew that the researcher was evaluating her or his behavior. Many people behave abnormally as a result of the contrived evaluation situation that many research projects create (remember the Hawthorne effect). By listening to participants' thoughts about the research process after the fact, a researcher can determine whether either of these problems has occurred.

THREATS TO EXPERIMENTAL VALIDITY

In this section, we examine six threats to the validity of an experiment, derived from the work by Campbell and Stanley (1963): historical flaw, maturation, testing flaw, regression to the mean, selection threat, and attrition.

Historical Flaw

The first threat to validity that can affect an experiment is the historical flaw. When a **historical flaw** occurs, some historical event has caused the sample to change in a way that is not measurable. For example, in a study conducted after September 11, 2001, terrorist attacks in the United States, a researcher who wanted to see how attuned participants were to crisis communication could have a sample more attuned to crisis communication than would have occurred normally. Often, historical flaws can be mentioned as a limitation, but other times, the historical flaw may not even be known to the researcher.

Maturation

A second threat to a study's validity is called maturation. **Maturation** involves changes to a sample that occur naturally as a result of time. The maturation threat occurs when a portion of the estimated change is not the result of our independent variable manipulations, but a result of the passage of time between the first measure of a dependent variable and following measures. Many experiments can last for decades as a researcher collects pertinent data. If a researcher has a sample over a long period of time, some natural changes may occur that are outside the scope of the experiment. For example, many studies that involve large-scale pharmaceutical variables last 5 to 10 years. In a 10-year period, people naturally change. A person who was active and fit at age 30, for example, may have gained weight and become a couch potato at age 40 and thus skew the results of the study. Overall, researchers must collect a number of data indicators at the beginning of a study to determine whether the participants have drastically changed by the time they reach the end of the study.

Testing Flaw

The third threat to validity that can exist in an experiment is a **testing flaw**. As we have discussed previously in this chapter, one way to determine whether an independent variable alters a dependent variable is to get a **baseline** score of the dependent variable at Time 1, manipulate the independent variable, and then get a second score of the dependent variable at Time 2. Unfortunately, changes in the score at Time 2 can occur simply because a score was taken at Time 1. So a researcher must be concerned with whether a score on a dependent variable occurs because of multiple administration of the dependent variable. We will look at a couple of experimental designs that attempt to control for this problem later in this chapter.

Regression to the Mean

The fourth threat to validity that can occur in an experiment is referred to as a regression to the mean. A **regression to the mean** is the tendency for extreme scorers on one measurement to move (regress) closer to the mean on a later measurement, causing a change that would normally not happen in the population. For example, imagine you are teaching a class. You have 10 students take a midterm examination (Time 1), and you get the following scores: 0, 84, 85, 79, 89, 85, 86, 87, 82, 100. You would have a mean of 77.7 and a standard deviation of 27.86. If you then gave the test a second time a week later (Time 2), you may naturally see a shift in the scores toward the mean (72, 85, 86, 79, 89, 86, 86, 88, 82, 100), which would give you a mean of 85.3 and a standard deviation of 7.20. Note that from Time 1 to Time 2, the standard deviation got smaller; this occurs because the scores on the test clumped more around the mean, or regressed to the mean.

In Figure 11.5, you can see the example in graph form. In the first graph, the sample is skewed to the right, whereas the second graph looks more bell shaped. The first time the students took the test, their scores were farther apart from the mean and regressed toward the mean the second time they took the test.

Selection Threat

The fifth threat to experimental validity is the selection threat. The **selection threat** asks whether the individuals who have been selected to participate in an experiment have some characteristic that could slant the findings of the study. For example, a lot of researchers rely on college students in need of extra credit for participation in research studies. Are people who desperately need extra credit the most accurate sample when trying to make generalizations about the general population?

FIGURE 11.5
Statistical Regression

Attrition

The last threat to validity that experiments can have is called attrition. **Attrition** is simply the number of participants who have left a study since it began. Although short-term studies are not generally affected by attrition, long-term studies often can be greatly affected by the dropout rate of the participants. One of the authors of this book started a study with 200 participants at Time 1 and was only able to get 36 participants to continue the study at Time 2. A researcher cannot generalize results from 36 out of an original 200 participants accurately because only 18% of the initial sample still agreed to participate at Time 2. Attrition is one of those factors that cannot be accurately predicted, but it can have a devastating impact on the overall outcome of a study. One of the major problems with attrition occurs if the participants who dropped out of a study are systematically different from those participants who remained in the study.

Other Threats to Experimental Validity

Although the six threats to validity discussed here are specifically related to experimental procedures, we should remind you of several other threats that we discussed in Chapter 8. All of the major threats to validity discussed in that chapter (inadequate preoperational explication of concepts, mono-operation bias, interaction of different treatments, interaction of testing and treatment, restricted generalizability across constructs, confounding constructs and levels of constructs, and social threats to validity) are also threats to the validity of experiments.

Replication

One of the biggest mistakes that non-scientists make when discussing research results is assuming that a single study "is scientific fact." The news media often trumpet studies that herald new and interesting results, but often those results do not stand up to scrutiny of the methods/results or replication. **Replication** involves conducting additional research on an existing topic for one of several reasons: (1) to determine whether the original results were by error or remain constant, (2) to examine the variable using new population characteristics, (3) to apply results from previous studies to new situations, and (4) to combine the results of two or more previous studies in developing new research directions.

Four primary types of replication are conducted. Each is distinguished by the researcher's decision to alter instrumentation or methods, samples, and data analysis procedures. **Literal replication** involves duplicating a previous study by keeping the instrumentation, experimental procedures, and sample as similar as possible to those of the original study. In **operational replication**, the researcher maintains similar samples and methods, but the instrumentation or surveys used in the study are changed. **Instrumental replication** involves measuring the dependent variable the same way as in the initial study, but changes in the independent variable are made to see whether a different operationalization of experimental procedures will yield similar results. Finally, **constructive replication** refers to a researcher's decision to use entirely new instrumentation, methods or procedures, samples, and data analysis techniques to duplicate the conceptual foundation of a previous study.

Replication is essential for testing and supporting various communication theories. Repeated studies focusing on the same variable or phenomenon assist communication scholars in building strong theoretical foundations for our discipline. Authors often provide suggestions for ways in which their studies can be replicated when discussing the limitations. However, few researchers attempt to replicate original studies. As students of research methods, you may want to consider ways in which you can replicate and build on previous research as you define your own interests.

COMMON EXPERIMENTAL DESIGNS

Now that we have explored some of the validity threats experiments can face, we focus our attention on some common experimental designs. There are three types of experimental designs that researchers work with: preexperimental, quasi-experimental, and true experimental. However, we must first introduce a few notation devices that researchers commonly use to aid a discussion of research designs.

Over the next few pages, you will be shown a series of characters that look like mathematical formulas followed by a paragraph example. The characters in the "formula" are there to help illustrate how a specific experimental design is conducted. The characters we will use to illustrate the experimental designs are O, X, R, and N. When you see the letter O in an illustrated experimental design, the O is an observation of the dependent variable being made by a researcher. When you see the letter X in an illustrated experimental design, the X is any time a researcher has manipulated the independent variable. You will often see X followed by a subscript 1 or 0. If the X is followed by a subscript 1 (X_1), then the independent variable has been manipulated and that line represents an experimental condition. If the X is followed by a subscript 0 (X_0), then the independent variable has not been manipulated. The letter R illustrates that people within that experimental design have been randomized into the different treatment conditions, whereas the letter N illustrates that people within that experimental design have not been randomized into the different treatment conditions.

Preexperimental Designs

Now that we have the basic terminology necessary for examining the different experimental designs, we can start by looking at the preexperimental designs. We will demonstrate how each different design can be used to answer one common research question in many different ways. The example used in the next few pages will be as follows: a researcher wants to find out whether attending a six-hour workshop on using humor in the classroom will affect how students perceive their teacher's communication competence.

ONE-SHOT CASE STUDY DESIGN

$$N X_1 \rightarrow O$$

In the one-shot case study design, a researcher uses a nonrandomized sample (N), manipulates the independent variable (X_1), and then measures how people score on the dependent variable (O). In this first example, the researcher would send a group of teachers to a six-hour workshop on using humor in the classroom (X_1) and then have the teachers' students fill out a communication competence scale on the teachers (O). The problem with this design is that we can never say with complete confidence that our manipulation of the independent variable caused the measurement of the dependent variable.

ONE-GROUP PRETEST–POSTTEST DESIGN

$$N O_1 \rightarrow X_1 \rightarrow O_2$$

In the one-group pretest–posttest design, a researcher uses a nonrandomized sample (N), gives the sample a pretest (O_1), manipulates the independent variable (X_1), and then gives the sample a posttest (O_2). In this example, a researcher would have a teacher's students fill out the communication competence (O_1), then send the teacher to the six-hour workshop on how to use humor in training (X_1), and then resurvey the students to see if their perception of the teacher has changed (O_2). This design is also somewhat problematic because it is easy for a researcher to miss the influence of intervening and confounding variables.

STATIC GROUP COMPARISONS DESIGN

$$N\ X_1 \to O$$

$$N\ X_0 \to O_1$$

In the static group comparisons design, a researcher uses a nonrandomized sample (N), manipulates the independent variable (X_1), and then measures how people score on the dependent variable (O). Furthermore, the researcher does not manipulate the independent variable of a second group or the control group (X_0), but does measure the dependent variable (O_1).

In this example, a researcher has two groups: an experimental group and a control group. The researcher would send one teacher through the six-hour workshop on using humor in the classroom (X_1), but not send another teacher through that workshop (X_0). After the teacher in the first group has gone through the workshop, the researcher has the students in both groups fill out a communication competence scale on both teachers (O_1). This manipulation is called a static group comparison because the two groups already exist and were not created for the experimental purpose. The problem with this design is the possibility of prior relationships between the teacher and students, a history of maturation, and other experimental flaws that could prevent a researcher from attaining clear, useful results. For example, if the teacher sent to the workshop was more communicatively competent to begin with, there would be no way to determine that using this preexperimental design.

Quasi-Experimental Designs

A **quasi-experimental design** mirrors an experimental design but lacks randomization (Cook & Campbell, 1979). The next four types of designs are different perspectives on how to design a quasi-experiment.

PRETEST–POSTTEST DESIGN

$$N\ O_1 \to X_1 \to O_2$$

$$N\ O_1 \qquad\qquad O_2$$

The purpose of the pretest–posttest design is to determine whether the effect of a pretest can account for the scores a person may achieve on a posttest. In this design, a researcher either creates two groups or uses two stagnant groups. In the manipulation group, a researcher measures the dependent variable (O_1), followed by a manipulation of the independent variable (X_1), and then follows that with another measurement of the dependent variable (O_2). In the control group, a researcher measures the dependent variable (O_1) and then measures the dependent variable (O_2) a second time without any kind of manipulation in between.

In the first group, the researcher measures the student perceptions of the teacher's communication competence (O_1), sends the teacher to the six-hour workshop on humor (X_1), and retests the student perceptions of the teacher's communication competence (O_2). In the control group, the researcher does not send the teacher to the workshop on humor. After the teacher in the first group has gone through the workshop, the researcher has the students in the control group fill out a communication competence scale again on the teacher (O_2) who had not attended the workshop.

TIME-SERIES DESIGN

$$N\ O_1 \rightarrow O_2 \rightarrow O_3 \rightarrow X_1 \rightarrow O_4 \rightarrow O_5 \rightarrow O_6$$

The time-series design is a way for researchers to establish a clear baseline score on a specific dependent variable and then determine whether the manipulation of the independent variable has lasting effects. In the time-series design, one group is nonrandomly established. The researcher measures the dependent variable the first time (O_1), measures the dependent variable a second time (O_2), and measures the dependent variable a third time (O_3). The researcher then performs the manipulation of the independent variable (X_1). After the manipulation of the independent variable, the researcher then measures the dependent variable a fourth time (O_4), followed by a fifth measurement of the dependent variable (O_5) and then a sixth measurement of the dependent variable (O_6). A time-series experimental design is not limited to six measurements of the dependent variable—it could just as easily have been eight or more measurements of the dependent variable. Multiple measurements of the dependent variable are useful because they help decrease the chance of a statistical regression to the mean validity threat by stabilizing outliers (participants with extreme scores).

In our example experiment, a researcher could measure a group of students' perceptions of the teacher's communication competence three times, then send the teacher to the six-hour workshop on how to use humor during training, and then measure the students' perception of the teacher's communication competence three more times. All in all, the teacher's communication competence would be measured six times. The major problem with this experimental design is that the researcher cannot determine whether the use of the same method for measuring the dependent variable (communication competence scale) or the manipulation of the independent variable is causing a change.

MULTIPLE TIME-SERIES DESIGN

$$N\ O_1 \rightarrow O_2 \rightarrow O_3 \rightarrow X_1 \rightarrow O_4 \rightarrow O_5 \rightarrow O_6$$
$$N\ O_1 \rightarrow O_2 \rightarrow O_3 \rightarrow X_0 \rightarrow O_4 \rightarrow O_5 \rightarrow O_6$$

The multiple time-series design is a way for researchers to establish a clear baseline score on a specific dependent variable and then determine whether the manipulation of the independent variable has lasting effects while controlling for multiple testing effects. In the multiple time-series design, two groups are nonrandomly established (N). In the first group, the researcher measures the dependent variable (O_1), measures the dependent variable a second time (O_2), and measures the dependent variable a third time (O_3). The researcher then performs the manipulation of the independent variable (X_1). After the manipulation of the independent variable, the researcher measures the dependent variable a fourth time (O_4), followed by a fifth measurement of the dependent variable (O_5) and then a sixth measurement (O_6). In the second group, the researcher measures the dependent variable six separate times ($O_1, O_2, O_3, O_4, O_5, O_6$), but does not attempt to manipulate the independent variable (X_0).

In our example experiment, a researcher could measure the experimental group of students' perception of the teacher's communication competence three times, then send the teacher to the six-hour workshop on how to use humor during training, and then measure the students' perception of the teacher's communication competence three more times. In the control group, the researcher simply measures the students' perception of the teacher's communication competence six different times. The purpose of the control group in this design is to determine whether the effect of measuring the dependent variable six different times causes any of the changes noted in the dependent variable. However, because this design is not random, it is always possible that the two groups had preexisting characteristics that could lead to a change seen in the experiment.

SWITCHING REPLICATIONS DESIGN

$$N\ O_1 \rightarrow X_1 \rightarrow O_2 \qquad\qquad O_3$$
$$N\ O_1 \qquad\qquad O_2 \rightarrow X_1 \rightarrow O_3$$

The switching replications design solves one of the basic problems that many people have with experimental designs—that is, the need to exclude some participants from the independent variable manipulation. For example, maybe you find a treatment for public speaking anxiety. You would not want to turn down people who could benefit from the treatment, would you? The new treatment clearly needs to be researched, but you could give half of your participants the treatment to begin with and then give the other half the treatment later, so both groups would still receive the treatment.

In this design, researchers create two nonrandom groups. The researcher starts off by observing the dependent variable in both groups (O_1), followed by a manipulation of the independent variable in the first group (X_1) while doing nothing in the second group, followed by an observation of the dependent variable a second time for both groups (O_2). The researcher then switches gears and manipulates the independent variable for the second group (X_1) while doing nothing in the first group. This is followed by a third observation of the dependent variable for both groups (O_3).

In our experimental example, we could use two groups that we create or that were previously established. To start our experiment, we would measure how the students in both groups perceive their teachers' communication competence. We then send the first teacher to the workshop on how to use humor in the classroom. After the workshop, we measure perceived teacher communication competence for both groups. We then send the second teacher to the workshop on how to use humor in the classroom. After that workshop, we then measure perceived teacher communication competence for both groups for the third, and final, time.

This design is strong and can determine whether changes in the dependent variable are happening by chance or as a result of the researcher's manipulation of the independent variable. However, because of its lack of randomization, it can still succumb to the validity threats discussed earlier in this chapter.

True Experimental Designs

True experimental designs are considered such because participants in the study are randomly placed into an experimental condition and the independent variable is actively manipulated (not just observed). In this section, we examine four different experimental designs.

PRETEST–POSTTEST DESIGN

$$R\ O_1 \rightarrow X_1 \rightarrow O_2$$

$$R\ O_1 \qquad\qquad O_2$$

The pretest–posttest design determines whether the effect of a pretest can account for the scores that a person may achieve on a posttest. In this design, a researcher randomly assigns a larger group of participants into two groups (R). In the first group, a researcher measures the dependent variable (O_1), followed by a manipulation of the independent variable (X_1), followed by another measurement of the dependent variable (O_2). In the control group, a researcher measures the dependent variable (O_1) the first time and then measures the dependent variable (O_2) a second time with no manipulation in between.

In our example experiment, a researcher would recruit a sample of research participants and then randomly assign them to one of two training conditions (use of humor or control). In the first group, the researcher would measure the student perceptions of the teacher's communication competence (O_1), then send the teacher to the six-hour workshop on humor (X_1), and then retest the student perceptions of the teacher's communication competence (O_2). In the control group, the teacher is not sent to the workshop on humor.

After the teacher in the first group has gone through the workshop, the researcher has the students in the control group fill out a communication competence scale again (O_2).

In this design, there still exists a possibility of a threat to the validity of the study caused by the pretest. Theoretically, the effect of the independent variable could be different when a pretest is present compared to when it is not.

TWO-GROUP POSTTEST-ONLY DESIGN

$$R\ X_1 \rightarrow O_1$$

$$R \qquad\quad O_1$$

In the two-group posttest-only design, a researcher uses a randomized sample (R), manipulates the independent variable (X_1), and then measures how people score on the dependent variable (O_1). Furthermore, the researcher only measures the dependent variable (O_1) for the second group. In this design, a researcher has two groups: an experimental group and a control group.

Using our experimental example, the researcher would send one teacher through the six-hour workshop on using humor in training sessions (X_1) and not send another teacher. After the teacher in the first group has gone through the workshop, the researcher would then have the students in both groups fill out a communication competence scale on both teachers (O_1).

This experimental design is economical, which is why it is often used in research. This experiment also eliminates the possibility of pre- and posttest interactions. However, without a baseline observance of the dependent variable, you always run the risk that the two groups were different to begin with.

RANDOMIZED SWITCHING REPLICATIONS DESIGN

$$R\ O_1 \rightarrow X_1 \rightarrow O_2 \qquad\qquad O_3$$

$$R\ O_1 \qquad\qquad O_2 \rightarrow X_1 \rightarrow O_3$$

The randomized switching replications design solves one of the basic problems of experimental designs—namely, the need to exclude some participants from the independent variable manipulation. In this design, researchers randomly place participants into one of two groups. The researcher starts off by observing the dependent variable in both groups (O_1), followed by a manipulation of the independent variable in the first group (X_1) while doing nothing in the second group, followed by an observation of the dependent variable a second time for both groups (O_2). The researcher then switches gears and manipulates the independent variable for the second group (X_1) while doing nothing in the first group. This is followed by a third observation of the dependent variable for both groups (O_3).

In our experimental example, we could use two groups that we create or that were previously established. To start our experiment, we find how the students in both groups perceive their teachers' communication competence. We then send the first teacher to the workshop on how to use humor in the classroom. After the workshop, we measure perceived teacher communication competence for both groups. We then send the second teacher to the workshop on how to use humor in the classroom. After that workshop, we measure perceived teacher communication competence for both groups for the third and final time. This design is good and can determine whether changes in the dependent variable are happening by chance or as a result of the researcher's manipulation of the independent variable.

SOLOMON FOUR-GROUP DESIGN

$$R\ O_1 \rightarrow X_1 \rightarrow O_2$$
$$R\ O_1 \qquad\qquad O_2$$
$$R \qquad X_1 \rightarrow O_2$$
$$R \qquad\qquad O_2$$

The Solomon four-group design is considered to be the "granddaddy" of all experimental research designs because it attempts to control for any major experimental flaws. In this design, a researcher separates her or his participants into a series of four different groups (R). In the first group, the researcher measures the dependent variable (O_1) at Time 1, manipulates the independent variable (X_1), and then measures the dependent variable (O_2) at Time 2. In the second group, the researcher observes the dependent variable (O_1) at Time 1 and then measures the dependent variable (O_2) at Time 2 but does not manipulate the independent variable. In the third group, the researcher does not measure the dependent variable at Time 1. Instead, the researcher starts the third group by manipulating the independent variable (X_1) and then measuring the dependent variable at Time 2 (O_2). In the fourth and final group, the researcher does not measure the dependent variable at Time 1 or manipulate the independent variable. The only thing the researcher receives from the fourth group is a measure of the dependent variable (O_2) at Time 2.

The first group in the Solomon four-group design measures the traditional pre- and posttest experimental design. The second group helps a researcher know whether there is a difference between a pretest and posttest score in general. The third group determines whether a pretest influences the outcome of the posttest. And the final group helps to determine whether a maturation effect is occurring and the change results from time and not the independent variable manipulation.

Ex Post Facto Design

Sometimes you may want to see the effects of an independent variable on a dependent variable, but manipulating that independent variable may be impossible (e.g., changing someone's height or someone's sight) or highly unethical (e.g., changing someone's weight, life experiences, or sexual orientation). For example, maybe you want to see whether someone's weight causes changes in how he or she reacts to a marketing campaign for dietary supplements. Although this design mirrors true experimental designs, it is not an experimental design in the strictest sense of the term. First, there is no random assignment of participants into control and tests groups. Second, there is manipulation of the independent variable because the participants already exist in the categories prior to the beginning of the study. For example, in our hypothetical marketing study, you could easily classify people based on the general body mass index (BMI) categories: underweight, normal weight, overweight, obese, and morbidly obese. When we assign people to one of these categories, we are doing so based on events that have happened in the past, which is where the name ex post facto (after the fact) comes from.

Although researchers can look for differences between the different groups within an ex post facto design (e.g., the BMI weight categories), researchers cannot establish time order because they are not manipulating anything. Instead, we can only examine differences that exist between or among the different groups. So yes, a researcher may find that participants in the different BMI groups view the dietary supplement marketing materials differently, but one must be careful not to overinterpret these results by saying that weight *causes* differences in how people view the marketing materials because we cannot establish time order.

FINAL THOUGHTS ON EXPERIMENTS

Experiments are useful and can help researchers determine the time effects or causal relationships between two variables. However, there are some problems with the experimental process in general: limited number of variables and generalizability problems.

Limited Number of Variables

First, a researcher can only examine a small number of independent variables in any given experiment. The more independent variables that a researcher attempts to manipulate, the more complex the design must become and the more participants a researcher will need. We suggest a minimum of 30 participants in each experimental condition. All of the experimental designs examined in this chapter were for one independent variable manipulation with two nominal levels, so if an experimenter is conducting a factorial experimental design (e.g., a 2 × 3 design), the experimental design becomes even more complex and cumbersome. Furthermore, the more advanced the statistical tests that a researcher wants to use, the more participants a researcher needs. For example, it is recommended that a researcher have a minimum of 300 participants to run multivariate statistical tests or statistical tests that use more than one dependent variable.

Generalizability Problems

A second major problem that occurs with experimental designs relates to the overall generalizability of the findings in an experiment. One of the basic questions that all researchers must ask themselves is whether their results can be generalized to the larger population. Can the results from one study be generalized to similar subject areas, time periods, or contexts? If an experiment is so finite in its generalizability, then its usefulness and meaning can be seriously called into question. Three factors have been shown to limit the generalizability of experimental research: overreliance on college students, overreliance on laboratory settings, and low in mundane realism.

OVERRELIANCE ON COLLEGE STUDENTS

First, researchers in every social scientific field have overly relied on college students as participant populations. Everyone will admit that college students are easy for researchers to get their hands on and are fairly cooperative (especially when extra credit is offered). But college students are the single most overstudied population in the United States. This is not to say that college students should not be studied, but that researchers must think outside of the box and find participant populations beyond the university walls.

OVERRELIANCE ON LABORATORY SETTINGS

Second, researchers have overly relied on laboratory settings when conducting experiments. Many researchers hold the belief that participants being studied in a laboratory environment will act differently than they would in a more natural environment. With that in mind, researchers would be wise to create more experimental designs using natural environments instead of laboratory ones.

LOW IN MUNDANE REALISM

The third reason many experiments have generalizability problems is that many experimental tasks are low in mundane realism. In one rather famous study, participants were asked to persuade people to sit in a room and turn pegs on a pegboard clockwise 25 degrees. As far as we can tell, there is no practical application of this experimental task. And although the finding from this study demonstrated that people commit to the persuasion task differently based on how much they are being paid to persuade someone to turn the pegs, the task cannot be generalized to any other task in the "real" world. Researchers must create experimental tasks that are similar to real tasks that a participant could face in her or his daily life.

Enhancing Generalizability

Having looked at three ways in which generalizability is limited, we can now discuss two ways to enhance generalizability. First, more researchers should attempt to conduct field experiments. Field experiments happen in the real world outside the confines of a laboratory. They are much more likely to reveal real behavior than laboratory experiments. Also, researchers should use more complex studies examining multiple independent variable manipulations. In most real-world phenomena, the effect of a single independent variable manipulation will not be that big. Researchers must develop more complex research designs that will enable them to achieve better understandings of how human communicative behavior occurs. Complexity in research design is a matter of sample size. Researchers and statistical tests can handle complex designs, but as designs become more complicated, additional research conditions are needed, which requires an ever-increasing sample size.

CONCLUSION

In this chapter, we have examined what experiments are and why we do them while exploring a variety of preexperimental, quasi-experimental, and true experimental study designs. In the next chapter, we will explore how to best sample a population to attain the most generalizable results possible.

KEY TERMS

Antecedent variables p. 339

Attrition p. 355

Baseline p. 354

Confederate p. 345

Confounding variables p. 350

Constructive replication p. 356

Control p. 339

Control group p. 344

Debriefing p. 352

Experiment p. 338

Experimental group p. 344

Experimenter effects p. 348

Extraneous variables p. 349

Factorial experimental design p. 346

Hawthorne effect p. 349

Historical flaw p. 353

Instrumental replication p. 356

Intervening variables p. 350

Literal replication p. 356

Lurker variables p. 350

Manipulation check p. 352

Manipulation of the independent variable p. 342

Maturation p. 353

Operational replication p. 356

Quasi-experimental design p. 358

Random assignment p. 340

Regression to the mean p. 354

Reinforcer variables p. 350

Replication p. 356

Selection threat p. 354

Suppressor variables p. 350

Testing flaw p. 354

Threshold effect p. 348

Time order p. 336

REFERENCES

Campbell, D. T., & Stanley, J. C. (1963). *Experimental and quasi-experimental designs for research*. Skokie, IL: Rand McNally.

Cook, T. D., & Campbell, D. T. (1979). *Quasi-experimental design and analysis issues for field settings*. Boston, MA: Houghton Mifflin.

Guéguen, N., & De Gail, M. A. (2003). The effect of smiling on helping behavior: Smiling and Good Samaritan behavior. *Communication Reports, 16*, 133–140.

Masling, J. (1966). Role-related behavior of the subject and psychologist and its effects upon psychological data. In D. Levine (Ed.), *Nebraska symposium on motivation* (pp. 67–103). Lincoln, NE: University of Nebraska Press.

Pertaub, D. B., Slater, M., & Barker, C. (2002). An experiment on public speaking anxiety in response to three different types of virtual audience. *Presence: Teleoperators and Virtual Environments, 11*, 68–78. doi: 10.1162/105474602317343668

Stewart, R. A. (1994). Perceptions of a speaker's initial credibility as a function of religious involvement and religious disclosiveness. *Communication Research Reports, 11*, 169–176.

Tamborini, R., Eastin, M. S., Skalski, P., Lachlan, K., Fediuk, T. A., & Brady, R. (2004). Violent virtual video games and hostile thoughts. *Journal of Broadcasting & Electronic Media, 48*, 335–357.

Weber, K., Fornash, B., Corrigan, M, & Neupauer, N. C. (2003). The effect of interest on recall: An experiment. *Communication Research Reports, 20*, 116–123.

Wiener, J. L., & Doescher, T. A. (1994). Cooperation and expectations of cooperation. *Journal of Public Policy & Marketing, 13*, 559–270.

Wrench, J. S., Millhouse, B., & Sharp, D. (2007). Laughing before takeoff: Humor, sex, and the preflight safety briefing. *Human Communication, 10*, 381–399.

FURTHER READING

Brown, S. R., & Melamed, L. E. (1990). *Experimental design and analysis*. Thousand Oaks, CA: Sage.

Field, A., & Hole, G. J. (2003). *How to design and report experiments*. Thousand Oaks, CA: Sage.

Levin, I. P. (2004). *Relating statistics and experimental design: An introduction*. Thousand Oaks, CA: Sage.

Ryan, T. P. (2007). *Modern experimental design*. New York, NY: Wiley.

Shadish, W. R., Cook, T. D., & Campbell, D. T. (2002). *Experimental and quasi-experimental designs for generalized causal inference*. Boston, MA: Houghton Mifflin.

Singleton, R. A., Jr., & Straits, B. C. (2017). *Approach to social research* (6th ed.). New York, NY: Oxford University Press.

Spector, P. E. (1981). *Research designs*. Newbury Park, CA: Sage.

12

Sampling Methods

CHAPTER OBJECTIVES

1. Distinguish between the terms *sampling* and *populations*.

2. Explain the central limits theorem.

3. Differentiate among the different probability and nonprobability samples.

4. Explain the general rules for determining a necessary sample size.

5. Describe the relationship between confidence intervals and sample sizes.

Selecting participants for a research study is one of the most crucial elements in the success of the project. Suppose a researcher wanted to answer the question, "What is the level of communication satisfaction between teachers and principals?" Who would you suggest that the researcher approach to be included in this study? The obvious answer is teachers and principals. However, there could be other characteristics of these two groups of participants that guide the research design. It would be important to include teachers from private and public schools, for example, and those at the elementary, junior high, and high school levels. Perhaps selecting teachers with a variety of years of teaching experience would be important in answering the question. As you can see, there are many factors to consider when selecting a sample for your research design.

Consider this: every time you complete an exam for a class, you are responding to questions that address a sample of the information learned in the class. If the instructor were to test you on each and every thing you had learned, the exam might be extremely long. Instead, a sample of concepts is selected to assess your knowledge.

This chapter discusses the various sampling methods used to identify who should be included in a research project. Different types of samples are identified, and questions about how many participants to include are answered.

WHY USE A SAMPLE?

Sampling is the term used to refer to selecting people or units to include in a research study. Scholars use samples because including all possible persons or units in a study is virtually impossible. And since it is not possible to include every person or unit in the research project, it is important that the sample chosen represents the entire group. To begin our discussion, we identify some key terms that will guide your understanding of the sampling process.

Population

Population refers to an entire set of objects, observations, or scores that have some characteristic in common. For example, all registered voters between the ages of 18 and 25 could be considered a population. In this instance, all members of the population have two characteristics of interest in common: voter eligibility and age. Suppose that the purpose of your research study is to identify the communication motives of college students who have visited their academic advisors. The population for this study would be extremely large. Thus, a sample of the population should be selected for the study to make data collection more manageable.

Sample

Sample is the term used to refer to the people or units that a researcher actually includes in the study. In Figure 12.1, you can see a possible population of 24 participants. The eight light-gray people in the population image represent the people who

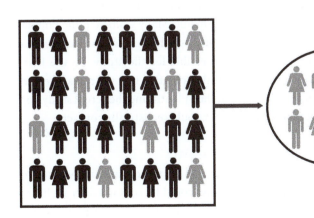

FIGURE 12.1
Populations and Samples

are randomly selected to become the sample (represented in the circle). Researchers choose samples because including all members of the population can be costly and time-consuming.

Have you ever wondered how marketers concluded that four of five dentists whose patients chew gum recommend Trident? They probably did not interview every dentist in the United States. More likely, they contacted a sample from the population of dentists and calculated a statistic that could be generalized. Consider our earlier example of the population of college students who have visited their academic advisors. Since it is impossible to contact all the college students who have done so, a researcher could select a sample of students and ask them to complete a survey about their communication motives.

At times, the terms *population* and *sample* may be confusing. To review, population refers to all possible people or units that could be included, and sample refers to those people or units who are selected to include in the study. The question then becomes: How does a researcher identify the population and select the sample to include in the study?

THE SAMPLING PROCESS

Ask any researcher what her or his goal is when selecting a sample to include in a study, and that researcher will likely respond that he or she wants a sample that will produce results that are generalizable to the population. The term *generalizable* refers to the notion that the results of studying a sample from a population can be assumed to be true of the entire population. To ensure generalizability, the researcher must take specific steps to make certain that the characteristics of the sample closely resemble those of the population. So the primary task at this stage of the research process involves identifying the appropriate sample. The sampling process involves several steps.

Identifying the Theoretical Population

Often, the population that is the focus of a study is not accessible. For example, conducting a study on the aggressive communication behaviors encountered by women in abusive relationships would be difficult. Many women in the population are apprehensive about reporting the abuse, so although they are members of the **theoretical population**, these women may not be accessible for the study. So the first step in sampling involves identifying the theoretical population that the researcher would like to generalize the results of the study to and then identifying the actual study population that includes participants that the researcher could realistically contact.

Identifying the Potential Participants

After selecting the study population, the second step involves identifying all members of that group and determining how each one could be contacted for inclusion in the study. Recall our earlier example regarding the communication motives of students who have visited their academic advisors. Suppose a researcher has determined that the accessible population includes students attending Eastern University. Members of the population could be identified by asking all academic advisors on campus to provide a list of the students who visited their offices during the previous two semesters. This list of all potential participants in the study population (students attending Eastern University) that are accessible to the researcher is referred to as the **sampling frame**. Remember, the sampling frame includes all members of the population accessible to the researcher, not all possible members of the theoretical population.

Say a study requires a researcher to conduct a survey of citizens' opinions about the credibility of a local politician. The local phone book could be used as a listing of the accessible population, but it could not be considered representative of the theoretical population. This is because various things could preclude a person from being listed in the phone book. Phone numbers may be unlisted, some members of the theoretical population may only use cell phones, and the listing typically includes the name of only one member of a household. Thus, although the phone book can be used to provide contact information for the accessible population, it does not provide information for the theoretical population.

Selecting the Sample

The final step of the sampling process involves identifying the method that will be used to select members of the accessible population for inclusion in the sample that is contacted for the study. Suppose that Eastern University is a large school and the academic advisors provided you with a list of more than 15,000 names. Contacting everyone on the list would be time-consuming, not to mention expensive. Thus, the researcher must identify the sample of students to be included in the study. A variety of sampling designs can be used to determine who will be contacted to participate in the study. Two primary designs involve probability sampling and nonprobability sampling. Each of these designs has a variety of sample methods available for a researcher to use.

SELECTING A SAMPLE DESIGN

When selecting the sample for a study, the researcher must decide whether to use probability or nonprobability designs when choosing participants. **Probability sampling** involves the random selection of participants that guarantees each member of the population an equal chance of being selected. Examples of probability methods for selecting participants include simple random samples, stratified random samples, cluster samples, and systematic samples. **Nonprobability sampling** involves selecting members of the accessible population in a nonrandom manner. Examples of nonprobability methods include convenience samples, volunteer samples, purposive samples, quota samples, and network samples.

Your decision of which design to use should consider your desire to predict the sampling error associated with the study. **Sampling error** refers to the random differences that exist between the sample and the population. By selecting a probability design, a researcher can calculate the sampling error, or the degree to which the sample might be different from the population it was selected to represent. Nonprobability samples do not enable a researcher to calculate the degree to which the sample differs from the population thus increasing the chances for this error to occur. We will inspect these sample designs and discuss how a researcher decides which sampling method to use.

Probability Sampling

Probability sampling involves randomly selecting participants from the population so that all potential participants have an equal chance of being selected for the study. Random selection methods eliminate any potential **sampling bias** by ensuring that each person in the population has an equal chance of being chosen. Chances are that you have used probability sampling at various times in your life and not realized it. The strategy of "drawing straws" for a task is one that involves random selection. Because the length of the straws is concealed from view and the selection of the straws is random, each person who takes a turn selecting a straw has an equal chance of drawing the short straw.

As we emphasized earlier, probability designs are used in situations where the researcher wants to calculate and report the sampling error. It makes sense that **probability theory** holds true in situations where probability samples are used—that is, the score that occurs most frequently in the sample will also be the score that should occur most often in the population. Probability samples produce scores that accurately reflect the most and the least common scores in the population. Probability methods allow the researcher to select a sample whose scores will be distributed in the shape of a normal distribution curve.

The central limits theorem is used to explain the relationship between probability samples and the population. According to this theorem, collecting data from repeated samples within the same population will produce a distribution of scores in the shape of a normal curve. In other words, the **central limits theorem** states that the mean of the scores obtained from the probability sample will be equal to the mean of the scores obtained from the population. Further, the central limits theorem states that the variance of the sample mean is equal to the variance of the population mean divided by the sample size (N). Thus, the more variance that exists between scores in the population, the more variance that will exist between scores in the sample used to represent that population. Finally, the central limits theorem states that the distribution of mean scores from the sample will more closely represent the distribution of mean scores of the population as the sample size (N) increases, which makes sense because probability samples provide equal opportunity for selection and the results thus are more likely to reflect the population.

As mentioned earlier, an advantage of probability sampling is that it enables the researcher to calculate sampling error, or how likely it is that the population mean differs from the sample mean. We will address the concept of sampling error in more detail later in this chapter.

Once the researcher determines that probability designs are preferred, the next step involves selecting the specific method that will be used to choose participants for the sample. These methods include the use of simple random samples, stratified random samples, cluster samples, and systematic samples,

SIMPLE RANDOM SAMPLES

Simple random samples are considered by many to be the "purest" method for collecting a probability sample. This method ensures that each member of the population has an equal chance of being selected for the study; the researcher makes a random decision of who will be included in the sample. For example, in Figure 12.1, the eight people in the population were randomly selected for inclusion in the final sample.

Various methods of randomization are used to select sample members, and these methods are selected to ensure the validity of the study. Two forms of randomization can be used in research: random samples and random assignment. Random sample refers to the selection of study participants from the population. Random assignment refers to how the researcher assigns the sample drawn from the population to various groups within the study. Suppose a researcher wants to examine the persuasive effect of language used in fear appeals. To ensure a representative sample, the researcher might select a simple random sample of 150 people from the target population. Next, members of the sample would be randomly assigned in groups of 50 to one of three conditions—high-intensity, medium-intensity, and low-intensity fear appeals. Thus, it is possible to design a study that utilizes both random sampling and random assignment. Random sampling allows a researcher to generalize the results to the population, thus enhancing the external validity of the study. Random assignment allows the researcher to strengthen the internal validity of the study by ensuring that participants are randomly assigned to the conditions being examined.

So how do researchers identify a simple random sample for a study? This task is often completed using a table of random numbers or some other computer-generated list that ensures random selection (see Figure 12.2 for an example from http://www.random.org/). Recall our earlier example of students who meet with academic advisors. The first step in securing a random sample requires the identification of the accessible population. To accomplish this, we would ask academic advisors to provide lists of students who had visited their office during the past two semesters. In the next step, we would identify the sample size desired for the project. Sample size will be discussed later in this chapter. For now, we will assume that 850 students were included on the lists provided by advisors, and that we want to survey 100 of these 850 students. One method for randomly selecting the participants might involve placing all 850 names in a hat and drawing 100 names to contact. Although this method would ensure that each person had an equal chance of being selected, it would also be time-consuming. A more efficient method for randomly selecting participants involves using a table of random numbers.

Computers have made the task of random number assignment much easier. Using the table of random numbers in Figure 12.2, we can collect a random sample for our study. First, assign each student on the list a number between 1 and 850. Then, close your eyes and randomly point to a spot on the chart. Suppose you randomly selected 46882 in Figure 12.2. We read that number as 468 (the first three digits) since 850 is a three-digit number. Thus, the student who was assigned the number of 468 is included in our sample list. Continue down the column to the next number, which is 02429. This is interpreted as 024, which means that student 24 is selected for the sample. Our next number on the chart is 85676. However, we only have 850 students on our list. Not a problem—simply skip that number and continue to the next number in the column. And continue through the chart until 100 students have been randomly selected for the sample.

As you can see, this task can be time-consuming for drawing large samples. However, computers have enabled researchers to carry out this task more efficiently. So for our study of students who visit advisors, another method for assigning random numbers to a list generated from the population can be accomplished using Microsoft Excel. In this method, we simply copy and paste the list of names into an Excel spreadsheet. In the column next to the list of names, the formula "=RAND()" is inserted in the cell to instruct Excel to assign a random number between 0 and 1 beside each name on the list. Be sure to copy and paste this formula throughout the entire selection of cells. Next, conduct a sort of both columns by instructing Excel to sort and arrange the list of random numbers from lowest to highest (or vice versa). Once this is completed, you simply select the first 100 names from your list of 850.

So what are the advantages and disadvantages of random samples? The primary advantage is the ability to calculate the statistical sampling error. Disadvantages include the need to have accurate lists representing the entire population and the time

FIGURE 12.2
Sample Table of
Random Numbers

61424	20419	86546	00517
46882	27993	04952	66762
02429	71146	97668	86523
85676	10005	07216	25906
19761	50349	15370	90222
78733	16447	27932	89990

involved in the process of random selection. In addition, by sheer luck, a researcher may find that the sample selected randomly does not provide an accurate representation of the population. Other probability sampling methods can be used to combat these concerns.

STRATIFIED RANDOM SAMPLES

In some instances when the population is extremely large, researchers may want to select participants based on criteria chosen specifically for the study. **Stratified random samples** enable researchers to divide the population into specific strata, also known as subsets of the population that have a common characteristic. Participants are randomly selected from the strata that have been identified.

Figure 12.3 is an example of a stratified random sample. Here, the researchers wanted to make sure that they had four females and four males. They grouped the men and women separately, and then randomly chose four from each strata (or biological sex group). Some examples of strata that could be examined in a study include males and females; full-time and part-time students; or Democrats, Republicans, and Independents. Once the strata have been identified, conduct a simple random sample of each group.

Stratified sampling is the preferred method in some studies because it reduces the potential for sampling error. Researchers often use this sampling method in situations where there is unequal representation of one group or stratum of a population compared to other groups. Consider our example of student motives for visiting academic advisors. If the list of names provided by advisors was disproportionate in terms of the number of freshmen, sophomores, juniors, and seniors, the researcher might decide to conduct a stratified random sample to ensure that information is gathered from all class ranks.

Once the strata have been identified, the next task involves determining the sample size for each group. As a general rule, the researcher should make sure that

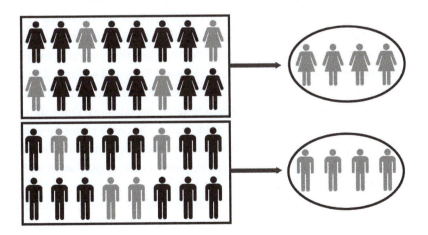

FIGURE 12.3
Stratified Random Sample

the number of participants selected from each stratum is proportionate to the group's size in the population. Suppose we know that of the 850 students included on the list, 300 are freshmen, 275 are sophomores, 175 are juniors, and 100 are seniors. Since there is a disproportionate amount of seniors in the population, it would be important to conduct a stratified sample to determine whether communication motives of seniors differ from those of freshmen and sophomores. To calculate the proportionate sample size for each stratum, we first must determine what percentage of the overall population is represented by each group. To determine the percentage, you divide the number of people in a group by the total number of students. For example, to find the percentage of freshman, we first multiply the number of freshmen (300) by 100 and then divide that number (30,000) by the total number of students (850), or 30,000/850 = 35.29 (when rounded). The population is composed of 35.29% freshman, 32.35% sophomores, 20.59% juniors, and 11.76% seniors. This means that of our sample of 100, we should survey 35 freshmen, 32 sophomores, 21 juniors, and 12 seniors.

The obvious advantage to stratified samples is their ability to make sure that various subgroups in the population are included in the study, which is especially important where there are minority groups who may not be selected for the study if simple random selection methods are used. Disadvantages to stratified sampling include the difficulty in identifying nonoverlapping strata and the additional time needed to organize groups for simple random selection.

CLUSTER SAMPLES

Suppose in your study of college students you want to collect information from colleges across the country. You would need a lot of time and money to complete the project if you began in California and surveyed students at various colleges until you arrived in Maine. An alternative method for ensuring that colleges have an equal chance of being selected, however, would involve using the cluster sample method.

Cluster samples occur when researchers identify naturally occurring clusters of participants who have a variable in common within the target population. In our example using colleges across the country, this method requires the researcher to first divide the country into regions: West, Southwest, Midwest, East, and so forth. Once all the colleges within each region are selected, the cluster sample method is used to randomly select the region of the country from which to select participants. Once the region is randomly selected, random sampling is conducted within each region to ensure that a probability sample is obtained. Another instance in which cluster sampling could be useful is if a researcher wanted to interview employees of an organization with offices around the nation or the world.

Figure 12.4 illustrates what a cluster sample would look like. In this case, the researchers found four existing clusters of people (represented by the people in squares.

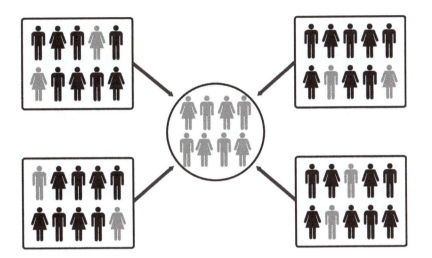

FIGURE 12.4
Cluster Sample

The researchers then randomly pick two people from each cluster (the light-gray people) to form the final sample. The final cluster sample is the one with all eight of the participants represented in the circle.

One apparent advantage of cluster sampling is the money and time that can be saved by contacting participants in a few areas rather than gathering data from all possible regions. A disadvantage of the method is that participants in the same geographic area or same organizational region might be similar to one another, and thus they could be less representative of the population than the researcher originally anticipated. A second important disadvantage to cluster samples is that the chance of sampling error (the random differences that exist between the sample and the population) will increase with each step (we will discuss this idea in more detail in a moment).

SYSTEMATIC SAMPLES

A final probability sampling method, **systematic samples**, involves selecting a sample by determining the sample size needed from the population and then selecting every "*nth*" person from the population for inclusion in the study. This method is as effective as simple random sampling so long as there is no systematic order to the listing of a population. In our student motives example, systematic sampling could be used as long as advisors were not instructed to submit their lists in order of class rank or grade point average. If any of the lists include a method for organizing or ordering population members, systematic sampling cannot be used.

Suppose you want to interview 15 employees from a population of 200. Divide 200 by 15 and you would discover that every 13th employee on the list should be included in your sample. To make sure that every employee has an equal chance of being chosen, choose a random number between 1 and 15 to determine your starting point. Then, select every 13th name on the employee list. If number 7 is the random number selected to start, employees 7, 20, 33, 46, and so forth would be included in the sample.

Systematic samples are often used because they are much easier to conduct compared to simple random samples. However, a potential disadvantage of this method is that results could be biased if there is a hidden order to the list of population members used to generate the sample. For example, say you get a list of addresses and you select every 10th house. If a city block has 10 houses, then you may be selecting every house that is right on a corner. And if you want to ask people about noise problems, those who live in a corner house may experience more noise than those who live in the middle of the block. You have unknowingly built error into your design.

Sampling Error

As stated earlier, one of the primary advantages of selecting probability sampling methods over nonprobability methods is the opportunity they afford the researcher to calculate the sampling error. Sampling error statistics provide the researcher with an idea of how accurate the sample will be in predicting similar results in the population. When the results of a study produce a low sampling error score, this indicates that there is little range or variability in the sample distribution of scores. A high sampling error score indicates wide variability.

How do you know what the sampling error is for the study? You can get a good idea by reviewing the sample standard deviation. The larger the standard deviation score is for the sample, the larger the sampling error that is present. This translates into a greater chance that discrepancies will be found when trying to generalize the results from the sample to the population.

Later in this chapter, we will discuss how to calculate sample size. Sample size is directly related to sampling error in that the larger the sample size, the less chance that sampling errors have occurred. It just makes sense—the larger the sample size, the greater chance that you have captured the characteristics representative of the population.

Nonprobability Samples

Samples that are not randomly selected are known as nonprobability samples. Because selection is not random, there is a greater chance for bias to exist in the results. Although nonprobability samples do not involve random selection, it is not necessarily the case that nonprobability samples are not representative of the population. Nonprobability samples may represent the population just as accurately as a probability sample. However, a researcher is not able to provide statistical support for the sampling error of a nonprobability sample. As a result, it is difficult to determine whether the results generated from the sample can be generalized to the population.

So why would a researcher choose to use nonprobability samples in lieu of a random sample? Several explanations might be offered for such a decision. In some instances a study might be examining a variable or phenomenon that is new. In this situation, it may be difficult to determine which population is most appropriate for the study. Other studies may focus on variables or characteristics that make it difficult to find participants. Recall the earlier example of a study designed to examine the verbal aggressiveness of women in abusive relationships. Finding participants for this sensitive topic may be difficult, and thus a researcher might be forced to engage in nonprobability sampling. A third reason for selecting this sampling method is related to the efficiency of cost and time associated with finding participants. Finally, nonprobability samples are used in instances where the characteristic being studied is not easily found.

Although these are all legitimate reasons for selecting nonrandom methods of sampling, the researcher must be aware of several cautions with their use. As we have already discussed, the chance of sampling error increases with nonprobability sampling. Of course, we can never be sure exactly what the error is, however, because random methods were not employed. Yet as a result of higher sampling error, the ability to generalize results to the population is limited. In these instances, the researcher must pay careful attention to addressing the sampling issues in the discussion section of the research paper when identifying limitations of the study. Sampling bias also is often associated with nonprobability samples. This bias is defined as a systematic difference between the population and the sample that results from failing to select representative cases.

There are five primary types of nonprobability sampling methods employed by communication scholars: convenience samples, volunteer samples, purposive samples, quota samples, and network samples. Here, we will examine each of these in turn.

CONVENIENCE SAMPLES

Convenience samples involve the selection of participants for the sample based on their availability. If you have ever been asked to complete a survey during class for a research project, chances are that you were part of a convenience sample. Are the results biased using this method? Absolutely! After all, only individuals who are enrolled in the class are included in the sample. Is this necessarily a bad thing? Not if the variable being examined is only applicable to those who are enrolled in the class.

Although some scholars may view results produced by convenience samples with skepticism, sometimes these samples can produce useful information. In a study designed to examine the nonverbal behaviors displayed in physician–patient interactions, Riddle et al. (2002) used a convenience sample of patients and physicians. Forty-seven patients who sought care at various clinics were approached and asked whether they would be willing to participate in the study. Their medical oncologists also agreed to participate. The clinic afforded the researcher the opportunity to solicit a convenience sample of the target population in an environment that ensured the participants met the criteria necessary for inclusion in the study. Soliciting a sample by randomly calling names in a phone book would be less efficient since one criterion for inclusion in the sample was that participants should have engaged in an interaction with a physician.

The major disadvantage with convenience sampling lies in the inability to generalize the results to the population. However, this method can be particularly useful in exploratory studies when a researcher has limited time or money to compile a random sample.

VOLUNTEER SAMPLES

In some instances, participants may volunteer to be a part of the study sample. **Volunteer samples** are often recruited by offering participants a reward in exchange for their time. Fans who cast their votes each week via phone on *American Idol* or *Dancing with the Stars* are examples of volunteer samples. The participants choose whether to be part of the sample of the population that selects the winner. Many media studies employ this method to obtain feedback from the population. Researchers find that it is often easier to have people volunteer to be a part of the study than to engage in other methods to locate participants.

An obvious disadvantage of this type of sampling method is that only those who are aware of the study would be available to volunteer. There is no mechanism for collecting information from those who are either unaware of the study or who choose not to participate. Advantages to volunteer sampling are that it is efficient to conduct the study in terms of cost and time, and that it is more likely participants who choose to participate have some level of knowledge or interest in the topic.

PURPOSIVE SAMPLES

Purposive sampling involves nonrandomly selecting participants to fulfill or meet a specific purpose the researcher has in mind. The sample is selected based on specific characteristics the researcher is investigating—generally, the participants meet some predetermined criteria that the researcher has used to determine eligibility.

Purposive sampling is used in both quantitative and qualitative studies. A primary strength of the purposive sample lies in its ability to select participants or cases that meet the criteria being examined in the study. Suppose that a researcher wanted to explore the perceived communication effectiveness of an organization following a crisis situation. It would make perfect sense to select a purposive sample of workers and businesses in the Gulf Coast region that were displaced from their facilities following Hurricane Katrina.

In a study examining intercultural perspectives taught in public relations courses, Bardhan (2003) used a purposive sample of students enrolled in his public relations course and asked them to provide responses to three open-ended questions. Because the goal was to examine perspectives taught in a public relations class, it was only logical that public relations students would be recruited for the purposive sample. In another study that examined the causes of job satisfaction among public relations practitioners, Grunig (1990) selected a total of 87 practitioners from 48 organizations, which represented one of four structural typologies. These organizations and their members were purposely selected so that there would be 12 organizations representing each of the four types of organization. To ensure that all four organization types would be equally represented in the study, a purposive sample of practitioners and organizations was chosen.

The primary advantage of purposive sampling is that it enables the researcher to collect information from the target sample more efficiently. Furthermore, it ensures that all participants selected for the study have a study variable in common. Disadvantages include the overrepresentation of the sample more easily accessed in the population and the tendency to obtain sample sizes that are not proportionate to the population size.

QUOTA SAMPLES

For **quota samples**, participants are separated into strata or groups based on a common characteristic or variable, and then participants from each group are selected nonrandomly to include in the study. It is important to note that although both quota and stratified samples identify strata for participant classification, stratified samples use random methods for selecting participants from each group and quote samples do not.

Quota samples can be proportionate or nonproportionate in relation to the population. **Nonproportionate quota samples** recruit volunteers until the determined number of participants has been reached. Suppose that you were conducting a study of 100 male and female employees to examine perceptions of their manager's communication style. Although the population of the organization consists of 80% females and 20% males, a nonproportionate quota sample could be drawn by simply interviewing the first 100 employees who enter the company cafeteria. Doing so may result in a sample population composed of 60% females and 40% males, but they all meet the group criteria of being an employee in the organization.

Proportionate quota samples are chosen to make sure that the number of volunteers recruited for the study is proportionate or equal to the number of group members in the population. Consider our earlier sample of 100 employees. Because the population consists of 80% women and 20% men and a total of 100 employees is needed for the sample, the researcher will continue to select participants until the percentage in each group matches the population percentage. In this instance, the researcher will stop interviewing women once 80 have been included in the sample. Even if additional female employees come along prior to soliciting 20 male employees, those women will be excluded from the study because a proportionate quota has been met.

The primary distinction between quota and stratified samples is their use of random or nonrandom procedures for selecting participants for the sample. Recall our earlier study of student motives for communicating with their advisor. A total of 100 students were identified as the target sample size for that study. Although stratified sampling methods might utilize a table of random numbers to select students from the list to fill the determined number of participants for each category, quota sampling methods might simply take the first 21 juniors and the first 12 seniors they contacted.

Many communication studies have employed quota sampling methods to identify samples. In a study examining children's comprehension of television advertising, Chan (2000) selected a quota sample of boys and girls to represent each class level from kindergarten to sixth grade. To ensure that each class level included an equal number of boys and girls, a total of 32 boys and 32 girls were selected from each grade. Thus, participants were selected to participate until the predetermined number in each group was obtained.

An advantage of quota samples is that they enable the researcher to identify a target number for each group or category of a population, thus ensuring that each group is equally represented. Furthermore, this sampling method is less costly and less time-consuming than stratified sampling. The obvious disadvantage lies in the nonprobability methods used for selecting participants. Not everyone has an equal chance of being selected for the study. Therefore, the study may produce results that are biased.

NETWORK SAMPLES

A final nonprobability sampling method used involves asking participants to refer researchers to other people who could serve as participants. Referrals from participants provide the researcher with a cost- and time-effective method for locating others who meet the study criteria. Earlier, we discussed a study that might examine the verbal aggressiveness of victims of domestic abuse. Because many victims are not willing to openly disclose their situation, a researcher might have to obtain a sample by asking each participant to refer another person who has experienced a similar situation. Known as **network samples**, these are often used in instances where a variable or characteristic being studied is rare or difficult to identify in a population.

Bruess and Pearson (2002) identified participants for their study of the functions of rituals in friendships and marriages using the network sampling method. The researchers used undergraduate students to recruit married couples to complete questionnaires and participate in interviews, which resulted in a total of 494 surveys from married individuals and a total of 489 surveys on friendships. Bruess and Pearson would have spent a considerable amount of time soliciting a sample size that large and that diverse without the assistance of network sampling.

One advantage of the network sample is that it enables researchers to recruit members of populations that are not easily identifiable (e.g., gay, lesbian, bisexual, and transgendered people; Internet porn addicts; or people with an identical twin). Another advantage is that it enables researchers to obtain larger sample sizes more quickly. The obvious disadvantage of the network sample lies in the inability to generalize findings to the population.

DETERMINING SAMPLE SIZE

Perhaps one of the first questions asked by students in research methods classes is "How many participants should I recruit for my sample?" As we discussed earlier, larger sample sizes typically produce results that are more generalizable to the population. However, it is important to assess your study. Samples that are too large could waste your time and money as a researcher. And a sample size that is too small can produce results that do not accurately reflect the larger population.

A quick analysis of the research design can help answer some initial questions regarding sample size. The more the population varies regarding the characteristics being examined, the larger the sample size should be to account for the variance. Suppose you wanted to do a study on Internet use in a region of the United States. Chances are that the patterns and motives for use would vary greatly depending on a person's age, sex, and employment or education status. Teens may be more likely to access the Internet than the elderly, and students may use their computers more for research purposes than do stay-at-home mothers. It is likely that the population will vary greatly, and thus a larger sample size is needed.

The first question a researcher must answer in determining the appropriate sample size is to identify the confidence level with which he or she wants to report the results. Confidence levels tell you how confident or sure you can be that the results are generalizable to the population and not simply a result of chance. As a general rule, if you want to produce results that are more precise, a larger sample size should be selected. The most frequently used confidence level in research is 95%. This means that the sample results should predict the population results with 95% accuracy.

A **confidence interval** provides additional information to interpret results. Confidence intervals are typically expressed in terms of plus or minus a specific number. When reporting on election exit poll results, for example, television networks may say that the polls indicate 62% of the population support Candidate A and cite a confidence interval (also referred to as the margin of error) of plus or minus 3%. This lets the audience know that between 59% and 65% of the population will likely vote for Candidate A. The range (59–65) is the confidence interval. In other words, the researchers can be 95% sure that the actual percentage of people voting for Candidate A will fall between 59% and 65%. Obviously, that is good news for Candidate A! For our purposes, however, it is important to note that the relationship between sample size and confidence interval is not necessarily linear in nature. Simply doubling the sample size will not necessarily reduce the confidence interval by half.

Many online and print resources are available to assist researchers in calculating sample size. Figure 12.5 shows a table for determining the sample size of a given

FIGURE 12.5
Determining Sample Size from a Given Population

N	*S	N	S	N	S
10	10	220	140	1,200	291
15	14	230	144	1,300	297
20	19	240	148	1,400	302
25	24	250	152	1,500	306
30	28	260	155	1,600	310
35	32	270	159	1,700	313
40	36	280	162	1,800	317
45	40	290	165	1,900	320
50	44	300	169	2,000	322
55	48	320	175	2,200	327
60	52	340	181	2,400	331
65	56	360	186	2,600	335
70	59	380	191	2,800	338
75	63	400	196	3,000	341
80	66	420	201	3,500	346
85	70	440	205	4,000	351
90	73	460	210	4,500	354
95	76	480	214	5,000	357
100	80	500	217	6,000	361
110	86	550	226	7,000	364
120	92	600	234	8,000	367
130	97	650	242	9,000	368
140	103	700	248	10,000	370
150	108	750	254	15,000	375
160	113	800	260	20,000	377
170	118	850	265	30,000	379
180	123	900	269	40,000	380
190	127	950	274	50,000	382
200	132	1,000	278	75,000	382
210	136	1,100	285	100,000	383

N = population size.

S = sample size.

* Confidence Interval = 5 & Confidence Level = 95%.

The entries in this table were computed by the authors.

population. To perform online calculations (http://statpages.org/javastat.html/ has many links to online calculators that could be useful), the researcher typically must identify specific criteria: the desired confidence level (typically either 95% or 99 %), the desired confidence interval, and an estimate of the population size. It is important to remember that sample size calculators assume that random sampling methods are being used in the study. Results obtained from these calculators cannot be used for nonrandom samples. Remember—random samples produce results that enhance the external validity of your study.

COMMON-SENSE SAMPLE RECRUITING

Recruiting samples can often be difficult and daunting. There is no one way that is the best way to recruit participants. Probably the single most common technique is the mass administration of surveys in a classroom environment. Why do people do this? Because it is fast and you get a lot of data quickly.

Unfortunately, you can spend a great deal of time attempting to recruit participants and end up with not much to show for your work. Earlier in this book, one of our coauthors told the story of how he sent out 200 surveys and got 26 back. What we didn't mention is that in the first part of the study he sent out thousands of surveys and only got 50 back. Our coauthor then collected another 150 to get that 200 using face-to-face methods. In both parts, people just didn't return the surveys in great numbers. As you can imagine, this was expensive for an endeavor that proved not to be fruitful. As such, it is important to really think through the best way to recruit your potential sample. To do so involves knowing your target population, choosing your recruitment approach, and making sure that your recruitment is ethical.

Know Your Target Population

First, you must know who your target population is and how you can possibly recruit them. For example, if you are doing research on college students' perceptions of their teachers, then using a college sample makes perfectly good sense. If, however, you are looking at people's reactions to internal branding in organizations, college students are probably not the best population to tap into. Yes, college students can be easy to access, but this does not mean they should be the only participants we use. When choosing your potential participants, think through how you can get access (and if you even can). In the past, we have had student researchers who used professional and volunteer firefighters, professionals in the New York City theater community, victims of workplace bullying, military personnel, and so on. Each of these groups made sense within the context of their individual studies. And each of these student researchers had connections that helped them to recruit participants.

Approaches to Recruitment

Second, determine how you will approach potential participants for recruitment. The most common methods are face-to-face (FtF), advertisement, letter, e-mail, and snowball. Today, in addition, samples can also be purchased.

FACE-TO-FACE

In the FtF recruitment strategy, you approach potential participants and ask them to participate in your study. You probably have been asked many times to participate in studies when hanging out at the mall. Sometimes the research was being conducted by professional research organizations, but other times, college students or academic researchers had gotten permission from the mall to recruit (always remember to get permission). FtF recruitment is probably the best way to recruit potential participants. When conducting FtF recruitment, approach the potential participant and ask politely whether he or she would take part in an academic research study. It is important to stress that you are a college student conducting an academic research study. We know that potential participants are less likely to say no when they are staring you in the face. At the same time, you must be ready to accept "no" from a potential participant without negatively responding. When a potential participant says "no," thank the individual for her or his time.

ADVERTISEMENT

The next way to recruit people is through advertisements. Go to any college campus and you will see signs advertising for study participants. The advertisement is often a sound approach to recruiting people. However, advertisements for research participation are still advertisements, so you should think strategically about the message you want to convey and where you think your potential participants will most likely see the advertisement. Besides the recruitment poster, some common advertisement venues are newspapers, radio, television, and the Internet. We know many student researchers who have effectively recruited using Facebook ads. Facebook ads can be short and to the point, but they can be relatively inexpensive, costing around $5 per day. One of our colleagues also used Facebook to recruit for a study. The original ad was bland and just comprised text. With the permission of her institutional review board (IRB), she changed the ad to include a picture of her son, who is quite attractive. Overnight, her recruitment numbers skyrocketed. Again, advertising for research is still advertising.

LETTER

Another common approach is to send out targeted letters to potential participants asking for their participation. Maybe you know that you want to recruit physicians in your geographic area for a study on physician responses to pharmaceutical representatives' marketing strategies. You could easily find a list of physician addresses in the phone book and send them letters this way. We should note that recruitment via letter can be difficult, however. Dillman, Smyth, and Christian (2014) have demonstrated that when a researcher tries multiple avenues of recruitment—send a postcard letting a person know that a survey is coming, send a follow-up letter with the survey, send a follow-up postcard reminding the person to complete the survey, send a registered letter with another copy of the survey, and so on—this will increase the overall response rate. However, this process can quickly become expensive, and it probably is not overly useful as a recruitment method for undergraduate or graduate research.

E-MAIL

Many organizations will sell you their member lists complete with e-mail addresses. As such, one other common way of recruiting people is through e-mail. This process is actually quite similar to the letter recruitment strategy. Figure 12.6 shows a possible sample e-mail that you could send to research participants.

SNOWBALL

The next common recruitment technique is the snowball technique. The snowball technique is called this because it resembles the process of making a snowball. When you make a snowball, you start small, you roll the ball in the snow, and it

Dear [Dr. /Mr. / Ms. LAST NAME],

My name is [*name*], and I am a [*undergraduate or graduate student*] from the [*department*] at [*college/university*]. I am writing to invite you to participate in my research study about [describe your research study]. I am conducting this research as part of my degree requirements under the direction of Dr./Professor [*name*]. The survey is an online survey and should not take up more than [*insert time frame*] of your valuable time.

If you decide to participate in this study, you will [*insert description of the study activities*].

Remember, your participation is completely voluntary. If you have any questions about the study, please contact me at [*insert contact information*].

Thank you very much.

Sincerely,

[*Principal Investigator*]

[*hyperlink to study*]

FIGURE 12.6
Sample Recruitment E-mail

gradually becomes larger and larger until you have the base of a potential snowman. With the snowball technique, the goal is to ask a small number of people to participate in your study and then forward the request for participation to others. You could easily add one sentence to Figure 12.6 to turn that recruitment e-mail into one requesting a snowball: "Please forward this message to any friends and/or family members who may also be interested in learning about this research study."

PURCHASING SAMPLES

Last, and the most recent version of recruitment, involves purchasing samples. Yes, in today's world, you can simply purchase research samples. In fact, selling research samples is a booming industry. Typically, you tell one of these corporations what types of people you are looking for to participate in your study. For example, you could say that you are looking for approximately 300 females and males between the ages of 30 and 50 with children. The company will then charge you a fee to recruit the targeted sample from their database of potential participants. Now, some companies will then offer those participants direct incentives on your behalf for their participation, but often, you will also need to consider what types of incentives you can offer to get them to participate. Other organizations are more general and just allow you to pay a prespecified amount to participants who complete a survey.

Ethical Recruitment

Participant recruitment must above all be ethical. If you have forgotten the main requirements for the ethical treatment of human subjects, reexamine Chapter 3. In this section, we talk about a few specific ways that you can try to recruit participants. However, please check with your campus's IRB for any specific requirements they may have about participant recruitment. Some campuses have strict recruitment policies that go above the minimal requirements set by the Office of Human Research Protections (OHRP), so you must make sure you always comply.

First, you must make sure that ALL of your recruitment strategies are approved by your IRB. For example, if you tell your local IRB that you will recruit female and male students on your campus, then you must only recruit female and male students on your campus. You cannot decide halfway through your project to also include faculty and staff, or even students on another campus. If you decide that you need to expand your initial sample, then you must request a modification to your original IRB protocol from the IRB itself. From an IRB perspective, the question becomes one of additional risk if you expand your sample.

Second, you cannot pressure people to participate in your study. Imagine you are a resident assistant in a dorm and you decide to walk around your floor recruiting people. If you do this as a peer and the questions involve nothing overly personnel or damaging, you are probably in a good place ethically. However, if you use your authority as a resident assistant to coerce people into completing your survey, then you are treating your participants in an unethical manner because they feel pressured to consent. We have often heard students say things like "I just forced all of my friends to fill out the survey" or "I gave them out in my sorority/fraternity and watched to make sure everyone completed it." One of the fundamental parts of research ethics is ensuring that participants can make an informed choice without consequences.

Third, make sure that all of your recruitment materials are honest. You cannot say that a survey will only take 10 minutes when you know it takes 50 minutes for the average person. Lying to get participants is simply not ethical unless there is a legitimate reason for the deception and your IRB has signed off on that reason.

CONCLUSION

There are many decisions that researchers must consider when identifying which sampling method to use. In this chapter, we have introduced you to a variety of sampling methods that can be used in designing your own research study. Probability and nonprobability sampling methods were discussed. As you decide which of these methods is most appropriate for your own research, consider the steps you can take to ensure that the results obtained from your sample are generalizable to the target population being examined. An important element in determining generalizability focuses on the selection of random or nonrandom samples in addition to the size of the sample selected for the study.

KEY TERMS

Central limits theorem p. 372

Cluster samples p. 376

Confidence interval p. 383

Convenience samples p. 379

Network samples p. 382

Nonprobability sampling p. 371

Nonproportionate quota samples p. 381

Population p. 369

Probability sampling p. 371

Probability theory p. 372

Proportionate quota samples p. 381

Purposive samples p. 380

Quota samples p. 381

Sample p. 369

Sampling p. 369

Sampling bias p. 372

Sampling error p. 372

Sampling frame p. 371

Simple random samples p. 373

Stratified random samples p. 375

Systematic samples p. 377

Theoretical population p. 370

Volunteer samples p. 380

REFERENCES

Bardhan, N. (2003). Creating spaces for international and multi(inter)cultural perspectives in undergraduate public relations education. *Communication Education, 52,* 164–172.

Bruess, C. J., & Pearson, J. C. (2002). The function of mundane ritualizing in adult friendship and marriage. *Communication Research Reports, 19,* 314–326.

Chan, K. (2000). Hong Kong children's understanding of television advertising. *Journal of Marketing Communications, 6,* 37–52.

Dillman, D. A., Smyth, J. D., & Christian, L. M. (2014). *Internet, phone, mail, and mixed-mode surveys: The tailored design method* (4th ed). Hoboken, NJ: Wiley.

Grunig, L. A. (1990). An exploration of the causes of job satisfaction in public relations. *Management Communication Quarterly, 3,* 355–375.

Riddle, D. L., Albrecht, T. L., Coovert, M. D., Penner, L. A., Ruckdeschel, J. C., Blanchard, C. G., . . . Urbizu, D. (2002). Differences in audiotaped versus videotaped physician–patient interactions. *Journal of Nonverbal Behavior, 26,* 219–239.

FURTHER READING

Fink, A. (2002). *How to sample in surveys* (2nd ed.). Thousand Oaks, CA: Sage.

Henry, G. T. (1990). *Practical sampling.* Thousand Oaks, CA: Sage.

Kalton, G. (1983). *Introduction to survey sampling.* Newbury Park, CA: Sage.

Thompson, S. K. (2002). *Sampling* (rev. ed.). New York, NY: Wiley.

Thompson, S. K., & Seber, G. A. F. (1996). *Adaptive sampling.* New York, NY: Wiley.

Hypothesis Testing

CHAPTER OBJECTIVES

1. Create both one-tailed and two-tailed hypotheses and directional and nondirectional research questions, and explain when they are appropriate to use in research.

2. Describe the mathematical nature of sampling error.

3. Explain the importance of a 95% confidence interval in scientific research.

4. Describe the process a researcher goes through for significance testing.

5. Describe both type I (α) and type II (β) errors.

DEFINING THE TERMS

Hypotheses

A hypothesis is the backbone of modern scientific study, whether it be in the physical or in the social sciences. A **hypothesis** is a statement about the relationship between independent and dependent variables. Good hypotheses must be testable, compatible with current knowledge, logically consistent, and simple.

First, a useful hypothesis is a statement about the relationship or difference between two or more variables that can be tested. A person can say after watching science-fiction movies, for example, that he or she believes all extraterrestrials will speak English, but unless he or she can sample all extraterrestrials, the statement is not a useful hypothesis because the statement cannot be tested. The key word when examining a hypothesis is "testable." A scientist must be able to perform a test of how two variables or phenomena might be related or differ.

A useful hypothesis also must be compatible with current knowledge about a specific topic. For example, Weber, Fornash, Corrigan, and Neupauer (2003) examined the effect that student interest has on the college classroom. Previous research found if a college student was interested in the examples in a textbook, that student could remember the material longer than a college student who was not interested in those examples. Although the authors had seen current issues addressed in college textbooks, no one had examined how interesting examples affect cognitive recall after a lecture. Based on this previous research, the authors hypothesized that if college instructors used examples that were interesting to the students, the students would perform better on a test after a lecture. Note how Weber et al. (2003) used what was previously seen in research to make an argument about what they would expect to see in a new, but related, context.

The Weber et al. (2003) hypothesis has the words "if" and "then," which are necessary in a formalized hypothesis. But not all if–then statements are hypotheses. For example, "If I gamble, then I will get rich" is not really a hypothesis—it is a simple prediction. In a formalized hypothesis, a relationship or difference is stated. For example, to turn the gambling case into a formalized hypothesis, one could test whether the frequency of winning is related to the amount of time spent playing slot machines. Here, the statement would read something like "If a person spends more time playing slot machines, then her or his odds of winning go up." If you always ask yourself whether one thing is related to another, then you should be able to test it.

Many hypotheses are also multilayered and have a number of "if" statements before the "then" statement in the hypothesis. For example, in the Weber et al. (2003) study, you could have the following if statements: (1) If student interest is important to cognitive recall with books and (2) if student interest functions the same way with lecturing and cognitive recall, then (3) student interest should relate to cognitive recall after a lecture. Note that without all three statements together, a clear argument could not be made. An author cannot make a leap in logic without clearly attempting to explain what he or she is thinking when writing a hypothesis.

A third factor of good hypotheses is that they are logically consistent. In other words, a hypothesis cannot contradict itself and actually be a hypothesis. If, when examining the literature, you find that studies consistently disagree on whether men or women are more ambivalent in the workplace, you will have problems generating a good hypothesis because your literature is inconsistent. If at any point you find yourself writing a justification for a hypothesis that says "it could be this or it could be that," then you really do not have a strong hypothesis, and that hypothesis should probably be rewritten as a research question.

Finally, good hypotheses are simple. Before each hypothesis is stated in a research study, a short explanation of the relationship between research studies in the literature is given to explain why the hypothesis can be justified. If this explanation becomes too long or too confusing, it is not simple and is more likely to be logically faulty. In the Weber et al. (2003) article, the authors wrote, "Based on what is known about the relationship between affective variables and cognitive learning [citations given in original] coupled with the literature on text-based interest [citations given in original] we could expect that interest would be positively related to recall of lecture material" (p. 118). This short, declarative statement clearly outlines the if–then statements and provides the basis for the actual hypothesis, which is "Lectures utilizing interest-based examples should result in participants with higher scores on subsequent tests of cognitive recall" (p. 118).

Although this section has introduced what a hypothesis is, we must also explain that there are two different types of hypotheses a person can make when writing a research study. These are one-tailed hypotheses and two-tailed hypotheses.

ONE-TAILED HYPOTHESES

The first type of hypothesis is called a **one-tailed hypothesis**, or a hypothesis that predicts the specific nature of the relationship or difference. In the previous example from Weber et al. (2003), the authors clearly indicated that lectures with interest-based examples would result in participants having higher scores on tests. This hypothesis predicted that students in classrooms where they heard interesting examples during lectures would score statistically significantly higher on cognitive recall (multiple-choice tests) than students in classrooms without interesting examples. Researchers can also write hypotheses to examine the relationship between two variables, like Chesebro (1999) did when he wrote, "A positive relationship exists between the [p]eople listening style and conversational sensitivity" (p. 235). In this hypothesis, Chesebro is expecting to see a positive relationship between two variables (people listening style and conversational sensitivity).

TWO-TAILED HYPOTHESES

The second type of hypothesis is called a **two-tailed hypothesis**, or a hypothesis that predicts that a significant difference or relationship exists but does not indicate the specific nature of that difference (which group would have a higher score) or relationship (positive or negative). For example, if we wanted to write the Weber et al. (2003) hypothesis as a two-way hypothesis, it would read "Lectures utilizing interest-based examples should result in different participant scores on subsequent tests of cognitive recall when compared to scores of participants who did not hear interest-based examples during lectures." In this case, all we did is take out the direction of the hypothesis and make it more general. To rewrite Chesebro's (1999) hypothesis and make it two way, we could write, "There will be a relationship between the people listening style and conversational sensitivity." In this case, we are no longer saying that we expect the relationship to be positive; rather, we are saying that we expect to see a relationship that could be either positive or negative.

CHOICE OF ONE-TAILED VERSUS TWO-TAILED HYPOTHESES

So how does one choose between one- and two-tailed hypotheses? Ideally, if you have a strong enough argument for the direction of the relationship (positive or negative) or for which nominal group will exhibit a variable to a greater degree (males or females; short or tall people; lower, middle, or upper socioeconomic status; etc.), you should make the argument in your hypothesis. However, if you write a hypothesis with a specific direction in mind, this alters the parameters of the statistical tests you will use. Many scholars argue that you should always be conservative and analyze the data for a one-tailed hypothesis as if it were a two-tailed hypothesis.

Research Questions

As mentioned earlier, a **research question** is an explicit question that researchers ask about variables of interest. Researchers often want to see whether there are differences or relationships between variables, so they ask a question about the possibility of that difference or relationship in the rationale section of the literature review. For example, maybe you want to know whether there is a difference between the overall scores of males and females on the Personal Report of Communication Apprehension–24. Although you could write your question like we just did, formal research has traditional ways of doing so.

When preparing to ask a research question, a researcher must thoroughly explain why he or she believes a question should be asked. A researcher must demonstrate that there is not enough evidence based on previous research to form a clear hypothesis. Just like a researcher has to explain the rationale for proposing a hypothesis, a researcher must explain her or his rationale for a research question as well. However, this rationale is not a formal argument establishing the possibility of a difference or relationship that is expected; rather, the rationale explains why there could be a difference or relationship between two or more variables.

Overall, when determining whether to use hypotheses or research questions, you must first determine whether you have the quality and quantity of previously conducted research to support a hypothesis. If you do not have the literature to form a clear argument for a hypothesis, then create a research question to examine the possible difference or relationship between two or more variables.

Just like hypotheses, there are two different types of research questions. These are directional and nondirectional.

DIRECTIONAL RESEARCH QUESTIONS

Directional research questions occur when a researcher asks whether there is either a specific significant difference between two or more variables or a positive or negative relationship between two or more variables. Suppose you wanted to see whether females or males consumed more alcohol in social settings. To test for a difference, you could run a study by asking this research question: "Do males drink significantly more than females in social situations?" And if you wanted to determine whether there is a relationship between the amount of alcohol consumed and an individual's perceptions of opposite sex attractiveness, you could propose a research question that reads "Is there a positive relationship between drinking alcohol and individual perceptions of attractiveness?" Most important, both of these statements are questions and not hypotheses.

NONDIRECTIONAL RESEARCH QUESTIONS

Nondirectional research questions occur when a researcher asks whether there is a difference or relationship between two or more variables. Most researchers who use research questions in a study will use a nondirectional research question. For example, you can write a nondirectional research question to test for differences in alcohol consumption by males and females: "Is there a difference between consumption of alcohol by females and males during social events?" This research question was written only to determine whether there was a difference between men and women and alcohol consumption during social events. This question does not predict a direction of the difference or that a difference will occur, only that there could be a difference. An example of a nondirectional research question for a relationship can be seen in Rocca and Vogl-Bauer's (1999) study. They asked, "What is the nature of the relationship between trait verbal aggression and sports fans' perceptions of appropriate communicative messages at sporting events?" In essence, this question wants to see how a fan's verbal aggression does or does not relate to her or his perceptions of appropriate communication at a sporting event. Note that no indication of the nature of this relationship is discussed in this research question.

Alternative and Null Hypotheses

An **alternative hypothesis** is the prediction that there is a relationship or that there is a difference that has not occurred by chance or random error. Although we differentiate between hypotheses and research questions in the creation of theoretical predictions based on previous research, there are no mathematical differences in how they are perceived. For this reason, both of the following predictions can be represented as alternative hypotheses:

H_1: There is a negative relationship between communication apprehension (CA) and an individual's belief that all students should take public speaking in college.

or

H_1: Females and males differ in their willingness to communicate (WTC).

From a research perspective, it is extremely important to understand that in statistics researchers never test an actual alternative hypothesis (or the one listed in a research article as H_1). Instead, researchers always test the **null hypothesis**—or the Null Monster!!! The null hypothesis (H_0) is almost always expressed as the "nil" hypothesis—namely, that there are zero differences or zero relationships (Cohen, 1994). According to traditional scientific standards, we must assume that the null hypothesis is true until a researcher can provide support to the contrary (or that her or his alternative hypothesis is true). Imagine that your hypothesis is the following:

H_1: There *is* a negative relationship between CA and an individual's belief that all students should take public speaking in college.

In this case, you are predicting that people who have higher levels of CA will be less likely to believe that all students in college should take public speaking. If this is your hypothesis (H_1), then your null hypothesis (H_0) must be the following:

H_0: There *is no* relationship between CA and an individual's belief that all students should take public speaking in college.

So why do we test the null hypothesis in statistics? Fisher (1935) posed the first argument for why we test the null hypothesis: we can never really prove anything as true using statistics; however, we can use statistics to prove that something is false. Based on this reasoning, we cannot prove a hypothesis, but we can prove that a null hypothesis is false. Imagine that we observed 100 people who all had blue eyes and then made the statement "Everyone has blue eyes." To disprove this statement, all we must do is find one person with brown eyes. More practically, the null hypothesis provides researchers with a more general base to make predictions. If researchers were going to test the hypothesis that females and males differ in their attitudes about the usefulness of public speaking, do you test the hypothesis that females and males differ by a small amount, a medium amount, or a large amount? By testing the null hypothesis, researchers do not have to have a specific magnitude of difference in mind; they just have to test the null hypothesis that there is no difference at all.

In shorthand notation, a null hypothesis is always written as H_0, and an alternative hypothesis is written as $H_{1, 2, ..., x}$, with x being an infinite number of study hypotheses. For example, in the Weber et al. (2003) study, H_1 is "Lectures utilizing interest-based examples *should* result in participants with higher scores on subsequent tests of cognitive recall," and H_0 is "Lectures utilizing interest-based examples *will not* result in participants with higher scores on subsequent tests of cognitive recall." In the Chesebro (1999) study, H_1 is "A *positive* relationship exists between the people listening style and conversational sensitivity," and H_0 is "*No* relationship exists between the people listening style and conversational sensitivity." Note that the words in italic make it either a hypothesis or the null hypothesis. The null version of Chesebro's hypothesis is not that there will be a negative relationship, but rather that no relationship will exist at all. If you rewrote the Chesebro hypothesis to read that there would be a negative relationship, you are just creating another hypothesis and not the null hypothesis. Remember, the null hypothesis is just the opposite of the actual hypothesis.

We should note here that both hypotheses and research questions that are generated for a study in one's rationale section have null hypothesis counterparts that say either there is not a relationship or there is not a difference. In Chapter 12, we discussed that our goal in research is to be able to determine whether our samples are consistent with their populations. The null hypothesis expresses expectations for what should occur within the population, so the null hypothesis allows researchers to determine the **probability** that the results we find in our samples are consistent with the overall population.

Although we have talked about the null hypothesis as being something that researchers generally avoid, this is not always the case. Researchers often hope that there is not a relationship or a difference in a study, or they want to accept the null hypothesis. For example, you may theorize that there is no relationship between an individual's CA and her or his IQ and form a hypothesis in a study predicting a lack of relationship. However, the alternative hypothesis always predicts that there is a relationship or difference:

H_1: There is a relationship between an individual's CA and her or his IQ.

However, the null hypothesis would predict that there is not a relationship:

H_0: There is no relationship between an individual's CA and her or his IQ.

In this case, the theoretical hypothesis made in our study suggests that we must accept the null hypothesis, which would have us reject the alternative hypothesis. **Hypothesis testing** then is the process a researcher goes through using inferential statistics to determine whether to reject or accept the null hypothesis.

HYPOTHESIS TESTING CASE STUDY

Now that we have explained the general concept of hypothesis testing, we will look at a case study to help us further understand the hypothesis-testing process.

Case Study Introduction

A team of researchers wanted to determine whether viewing of televangelists positively or negatively influenced nonreligious individuals' perceptions of religion. The researchers used a phone bank that randomly called a large number of potential participants in a major city and asked whether they would participate in a study, and 80% agreed to help. The researchers then mailed a series of scales and asked the participants to fill out and return them in the self-addressed stamped envelope provided. This initial packet contained a short survey asking the participants about their perceptions of various religious organizations.

When the researchers received the completed first survey packet, the participant was sent a second survey packet (sealed in a secondary envelope) with a set of instructions attached. The researchers asked the participants not to open the survey packet until they had watched a televangelist from a religion different from their own. Once a participant had watched a televangelist, he or she opened the secondary survey packet and filled out the survey, which asked the participants to rate their attitudes toward the religion of the televangelist they had watched. The participants also supplied information about the television show they had watched. When the survey was completed, the participants sent the survey back to the researchers.

In essence, each participant rated the televangelist's religion two different times. The measurement of the dependent variable (perception of a religion) occurred in the first survey packet, since participants supplied their attitudes about a wide range of religious groups. The second measurement of the dependent variable (perception of religion) occurred more specifically toward the specific religion of the televangelist they had watched. However, since attitudes about a religious faith were gathered at both Time 1 (T_1; first survey packet) and Time 2 (T_2; second survey packet), this is a clear experimental procedure. To make sure that the study did not have a time effect on the participants' filling out the surveys, the researchers also had a control group who filled out the survey packet at Time 1 and again at Time 2, but were not asked to watch a televangelist from a differing religion. In this control group, the means on the religious attitude scales were virtually identical (MT_1 = 53.69; MT_2 = 53.56). In the manipulation group (filled out the scales in T_1, watched the televangelist, and then filled out the survey packet in T_2), the means are a little different (MT_1 = 52.9; MT_2 = 48.9).

If we were just eyeballing this finding, we might say that there is almost a four-point drop from Time 1 to Time 2, so clearly people end up not liking a religion after viewing a televangelist. In statistics, however, we simply cannot eyeball a difference in means and say that the change is statistically meaningful. For this reason, we use hypothesis testing to determine whether a difference or relationship between two means is meaningful or is occurring as a result of random chance.

Hypothesis Testing in the Case Study

As defined in Chapter 2, a hypothesis is a tentative statement about the relationship between independent and dependent variables. In this chapter, we discuss IVs and

DVs together under the heading of "hypothesis testing" because we are talking about mathematical hypothesis testing, not a hypothesis derived as a result of your literature review. For our case study, the alternative and null hypotheses would be as follows:

H_1: There is a difference between people who view a televangelist and people who do not and their perceptions of a televangelist's religion.

H_0: There is no difference between people who view a televangelist and people who do not and their perceptions of a televangelist's religion.

In this example, we want to determine whether there is a difference between the mean score on the religious attitude scale for Time 1 (before they watched the televangelist) and the mean score on the religious attitude scale for Time 2 (after they watched the televangelist). The mathematical notion for this would then be

H_1: $\mu_{Time1} \neq \mu_{Time2}$

This statement says that the mean of Time 1 is not equal to the mean of Time 2, or that there is a difference between them.

In this example, our null hypothesis would state that the mean score on the religious attitude scale for Time 1 (before they watched the televangelist) and the mean score on the religious attitude scale for Time 2 (after they watched the televangelist) were the same, or no difference exists. The mathematical notion for this would then be

H_0: $\mu_{Time1} = \mu_{Time2}$

This statement says that the mean of Time 1 is equal to the mean of Time 2, or that there is not a difference between them. Note how the alternative hypothesis and null hypothesis would be the same whether you developed a hypothesis or research question out of your literature review.

FROM RANDOM SAMPLES TO A WHOLE POPULATION

One of the most interesting and complex aspects of empirical social scientific research is that it deals with people and numbers. As a result, a certain amount of error naturally occurs. Ideally, researchers could gather data from an entire population. This is not realistic, however, so we must rely on samples as discussed in Chapter 12.

Sampling Error

When researchers rely on samples, a certain amount of error occurs, which is called **sampling error**, or the degree to which a sample *probably* differs with respect to a specific variable from a population. Imagine that our example study in this chapter had only 10 participants. If we attained the mean on the religious attitude scale for each of the 10 participants, we would see that not everyone's score was identical, so we would have what is called a sampling distribution. And as we know, the mean of a sampling distribution can be calculated by adding up all of the 10 individual scores on the religious attitude scale and dividing that number by 10 (number of participants; $N = 10$). If in our sample we got the 10 following scores—57, 58, 62, 23, 54, 56, 55, 54, 51, and 59 at Time 1 and 55, 57, 60, 20, 50, 52, 53, 55, 48, and 39 at Time 2—we would get means and standard deviations for Time 1 of ($MT_1 = 52.9$, $SD = 10.94$) and for Time 2 of ($MT_2 = 48.9$, $SD = 11.67$).

If we wanted to determine how much error was in our sampling distribution (how much our random sample means differ from the overall mean of Time 1 52.9), we simply divide the standard deviation by the square root of N (sample size of 10). So first, we must calculate the square root of 10, which is 3.16227766. We can then divide our standard deviation (10.94) by 3.16227766 and we get 3.45953176. The standard error of the mean (SE_M) in our example is roughly 3.46. In other words, our sample has an inherent amount of error, which is always expected in statistics.

Sampling error must be taken into account when attempting to determine whether a statistical difference or relationship exists. Since we calculated that our sample has a standard error of the mean of 3.46 in the first mean, this indicates that we can guess that the actual population mean (everyone who could have participated in the study) should exist between 56.36 and 49.44. We get this interval of possible choices because we take the calculated mean we had in our sample at Time 1 (52.9) and then add and subtract the SE_M (3.46) from that mean. As we will discuss in more detail in Chapter 14, anything that falls within ±1 standard deviation of the mean (10.94 in our example) is said to account for approximately 68.26% of the individual means in a sample. Using our SE_M of ±3.46, we know that our population mean will fall between 56.36 and 49.44, but this also means that about 31.74% of the time the actual population mean will not fall between 56.36 and 49.44. I don't know about you, but I want something that will be accurate more than 68.26% of the time.

95% Confidence

Researchers do not want to rely on results that are only accurate 68.26% of the time, so they have decided that for something to be considered statistically significant, an interval of numbers (e.g., 56.36 to 49.44) should be accurate at least 95% of the time. Hence, 95.44% of all sample means will fall between two standard deviations away from the mean or ±2SD; the same is also true for the standard error of the mean (more on this in Chapter 14). In our example, the SE_M is ±3.46, so if we multiply 3.46 × 2, we get 6.92. If we take this number and then add it to and subtract it from our mean, 52.9, we can say that 95% of all of our scores fall between 45.98 and 59.82, which is a range of 13.84. This range of scores of random sample means associated with a **confidence level** is called a **confidence interval**, so at the 95% confidence level (or possibility of a 5% chance that we are wrong), our population mean would fall between 45.98 and 59.82. So all in all, how confident should a researcher be?

Researchers generally agree that we should be at least 95% confident or have a 95% confidence interval, which means that researchers expect their results to be inaccurate 5% of the time. To achieve a confidence interval of 95%, we know that the SE_M (3.46) must be multiplied by ±1.96 (see Chapter 14 for a discussion of this), which would be 6.782. In other words, we can be 95% confident that the population mean from which our sample mean (the 10 people in the study, $M = 52.9$) will lie between 46.118 and 59.682.

Confidence Levels Across Research Fields

You may be wondering whether this is something that only social scientific researchers do—it is not. In fact, most research, from medicine to physics to communication, uses the 95% confidence interval as the standard to judge statistics. Think of it like this: imagine a drug company wants to find out whether their drug kills people. At the 95% confidence rate, the drug would kill 1 in 20 people. Occasionally, medical studies will increase the confidence rate to 99.99%, which would mean that only 1 of every 10,000 people who take the drug would die as a result. However, the 95% confidence interval is still standard for most statistically based research.

Most research studies do not rely on just one variable's confidence interval, however, so other techniques have been developed to help us determine how confident researchers are when examining multiple variable means. When examining multiple variables, researchers pool these individual variables and use them as a single random sample (both Time 1 and Time 2 together) to stand for the large number of random samples that are being examined (both Time 1 and Time 2 separately). By doing this and following the same steps we performed above looking at the combined $\pm 1.96 SE_M$, researchers can create a confidence interval, and this confidence interval allows researchers to know what kind of sampling error, or "margin of error," actually exists. For example, what if we found out that in our example the means for Time 1 (before watching the televangelist) and Time 2 (after watching the televangelist) were different only at a confidence interval of ±20%? Would you then be willing to say that these two means were different from each other? If you said a 60% confidence interval is acceptable, then you are saying that 40 of every 100 times, the findings of your study would be false. Essentially, your study's results are meaningless. If, however, we found that the means for Time 1 and Time 2 were different with a confidence interval of ±2.5%, then we could say that the two variables were different at a 95% confidence level.

TESTING FOR SIGNIFICANCE

In the previous section, we introduced the concept of confidence intervals and the importance of a 95% confidence level. In this section, we look at how we can determine whether a difference or relationship between two variables has occurred by chance. The process to determine whether chance causes a difference or relationship is called significance testing.

In significance testing, the goal is to determine whether our null hypothesis (H_0: μ_{Time1} = μ_{Time2}) is accurate. As mentioned earlier, we are always concerned with testing the null hypothesis, so significance testing is the process of analyzing quantitative data to determine whether a null hypothesis is probably true or probably false. And in this definition, note that we are examining whether the null is *probably* true or false, which indicates that there is always a possibility of error occurring when conducting a significance test. **Significance testing**, then, is determining whether you can accept the null hypothesis (there is no difference between the participants' religious attitudes before they watched a televangelist and after they watched a televangelist) or must reject the null hypothesis (there is a difference between the participants' religious attitudes before they watched a televangelist and after they watched a televangelist).

In significance testing, we often refer to the "probability level" when discussing how confident we are about our results. To determine the **probability level**, simply take the percentile number (95) and subtract it from 1, or $1 - 0.95 = 0.05$. The probability level is also sometimes called a *p* value, or **probability value**, and is also referred to by the Greek letter alpha (α). So, if you wanted to be 99% confident, your *p* value would be 0.01 ($1 - 0.99 = 0.01$), and so on. As a quick side note to the use of the Greek letter α, this is not the same alpha referred to earlier in this book with regard to scale reliability. Statisticians often use the same Greek letter to represent a number of different functions, depending on which statistical formula is being discussed.

We should also note that sampling error is one of the major reasons why replication of studies is important. If a study's findings are accurate 95% of the time, then there is a 5% chance that the results obtained in that study happened because of error. Scientists often will replicate a study or research the same patterns of variables multiple times to make sure the results are consistent. Researchers often find contradictory results even when the research process, measures, and participants are identical. An advanced statistical procedure known as a meta-analysis can be used to combine a number of different studies looking at the same phenomenon to achieve stronger support for the existence of a relationship or difference or the lack of a relationship or difference.

Now that we have explained what a probability value is, we will examine the steps necessary in significance testing: setting the probability level, conducting a statistical test, and comparing calculated and critical values.

Step 1: Set the Probability Level

Before you can perform any statistical tests to determine whether there are differences or relationships in your study, you must first decide how confident you must be. As discussed earlier with confidence intervals, researchers prefer to be at least 95% confident. A 95% confidence in significance testing indicates that a researcher could expect to see a difference or relationship occurring in her or his results by accident, as a result of chance, about 5 times out of 100. This may sound like a lot, but it is the standard used by all scientists when determining whether something is an actual difference or relationship.

If you were conducting a study that could have a chance of killing someone (like many pharmaceutical studies), however, you may want to be more than 95% confident in your results. Maybe in a pharmaceutical company you would pick a probability level of 0.0005, indicating that you are 99.95% confident in the finding of a difference or a relationship between a set of variables.

Ultimately, what level of probability you establish for your study will determine whether a difference exists. The lower your p value, the harder it is to be significant at that level. Maybe in our example we find out we are significant at $p < 0.10$ but are not significant at $p < 0.05$. In this case, if we had previously established that for a difference to exist we would have to be 95% confident, then the difference found between the pretest (before the participant watched the televangelist) and the posttest (after the participant watched the televangelist) would not be statistically significant. If, however, we had established a 90% confidence interval, then our study would be significant at $p < 0.10$. Although some researchers will raise their confidence interval to 90%, we strongly encourage you not to do this because you also increase the probability of type II error (i.e., we accept the null hypothesis based on our sample, but the null hypothesis is actually false in the population), which we will examine later in this chapter.

Step 2: Conduct a Statistical Test

The second part of significance testing is to conduct a statistical test. Every statistical test ultimately generates a value called the **calculated value**, which is simply the end result that a researcher receives when he or she has completed a mathematical formula related to a specific statistical test. This part of significance testing is often the most complicated and time-consuming if completed by hand. Researchers often prefer to work with computer packages (e.g., Statistical Package for the Social Sciences [SPSS]) that determine the calculated value for them.

Step 3: Compare Calculated and Critical Values

The third part of conducting a significance test is to compare the calculated value (the answer one achieves through arithmetic) to a **critical value** (a predetermined value calculated by statisticians that a calculated value must be greater than). In the example for this chapter, we obtained a calculated value of 2.176 and the critical value associated with the 0.05 probability level we had to beat was 2.262; our calculated value is smaller, so it does not beat the threshold. If our calculated value is not greater than the critical value, then we cannot say that we are significant at that level. In other words, the probability of a relationship or difference existing is less than the probability level (less than 95%). We will spend a lot more time exploring this concept as we look at various statistical tests in the next five chapters.

Critical values are determined based on the size of sample, the number of variables being compared, and the type of statistical test being used. Each statistical test has its own unique set of critical values. These critical values ultimately allow researchers to determine whether a calculated value is greater than a specific critical value that indicates that the calculated value is significant at the ±1.96 *SD* away from the mean. Remember that we can be 95% confident in a result if that result beats the ±1.96 *SD* threshold for determining whether something is confident at that level. Figure 13.1 shows the bell

FIGURE 13.1
Bell Curve

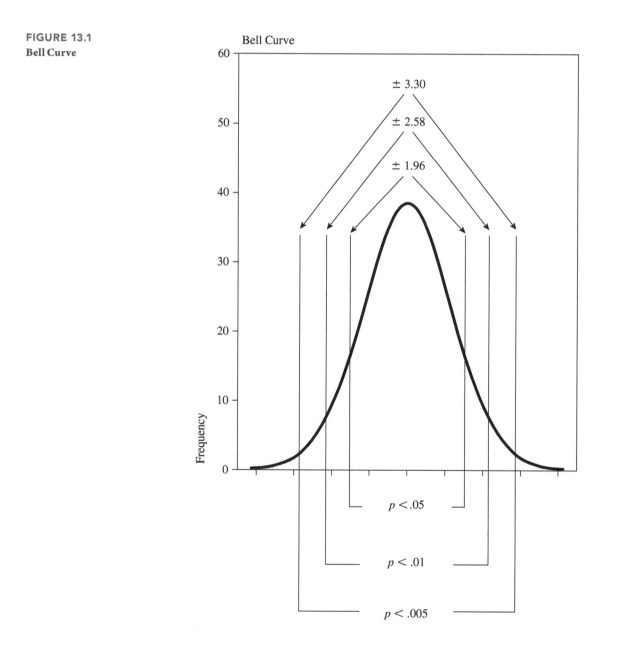

curve with the standard deviation estimates for determining the critical values at the $p < 0.05$, $p < 0.01$, and $p < 0.005$ levels.

As we know from our example, the critical value to beat in order to obtain a 95% confidence in our results is 2.262 and the value we calculated was 2.176. (We used a paired t test to statistically test for a significant difference between the two means. Paired t tests are discussed later in Chapter 16.) Figure 13.2 shows three sets of critical values to beat in order to obtain significance at $p < 0.05$, $p < 0.01$,

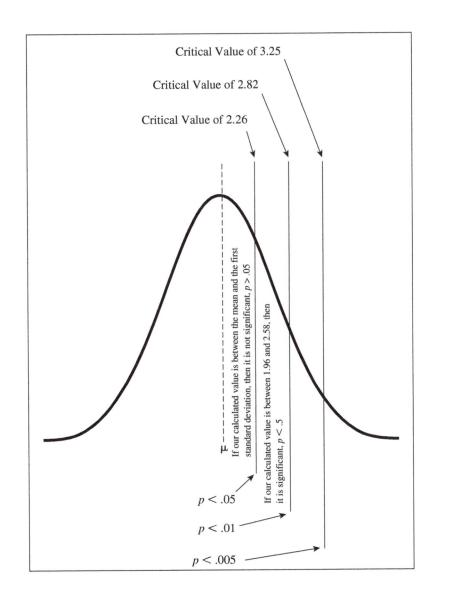

FIGURE 13.2
Curve with
Significant Values

and $p < 0.005$. With our calculated value of 2.176, we fall between the mean and the first critical value (±1.96, or 2.262). If, however, we had a calculated value of 2.367, we would have fallen between the 0.05 and 0.01 confidence intervals and thus would have been significant at $p < 0.05$. Ultimately, this is how significance testing is completed.

TESTING FOR POWER

In addition to making sure that a difference or relationship is statistically significant, it is also important to make sure that a statistical test has power. The purpose of statistical **power** is to determine whether a researcher can reject a false null hypothesis. Power allows a researcher to determine how sensitive a statistical test will be in detecting relationships and differences of a specific size. If a study is powerful, then a researcher will be able to correctly find even small differences and relationships, but if a study is not powerful, a researcher may miss small differences and relationships. For example, a researcher could conclude that there is no relationship between an individual's level of CA (anxiety about real or perceived communication) and her or his WTC (desire to initiate communication) based on her or his sample. However, previous research consistently shows that there should be a negative relationship between CA and WTC (as someone's CA goes up, her or his WTC goes down, and vice versa).

There are three reasons why a researcher may accept a false null hypothesis (i.e., there is no relationship between CA and WTC). First, the type of test a researcher uses to examine the relationship is relevant. Some tests are less "sensitive," or less likely to note actual relationships or differences even when they do exist. We will talk about these issues in the next six chapters.

Second, it is harder to attain statistical differences using two-tailed hypotheses. As we discussed earlier in this chapter, two-tailed hypotheses leave open the direction of a difference or relationship, whereas one-tailed hypotheses are specific about the direction of the difference or relationship. Figure 13.3 illustrates the problem that can often occur when examining one- and two-tailed hypotheses. To be significant at the 0.05 probability level using a one-tailed test, a calculated value must be greater than a lower critical value (located $+1.65$ or -1.65, but not ±1.65, standard deviations away from the mean). However, to be significant at the 0.05 probability level using a two-tailed test, we test in both directions on the number line, so the critical value is higher (±1.96).

If you have a clear reason for using a one-tailed test, it is perfectly appropriate to do so. However, one-tailed hypothesis testing is often misused as a way of gaining

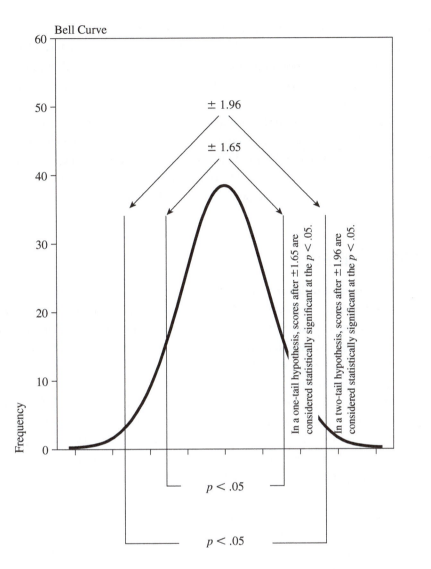

FIGURE 13.3
**One- and Two-Tailed
Tests**

significance even when a research question does not call for the test. Use one-tailed hypothesis testing sparingly, but understand that some circumstances do warrant its use.

Finally, small sample sizes often make it impossible for a statistical device to determine when a null hypothesis should be rejected. Many researchers attempt to calculate complicated statistics based on small sample sizes. Much medical and social scientific research is conducted with sample sizes of less than 20 participants.

Ideally, no sample should be smaller than 200 unless the entire population from which the sample is drawn is smaller than 200. When a sample has 200 or more participants, the likelihood of finding statistically significant small differences and relationships increases, which in turn decreases the incidence of type II error, as we will see in a moment.

To increase the likelihood that a statistical test will be able to reject a null hypothesis when it should, a researcher should use appropriate statistical tests, use one- and two-tailed tests appropriately, and have a large sample. Power, when it is measured, exists on a continuum from 0 to 1. However, statistical power should never be lower than 0.8, or you risk the chance of missing actual relationships and differences that really exist.

EFFECT SIZES

Along with power, another important characteristic to understand is the effect size of a statistical finding. An effect size is like a thermometer. If there has been a change to one or two degrees cooler, you may not even notice it has gotten colder. So although this may be a significant difference in the heat, it may not be large enough for it to really matter. If the temperature decreases by 50 degrees, however, you will be hunting around your house for an electric blanket.

An **effect size** is the strength of a relationship or the magnitude of a difference occurring between two variables, or the degree to which a null hypothesis is false. There are three types of effect sizes that can be seen in statistics (small, medium, and large). Each difference test discussed in this book has a corresponding effect size that is important to understand, so we will discuss this concept in greater detail later.

In Figure 13.4, the first set of bell curves illustrates what we mean by a small effect size. In this case, we are examining the difference between two means (indicated by the dashed lines). Note that the means are closer together. Although the means may be significantly different, researchers cannot conclude that means are drastically different. A lot of research done on sex differences runs into this problem. Basically, little research that examines differences between male and female behavior (if the difference is significant) is beyond a small effect. In case of small effects, researchers must be honest about these effect sizes. Although the difference may be significant, it may not mean much. The second graph in the chart in Figure 13.4 represents what a medium effect may look like if we graphed it. In this case, the mean differences are farther apart than we saw in the first graph, but still closer together than we see in the third graph, which represents a large effect. All in all, it is important to realize that although something may be statistically significant, the effect size associated with that significance is also extremely important.

FIGURE 13.4
Effect Size

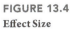

UNDERSTANDING ERROR

The last part of this chapter explores a concept that we already hinted at previously, which is error. The chart that we are going to use to explain error is in Figure 13.5.

To understand this chart, we will look at and provide an example illustrating each quadrant. Along the top of the chart are two columns: "Null Hypothesis Is True" and

In the Whole Population → What ↓ We conclude Based on Our Sample	**Null Hypothesis Is True** In reality… • There is no difference or relationship • Our theory is wrong	**Null Hypothesis Is False** In reality… • There is a difference or relationship • Our theory is correct
Accept the Null Hypothesis We <u>say</u>… • There is no difference or relationship • Our theory is wrong	$1 - \alpha$ The Confidence Interval The odds of saying there is <u>no</u> effect or gain when in fact there is none No. of times out of 100 when there is no effect, we'll say there is none	β Type II Error The odds of saying there is <u>no</u> effect or gain when in fact there is one No. of times out of 100 when there <u>is</u> an effect, we'll say there is none
Reject the Null Hypothesis We <u>say</u>… • There is a difference or relationship • Our theory is correct	α Type I Error The odds of saying there <u>is</u> an effect or gain when in fact there is none. No. of times out of 100 when there is <u>no</u> effect, we'll say there is one	$1 - \beta$ Power The odds of saying there <u>is</u> an effect or gain when in fact there is one. No. of times out of 100 when there <u>is</u> an effect, we'll say there is one

FIGURE 13.5
Type I (α) and Type II (β) Errors

"Null Hypothesis Is False." These two columns refer to what actually happens in the real world. Maybe you predicted that men and women will have differing levels of humor, but in reality there is no difference between men and women and their use of humor. In this case, the null hypothesis is true in the real world. By contrast, often a null hypothesis is false. If you were examining men and women and differing levels of verbal aggression, men are more verbally aggressive in the real world, so the null hypothesis is false in the real world (or your actual hypothesis—that men have higher verbal aggression scores than women—is true).

As mentioned in both of these examples, what we expect to happen when we create a mathematical hypothesis often is correct but also often is wrong. For this reason, we must understand whether we have accepted the null hypothesis after we get our results, which the two rows ("Accept the Null Hypothesis" and "Reject the Null Hypothesis") address. If we accept the null hypothesis, we are basically saying that our original hypothesis was incorrect. If, for example, we had predicted that there would be a positive relationship between nonverbal immediacy and assertiveness and the results indicated there was not a significant relationship, then we would accept the null hypothesis. By contrast, if we had predicted that there was a relationship between humor assessment and nonverbal immediacy and the results indicated there was a significant relationship, then we could reject the null hypothesis (or affirm our actual hypothesis).

We realize that this sounds backward and almost like we are talking out of both sides of our mouths, but remember what we said in the beginning of this chapter—in statistics, we are not testing hypotheses; we are testing null hypotheses. When we talk about error, many people get confused because it sounds logically backward compared to how most people think.

Now that we have looked at what the columns mean and what the rows mean, we can examine the four quadrants indicated by both reality and what we conclude. These first two quadrants represent what we hope will happen when we use statistics to analyze quantitative data. The third and fourth quadrants, however, represent two types of errors that occur when people use statistics to analyze quantitative data.

The Confidence Interval

In the first quadrant, "The Confidence Interval," we have a case where in "reality" (or in the actual population) the null hypothesis is true and through our statistical testing we accept the null hypothesis. Imagine that you predicted there would be a relationship between responsiveness and the attitude people have toward college. However, when you conduct a test with your sample to see whether this relationship exists, you do not find a significant relationship. At the same time, in the larger population, this relationship does not exist as well. In other words, you accepted the null (there is no relationship between responsiveness and attitude toward college), and the null is true (in the real world, there is no relationship between responsiveness and attitude toward college).

In this case, you get a confidence interval. As discussed earlier in this chapter, a confidence interval lets you know how many times out of 100 that your results will say there is no effect (difference or relationship) and there really is no effect (difference or relationship) in the real world. The confidence interval is represented by 1 – alpha (α). If your alpha reliability (or p value) is 0.0001, then your confidence interval is 1 – 0.0001 = 0.9999, or a 99.99% confidence interval. Generally speaking, when reporting alphas it is always important to round up and not down. For example, the paired t-test case example used in this chapter had a calculated p-value of 0.058, so this test would not be considered significant at 0.05 because 0.058 is greater than 0.05. Also, it is often best to report alpha levels on half-step intervals like 0.05, 0.01, 0.005, 0.001, 0.0005, and 0.0001. So, if you found that the calculated value for p was 0.0047, the easiest way to report this alpha would be to say that the test was significant at 0.005 since this is the nearest half-step interval rounded up. (To help you think about p values in terms of a number line, see Figure 13.6. Remember, the goal is for the probability value (p value) to be less than 0.05 in order to reach statistical significance. In the case of Figure 13.6, those p values to the left of 0.05 would be statistically significant, and those values to the right of 0.05 would not be statistically significant.)

When looking at computer printouts, SPSS provides you with calculated alpha levels. However, there is some disagreement as to how to report alpha levels that are below 0.000. Levine and Atkin (2004) argue that when a computer prints out a 0.000 alpha level (this occurs with SPSS), it is most correct to report this alpha level as 0.0005 (99.95% confident).

The sixth edition of the American Psychological Association (APA) style manual established some clear-cut guidelines for reporting p values in academic research:

> When reporting p values, report exact p values (e.g., $p = .031$) to two or three decimal places. However, report p values less than .001 as $p < .001$. The tradition of reporting p values in the form of $p < .10$, $p < .05$, $p < .01$, and so forth, was appropriate in a time when only limited tables of critical values were available. However, in tables the "$p <$" notation may be necessary for clarity (see section 5.16). (p. 114)

For those of you new to APA style, this may not seem like a huge deal, but to those of us who have been using APA style for a few decades (or more), this is a big change in how we report p values. Although we are talking about this issue here, you will see where this becomes important in the next six chapters as we explore various statistical tests.

FIGURE 13.6
Statistical Significance Number Line

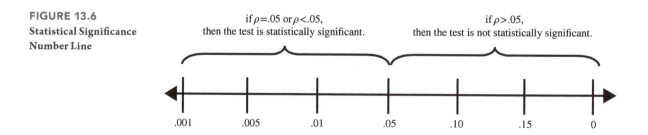

Power

In the quadrant diagonal to "The Confidence Interval" is the quadrant labeled "Power." In this case, you reject the null hypothesis based on the results from your statistical analysis, and the null hypothesis is actually rejected in the real world. For example, maybe you predicted that there would be a positive relationship between nonverbal immediacy and responsiveness. To test this question, you run a statistical analysis and find out that there is a relationship, and then this relationship actually exists in the real world. In this case, your statistical test rejected the null hypothesis and the null hypothesis should be rejected. When this occurs, the result is called power.

Power is the odds of saying there is a difference or relationship when in fact there is one. In essence, power is the number of times out of 100 when there is a relationship or difference in a study and there is a relationship or difference that actually exists in the real world. Power is represented by $1 -$ beta (β). If your beta is equal to 0.05, then your power is $1 - 0.05 = 0.95$. As mentioned earlier, power should be greater than 0.80 to successfully reject the null hypothesis when the null hypothesis is rejected in the larger population.

Type I Error

A **type I error** (or **α error**) occurs when a researcher rejects a null hypothesis (says that the alternative hypothesis was true) based on a sample when the null hypothesis should be accepted (the alternative hypothesis was false in the real world). In other words, suppose you run a test to see whether an individual's level of interpersonal humor (humor assessment) is related to nonverbal sensitivity (ability to pick up on other people's nonverbal behavior). You find a positive relationship between humor assessment and nonverbal sensitivity in your sample, but in the real world, this relationship does not exist. When this occurs, you have a type I error.

A type I error is the odds of finding a difference or relationship when in fact there is not one. This probability is represented by Greek letter alpha, or your probability value. If a finding is significant at $p < 0.05$, then there is a 5% chance that you will reject your null hypothesis (or affirm your hypothesis or research question) when in the actual population you would not reject your null hypothesis.

Type II Error

A **type II error** (or **β error**) occurs when a researcher accepts the null hypothesis (says that the alternative hypothesis was not true) based on a sample when the null hypothesis should be rejected (the alternative hypothesis was true in the real world). We can take the flip side of the example discussed under type I error. You run a test to see whether an individual's level of interpersonal humor (humor assessment) is related to nonverbal sensitivity (ability to pick up on other people's nonverbal behavior). You do not find a relationship between humor assessment and nonverbal sensitivity in your sample, but in the real world (or actual population), this relationship exists. When this occurs, you have a type II error.

A type II error is the odds of finding there is no difference or relationship when in fact there is one. Type II error is represented by the Greek letter β. If in a study you find that $\beta = 0.05$, then there is a 5% chance you will accept the null hypothesis (or reject your hypothesis or research question) when in the actual population you would reject your null hypothesis (or affirm your hypothesis or research question).

Minimizing Error

One of the basic goals of empirical research is to limit both type I and type II errors as much as possible. To limit type I error, the best thing to do is to increase your confidence interval from, say, 95% confidence (5 times out of 100 you are wrong) to, say, 99% confidence (1 time out of 100 you are wrong). Do not think, however, this means that researchers should just neglect the 95% confidence interval for a more conservative 99% confidence interval all the time. Unfortunately, if you try to protect against type I errors (rejecting a null hypothesis that is probably true, or a false positive), you often enable type II errors instead (accepting a null hypothesis that is probably false, or a false negative). In other words, type I errors (α errors) and type II errors (β errors) are inversely related. The more stringent the probability level, the more likely you will commit a type II error, and the more stringent the power, the more likely you will commit a type I error.

In an ideal world, a fair balance can be struck between type I and type II errors, but researchers often must err on one side or the other. However, increasing the sample size does allow a researcher to achieve both low α and high β values. To prevent both type I and type II errors, researchers are encouraged to recruit fairly large samples (at least 200 participants). Ultimately, the number of participants needed for a study is based on a variety of factors related to how many groups you want to compare and the size of the differences and relationships you hope to obtain.

CONCLUSION

This chapter has introduced you to three major concepts that will be seen again and again in the chapters to come—namely, significance, power, and effect size. Remember, just because two means may appear different does not indicate that the difference is statistically significant. For instance, we have used an example throughout the entire chapter about 10 participants in a study to determine whether a difference occurs in an individual's attitude toward a religion after watching a televangelist. Based on the numbers described in the first part of a chapter, there was not a significant difference between Time 1 (before watching the televangelist) and Time 2 (after watching the televangelist). In fact, the calculated p value was 0.058, so the difference was not significant at the 0.05 level. (How this was tested will be discussed in Chapter 16.)

KEY TERMS

Alternative hypothesis p. 395

Calculated value p. 403

Confidence interval p. 400

Confidence level p. 400

Critical value p. 403

Directional research questions p. 395

Effect size p. 408

Hypothesis p. 391

Hypothesis testing p. 397

Nondirectional research questions p. 395

Null hypothesis p. 396

One-tailed hypothesis p. 393

Power p. 406

Probability p. 397

Probability level p. 402

Probability value (p value) p. 402

Research question p. 394

Sampling error p. 399

Significance testing p. 402

Two-tailed hypothesis p. 393

Type I error (α error) p. 413

Type II error (β error) p. 413

REFERENCES

American Psychological Association. (2010). *Publication manual of the American Psychological Association* (6th ed.). Washington, DC: American Psychological Association.

Chesebro, J. (1999). The relationship between listening styles and conversational sensitivity. *Communication Research Reports, 16,* 233–238.

Cohen, J. (1994). The earth is round (*p* < .05). *American Psychologist, 49,* 997–1003.

Fisher, R. A. (1935). *The design of experiments.* Edinburgh, Scotland: Oliver & Boyd.

Levine, T. R., & Atkin, C. (2004). The accurate reporting of software-generated *p*-values: A cautionary research note. *Communication Research Reports, 21,* 324–327.

Rocca, K. A., & Vogl-Bauer, S. (1999). Trait verbal aggression, sports fan identification, and perceptions of appropriate sports fan communication. *Communication Research Reports, 16,* 239–248.

Weber, K., Fornash, B., Corrigan, M, & Neupauer, N. C. (2003). The effect of interest on recall: An experiment. *Communication Research Reports, 20,* 116–123.

FURTHER READING

Chow, S. L. (1997). *Statistical significance: Rationale, validity, and utility.* Thousand Oaks, CA: Sage.

Gravetter, F. J., & Wallnau, L. B. (2000). *Statistics for the behavioral sciences* (5th ed.). Belmont, CA: Wadsworth/Thomson Learning.

Howell, D. C. (1997). *Statistical methods for psychology* (4th ed.). Belmont, CA: Duxbury Press.

Huff, D. (1954). *How to lie with statistics.* New York, NY: Norton.

Keller, D. K. (2006). *The Tao of statistics: A path to understanding (with no math).* Thousand Oaks, CA: Sage.

Lehmann, E. L. L., & Romano, J. P. (2005). *Testing statistical hypothesis* (3rd ed.). New York, NY: Springer-Verlag.

Mohr, L. B., & Lewis-Beck, M. S. (1990). *Understanding significance testing.* Thousand Oaks, CA: Sage.

Salkind, N. J. (2012). *100 questions (and answers) about research methods.* Los Angeles, CA: Sage.

Salkind, N. J. (2017). *Statistics for people who (think they) hate statistics* (6th ed.). Thousand Oaks, CA: Sage.

Singleton, R. A., Jr., & Straits, B. C. (2017). *Approach to social research* (6th ed.). New York, NY: Oxford University Press.

Tabachnick, B. G., & Fidell, L. S. (2013). *Using multivariate statistics* (6th ed.). Boston, MA: Pearson.

Trochim, W. M. K. (2000). *The research methods knowledge base* (2nd ed.). Cincinnati, OH: Atomic Dog. Retrieved from http://www.socialresearchmethods.net/

14

Descriptive Statistics

CHAPTER OBJECTIVES

1. Define the term *statistic*, and discriminate between descriptive and inferential statistics.

2. Explain and calculate the measures of central tendency discussed in the chapter (mean, median, and mode).

3. Explain the purpose of skewness and kurtosis.

4. Calculate and explain the measures of variability discussed in the chapter (range, sum of squares, variance, and standard deviation).

5. Evaluate the measures of central tendency and measures of variability for the variables collected in the textbook's dataset.

Statistics is a term that conjures up many meanings in the minds of students. The majority of students we have worked with express a high level of anxiety and apprehension about taking a course in research methods because of a fear of statistics. Be honest—were you excited at the prospect of taking this class? Our guess is that if given the choice, most of you would have preferred to take a different course. In fact, this is a good example of a statistic—the "majority."

Imagine we could have everyone in the world fill out the Personal Report of Communication Apprehension–24 (PRCA- 24) scale. The average we would get for the entire world population on the PRCA-24 would be called a parameter because the average would refer to the entire population. Parameters are almost never achieved, however, because having an entire population fill out a scale is almost impossible unless the target population is small. Instead, we often use smaller groups from within the entire population called samples. Although we discussed how to get samples in great detail in Chapter 12, just understand here that a sample is a subset from within the whole population that allows researchers to make generalizations

417

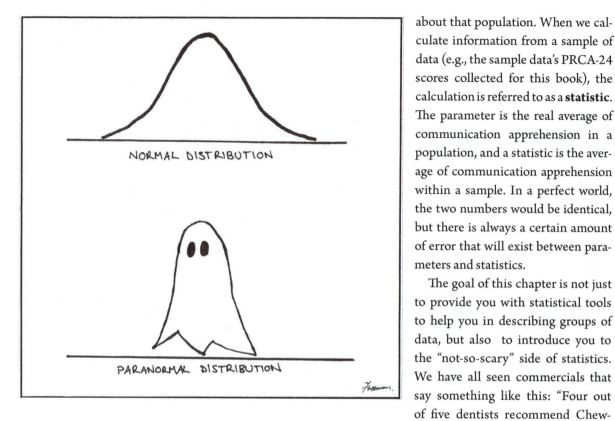

NORMAL DISTRIBUTION

PARANORMAL DISTRIBUTION

▲ A Visual Comparison of Normal and Paranormal Distributions

Source: Reproduced from the *Journal of Epidemiology & Community Health*, Matthew Freeman, Volume 60(1), 2006, with permission from BMJ Publishing Group Ltd.

about that population. When we calculate information from a sample of data (e.g., the sample data's PRCA-24 scores collected for this book), the calculation is referred to as a **statistic**. The parameter is the real average of communication apprehension in a population, and a statistic is the average of communication apprehension within a sample. In a perfect world, the two numbers would be identical, but there is always a certain amount of error that will exist between parameters and statistics.

The goal of this chapter is not just to provide you with statistical tools to help you in describing groups of data, but also to introduce you to the "not-so-scary" side of statistics. We have all seen commercials that say something like this: "Four out of five dentists recommend Chewing Gum Brand X for their patients who chew gum." The advertisement uses a statistic to illustrate that 80% of dentists would recommend Chewing Gum Brand X. This is much more effective than simply stating, "Most dentists prefer Chewing Gum Brand X." When information is presented using words like "most," "many," and "substantial," consumers are often skeptical and want to know the exact amount. Generally, we seek proof for claims that are made, and statistics lends credibility. Consider the grades you earn in your classes. Suppose you take an exam and the instructor indicates that you "passed." Typically, the first question asked is "What percentage did I earn?" Students think statistics is scary, but when you stop to consider, we encounter statistics every day of our lives.

THE BENEFITS OF STATISTICS

When considering the usefulness of statistics for communication researchers, three primary benefits are identified. Statistics can be thought of as tools used to describe, organize, and interpret information.

First, statistics allows us to summarize or describe data, and it enables researchers to make predictions and make sense of the world around us. The ability of statistics to help us summarize data is incredible! For example, the 2010 US Census collected information from over 308 million people (http://factfinder2. census.gov/). Statistics were used to summarize massive amounts of information and enable researchers to describe the general US population. For example, we know that 37,253,956 residents who took part in the census live in California. That is 12.07% of the total US population in 2010. Statistics helps paint a picture of our nation's population by summarizing data from millions of participants and describing those data in a way that makes sense.

Second, statistics enables us to organize information in a meaningful way to make predictions. If information about a sample group is known, those data can be organized and used to make predictions about the general population. For example, in her study of teachers' use of humor to gain student compliance, Punyanunt (2000) found that students were more likely to comply with requests that were humorous (this article is on the textbook's website, https://oup-arc.com/wrench). By organizing these data, we can predict that if other teachers want to be effective in their compliance-gaining attempts, they should employ a humorous tone. Referring back to the earlier example for Chewing Gum Brand X, you could predict that your dentist would likely recommend Chewing Gum Brand X if you were to ask what brand of gum you should chew.

Finally, statistics helps us in understanding and interpreting the world around us. We doubt that you could go through one day without encountering or using statistics in some way. Sports fans depend on statistics to understand where their favorite team is ranked, and consumers interpret the nutritional values on packages to assist them when making product choices in supermarkets. If you are a frequent reader of *USA Today*, you have probably noticed the "Snapshots" boxes located in the bottom corner on the cover page of each section. Topics explored in these quantitative surveys include everything from favorite food duos (e.g., macaroni and cheese vs. cereal and milk) to sources that influence decisions to buy products (e.g., word-of-mouth vs. in-store promotions). Daily weather forecasts also usually include statistical predictions, such as "There is a 60% chance of scattered thundershowers for the region today." Even your very existence as a college student revolves around a statistic known as your grade point average. When you stop to think about it, you really know more about statistics than you thought.

DESCRIPTIVE VERSUS INFERENTIAL STATISTICS

As stated earlier, one of the benefits of statistics is that they allow us to describe or summarize information. **Descriptive statistics** is used to organize and summarize information or data. Essentially, descriptive statistics allows a researcher to provide a description of what actually "exists" in the data. **Data** can be defined as any record or observation. Examples of data include the number of years employed, grade point average, annual income, gender, or the number of hours spent watching television each day. Researchers use descriptive statistics to help reduce large amounts of data to a more manageable size.

Perhaps one of the most commonly used descriptive statistics is percentages. Consider the following example—one way that a university could use descriptive statistics is to summarize students in a particular class. For example, the class could be 60% female; 4% freshmen, 19% sophomores, 52% juniors, and 25% seniors; or 42% traditional students and 58% nontraditional students. A variety of data can be collected to describe different characteristics of the group. With the individual pieces of information (or data) collected from each student, a summary of the entire class can be calculated.

Whereas descriptive statistics describes or summarizes data, **inferential statistics** is often the next stage in data analysis. Once the researcher has summarized and described the data in terms of percentages or averages, the data can be further analyzed to make inferences from the smaller group of data (also known as the sample) to a larger group of data (also referred to as the **population**). Inferential statistics is used when a researcher wants to make predictions. To make predictions, researchers often (but not always) take the process of statistical analyses to the next level and use inferential statistics to draw conclusions and make predictions about a larger group based on a smaller group of data. And it is important to reiterate here the distinction between these two groups—the smaller group of participants that were selected for the study is referred to as the sample. A **sample** is defined as a subset of the larger population, or all the possible persons who could fall into a particular category. Because it is usually improbable that a researcher would be able to access all possible participants in the population, samples of participants are selected to best represent the entire group. Students in a communication research methods class at a university could be considered a sample of the population of all communication majors currently enrolled at that campus. (Methods for selecting samples are discussed in more detail in Chapter 12).

Suppose your university requires all students to complete a public speaking class prior to graduation. To determine whether this requirement is beneficial in preparing students for their careers, they decide to survey a sample of communication alumni from your school. Depending on the size of the school, surveying every graduate might be a difficult and time-consuming task. Instead, a sample of alumni might be used to determine their perceptions about the usefulness of the public speaking requirement. Various statistics could be calculated for this sample of alumni. Suppose you asked alumni the following question: "On a scale of 1 to 10 (1 *being lowest* and 10 *being highest*), please indicate how valuable you perceive your public speaking class to be in preparing for your current career." Descriptive statistics could be used to provide an average rating for the perceived value of public speaking as reported by alumni in the sample.

What if you wanted to take your analyses to the next level and compare the results of those graduates who are frequently required to make presentations in their careers with those who do little or no public speaking? Inferential statistics could be used to make comparisons between these two groups and identify whether they differ in their perceptions about the value of the public speaking requirement. The concept of inferential statistics will be discussed in more depth in later chapters. For now, we will focus our attention on using statistics to describe data.

MEASURES OF CENTRAL TENDENCY

One of the first questions typically asked when analyzing data from a group is "What is the average score?" Recall the last time you received an exam back from an instructor. If you scored a 72% on the exam, your initial reaction might be disappointment. However, suppose the instructor announces that the class average on the exam was a 63%, so she is going to add points to the grades. Your disappointment now turns to elation simply as the result of a statistic that is mentioned. No longer is your score considered "slightly below the average grade" (in this case, 75%, which typically represents a grade of "C"). Rather, you learn that your grade is now considered well above the average for the class.

To measure the "center" or "middle" score in a group of data, researchers use what are commonly referred to as measures of central tendency. Three **measures of central tendency** that can be examined on a frequency distribution are the mean, median, and mode. We will discuss each of these in turn, then examine frequency distributions themselves as well as skewness and kurtosis.

Mean

The **mean**, or average, is typically defined as the value that represents an entire group of scores. To calculate the mean, add all of the scores in the category you wish to summarize and then divide the total by the number of scores. Researchers use two different types of means to describe data. If data have been collected from the entire population, the population mean is the best descriptor of the average score. The formula for calculating the population mean can be seen in Figure 14.1.

Because only rarely can a researcher get data from all possible members of a population, the sample is used to best represent the entire group. Suppose a researcher wants to gauge student satisfaction with campus activities. It is highly unlikely that data could

$$\mu = \Sigma X \div N$$

μ = Population mean

ΣX = Sum of all scores within a population

N = Number of scores within a population

FIGURE 14.1
Population Mean

FIGURE 14.2
Sample Mean

$$\bar{x} = \Sigma x \div n$$

$\bar{x}$ = Sample mean

Σx = Sum of all scores within a sample

n = Number of scores within a sample

be collected from every student. Instead, a sample of students could be collected by visiting a sample of classes across different majors. The formula used to compute the sample mean is seen in Figure 14.2.

Although the mean is a solid measure of central tendency for datasets that have a relatively normal distribution curve, it can be deceiving for data that are not symmetrically distributed because of extreme scores. Suppose that you want to assess the average level of apprehension of five students who completed the PRCA-24 scale and whose scores were 98, 56, 49, 42, and 39. Simply by looking at the list of scores, it is evident that 98 is different from the other four scores—thus, it is often referred to as an "extreme" score, or an outlier. Here, we calculate the mean for the sample of PRCA-24 scores.

The first step to computing a sample mean is to add all of the numbers of a sample together. In our example, we add the five numbers (Σx) together and receive a summed total of 284:

$$98 + 56 + 49 + 42 + 39 = 284$$

The second step in computing a sample mean is to take the summed total (Σx) from step 1 and divide the sum (Σx) by the number of scores in the group (n). In our example, we received a Σx of 284, and we have five participants (n = 5), so we divide 284 by 5, or

$$284/5 = 56.8$$

So the mean of the five scores is 56.8, which turns out to be higher than the scores reported for four of the five team members. In this instance, the mean is not representative of the distribution.

Median

In cases where the mean score is biased or skewed by extreme scores, other measures of central tendency may offer a better summary of the data. One statistic that could be used in this instance is the median.

The **median** is defined as the middle value in a list of data. To calculate the median, first list the data in order from smallest to largest. After you have sorted data in ascending order, identify the number that lies at the exact midpoint of the list. If the list has an odd number of items, the median is the middle entry in the list. If the list has an even number of items, add the two middle numbers and then divide by two.

One way of thinking about the median is to consider it a representation of percentile. A score that falls at the 75th percentile will lie at or above 75% of all the other scores in the distribution. The median is known as the true "50th percentile" score, or the point at which half of the scores fall above and the remaining half of the scores fall below.

Recall our earlier example, which examined a series of PRCA-24 scores. In a set of scores where one or more scores fall at an extreme end of the distribution, the median is perhaps the best choice for representing the middle value of the dataset. Let's calculate the median for the sample of PRCA-24 scores.

The first step in finding a median in a set of data is to list all the scores in order from smallest to largest:

$$39 \qquad 42 \qquad 49 \qquad 56 \qquad 98$$

The second step in finding a median in a set of data is to identify whether the data consist of an even or an odd number of scores. If there are an odd number of scores (three scores, five scores, seven scores, etc.), simply find the midpoint of all the scores, which is your median. In our example, we have five scores, which is an odd number, so when we look at the third number in the set of five, we have the number "49." So in this case, our median is 49.

Often, however, sets of data will have an even number of scores (two scores, four scores, six scores, eight scores, etc.), so in these cases, a different technique is needed for determining the median. If there is an even number of scores, add the two middle scores and then divide them by the number "2" to find the median score. For example, suppose the dataset from the example had looked like this after you rearranged the numbers from least to greatest:

$$39 \qquad 42 \qquad 49 \qquad 51 \qquad 56 \qquad 98$$

To calculate the median in this case, you would first find the scores in the middle of the data. Here, we have six data points, so the two middle numbers would be the third and fourth numbers, or 49 and 51. So to find the median, we first need to add the two middle numbers:

$$49 + 51 = 100$$

Once we have the summed total, we divide the number by 2 (since there are two numbers involved in the sum total):

$$100/2 = 50$$

So the median for this example would be 50.

As mentioned earlier, the median is a better descriptive statistic to use when reporting on the average for data with extreme scores. Often, the median will be stated as,

Bloomberg and the Mean

When examining descriptive statistics, it is important to examine both the mean and the median to get a realistic portrayal of a sample. The mean gives us the general average of a group, whereas the median lets us know the middlemost value. For illustrative purposes, imagine you are sitting at a bar with a couple of your friends. You have a bank balance of $2,100, Friend 1 has a balance of $1,692, and Friend 2 has a balance of $1,553. Among the three of you, the average current bank account balance is $1,781.67, with a median of $1,692. In this case, the mean and the median are not drastically far away from each other numerically. However, imagine if out of nowhere Michael Bloomberg walks into the bar, sits down, and joins you for a drink. In 2018, he was worth approximately $51.7 billion. Magically, the average net worth for the people sitting at the bar is now $12,750,000,000.00. Would you think this is a great way of representing these numbers? Probably not. In this case, the mean is far from a great tool for understanding the actual net worth of the people in the bar. Instead, the median, which is now $1,896, is going to be considerably more important. This little averaging trick is often used by people to inflate the mean incomes of workers.

"The median income of the average American family is . . ." The median allows a more accurate representation of the data in situations like this.

Mode

Perhaps the least frequently cited descriptive statistic is the mode. The **mode** is defined as the value that occurs most frequently in a dataset. An easy way to remember the definition for mode is to recall the phrase "mode is the most." After all, it is the most general and most imprecise of all descriptive statistics. To calculate the mode, we will use the data from the even median example discussed earlier.

The first step in finding the mode is to create a list of the values that occur in a dataset. Be sure to list each value only once!

39	42	42	49	51	56	98

Next, create a tally of the number of times that each score appears. In our example, the number "39" appears once, the number "42" appears twice, the number "49" appears once, the number "51" appears once, the number "56" appears once, and the number "98" appears once.

The score or value that appears most often is the mode. In our example, the numbers "39," "49," "51," "56," and "98" appear only one time. However, the number "42" appears twice, so we would consider the number "42" our mode because it is the number seen most often within our data.

Now, suppose we wanted to examine the dataset for political affiliation from the first edition of this book. (We'll get to the current edition's dataset in a moment.)

After calculating the frequency of political affiliations for the first edition's dataset, the following data would be reported:

Republican   144
Democrat   117
Other   39
Not registered   21

What would the mode be for this dataset? Be careful—your first instinct might be to indicate that "144" is the mode, but this is incorrect. "Republican" is the mode for the variable of political affiliation because it is the most frequently occurring value.

As mentioned earlier, a dataset can have more than one mode. In instances where two values occur with equal frequency, the dataset is defined as being bimodal. In the actual dataset that accompanies this edition of the text, we ended up with exactly 220 Democrats and 220 Republicans, so our dataset is bimodal. When a dataset has more than two values that occur with the same frequency, the data are defined as being multimodal. Figure 14.3 provides you with one more look at how the mean, median, and mode compare for a set of scores measuring the level of CA.

Choosing a Measure of Central Tendency

So which statistic should you use to represent a dataset? Let's use the example of reporting annual salaries for an organization. Suppose an organization employs 10 people who each earn an annual salary of $25,000. The production manager earns $50,000, whereas the supervisor earns $100,000. The mode ($25,000) would be the most accurate statistic to represent the salary that most people in the organization earn. However, if your goal is to make a strong impression on potential employees, you might decide that it is to your advantage to use the mean of $33,333 to attract more applicants. The decision is yours!

Often, the decision of which measure of central tendency to use depends on the available dataset. The mode is the best statistic for representing qualitative data such as

Variable	CA	Represented as $\overline{X}$
	39	
	42	
	42	Mode (occurs most frequently)
	49	Median (midpoint of data)
	51	
	56	
	98	
n	7	Number of cases
$\Sigma\overline{X}_i$	377	Total or sum of all scores (ages)
$\overline{X}$	53.86	Mean or average score (age)

FIGURE 14.3
Mean, Median, and Mode for a Sample of PRCA-24 Scores

political affiliation, sex, or class rank. Calculating an average for these types of data would be inaccurate. After all, it would not make sense to say that the average score for biological sex is 1.2—a participant is either female or male. It also would not make sense to report that "of 325 respondents, most (144) indicated that they are unemployed." Unfortunately, Statistical Package for the Social Sciences (SPSS) will not tell if you are running an incorrect statistical test, so you must be smarter than the computer program or you will run statistical tests that mean nothing. Without fail, at least one student will fall into this trap every time we teach research methods. They will think that because the computer lets them run a mean for biological sex, this mean is somehow meaningful, but it is not. Numbers can be computed for almost anything, but not all of these numbers are meaningful.

Quantitative data, on the other hand, require a researcher to use either the mean or the median to report the measure of central tendency. As stated earlier, the median is best in situations where extreme scores exist so that the average score is not misrepresented. The mean is the appropriate statistic for datasets where there are not extreme scores.

Frequency Distributions

Measures of central tendency are often visually depicted by constructing a frequency distribution. These frequency charts allow researchers to summarize and organize a set of data and enable them to identify trends. To create a **frequency distribution**, simply record the number of occurrences for each value in the dataset. Although the statistics could be computed by hand like we did earlier, it is not time efficient to do so. For this reason, a variety of computer programs have been created to aid in this process.

One commonly used statistical software package used by communication researchers is SPSS. If you look on the textbook's website, you will find a link for "Book Datasets." In this folder, you will find folders for SPSS datasets, Excel datasets, STATA datasets, and Notepad datasets. The SPSS datasets can be used only by SPSS (along with PSPP, JASP, and R), and the Excel dataset can used in Microsoft Excel. If you do not have a statistical software package other than SPSS, you can use the Notepad datasets to import the data into whatever program you are using. For example, if you would prefer to use STATA, we would recommend reading Acock (2018). We will only be discussing how to read and interpret results from SPSS in this book. However, we do have videos online that demonstrate conducting these tests in a range of different statistical software packages.

We should mention here, again, that we specifically used SPSS 24.0 in the conducting of the statistical tests in this book. We mention this because earlier or later versions of the software may display more or less information in similar or different ways. Although the steps in conducting the tests will be the same for various versions of the software packages, often the display gets altered. For this reason, if you are using an earlier version (or later version) of either SPSS, you may want to consult the software guide that accompanied the software package. Mostly, these changes are minor, but for students new to dealing with statistical software packages the changes may be confusing.

SPSS AND FREQUENCY DISTRIBUTIONS

When using SPSS to calculate frequency distributions, you use the "Crosstabs" function. For this example, open the SPSS dataset called "Textbook Data Set" on the textbook's website. Once you open the dataset (Figure 14.4), you must create a frequency table. To get to the "Frequencies" function, go to the menu bar at the top of your screen and click on "Analyze." When you click on Analyze, a drop-down menu will appear (Figure 14.5). Go to the second category on this menu, "Descriptive Statistics," scroll over the arrow, and another menu will appear to the right. In this menu, search for the "Frequencies" option and left click on it. At this point, the "Frequencies" dialogue box will appear (Figure 14.6a).

To create a frequency table in SPSS, first you must select the variable that you want to create the table for by highlighting it (click on it once). Scroll through the list of variables in the "Textbook Data Set," and right click on "Biological Sex [sex]." When you right click on Biological Sex [sex], the variable is highlighted in blue (Figure 14.6a). You now want to click the arrow button to move Biological Sex [sex] to the "Variable(s)" list (Figure 14.6b), which is the list of variables to be analyzed. When you click on the arrow button, the variable Biological Sex [sex] will be transferred from the left column

FIGURE 14.4
Main SPSS Screen Shot

Analyze	Direct Marketing	Graphs	Utilities	Add-ons	Wi
Reports	▶				
Descriptive Statistics	▶		Frequencies...		
Tables	▶		Descriptives...		
Compare Means	▶		Explore...		
General Linear Model	▶		Crosstabs...		
Generalized Linear Models	▶		Ratio...		
Mixed Models	▶		P-P Plots...		
Correlate	▶		Q-Q Plots...		
Regression	▶				
Loglinear	▶	5.00	5.00		
Neural Networks	▶	2.00	2.00		
Classify	▶	3.00	2.00		
Dimension Reduction	▶	3.00	2.00		
Scale	▶	5.00	5.00		
Nonparametric Tests	▶	3.00	2.00		
Forecasting	▶	5.00	2.00		
Survival	▶	4.00	4.00		
Multiple Response	▶	2.00	3.00		
Missing Value Analysis...		1.00	1.00		
Multiple Imputation	▶	1.00	1.00		
Complex Samples	▶	1.00	2.00		
Quality Control	▶	4.00	3.00		
ROC Curve...		3.00	3.00		
IBM SPSS Amos...		4.00	1.00		
3.00	3.00	3.00	4.00		

FIGURE 14.5
Frequencies
Drop-Down Menu

(variables in the data set) to the right column (variables you want frequency tables for; Figure 14.6c). At this point, all you need to do to achieve a frequency window is to click on "OK" on the right side of the screen because, when you initially open the Frequencies dialogue box, the frequency tables option is always preselected for you (Figure 14.6d). When you do this, the data in Figure 14.7 will appear.

We have provided all of the frequency information for three other variables in the "Textbook Data Set" in Figure 14.8 (Biological Sex, Political Affiliation, Year in School, and Time Spent Online). We will discuss how to calculate means, medians, and modes using SPSS later in this chapter.

FREQUENCY DISTRIBUTIONS AND CHARTS

Once a frequency distribution has been constructed, the data can also be graphically represented by creating a histogram. A histogram is a bar chart that represents the frequency with which each value for a variable occurs. Suppose that we wanted to create a histogram for the following scores obtained on a statistics exam. A frequency distribution for the data would look like Figure 14.9. Using this information, a histogram (or bar graph) can be constructed to assist the researcher in identifying the shape of the data, the symmetry, and the presence of **outliers** (extreme scores). Each test score is included along the *x* axis in ascending order, and the frequency with which each score occurs is plotted on the *y* axis (Figure 14.10).

FIGURE 14.6A
Dialogue Box as It Loads

FIGURE 14.6B
Moving Biological Sex to the Variable(s): Box

FIGURE 14.6C
Biological Sex in the Variable(s): Box

FIGURE 14.6D
Display Frequency Tables (Check Box)

Statistics

Biological Sex

N	Valid	641
	Missing	13

FIGURE 14.7
Frequency Table for
Biological Sex

Biological Sex

		Frequency	Percent	Valid Percent	Cumulative Percent
Valid	Male	320	48.9	49.9	49.9
	Female	321	49.1	50.1	100.0
	Total	641	98.0	100.0	
Missing	System	13	2.0		
Total		654	100.0		

By glancing at the histogram, a researcher can determine whether the set of data is normally distributed. The score with the highest frequency (in this case, 70) falls at the middle of the normal distribution. Scores with lower frequencies are on either side of the mean. If the scores are distributed normally, the curve forms a bell shape. A closer look at the information provided in the SPSS output in Figure 14.10 shows that the mean, median, and mode are all the same for this dataset. In fact, statisticians refer to any distribution where the mean, median, and mode are the same as a bell curve.

So why should a researcher be concerned with the shape of the histogram? Normality of data is a condition for certain statistical analyses associated with hypothesis testing, which was discussed in Chapter 13. Although formal statistical tests can be used to test whether a distribution for a dataset is normal, a simple glance at the histogram

Political Affiliation

		Frequency	Percent	Valid Percent	Cumulative Percent
Valid	Democrat	220	33.6	34.6	34.6
	Republican	220	33.6	34.6	69.3
	Other	131	20.0	20.6	89.9
	Not Registered to Vote	64	9.8	10.1	100.0
	Total	635	97.1	100.0	
Missing	System	19	2.9		
Total		654	100.0		

School Classification

		Frequency	Percent	Valid Percent	Cumulative Percent
Valid	First Year Student	52	8.0	8.2	8.2
	Sophomore	107	16.4	16.8	24.9
	Junior	231	35.3	36.2	61.1
	Senior	244	37.3	38.2	99.4
	Other	4	.6	.6	100.0
	Total	638	97.6	100.0	
Missing	System	16	2.4		
Total		654	100.0		

Time Spent Online

		Frequency	Percent	Valid Percent	Cumulative Percent
Valid	0-.5 hour	15	2.3	2.3	2.3
	.5-1 hour	20	3.1	3.1	5.5
	1-2 hours	58	8.9	9.1	14.6
	2-5 hours	183	28.0	28.6	43.2
	5-10 hours	142	21.7	22.2	65.4
	10-15 hours	93	14.2	14.6	80.0
	15-20 hours	64	9.8	10.0	90.0
	25 + hours	64	9.8	10.0	100.0
	Total	639	97.7	100.0	
Missing	System	15	2.3		
Total		654	100.0		

FIGURE 14.8
Frequency Table for All Nominal and Ordinal Variables in the Data Set

Letter Grade	Score	Frequency
A	90	1
B	80	2
C	70	4
D	60	2
F	50	1

FIGURE 14.9
Frequency Distribution of Exam Scores

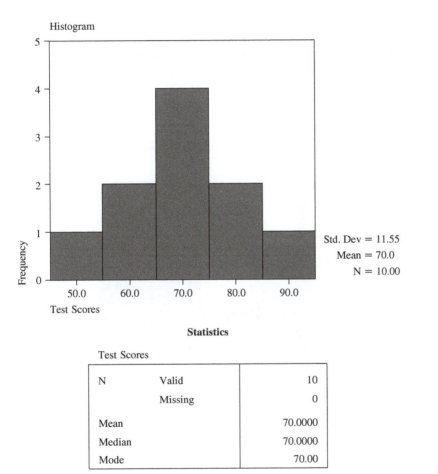

FIGURE 14.10
Histogram and SPSS Statistics for a Normal Distribution of Exam Scores

Histogram

Std. Dev = 11.55
Mean = 70.0
N = 10.00

Statistics

Test Scores

N	Valid	10
	Missing	0
Mean		70.0000
Median		70.0000
Mode		70.00

can speak volumes. It is important to note, however, that not all distribution curves are normal or bell shaped. Earlier, we mentioned that a dataset can have more than one mode. Remember—the mode is the value that occurs most often. If the midpoint in the curve is represented by the mode score, a dataset that is bimodal would produce a shape that resembles an inverted bell curve. Consider the following hypothetical exam scores:

$$50, 50, 50, 60, 60, 70, 80, 80, 90, 90, 90$$

Note that the scores of "50" and "90" occur with the same frequency—each appears three times in the list. Thus, the dataset is **bimodal**. A histogram for this set of scores would look like Figure 14.11.

A closer look at the information provided in the SPSS output in Figure 14.11 shows that the mean and median scores are the same for this dataset, but that multiple modes exist. (Note: SPSS only reports the smallest value for the mode.) You will also note that SPSS will report multimodal distributions by placing a superscript letter "a" next to the mode on the SPSS printout.

FIGURE 14.11
Histogram and SPSS Statistics for a Bimodal Distribution of Exam Scores

Histogram

Std. Dev = 16.73
Mean = 70.0
N = 11.00

Statistics

Test Scores

N		
	Valid	11
	Missing	0
Mean		70.0000
Median		70.0000
Mode		50.00[a]

[a] Multiple modes exist. The smallest value is shown.

Skewness and Kurtosis

More often than not, the dataset you are analyzing will produce a curve that is asymmetrical, and this asymmetry in a set of data points is known as a dataset's **skewness**. A curve can be either positively skewed or negatively skewed. A positively skewed curve is one in which the tail of the curve is longer on the right side of the distribution. The majority of scores are low, causing the curve to be asymmetrical, with a long tail in the positive direction on a number line. The mean for a sample whose scores are positively skewed will be greater than the median or mode (Figure 14.12).

The opposite is true for a dataset with negatively skewed scores. In this instance, the tail of the distribution curve is longer on the left side. The majority of the scores are high, creating a long tail in the negative direction on a number line. A mean for a sample that is negatively skewed will be less than the median or mode (Figure 14.13).

SPSS can also provide a statistical score regarding the skewness of a distribution. When computing frequencies for a variable, select the "Statistics" button, and click on "Skewness." If the sample has a normal distribution, the skewness score will be equal to "0." A positively skewed sample will result in a positive score for skewness, and a negatively skewed score will result in a negative score.

SPSS can also calculate the kurtosis of the distribution curve. **Kurtosis** refers to the degree of peakedness of a distribution of scores. A kurtosis score greater than zero indicates a high, peaked curve with thin tails where the majority of values are in the peak of the curve and few are located in the tails of the distribution. A negative kurtosis

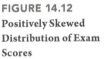

Std. Dev = 19.93
Mean = 41.6
N = 25.00

FIGURE 14.12
Positively Skewed Distribution of Exam Scores

FIGURE 14.13
Negatively Skewed
Distribution of Exam
Scores

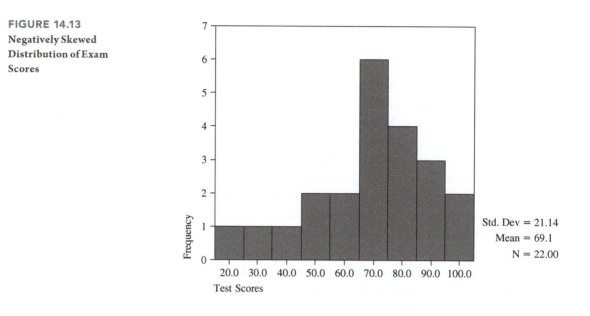

Std. Dev = 21.14
Mean = 69.1
N = 22.00

FIGURE 14.14
SPSS Frequency
Distribution with
Skewness and Kurtosis
Scores

Statistics

Test Scores

N	Valid	21
	Missing	0
Mean		67.6190
Median		70.0000
Mode		70.00
Std. Deviation		20.4707
Skewness		–.766
Std. Error of Skewness		.501
Kurtosis		.289
Std. Error of Kurtosis		.972
Range		80.00
Minimum		20.00
Maximum		100.00

score signals that the distribution curve is flat with several cases of scores located in the tails.

If you look at the results in Figure 14.14, you will find a distribution where the mean is 67.62, the median is 70, the mode is 70, the skewness is –0.766, and the kurtosis is 0.289. With reference to skewness and kurtosis, the sample is negatively skewed (skewness is a negative number) and minimally peaked (kurtosis > 0).

MEASURES OF VARIABILITY

As previously stated, measures of central tendency are the statistics most commonly used by consumers. However, averages only provide us with half of the information needed to describe the scores in a sample—the other half involves measures of variability.

Variability reflects how scores differ from one another. Also referred to as "measures of dispersion," variability refers to how different each score is from the mean score. Four measures of variability can be used to assess the differences in scores: range, sum of squares, variance, and standard deviation.

Range

The most general measure of variability is the range. Simply stated, the **range** represents how far apart scores are from one another, or the distance between the largest value and the smallest value in the dataset. The range is calculated by subtracting the lowest score in the distribution from the highest score:

$$\text{Range} = X_{max} - X_{min}$$

Suppose that the highest score obtained on an exam was 96 and the lowest score was 53. To find the range, you subtract X_{min} from X_{max}, or the smallest score from the largest score. In our example, 53 is the smallest score and 96 is the largest score, so to find the range you subtract 53 from 96, or

$$96 - 53 = 43$$

In this example, our range is 43.

It should be noted here that although this score tells us the gap between the high and low score, it does not provide any insight into how each score in the distribution differs from the mean or average score.

Sum of Squares

The sum of squares is a concept seen quite often in both descriptive statistics (statistical tools used to describe a dataset—what we are examining in this chapter) and inferential statistics (statistical tools that allow researchers to make inferences about some unknown aspect of a population from a sample—Chapters 15 through 19 will examine inferential statistics). In social scientific research, people differ from one another, which makes it impossible for social scientists to make universal statements about all people. These individual differences, however, make up the bulk of what social scientists study. In fact, Thompson (2006) defines the **sum of squares** as the "information about both the amount and the origins of individual differences" (p. 60). Ultimately, the more individual scores in a dataset differ from one another, the greater

FIGURE 14.15
Sum of Squares
Equation

$$SS = \Sigma X^2 - \frac{(\Sigma X)^2}{N}$$

the sum of squares will become. Overall, the sum of squares is used in the calculating of many statistical tests, so understanding how it is computed is extremely important. Figure 14.15 contains the formula for the sum of squares.

The formula for the sum of squares is easy to compute when you understand what the various parts in the formula mean. The first symbol (Σ) should be familiar to you by this point in the chapter because it stands for the "sum of" something, or all of the numbers added together. The second symbol (X^2) is the squaring of an individual number. Do not confuse this symbol with the next symbol $[(\Sigma X)^2]$, which is the sum of all of the numbers added together first and then the sum squared. The last symbol in the equation (N) is the number of people in the population.

Because calculating the sum of squares is complicated, we will use a small sample in this example. Say we ask four people how many hours they spend watching television daily and we get the following responses: 1 hour, 0 hours, 6 hours, and 1 hour. Now, let's calculate the sum of squares for this sample.

The first step in computing the sum of squares is to find what is referred to as the sum of all of the X numbers squared (ΣX^2). To find ΣX^2, we first must find each score's squared value. The first person in our sample indicated that he watched only 1 hour of television daily, and the squared value for 1 is 1 (1 * 1 = 1). The second person in our sample indicated that she watched 0 hours daily, and the squared value for 0 is 0 (0 * 0 = 0). The third person in our sample indicated that he watched 6 hours daily, and the squared value for 6 is 36 (6 * 6 = 36). The final person in our sample indicated that she watched 1 hour daily, and the squared value for 1 is 1 (1 * 1 = 1). We now have the squared values for each X. And to solve for ΣX^2, we simply need to add the four X^2 values together:

$$\Sigma X^2 = 1 + 0 + 36 + 1$$
$$\Sigma X^2 = 38$$

The second step to computing the sum of squares is to determine the sum of all the X numbers squared $[(\Sigma X)^2]$. To find $(\Sigma X)^2$, we first must determine the value for the sum of X (ΣX), which is just a mathematical way of saying we must add the individual scores together (1 + 0 + 6 + 1 = 8), so $\Sigma X = 8$. Once we know what the ΣX is, we simply square this value to find $(\Sigma X)^2$, so 8 * 8 = 64.

The complicated math is complete, so we just need to plug the numbers into the equation in Figure 14.15 and compute the formula. We have already determined that

$\Sigma X^2 = 38$, $(\Sigma X)^2 = 64$, and $N = 4$. Let's complete the part of the formula to the right of the minus sign in the equation, or $(\Sigma X)^2/N$:

$$(\Sigma X)^2/N$$
$$64/4$$
$$16$$

So $(\Sigma X)^2/N = 16$.

We can now perform the subtraction part of the formula, $\Sigma X^2 - [(\Sigma X)^2/N]$. Here, we know that $\Sigma X^2 = 38$ and $[(\Sigma X)^2/N] = 16$, so we just subtract 16 from 38, or $38 - 16 = 22$. At this point, we have calculated the sum of square, and the answer is 22.

Variance

Variance measures how wide or spread out a distribution is, or the average distance of the scores for an interval or ratio scale from the mean in squared units. Because our variance is dependent on the sum of squares, we know that as our scores become more different, the variance will increase. The opposite is also true—as the scores become more similar, the variance will decrease. The formula in Figure 14.16 is used to compute the variance of a sample of scores.

$$S^2 = \frac{SS}{N-1}$$

FIGURE 14.16
Variance Equation

When you look at this formula, you will note that to calculate variance you must know two basic pieces of information: the sum of squares (SS) and the number of participants (N). Using the data used in the previous example (1, 0, 6, 1), we have already determined that the sum of squares is 22 and the number of participants is 4, so to calculate the variance (s^2) we need to plug the numbers into the appropriate places and solve:

$$s^2 = SS/(N-1)$$
$$s^2 = 22/(4-1)$$
$$s^2 = 22/3$$
$$s^2 = 7.3333$$

So the variance for the sample (1, 0, 6, 1) is 7.3333.

Standard Deviation

The **standard deviation** of a sample is directly related to the variance of a sample. When we report variance, we are dealing with what is called a "squared metric" because the variance stems from the sum of squares. However, most people are not good at understanding squared metrics by looking at them, so the standard deviation is the square root of the variance, which forms the descriptive statistic in a number that can be more easily applied to our sample scores.

The standard deviation tells us on average how far each score differs from the average score. A standard deviation score of 3.12 indicates that, on average, each score in the distribution deviates plus or minus 3.12 points from the mean score. The larger the standard deviation score, the greater the distance between each score and the mean and the more different the scores are from one another. The formula for calculating a standard deviation can be seen in Figure 14.17.

FIGURE 14.17
Standard Deviation
Equation

$$SD = \sqrt{\frac{SS}{N-1}}$$

If the formula for the standard deviation looks familiar, it is; the standard deviation can be calculated simply by taking the square root of the variance. Previously, we determined that the variance for the sample (1, 0, 6, 1) was 7.3333. To determine the standard deviation, we simply take the square root of 7.3333, which is 2.708, or 2.71 after rounding.

Recall our earlier discussion of the normal distribution of scores. If a researcher is able to calculate the mean and standard deviation for a sample that has a normal distribution, then a percentile score can be reported for the sample. In a normal distribution, approximately 68% of the scores are within one standard deviation of the mean score (Figure 14.18). Overall, nearly 95% of the scores fall within two standard deviations from the mean. So, in a normal distribution, most scores are relatively close to the mean score.

FIGURE 14.18
Standard Deviations
and Percentiles

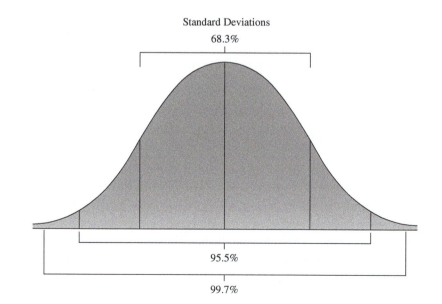

Standard Deviations
68.3%

95.5%

99.7%

SPSS and Measures of Variability

In most research studies, the sample size is too large for many of the statistics described in this chapter to be calculated by hand. We depend on statistical packages like SPSS to calculate the variance and the standard deviation for us. To calculate the variance and standard deviation using SPSS for the variable communication apprehension, you start by going to the same "Frequencies" dialogue box previously discussed in this chapter and seen in Figures 14.4 and 14.5). Once you are at the Frequency dialogue box, find the variable "Communication Apprehension," and switch it to the "Variables:" box (Figure 14.19a). Deselect the "Display Frequency Tables" option because you will end up with a list of every score you achieve from 24 to 120, which is not useful for you (Figure 14.19b). Do not be alarmed when the pop-up warning appears (Figure 14.19c). Just click "OK," and select the "Statistics" button on the frequencies dialogue box (Figure 14.19d). The "Frequencies: Statistics" dialogue box will then appear (Figure 14.19e). Note that you have many different options you can select in this dialogue box. In fact, all of the descriptive statistics discussed

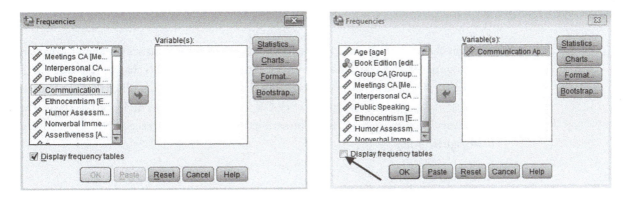

FIGURE 14.19A
Highlight Communication Apprehension

FIGURE 14.19B
Deselect Display Frequency Tables

FIGURE 14.19C
Pop-Up Warning

FIGURE 14.19D
Select Statistics Button

FIGURE 14.19E
"Frequencies Statistics" Dialogue Box

FIGURE 14.19F
Selecting Statistics

in this chapter can be found in this dialogue box. Select the statistics you want to analyze. For our purposes, I selected all the ones we have discussed in this chapter (Figure 14.19f). Once you have selected your statistics, click the "Continue" button. When the Frequencies: Statistics dialogue box disappears, click OK, on the Frequencies dialogue box to run the analysis. The SPSS printouts can be seen in Figure 14.20. will receive the printout seen in Figure 14.20.

FIGURE 14.20
Descriptive Statistics
for CA

Statistics

Communication Apprehension Total

N	Valid	644
	Missing	10
Mean		63.6630
Median		64.0000
Mode		67.00
Std. Deviation		17.00407
Variance		289.138
Skewness		.203
Std. Error of Skewness		.096
Kurtosis		.335
Std. Error of Kurtosis		.192
Range		96.00
Minimum		24.00
Maximum		120.00

You can also watch videos on the website that will show you how to perform these tests in a number of different statistical software packages.

DATASET VARIABILITY

In Chapter 6, we introduced you to the variables available in the dataset that accompanies this book. In Figure 14.21, you will see a detailed description for reading descriptive statistics produced in SPSS. In Figure 14.22, you will find the SPSS frequency lists for the nominal and ordinal variables in the data and the measures of variability for the interval and ratio variables.

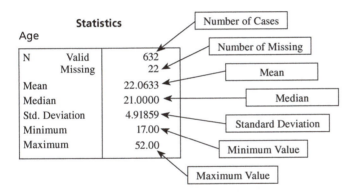

FIGURE 14.21
Descriptive Statistics in SPSS

Statistics

		Group CA	Meetings CA	Interpersonal CA	Public Speaking CA	Communication Apprehension Total
N	Valid	646	645	645	645	644
	Missing	8	9	9	9	10
Mean		15.0402	15.5628	14.4202	18.6140	63.6630
Median		15.0000	15.0000	14.0000	18.0000	64.0000
Std. Deviation		5.04383	4.98861	4.53303	5.71867	17.00407
Minimum		6.00	6.00	6.00	6.00	24.00
Maximum		30.00	30.00	30.00	30.00	120.00

FIGURE 14.22
SPSS Dataset Information

Figure 14.22 Continued

Statistics

		Ethnocentrism	Humor Assessment	Nonverbal Immediacy	Assertiveness	Responsiveness
N	Valid	650	646	640	645	646
	Missing	4	8	14	9	8
Mean		31.7369	63.2492	96.5188	35.3302	40.3297
Median		31.0000	63.0000	96.0000	36.0000	40.0000
Std. Deviation		9.10274	9.52523	13.35466	6.30570	6.28210
Minimum		15.00	34.00	48.00	16.00	16.00
Maximum		62.00	80.00	130.00	50.00	50.00

Statistics

		Group WTC	Meetings WTC	Interpersonal WTC	Public Speaking WTC	Stranger WTC	Acquaintance WTC	Friend WTC	Willingness to Communicate Total
N	Valid	625	624	625	624	625	624	624	622
	Missing	29	30	29	30	29	30	30	32
Mean		73.4949	65.3446	73.3339	65.0139	45.7556	74.5938	87.5761	68.9518
Std. Deviation		17.36078	21.60458	17.11978	20.90989	25.62502	20.00382	14.00961	15.70704
Minimum		5.00	.00	10.67	.00	.00	.00	25.00	15.45
Maximum		100.00	100.00	100.00	100.00	100.00	100.00	100.00	100.00

Statistics

		Everyone should be required to take public speaking in college.	Attitude about Higher Education
N	Valid	623	625
	Missing	31	29
Mean		23.3836	35.7296
Median		25.0000	38.0000
Std. Deviation		9.20395	6.67435
Minimum		5.00	11.00
Maximum		35.00	42.00

CONCLUSION

For most of you, the initial thought of calculating statistics for a sample was overwhelming. Throughout this chapter, we have provided a description of the sample and identified how diverse or spread out those scores are from the average. Statistics such as those discussed in this chapter are often referenced in everyday life. Now, you can understand and interpret these statistics with confidence.

KEY TERMS

Bimodal p. 432

Data p. 419

Descriptive statistics p. 419

Frequency distribution p. 426

Inferential statistics p. 420

Kurtosis p. 433

Mean p. 421

Measures of central
tendency p. 421

Median p. 422

Mode p. 424

Outliers p. 428

Population p. 420

Range p. 435

Sample p. 420

Skewness p. 433

Standard deviation p. 437

Statistic p. 418

Sum of squares p. 435

Variance p. 437

REFERENCES

Acock, A. C. (2018). *A gentle introduction to Stata* (6th ed.). College Station, TX: Stata Press.

Punyanunt, N. M. (2000). The effects of humor on perceptions of compliance-gaining in the college classroom. *Communication Research Reports, 176*, 30–38.

Thompson, B. (2006). *Foundations of behavioral statistics: An insight-based approach.* New York, NY: Guilford.

FURTHER READING

Abramson, J. H., & Abramson, Z. H. (2001). *Making sense of data: A self-instruction manual on the interpretation of epidemiological data* (3rd ed.). New York, NY: Oxford University Press.

Bruning, J. L., & Kintz, B. L. (1997). *Computational handbook of statistics* (4th ed.). New York, NY: Longman.

Gravetter, F. J., & Wallnau, L. B. (2000). *Statistics for the behavioral sciences* (5th ed.). Belmont, CA: Wadsworth/Thomson Learning.

Green, S. B., & Salkind, N. J. (2004). *Using SPSS for Windows and Macintosh: Analyzing and understanding data* (4th ed.). Upper Saddle River, NJ: Prentice Hall.

Hocking, J. E., Stacks, D. W., & McDermott, S. T. (2003). *Communication research* (3rd ed.). Boston, MA: Allyn & Bacon.

Howell, D. C. (1997). *Statistical methods for psychology* (4th ed.). Belmont, CA: Duxbury Press.

Huff, D. (1954). *How to lie with statistics*. New York, NY: Norton.

Keller, D. K. (2006). *The Tao of statistics: A path to understanding (with no math)*. Thousand Oaks, CA: Sage.

Pyrczak, F. (1999). *Statistics with a sense of humor: A humorous workbook and guide to study skills* (2nd ed.). Los Angeles, CA: Pyrczak.

Salkind, N. J. (2017). *Statistics for people who (think they) hate statistics* (6th ed.). Thousand Oaks, CA: Sage.

Singleton, R. A., Jr., & Straits, B. C. (2017). *Approach to social research* (6th ed.). New York, NY: Oxford University Press.

Trochim, W. M. K. (2000). *The research methods knowledge base* (2nd ed.). Cincinnati, OH: Atomic Dog. Retrieved from http://www.socialresearchmethods.net/

Chi-Square (χ^2) Test of Independence

CHAPTER OBJECTIVES

1. Explain the purposes of a chi-square (χ^2) statistical test.

2. Calculate a chi-square test by hand.

3. Conduct a chi-square test using Statistical Package for the Social Sciences (SPSS).

4. Analyze the use of the chi-square test in the article by Brummans and Miller (2004).

5. Explain the purpose of phi (Φ), how one calculates phi by hand, and how to interpret phi.

In this chapter, we explore the **chi-square** (χ^2) test of independence. The term *chi-square* has two different meanings in statistics, which often confuses new researchers. First, researchers refer to a specific type of mathematical distribution that occurs with no necessary referent outside of mathematics. Although this distribution is beyond the scope of this textbook, understand that it is important to a number of statistical tests. In this chapter, we are more concerned with the second meaning of a chi-square, which is a specific statistical test. However, this statistical test (i.e., χ^2 test of independence) is related to the first definition. The chi-square test examines whether scores obtained from a group of people is like, or different from, the scores expected if the numbers were evenly distributed along the chi-square distribution.

445

Say you want to determine whether females and males differ in their preference for two soft drinks (A and B). In an ideal world, we would have four categories (females who like soft drink A, females who like soft drink B, males who like soft drink A, and males who like soft drink B). Note that both categories (biological sex and soft drink preference) are nominal variables. If we set up a taste test using 200 people (100 females and 100 males), then in an ideal world we would expect there to be 50 people in each of the four categories. Unfortunately, the "ideal world" rarely happens, and scores often are not distributed evenly among available categories. Maybe 70 females prefer soft drink A and only 30 females prefer soft drink B. When this lopsidedness happens, the question becomes one of what researchers would expect to see versus what researchers are seeing.

The purpose, then, of a chi-square is to examine the balance between observed frequencies, or the number of times participants fell into a specific category (in this case, how many females and males picked each of the soft drinks), and expected frequencies, or the number of times one would expect participants to fall into a specific category. If the observed and expected frequencies are equal, then the chi-square statistic will always equal zero because there is not a difference between the two numbers. The greater the difference between the observed and expected frequencies, however, the larger the chi-square statistic will be. And as the chi-square statistic increases, so does the likelihood that a statistically significant difference exists between the observed and expected frequencies.

CASE STUDY INTRODUCTION

Now that we have explained the basic purpose of a chi-square statistic, let's look at an example. Pretend that you are working in a communication studies department and have been asked to analyze when females and males take public speaking during their academic careers. If you remember Chapter 6, female and male is an example of a nominal variable. Remember, nominal variables are categorical, or people that can be clearly placed into one category (female) or the other (male), but not both. Your department chair has also given you another variable to examine—school classification. For school classification, your department chair has given you five categories: precollege, first-year student, sophomore, junior, and senior. Yet again, the school classification variable is also a nominal variable because you cannot be a sophomore and a senior at the same time. If you go back and look at Figure 6.10, you will note that if you have two nominal variables, the appropriate statistic to examine differences is a chi-square test of independence.

After discussing this project with you, your department chair hands you a table of when students are taking public speaking in the department (Figure 15.1). In this

FIGURE 15.1
**When Students Take
Public Speaking**

	Precollege students	First-year students	Sophomores	Juniors	Seniors	N
Male	6	8	10	1	25	50
Female	7	20	9	8	6	50

table, we have what is called a 2 × 5 table. This means that we have two rows (male and female) by five columns (precollege, first-year student, sophomore, junior, and senior). Where a row intersects with a column, we have cells. For example, on row "female" in column "junior," the number 8 appears in the cell. The last column has the letter N above it and contains the sum total of students for each row. For our example, the male row has 50 students and the female row has 50 students. This chapter will illustrate how you can use the chi-square test of independence to determine whether females and males differ in their school classification when they take public speaking.

CHI-SQUARE BACKGROUND INFORMATION

The one-sample chi-square test evaluates whether the proportions of individuals who fall into categories of two or more nominal variables are equal to hypothesized values. In an ideal world, again, you would have equal numbers of females and males taking public speaking in each school classification category. For example, if you had 50 females and 50 males in a school, you would expect that there would be 10 females and 10 males taking public speaking in the precollege category, 10 females and 10 males taking public speaking in the first-year student category, and so on. However, the real world rarely works this smoothly. Maybe 15 male students were all friends and decided to take public speaking together during one semester or quarter. This would prevent our perfect world of 10 females and 10 males in every class.

Chi-Square Assumptions

To use the chi-square test of independence, some basic assumptions that must be met:

1. Both variables being analyzed must be nominal in nature (biological sex, school classification, etc.).
2. Participants contributing data should represent a random sample drawn from the population of interest (this is an assumption of most statistical tests—see Chapter 11 for an explanation of the importance of randomization).
3. One participant's appearance in a category (e.g., a female taking public speaking during her senior year) should not affect the probability of another participant's

appearance in another cell (e.g., a male taking public speaking during his sophomore year).

4.   If you have a 2 × 2 table, there should be no fewer than five cases in every cell. However, if you have a larger table (e.g., the 2 × 5 table like the one in our example), 20% of the cells should be no fewer than five cases in every cell.

Chi-Square and Statistical Significance

The one-sample chi-square test is more likely to yield significance if the sample proportions for the categories differ greatly from the hypothesized proportions and if the sample size is large. If all the females were able to take public speaking in the first two-and-a-half years and all the males took public speaking in the last two-and-a-half years, we would see a large difference. However, as we see in Figure 15.1, there are differences in our example, but whether these differences are truly statistically significant is not known. For this reason, the chi-square test of independence was created to help us determine whether statistically significant differences exist in examples such as the one we have here.

Before a researcher ever starts calculating a statistical test, he or she must first set the significance level of the test. In Chapter 13, we discussed why researchers set the significance level at 95% confidence level, or $p = 0.05$. The reason that we set the significance level before conducting the test is ethical. In some cases, less than scrupulous researchers have lowered their significance level to 90%, or $p = 0.10$, because their results were not significant at the 95% confidence level. If you remember back to our discussion of research ethics in Chapter 3, we discussed the problem of post hoc revisions of hypotheses (changing your hypothesis when the study was completed to match the results you found). The discussion we had for post hoc revisions of hypotheses is akin to changing our confidence level after the fact. The need to set your confidence level prior to conducting a statistical test is true for all statistical tests. Once you have set your confidence level, you can then calculate your chi-square.

Chi-Square Formula

Figure 15.2 depicts the mathematical formula for completing the chi-square test of independence. We know this formula looks scary, but it is not hard to understand what it is saying. First, f_o stands for the frequency observed, which is the technical term for what was discussed in Figure 15.1. Second, f_e stands for the frequency expected. But before we can discuss frequency expected, we must going step by step through our computation of the chi-square statistic.

FIGURE 15.2
Chi-Square Formula

$$\chi^2 = \Sigma \frac{(f_o - f_e)^2}{f_e}$$

STEP-BY-STEP APPROACH TO THE CHI-SQUARE TEST OF INDEPENDENCE

Step 1

The first step in computing the chi-square test of independence is to add the totals from each row separately. For example, to obtain the total for the male row, you must add $6 + 8 + 10 + 1 + 25$, which gives you a row total of 50. You then repeat this process for the female row $(7 + 20 + 9 + 8 + 6)$, which also gives you a row total of 50. You do this again for each of the five columns (precollege, first-year student, sophomore, junior, and senior) as well. For the precollege column, you will add $6 + 7$, which gives you a total of 13. In Figure 15.3, you can see that we have provided row and column totals for you in an easy-to-use table because we will need these numbers in the next step.

Step 2

The second step is slightly more complicated than the first and requires that you carefully keep track of where you are getting your numbers. As mentioned earlier, the second part of the formula requires us to examine the expected frequency (f_e), so this step will help us generate these numbers.

The expected frequency is a simple calculation to help define an ideal hypothetical distribution that would be in agreement with the null hypothesis. In other words, based on the data that you have, what is the frequency for upholding the null hypothesis (i.e., that there is no difference between females and males regarding when they take public speaking in college)? To obtain these values, you use the following simple formula:

Expected frequency = (total column × total row)/overall total

So, let's compute the first expected frequency for males in precollege. The column total for precollege, as seen in Figure 15.3, is 13. The row total for males is 50. And the overall total for the population, or N, is 100. To obtain the expected frequency for males in precollege, we then plug these numbers into the formula: $(13 \times 50)/100 = 6.5$. Based on this result, we can say that to reject the null hypothesis that females and males take public speaking at the same points in college, the expected frequency for males in precollege would have to be 6.5. Obviously, you cannot have a 0.5 person, so this number

	Precollege students	First-year students	Sophomores	Juniors	Seniors	TOTAL
Male	6	8	10	1	25	50
Female	7	20	9	8	6	50
Total	13	28	19	9	31	100

FIGURE 15.3
Adding Row and Column Totals

FIGURE 15.4
Expected Frequencies

	Total column		Total row		Overall total		Expected frequency
Males in precollege	13	*	50	/	100	=	6.5
Male first-year students	28	*	50	/	100	=	14.0
Male sophomores	19	*	50	/	100	=	9.5
Male juniors	9	*	50	/	100	=	4.5
Male seniors	31	*	50	/	100	=	15.5
Females in precollege	13	*	50	/	100	=	6.5
Female first-year students	28	*	50	/	100	=	14.0
Female sophomores	19	*	50	/	100	=	9.5
Female juniors	9	*	50	/	100	=	4.5
Female seniors	31	*	50	/	100	=	15.5

is hypothetical. In reality, we must look at all of the expected frequencies for each biological sex in each school classification to get a full picture of the numbers necessary to reject the null hypothesis. In Figure 15.4, we have computed all of the expected frequencies for you, just repeating the computational process for each category.

Step 3

At this point, we can once again look at the formula given in Figure 15.2. The basic formula for the chi-square test of independence can be said to be the following:

$$\text{Chi-square} = \text{sum of } ((\text{observed frequencies} - \text{expected frequencies})^2 / \text{expected frequencies})$$

Note that we are looking at the Σ, or sum of the equation. This basically means that we must compute that formula for each and every one of the cells in the table and then add up the values that we obtain.

Let's compute the first portion of the chi-square statistic for males in precollege. The observed frequency score for males, as seen in Figure 15.1, is 6. And the expected frequency score for males, as seen in Figure 15.4, is 6.5. So to obtain the portion of the chi-square statistic represented by males in precollege, we then plug these numbers into the formula: $(6 - 6.5)^2/6.5 = 0.038462$. In Figure 15.5, we have computed all of the parts of the chi-square statistic.

Step 4

Because the sigma was in front of the formula, now we just add all of the values from step 3 together:

0.038462 + 2.571429 + 0.026316 + 2.722222 + 5.822581 + 0.038462 +
2.571429 + 0.026316 + 2.722222 + 5.822581

	Observed frequency		Expected frequency		Expected frequency		Chi-square (χ^2) statistic
Males in precollege	(6	–	6.5) ^{2}	/	6.5	=	0.038462
Male first-year students	(8	–	14) ^{2}	/	14.0	=	2.571429
Male sophomores	(10	–	9.5) ^{2}	/	9.5	=	0.026316
Male juniors	(1	–	4.5) ^{2}	/	4.5	=	2.722222
Male seniors	(25	–	15.5) ^{2}	/	15.5	=	5.822581
Females in precollege	(7	–	6.5) ^{2}	/	6.5	=	0.038462
Female first-year students	(20	–	14) ^{2}	/	14.0	=	2.571429
Female sophomores	(9	–	9.5) ^{2}	/	9.5	=	0.026316
Female juniors	(8	–	4.5) ^{2}	/	4.5	=	2.722222
Female seniors	(6	–	15.5) ^{2}	/	15.5	=	5.822581
			χ^2 Calculated value	=	22.362		

FIGURE 15.5
Chi-Square (χ^2) Statistics

This sum indicates that the **calculated value** that we obtained for chi-square is 22.362. However, we still have a couple of steps to go before we can say that we are truly finished with this example.

Step 5

In this step, we must calculate the degrees of freedom for the chi-square computed in this example. **Degrees of freedom** is defined as the number of participant scores in a sample that can or are free to vary. Because this is an important concept, we will think of it in terms of a car lot. Imagine that you are a car salesperson and that you have five cars to sell. All of the cars are the same make and model, but they have different colors: yellow, blue, green, red, and white. One day, five customers come to your showroom to buy cars. The first person looks at the five cars and selects the blue one. This person had the ability to choose among five cars, but the next person who comes to the dealership can only choose among four cars (yellow, green, red, and white) because the blue car has already been sold. The second person picks the yellow car. The third person only has three choices then and picks the red car. The fourth person who comes in now only has the freedom to choose between two cars and selects the white car. The fifth person who comes into the showroom now has no ability to choose at all and must select the green car or go elsewhere. Each of these customers had the ability to vary her or his choice until the last customer.

Because in the chi-square example we are dealing with two different nominal variables (sex and classification in school), the formula is a little different: $(r - 1)$ $(c - 1)$, or (number of rows – 1)(number of columns – 1). In this example, we have two rows (male and female) and five columns (precollege, first-year student, sophomore, junior, and senior). So the degrees of freedom for our chi-square example would be

$(2-1)(5-1)$, or $(1)(4)$, which is equal to 4. So in our example, the degree to which the frequencies had the freedom to vary was 4.

Step 6

Figure 15.6 is what is called a critical value table. A **critical value** table is a table that has been previously created to determine when specific chi-square calculated values are statistically significant (for a discussion of statistical significance, see Chapter 13). On the left side is the column for the degrees of freedom. In our study, our degrees of freedom value, as calculated in step 5, was 4, so we must compare the number we calculated for the chi-square statistic in step 4, or 22.362, against the numbers in row 4 on this chart. If 22.362 is greater than the number listed in the columns, our chi-square is statistically significant at that p value (shown at the top of each column). The first column represents $p < 0.10$, which is not statistically significant, as discussed in Chapter 13. The critical value in this column was 7.78, and our calculated chi-square statistic was 22.362, which is greater than 7.78, so we would consider our chi-square significant at the $p < 0.10$ level. However, 0.10 does not meet the 95% confidence interval discussed in Chapter 13, so we would not consider a chi-square statistically significant at this p-value. The second column represents $p < 0.05$, which meets the 95% confidence interval, so if our

FIGURE 15.6
Probability Values of the Chi-Square Distribution

df	0.10	0.05	0.01	0.005	0.001
1	2.71	3.84	6.64	7.88	10.83
2	4.61	5.99	9.21	10.60	13.82
3	6.25	7.82	11.34	12.84	16.27
4	7.78	9.49	13.28	14.87	18.47
5	9.24	11.07	15.09	16.75	20.52
6	10.65	12.59	16.81	18.55	22.46
7	12.02	14.07	18.48	20.28	24.32
8	13.36	15.51	20.09	21.95	26.12
9	14.68	16.92	21.67	23.59	27.88
10	15.99	18.31	23.21	25.19	29.59
11	17.28	19.68	24.72	26.76	31.26
12	18.55	21.03	26.22	28.30	32.91
13	19.81	22.36	27.69	29.82	34.53
14	21.06	23.69	29.14	31.32	36.13
15	22.31	24.99	30.58	32.80	37.70
16	23.54	26.30	32.00	34.27	39.26
17	24.77	27.59	33.41	35.72	40.80
18	25.99	28.87	34.81	37.16	42.32
19	27.20	30.14	36.20	38.59	43.83
20	28.41	31.41	37.57	40.00	45.32

If the observed chi-square is greater than or equal to the tabled value for the desired probability level and degrees of freedom, we should reject the null hypothesis.

The entries in this table were computed by the authors.

computed value is greater than the critical value, we would consider a chi-square statistically significant at this p value. The critical value in the $p = 0.05$ column is 9.49, and our calculated chi-square statistic is 22.362, which is greater than 9.49, so we would consider our chi-square significant at the $p < 0.05$ level. Our example is clearly larger than the critical value of 9.49 shown in the table, so we can reject the null hypothesis and affirm the claim that female and male undergraduates differ in the year in college when they take public speaking. In fact, if you examine the critical values table further, we can reject the null hypothesis at the $p < 0.01$, $p < 0.005$, and $p < 0.001$ levels as well.

COMPUTER PRINTOUTS OF THE CHI-SQUARE TEST OF INDEPENDENCE

Most researchers no longer compute statistics by hand. In fact, computing statistics by hand is dangerous because humans make errors easily when handling large quantities of data. In this example, we only had 100 people in the 10 cells in the 2×5 table. Imagine if we had used 4,000 people. Although the statistics could be computed by hand as we did earlier, it just is not time-efficient to do so. For this reason, a variety of computer programs have been created to aid in this process.

If you look online at the textbook's website (https://oup-arc.com/wrench), you will find a link for "Book Datasets." In this folder, you will find subfolders for Statistical Package for the Social Sciences (SPSS) datasets, Excel datasets, STATA datasets, and Notepad datasets. The SPSS datasets can be used by SPSS along with PSPP, JASP, & R. The STATA files can only be used in STATA, and Excel the dataset can be used in Microsoft Excel. You can use the Notepad datasets to import the data into whatever program you prefer to use.

In this book, we will only be discussing how to read and interpret results from SPSS. However, we do have videos online that demonstrate conducting these tests in a range of different statistical software packages. If you would prefer to use STATA, we would also recommend reading Acock (2018).

In addition, we will again mention, for this chapter and those that follow, that we specifically used SPSS 24.0 when conducting the statistical tests in this book. As you remember, earlier or later versions of the software may display more or less information in similar or different ways. Although the steps in conducting the tests will be the same for various versions of the software package, the display often gets altered. For this reason, if you are using an earlier (or later) version of SPSS, you may want to consult the software guide that accompanied the software package. Mostly, these changes are minor, but for students new to dealing with statistical software packages, the changes may be confusing.

SPSS and Chi-Square

Open the SPSS datasets folder and select the file "Chi-square." *When you select this file, SPSS will automatically import the data into the front page of the software program.* When using SPSS to calculate a chi-square, you use the "Crosstabs" function.

To get to the Crosstabs function, go to the menu bar at the top of your screen and click on "Analyze" (Figure 15.7). When you click Analyze, a drop-down menu will appear. Go to the second category on this menu, "Descriptive Statistics," scroll over the arrow, and another menu will appear to the right. In this menu, click on "Crosstabs" (Figure 15.8). When you do this, the Crosstabs dialogue box appears (Figure 15.9a). On the left side of the screen, you will find a box that lists all of the variables in the dataset. If you have opened the chi-square file from the textbook's website, you will see two variables listed (sex and class).

To compute a chi-square using SPSS, highlight the sex variable, and click on the right arrow to the left of the box labeled "Row(s)" (Figure 15.9b). If you have done this correctly, you will see that the sex variable has not been placed in the "Row(s)" box on the right side of the dialogue box. Next, highlight the class variable, and click on the right arrow to the left of the box labeled "Column(s)" (Figure 15.9c). If you have done this correctly, you will see that the class variable has been placed in the "Column(s)" box on the right side of the dialogue box.

FIGURE 15.7
Chi-Square Main Page

In the upper right of the Crosstabs dialogue box, you will see three buttons: "Statistics," "Cells," and "Format." Click on the Statistics button. A new dialogue box called "Crosstabs: Statistics" will appear (Figure 15.9d). In this box, you will see a variety of different statistical procedures that can be completed. However, we are only interested in the one on the top left called "Chi-square." When you click on the white box next to the word "Chi-square," you will see a little black checkmark appear in the box. Do the same for the statistics "Phi and Cramér's V" (Figure 15.9e). Now, click the button "Continue" at the bottom of the dialogue box.

Next, we are going to go click on the Cells button. A new dialogue box will open called "Crosstabs: Cell Display" (Figure 15.9f). When this dialogue box first appears, the only box that will have a checkmark in it is next to the word "Observed," which is the same thing as frequency observed. Right under "Observed" is "Expected." Click on this as well (Figure 15.9g), and then click Continue. At this point, you can click OK at the bottom of the Crosstabs dialogue box. Figure 15.10 shows the actual results you will see from SPSS.

When looking at the SPSS printouts, you will see four boxes, three of which we discuss here. The first box is labeled the "Case Processing Summary" box and lets you know how many cases (or participants) were used in this test. Just like when we did it by hand, 100 participants were used in this statistical test. The second box is the "sex*class Crosstabulation" box. This box is similar to the table seen in Figure 15.3, but it also has both the observed and the expected values. Note that all of the numbers we calculated by hand match up perfectly to those in this box. The third box in the SPSS printouts, the "Chi-Square Tests" box, is the important one for understanding whether the chi-square was statistically significant. Although three tests are represented in this box, the one to be concerned about for a basic chi-square is the first test, the "Pearson Chi-Square." Look at the "Pearson Chi-Square" row, and you will see three columns: "Value," "df," and "Asymp. Sig. (2-sided)." The first column is the calculated value for the chi-square. And just like the value obtained when we calculated chi-square by hand, the computer also found this value to be 22.362 and the degrees of freedom to be 4. However, the computer is able to obtain a much more exact p value than we could by looking at a critical value chart. In this case, the chi-square was found to be significant at the $p < 0.001$ level. The printout just says that the significance is 0.000; however, this means that the significance is lower than this level, however the 6th edition of the APA Style Manual says to only report out to $p < .001$, which is what we would do in this case. (Keep this in mind whenever you see 0.000 printout in the chapters that follows.)

FIGURE 15.8
Crosstabs Menu

FIGURE 15.9A
Main Dialogue Box

FIGURE 15.9B
Place Variable "Sex" in the Row(s) Box

FIGURE 15.9C
Place Variable "Class" in the Column(s) Box

FIGURE 15.9D
"Crosstabs: Statistics" Dialogue Box

FIGURE 15.9E
Select Statistics to Run

FIGURE 15.9F
"Crosstabs: Cell Display" Dialogue Box

FIGURE 15.9G
Select "Expected"

Cramér's Phi (Φ)

The fourth box of the printout shown in Figure 15.10 includes one other statistic that we have not discussed: **Cramér's phi (Φ)**. All a chi-square test of independence can do is tell you that a difference exists; Cramér's phi is used to determine how much of

Case Processing Summary

	Cases					
	Valid		Missing		Total	
	N	Percent	N	Percent	N	Percent
sex * class	100	100.0%	0	0.0%	100	100.0%

sex*class Crosstabulation

			class					Total
			Pre-college	First-Year Student	Sophomore	Junior	Senior	
sex	male	Count	6	8	10	1	25	50
		Expected Count	6.5	14.0	9.5	4.5	15.5	50.0
	female	Count	7	20	9	8	6	50
		Expected Count	6.5	14.0	9.5	4.5	15.5	50.0
Total		Count	13	28	19	9	31	100
		Expected Count	13.0	28.0	19.0	9.0	31.0	100.0

Chi-Square Tests

	Value	df	Asymp. Sig. (2-sided)
Pearson Chi-Square	22.362[a]	4	.000
Likelihood Ratio	24.153	4	.000
Linear-by-Linear Association	9.541	1	.002
N of Valid Cases	100		

[a] 2 cells (20.0%) have expected count less than 5. The minimum expected count is 4.50.

Symmetric Measures

		Value	Approx. Sig.
Nominal by Nominal	Phi	.473	.000
	Cramer's V	.473	.000
N of Valid Cases		100	

[a] Not assuming the null hypothesis.
[b] Using the asymptotic standard error assuming the null hypothesis.

FIGURE 15.10
Chi-Square Results

FIGURE 15.11
Cramér's Phi Statistic

$$\Phi = \sqrt{\frac{\chi^2}{N\,(k-1)}}$$

the difference in one variable can be accounted for by the variance in another variable (i.e., the effect size). To obtain Cramér's phi, the formula in Figure 15.11 is used.

To understand this formula, you must have a calculated value for a chi-square (22.362) and remember that N = total number of observations (N = 100) and k = the smaller of the number of rows or columns (k = 2). In other words:

$$\Phi = \sqrt{(22.362/(100\,(2-1)))},$$

$$\Phi = \sqrt{(22.362/(100\,(1)))},$$

$$\Phi = \sqrt{(22.362/(100))}$$

$$\Phi = \sqrt{(22.362/100)}$$

$\Phi = \sqrt{0.22362} \leftarrow$ This number is the percent of variability in the dependent variable (effect) accounted for by the independent variable (ambiguity).

$\Phi = 0.472884764 \leftarrow$ This is the number that would be reported in your results section.

Cramér's phi in this case was 0.47, and the biological sex of a participant (female or male) accounted for approximately 22% of the variability in when a college student takes public speaking in college. Note that this is the same result we see in the previous SPSS results in Figure 15.10. Overall, this is a good example of how the chi-square test of independence can be used to answer a research question.

APA Write-Up

A chi-square was conducted to assess whether females and males take public speaking at different stages in their educational career. The result for this test was significant: $\chi^2(4, N = 100) = 22.36, p < 0.001$. Cramér's phi was 0.47, which indicates that biological sex of a participant (female or male) accounted for approximately 22% of the variability in when a college student takes public speaking in college.

You will note that in this APA write-up, everything is simply stated. The actual statement written is simple: χ^2 = (degrees of freedom, number of people in sample) = calculated value, level of statistical significance. Note that the p value is reported at $p < 0.001$ because the *APA Style Manual* recommends this reporting with p values that are less than 0.001. In the future, when analyzing a chi-square, all you really need to see is this one line to determine what was done and what results were found by the researchers. Also note that APA requires that we round results to the nearest hundredth (two decimal places) for all results except your p value.

Discussion of Findings

By this point, you are probably wondering what the result means. To really grasp what we have found in this chi-square, you must go back to what we said about the chi-square in the beginning of this chapter. A chi-square is a difference test. All you basically get in a chi-square test is whether a difference occurs between the two groups. In this example, based on the basic chi-square, we can say that a statistically significant difference occurs between females and males and when they take public speaking in college. However, we cannot say exactly when that difference occurs. We cannot eyeball Figure 15.1, for example, and say that more females take public speaking during their first year in college than men because we did not conduct a test to determine whether this is true. Based on a simple chi-square test of independence, all you can legitimately say is that a difference exists.

To find out where this difference exists, you must conduct a multiple comparison procedure. You only need to conduct a multiple comparison procedure if the overall chi-square is significant. Although a chi-square multiple comparison procedure is useful, it is not the most statistically accurate way to obtain results. In a chi-square multiple comparison procedure, you compare all the parts of the smaller variable (sex) with all the parts of the larger variable (year in school). Because sex only has two levels (male and female), we do not have to worry about changing anything for it. However, because year in school has five levels, we have to conduct 10 comparison tests. To determine how many comparison tests are necessary, you can use the following formula: $(K(K-1))/2$, with K being the number of groups being compared. In this case, we have five groups being compared (precollege, first-year student, sophomore, junior, and senior). So the formula would be solved like this:

$$(5(5-1))/2$$
$$(5(4))/2$$
$$20/2$$
$$10$$

To perform a multiple comparison test, you simply select two categories from the larger variable (year in school) that you want to compare (e.g., precollege and first-year student) and then compare them by conducting a chi-square. In SPSS, you open the chi-square file, go to the menu bar on the top of your screen, and click on "Data." When you click Data, a drop-down menu will appear. Scroll down and click on "Select Cases." The Select Cases dialogue box will appear. On the left side of the box you will see your variables listed, and on the right side you will see that the radio button "All Cases" currently has a black dot filling the button. Click on the radio button that corresponds to the phrase "If condition is satisfied." Next, click on the button "If" immediately below. When you click on this button, the "Select Cases: If" dialogue box will appear. In this window, you will see your variables in a box on a left side, an empty box on the top right, a calculator in the center, and some mathematical expressions on the bottom right. The only box you will need to be worried about at this time is the empty box on the top right. Type in this empty box *class = 1 or class = 2*. Click Continue at the bottom of the Select Cases: If dialogue box, and then click OK button at the bottom of the Select Cases dialogue box. When you do this, a new variable called "filter_$" appears. Many of your cases now have a slash mark through the case number on the left side of the main SPSS screen. You have told SPSS that you are only going to pay attention to the first two parts of the "class" variable (precollege and first-year students). You then will compute a chi-square test of independence just like we did earlier. This time, however, the only variables being compared will be a 2 × 2 table, or sex (male and female) by class (precollege and first-year students). This process will then be repeated nine more times, comparing each set of variables in the chi-square itself (precollege with sophomores, precollege with juniors, precollege with seniors, sophomores with juniors, etc.). When all 10 chi-squares have been calculated, you end up with the results shown in Figure 15.12 and summarized in Figure 15.13.

Chi-Square Tests - Precollege vs. First-year

	Value	df	Asymp. Sig. (2-sided)	Exact Sig. (2-sided)	Exact Sig. (1-sided)
Pearson Chi-Square	1.221[b]	1	.269		
Continuity Correction[a]	.564	1	.453		
Likelihood Ratio	1.196	1	.274		
Fisher's Exact Test				.307	.225
Linear-by-Linear Association	1.191	1	.275		
N of Valid Cases	41				

[a] Computed only for a 2 × 2 table
[b] 1 cells (25.0%) have expected count less than 5. The minimum expected count is 4.44.

Chi-Square Tests - Precollege vs. Sophomore

	Value	df	Asymp. Sig. (2-sided)	Exact Sig. (2-sided)	Exact Sig. (1-sided)
Pearson Chi-Square	.130[b]	1	.719		
Continuity Correction[a]	.000	1	1.000		
Likelihood Ratio	.130	1	.719		
Fisher's Exact Test				1.000	.500
Linear-by-Linear Association	.126	1	.723		
N of Valid Cases	32				

[a] Computed only for a 2 × 2 table
[b] 0 cells (.0%) have expected count less than 5. The minimum expected count is 6.50.

FIGURE 15.12
Multiple Comparison Tests

FIGURE 15.12
Continued

Chi-Square Tests - Precollege vs. Junior

	Value	df	Asymp. Sig. (2-sided)	Exact Sig. (2-sided)	Exact Sig. (1-sided)
Pearson Chi-Square	3.010[b]	1	.083		
Continuity Correction[a]	1.612	1	.204		
Likelihood Ratio	3.298	1	.069		
Fisher's Exact Test				.165	.101
Linear-by-Linear Association	2.874	1	.090		
N of Valid Cases	22				

a. Computed only for a 2 × 2 table

b. 2 cells (50.0%) have expected count less than 5. The minimum expected count is 2.86.

Chi-Square Tests - Precollege vs. Senior

	Value	df	Asymp. Sig. (2-sided)	Exact Sig. (2-sided)	Exact Sig. (1-sided)
Pearson Chi-Square	5.234[b]	1	.022		
Continuity Correction[a]	3.709	1	.054		
Likelihood Ratio	5.006	1	.025		
Fisher's Exact Test				.033	.029
Linear-by-Linear Association	5.115	1	.024		
N of Valid Cases	44				

a. Computed only for a 2 × 2 table

b. 1 cells (25.0%) have expected count less than 5. The minimum expected count is 3.84.

Chi-Square Tests - First-year vs. Sophomore

	Value	df	Asymp. Sig. (2-sided)	Exact Sig. (2-sided)	Exact Sig. (1-sided)
Pearson Chi-Square	2.773[b]	1	.096		
Continuity Correction[a]	1.848	1	.174		
Likelihood Ratio	2.767	1	.096		
Fisher's Exact Test				.130	.087
Linear-by-Linear Association	2.714	1	.099		
N of Valid Cases	47				

a. Computed only for a 2 × 2 table

b. 0 cells (.0%) have expected count less than 5. The minimum expected count is 7.28.

Chi-Square Tests - First-year vs. Junior

FIGURE 15.12
Continued

	Value	df	Asymp. Sig. (2-sided)	Exact Sig. (2-sided)	Exact Sig. (1-sided)
Pearson Chi-Square	1.128[b]	1	.288		
Continuity Correction[a]	.379	1	.538		
Likelihood Ratio	1.272	1	.259		
Fisher's Exact Test				.403	.280
Linear-by-Linear Association	1.098	1	.295		
N of Valid Cases	37				

[a.] Computed only for a 2 × 2 table
[b.] 1 cells (25.0%) have expected count less than 5. The minimum expected count is 2.19.

Chi-Square Tests - First-year vs. Senior

	Value	df	Asymp. Sig. (2-sided)	Exact Sig. (2-sided)	Exact Sig. (1-sided)
Pearson Chi-Square	16.185[b]	1	.000		
Continuity Correction[a]	14.142	1	.000		
Likelihood Ratio	16.994	1	.000		
Fisher's Exact Test				.000	.000
Linear-by-Linear Association	15.911	1	.000		
N of Valid Cases	59				

[a.] Computed only for a 2 × 2 table
[b.] 0 cells (.0%) have expected count less than 5. The minimum expected count is 12.34.

Chi-Square Tests - Sophomore vs. Junior

	Value	df	Asymp. Sig. (2-sided)	Exact Sig. (2-sided)	Exact Sig. (1-sided)
Pearson Chi-Square	4.414[b]	1	.036		
Continuity Correction[a]	2.845	1	.092		
Likelihood Ratio	4.955	1	.026		
Fisher's Exact Test				.049	.042
Linear-by-Linear Association	4.256	1	.039		
N of Valid Cases	28				

[a.] Computed only for a 2 × 2 table
[b.] 1 cells (25.0%) have expected count less than 5. The minimum expected count is 3.54.

Continued

FIGURE 15.12
Continued

Chi-Square Tests - Sophomore vs. Senior

	Value	df	Asymp. Sig. (2-sided)	Exact Sig. (2-sided)	Exact Sig. (1-sided)
Pearson Chi-Square	4.402[b]	1	.036		
Continuity Correction[a]	3.169	1	.075		
Likelihood Ratio	4.337	1	.037		
Fisher's Exact Test				.056	.038
Linear-by-Linear Association	4.314	1	.038		
N of Valid Cases	50				

[a.] Computed only for a 2 × 2 table
[b.] 0 cells (.0%) have expected count less than 5. The minimum expected count is 5.70.

Chi-Square Tests - Junior vs. Senior

	Value	df	Asymp. Sig. (2-sided)	Exact Sig. (2-sided)	Exact Sig. (1-sided)
Pearson Chi-Square	14.824[b]	1	.000		
Continuity Correction[a]	11.925	1	.001		
Likelihood Ratio	15.054	1	.000		
Fisher's Exact Test				.000	.000
Linear-by-Linear Association	14.453	1	.000		
N of Valid Cases	40				

[a.] Computed only for a 2 × 2 table
[b.] 1 cells (25.0%) have expected count less than 5. The minimum expected count is 3.15.

Based on these results, we can safely say that females and males differ when they take public speaking between precollege and seniors, first-year students and seniors, sophomores and juniors, sophomores and seniors, and juniors and seniors. We can make these claims because the chi-square tests of independence were significant for these pairwise comparisons. However, this is a liberal or loose conclusion. With any statistical test, there occurs a certain amount of error, as discussed in Chapter 13. The more statistical tests one runs, the more the error is compounded, and the greater the chance of type I error. For this reason, statisticians recommend being conservative. And one way to be conservative and prevent type I error is to lower the significance level. Although there are many tests to help you lower your significance level, one we commonly use is the **Dunn–Sidak test**. Using the formula $1 - (1 - \alpha)^{1/k}$, where k is the number of comparisons being made (which, as we discussed earlier, is 10 in this case), a lower alpha level can be calculated. Because this hypothesis was examining 10 different chi-square tests, k was equal to 10 and alpha,

Pairwise Comparison	N	df	χ^2	p
Precollege vs. First-year Student	41	1	1.22	.27
Precollege vs. Sophomore	32	1	1.30	.72
Precollege vs. Junior	22	1	3.01	.08
Precollege vs. Senior	44	1	5.23	.02
First-year Student vs. Sophomore	47	1	2.77	.10
First-year Student vs. Junior	37	1	1.23	.29
First-year Student vs. Senior	59	1	16.19	.0005*
Sophomore vs. Junior	28	1	4.41	.04
Sophomore vs. Senior	50	1	4.40	.04
Junior vs. Senior	40	1	14.82	.0005*

Significant at the .005 level after a Dunn-Sidak correction.

FIGURE 15.13
Pairwise Comparisons

as discussed in Chapter 13 is usually set at $p < 0.05$, so the Dunn–Sidak test would look something like this:

$$1 - (1 - 0.05)^{1/10}$$
$$1 - (0.95)^{1/10}$$
$$1 - (0.9948838031)$$
$$0.0051161969$$

For the 10 pairwise comparisons to be considered statistically significant, the computed alpha level must now be less than 0.005. For example, by normal standards there is a significant difference between precollege and seniors because alpha was computed at $p = 0.022$; however, at the new alpha level of 0.005, $p = 0.022$ is not considered significant because it is greater than $p < 0.005$. With this more conservative alpha level, only two pairwise comparisons are now significant: first-year students and seniors, and juniors and seniors.

Post Hoc APA Write-Up

Here is how you would write up this part of your report in American Psychological Association (APA):

As a post hoc analysis, 10 pairwise comparisons were calculated to determine where the actual differences are. To correct for type I error in this procedure, a Dunn–Sidak procedure was conducted to correct for possible compounded error resulting from the 10 pairwise comparisons. The new calculated alpha value is $p = 0.005$. Based on the new alpha value, only two pairwise comparisons were found to be statistically significant: first-year students and seniors, and juniors and seniors. Figure 15.13 contains the chi-square statistics for all the pairwise comparisons.

BIOLOGICAL SEX AND BOOK EDITION

Now that we have calculated a complete chi-square by hand, we examine a chi-square based on data actually collected with a real sample population. In this example, we wanted to see whether the numbers of female and male participants differed between the first and second editions of this book. In this case, we created a nominal variable for book edition: first edition versus second edition. Figure 15.14 represents the findings from the SPSS results.

APA Write-Up

The APA write-up would be as follows:

> A chi-square was conducted to assess whether the numbers of female and male participants differed between the first and second editions of Wrench, Thomas-Maddox, Richmond, and McCroskey's (2008, 2013) *Quantitative Research Methods for Communication: A Hands-On Approach* (first edition: females [n = 139], males [n = 183]; second edition: females [n = 182], males [n = 137]). The result for this test was not significant: χ^2(1, N = 641) = 12.36, p < 0.001. Cramér's phi was 0.14, which indicates that the book edition (first or second) accounted for approximately 1.9% of the variability in biological sex within the dataset sample.

Discussion

We should note that the similarity between the number of females and males from edition to edition was remarkably similar, but flipped. In the first edition, we had 139 females, and in the second, we had 137 males. However, in the first edition, we had 183 males, and in the second, we had 182 females. Although these numbers are interesting, they happened by chance. So what does this result actually tell us? When you look at the basic numbers, we can clearly see that we had significantly more males in the first-edition sample and significantly more females in the second-edition (and vice versa). Overall, however, we had roughly the same number of females (n = 321) and males (n = 320) when we combine both samples. This balance was not attempted or strived for; it just naturally happened through our data-collecting efforts.

Crosstabs

Case Processing Summary

	Cases					
	Valid		Missing		Total	
	N	Percent	N	Percent	N	Percent
Biological Sex * Book Edition	641	98.0%	13	2.0%	654	100.0%

Count

Biological Sex * Book Edition Crosstabulation

		Book Edition		Total
		1st Edition – 2008	2nd Edition – 2012	
Biological Sex	Male	183	137	320
	Female	139	182	321
Total		322	319	641

Chi-Square Tests

	Value	df	Asymp. Sig. (2-sided)	Exact Sig. (2-sided)	Exact Sig. (1-sided)
Pearson Chi-Square	12.359[a]	1	.000		
Continuity Correction[b]	11.810	1	.001		
Likelihood Ratio	12.399	1	.000		
Fisher's Exact Test				.001	.000
Linear-by-Linear Association	12.340	1	.000		
N of Valid Cases	641				

[a]. 0 cells (0.0%) have expected count less than 5. The minimum expected count is 159.25.

[b]. Computed only for a 2 X 2 table

Symmetric Measures

		Value	Approx. Sig.
Nominal by Nominal	Phi	.139	.000
	Cramer's V	.139	.000
N of Valid Cases		641	

[a]. Not assuming the null hypothesis.

[b]. Using the asymptotic standard error assuming the null hypothesis.

FIGURE 15.14
SPSS Printout for Sex × Book Edition

DISCUSSION OF BRUMMANS AND MILLER'S ARTICLE

To help further your understanding of chi-square tests for independence, the 2004 article by Boris Brummans and Katherine Miller entitled "The Effect of Ambiguity on the Implementation of a Social Change Initiative" can be found on the textbook's website in the folder titled "Articles." To view this article, you will need to download a copy of the free Adobe Acrobat Reader (https://get.adobe.com/reader/) if you do not already have this program installed on your computer. We strongly encourage you to read the article first and then read our analysis of the article. The goal of this process is to make sure you understand how to read and interpret research results related to chi-squares.

Article Purpose

In 1992, the Kellogg Foundation set out to influence health care in three Michigan communities through its Comprehensive Community Health Models Initiative. To do this, the Kellogg Foundation sought to "legitimize the problem of community health" and "provide resources and infrastructure for change" (Brummans & Miller, 2004, p. 4). The goal of the Brummans and Miller (2004) article was to see whether people involved with the implementation of the initiative found the ambiguity of the term *collaborative community health improvement* detrimental or beneficial to the implementation of the initiative.

Methodology

The research team involved in this project interviewed 48 "key participants" in three small group settings. After the interviews, the research team searched for specific ambiguity-oriented language (see the last sentence of the first paragraph on page 6 in the article) and broke the dialogue into research units. These units were then classified as either high ambiguity or low ambiguity, which is the independent variable in this study, by two independent coders. If you remember the section on Cohen's kappa from Chapter 10, you will note that 0.86 is above the 0.70 designation described as necessary to be considered satisfactorily reliable for coders. The coders also determined whether the participant perceived the ambiguity as either beneficial or detrimental to the Comprehensive Community Health Model initiative's implementation, which is the dependent variable in this study. Ultimately, the coders created a 2 × 2 table ((high ambiguity and low ambiguity) × (detrimental effects and beneficial effects)). The actual 2 × 2 table can be seen on page 7 of the article.

Results

The goal of this study was to see whether there was a difference in perception of the effects based on the level of ambiguity. Pearson's chi-square was reported as ($\chi^2 = 117.05$, 1 df, $p < 0.01$). Note that this format for presenting the chi-square information is slightly different than the one discussed in the APA write-ups. However, all of the same information is presented (*N* can be found in the table on page 7). So based on the results, people do perceive the effects of the implementation with regard to their perception of the ambiguity of the term *collaborative community health improvement*.

RESEARCH OUTSIDE THE WALLS OF ACADEMIA

Chi-squares are fairly simple tests that actually have a number of benefits outside traditional academic research. Say you worked for an auto dealership and wanted to know whether biological sex influenced the model of a car that a customer buys. This is a clear case where you would have different categories (biological sex: female and male) and car model (every different auto manufacturer has a line of different models). Both variables also would clearly be nominal, so the chi-square would be a great test to determine this outcome. These results could then be used to target customers. For example, if you learn that male customers are more likely to buy one model of car than female customers, then spending a lot of time trying to sell a female customer that other model of car may not be the best sales approach.

Another example of a chi-square outside of academia is determining whether different products sell better in different geographic locations. In fact, some companies are interested in product type, geographic location, and store location. Although we have added a third nominal variable here, the appropriate test would still be a chi-square. For example, maybe we want to see whether five different types of plants sell differently based on geographic location (north, south, east, and west), based on whether those plants are in the front of the store or in a garden section. You can quickly see that we have a series of three nominal variables.

Overall, any time you want to test a business analytics problem that utilizes two or more sets of nominal variables, then the chi-square test will be a useful tool. The results one gains from these tests can really help an organization grow and thrive.

CONCLUSION

In this chapter, we have examined how to compute a chi-square statistic by hand, how to compute and interpret computer results of a chi-square statistic in SPSS, and how to write up a chi-square test using APA style. We have also seen the chi-square statistic used in several different examples. In the next chapter we will discuss how to calculate *t* tests.

KEY TERMS

Calculated value p. 451

Chi-square (χ^2) p. 445

Cramér's phi (Φ) p. 457

Critical value p. 452

Degrees of freedom p. 451

Dunn–Sidak test p. 464

REFERENCES

Acock, A. C. (2018). *A gentle introduction to Stata* (6th ed.). College Station, TX: Stata Press.

Brummans, B. H. J. M., & Miller, K. (2004). The effect of ambiguity on the implementation of a social change initiative. *Communication Research Reports, 21*, 1–10.

FURTHER READING

Abramson, J. H., & Abramson, Z. H. (2001). *Making sense of data: A self-instruction manual on the interpretation of epidemiological data* (3rd ed.). New York, NY: Oxford University Press.

Bruning, J. L., & Kintz, B. L. (1997). *Computational handbook of statistics* (4th ed.). New York, NY: Longman.

Gravetter, F. J., & Wallnau, L. B. (2016). *Statistics for the behavioral sciences* (10th ed.). Boston, MA: Cengage.

Green, S. B., & Salkind, N. J. (2017). *Using SPSS for Windows and Macintosh: Analyzing and understanding data* (8th ed.). New York, NY: Pearson.

Greenwood, P. E., & Nikulin, M. S. (2004). *A guide to chi-square testing.* New York, NY: Wiley.

Hocking, J. E., Stacks, D. W., & McDermott, S. T. (2003). *Communication research* (3rd ed.). Boston, MA: Allyn & Bacon.

Hogan, T. P. (2010). *Bare-bones R: A brief introductory guide.* Los Angeles, CA: Sage.

Howell, D. C. (2013). *Statistical methods for psychology* (8th ed.). Belmont, CA: Wadsworth.

Huff, D. (1954). *How to lie with statistics.* New York, NY: Norton.

Keller, D. K. (2006). *The Tao of statistics: A path to understanding (with no math).* Thousand Oaks, CA: Sage.

Muenchen, R. A. (2009). *R for SAS and SPSS users.* New York, NY: Springer.

Pyrczak, F. (1999). *Statistics with a sense of humor: A humorous workbook and guide to study skills* (2nd ed.). Los Angeles, CA: Pyrczak.

Reynolds, H. T. (1984). *Analysis of nominal data* (2nd ed.). Newbury Park, CA: Sage.

Salkind, N. J. (2017). *Statistics for people who (think they) hate statistics* (6th ed.). Thousand Oaks, CA: Sage.

Singleton, R. A., Jr., & Straits, B. C. (2017). *Approach to social research* (6th ed.). New York, NY: Oxford University Press.

Trochim, W. M. K. (2000). *The research methods knowledge base* (2nd ed.). Cincinnati, OH: Atomic Dog. Retrieved from http://www.socialresearchmethods.net/

16

Independent Samples *t* Tests

CHAPTER OBJECTIVES

1. Explain the purposes of a *t* test.

2. Calculate a *t* test by hand.

3. Conduct a *t* test using Statistical Package for the Social Sciences (SPSS).

4. Analyze the use of the *t* test in the article by Weber, Fornash, Corrigan, and Neupauer (2003).

5. Explain the purpose of Cohen's *d* (statistic for the effect size of a *t* test), how one calculates Cohen's *d* by hand, and how to interpret Cohen's *d*.

When we conducted a chi-square test in the last chapter, both of the variables we analyzed had to be nominal or categorical variables (if you do not remember what this means, please reread Chapter 6 before continuing). In contrast, an **independent samples *t* test**, or Student's *t* test, examines one nominal variable with two categories (two independent groups) and their scores on one dependent interval/ratio variable.

The nominal variable in a *t* test is the independent variable, and the interval/ratio variable is the dependent variable. A group is considered to be independent when a participant's place in one group influences no other participant's placement within that group or another group. In essence, the two groups are not related to each other. For example, one common nominal variable used in *t* tests is biological sex. With the nominal variable, biological sex, we have two groups: females and males. If the first participant in the sample is male, then the second participant in the sample could equally be either female or male because the first participant's biological sex has no impact on the second participant's biological sex.

Besides the two groups being independent from each other, every participant should have scores on two variables: the grouping/nominal variable (biological sex) and a test/dependent variable. With an independent samples *t* test, the goal is to determine whether two groups' means differ on an interval/ratio variable of some kind. The groups function as the independent variable, and the interval/ratio variable is the dependent variable. For example, maybe we wanted to determine whether females and males (independent variable) differ in their levels of nonverbal sensitivity (dependent variable).

CASE STUDY INTRODUCTION

Now that we have explained the basic purpose of an independent samples *t* test, let's consider an example. Imagine that you are teaching an interpersonal communication seminar to two different classes with five students in each class ($n = 5$). In one class, you wear stylish clothing (Class A), and in the other class, you wear clothes from the 1970s (Class B). You want to determine whether the style of clothing you wear affects the performance of your class on a test. You formulate a hypothesis predicting that your wardrobe (stylish clothing vs. outdated clothing) influences the midterm examination grades of Class A and Class B.

Based on this description, you have one nominal variable (stylish clothing vs. outdated clothing) and one ratio variable (grades on a midterm). You might ask yourself why the grades on the midterm variable is considered a ratio variable. If a student answers none of the questions correctly on a test, then he or she could receive an absolute zero (assuming the professor does not give points for correctly spelling one's name). If you look on the Figure 6.10 (on page 188) in this book, you will note that if you have one nominal variable and one interval/ratio variable, the correct statistical test to determine whether a difference exists is an independent *t* test.

INDEPENDENT SAMPLES *t* TEST BACKGROUND INFORMATION

The independent samples *t* test allows a researcher to examine the differences on an interval or ratio variable between two nominal variables. The nominal variables always function as the independent variables in the *t* test. For example, maybe you wanted to determine the level of communication apprehension (CA) between females and males. The biological sex nominal variable (females and males) would be the independent variable, and CA would be the dependent variable. If your nominal variable has more than two levels (e.g., political affiliation—Democrat, Republican, independent voter, or not registered to vote), you cannot use an independent samples *t* test to ascertain differences; instead, the one-way analysis of variance, which will be discussed in the next chapter, should be used.

t Test Assumptions

Now that we have discussed the basic aspects of the independent samples *t* test itself, let's look at the underlying assumptions of the test:

1. The dependent variable must be an interval or ratio variable.
2. The independent variable must be a nominal variable.
3. The dependent variable (e.g., grade) should be normally distributed in both of the independent variable levels (e.g., stylish clothing vs. outdated clothing). Specifically, the distributions for both populations should not have a high skewness or kurtosis. In a real-world situation, it is recommended that each nominal category have at least 30 participants. (Because we are only performing an example in this chapter, we do not have 30 participants in each category, to make the math easier to compute.)
4. A sample should be drawn from populations with equal variances on the dependent variable (e.g., midterm grade). Variance in the *t* statistic formula is obtained by averaging the variance for both of the independent variables (e.g., stylish clothing vs. outdated clothing). Because the variance is obtained by averaging the variance of both independent variables, it makes sense that both values should estimate the same population variance. If the independent variables are both estimating the same population variance, then you are said to have achieved the homogeneity of variance assumption (we will see this assumption again in the next chapter).
5. Finally, the participants contributing data should represent a random sample drawn from the population of interest (this is an assumption of most statistical tests).

The assumptions are extremely important because if even one assumption is violated, the meaning of the *t* test is lost.

t Test Formula

Now that we have explained what a *t* test is and what the basic assumptions of the *t* test are, we can look at the basic *t* test formula given in Figure 16.1. For some, this formula looks scary. However, most of the formula is simply computing some basic descriptive statistics, as we did in Chapter 15, and then plugging those answers into the formula as we go along.

$$t = \frac{(\overline{X}_1 - \overline{X}_2) - (\mu_1 - \mu_2)}{\sqrt{\left[\dfrac{\sum X^2_1 - \dfrac{(\sum X_1)^2}{n_1} + \sum X^2_2 - \dfrac{(\sum X_2)^2}{n_2}}{n_1 + n_2 - 2}\right]\left(\dfrac{1}{n_1} + \dfrac{1}{n_2}\right)}}$$

FIGURE 16.1
t Test Formula

How Beer Created the *t* Test

Ever heard of William Sealy Gosset? We are going to bet that you probably have not. Gosset is an important statistician, however, and many of you have probably sampled the fruits of his labor without even knowing that you have him to thank. After graduating from New College, Oxford, with degrees in chemistry and mathematics, Gosset worked for Arthur Guinness & Son in Dublin, Ireland. Yep, that Guinness! You see, Gosset was attempting to develop a statistical tool that could help Guinness achieve the best selection and yield of barley. Working with one of his contemporaries, Karl Pearson (of correlation fame), the two created the *t* test. But why is it called the Student's *t* test and not the Gosset *t* test? Well, Guinness was afraid that their competitors could use Gosset's mathematical formula to get the same advantage they had received, so they decided Gosset should publish the article under the pseudonym "Student."

STEP-BY-STEP APPROACH TO THE INDEPENDENT *t* TEST

As we discussed earlier, the basic hypothesis in our example is that there is a difference between Class A (fashionable dress) and Class B (outdated dress) in terms of student performance on their midterm examinations. Figure 16.2 portrays the midterm test scores from all 10 student participants.

Step 1

The first step to solving the independent *t* test is to find the ΣX_1 (all five grades in Class A added together), $\overline{X}_1$ (average for Class A), and the ΣX_1^2 (sum of squares for Class A). To find the ΣX_1, you must add all five scores for the midterm examination

FIGURE 16.2
t Test Sample Data

Summary of Data (Scores Out of 100)			
Class A (Fashionable Dress) Condition$_1$ ($n = 5$)		**Class B** (1970s Dress) Condition$_2$ ($n = 5$)	
Participant	**X$_1$**	**Participant**	**X$_2$**
1. Natalie	90	1. Dave	83
2. Louise	85	2. Tad	71
3. Jimmy	88	3. Penny	96
4. Tika	98	4. Kevin	52
5. Kirsten	90	5. Brenda	62

for Class A together ($90 + 85 + 88 + 98 + 90 = 451$). To find $\overline{X}_1$, take the sum you found for ΣX_1 (451) and divide it by n, which is the number of people in Class A ($451/5 = 90.2$). To get the ΣX_1^2 value (student grades in Class A), you start by first squaring each X value on the chart. For example, Natalie got a 90 on her test, so you take 90^2, or 90×90, and get 8,100. You then repeat this process for each student in Class A. Louise obtained an X^2 value of 7,225, Jimmy had a 7,744, Tika had a 9,604, and Kristen had an 8,100. You then add all of these X^2 values together to obtain the ΣX_1^2 ($8,100 + 7,225 + 7,744 + 9,604 + 8,100 = 40,773$). Once you have completed this process for Class A or X_1, you then repeat the process for Class B or X_2. Figure 16.3 has the mathematical values for Class A (X_1) and Class B (X_2) necessary for computing the t test.

Step 2

As with any formula, you must start by doing things within parentheses and brackets first. The part we will solve for in Step 2 is shown in bold in Figure 16.4. These portions of the formula involve the ΣX_1 (451) and the ΣX_2 (364).

	Summary of Data (Scores Out of 100)					
	Class A (Fashionable Dress) Condition$_1$ ($n = 5$)			**Class B** (1970s Dress) Condition$_2$ ($n = 5$)		
Participant	X_1	X_1^2	Participant	X_2	X_2^2	
1. Natalie	90	8100	1. Dave	83	6889	
2. Louise	85	7225	2. Tad	71	5041	
3. Jimmy	88	7744	3. Penny	96	9216	
4. Tika	98	9604	4. Kevin	52	2704	
5. Kirsten	90	8100	5. Brenda	62	3844	
	$\Sigma X_1 = 451$ $\overline{X}_1 = 90.2$	$\Sigma X_1^2 = 40773$		$\Sigma X_2 = 364$ $\overline{X}_2 = 72.8$	$\Sigma X_2^2 = 27694$	

FIGURE 16.3
Summary Data Table for t Test Example

$$ t = \frac{(\overline{X}_1 - \overline{X}_2) - (\mu_1 - \mu_2)}{\sqrt{\left[\dfrac{\Sigma X_1^2 - \dfrac{(\Sigma X_1)^2}{n_1} + \Sigma X_2^2 - \dfrac{(\Sigma X_2)^2}{n_2}}{n_1 + n_2 - 2}\right]\left(\dfrac{1}{n_1} + \dfrac{1}{n_2}\right)}} $$

FIGURE 16.4
t Test Computation (Step 2)

The actual formula for this first part is $(\Sigma X_1)^2/n_1$. Remember, the lowercase *n* stands for the number of students in each class, or the number 5 in this example. So the solution for this part of the formula would be this:

$$\left(\Sigma X_1\right)^2/n_1$$
$$(451)^2/5$$
$$(203,401)/5$$
$$40,680.2$$

So $(\Sigma X_1)^2/n_1 = 40,680.2$.

We can now just repeat these steps for $(\Sigma X_2)^2/n_2$ to find the result:

$$\left(\Sigma X_2\right)^2/n_2$$
$$(364)^2/5$$
$$(132,496)/5$$
$$26,499.2$$

So $(\Sigma X_2)^2/n_2 = 26,499.2$.

Step 3

We can do everything within the brackets on the top side of the numerator bar, which is shown in bold in Figure 16.5.

First, we must bring back our sum of square calculations for both Class A (X_1) and Class B (X_2). The sum of square calculation for Class A was $\Sigma X_1^2 = 40,773$, and the sum of square calculation for Class B was $\Sigma X_2^2 = 27,694$. In this part of the formula, we are subtracting the sum of square for X_1 from the portion of the formula for X_1 that was computed in step 2 $[(\Sigma X_1)^2/n_1 = 40,680.2]$. Thus, we are subtracting 40,680.2 from 40,773:

$$\Sigma X_1^2 - [(\Sigma X_1)^2/n_1]$$
$$40,733 - 40,680.2 = 92.8$$

FIGURE 16.5
t **Test Computation**
(Step 3)

$$t = \frac{(\overline{X}_1 - \overline{X}_2) - (\mu_1 - \mu_2)}{\sqrt{\left[\dfrac{\Sigma X_1^2 - \dfrac{(\Sigma X_1)^2}{n_1} + \Sigma X_2^2 - \dfrac{(\Sigma X_2)^2}{n_2}}{n_1 + n_2 - 2}\right]\left(\dfrac{1}{n_1} + \dfrac{1}{n_2}\right)}}$$

We then repeat this part of the formula for X_2. Here, we subtract the sum of square for X_2 from the portion of the formula for X_2 that was computed in step 2 $[(\Sigma X_2)^2/n_2 = 26{,}499.2]$. Thus, we are subtracting 26,499.2 from 27,694.

$$\Sigma X_2^2 - [(\Sigma X_2)^2/n_2]$$
$$27{,}694 - 26{,}499.20 = 1{,}194.8$$

Step 4

Step 4 is threefold, but it is easy. First, we add both of the numbers calculated in Step 3 together $(92.8 + 1{,}194.8 = 1{,}287.6)$. Second, we complete the formula immediately below what we just completed doing $(n_1 + n_2 - 2)$. If you remember from above, $n_1 = 5$, which shows that there are five students in Class A, and $n_2 = 5$, which shows that there are five students in Class B. To complete the formula, you do the mathematical computation $(5 + 5 - 2 = 8)$. Finally, we divide the first number calculated in this step $(1{,}287.6)$ by the second number calculated in this step (8): $1{,}287.6/8 = 160.95$.

Step 5

In the fifth step of this equation, we must calculate everything in the big parentheses to the right of the part of the equation we just finished computing. This part of the equation reads $(1/n_1) + (1/n_2)$. As we know, $n_1 = 5$ and $n_2 = 5$, so we just need to compute the formula:

$$(1/n_1) + (1/n_2)$$
$$(1/5) + (1/5)$$
$$(0.2) + (0.2)$$
$$0.4$$

So $(1/n_1) + (1/n_2) = 0.4$.

Step 6

In this step, take the number calculated in the third part of Step 4 (160.95) and multiply it by the number calculated in Step 5 (0.4):

$$160.95 * 0.4 = 64.38$$

We then take this newly calculated number (64.38) and find its square root: $\sqrt{64.38} = 8.0237$. We have now calculated everything on the bottom part of this formula.

FIGURE 16.6

t Test Computation
(Step 7)

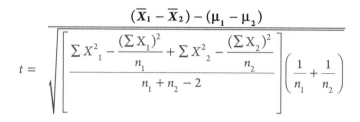

$$t = \cfrac{(\overline{X}_1 - \overline{X}_2) - (\mu_1 - \mu_2)}{\sqrt{\left[\cfrac{\sum X^2_{1} - \cfrac{(\sum X_1)^2}{n_1} + \sum X^2_{2} - \cfrac{(\sum X_2)^2}{n_2}}{n_1 + n_2 - 2}\right]\left(\cfrac{1}{n_1} + \cfrac{1}{n_2}\right)}}$$

Step 7

The seventh step will calculate the top portion of the formula, or the part that is in bold in Figure 16.6. This part of the formula $(\overline{X}_1 - \overline{X}_2) - (\mu_1 - \mu_2)$ can be understood as the sample mean difference minus the population mean difference. As previously explained, one assumption of the basic *t* test is the homogeneity of variance, so the population mean difference should equal 0. All that must be computed in this part is $(\overline{X}_1 - \overline{X}_2)$. As stated in Figure 16.3, $\overline{X}_1 = 90.2$ and $\overline{X}_2 = 72.8$. We just need to complete this part of the formula:

$$(\overline{X}_1 - \overline{X}_2) - (\mu_1 - \mu_2)$$
$$(90.2 - 72.8) - (0)$$
$$17.4 - 0$$
$$17.4$$

So, $(\overline{X}_1 - \overline{X}_2) - (\mu_1 - \mu_2) = 17.4$

Step 8

The final step in computing the *t* statistic is divide the value calculated in step 7 (17.4) by the value calculated in step 6 (8.0237), or

$$17.4/8.0237 = 2.168575595$$

This shows that the calculated value that we obtained for *t* is 2.169. However, we still have two steps to go before we are finished with this example.

Step 9

In this step, we must calculate the degrees of freedom for the *t* computed in this example. The formula for the degrees of freedom for the *t* test is simple. In fact, we have already computed it as part of the *t* test formula in step 4. The formula for the *t* test degrees of freedom is $(df = n_1 + n_2 - 2)$, or $(df = 5 + 5 - 2)$, or 8.

Step 10

Figure 16.7 has the independent samples *t* test critical value table. Note that this critical value table is different from that used to test for chi-square significance in the previous chapter. On the left side is the column for the degrees of freedom. In our study, our degrees of freedom value, as calculated in step 9, was 8, so we must compare the number we calculated for the *t* statistic in step 8, 2.169, against the numbers in row 8 on this chart. If 2.169 (the calculated value) is greater than the number listed in the columns (the critical value), then our *t* test is statistically significant at that *p* value level (shown at the top of each column). The first column represents $p < 0.10$, which is not statistically significant, as discussed in Chapter 13. The critical value in this column was 1.86, and our calculated *t* statistic was 2.169, which is greater than 1.86, so we would consider our *t* significant at the $p < 0.10$ level. However, $p < 0.10$ does not meet the 95% confidence interval discussed in the previous chapter, so we would not consider a *t* test statistically significant at this *p* value. The second column represents $p < 0.05$, which is statistically significant, as discussed in Chapter 13. The critical value in this column was 2.31, and our calculated *t* statistic was 2.169, which is not greater than 2.31, so our *t* test is not statistically significant at the $p < 0.05$ level. Therefore, our *t* test is not statistically significant. We cannot be 95% confident that there is a difference between the two classes and their midterm examination scores, which means that we must accept the null hypothesis that style of dress (fashionable vs. 1970s dress) did not affect the students' scores on the midterm examination.

df	0.10	0.05	0.01	0.005	0.001
1	6.31	12.71	63.66	636.62	363.62
2	2.92	4.30	9.93	31.60	31.60
3	2.35	3.18	5.84	12.94	12.92
4	2.13	2.78	4.60	8.61	8.61
5	2.02	2.57	4.03	6.86	6.87
6	1.94	2.45	3.71	5.96	5.96
7	1.90	2.37	3.50	5.41	5.41
8	1.86	2.31	3.36	5.04	5.04
9	1.83	2.26	3.25	4.78	4.78
10	1.81	2.27	3.17	4.59	4.59
11	1.80	2.20	3.12	4.44	4.44
12	1.78	2.18	3.06	4.32	4.32
13	1.77	2.16	3.01	4.22	4.22
14	1.76	2.15	2.98	4.14	4.14
15	1.75	2.13	2.95	4.07	4.07
16	1.75	2.12	2.92	4.02	4.02
17	1.74	2.11	2.90	3.97	3.97
18	1.73	2.10	2.88	3.92	3.92
19	1.73	2.09	2.86	3.88	3.88
20	1.73	2.09	2.85	3.85	3.85

FIGURE 16.7
t Test Critical Value Table (Two-Tailed Test)

The entries in this table were computed by the authors.

COMPUTER PRINTOUTS OF THE INDEPENDENT *t* TEST

Now that we have examined how the independent *t* test can be calculated by hand, we examine what output from Statistical Package for the Social Sciences (SPSS) looks like as well.

SPSS and *t* Tests

Using SPSS to compute an independent *t* test is fairly easy as long as you know how to follow instructions, so let's get started. Remember, however, that the specific version of the software you have may display more or less information in similar or different ways than shown here.

First, open your SPSS software, and then locate the file on the textbook's website (https://oup-arc.com/wrench) in the SPSS folder called "*t*-test" (Figure 16.8). When you open this file, you will see two variables listed, "class" and "score." "Class" is the variable name given to either Class A (fashionable dress) or Class B (1970s dress). The classes are only represented by the numbers 1 (Class A) and 2 (Class B). Remember, a statistics program can only understand numbers, so it is up to you as

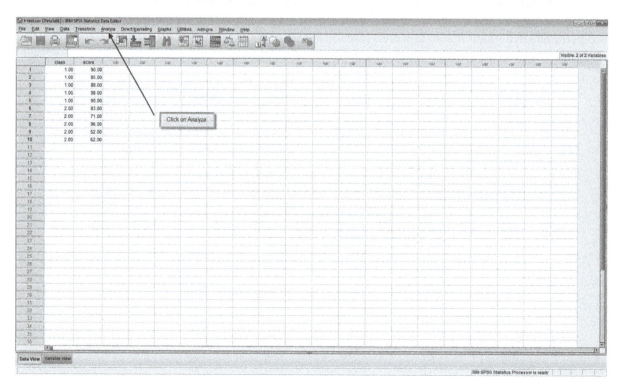

FIGURE 16.8
t Test Main Page

a researcher to remember how you classified the two groups when you are inputting the data. The "score" variable is the score that each participant received on the midterm examination.

To conduct the *t* test, go to the menu bar at the top of your screen and click "Analyze." When you click Analyze, a drop-down menu will appear. Go to the "Compare Means" category on this menu, scroll over the arrow, and another menu will appear to the right. In the "Compare Means" menu, click on "Independent Samples T Test" (Figure 16.9). At this point, the "Independent Samples T Test" dialogue box will appear on your screen (Figure 16.10a). This screen has three major boxes on it. On the left side is a box with your variables already listed. On the upper right is a box labeled "Test Variable(s)," and below that is a small box labeled "Grouping Variable." Any dependent variables that you are attempting to analyze are placed in the "Test Variable(s)" box. Click on the dependent variable for this example, score. When score is highlighted blue, click the right arrow between the variable list box and the Test Variable(s) box (Figure 16.10b). After clicking the right arrow, score should now appear in the Test Variable(s) box. Next, we must send our independent variable class to the Grouping Variable box as well. When conducting a *t* test, your independent variable will always be placed in the Grouping Variable box, and your dependent variable(s) will always be placed in the Test Variable(s) box (Figure 16.10c).

You cannot click OK yet because you have not finished telling the computer what to do. Click on the word class in the Grouping Variable box if it is not already highlighted blue. In the Grouping Variable box, click the button labeled "Define Groups." When you click Define Groups, the "Define Groups" dialogue box will pop up (Figure 16.10d). In the Define Groups dialogue box, you must tell the computer which two numbers in the variable class you are comparing. Remember, a *t* test can only be used

FIGURE 16.9
t Test Menu

FIGURE 16.10A
Main Dialogue Box

FIGURE 16.10B
Dependent Variable to the "Test Variable(s):" Box

if a nominal variable has two levels, so you must tell your computer what numbers you chose to represent those two levels. As mentioned above, we have chosen the numbers 1 and 2 to represent Class A (1) and Class B (2). We could have chosen 0 and 1, or 8 and 9—the numbers do not matter to the computer; what matters is that we clearly identify them to the computer. So, in the Define Groups dialogue box, you will note two places for you to enter information beside "Group 1" and "Group 2." Next to Group 1, type the number "1" in the box, and next to Group 2, type the number "2" in the box (Figure 16.10e). Once you have labeled the groups, click on the "Continue" button, and you will now be looking again at the Independent Samples T Test dialogue box. Now, you can click OK, the results from SPSS will appear (Figure 16.11). If for some reason you cannot click "OK," you have not entered your grouping variables correctly, so repeat the steps above and attempt to find out where you made your mistake.

Interpreting SPSS Results

FIGURE 16.10C
Independent Variable to the "Grouping Variable:" Box

The first box that you will see in the results is simply a "Group Statistics" box. In this box, you will see the *N*, mean, standard deviation, and standard error of the means listed for both Class A and Class B. The second box, or the "Independent Samples Test" box, is where the primary information about the *t* test itself is located. The first thing we must

do when analyzing our computer printouts is to determine whether we have met the assumption discussed earlier, called the homogeneity of variance assumption, for *t* tests. And the second column in the Independent Samples Test box is labeled "Levene's Test for Equality of Variances." Levene's test examines the homogeneity of variance assumption. If Levene's test is statistically significant, then the assumption has not been met. Remember, the assumption states that the variances

FIGURE 16.10D
"Define Groups" Dialogue Box

FIGURE 16.10E
Defined Groups

would be equal, so when the two groups' variances are not equal, the assumption is not met. In the Levene's Test for Equality of Variances column, you will see two subcolumns, "F" and "Sig." If "Sig." is below 0.05, then Levene's test for equality of variances is significant and the basic assumption of the *t* test has been violated, so equal variances cannot be assumed, which is the second row listed.

t **Test**

Group Statistics

	Class	N	Mean	Std. Deviation	Std. Error Mean
Test Scores	Class A	5	90.2000	4.8166	2.1541
	Class B	5	72.8000	17.2829	7.7292

Independent Samples Test

		Levene's Test for Equality of Variances		*t* test for Equality of Means							
										95% Confidence Interval of the Difference	
		F	Sig.	t	df	Sig. (2-tailed)	Mean Difference	Std. Error Difference	Lower	Upper
Test Scores	Equal variances assumed	6.053	.039	2.169	8	.062	17.4000	8.0237	–1.1027	35.9027
	Equal variances not assumed			2.169	4.618	.087	17.4000	8.0237	–3.7501	38.5501

FIGURE 16.11
SPSS Results for *t* Test Example

So what does it mean when your *t* test indicates that equal variances cannot be assumed? It means that the *t* test we calculated by hand in the example must be tweaked since this assumption was violated. If you look at the Independent Samples Test box, you will see that there are *t* test results for both "Equal variances assumed" and "Equal variances not assumed." If our Levene's test for equal variances is statistically significant ($p < 0.05$), we must report the *t* test on the lower level. However, the biggest change that occurs is how we report our degrees of freedom. By lowering the degrees of freedom from 8 (like we calculated) to 4.618 (as seen for the "Equal variances not assumed"), we make it harder for a *t* test to be statistically significant in order to protect against possible type I errors. If you look at the significance levels for "Equal variances assumed" ($p = 0.062$) and "Equal variances not assumed" ($p = 0.087$), you will see that the *p* value for equal variances being assumed is lower (greater chance of reaching statistical significance) than the *p* value for equal variances cannot be assumed (less of a chance of reaching statistical significance). Additionally, you will see that the *t* value, the "Mean Difference," and the "Std. Error Difference" are all identical; the only values that are affected by the homogeneity of variance assumption are the "df" and "Sig." values.

APA Write-Up

Here is how you would write up this part of your report in American Psychological Association (APA) format:

> An independent *t* test was conducted to determine whether an instructor's dress in a classroom (fashionable [*M* = 90.20, *SD* = 4.82] vs. out-of-date dress [*M* = 72.80, *SD* = 7.73]) affected the scores students received on their midterm examinations. Levene's test for equality of variances was significant (*F* = 6.05, $p < 0.04$), so equality of variances cannot be assumed, *t*(4.62) = 2.17, $p = 0.06$.

Discussion of Findings

Now that we have completed the APA write-up, you may wonder what the results tell us. To understand what the *t* test tells us, we must go back to the original purpose we had for conducting this test. In our example, we had a teacher who wanted to determine whether altering her dress between modern fashions in one class and outdated clothing from the 1970s in the other class would affect student learning. To test student learning, the teacher used the midterm examination as a benchmark. Based on the *t* test that we conducted, no difference was noted on the students' midterm examinations between the two classes. In a difference test, when we say that something is not significant or greater than $p = 0.05$, we are saying that a difference did not occur within our sample. In this case, the teacher's dress, whether fashionable or from the 1970s, did not change how students performed on the midterm examination.

BIOLOGICAL SEX AND COMMUNICATION APPREHENSION

In this example, we wanted to determine whether females and males differed in their reported CA levels. To analyze this question, we used the dataset that was collected for this textbook and found on the book website. To test for a difference between females and males on the Personal Report of Communication Apprehension–24 (PRCA-24), we used the nominal variable biological sex and the interval variable CA. Figure 16.12 shows the findings from the SPSS results.

APA Write-Up

For this example, your write-up in APA format would look like this:

An independent t test was conducted to determine whether female (M = 65.60, SD = 18.16) and male (M = 61.62, SD = 15.49) reported levels of CA differed. Levene's test for equality of variances was significant (F = 4.85, p < 0.05), so equality of variances cannot be assumed: $t(615.46)$ = –2.96, p = 0.003.

t Test

Group Statistics

	Biological Sex	N	Mean	Std. Deviation	Std. Error Mean
Communication Apprehension Total	Male	314	61.6178	15.49195	.87426
	Female	317	65.5962	18.16314	1.02014

Independent Samples Test

		Levene's Test for Equality of Variances		t test for Equality of Means						95% Confidence Interval of the Difference	
		F	Sig.	t	df	Sig. (2-tailed)	Mean Difference	Std. Error Difference		Lower	Upper
Communication Apprehension Total	Equal variances assumed	4.850	.028	–2.959	629	.003	–3.97838	1.34452		–6.61868	–1.33808
	Equal variances not assumed			–2.961	615.457	.003	–3.97838	1.34351		–6.61680	–1.33996

FIGURE 16.12
SPSS Results of Sex and CA *t* Test

Discussion

Let's examine this APA write-up in detail. First, note that when we described the two groups being compared, we also reported the group's means and standard deviations for the dependent variable (CA). We do this because we want to make the results easy to interpret. If the *t* test is significant, then the group with the higher mean has statistically significant higher levels on the dependent variable. In the case in front of us, females were shown to have higher levels of CA when compared to males. However, at this point, we still do not know how big this difference is, which is why we must calculate the effect size.

CALCULATING EFFECT SIZES

As mentioned in Chapter 13, one of the most important aspects related to difference research is the effect size, or the size of the difference. Although statistics allows researchers to find small differences between two groups, the size of this difference is not always known. In the example given earlier, females were shown to have significantly higher levels of CA when compared to males. As researchers, we must ask ourselves: Is a difference between 65.60 and 61.62 that big? Statistically, the relationship may be meaningful, but how big a difference are we really talking about? For this reason, it is important to calculate an effect size whenever one is calculating a difference using an independent *t* test. To test for an independent samples effect size, we use the **Cohen's *d*** formula:

$$d = t\sqrt{\frac{N_1 + N_2}{N_1 N_2}}$$

You will note that all the information we need to compute the effect size for the *t* test is located within the APA write-up itself. First, we need the computed *t* value, which was 2.961 in the study (for the purposes of this test, we need not worry about the negative sign). Second, we need the number of participants in the study ($N = 631$). Third, we must know how many people were in each group: $N_{1(female)} = 317$ and $N_{2(male)} = 314$. Once we have both of these pieces of information, it is simply a matter of completing the formula.

Step 1

The first step for computing *d* is to handle everything within the square-root function first. So we will solve the information in the numerator ($N_1 + N_2$):

$$N_1 + N_2$$

$$317 + 314 = 631$$

Next, we want to solve the information within the denominator ($N_1 N_2$):

$$N_1 N_2$$

$$317 * 314 = 99{,}538$$

Interpreting Cohen's *d*

To interpret *t* test effect sizes, use the following scale (Green & Salkind, 2004):

  0.2—small effect size

  0.5—medium effect size

  0.8—large effect size

Then, we divide our first result (631) by our second result (99,538):

$$(N_1 + N_2)/(N_1 N_2)$$

$$631/99{,}538 = 0.00633932875$$

Finally, we take the square root of this result:

$$\sqrt{\left(N_1 + N_2\right)/\left(N_1 N_2\right)}$$

$$\sqrt{0.00633932875} = 0.0796196427$$

Step 2

The second step is to take the calculated *t* test value reported in the example (2.961) and multiply it by the number we found in the last part of step 1 (0.0796196427). You'll notice that for mathematical purposes, the negative sign is dropped from the equation:

$$2.961 \times 0.0796196427 = 0.235753762$$

$$\text{or, Cohen's } d = 0.24$$

Based on the information in "Interpreting Cohen's *d*," the effect found (Cohen's *d* = 0.24) for the CA score differences between females (*M* = 65.60) and males (*M* = 61.62) is small.

DISCUSSION OF THE WEBER, FORNASH, CORRIGAN, AND NEUPAUER ARTICLE

To help you further understand the concept of the independent samples *t* test, we have included an article on the textbook's website that uses this statistical test. The 2003 article by Keith Weber, Bennie Fornash, Michael Corrigan, and Nicholas Neupauer entitled "The Effect of Interest on Recall: An Experiment" can be found in the folder titled "Articles." To view this article, you must download a copy of the free Adobe Acrobat Reader (https://get.adobe.com/reader/) if you do not already have this program installed on your computer. We strongly encourage you to read the article first and then read our analysis of the article. The goal of this process is to make sure you understand how to read and interpret research results related to *t* tests.

Article Purpose

Have you ever had to sit through a lecture in which the professor used examples that were outdated and did not mean a lot to you? Apparently, these researchers had as well, and they wanted to determine whether these outdated examples affected student learning. The basic goal of this project was to determine whether presenting interest-based examples (examples that are meaningful to the student, are something the students know about so they can actually discuss the examples openly, and are examples that clearly make a difference in everyday life) create more interested students in the classroom and result in students who perform better on subsequent tests.

Methodology

In this study, the researchers divided participants into two groups and showed each group a 10-minute video with a lecturer talking about public relations. In one video, the instructor (a male in his mid-30s) used examples that are not current but exist in most public relations textbooks (P. T. Barnum, Edward Bernays, and Ivy Ledbetter Lee). In the second video, the instructor (the same person as in the first video) used contemporary personalities such as Vince McMahon (wrestling promoter), Ray Lewis (professional football player), and Sean "Puffy" Combs (musician/entertainer/entrepreneur). The goal of this second video was to use examples that students would be familiar with and therefore, theoretically, cause them to be more interested in the course content as well.

After both groups watched the 10-minute videos, participants were given a seven-item, multiple-choice "quiz" to test their ability to understand the actual content from the videos. The groups also filled out the Learner Empowerment Scale that measures the three concepts that represent interest-based examples: meaningfulness, competence, and impact.

The participants also filled out a nonverbal immediacy test to determine whether one group perceived the lecturer from the video as being more nonverbally immediate (and thus skewing the results from the examples). To test this notion, the researchers conducted an independent *t* test and did not find a significant difference between the lecturer's nonverbal immediacy when using textbook examples and when using modern examples. This indicates that the lecturer did not alter his nonverbal communication significantly between the taping of one video and the next.

Results

The first hypothesis in this study stated that "lectures utilizing interest-based examples should result in more interested participants" (p. 118). To examine this hypothesis, the researchers conducted an independent t test to determine whether students' interest in the videos (dependent variable) was different based on whether they watched the textbook-example lecture versus the contemporary-example lecture (independent variable). The researchers reported that the students who watched the video with the contemporary examples scored significantly higher on the interest scale than those students who watched the video with the traditional textbook examples. Students are more interested in lectures that have examples they can relate to in a classroom.

If you look at the way the authors of the article presented their results, you will note that they presented the t test as we previously discussed in this chapter and then presented the actual means for each group since the difference was significant. Although presenting the means is necessary, we strongly encourage you to always present both the mean and the standard deviation because they influence the meaningfulness of the findings. When presenting means in an article, it should look something like this (M = #, SD = #). Note that "M" and "SD" are both capitalized and italicized when presenting them in a research article.

The second hypothesis in this study predicted that "lectures utilizing interest-based examples should result in participants with higher scores on subsequent tests of cognitive recall" (p. 118). To examine this hypothesis, the researchers conducted an independent t test to determine whether students' scores on the seven-item quiz (dependent variable) were different based on whether they watched the textbook-example lecture versus the contemporary-example lecture (independent variable). The researchers reported that the students who watched the video with the contemporary examples scored significantly higher on the quiz than those students who watched the video with the traditional textbook examples. Students will remember more and be able to recall it on a quiz when they listen to lectures that have examples they can relate to in a classroom.

The researchers then break the first hypothesis down and look at all three aspects of interest separately in three post hoc (after the fact) tests. In the post hoc analysis, the researchers conducted three more independent t tests examining the three factors of interest-based examples (competence, meaningfulness, and impact). The researchers report that they found differences between the two lecture groups on competence and meaningfulness, but not on impact. These results indicate that students in classrooms with modern examples feel that the examples are more meaningful to them and therefore are more competent to discuss these examples than students who listened to examples that came from traditional textbooks. However, the impact of both the contemporary and the textbook examples did not differ between the two groups.

Overall, this article is helpful because it emphasizes that college professors must stay on top of current events if they want to be effective and affective teachers in the classroom. Sticking with examples that exist in the textbook and dismissing the notion that modern examples are needed will only do a disservice to the learning environment.

PAIRED *t* TESTS

The majority of this chapter has been concerned with the independent samples *t* test or Student's *t* test. However, there is another type of *t* test that we think you should be aware of at this point. A **paired *t* test** is used to compare two interval/ratio level scores that are taken from the same group at two distinct time periods. Imagine you have run an experiment looking at an individual's level of CA after interacting with a robot. To see whether interacting with a robot can decrease participant levels of CA with a robot, you take a baseline score of their Robot-CA (Time 1) and then take a second score after the interaction (Time 2). A paired *t* test can then be used to determine whether these two scores differ from one another. Because of the paired *t* test's ability to measure differences in this fashion, it is most commonly used in conjunction with experiments.

RESEARCH OUTSIDE THE WALLS OF ACADEMIA

As we discussed earlier in this chapter, the *t* test was created to help solve a practical problem that Guinness was facing. From its inception, the *t* test helped solve a real organizational problem. And today, many organizations use *t* tests for a variety of different reasons. Whenever an individual has two groups that he or she wants to compare on an interval or ratio variable, then the *t* test is the most appropriate test to use. If you want to see whether female and male viewers have the same responses while watching a commercial, you will probably want to use a *t* test. In fact, a lot of research that examines sex differences in the worlds of marketing and media rely heavily on the *t* test. In corporate training and development, a *t* test is often used to determine whether face-to-face and online training courses lead to similar levels of learning. You could also use a *t* test to examine a variety of business indicators against data from your organization's main rival. Whether you wanted to test issues like efficiency, productivity, or error rates against those of your competitor, a *t* test would be the tool to use.

CONCLUSION

In this chapter, we have examined how to compute a *t* test by hand, how to compute and interpret computer results of a *t* test in SPSS, and how to write up a *t* test using APA style. We have seen the *t* test used in several different examples and have discussed how to compute a *t* test effect size.

KEY TERMS

Cohen's *d* p. 486   Independent samples *t* test p. 471   Paired *t* test p. 490

REFERENCES

Green, S. B., & Salkind, N. J. (2017). *Using SPSS for Windows and Macintosh: Analyzing and understanding data* (8th ed.). New York, NY: Pearson.

Weber, K., Fornash, B., Corrigan, M, & Neupauer, N. C. (2003). The effect of interest on recall: An experiment. *Communication Research Reports, 20,* 116–123.

FURTHER READING

Abramson, J. H., & Abramson, Z. H. (2001). *Making sense of data: A self-instruction manual on the interpretation of epidemiological data* (3rd ed.). New York, NY: Oxford University Press.

Bruning, J. L., & Kintz, B. L. (1997). *Computational handbook of statistics* (4th ed.). New York, NY: Longman.

Cohen, J. (1988). *Statistical power analysis for the behavioral sciences* (2nd ed.). Hillsdale, NJ: Erlbaum.

Gravetter, F. J., & Wallnau, L. B. (2000). *Statistics for the behavioral sciences* (5th ed.). Belmont, CA: Wadsworth/Thomson Learning.

Hocking, J. E., Stacks, D. W., & McDermott, S. T. (2003). *Communication research* (3rd ed.). Boston, MA: Allyn & Bacon.

Hogan, T. P. (2010). *Bare-bones R: A brief introductory guide.* Los Angeles, CA: Sage.

Howell, D. C. (1997). *Statistical methods for psychology* (4th ed.). Belmont, CA: Duxbury Press.

Huff, D. (1954). *How to lie with statistics.* New York, NY: Norton.

Keller, D. K. (2006). *The Tao of statistics: A path to understanding (with no math).* Thousand Oaks, CA: Sage.

Muenchen, R. A. (2009). *R for SAS and SPSS users.* New York, NY: Springer.

Pyrczak, F. (1999). *Statistics with a sense of humor: A humorous workbook and guide to study skills* (2nd ed.). Los Angeles, CA: Pyrczak.

Salkind, N. J. (2017). *Statistics for people who (think they) hate statistics* (6th ed.). Thousand Oaks, CA: Sage.

Singleton, R. A., Jr., & Straits, B. C. (2017). *Approach to social research* (6th ed.). New York, NY: Oxford University Press.

Tabachnick, B. G., & Fidell, L. S. (2013). *Using multivariate statistics* (6th ed.). Boston, MA: Pearson.

Trochim, W. M. K. (2000). *The research methods knowledge base* (2nd ed.). Cincinnati, OH: Atomic Dog. Retrieved from http://www.socialresearchmethods.net/

17

One-Way Analysis of Variance

CHAPTER OBJECTIVES

1. Explain the purposes of a one-way analysis of variance (ANOVA).

2. Calculate a one-way ANOVA by hand.

3. Conduct a one-way ANOVA using Statistical Package for the Social Sciences (SPSS).

4. Analyze the use of the one-way ANOVA in the article by Boiarsky, Long, and Thayer (1999).

When we conducted a *t* test in the previous chapter, we examined one nominal variable with only two independent groups and their scores on one dependent interval/ratio variable. A **one-way analysis of variance** (ANOVA), by contrast, examines one nominal variable with two or more independent groups and their scores on one dependent interval/ratio variable. Once again, the nominal variable (with two or more groups) is the independent variable, and the interval/ratio variable is the dependent variable.

A group is considered to be independent when one participant's place in one group being tested influences no one else's placement within that group or another group. In essence, the groups being tested are not related to each other. For example, one common nominal variable used in one-way ANOVA is political affiliation. With the nominal variable political affiliation, as we have defined it in this text, there are four groups: Democrat, Republican, other political party affiliation, and not registered to vote. If the first participant in the sample is a Democrat, then the second participant in the sample could equally be a Democrat, Republican, other political party affiliation, or not registered to vote because the first participant's political affiliation has no impact on the second participant's political affiliation.

Besides the two or more groups being independent from each other, every participant should have scores on two variables: the grouping/nominal variable (political affiliation) and a test/dependent variable. In the case of a one-way

492

ANOVA, the goal is to determine whether the two or more groups' means differ on an interval/ratio variable of some kind. The groups function as the independent variable, and the interval/ratio variable is the dependent variable. For example, maybe we wanted to determine whether people differ based on political affiliation (independent variable) in their levels of ethnocentrism (dependent variable).

The one-way ANOVA is part of the family of statistical tests that belong to the **general linear model** (GLM) family. Although we want to mention here that the one-way ANOVA is a GLM test, we will discuss what the GLM is and how it functions when we talk about regressions in Chapter 19. Now that we have explained the basic purpose of a one-way ANOVA, we will look at an example of a one-way ANOVA.

CASE STUDY INTRODUCTION

Have you ever noticed how some rooms just make you feel sleepy or physically drained? What if the color of the room caused this kind of reaction? In this example, a nonverbal communication researcher wants to find out whether the color of a room affects the speed with which a person can take a standard 10-item test. So, using the same 10-item test, the researcher places 12 participants randomly into one of three rooms: white, yellow, and blue. When all is said and done, the researcher tests the time (in minutes) for the four participants in the white room, the four participants in the yellow room, and the four participants in the blue room.

In the previous chapter, we examined what was necessary to find a difference between a nominal variable with two levels (e.g., female and male) on an interval/ratio variable (communication apprehension). In this chapter, we examine what is necessary to find a difference between a nominal variable with two or more levels (white, yellow, and blue) on an interval or ratio variable of some kind (time in minutes to complete the test). To perform this type of test, we calculate a one-way ANOVA.

ONE-WAY ANOVA BACKGROUND INFORMATION

The one-way ANOVA allows researchers to compare two or more groups on an interval variable using one test. If we attempted to do the example here using t tests, we would have to conduct three t tests with three unique null hypotheses:

H_0: $\mu_{white} = \mu_{yellow}$ ← mean time (in minutes) to take a test in the white room is equal to the mean time (in minutes) to take a test in the yellow room.

H_0: $\mu_{white} = \mu_{blue}$ ← mean time (in minutes) to take a test in the white room is equal to the mean time (in minutes) to take a test in the blue room.

H_0: $\mu_{yellow} = \mu_{blue}$ ← mean time (in minutes) to take a test in the yellow room is equal to the mean time (in minutes) to take a test in the blue room.

Although three groups and three *t* tests may not sound like a bad proposition, if we were comparing seven groups, for example, we would need 21 separate *t* tests. Not only would 21 tests be time-consuming, but also, completing 21 statistical tests would be inherently flawed because in each *t* test we accept a 5% chance of our conclusion being wrong (when we test for *p* = 0.05). So, in 21 tests, we would *expect* (by probability) that one test would give us a false result. And frankly, we do not like those odds at all.

In a one-way ANOVA, the null hypothesis reads like this:

H_0: $\mu_{white} = \mu_{yellow} = \mu_{blue}$ ← mean time (in minutes) to take a test in the white room is equal to the mean time (in minutes) to take a test in the yellow room, which is equal to the mean time (in minutes) to take a test in the blue room.

Your hypothesis would then predict that at least one pair (white and yellow, white and blue, and yellow and blue) is not equal, or

$$H_1: \mu_{white} \neq \mu_{yellow} \neq \mu_{blue}$$

So instead of doing 3 tests or 21 tests, the one-way ANOVA lets us perform one simple test to examine differences.

One-Way ANOVA Assumptions

Now that we have discussed the basic aspects of the one-way ANOVA itself, we will look at the underlying assumptions of the one-way ANOVA:

1. The dependent variable must be an interval/ratio variable.
2. The independent variable must be a nominal variable.
3. The dependent variable (in this case, time to take the test in minutes) should be normally distributed in the independent variable levels (white room, yellow room, and blue room). Specifically, the distributions for all of the populations should not have a high skewness or kurtosis. In a real-world situation, it is recommended that each nominal category have at least 30 participants. (Because we are only performing an example in this chapter, we do not have 30 participants in each category to make the math easier to compute.)
4. The populations for all groupings in the independent variable (white room, yellow room, and blue room) should have equal variances. If the population in the largest group has no more than 1.5 times the number of participants than the number of participants in the smallest group, you will not violate the homogeneity assumption (Stevens, 1986).
5. Finally, the participants contributing data should represent a random sample drawn from the population of interest.

These assumptions are extremely important because if even one assumption is violated, the meaning of the one-way ANOVA is lost.

FIGURE 17.1
One-Way ANOVA
Formula

$$SS_{total} = \sum x^2 - \frac{G^2}{N} \qquad df_{total} = N - 1$$

$$SS_{between} = \frac{\sum T^2}{n} - \frac{G^2}{N} \qquad df_{between} = k - 1$$

$$SS_{within} = \sum SS_{inside\ each\ treatment} \qquad df_{within} = N - k$$

$$F = \frac{MS_{between}}{MS_{within}} \quad \text{Where each } MS = \frac{SS}{df}$$

One-Way ANOVA Formula

Now that we have explained what a one-way ANOVA is and what the basic assumptions of the one-way ANOVA are, we can look at the basic one-way ANOVA formula given in Figure 17.1. Do not be scared by this formula. It is just as easy to calculate a one-way ANOVA as it was to calculate a chi-square or t test. Most of the one-way ANOVA formula is simply computing some basic descriptive statistics, like we did in Chapter 15, and then plugging those answers into the formula as we go along. We do want to mention that in this formula you'll see two new letters T (treatment) and G (group). Treatment essentially means that we're examining the summed scores for each of the three classrooms separately (white score, yellow score, and blue score). Group means that we're looking at the total sum of the three separate classrooms (white, yellow, and blue).

STEP-BY-STEP APPROACH TO THE ONE-WAY ANOVA

As we discussed earlier, the basic hypothesis being examined in this example is that there is a difference in the time it takes participants to complete a test in a white room versus a yellow room versus a blue room. Figure 17.2 portrays the raw data from all 12 participants in this study.

Step 1

The first step in computing a one-way ANOVA is to determine the X for each of the three groups. To find the *sum* or T for each group, you add up each participant's score (in minutes). Figure 17.3 illustrates how this is accomplished.

White	Yellow	Blue
5	5	8
6	6	10
5	10	10
4	7	8

FIGURE 17.2
Participant Scores from
Chapter Example

FIGURE 17.3
One-Way ANOVA
(Step 1)

	White	Yellow	Blue
	5	5	8
	6	6	10
	5	10	10
	4	7	8
T =	$5 + 6 + 5 + 4 = 20$	$5 + 6 + 10 + 7 = 28$	$8 + 10 + 10 + 8 = 36$

FIGURE 17.4
Sum of Squares
Between Formula

$$SS_{between} = \frac{\sum T^2}{n} - \frac{G^2}{N} \quad df_{between} = k - 1$$

Step 2

In this step and the next, you will calculate the part of the formula represented in Figure 17.4. The computed value you will attain in this step is called the **sum of squares between** ($SS_{between}$). The $SS_{between}$ measures two different phenomena: (1) the differences between the groups that have been caused by the treatment effects (i.e., the difference in time it takes the participants to complete the 10-item test caused by being in a white, yellow, or blue room) and (2) the differences between the treatments that are simply a result of chance. In this step, we calculate the first part of the $SS_{between}$ formula ($\sum T^2/n$).

To compute this formula, simply take the T values computed in Figure 17.4, square them, and then divide them by the number of participants in each column (4). So, to compute the formula ($\sum T^2/n$) for the white room group, you take the T value found in step 1 (20) and square that value ($20 \times 20 = 400$). You then take 400 and divide it by n (the number of participants in the group or 4), or $400/4 = 100$. So, for the white group, $\sum T^2/n = 100$. You now compute this number for the other two groups as well:

$$\sum T^2/n$$
$$\left((20)^2/4\right) + \left((28)^2/4\right) + \left((36)^2/4\right)$$
$$(400/4) + (784/4) + (1,296/4)$$
$$100 + 196 + 324$$
$$620$$

So, $\sum T^2/n = 620$.

Step 3

We now need to compute the part of the $SS_{between}$ formula that is represented by G^2/N. G is calculated by taking the T values found in step 1 and adding them together to create a summed total. The T score for the white room group was 20; the T score for the yellow group was 28; and the T score for the blue group was 36. When you add these three numbers together ($20 + 28 + 36$), you get a total of 84. Now that we have attained G, we must square that number ($84^2 = 7,056$). The number we get for G^2 is then divided by the total number of participants in the study ($N = 12$), or $7,056/12 = 588$.

Step 4

The next step of the one-way ANOVA will give us the actual value for $SS_{between}$. To compute $SS_{between}$, you must take the value created in step 2 (620) and subtract it from the value created in step 3 (588):

$$(\Sigma T^2/n) - (G^2/N)$$

$$620 - 588 = 32$$

So, for our example, $SS_{between} = 32$.

Step 5

In this step, we determine another important part of the one-way ANOVA puzzle called the **sum of squares within** (SS_{within}). Figure 17.5 is the formula portion for the SS_{within}.

Inside each condition or group tested in a one-way ANOVA, we have participants who are treated exactly the same. In other words, the researcher treats all of the participants who take the test in the white room, for example, the same, so the researcher does nothing that could cause the individuals to have different scores within that room. When you look at the scores from Figure 17.2, you will see that people in the white room took the test at different speeds. Why did the four people in the white room take the test at different speeds? Well, the only answer that is plausible is that the people in the white room took the test at different speeds purely by chance. The SS_{within} provides a measure of how much difference in the time it took to take the 10-item test used in this study is simply a result of chance.

To calculate SS_{within}, you must first find the mean for each group. Take the T value computed for each group in Figure 17.3 and then divide the T value by the number of participants in that group ($n = 4$). For example, in the white group, the T value is equal to 20 and there were 4 participants in the group, so to find the mean, you simply divide 20 by 4 (20/4 = 5). You then repeat this procedure for the other two groups: yellow (28/4 = 7) and blue (36/4 = 9).

Once you have the averages computed, you then subtract the individual scores for each participant in a group from the group average and then square that number (like we did in Chapter 14 when we first introduced the sum of squares concept). So, for the white group you take the first participant's score (5) and subtract that score from the mean score (5), or 5 – 5 = 0. You then take this score (0) and square it. Of course, 0 × 0 is always going to equal 0. Let's follow the same procedure for the second participant in the white group. Take the second participant's score (6) and subtract that from the mean score (5), or 5 – 6 = –1. You then take this score (–1) and square it. Of course, –1 * –1 is always going to equal 1. Do not forget, when you multiply a negative number by a negative number,

$$SS_{within} = \Sigma SS_{inside\ each\ treatment} \qquad df_{within} = N - k$$

FIGURE 17.5
Sum of Squares Within Formula

the two negatives cancel each other out. Let's now take the third participant's score (5) in the white group and subtract that from the mean score (5), or $5 - 5 = 0$. You then take this score (0) and square it. Of course, 0×0 is always going to equal 0. Last, we can take the fourth participant's score (4) in the white group and subtract it from the mean score (5), or $5 - 4 = 1$. You then take this score (1) and square it. Of course, 1×1 is always going to equal 1. You then add these four scores together: $0 + 1 + 0 + 1 = 2$, so the sum of squares for the white room is 2. You can now repeat these steps for both the yellow and the blue room groups. This process has been completed in Figure 17.6.

To compute the overall score for the SS_{within}, you simply take the three scores calculated in Figure 17.6 and add them together $(2 + 14 + 4 = 20)$. In our example, $SS_{within} = 20$.

Step 6

In this step, we determine the sum of squares total (SS_{total}). To calculate SS_{total}, you simply add $SS_{between}$ from step 4 (32) and SS_{within} from step 5 (20) together:

$$SS_{total} = SS_{between} + SS_{within}$$

$$32 + 20 = 52$$

So for this example, $SS_{total} = 52$.

FIGURE 17.6
Computing the Sum of Squares Within

	Group Average		Participant's Score				
White Room	5	–	5	=	0^2	=	0
	5	–	6	=	-1^2	=	1
	5	–	5	=	0^2	=	0
	5	–	4	=	1^2	=	1
					Sum		2

	Group Average		Participant's Score				
Yellow Room	7	–	5	=	2^2	=	4
	7	–	6	=	1^2	=	1
	7	–	10	=	-3^2	=	9
	7	–	7	=	0^2	=	0
					Sum		14

	Group Average		Participant's Score				
Blue Room	9	–	8	=	1^2	=	1
	9	–	10	=	-1^2	=	1
	9	–	10	=	-1^2	=	1
	9	–	8	=	1^2	=	1
					Sum		4

Step 7

Now, we must compute the degrees of freedom for the one-way ANOVA. The one-way ANOVA has two different types of degrees of freedom: **degrees of freedom between** (df between) and **degrees of freedom within** (df within). To calculate the df between, the formula is $K - 1$, or the number of groups (white, yellow, and blue) being examined in your study minus one ($3 - 1 = 2$). So, in this example, the df between = 2. To calculate the df within, the formula is $N - K$, or the total number of participants in a study (12 in our example) minus the number of groups (3 in our example) being examined in your study ($12 - 3 = 9$). So, in this example, the df within = 9.

Step 8

We can now calculate the two mean squares (MS) in this example. To calculate the **mean squares between** ($MS_{between}$), you divide $SS_{between}$ calculated in step 4 (32) by the df between calculated in step 7 (2), or $32/2 = 16$. So, in this example, $MS_{between} = 16$. To calculate the **mean squares within** (MS_{within}), you divide SS_{within} calculated in step 5 (20) by the df between calculated in step 7 (9), or $20/9 = 2.22$. So, in this example, $MS_{within} = 2.22$.

Step 9

Once we have $MS_{between}$ and MS_{within}, we can calculate what is called the F ratio, or **F test** value. To calculate the F ratio, we simply divide MS_{within} (2.22) from $MS_{between}$ (16):

$$F = MS_{between} / MS_{within}$$
$$16/2.22 = 7.21$$

So, for our current example, the F value = 7.21.

The F value lets us know that the differences among the three groups (white room, yellow room, and blue room) and the time it took the participants to take a 10-item test is more than 7% larger than we would expect to see randomly occurring. This could indicate that, yes, the participants took the test at different speeds in the differently colored rooms (white, yellow, and blue). However, to truly determine whether a difference exists, we must determine whether the one-way ANOVA is statistically significant.

Step 10

Figure 17.7 contains the critical value table for the F distribution. You will notice that this critical value table is different than the others we have already seen. On this chart, the df numbers run along the top and down the left side of the table. The df numbers that run along the top of the chart (or the columns) represent the degrees of freedom numerator (df between), and the df numbers that are on the left-hand side of the chart (or the rows) represent the degrees of freedom denominator (df within).

There are two separate charts presented in Figure 17.7. The first chart examines the critical values at $p < 0.05$, and the second chart examines the critical values at $p < 0.01$. To analyze this chart, we need to remember the df between (2) and df within (9) we calculated in step 7. To determine our critical value to compare to our calculated value (7.20), we must go to the second column (df between) and then go down to the ninth row (df within). So our critical value for F at $p < 0.05$ is 4.26. Since our calculated F value (7.20) is larger than the critical value of 4.26, we are statistically significant at the $p < 0.05$ level. To determine whether we are statistically significant at the $p < 0.01$ significance level (the second chart in Figure 17.7), we again go to the second column (df between) and then go down to the ninth row (df within) to find the critical value, which is 8.02. Because our calculated F value (7.20) is smaller than the critical value of 8.02, we are not statistically significant at the $p < 0.01$ level.

Step 11

The last step of the one-way ANOVA calculation is to create an ANOVA summary table. Figure 17.8 is the ANOVA summary table for this example.

The ANOVA summary table arranges the information that you have calculated in an easy-to-understand chart format. All of the basic information you need about the calculation of a one-way ANOVA can be found on this chart.

$\alpha = .05$									
	1	2	3	4	5	6	7	8	9	10
1	161.00	200.00	216.00	225.00	230.00	234.00	237.00	239.00	241.00	242.00
2	18.51	19.00	19.16	19.25	19.30	19.33	19.36	19.37	19.38	19.39
3	10.13	9.55	9.28	9.12	9.01	8.94	8.88	8.84	8.81	8.78
4	7.71	6.94	6.59	6.39	6.26	6.16	6.09	6.04	6.00	5.96
5	6.61	5.79	5.41	5.19	5.05	4.95	4.88	4.82	4.78	4.74
6	5.99	5.14	4.76	4.53	4.39	4.28	4.21	4.15	4.10	4.06
7	5.59	4.74	4.35	4.12	3.97	3.87	3.79	3.73	3.68	3.63
8	5.32	4.46	4.07	3.84	3.69	3.58	3.50	3.44	3.39	3.34
9	5.12	4.26	3.86	3.63	3.48	3.37	3.29	3.23	3.18	3.13
10	4.96	4.10	3.71	3.48	3.33	3.22	3.14	3.07	3.02	2.97
11	4.84	3.98	3.59	3.36	3.20	3.09	3.01	2.95	2.90	2.86
12	4.75	3.88	3.49	3.26	3.11	3.00	2.92	2.85	2.80	2.76
13	4.67	3.80	3.41	3.18	3.02	2.92	2.84	2.77	2.72	2.67
14	4.60	3.74	3.34	3.11	2.96	2.85	2.77	2.70	2.65	2.60
15	4.54	3.68	3.29	3.06	2.90	2.79	2.70	2.64	2.59	2.55
16	4.49	3.63	3.24	3.01	2.85	2.74	2.66	2.59	2.54	2.49
17	4.45	3.59	3.20	2.96	2.81	2.70	2.62	2.55	2.50	2.45
18	4.41	3.55	3.16	2.93	2.77	2.66	2.58	2.51	2.46	2.41
19	4.38	3.52	3.13	2.90	2.74	2.63	2.55	2.48	2.43	2.38
20	4.35	3.49	3.10	2.87	2.71	2.60	2.52	2.45	2.40	2.35

FIGURE 17.7
Critical Values of the F Distribution

	1	2	3	4	5	6	7	8	9	10
					$\alpha = .01$					
1	4052.00	4999.00	5403.00	5625.00	5764 .00	5859.00	928.00	5981.00	6022.00	6056.00
2	98.49	99.01	99.17	99.25	99.30	99.33	99.34	99.36	99.38	99.40
3	34.12	30.81	29.46	28.71	28.24	27.91	27.67	27.49	27.34	27.23
4	21.20	18.00	16.69	15.98	15.52	15.21	14.98	14.80	14.66	14.54
5	16.26	13.27	12.06	11.39	10.97	10.67	10.45	10.27	10.15	10.05
6	13.74	10.92	9.78	9.15	8.75	8.47	8.26	8.10	7.98	7.87
7	12.25	9.55	8.45	7.85	7.46	7.19	7.00	6.84	6.71	6.62
8	11.26	8.65	7.59	7.01	6.63	6.37	6.19	6.03	5.91	5.82
9	10.56	8.02	6.99	6.42	6.06	5.80	5.62	5.47	5.35	5.26
10	10.04	7.56	6.55	5.99	5.64	5.39	5.21	5.06	4.95	4.85
11	9.65	7.20	6.22	5.67	5.32	5.07	4.88	4.74	4.63	4.54
12	9.33	6.93	5.95	5.41	5.06	4.82	4.65	4.50	4.39	4.30
13	9.07	6.70	5.74	5.20	4.86	4.62	4.44	4.30	4.19	4.10
14	8.86	6.51	5.56	5.03	4.69	4.46	4.28	4.14	4.03	3.94
15	8.68	6.36	5.42	4.89	4.56	4.32	4.14	4.00	3.89	3.80
16	8.53	6.23	5.29	4.77	4.44	4.20	4.03	3.89	3.78	3.69
17	8.40	6.11	5.18	4.67	4.34	4.10	3.93	3.79	3.68	3.59
18	8.28	6.01	5.09	4.58	4.25	4.01	3.85	3.71	3.60	3.51
19	8.18	5.93	5.01	4.50	4.17	3.94	3.77	3.63	3.52	3.43
20	8.10	5.85	4.94	4.43	4.10	3.87	3.71	3.56	3.45	3.37

The entries in this table were computed by the authors.

FIGURE 17.7
Continued

Source	df	SS	MS	F	p
Between	2	32	16	7.20	.05
Within	9	20	2.22		
Total	11	108			

FIGURE 17.8
ANOVA Summary
Table

COMPUTER PRINTOUTS OF THE ONE-WAY ANOVA

Now that we have conducted a one-way ANOVA by hand, we will examine what output from SPSS looks like.

Using SPSS to compute a one-way ANOVA is fairly easy as long as you follow the instructions, so let's get started. First, open SPSS and then locate the file on the textbook's website (https://oup-arc.com/wrench) in the SPSS folder called "One-Way ANOVA." When you open this file you will see two variables listed: "color" and "time." Color is the name given to the variable that contains the three room colors. Note, however, that the colors are only represented by the numbers 1 (white), 2 (yellow), and 3 (blue). Remember, a statistics program can only understand numbers, so it is up to you as a researcher to remember how you classified the two groups when you are

FIGURE 17.9
One-Way
ANOVA Main

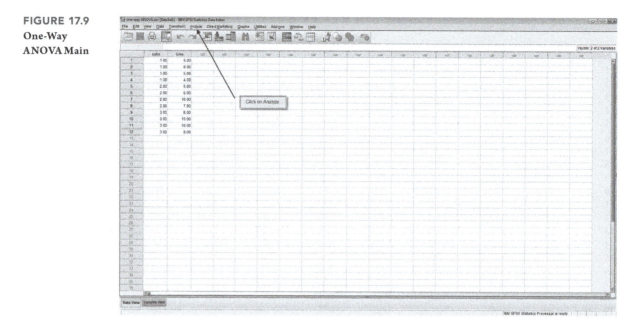

FIGURE 17.10
Univariate GLM Menu

inputting the data. The time variable is the amount of time in minutes that it took each participant to complete the 10-item quiz.

To conduct the one-way ANOVA, go to the menu bar at the top of your screen, and click on "Analyze" (Figure 17.9). When you click Analyze, a drop-down menu will appear. Go to the category "General Linear Model" on this menu, scroll over the arrow, and another menu will appear to the right. The first option on the General Linear Model menu is "Univariate"; click on it (Figure 17.10). The "Univariate" dialogue box then appears on your screen (Figure 17.11a). On this screen, you will see six boxes. The first box, on the left side of the Univariate dialogue box, will contain your variables. To the right, on top, is the "Dependent Variable" box, which is where dependent variables are placed (in this case, time). To place the variable "time" in this box, click and highlight in blue the variable time. When time is highlighted blue, click the right arrow button next to the Dependent Variable box (Figure 17.11b). Below that box is the "Fixed Factor(s)" box, which is where you place your nominal independent variable (color). To place the variable "color" in this box, click and highlight in blue the variable color. When color is highlighted blue, click the right arrow button next to the "Fixed Factor(s)" box (Figure 17.11c).

To the right of those boxes, you will see the buttons "Model," "Contrasts," "Plots," "Post Hoc," "Save," and "Options." Click on Post Hoc. The "Univariate: Post Hoc Multiple Comparisons for Observed Means" dialogue box then appears on your screen (Figure 17.11d). First, you must choose the Factor(s) you want to compute a post hoc analysis for by selecting the variable (color) and clicking the arrow between the "Factor(s)" box and the "Post Hoc Tests for" box. After you have sent your Factor

FIGURE 17.11A
Main Dialogue Box

FIGURE 17.11B
Move the Dependent Variable (DV) to the DV Box

FIGURE 17.11C
Move the Independent Variable to the "Fixed Factor(s)" Box

FIGURE 17.11D
Univariate Post Hoc Dialogue Box

variable over to the Post Hoc Tests for box, you will note that the various post hoc tests are now active (Figure 17.11e). In this box, there are two groupings for post hoc tests. One grouping is for "Equal Variances Assumed," and one is for "Equal Variances Not Assumed." We will go into more detail in a few minutes about post hoc tests, but for now, put a checkmark in the box next to the "Tukey" post hoc test under the "Equal Variances Assumed" list (it is the second one in the second column). Once "Tukey" is checked (Figure 17.11f), you can click the button at the bottom of the screen marked "Continue."

You should now have returned to the "Univariate" dialogue box shown in Figure 17.11c. Press the button at the right side of the dialogue box marked "Options." In the "Options" dialogue box that now appears, you will find two boxes on top and a variety of options at the bottom (Figure 17.11g). To have any options performed, you must select the variable (color) you want options for on the left in the "Factor(s) and Factor Interactions" box and then send the variable over to the "Display Means for" box on the right by selecting the variable and pushing the arrow button between the two boxes. Once the variable color is in the Display Means for box, we can then select a variety of options at the bottom (Figure 17.11h). The bottom box is called the "Display" box and contains two items we must check at this point: "Descriptive Statistics" and "Estimates of effect size." Once you have selected these (Figure 17.11i), click on the "Continue" button. Once you are back to the Univariate dialogue box, click the "OK" button to run the results, which results (excluding the post hoc) can be seen in Figure 17.12.

The results for the SPSS printouts are straightforward at this point. If you examine the three tables printed in Figure 17.12, you will see that the first table contains information

FIGURE 17.11E
Shift Independent Variable to "Post Hoc Tests for:" Box

FIGURE 17.11F
Select Desired Post Hoc Analyses

FIGURE 17.11G
"Univariate Options" Dialogue Box

FIGURE 17.11H
Send Independent Variable (Color) to "Display Means for:" Box

about the independent variable, the second table contains simple descriptive statistics for the dependent variable, and the third table contains much of the same information as the ANOVA summary table we created in step 11 earlier in this chapter. The third row, "COLOR," is the row that contains the information we calculated by hand earlier in this chapter. The major difference between the information contained in the SPSS ANOVA summary table and the one in Figure 17.8 is that the SPSS table gives you an

FIGURE 17.11I
Select Desired Options

exact calculation of the significance level ($p = 0.014$) and also calculates the effect size for the difference seen in the test ($\eta^2 = 0.615$). **Eta-square (η^2)** ranges from 0 to 1, with 0 indicating that there is no difference and 1 indicating that there is a difference between the groups but not a difference in scores within the groups.

In this example, our effect size was 0.62, so we could say that there is a large proportion of the variance within the dependent variable (time it took to take the test) related to one of the groups (white, yellow, or blue). Based on this, we can conclude that a large portion of the time it took someone to fill out the survey was dependent on the color of room the participant was in. However, at this point, we cannot say which room had the most impact, so a multiple comparison test is needed.

Univariate Analysis of Variance

Between-Subjects Factors

		Value Label	N
Room	1.00	White	4
Color	2.00	Yellow	4
	3.00	Blue	4

Descriptive Statistics

Dependent Variable: Time (in minutes) to finish the test.

Room Color	Mean	Std. Deviation	N
White	5.0000	.8165	4
Yellow	7.0000	2.1602	4
Blue	9.0000	1.1547	4
Total	7.0000	2.1742	12

Test of Between-Subjects Effects

Dependent Variable: Time (in minutes) to finish the test.

Source	Type III Sum of Squares	df	Mean Square	F	Sig.	Eta Squares
Corrected Model	32.000[a]	2	16.000	7.200	.014	.615
Intercept	588.000	1	588.000	264.600	.000	.967
COLOR	32.000	2	16.000	7.200	.014	.615
Error	20.000	9	2.222			
Total	640.000	12				
Corrected Total	52.000	11				

[a]. R Squared = .615 (Adjusted R Squared = .530)

FIGURE 17.12
SPSS One-Way ANOVA Results

Interpreting Eta-Square (η^2)

According to IBM, the makers of SPSS, here is how you should interpret η^2:

$\eta^2 \leq 0.04$ —,statistically significant, but small or weak

$0.04 < \eta^2 \leq .36$ —medium or moderate effect size

$\eta^2 > 0.36$ <—large or strong effect size

MULTIPLE COMPARISON TESTS

One part of the one-way ANOVA that we did not calculate by hand is the **multiple comparison test**. All we know is that our one-way ANOVA test is significant (people take tests in different colored rooms at different speeds), but we do not know where those differences are. Maybe people in white rooms take tests slower than people in blue rooms but not slower than people in yellow rooms. Maybe people in yellow rooms take tests at similar speeds to people in blue rooms, but people in white rooms take tests faster than people in blue rooms. If you remember the null hypothesis we created at the beginning of this chapter, we wrote: "H_0: $\mu_{white} = \mu_{yellow} = \mu_{blue}$ ← mean time (in minutes) to take a test in the white room is equal to the mean time (in minutes) to take a test in the yellow room, which is equal to the mean time (in minutes) to take a test in the blue room." Your hypothesis would then predict that *at least one of the pairs* (white and yellow, white and blue, and yellow and blue) is not equal, or "H_1: $\mu_{white} \neq \mu_{yellow} \neq \mu_{blue}$." (Note that the italic portion in the last sentence emphasizes that at least one pair will be different, but not all three different from each other.)

In the *t* test, we compared the two groups directly to each other, which we can also do with a one-way ANOVA if, and only if, the nominal variable being used as the independent variable has two groups (e.g., females and males). If the nominal variable has more than two groups (like our example), the one-way ANOVA will determine whether at least one pair within a group differs from each other in their means on a dependent variable. However, the one-way ANOVA will not say that people in the white room took more time to take the test than people in the blue room. To determine where the difference lies, a second test, the post hoc (after the fact) multiple comparison test, is conducted, which compares white and yellow, white and blue, and yellow and blue.

Remember from the SPSS discussion earlier that when you entered into the "One-Way ANOVA: Post Hoc Multiple Comparisons" dialogue box, SPSS provides you with 18 different types of multiple comparison tests broken into two groups: "Equal Variances Assumed" and "Equal Variances Not Assumed." The four most common post hoc tests for a one-way ANOVA are **Fisher's least significant difference (LSD)**, **Student Newman-Keuls (SNK)**, **Tukey's honestly significant difference test (HSD)**, and **Scheffé (Scheffé)**. The order presented here (LSD, SNK, Tukey HSD, and Scheffé) is a continuum from liberal to conservative post hoc tests. Liberal tests are called such because they make it easier to find significant differences between groups (white room, yellow room, and blue room). With liberal tests, however, your chance of type I error also increases, so they should always be used with caution. Conservative tests make it harder to find significant differences between groups, but you also have less chance of a type I error.

We will briefly explain the four post hoc tests. First, Fisher's LSD is the equivalent of running a series of paired *t* tests, but the alpha level is not controlled for, so the chance of compounded error is great. Second, SNK is a stepwise test for ordered means where the alpha level depends on the number of "steps apart" that each of the means are from each other. This test is great when your data consist of ranges, but it is not useful for pairwise

FIGURE 17.13
SPSS One-Way ANOVA
Post Hoc Results

Post Hoc Tests

Room Color

Multiple Comparisons

Dependent Variable: Time (in minutes) to finish the test.
Tukey HSD

(I) Room Color	(J) Room Color	Mean Difference (I-J)	Std. Error	Sig.	95% Confidence Interval	
					Lower Bound	Upper Bound
White	Yellow	−2.0000	1.0541	.195	−4.9431	.9431
	Blue	−4.0000*	1.0541	.011	−6.9431	−1.0569
Yellow	White	2.0000	1.0541	.195	−.9431	4.9431
	Blue	−2.0000	1.0541	.195	−4.9431	.9431
Blue	White	4.0000*	1.0541	.011	1.0569	6.9431
	Yellow	2.0000	1.0541	.195	−.9431	4.9431

Based on observed means.
  * The mean difference is significant at the .05 level.

Homogeneous Subsets

Time (in minutes) to finish the test.

Tukey HSD[a,b]

Room Color	N	Subset	
		1	2
White	4	5.0000	
Yellow	4	7.0000	7.0000
Blue	4		9.0000
Sig.		.195	.195

Means for groups in homogeneous subsets are displayed.
Based on Type III Sum of Squares
The error term is Mean Square(Error) = 2.222.
  [a] Uses Harmonic Mean Sample Size = 4.000.
  [b] Alpha = .05.

comparisons. Furthermore, the SNK post hoc has more power, so you are more likely to find significant pairwise comparisons (Seaman, Levin, & Serlin, 1991). However, when you attempt to increase power, you risk increasing your risk of type I error. Third, unlike the SNK, the Tukey HSD is able to test for pairwise comparisons while controlling your type I error and generating confidence intervals (Seaman et al., 1991). Finally, the Scheffé post hoc test assumes that you wish to test all possible pairs and all possible combinations of means. For example, if you have three means, then there are six possible comparisons (white vs. blue, white vs. yellow, blue vs. yellow, white + blue vs. yellow, white + yellow vs. blue, and yellow + blue vs. white). The only real reason to use the Scheffé post hoc test is if you really need to examine all six combinations. We generally recommend using the Tukey HSD. The results for the post hoc analysis we selected earlier (Tukey HSD) can be seen in Figure 17.13.

In the "Multiple Comparisons" box in Figure 17.13, we see the three colors compared to each other. The first row compares people who took the test in the white room to people who took the test in the yellow and blue rooms. The second column in the box is labeled "Mean Difference (I-J)," with "I" being the white room and "J" being both people in the yellow room and people in the blue room. In essence, what this first row is testing is whether people in the white room took more or less time to complete the 10-item test than people in the yellow room and whether people in the white room took more or less time to complete the 10-item test than people in the blue room. The first room that the white room is compared to is the yellow room. If you look in the Mean Difference column, you will note a mean difference between the two of -2.0000. If a mean difference is negative, then the mean time spent taking the 10-item test in the group in the I part of the column (in this case people in the white room) is less than the group it is being compared to in the J part of the column (or yellow). However, people in the white room took less time to complete the test than people in the yellow room. And the mean difference of -2.0000 means that people in the white room took the test on average 2 minutes faster than people in the yellow room. The fourth column in the printout box indicates that the significance is $p = 0.195$, which is not statistically significant. There is not a significant difference between the time it took people in the white and yellow rooms to complete the 10-item test.

We have used the first row on the Multiple Comparisons SPSS printout box to compare people in white rooms with people in yellow rooms. We now need to compare people in white rooms with people in blue rooms. On the first row, the second variable listed under "(J) Room Color" is blue. If you look in the Mean Difference column, you will see that there is a mean difference between white and blue of -4.0000. Again, this means that people in the white room took the test on average 4 minutes faster than the people in the blue room. You will note that next to the -4.0000 beside blue in the Mean Difference column is an asterisk (*). SPSS automatically flags significant multiple comparisons if they are at the $p < 0.05$ level. In this case, the significance level listed in the fourth column of the printout box was $p = 0.011$. At this point, we have found out that people in the white and yellow rooms did not complete the test at significantly different rates, but that people in the white room did complete the test significantly faster than people in the blue room. And now, there is only one other pairing that we have not examined: whether people in yellow and blue rooms took the test at different speeds.

The second row in the Multiple Comparisons SPSS printout box now has yellow in the "(I) Room Color" column and white and blue in the "(J) Room Color" column. The first comparison that can be made compares yellow to white. However, we did this comparison already, and we are not concerned with it here. All of the comparisons are done twice in the printout, so be careful not to report both sets of multiple comparisons. Once you have reported the comparison between white and yellow, you need not report it a second time. Here, we are only interested in the comparison between yellow and blue. Yet again, the mean difference between yellow and blue is –2.0000, which indicates that people in the yellow room took the test on average 2 minutes faster than people in the blue room; however, this is not a significant difference, $p = 0.195$.

APA Write-Up (Without Chart)

The write-up in American Psychological Association (APA) style for these calculations, not including a chart, would be as follows:

> This research question wanted to determine whether there was a significant difference in the color of a room (white, yellow, and blue) and the length of time (in minutes) that it took the participant to finish a 10-item test. A one-way ANOVA was calculated using the color of the room as the independent variable and length of time to finish the test (in minutes) as the dependent variable. A significant difference was noted: $F(2, 9) = 7.20$, $p = 0.014$, $\eta^2 = 0.62$. In a follow-up to this question, a Tukey HSD post hoc was conducted. The Tukey HSD post hoc indicated that there was a significant difference between people in the white room ($M = 5$, $SD = 0.82$) and people in the blue room ($M = 9$, $SD = 1.15$). However, the Tukey HSD post hoc test did not find a significant difference between people who took the test in the white room ($M = 5$, $SD = 0.82$) and people who took the test in the yellow room ($M = 7$, $SD = 2.16$), and the Tukey HSD also did not find a significant difference between people in the yellow room ($M = 7$, $SD = 2.16$) and people in the blue room ($M = 9$, $SD = 1.15$).

APA Write-Up (With Chart)

The write-up in APA style for these calculations, including a chart, would be as follows:

> This research question wanted to determine whether there was a significant difference in the color of a room (white, yellow, and blue) and the length of time (in minutes) it took the participant to finish a 10-item test. A one-way ANOVA was calculated using the color of the room as the independent variable and length of time to finish the test (in minutes) as the dependent variable. A significant difference was noted: $F(2, 9) = 7.20$, $p = 0.014$, $\eta^2 = 0.62$. In a follow-up to this question, a Tukey HSD post hoc was conducted. The unnumbered figure at the end of this chapter examines the exact differences that were noted.

Discussion of Findings

After all of the work that we have done so far in this chapter, this is the point where we get to try to make some sense out of the results. To do this, let's go back to the initial question we asked. We wanted to determine whether the color of a room (white, yellow, or blue) caused people to take a 10-item test at different speeds. After calculating the one-way ANOVA, we found that the color of a room causes people to take a 10-item test at different speeds. Based on this information, we performed a Tukey HSD post hoc analysis to see where that difference actually existed. Based on the Tukey HSD, we can say that people in white rooms and yellow rooms will take tests at roughly the same speed. We can also say that people in yellow rooms and blue rooms will take tests at roughly the same speed. However, we found out that people in white rooms finish tests faster than people in blue rooms. Now that we have completed a hypothetical example of a one-way ANOVA, we will examine results from an actual sample.

POLITICAL AFFILIATION AND HUMOR ASSESSMENT

For this example, we are using the large dataset that was collected for this book and can be found on the textbook website. The purpose of this example was to see whether differences existed among political affiliations (Democrat, Republican, other, or not registered to vote) and an individual's humor assessment. Call this an "Are Democrats really funnier than Republicans?" question. To test for a possible difference among Democrats, Republicans, people belonging to other political parties, and people not registered to vote on the humor assessment inventory, we used the nominal variable politics (independent variable) and the interval variable humor assessment (dependent variable). Figure 17.14 represents the findings from the SPSS results.

APA Write-Up
The write-up in APA style for this example would be as follows:

> This research question tests for a possible difference among Democrats, Republicans, people belonging to other political parties, and people not registered to vote on their reported levels of humor assessment. A one-way ANOVA was calculated using the four political party groupings as the independent variable and humor assessment as the dependent variable. The test was not significant: $F(3, 312) = 0.37$, $p = 0.78$.

Discussion
For the test examining political affiliation and humor assessment, the p value was greater than 0.05, so the test was not statistically significant. It is important to note that once a test is reported as not statistically significant, we report neither the eta-square nor the post hoc analysis. We do not report the eta-square because it is an effect size. And when we say that the test is not statistically significant, we say that there is no effect, so reporting the effect size is meaningless. The same is also true for why we do not report post hoc analyses. We only run a post hoc analysis if the overall model is statistically significant. Once the one-way ANOVA model is shown to be not statistically significant, there is no reason to run a post hoc analysis.

Univariate Analysis of Variance

Between-Subjects Factors

		Value Label	N
Political Affiliation	1.00	Democrat	217
	2.00	Republican	217
	3.00	Other	131
	4.00	Not Registered to Vote	63

Descriptive Statistics

Dependent Variable: Humor Assessment

Political Affiliation	Mean	Std. Deviation	N
Democrat	63.7373	9.63405	217
Republican	62.8940	9.84523	217
Other	63.4198	9.08418	131
Not Registered to Vote	62.7143	8.84532	63
Total	63.2771	9.50646	628

Tests of Between-Subjects Effects

Dependent Variable: Humor Assessment

Source	Type III Sum of Squares	df	Mean Square	F	Sig.	Partial Eta Squared
Corrected Model	100.434[a]	3	33.478	.369	.775	.002
Intercept	1952449.491	1	1952449.491	21539.183	.000	.972
politics	100.434	3	33.478	.369	.775	.002
Error	56563.355	624	90.646			
Total	2571168.000	628				
Corrected Total	56663.790	627				

[a] R Squared = .002 (Adjusted R Squared = -.003)

Estimated Marginal Means

Political Affiliation

Dependent Variable: Humor Assessment

Political Affiliation	Mean	Std. Error	95% Confidence Interval	
			Lower Bound	Upper Bound
Democrat	63.737	.646	62.468	65.007
Republican	62.894	.646	61.625	64.163
Other	63.420	.832	61.786	65.053
Not Registered to Vote	62.714	1.200	60.359	65.070

FIGURE 17.14

SPSS Results of Political Affiliation with Humor Assessment

DISCUSSION OF THE BOIARSKY, LONG, AND THAYER ARTICLE

To help you further understand the concept of the one-way ANVOA, we have included an article on the textbook's website that utilizes the one-way ANOVA in a unique way. The 1999 article by Greg Boiarsky, Marilee Long, and Greg Thayer entitled "Formal Features in Children's Science Television: Sound Effects, Visual Pace, and Topic Shifts" can be found in the folder titled "Articles." To view this article, you will need to download a copy of the Adobe Acrobat Reader (https://get.adobe.com/reader/) if you do not already have this program installed on your computer. We strongly encourage you to read the article first and then read our analysis of the article. The goal of this process is to ensure you understand how to read and interpret research results related to one-way ANOVAs.

Article Purpose

Children love television. And most of us have been raised on some form of child-centric TV. Whether it was the *Muppets, Sesame Street, Mr. Rogers,* or *Captain Kangaroo,* we all enjoyed entertainment with a lesson. More recently, a new breed of children's television has surfaced known as children's science television. The purpose of this study was to determine whether four different children's television shows (*Beakman's World, Bill Nye the Science Guy, Magic School Bus,* and *Newton's Apple*) differed in their use of sound effects per minute, cuts per minute, fades/dissolves per minute, wipes per minute, and topic shifts per minute.

Methodology

In this study, the researchers analyzed a sampling of the four children's science television shows during the 1995–1996 season. The shows were then coded to examine sound effects per minute, cuts per minute, fades/dissolves per minute, wipes per minute, and topic shifts per minute. To test for reliable program attribute coding, two independent researchers coded content pacing, sound effects, and visual pacing with Cohen's kappas ranging from 0.77 to 1.0. Although the 0.77 (content pacing's Cohen's kappas ranged from 0.77 to 0.87) is somewhat suspect (see Chapter 10 for information on intercoder reliability), all the other coding was strong.

Results

The researchers ran a series of five one-way ANOVAs using the four children's television shows (*Beakman's World, Bill Nye the Science Guy, Magic School Bus,* and *Newton's Apple*) as the independent variable and the program attributes (sound effects per minute, cuts per minute, fades/dissolves per minute, wipes per minute, and topic shifts per minute) as the dependent variables. All five of their one-way ANOVAs were significant.

One problem with this article is seen in the reporting of the post hoc analyses. Although the authors do a good job explaining which television shows they perceive to have higher levels of specific program attributes, they do not explain what type of post hoc analysis was completed. Although this article was set up nicely overall, its discussion of the post hoc analyses used needed some help.

RESEARCH OUTSIDE THE WALLS OF ACADEMIA

One-way ANOVAs are a common statistical tool for researches both inside and outside of academia. Maybe you are the head of a training and development department and you want to determine whether the time it takes to complete a task differs based on the type of training an employee has taken. For our purposes, you offer three different types of training: fully face-to-face, fully online, and a blended approach of both online and face-to-face training (one nominal variable with three levels). After people have completed their training, you could then examine the time it takes to complete a task (dependent variable).

Another example of using one-way ANOVAs outside of academia could be to test all of the major types of produce (apples, oranges, bananas, pears, other) and their sales rates. Through this one-way ANOVA, you could determine which form of produce is selling the best at your store if there is a statistical difference, or you could find out that your customers purchase produce in fairly equal amounts, when no statistical difference is found. Another use for one-way ANOVAs in corporate America is to see if different merchandise sells better. For example, you have three shirts that you're selling and you can see if the three differ in their sales. When you have a limited amount of shelf space, knowing what your customers want can be beneficial.

A third example of using a one-way ANOVA outside of academia would be to determine whether different groups within an organization (lower-level workers, upper-level workers, mid-level management, and upper-level management) differ in their perceptions of any number of **key performance indicators**, or quantifiable measures that help organizational decision makers evaluate organizational performance (e.g., meeting or exceeding strategic and organizational goals). For example, you could look for differences among these four groups on job satisfaction, employee motivation, productivity, and so on.

Post Hoc Analysis of Test Time and Room Color

Room Color	N	M	SD	White	Yellow
White	4	5.0	0.82		
Yellow	4	7.0	2.16	NS	
Blue	4	9.0	2.17	*	NS

Note: NS = nonsignificant differences between pair means; * = significance using the Tukey HSD procedure.

CONCLUSION

In this chapter, we have examined how to compute a one-way ANOVA by hand, how to compute and interpret computer results of a one-way ANOVA in SPSS, and how to write up a one-way ANOVA using APA style. We have seen the one-way ANOVA used in several different examples. Appendix E (available on the textbook's website) includes further discussion of the different types of ANOVAs.

KEY TERMS

Degrees of freedom (df) between p. 499

Degrees of freedom (df) within p. 499

Eta-square (η^2) p. 505

F test p. 499

Fisher's least significant difference p. 507

General linear model p. 493

Key performance indicators p. 514

Mean squares between p. 499

Mean squares within p. 499

Multiple comparison tests p. 507

One-way analysis of variance p. 492

Scheffé p. 507

Student Newman–Keuls p. 507

Sum of squares between p. 496

Sum of squares within p. 497

Tukey's honestly significant difference test p. 507

REFERENCES

Boiarsky, G., Long, M., & Thayer, G. (1999). Formal features in children's science television: Sound effects, visual pace, and topic shifts. *Communication Research Reports, 16,* 185–192.

IBM (n..d.). Eta-squared. Retrieved from https://www.ibm.com/support/knowledgecenter/en/SS4QC9/com.ibm.solutions.wa_an_overview.2.0.0.doc/etasquared.html

Seaman, M. A., Levin, J. R., & Serlin, R. C. (1991). New developments in pairwise multiple comparisons: Some powerful and practicable procedures. *Psychological Bulletin, 110,* 577–586.

Stevens, J. (1986). *Applied multivariate statistics for the social sciences.* Hillsdale, NJ: Erlbaum.

FURTHER READING

Abramson, J. H., & Abramson, Z. H. (2001). *Making sense of data: A self-instruction manual on the interpretation of epidemiological data* (3rd ed.). New York, NY: Oxford University Press.

Bruning, J. L., & Kintz, B. L. (1997). *Computational handbook of statistics* (4th ed.). New York, NY: Longman.

Cortina, J. M., & Nouri, H. (1999). *Effect size for ANOVA designs.* Thousand Oaks, CA: Sage.

Fox, J., & Weisberg, S. (2011). *An R companion to applied regression* (2nd ed.). Los Angeles, CA: Sage.

Gravetter, F. J., & Wallnau, L. B. (2000). *Statistics for the behavioral sciences* (5th ed.). Belmont, CA: Wadsworth/Thomson Learning.

Green, S. B., & Salkind, N. J. (2017). *Using SPSS for Windows and Macintosh: Analyzing and understanding data* (8th ed.). New York, NY: Pearson.

Hocking, J. E., Stacks, D. W., & McDermott, S. T. (2003). *Communication research* (3rd ed.). Boston, MA: Allyn & Bacon.

Hogan, T. P. (2010). *Bare-bones R: A brief introductory guide.* Los Angeles, CA: Sage.

Howell, D. C. (1997). *Statistical methods for psychology* (4th ed.). Belmont, CA: Duxbury Press.

Iversen, G. R., & Norpoth, H. (2004). *Analysis of variance* (2nd ed.). Thousand Oaks, CA: Sage.

Keller, D. K. (2006). *The Tao of statistics: A path to understanding (with no math).* Thousand Oaks, CA: Sage.

Muenchen, R. A. (2009). *R for SAS and SPSS users.* New York, NY: Springer.

Salkind, N. J. (2017). *Statistics for people who (think they) hate statistics* (6th ed.). Thousand Oaks, CA: Sage.

Scheffé, H. (1959). *The analysis of variance.* New York, NY: Wiley.

Singleton, R. A., Jr., & Straits, B. C. (2017). *Approach to social research* (6th ed.). New York, NY: Oxford University Press.

Tabachnick, B. G., & Fidell, L. S. (2013). *Using multivariate statistics* (6th ed.). Boston, MA: Pearson.

Trochim, W. M. K. (2000). *The research methods knowledge base* (2nd ed.). Cincinnati, OH: Atomic Dog. http://www.socialresearchmethods.net/

Turner, J. R., & Thayer, J. (2001). *Introduction to analysis of variance: Design, analysis, & interpretation.* Thousand Oaks, CA: Sage.

Weiss, D. J. (2005). *Analysis of variance and functional measurement: A practical guide.* New York, NY: Oxford University Press.

18

Correlation

CHAPTER OBJECTIVES

1. Describe the different types of relationships (positive, negative, curvilinear, and neutral).

2. Calculate a correlation by hand.

3. Conduct a correlation using Statistical Package for the Social Sciences (SPSS).

4. Interpret large correlation tables.

5. Analyze the use of the correlations in the articles by Chesebro (1999) and Punyanunt (2000).

In the previous chapter, we examined one-way analysis of variance (ANOVA), which used one nominal variable (with two or more groups) and one interval/ratio variable. In fact, the first three tests that we have examined (chi-square, t test, and one-way ANOVA) all used nominal variables to examine differences between groups. The correlation, however, is not a difference test, so it does not use nominal variables at all. Instead, the Pearson product-moment **correlation** (**r**) uses two interval/ratio variables.

The Pearson product-moment correlation coefficient (r) is a measure of the degree to which two quantitative variables (Likert/ratio) are linearly related in a sample (i.e., changes in one variable correspond to changes in another variable). To conduct a Pearson product-moment correlation, a researcher must obtain two scores (one for each variable) from each participant. If the correlation coefficient (r) is significant, then some type of relationship between the two variables exists. However, if the correlation coefficient (r) is not significant, then we cannot draw any conclusions about the nature of the relationship between the two variables.

CASE STUDY INTRODUCTION

Let's look at a communication-related example in which the Pearson product-moment correlation could be used. Many people around the world suffer from communication apprehension (CA). As we talked about in Chapter 6, CA can affect people in their interpersonal relationships, in health care, in organizations, and in their intimate relationships. One area that CA clearly affects is one's ability to give speeches in a public setting. So in this example, we have a researcher who is studying the relationship between a participant's score on the Personal Report of Communication Apprehension–24 (PRCA-24) and her or his change in heart rate while giving an impromptu speech—that is, a speech with no time for preparation.

The researcher first has the participants fill out the PRCA-24. Next, the participants are hooked up to a machine that monitors and records their heart rates. The participants are then asked to speak for 5 minutes about why they did or did not vote in the last election. The researcher records the participants' heart rates at the beginning of their speeches and throughout the speech, and notes the highest heart rate achieved while speaking. After the fact, the researcher takes the highest heart rate and subtracts the baseline heart rate to obtain a figure called heart rate change. The researcher is determining whether people who have higher scores on the PRCA-24 (interval variable) have faster heart rates (ratio variable because heart rate change could be equal to 0) while giving a speech than people who have lower levels of CA while giving a speech.

CORRELATION BACKGROUND INFORMATION

Before we can calculate the correlation between CA and heart rate change, some basic concepts related to correlations must be discussed. The purpose of a correlation is to determine the relationship between two independent variables. The purpose of a correlation is to measure whether as the score on one variable changes (goes up or down), the score on a second variable also changes (goes up or down). The four types of relationships are illustrated in Figure 18.1.

Types of Relationships

In statistics, four types of relationships are theoretically possible. These are positive, negative, curvilinear, and neutral.

The first relationship a researcher can find between two variables is called a **positive relationship**, or positive correlation. Figure 18.1a is an example of a positive correlation for two variables: humor assessment and popularity. This example is a

(a) Positive Relationship

(b) Negative Relationship

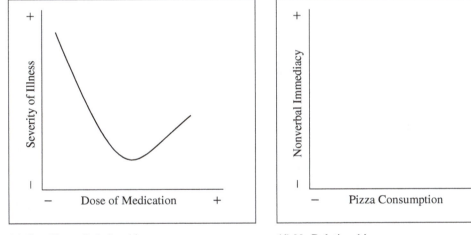

(c) Curvilinear Relationship

(d) No Relationship

FIGURE 18.1
Four Types of Relationships

positive relationship because as a person's use of interpersonal humor increases, so does her or his popularity. In other words, this relationship shows that the more humorous a person is, the more popular he or she will be, which is a positive relationship or correlation.

The second relationship, seen in Figure 18.1b, is a negative relationship. A **negative relationship** exists when the score on one variable goes up and the score on the other variable goes down. In Figure 18.1b, we are examining the relationship between CA and self-esteem. As a person's level of CA goes up, her or his self-esteem goes down.

The converse is also true: as a person's level of self-esteem goes up, her or his level of CA goes down.

The third example of a relationship, seen in Figure 18.1c, is called a curvilinear relationship. A **curvilinear relationship** is a relationship that is either positive or negative to a certain point and then goes in the other direction. In the example in Figure 8.1c, we have the severity of an illness and the dose of medication. In an ideal world, the severity of an illness will go down as the dose of medication goes up. However, there does come a point when you can actually take too much medication for an illness (called an overdose), and the severity of your illness will then go up. This is a good example of a curvilinear relationship.

Finally, as seen in Figure 18.1d, some variables are simply not related to each other at all, or have a **neutral relationship**. In this example, we are looking at an individual's pizza consumption and her or his nonverbal immediacy. These two variables simply do not make sense together in the first place, so as one variable's score goes up or down, there should be no clear change in the score of the other variable.

Correlation Not Causation

Now that we have explained what the four basic types of relationships are, we must make one thing clear—correlation does not mean causation. Being more humorous does not cause popularity, low self-esteem does not cause high levels of CA, and more medication does not cause the severity of the illness to change. You might think "Of course medication causes the severity of the illness to change," which might even be true. However, the statistical tool called a correlation only examines whether two variables are linearly related to each other, *not* if the change in one variable causes the change to occur in the other variable.

A published example of the "relationship versus **causation**" issue came from Eugene Volokh (2004), a professor in the UCLA School of Law, who conducted a study examining the relationship between ice cream consumption and the incidence of rape. In his study, Volokh (2004) used "2000 data from the Federal Bureau of Investigation's Uniform Crime Reports, and 2000 data from the international Dairy Foods Association's Dairy Facts publication; the correlation was 0.84, which is very high" (para. 2). The two variables were strongly related to each other. And an untrained person might say this finding indicates that eating ice cream causes people to go out and rape others, but this is obviously a fairly idiotic statement. Instead, when one looks at the data more closely, there is a clear spike in the amount of ice cream consumed and the number of rapes that occur during the summer months. People eat more ice cream when it is hot, and people are outside more during the summer, which makes them more vulnerable to rape.

Another example of the problem with trying to create causation from correlation can be found in the study conducted by Janis Walworth (2001), who wanted to see whether there was a relationship between the number of Protestants living in a state and the incidence of tornados. Although there was no relationship between the number of Jews and Catholics living in a state and the number of tornados that a state reported, this could not be said for Protestants. In fact, the relationship between the number of self-reported Protestants in a state and the number of tornados was strong ($r = 0.71$ for the statistically inclined). Walworth further analyzed this phenomenon by examining the differences between reported categories of Protestantism (Lutheran, Methodist, and Baptist) and the number of tornados. Lutherans apparently did not annoy God enough to spite them with a natural disaster because there was not a statistical relationship between the number of Lutherans living in a state and the number of tornados a state experiences. However, the numbers of both Methodists ($r = 0.52$) and Baptists ($r = 0.68$) were positively related to the number of tornados a state has annually. Walworth concluded by saying, "[T]his means that Texas could cut its average of 139 tornados per year in half by sending a few hundred thousand Baptists elsewhere (Alaska maybe?)" (p. 5).

Obviously, Walworth was joking in this article. However, we do see the interesting phenomenon that can occur if someone tries to create causal inferences from statistical relationships. One reason there may be a strong relationship between the number of Methodists and Baptists and the number of tornados is that more Methodists and Baptists live in the region of the United States known as Tornado Alley. Although there is a strong relationship, having Methodists and Baptists in a state clearly does not cause tornado activity.

Spurious Correlations

Need more evidence that correlation does not equal causation? Here are a number of actual correlations that research scientists have discovered:

- Pirate shortages and global temperature rates.
- The number of people who drowned in a year and the number of Nicholas Cage films.
- Per capita consumption of cheese and the number of people dying from tangled bed sheets.
- Per capita consumption of margarine and the death rate in Maine.
- Age of Miss America and the number of people dying from steam, hot vapors, and hot objects.

- Per capita consumption of chicken and US crude oil imports.
- Quality of M. Night Shyamalan movies and newspaper purchasing rates.
- Market share of Internet Explorer and murder rates.

Sources: http://stats.stackexchange.com/questions/36/examples-for-teaching-correlationdoes-not-mean-causation; http://www.tylervigen.com/; http://www.buzzfeed.com/kjh2110/the-10-most-bizarre-correlations/; Vigen, T. (2015). *Spurious correlations: Correlation does not equal causation*. New York, NY: Hachette.

FIGURE 18.2
**Pearson Product-
Moment Correlation
Formula**

$$r = \frac{N\Sigma xy - (\Sigma x)(\Sigma y)}{\sqrt{[N\Sigma x^2 - (\Sigma x)^2][N\Sigma y^2 - (\Sigma y)^2]}}$$

Correlation Assumptions

Now that we have examined some basic information about what a correlation is, we can turn our attention to the basic assumptions of the correlation:

1. Both the independent variable and the dependent variable should be interval (in the example for this chapter, CA) or ratio (heart rate change).
2. A sample should be random.
3. Scores for both of the variables being compared must be obtained from each participant.
4. The relationship between the two scores should be linear (positive or negative) because the Pearson product-moment correlation (the test we will conduct) does not test for curvilinear relationships.
5. To avoid having an abnormal distribution, the Pearson product-moment correlation should have no fewer than 25 participants. (To make the math easy for this example, our example has fewer than 25 participants.)

These assumptions are extremely important, because if even one assumption is violated, the meaning of the Pearson product-moment correlation is lost.

Correlation Formula

Now that we have explained what a correlation is and what the basic assumptions of the correlation are, we can look at the basic correlation formula given in Figure 18.2. In this formula, we are solving for the mysterious "*r*" value. When you see an "*r*" reported in research, you can be guaranteed that you are seeing a Pearson product-moment correlation. And although the formula may look somewhat scary, it is just as easy as the other formulas previously computed in this book.

STEP-BY-STEP APPROACH TO THE PEARSON PRODUCT-MOMENT CORRELATION

In our example, a researcher wants to determine whether an individual's level of CA (independent variable) relates positively or negatively to a participant's change in heart rate during an impromptu speaking situation. Figure 18.3 represents the raw data for this study. In this figure, PRCA scores are referred to as *x* scores and heart rate change as *y* scores.

Participant	Communication Apprehension (X)	Change in Heart Rate (Y)
1	120	5.5
2	71	4.6
3	72	3.8
4	118	5
5	58	3.2
6	60	3.1
7	72	3.8
8	55	2
9	115	4.9
10	70	3.7
11	68	3.5
12	24	0
13	72	3.7
14	65	3.3
15	70	3.4
16	92	4
17	95	4.1
18	90	3.8
19	63	3.4
20	24	0

FIGURE 18.3

Raw Data for Correlation Example

Step 1

Before we can complete any of the parts of the formula, we must do some simple descriptive statistics. First, we must find the sum of x multiplied by y (Σxy). To do this, we multiply everyone's x score (PRCA-24 score) by her or his y score (heart rate change). For example, the first participant's x score is 120, and her or his y score is 5.5. To obtain xy, we simply multiply 120 times 5.5, or $120 \times 5.5 = 660$. Once you have computed all of the xy scores, you simply add them up to achieve the Σxy, which is equal to 5,698.5. (We have multiplied all of the xy scores in Figure 18.4, as seen in the third column.)

Next, we must determine the sum of squares x and then the sum of squares y. As discussed in Chapter 14, to find the sum of squares x (Σx^2), you simply square each x value (individual's PRCA-24 score) and then add those values. For example, to square the first participant's score, you simply take her or his PRCA-24 score (120) and multiply it by itself ($120 \times 120 = 14,400$). After you have done this for all of the participants' x scores, you simply add the scores up to obtain the sum of squares x (Σx^2), which can be seen in the fourth column in Figure 18.4. Finally, you repeat the process for each participant's y scores (heart rate change) and then add these totals together to obtain the sum of squares y (Σy^2), which can be seen in the fifth column of Figure 18.4.

To complete the Pearson product-moment correlation formula, we must know the sum of x ($\Sigma x = 1,474$), the sum of x-square ($\Sigma x^2 = 121,490$), the sum of y ($\Sigma y = 68.8$), the sum of y-square ($\Sigma y^2 = 274.04$), the sum of xy ($\Sigma xy = 5,698.5$), and the number of

FIGURE 18.4

Descriptive Statistics for the Correlation Formula

Participant	CA (x)	HR Change (y)	x*y	x*x	y*y
1	120	5.5	660	14400	30.25
2	71	4.6	326.6	5041	21.16
3	72	3.8	273.6	5184	14.44
4	118	5	590	13924	25
5	58	3.2	185.6	3364	10.24
6	60	3.1	186	3600	9.61
7	72	3.8	273.6	5184	14.44
8	55	2	110	3025	4
9	115	4.9	563.5	13225	24.01
10	70	3.7	259	4900	13.69
11	68	3.5	238	4624	12.25
12	24	0	0	576	0
13	72	3.7	266.4	5184	13.69
14	65	3.3	214.5	4225	10.89
15	70	3.4	238	4900	11.56
16	92	4	368	8464	16
17	95	4.1	389.5	9025	16.81
18	90	3.8	342	8100	14.44
19	63	3.4	214.2	3969	11.56
20	24	0	0	576	0
Sum =	**1474**	**68.8**	**5698.5** $= \Sigma xy$	**121490** $= \Sigma x^2$	**274.04** $= \Sigma y^2$
Mean =	**73.7**	**3.44**	**284.925** $= \Sigma xy$	**6074.5** $= \Sigma x^2$	**13.702** $= \Sigma y^2$

participants ($N = 20$). Figure 18.4 presents all of these totals for us. And with these six numbers, we can now fill in every part of the correlation formula.

Step 2

The first part of the formula in Figure 18.2 we are going to complete is the part above the division line, $N\Sigma xy - (\Sigma x)(\Sigma y)$. At this point, we simply have to plug the results from step 1 into the formula and perform the calculation. Specifically, this formula asks us to multiply the number of participants ($N = 20$) by the sum of xy ($\Sigma xy = 5,698.5$) and then subtract this total from the sum of x ($\Sigma x = 1,474$) multiplied by the sum of y ($\Sigma y = 68.8$):

$$(20 \times 5,698.5) - (1,474 \times 68.8)$$
$$(113,970) - (101,411.2)$$
$$12,558.8$$

So $N\Sigma xy - (\Sigma x)(\Sigma y) = 12,558.8$.

Step 3

Next, we compute the part of the formula under the division line that appears in the left bracket, $[N\Sigma x^2 - (\Sigma x)^2]$. Once again, this is a matter of plugging in the results we computed in step 1. For this equation, we must multiply the number of participants

($N = 20$) by the sum of x-square ($\Sigma x^2 = 121{,}490$) and then subtract this total from the sum of x ($\Sigma x = 1{,}474$) squared:

$$(20 \times 121{,}490) - (1{,}474)^2$$
$$(2{,}429{,}800) - (2{,}172{,}676)$$
$$257{,}124$$

So $[N\Sigma x^2 - (\Sigma x)^2] = 257{,}124$.

Step 4

Now, we compute the formula under the division line by working on the part of the formula that appears in the right bracket, $[N\Sigma y^2 - (\Sigma y)^2]$. Once again, this is simply a matter of plugging in the results we computed in step 1. For this equation, we must multiply the number of participants ($N = 20$) by the sum of y-square ($\Sigma y^2 = 274.04$) and then subtract this total from the sum of y ($\Sigma y = 68.8$) squared:

$$(20 \times 274.04) - (68.8)^2$$
$$(5{,}480.8) - (4{,}733.44)$$
$$747.36$$

So $[N\Sigma y^2 - (\Sigma y)^2] = 747.36$.

Step 5

We are now going to complete two basic computations. First, we must multiply the answer from step 3 (257,124) by the answer from step 4 (747.36), or $257{,}124 \times 747.36 = 192{,}164{,}192.6$. Once we have done this, we simply take the square root of that number, $\sqrt{192{,}164{,}192.6} = 13{,}862.32998$.

Step 6

We have now calculated everything above the division line (12,558.8) and everything below the division line (13,862.32998). All we have to do now to obtain our r value is to divide 12,558.2 by 13,862.32998:

$$12{,}558.2/13{,}862.32998 = 0.905922743$$

So, for this example $r = 0.91$.

We should note here that all Pearson product-moment correlation coefficients (r) exist on a scale from 0 to 1 or 0 to –1. The closer a correlation coefficient is to 1 or –1, the stronger the relationship is. To understand what r means, we must explore a concept called practical significance. Practical significance is not the same thing as statistical significance. Practical significance is an indicator of the strength of the relationship. The generally agreed-on practical significance for an r value is that if it is under 0.30 (or –0.30), then it is a weak relationship (and somewhat questionable); if

Interpreting Correlations (r)

Positive Correlations

0 to 0.30—Weak Relationship

0.30 to 0.59—Moderate Relationship

0.60 to 1.0—Strong Relationship

Negative Correlations

0 to −0.30—Weak Relationship

−0.30 to −0.59—Moderate Relationship

−0.60 to −1.0—Strong Relationship

r is between 0.30 and 0.59 (or −0.30 to −0.59), then it is a moderate relationship (there is a clear relationship, but it is not strong); and if r is above 0.60 (or −0.60), then it is a strong relationship (there is a clear, strong relationship between the two variables). In our example, we achieved an r value of 0.91, so there is a clear, strong, positive relationship between the two variables. However, practical significance means nothing unless it is statistically significant.

Step 7

In this step, we determine whether our r value (0.91) is statistically significant. Before we can determine this, however, we must calculate the degrees of freedom (df) for the correlation. The formula for calculating the Pearson product-moment correlation df is $N - 2$, or the number of participants in a study (20) minus 2 ($20 - 2 = 18$). So, for our example, the degree of freedom is 18.

On the left side of Figure 18.5 are the df values for the Pearson product-moment correlation. Because our df calculated for this example was 18, we must go to the row for the number 18. In this row, you will find the critical values listed for the calculated r value. As we have seen in previous chapters when examining a critical value table, if the calculated r is larger than the value in a column at a specific p value, then the r value is significant at that p value. For example, in the first column in row 18 is the critical value 0.3783. Because the calculated value for r (.91) is larger than the critical value (0.3783), then we can say the correlation is significant at $p < 0.10$. However, 0.10 does not meet the 95% confidence interval discussed in Chapter 13, so we would not consider a correlation statistically significant at this p value. However, if you look across this entire row of p values listed on the critical value chart (0.05, 0.01, and 0.001), the calculated r in this example (0.91) is larger than all three of the critical values (0.4438, 0.5614, and 0.6787, respectively). The lowest p value listed in the chart is 0.001, so we would have to declare 0.001 as the significance level since we do not have a more accurate significance level. However, it is probably significant at an even lower significance level, so we will examine how correlations are reported by Statistical Package for the Social Sciences (SPSS).

df N − 2	Level of Significance for a nondirectional two-tailed test			
	0.10	0.05	0.01	0.001
1	0.9877	0.9969	0.9999	1.0000
2	0.9000	0.9500	0.9900	0.9990
3	0.8054	0.8783	0.9587	0.9912
4	0.7293	0.8114	0.9172	0.9741
5	0.6694	0.7545	0.8745	0.9507
6	0.6215	0.7067	0.8343	0.9249
7	0.5822	0.6664	0.7977	0.8982
8	0.5494	0.6319	0.7646	0.8721
9	0.5214	0.6021	0.7348	0.8471
10	0.4973	0.5760	0.7079	0.8233
11	0.4762	0.5529	0.6835	0.8010
12	0.4575	0.5324	0.6614	0.7800
13	0.4409	0.5139	0.6411	0.7603
14	0.4259	0.4973	0.6226	0.7420
15	0.4124	0.4821	0.6055	0.7246
16	0.4000	0.4683	0.5897	0.7084
17	0.3887	0.4555	0.5751	0.6932
18	0.3783	0.4438	0.5614	0.6787
19	0.3687	0.4329	0.5487	0.6652
20	0.3598	0.4227	0.5368	0.6524
25	0.3233	0.3809	0.4451	0.5974
30	0.2960	0.3494	0.4093	0.5541
35	0.2746	0.3246	0.3810	0.5189
40	0.2573	0.3044	0.3578	0.4896
45	0.2428	0.2875	0.3384	0.4648
50	0.2306	0.2732	0.3218	0.4433
60	0.2108	0.2500	0.2948	0.4078
70	0.1954	0.2319	0.2737	0.3799
80	0.1829	0.2172	0.2565	0.3568
90	0.1726	0.2050	0.2422	0.3375
100	0.1638	0.1946	0.2301	0.3211

FIGURE 18.5
Critical Values Table for the Pearson Product-Moment Correlation

The entries in this table were computed by the authors.

COMPUTER PRINTOUTS OF THE PEARSON PRODUCT-MOMENT CORRELATION

Now that we have examined how the Pearson product-moment correlation can be calculated by hand, we will examine output from SPSS.

SPSS and Pearson Product-Moment Correlations

Using SPSS to compute a Pearson product-moment correlation is fairly easy as long as you follow instructions, so let's get started. First, open your SPSS software, and locate the file on the textbook's website (https://oup-arc.com/wrench) in the SPSS folder called "Correlation." When you open this file, you will see two variables listed: "ca" and "hrchange." Here, "ca" is the variable name for the participants' scores on the PRCA-24 (i.e., CA), and "hrchange" is the variable name for the participants' change in heart rates while giving the impromptu speech (Figure 18.6).

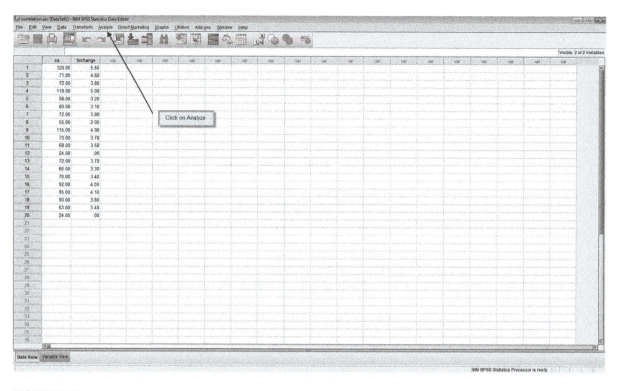

FIGURE 18.6
Correlation Main

To conduct a Pearson product-moment correlation using SPSS, go to the menu bar at the top of your screen, and click on "Analyze." When you click on Analyze, a drop-down menu will appear. On this menu, go to "Correlate," scroll over the arrow, and another menu will appear to the right. In that list, scroll over "Bivariate," and click on it (Figure 18.7). The "Bivariate Correlations" dialogue box now appears (Figure 18.8a). In this dialog box are two white boxes, one on the left side of the screen (with your variables listed) and an empty one on the right side of the screen labeled "Variables." Highlight both variables (CA and heart rate change), and transfer them to the Variables box (Figure 18.8b).

Note that some correlation functions have been preselected. The SPSS "Bivariate Correlations" dialogue box allows you to perform three different types of correlations (Pearson's product-moment, Kendall's tau-b, and Spearman). When you enter into the "Bivariate Correlations" dialogue box, "Pearson" is automatically checked because it is the most common form of correlation conducted by researchers. Below the three types of correlations, you can choose either a two-tailed significance test or a one-tailed significance test. Remember from our discussion of significance in Chapter 13 that you can use a one-tailed test if you have made a prediction about the direction of a correlation; however, it is recommended that you always use a two-tailed test since it is more conservative and less likely to cause type I errors. SPSS automatically selects a two-tailed significance test unless told otherwise. Finally, you will see that SPSS has selected the "Flag Significant Correlations" box. When you look at the SPSS correlation printout, you will see an asterisk (*) next to any significant correlation.

To run the correlation using SPSS, click on "OK." The results for the SPSS results can be seen in Figure 18.9.

Interpreting SPSS Correlation Results

When SPSS produces a correlation result, it correlates all of the variables listed as both the independent variable and the dependent variable. In a correlation table, each result will be presented twice. The computer program also correlates each variable with itself. If you correlate a thing with itself, then you will have a perfect correlation of 1.0. Looking at the answer listed in the first column and the first row of Figure 18.9 (CA correlated with CA), you will note that they list 1.0 as the correlation coefficient. You will also note that in column 2 and row 2, SPSS correlated heart rate change with heart rate change and reported a 1.0 correlation coefficient. You will always end up with a diagonal line going through a correlation table where the program has correlated each variable with itself. On either side of that diagonal of 1.0 correlation coefficients will appear the exact same set of results. We recommend that you select one side of the line just to make sure you only report correlation results once.

In this example, you will see that the *r* value listed in the SPSS chart is identical (with rounding) to the one we computed by hand earlier in this chapter. You will also note that immediately under the *r* value is the significance (0.000) level, and immediately under that is the number of participants used in the correlation (20). The computer is able to obtain a much more exact *p* value than we could by looking at a critical value chart. The printout just says that the significance is 0.000. However, American Psychological Association (APA) style informs us that we only report *p* values as low as $p < 0.001$.

FIGURE 18.7
Correlate Bivariate Menu

APA Write-Up

The write-up in APA style for these calculations would be as follows:

> This research question tested for a relationship between an individual's level of CA and her or his increase in heart rate during an impromptu speaking situation, $r(20) = 0.91$, $p < 0.001$, which is considered a strong relationship.

FIGURE 18.8A
Correlation
Dialogue Box

FIGURE 18.8B
Correlation Dialogue
Box – Items Sent to the
Variables Box

Discussion

After all of the work we have done so far in this chapter, this is the point where we try to make some sense out of our results. Let's go back to the initial research question we asked. The goal of this example was to see whether a person's level of CA related to a person's heart rate change while giving an impromptu speech. We found a strong, significant relationship between CA and heart rate change: as a person's level of CA went up, so did her or his heart rate while giving a speech. Remember, this does not mean that an individual's CA caused the heart rate change, only that the two variables are positively related to each other. As another reminder, when dealing with numbers in APA style, we always round to the hundredth, or two numbers following the decimal. The only exception to this rule is the reporting of your *p* value.

RELATIONSHIPS AMONG CA, WTC, AND BELIEFS ABOUT PUBLIC SPEAKING

The purpose of this example is to determine the relationships between an individual's CA, willingness to communicate (WTC), and belief that all students should be required to take public speaking in college (BELIEF). To analyze this question, we conducted three correlations: CA with WTC, CA with BELIEF, and WTC with BELIEF. Because we can calculate all these correlations in one printout, Figure 18.10 shows the SPSS printout.

In this example, you will note that SPSS has indicated significant relationships between the three variables. To make it somewhat easier to see the results, we have boldfaced the diagonal line of 1.0 correlation coefficients where the program correlates each variable with itself. You should only look at the results either to the right or the left of this diagonal line in order to make it easier to interpret your results. It does not matter if you look to the left or right of the diagonal line because the results are identical.

Correlations

Correlations

		Communication Apprehension	Heart Rate Change
Communication Apprehension	Pearson Correlation	1.000	**.906****
	Sig. (2-tailed)	.	.000
	N	20	20
Heart Rate Change	Pearson Correlation	.906**	1.000
	Sig. (2-tailed)	.000	.
	N	20	20

** Correlation is significant at the 0.01 level (2-tailed).

FIGURE 18.9
SPSS Results for CA
and Heart Rate Change

Correlations

Correlations

		Communication Apprehension Total	Willingness to Communicate Total	Everyone should be required to take public speaking in college
Communication Apprehension	Pearson Correlation	1	.407**	**−.301****
	Sig. (2-tailed)		.000	.000
	N	**644**	614	615
Willingness to Communicate Total	Pearson Correlation	−.407**	1	.141**
	Sig. (2-tailed)	.000		.001
	N	614	**622**	599
Everyone should be required to take public speaking in college	Pearson Correlation	**−.301****	.141**	1
	Sig. (2-tailed)	.000	.001	
	N	615	599	**623**

**. Correlation is significant at the 0.01 level (2-tailed).

FIGURE 18.10
SPSS Results for WTC,
CA, and BELIEF

APA Write-Up

The write-up in APA style for these calculations would be as follows:

This research question examined the relationships between an individual's CA, WTC, and the belief that all students should be required to take public speaking in college. To conduct this analysis, three Pearson product-moment correlations were conducted. CA was found to be negatively related to an individual's WTC, $r(614) = −0.41$, $p < 0.001$, which is considered a moderate relationship. CA was found to be negatively related to an individual's belief that all students should be required to take public speaking in college, $r(615) = −0.30$, $p < 0.001$, which is considered a moderate relationship. Finally, WTC was found to positively relate to an individual's belief that all students should be required to take public speaking in college, $r(599) = 0.14$, $p = 0.001$, which is considered a minimal relationship.

READING LARGE CORRELATION TABLES

Because correlations are probably the most common statistical tool used by social scientists, understanding how to read a correlation table is extremely important. We have taken all of the variables from the real sample dataset on the textbook's website (CA, ethnocentrism, humor assessment, nonverbal immediacy, assertiveness, responsiveness, WTC, belief that everyone should take public speaking in college, and attitude toward higher education) and run the correlations. To find how many correlations you must report, you can use the following formula: $[(N \times (N - 1))/2]$, with N being the number of variables you want to correlate. In the sample dataset, we have nine unique variables, so the formula would be:

$$(9 \times (9 - 1))/2$$
$$(9 \times 8)/2$$
$$72/2$$
$$36$$

So, the correlation table will have 81 (36 correlations you must report on one side of the diagonal, 36 correlations that are replicated on the other side of the diagonal, and 9 correlations where the variable is correlated with itself), but only 36 of them are unique correlations. See Figure 18.11 for the SPSS results.

On the SPSS printout, we have placed a big black line down the diagonal to point this out clearly. Also, we put a big black "X" through the left side of the diagonal, so we will only focus on those results found on the right side of the "X." Remember, the results on the left and the right side of the diagonal of 1.0 are identical. To find the relationship between two variables, select a variable name from the top (columns) and one from the right side (rows). Where the column and row intersect, you will find the correlation information for the relationship between those two variables. For example, let's find the relationship between ethnocentrism and responsiveness. To do this, find the ethnocentrism row and then find the responsiveness column. The correlation you find at this intersect is $r(643) = -0.32$, $p < 0.001$. In other words, there is a moderate, but negative, relationship between ethnocentrism and responsiveness. Therefore, as a person's ethnocentrism goes up, her or his responsiveness goes down. Just a quick reminder from Chapter 13. You'll notice on the printout that the p-value was listed as .000. However, with the 6th edition of the APA style manual, the lowest p-value that should be reported is .001, which is why .000 gets reported as $p < .001$

Correlations

		Communication Apprehension Total	Ethnocentrism	Humor Assessment	Nonverbal Immediacy	Assertiveness	Responsiveness	Willingness to Communicate Total	Everyone should be required to take public speaking in college.	Attitude about Higher Education
Communication Apprehension Total	Pearson Correlation	1	.157**	-.258**	-.331**	-.309**	-.072	-.407**	-.301**	-.094*
	Sig. (2-tailed)		.000	.000	.000	.000	.071	.000	.000	.020
	N	644	641	637	631	636	637	614	615	617
Ethnocentrism	Pearson Correlation	.157**	1	-.291**	-.331**	.091*	-.322**	-.124**	-.138**	-.190**
	Sig. (2-tailed)	.000		.000	.000	.021	.000	.002	.001	.000
	N	641	650	643	631	642	643	619	620	622
Humor Assessment	Pearson Correlation	-.258**	-.291**	1	.419**	.175**	.208**	.219**	.098*	.214**
	Sig. (2-tailed)	.000	.000		.000	.000	.000	.000	.015	.000
	N	637	643	646	639	641	642	617	617	619
Nonverbal Immediacy	Pearson Correlation	-.331**	-.360**	.419**	1	.117**	.386**	.334**	.125**	.281**
	Sig. (2-tailed)	.000	.000	.000		.003	.000	.000	.002	.000
	N	631	637	639	640	637	638	614	612	613
Assertiveness	Pearson Correlation	-.309**	.091*	.175**	.117**	1	.112**	.267**	.067	.145**
	Sig. (2-tailed)	.000	.021	.000	.003		.004	.000	.099	.000
	N	636	642	641	637	645	644	618	616	618
Responsiveness	Pearson Correlation	-.072	-.322**	.208**	.386**	.112**	1	.203**	.081*	.188**
	Sig. (2-tailed)	.071	.000	.000	.000	.004		.000	.045	.000
	N	637	643	642	638	644	646	618	617	619
Willingness to Communicate Total	Pearson Correlation	-.407**	-.124**	.219**	.334**	.267**	.203**	1	.141**	.156**
	Sig. (2-tailed)	.000	.002	.000	.000	.000	.000		.001	.000
	N	614	619	617	614	618	619	622	599	598
Everyone should be required to take public speaking in college.	Pearson Correlation	-.301**	-.138**	.098*	.125**	.067	.081*	.141**	1	.109**
	Sig. (2-tailed)	.000	.001	.015	.002	.099	.045	.001		.007
	N	615	620	617	612	616	617	599	623	617
Attitude about Higher Education	Pearson Correlation	-.094*	-.190**	.214**	.281**	.145**	.188**	.156**	.109**	1
	Sig. (2-tailed)	.020	.000	.000	.000	.000	.000	.000	.007	
	N	617	622	619	613	618	619	598	617	625

**. Correlation is significant at the 0.01 level (2-tailed).

*. Correlation is significant at the 0.05 level (2-tailed).

FIGURE 18.11

Reading Large SPSS Correlation Tables

DISCUSSION OF THE CHESEBRO ARTICLE

To help you understand how correlations appear in research, we now examine the 1999 article by Joe Chesebro entitled "The Relationship Between Listening Styles and Conversational Sensitivity," which can be found on the textbook's website in the folder titled "Articles." To view this article, you will need to download a copy of the Adobe Acrobat Reader (https://get.adobe.com/reader/) if you do not already have this program installed on your computer. We strongly encourage you to read the article first and then read our analysis of the article. The goal of this process is to ensure you understand how to read and interpret research results related to the Pearson product-moment correlation.

Article Purpose

Have you ever noticed that you can let a group of people watch a video and everyone will come away with something completely different? One reason this occurs is because of listening styles. In this article, Chesebro talks about four listening styles (people, action, content, and time). People-oriented listeners listen for information-related feelings and emotions and areas of common interest. Action-oriented listeners like short, simple messages where people get to the point. Content-oriented listeners enjoy complex messages they can evaluate and sink their teeth into. Finally, time-oriented listeners are more focused on their watches than on the messages. The purpose of this study was to see whether the four types of listener styles (people, action, content, and time) related to an individual's conversational sensitivity, or the degree to which an individual is attentive and responsive during a conversation.

Methodology

Chesebro had 239 participants in an introduction to communication course fill out scales. The set of scales the participants filled out measured listening styles and conversational sensitivity along with basic demographic information.

Results

If you look at the results on page 236 in Chesebro's article, they are straightforward. Chesebro used two different types of correlation (Pearson and partial correlations) in the article. A partial correlation is an advanced correlation tool. It (r_p) allows a researcher to determine actual relationships between variables that are highly interrelated. For example, the four listening styles are highly related constructs because they all involve listening and are measured using the same scale. To control for interference between the measurement of conversational sensitivity and one listening type (people), you can rule out the interference of the other variables (action, content, and time). Although this is by no means a complete description of what a partial correlation is, it should suffice to examine the results of this study.

The goal of this study was to examine the relationship between the independent variables (people, action, content, and time) and the dependent variable (conversational sensitivity). Looking at just the Pearson product-moment correlations, the people listening style is the only listening style that significantly relates to conversational sensitivity. Although two of the other listening styles related significantly when examining the partial correlations, the correlations were minimal and so probably not overwhelmingly meaningful.

DISCUSSION OF THE PUNYANUNT ARTICLE

The 2000 article by Narissra Punyanunt entitled "The Effects of Humor on Perceptions of Compliance-Gaining in the College Classroom" can be found on the textbook's website in the folder titled "Articles." To view this article, you will need to download a copy of the Adobe Acrobat Reader (https://get.adobe.com/reader/) if you do not already have this program installed on your computer. We strongly encourage you to read the article first and then read our analysis of the article. The goal of this process is to ensure you understand how to read and interpret research results related to the Pearson product-moment correlation.

Article Purpose

The purpose of this article was to find the relationships between a student's perception of her or his teacher's use of humor (whether the teacher was effective at it) and how the teacher attempts to gain compliance and change behavior through communication in the college classroom (using behavioral alteration techniques BATs). According to the article, a teacher in a college classroom can use 22 possible BATs to gain compliance and change behavior. The BATs are listed on page 34 of the Punyanunt article.

Methodology

The 428 participants in this study were all students attending a large southwestern university. The participants were asked to fill out a modified version of the BATs scale. The first column added to the scale asked participants to rate whether they thought their teacher employed humor when using a specific BAT. This was measured using a five-point Likert scale from 1 = *never* to 5 = *always*. The second column added to the scale asked participants whether they thought their instructor was effective at using humor to deliver the specific BAT. This was measured using a five-point Likert scale from 1 = *very ineffective* to 5 = *very effective*.

Results

To examine the relationship among a teacher's use of humor, its effectiveness, and the use of a specific behavior alteration technique, Punyanunt correlated the BAT scores for each BAT with the use of humor and the effectiveness of the use of humor questions. The results from these analyses can be seen in the charts on pages 34–35 of the article. These results demonstrated that teachers do use humor when trying to alter students' behavior in the classroom. However, these results indicate that using humor to guilt students into doing something may not be as effective as using humor to enhance a student's self-esteem.

RESEARCH OUTSIDE THE WALLS OF ACADEMIA

You probably hear about correlations more than any other statistic because reporters often "think" they understand correlations and what they mean. We use the quotation marks around the word "think" because reporters often fall into the "correlation equals causation" trap when reporting on data that are purely correlational. However, correlations can be important. For example, you may want to determine whether the number of new customers is positively related to sales rates. It is entirely possible that if you increase the number of people coming through your front door or website, you may see the same levels of purchases or even a dip in purchases. Ultimately, the question at hand here is do certain business practices actually lead to increased profits?

Do you want to know how an organization like Netflix makes recommendations for your next movie? Correlations. Basically, when you rate whether you liked a movie using their simple rating system of five stars, Netflix examines your ranking of that movie and looks for other people who ranked the same movie. Let's say you ranked *Star Wars* with five stars. Netflix is going to find all of those people who also ranked *Star Wars* with five stars and then use correlations to see what other movies that whole giant group of *Star Wars* fans also ranks highly. Admittedly, the correlational models for this process can become extremely complex, but they are built on the basic backbone of a correlation.

In fact, much of what we discuss in terms of Big Data in Appendix D (available on the textbook's website) is often based on correlational analyses. In an article published in *The New York Times Magazine* titled "How Companies Learn Your Secrets," Charles Duhigg (2012) discusses how organizations are using huge datasets to make some interesting and amazing predictions about people. This article has often been cheekily called the "Target Knows When You're Pregnant" article because Duhigg discusses how Target has created a data model (based on correlations) that can help them predict when women are pregnant based on purchasing different products. The article recalls the story of a father whose daughter started receiving pregnancy-related advertising at home before he knew she was even pregnant. He went so far as to complaining to Target that they were sending his daughter these advertisements encouraging her to get pregnant and that Target was out of line. When he later found out from his daughter that she was indeed pregnant, he apologized to Target.

CONCLUSION

In this chapter, we have examined how to compute a Pearson product-moment correlation by hand, how to compute and interpret computer results of a Pearson product-moment correlation in SPSS, and how to write up a Pearson product-moment correlation using APA style. We have also seen the Pearson product-moment correlation used in several different examples.

KEY TERMS

Causation p. 520	Curvilinear relationship p. 520	Neutral relationship p. 520
Correlation (r) p. 517	Negative relationship p. 519	Positive relationship p. 518

REFERENCES

Chesebro, J. (1999). The relationship between listening styles and conversational sensitivity. *Communication Research Reports, 16*, 233–238.

Duhigg, C. (2012, February 16). How companies learn your secrets. *The New York Times Magazine*, p. MM30. Retrieved from http://www.nytimes.com/2012/02/19/magazine/shopping-habits.html?_r=3&pagewanted=1&hp/

Punyanunt, N. M. (2000). The effects of humor on perceptions of compliance-gaining in the college classroom. *Communication Research Reports, 176*, 30–38.

Volokh, E. (2004, July 13). *Ice cream production is closely correlated with the rate of forcible rape* [blog]. Message posted to http://volokh.com/2004/07/13/academic-study-reveals/

Walworth, J. (2001, September/October). Does God punish gays? A statistical approach. *Gay & Lesbian Review Worldwide, 8* (5), 5.

FURTHER READING

Abramson, J. H., & Abramson, Z. H. (2001). *Making sense of data: A self-instruction manual on the interpretation of epidemiological data* (3rd ed.). New York, NY: Oxford University Press.

Bruning, J. L., & Kintz, B. L. (1997). *Computational handbook of statistics* (4th ed.). New York, NY: Longman.

Chen, P. Y., & Popovich, P. M. (2002). *Correlation: Parametric and nonparametric measures.* Thousand Oaks, CA: Sage.

Fox, J., & Weisberg, S. (2011). *An R companion to applied regression* (2nd ed.). Los Angeles, CA: Sage.

Gravetter, F. J., & Wallnau, L. B. (2000). *Statistics for the behavioral sciences* (5th ed.). Belmont, CA: Wadsworth/Thomson Learning.

Green, S. B., & Salkind, N. J. (2017). *Using SPSS for Windows and Macintosh: Analyzing and understanding data* (8th ed.). New York, NY: Pearson.

Hocking, J. E., Stacks, D. W., & McDermott, S. T. (2003). *Communication research* (3rd ed.). Boston, MA: Allyn & Bacon.

Hogan, T. P. (2010). *Bare-bones R: A brief introductory guide.* Los Angeles, CA: Sage.

Howell, D. C. (1997). *Statistical methods for psychology* (4th ed.). Belmont, CA: Duxbury Press.

Huff, D. (1954). *How to lie with statistics.* New York, NY: Norton.

Keller, D. K. (2006). *The Tao of statistics: A path to understanding (with no math).* Thousand Oaks, CA: Sage.

Muenchen, R. A. (2009). *R for SAS and SPSS users.* New York, NY: Springer.

Pyrczak, F. (1999). *Statistics with a sense of humor: A humorous workbook and guide to study skills* (2nd ed.). Los Angeles, CA: Pyrczak.

Salkind, N. J. (2017). *Statistics for people who (think they) hate statistics* (6th ed.). Thousand Oaks, CA: Sage.

Singleton, R. A., Jr., & Straits, B. C. (2017). *Approach to social research* (6th ed.). New York, NY: Oxford University Press.

Trochim, W. M. K. (2000). *The research methods knowledge base* (2nd ed.). Cincinnati, OH: Atomic Dog. http://www.socialresearchmethods.net/

Regression

CHAPTER OBJECTIVES

1. Explain the purposes of a linear regression.

2. Calculate a linear regression by hand.

3. Conduct a linear regression using the Statistical Package for the Social Sciences (SPSS).

4. Explain the purposes of a multiple linear regression.

5. Analyze the use of regressions in the articles by Wrench and Booth-Butterfield (2003) and Rocca and Vogl-Bauer (1999).

Remember when you first learned how to graph a line in high school algebra? We all learned that the formula for graphing a line is $Y = mX + b$. For a practical example, imagine that you were asked to tutor students in public speaking during the next semester/quarter. Before you will tutor anyone, you get paid $20 to assess their skills, and then you charge $10 per hour of tutoring thereafter. One student, Fatwah, wants you to tutor her for five hours. To determine how much you would get paid, you can plug it into the linear formula, with m equaling the charge per hour, X equaling the number of hours, and b equaling your $20 assessment fee, or $Y = (10 \times 5) + 20$, or $70. If your next student, Bob, wants to be tutored for eight hours, you can still use the same formula, $Y = (10 \times 8) + 20$, or $100. And the relationship between Fatwah's cost and Bob's cost would be a perfect relationship ($r = 1.0$). Furthermore, both scores would exist on a straight line if you graphed them because you are using the same formula to determine their overall cost. If Tika then comes to you and only wants to receive two hours of tutoring, you can once again use the formula to determine how much she would be charged, $Y = (10 \times 2) + 20$, or \$40.

Figure 19.1 shows these three situations on a graph. Remember, b values are points where the line intercepts the y axis. Note in this graph that the three points form a perfect line or have an r value of 1.0. Unfortunately, most relationships are not perfect ($r = 1.0$), so seeing perfect lines does not happen often in research. However, a simple linear regression can let us know how close to the perfect line the relationship between two variables is.

As mentioned in Chapter 17 on one-way analysis of variance (ANOVA), there is a series of statistical tests that all fall in the general category of the **general linear model** (GLM), which includes regression. The easiest way to understand the GLM is through the discussion we had earlier regarding how two variables (time tutoring and amount paid) are linearly related to each other. Throughout this chapter we will be discussing the importance of linearity with reference to bivariate regression and multiple linear regression equations. Before we get into too much detail about linear equations, we will revisit the example from the previous chapter.

FIGURE 19.1
Simple Regression Graph

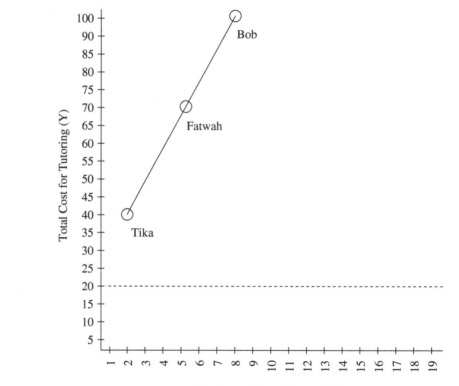

CASE STUDY INTRODUCTION

In the previous chapter, we examined the relationship between an individual's score on the Personal Report of Communication Apprehension–24 (PRCA-24) and her or his change in heart rate while giving an impromptu speech in public. We found that there was a significant correlation between the two variables: $r(20) = 0.91$, $p < 0.001$. This finding indicates that there is a strong, positive linear relationship between an individual's level of communication apprehension (CA) and her or his increase in heart rate (HR change) while giving an impromptu speech. This chapter will take the same example, but further develop the nature of the linear relationship between CA and HR change.

Let's compare the perfect line seen in Figure 19.1 to the line between CA and HR change from Chapter 18, which can be seen in Figure 19.2. The line drawn in on top of the scatterplot (type of graph that illustrates where participants' scores on the x axis value [HR change] and the y axis value [CA] intersect) runs through the means of both variables to demonstrate where the linear relationship exists. Note that most of the participants' scores for CA and HR change do not fall on the line perfectly. When this occurs, the predictive nature of the linear relationship also is not perfect, and we have

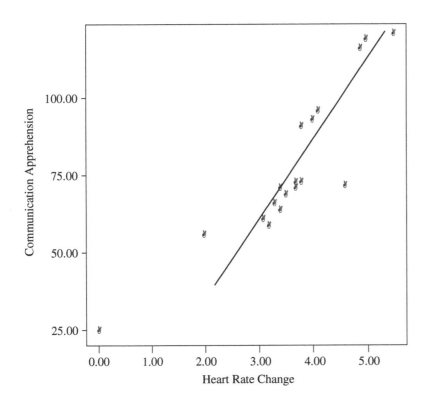

FIGURE 19.2
CA with HR Change Line

FIGURE 19.3
Regression Equation

$$Y = m_{slope} \, X + b_{constant}$$

$$m = \frac{\sum xy - (N * \mu x * \mu y)}{\sum X^2 - N\mu_{x^2}}$$

$$b = \mu_y - m\mu_x$$

some amount of error. Therefore, the formula for examining regressions must include an error term as seen in Figure 19.3.

REGRESSION ASSUMPTIONS

Now that we have examined basic information about what a **regression (R)** is, we can turn our attention to the basic assumptions of the linear regression, applying them to our example:

1. Both the independent variable(s) and the dependent variable should be interval (CA) or ratio (HR change).
2. Your sample should be random.
3. Scores for both variables being compared must be obtained from each participant.
4. The cases represent scores (on CA and HR change) that are independent of each other from one participant in your sample to the next participant. In other words, Jerry's level of CA cannot impact Heather's HR change.
5. The dependent variable (HR change) must be normally distributed in the population for each level of the independent variable. To ensure normal distributions, adequate sample sizes are necessary. Small samples may produce p values that are invalid.
6. The population variances of the dependent variable (HR change) are the same for all levels of the independent variable. If this assumption is violated, then the resulting p value for the overall F test is not trustworthy.

These assumptions are extremely important because if one assumption is violated, the meaning of the linear regression is lost.

Although a correlation does not require that you determine independent and dependent variables, a regression requires that you know which variable is independent and which variable is dependent. In our example, we predict that a person's CA (independent variable) can account for why a person's heart rate increases while giving an impromptu speech (dependent variable). You should also remember that independent variables and dependent variables often are not interchangeable. For example, it would not make sense to say that a person's HR change while giving an impromptu speech causes her or his preexisting level of CA. With these two variables, there is clearly only one direction in which the linear equation can occur. Remember, correlations just test for relationships—regressions are creating predictive equation lines. And it is the hope of the regression that if you are able to supply a person's CA score, then you can determine how much her or his heart rate will increase. If the correlation between two variables was 1.0, then the predictive nature of the line would be perfect. However, since our correlation between CA and HR change was 0.91, there will be some amount of error in our ability to predict a person's HR change from her or his CA score.

STEP-BY-STEP APPROACH TO A LINEAR REGRESSION

In our example, a researcher wants to determine the nature of the **linear relationship** between an individual's level of CA (independent variable) and her or his HR change during an impromptu speaking situation. The goal is to find the "best-fitting" straight line that was drawn in Figure 19.2 for the correlation data discussed in Chapter 18. This line is called a regression line.

So what do we mean by "best fit?" For any set of data, it is possible to draw hundreds of lines that will pass through the data and appear meaningful. However, only one line is the best line to represent the relationship between the data and the actual relationship between the two variables, and this line is said to provide the "best fit" for the actual data points in a study.

Before we can complete the linear aspect of the regression equation (see Figure 19.3), however, we must retrieve some information from Chapter 18. We must know the sum of x ($\Sigma x = 1,474$), the sum of x-squared ($\Sigma x^2 = 121,490$), the sum of y ($\Sigma y = 68.8$), the sum of y-squared ($\Sigma y^2 = 274.04$), the sum of $x \times y$ ($\Sigma xy = 5,698.5$), and the number of participants ($N = 20$). If you forgot how these numbers were calculated, please refresh your memory by rereading the first part of Chapter 18.

Step 1
In this step, we must find the mean of x (CA) and the mean of y (HR change). To find the mean of x (μ_x), we simply take the sum of x (1,474) and divide it by N (20), or 1,474/20 = 73.7. Next, we repeat this process for the mean of y (μ_y), or 68.8/20 = 3.44.

Step 2
In this step, we compute the top portion of the formula for m, or $\Sigma xy - (n \times \Sigma\mu_x \times \Sigma\mu_y)$. We already know the sum of $x \times y$ ($\Sigma xy = 5,698.5$), the number of participants in the study ($N = 20$), the mean of x ($\mu_x = 73.7$), and the mean of y ($\mu_y = 3.44$). Since we have already calculated each of these numbers, all we have to do is complete the formula as follows:

$$\Sigma xy - (n \times \mu_x \times \mu_y)$$
$$5,698.5 - (20 \times 73.7 \times 3.44)$$

$$5{,}698.5 - 5{,}070.56$$
$$627.94$$

So, $\Sigma xy - (n \times \mu_x \times \mu_y) = 627.94$.

Step 3

Now, we must calculate the part of the equation for m under the division bar, $\Sigma x^2 - N\mu_x^2$. Again, we have already calculated the sum of x-squared ($\Sigma x^2 = 121{,}490$), the number of people in the sample ($N = 20$), and the mean of x ($\mu_x = 73.7$). Since we have already calculated each of these numbers, all we have to do is complete the formula as follows:

$$\Sigma x^2 - N\mu_x^2$$
$$121{,}490 - (20 \times 73.7^2)$$
$$121{,}490 - (20 \times 5{,}431.69)$$
$$121{,}490 - 108{,}633.8$$
$$12{,}856.2$$

So, $\Sigma x^2 - N\mu_x^2 = 12{,}856.2$.

Step 4

In this step, we need to complete the equation for m by dividing the finding for step 2 (627.94) by the finding in Step 3 (12,856.2), or $627.94/12{,}856.2 = 0.0488433596$. The slope of the linear relationship between CA and HR change is $m = 0.0488433596$.

Step 5

Now that we have found m, we must switch gears and find the constant, or b. To find b, we simply have to fill in the following equation: $b = \mu_y - b\mu_x$. We already know the mean of y ($\mu_y = 3.44$), the slope of the line ($m = 0.0488433596$), and the mean of x ($\mu_x = 73.7$), so we just need to fill in the formula:

$$\mu_y - b\mu_x$$
$$3.44 - (0.0488433596 \times 73.7)$$
$$3.44 - 3.599755603$$
$$-0.159755603$$

So, $b = -0.159755603$.

Step 6

Now, we have all the parts needed to complete the linear equation of $Y = mX + b$. So, the linear equation for the "best-fit" line between CA and HR change is

$$Y = mX + b$$
$$Y = 0.0488433596X + -0.159755603$$

COMPUTER PRINTOUTS OF THE LINEAR REGRESSION

Now that we have examined how the linear regression line can be calculated by hand, we can turn our attention to the results from the computer to determine whether this "best-fit" line between CA and HR change is significant. Specifically we examine the output from Statistical Package for the Social Sciences (SPSS).

SPSS and Simple Linear Regressions

Using SPSS to compute a simple linear regression is easy, so let's get started. First, open your SPSS student version, and then locate the file on the textbook's website (https://oup-arc.com/wrench) in the SPSS folder called "Regression." When you open this file, you will see two variables listed, "ca" and "hrchange." Here, "ca" stands for "CA" and is the variable name for individuals' scores on the PRCA-24, and "hrchange" stands for "HR Change" and is the variable name for an individual's change in heart rate while giving the impromptu speech (Figure 19.4). You could also use the file from the last chapter labeled "Correlation" since the data are identical.

FIGURE 19.4
Regression Main

Analyze	Direct Marketing	Graphs	Utilities	Add-ons	Window	Help

Reports	►
Descriptive Statistics	►
Tables	►
Compare Means	►
General Linear Model	►
Generalized Linear Models	►
Mixed Models	►
Correlate	►
Regression	►
Loglinear	►
Neural Networks	►
Classify	►
Dimension Reduction	►
Scale	►
Nonparametric Tests	►
Forecasting	►
Survival	►
Multiple Response	►
Missing Value Analysis...	
Multiple Imputation	►
Complex Samples	►
Quality Control	►
ROC Curve...	
IBM SPSS Amos...	

Regression submenu:
- Automatic Linear Modeling...
- Linear...
- Curve Estimation...
- Partial Least Squares...
- Binary Logistic...
- Multinomial Logistic...
- Ordinal...
- Probit...
- Nonlinear...
- Weight Estimation...
- 2-Stage Least Squares...
- Optimal Scaling (CATREG)...

FIGURE 19.5
Regression
Bivariate Menu

To conduct a linear regression, go to the menu bar at the top of your screen and click on Analyze. When you click Analyze, a drop-down menu will appear. Go to the ninth category on this menu, "Regression," and then scroll over the arrow. Another menu will appear to the right. Scroll over the second option in this list, "Linear," and click on it (Figure 19.5). The "Linear Regression" dialogue box will then appear (Figure 19.6a). As we have previously noted, in this example a person's CA is the independent variable, so it should be placed in the second box down, labeled "Independent(s)." To do this, highlight the variable "Communication Apprehension" and then click the right arrow next to the box labeled "Independent(s)" (Figure 19.6b). Next, we must place the HR change variable in the "Dependent" box by highlighting the variable "Heart Rate Change" and then clicking the right arrow next to the box labeled "Dependent" (Figure 19.6c). Once you have moved the variables, simply click OK, and SPSS will produce the results that you see in Figure 19.7.

In the first box, SPSS tells you which variable(s) are the independent variables (in the "Variables Entered" box) and which variable was the dependent variable, listed as "b" under the box itself. The second box of statistics is extremely important. The first column of results reports the R value for this linear regression. Since this is a bivariate linear regression (meaning we only looked at two variables—CA and HR change), the R value is the same computational value received for r in the last chapter, so $R = 0.91$.

The second box indicates the **R-squared** (R^2) value. R^2 is an important concept to understand when talking about regressions. Because it is a coefficient of determination, R^2 determines what proportion of the variability in Y or your dependent variable (HR change) can be predicted by its relationship with X or your independent variable (CA). In our example, $R^2 = 0.821$, which indicates that 82% of the variance in an individual's HR change while giving an impromptu speech can be predicted by an individual's level of CA.

With that said, we should remember that to find out how much of the variance is not accounted for by our linear regression, we simply subtract R^2 from 1 (1 – 0.821 = 0.179). In other words, 17.9% of an individual's change in her or his heart rate while giving an impromptu speech cannot be predicted by the linear relationship

FIGURE 19.6A
Highlight Dependent Variable

FIGURE 19.6B
Send CA to "Independent(s):" Box

with CA. Not all the increase in an individual's heart rate during an impromptu speech can be accounted for by her or his level CA, after all.

The next column in the second box, "Adjust R Square," is a mathematical adjustment to R^2 that attempts to more accurately reflect the goodness of fit in the overall linear regression. Researchers may attempt to conduct a regression when they have enough participants to justify the number of independent variables they are using. When this happens, the adjusted R^2 is a more accurate portrayal of the variance accounted for. Datasets that use small samples and a large number of independent variables will see the greatest differences between R^2 and adjusted R^2.

FIGURE 19.6C
Send HR Change to "Dependent:" Box

The last column in the second box, "Std. Error of the Estimate," provides a measure of how accurately the regression equation predicts dependent variable values. The smaller your standard error of the estimate is, the better you can predict that the independent variable(s) accounts for variance in the dependent variable. In this case, the standard distance between the actual data points seen in this example and the regression line is 0.61, which would indicate that the actual data points are fairly close to the regression line. The higher the standard error, the lower your R value will be.

The next table of results is also important because it is a traditional ANOVA summary table akin to the one we saw in Chapter 17 when we examined one-way ANOVAs. The reason we get an ANOVA summary table for a regression is because regressions, like one-way ANOVAs, are based on the GLM, so the F test allows us to determine whether

FIGURE 19.7
SPSS Regression
Results for CA and
HR Change

Regression

Variables Entered/Removed[b]

Model	Variables Entered	Variables Removed	Method
1	Communication Apprehension[a]		Enter

[a.] All requested variables entered.
[b.] Dependent Variable: Heart Rate Change

Model Summary

Model	R	R Square	Adjusted R Square	Std. Error of the Estimate
1	.906[a]	.821	.811	.6100

[a.] Predictors: (Constant), Communication Apprehension

ANOVA[b]

Model		Sum of Squares	df	Mean Square	F	Sig.
1	Regression	30.671	1	30.671	82.432	.000[a]
	Residual	6.697	18	.372		
	Total	37.368	19			

[a.] Predictors: (Constant), Communication Apprehension
[b.] Dependent Variable: Heart Rate Change

Coefficients[a]

Model		Unstandardized Coefficients		Standardized Coefficients	t	Sig.
		B	Std. Error	Beta		
1	(Constant)	−.160	.419		−.381	.708
	Communication Apprehension	4.884E-02	.005	.906	9.079	.000

[a.] Dependent Variable: Heart Rate Change

our linear regression is statistically significant. If you need a refresher course in reading an ANOVA summary table, reread the discussion in Chapter 17 on how to create them.

The fourth box in the SPSS results, "Coefficients," is extremely important for regressions, but not necessarily for a simple linear bivariate regression like the example we've been using so far here. We will examine a more complicated regression model called a multiple linear regression later in this chapter and spend more time discussing this box at that point. However, we do want to point out that it contains the information you need for creating your line formula, $Y = mX + b$. The second column in this box is labeled "Unstandardized Coefficients," and in this column is the letter

B. The first number listed under B is your constant (b) or y axis number (–0.160). The second number needed to create your linear equation is in the "Communication Apprehension" row (4.884E-02), which is scientific notation for 0.04884 or 0.05 (when you round up). When you put these two numbers together, you achieve the same linear formula we calculated by hand earlier, $Y = 0.05X + -0.16$.

APA Write-Up

The write-up in American Psychological Association (APA) style for these calculations would be as follows:

> A bivariate linear regression was conducted to evaluate the prediction of heart rate change during an impromptu speech from an individual's level of communication apprehension (CA). The regression equation for predicting an individual's hear rate change is
>
> $$\text{Change in heart rate} = (0.05 \times \text{CA}) + -0.16$$
>
> The linear combination of CA and heart rate change was significant: $F(1, 18) = 82.43$, $p < 0.001$. The sample multiple correlation coefficient (R) was 0.91, which indicates that approximately 82% of the variance in heart rate change in the sample can be accounted for by an individual's level of CA.

Discussion

We have now looked at this example for two complete chapters, so you are probably tired of trying to further your understanding of CA and the effect it has on HR change while a person delivers an impromptu speech. However, this simple example has illustrated both how a Pearson product-moment correlation could be conducted and how a bivariate linear regression could be conducted. And the regression finding indicates that there is a certain predictive nature between a person's level of CA and the change we could expect to see in her or his heart rate during an impromptu speech. Let's pretend that Pam has a CA score of 90. Using the equation generated by this example, we can predict how much Pam's heart rate will increase while giving an impromptu speech. We simply plug in Pam's CA score for X:

$$\text{Change in heart rate} = (0.05 \times \text{CA}) + -0.16$$
$$\text{Change in heart rate} = (0.05 \times 90) + -0.16$$
$$\text{Change in heart rate} = (4.5) + -0.16$$
$$\text{Change in heart rate} = 4.34$$

Given this finding, we would expect that Pam's heart rate would increase by 3.44 beats per minute during an impromptu speech. Admittedly, this is just an example and not based on actual research findings, but it illustrates how regression equations can be used to make predictions.

RELATIONSHIPS BETWEEN CA AND BELIEFS ABOUT PUBLIC SPEAKING

Here, we present an example based on actual research collected from a college sample. In this research question, we want to see whether an individual's level of CA (independent variable) can predict an individual's belief that public speaking should be a required course for all college students. The findings for this linear regression can be seen in Figure 19.8 for the SPSS printout.

FIGURE 19.8
SPSS Results for Linear Regression of CA and Belief

Regression

Variables Entered/Removed[a]

Model	Variables Entered	Variables Removed	Method
1	Communication Apprehension Total[b]	.	Enter

[a.] Dependent Variable: Everyone should be required to take public speaking in college.
[b.] All requested variables entered.

Model Summary

Model	R	R Square	Adjusted R Square	Std. Error of the Estimate
1	.301[a]	.091	.089	8.77707

[a.] Predictors: (Constant), Communication Apprehension Total

ANOVA[b]

Model		Sum of Squares	df	Mean Square	F	Sig.
1	Regression	4708.105	1	4708.105	61.115	.000[b]
	Residual	47223.693	613	77.037		
	Total	51931.798	614			

[a.] Dependent Variable: Everyone should be required to take public speaking in college.
[b.] Predictors: (Constant), Communication Apprehension Total

Coefficients[a]

Model		Unstandarized Coefficients		Standardized Coefficients		
		B	Std. Error	Beta	t	Sig.
1	(Constant)	33.746	1.370		24.636	.000
	Communication Apprehension Total	−.162	.021	−.301	−7.818	.000

[a.] Dependent Variable: Everyone should be required to take public speaking in college.

APA Write-Up

The APA write-up for this example would be as follows:

A bivariate linear regression was conducted to evaluate the prediction of an individual's belief that all college students should be required to take public speaking from her or his level of CA. The regression equation for predicting an individual's belief that all college students should be required to take public speaking is

$$\text{Belief about public speaking} = (-0.16 \times CA) + 33.75$$

The linear combination of CA and belief about public speaking was significant: $F(1, 613) = 61.12$, $p < 0.001$. The sample multiple correlation coefficient (R) was $-.30$, which indicates that approximately 9.1% of the variance in a person's belief that all college students should be required to take public speaking in the sample can be accounted for by an individual's level of CA.

Discussion

After all of the work we have done so far in this chapter, this is the point where we try to make some sense out of our results. Let's go back to the initial research question we asked. The goal of this example was to see whether a person's level of CA related to a person's heart rate change while giving an impromptu speech. We found a significant, positive linear relationship between CA and heart rate change: as a person's level of CA went up, so did her or his heart rate while giving a speech. Remember, this does not mean that an individual's CA caused the heart rate change, only that the two variables are positively related to each other. Instead, we can say that approximately 9.1% of the increase in someone's heart rate while giving a speech can be accounted for by her or his level of CA. This means there's still 90.9% of this equation that is not accounted for by it's linear relationship with CA.

UNDERSTANDING MULTIPLE LINEAR REGRESSIONS

Multiple linear regressions allow researchers to determine how a number of independent variables collectively account for the variance in a single dependent variable. For example, perhaps we wanted to go further than just CA and see how an individual's level of willingness to communicate (WTC), assertiveness, responsiveness, and CA accounted for the variance in her or his belief that all college students should take public speaking. Figure 19.9 is a pictorial representation of what we are asking in a multiple linear regression.

FIGURE 19.9
**Pictorial Example
of Multiple Linear
Regression**

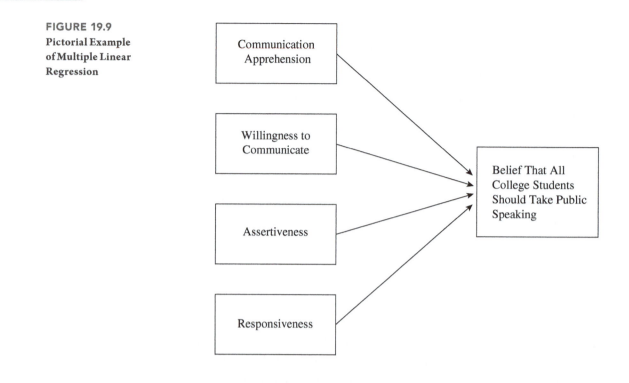

When we ran this research question in SPSS, we indicated that there were multiple independent variables (CA, WTC, assertiveness, and responsiveness) instead of just one, like we did in the previous two examples in this chapter, and one dependent variable (student belief about college). The results for what a multiple linear regression would look like can be seen in Figure 19.10 (SPSS).

Note that although output has not changed in how it is presented, there is now more information presented in the "Coefficients" box in the SPSS printout. First, the column marked "B" in SPSS represents the same linear equation as seen in the bivariate linear regression in the previous two examples, but this one is more complex:

$$Y = -0.17X_{CA} + 0.00X_{WTC} + -0.09X_{ASSERTIVENESS} + -0.06X_{RESPONSIVENESS} + 33.69$$

This is still the same linear $Y = mX + b$, but you now have four mX statements—one for each independent variable you are examining. Ultimately, this is where the true power of the GLM comes into play for researchers.

The next column is your standardized error for the "Unstandardized Coefficients" in SPSS, and this is followed by the "Standardized Coefficients" column. The values represented in this column can be interpreted as correlation coefficients and are called beta weights. However, for a beta weight to be significant, the t value must be significant. For example, CA has a **beta (β) weight** of -0.307, a t value of -6.904, and a p-value of 0.000. This indicates that CA significantly accounts for a portion of the unique variance in a

Regression

FIGURE 19.10
SPSS Results for
Multiple Linear
Regression

Variables Entered/Removed[a]

Model	Variables Entered	Variables Removed	Method
1	Responsiveness, Assertiveness, Willingness to Communicate Total, Communication Apprehension Total[b]	–	Enter

[a.] Dependent Variable: Everyone should be required to take public speaking in college.
[b.] All requested variables entered.

Model Summary

Model	R	R Square	Adjusted R Square	Std. Error of the Estimate
1	.301[a]	.096	.090	8.83841

[a.] Predictors: (Constant), Responsiveness, Assertiveness, Willingness to Communicate Total, Communication Apprehension Total

ANOVA[b]

Model		Sum of Squares	df	Mean Square	F	Sig.
1	Regression	4849.869	4	1212.467	15.521	.000[b]
	Residual	45464.418	582	78.118		
	Total	50314.286	586			

[a.] Dependent Variable: Everyone should be required to take public speaking in college.
[b.] Predictors: (Constant), Responsiveness, Assertiveness, Willingness to Communicate Total, Communication Apprehension Total

Coefficients[a]

Model		Unstandarized Coefficients		Standardized Coefficients		
		B	Std. Error	Beta	t	Sig.
1	(Constant)	33.689	4.183		8.054	.000
	Communication Apprehension Total	−.165	.024	−.307	−6.904	.000
	Willingness to Communicate Total	.001	.001	.026	.578	.563
	Assertiveness	−.091	.063	-.061	−1.442	.150
	Responsiveness	.062	.062	.040	.999	.318

a. Dependent Variable: Everyone should be required to take public speaking in college.

person's belief that public speaking should be required of all college students. However, if you look at responsiveness, the results indicate that it has a beta weight of 0.040, a t value of 0.999, and a p-value of 0.318, which would indicate that responsiveness does not account for a portion of the unique variance in a person's belief that public speaking should be required for all college students. Beta weights are actually just standardized ways of examining the "Standardized Coefficients," which are actually unstandardized regression coefficients (B) or partial regression coefficients.

APA Write-Up

The APA write-up for this would be as follows:

> A multiple linear regression was conducted to evaluate how well the independent variables (CA, WTC, assertiveness, and responsiveness) could predict the dependent variable (an individual's belief that all college students should be required to take public speaking). The linear combination of the independent variables was significantly related to an individual's belief that all college students should be required to take public speaking: $F(4, 582) = 15.52$, $p < 0.001$. The sample multiple correlation coefficient, R, was 0.301, which indicates that approximately 9.6% of the variance of an individual's belief that all college students should be required to take public speaking could be accounted for by the linear combination of CA, WTC, assertiveness, and responsiveness. However, only CA ($t = -6.904$, $p < 0.001$, $\beta = -0.31$) accounted for any of the unique variance in an individual's belief that all college students should be required to take public speaking.

Discussion

So, what does this mean? A multiple linear regression allows us to see whether the linear combination of a variety of variables (CA, WTC, assertiveness, and responsiveness) can help predict a dependent variable (belief that all college students should be required to take public speaking). In this case, we found that only an individual's CA actually helps to predict her or his belief that all college students should be required to take public speaking. WTC, assertiveness, and responsiveness, by contrast, were not shown to add anything to one's ability to predict a person's belief that all college students should be required to take public speaking. As usual, the statistical process may be complex and unnerving at times, but the findings are generally straightforward.

Just a quick reminder from Chapter 13. You'll notice on the printout that the F-test p-value is listed as .000 (see the ANOVA summary table). However, with the 6th edition of the APA Style Manual, the lowest p-value that should be reported is .001, which is why .000 gets reported as $p < .001$. This conversion from .000 to $p < .001$ is also true when you report the unique variance t-test between CA and belief in public speaking.

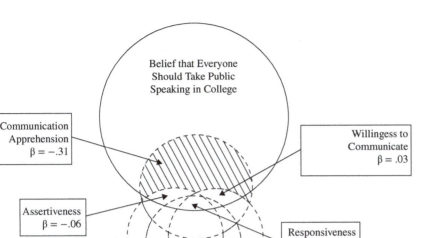

FIGURE 19.11
Multiple Linear Regression Venn Diagram

To help us understand what is going on, let's look at this in terms of a Venn diagram. Figure 19.11 has an exaggerated replication of what we are seeing in this regression equation. In this Venn diagram, the larger, solid circle represents the dependent variable (belief that everyone should take public speaking in college). The dashed circles represent the independent variables used in this model (CA, WTC, assertiveness, and responsiveness). Although this is not exactly how it would really look if we plotted with 100% accuracy, this diagram is useful for understanding what unique variance is. For our purposes, unique variance is represented by that part of CA that is shaded in the diagram. You will note that all four of the independent variables overlap with the dependent variable, but only CA is overlapping in a section of the dependent variable by itself. The other three variables, while overlapping with the dependent variable, do not overlap with the dependent variable in a unique fashion.

DISCUSSION OF THE WRENCH AND BOOTH-BUTTERFIELD ARTICLE

Because regressions are commonly used in communication research, we are going to examine two studies that have utilized regressions in this chapter. The article by Jason Wrench and Melanie Booth-Butterfield (2003) entitled "Increasing Patient Satisfaction and Compliance: An Examination of Physician Humor Orientation, Compliance-Gaining Strategies, and Perceived Credibility" can be found on the textbook's website in the folder titled "Articles." To view this article, you will need to download a copy of the Adobe Acrobat Reader (https://get.adobe.com/reader/) if you do not already have this program installed on your computer. We strongly encourage you to read the article first and then read our analysis. The goal of this process is to make sure that you understand how to read and interpret research results related to the linear and multiple linear regressions.

Article Purpose

Have you ever noticed that some physicians have a good sense of humor when interacting with their patients and some simply do not? The authors of this study noticed, and they wanted to determine how a physician's humor orientation (use of jokes and humorous story telling during interpersonal interactions) related to patient perceptions of credibility (competence, caring/goodwill, and trustworthiness), patient satisfaction (affective, behavioral, and cognitive), use of compliance-gaining strategies (expectancies/consequences, relationship/identification, and values/obligations), and actual patient compliance. (See the original article for a more detailed explanation of what each of these variables actually entails.)

Methodology

Participants in this study were college students (N = 44), professional educators in a Master's program (N = 48), people shopping at a mall (N = 142), and people online (N = 26). All participants were asked to fill out a variety of scales measuring the study variables using either a pen-and-paper test or an Internet-based survey.

Results

The results from this study indicated that physician humor can help to predict a patient's satisfaction (affective, behavioral, and cognitive) and a patient's perception of a physician's credibility (competence, trustworthiness, and caring/goodwill). In a multiple linear regression analysis using physician humor orientation, credibility, use of compliance-gaining strategies, and patient satisfaction as the independent variables and actual patient compliance as the dependent variable, 11% of the variance in compliance was accounted for by two compliance-gaining strategies (expectancies/consequences and values/obligations) and two forms of patient satisfaction (cognitive and behavioral).

Although humor was a strong predictor of satisfaction and patients' perceptions of physician credibility, it did not affect whether a patient would actually comply with a physician's treatment plan. We chose this article because the regression analyses are straightforward and are designed in a way that follows the reporting format that we have shown you in this chapter. You will also see that this article reported results for correlations and a one-way ANOVA as well, which is often the case in actual research. Most research does not rely on single statistical tests like the articles we have selected for inclusion on the textbook's website.

DISCUSSION OF THE ROCCA AND VOGL-BAUER ARTICLE

The 1999 article by Kelly Rocca and Sally Vogl-Bauer entitled "Trait Verbal Aggression, Sports Fan Identification, and Perceptions of Appropriate Sports Fan Communication" can be found on the textbook's website in the folder titled "Articles." Again, we strongly encourage you to read the article first and then read our analysis. The goal of this process is to ensure you understand how to read and interpret research results related to the linear and multiple linear regressions.

Article Purpose

Let's face it, sports fans are nuts!!! We don't mean the average sports enthusiast (the person who enjoys a good game on a Sunday afternoon or Monday night). No, we are talking about the cheese head–wearing, body-painting, screaming, and yelling types that are often broadcast into our living rooms while we are watching any kind of athletic competition. Sometimes these sports fans can get out of control. Fans have assaulted the fans of other teams, destroyed property, caused riots, and exhibited other antisocial forms of behavior. After noticing this phenomenon, Rocca and Vogl-Bauer wanted to determine what fans saw as appropriate forms of sports fan communication.

To do this, Rocca and Vogl-Bauer created a new scale for measuring fan behavior. The scale consists of three subscales: verbal response (yelling at officials, taunting the opposing team, openly criticizing players and coaches, etc.), fan display (wearing clothing with team logos, wearing jewelry with team logos, buying a newspaper to read about the team, etc.), and violent response (destroying objects while watching a game, hitting someone during an intense game, being more violent than normal during a game, etc.). Ultimately, Rocca and Vogl-Bauer wanted to determine how fan display, verbal response, and physical response related to sports spectator identification (degree of connection a person feels with a specific sports team) and verbal aggression (personality construct where people use character attacks, competence attacks, insults, maledictions, teasing, profanity, and threats to attack the self-concept or self-esteem of another person).

Methodology

Participants in this study were undergraduates from either a large Eastern university ($N = 213$) or a medium-sized Midwestern university ($N = 194$). The participants were asked to fill out three scales (verbal aggression, fan identification, and a revised version of the sports identification behavior scale).

Results

This study had only two basic research questions. The first research question examined the relationship between sports fans' verbal aggression and sports fans' perceptions of appropriate communicative messages at a sporting event (behavioral identification, verbal response, and physical violence). The researchers examined how participants' perceptions of appropriateness of communicative behavior (behavioral identification, verbal harassment, and physical violence) could account for an individual's level of verbal aggression (dependent variable). The independent variables accounted for 12% of the variance in an individual's verbal aggression. Rocca and Vogl-Bauer found that fan display related negatively to verbal aggression ($\beta = -0.12$) and that verbal response related positively to verbal aggression ($\beta = 0.28$), but violence did not significantly account for any of the unique variance in an individual's level of verbal aggression.

The second research question examined how participants' perceptions of appropriateness of communicative behavior (behavioral identification, verbal harassment, and physical violence) could account for an individual's sport spectator identification (dependent variable). The independent variables accounted for 9% of the variance in an individual's sport spectator identification. Both verbal response ($\beta = 0.27$) and fan display ($\beta = 0.17$) related positively to sports spectator identification, but violence did not significantly account for any of the unique variance in an individual's level of sport spectator identification.

The regression equations used in this article are written up using APA style, which is slightly different from those used in the Wrench and Booth-Butterfield article discussed earlier. This does not mean that one format is better than another, just that they are different. One of the things you will learn as you continue doing social scientific research is that there are a variety of ways to present the same information.

RESEARCH OUTSIDE THE WALLS OF ACADEMIA

By this point in life, you have probably come to know that everyone has a credit score, and this credit score determines the types of credit card, car, house, and loans that one can get. Your credit rating also determines how much interest the credit lenders will throw on top of your loan as well. These credit ratings are based largely on regression models that help lenders determine whether an individual is a good investment or will ultimately default on her or his loans. A wide range of different factors are examined. In fact, approximately 100 common variables are used to determine your credit score, but the major credit companies also stockpile huge amounts of other consumer information as well. One of the three large credit bureaus, Experian, says that they have 310 different variables in their dataset that can be utilized to make financial predictions (Experian, 2004). As you can imagine, this is a lot of data the company has at its disposal to create large regression models.

Besides determining your credit score, regressions are also beneficial in your daily life. In the business world, regressions are often used for a process called forecasting, or using historical data to make predictions about the future. Maybe an organization wants to predict how many products it must manufacture this year. Many variables can impact customer purchases: economy, competitor sales, previous sales records, interest rates, and so on. Any changes in these different variables could have huge impacts on the market's desire for your product. For example, during the economic crisis that hit the world starting in 2008, many organizations suddenly found the public's desire for their products dry up as it became more difficult for people to get loans with low interest rates. In parts of the United States, giant home, condo, and apartment complex projects were halted for years because no one was making those types of large purchases. Being able to predict different possible scenarios that an organization may face is an important use of the regression.

There are an endless supply of reasons to use multiple linear regressions in the modern business world. Want to find out what factors lead to employee burnout in your organization? Use a regression. Want to find out what website factors increase sales? Use a regression. Want to find out which recruitment mechanisms lead to the best job applicants? Use a regression. The possibilities are endless with multiple linear regressions.

CONCLUSION

In this chapter, we discussed simple linear regressions and multiple linear regressions. If you go back and look at the math we used to understand regressions, it's the same basic math we've used in each of the previous five chapters. Many students find the math to be one of the easiest parts of quantitative research methods because it's familiar and follows a pretty logical sequence of steps. As we discussed in the last six chapters (including this one), learning about quantitative research methods is about learning how to interpret what the math means and how it helps us understand real communicative behavior.

This is not to say that we have taught you everything there is to know about any one test. In fact, there are graduate-level courses in ANOVAs and regressions alone, so the information presented here is to help you learn the basic terminology of statistics, see how simple statistics can be employed to answer real research questions, and provide enough information to allow you to read actual research in any field that employs social scientific statistical procedures.

The last six chapters introduced you to a range of descriptive and inferential statistical tests, but we've only scratched the surface regarding statistical tests commonly seen in today's academic journals than we've covered here. To learn more about advanced statistical tests, check out Appendix E online at https://oup-arc.com/wrench. And in the next chapter, we will examine what to do with your research study when you are done with the paper/project.

KEY TERMS

Beta (β) weight p. 552

General linear model p. 540

Linear relationship p. 543

Regression (R) p. 542

R-squared (R^2) p. 546

REFERENCES

Experian. (2004). *Summarized credit statistics*. Retrieved from http://www.experian.com/assets/marketing-services/product-sheets/summarized-credit-stat.pdf/

Rocca, K. A., & Vogl-Bauer, S. (1999). Trait verbal aggression, sports fan identification, and perceptions of appropriate sports fan communication. *Communication Research Reports, 16,* 239–248.

Wrench, J. S., & Booth-Butterfield, M. (2003). Increasing patient satisfaction and compliance: An examination of physician humor orientation, compliance-gaining strategies, and perceived credibility. *Communication Quarterly, 51,* 482–503.

FURTHER READING

Abramson, J. H., & Abramson, Z. H. (2001). *Making sense of data: A self-instruction manual on the interpretation of epidemiological data* (3rd ed.). New York, NY: Oxford University Press.

Achen, C. H. (1982). *Interpreting and using regression*. Newbury Park, CA: Sage.

Bruning, J. L., & Kintz, B. L. (1997). *Computational handbook of statistics* (4th ed.). New York, NY: Longman.

Chatterjee, S., Hadi, A. S., & Price, B. (2000). *Regression analysis by example* (3rd ed.). New York, NY: Wiley.

Gravetter, F. J., & Wallnau, L. B. (2000). *Statistics for the behavioral sciences* (5th ed.). Belmont, CA: Wadsworth/Thomson Learning.

Green, S. B., & Salkind, N. J. (2017). *Using SPSS for Windows and Macintosh: Analyzing and understanding data* (8th ed.). New York, NY: Pearson.

Hocking, J. E., Stacks, D. W., & McDermott, S. T. (2003). *Communication research* (3rd ed.). Boston, MA: Allyn & Bacon.

Howell, D. C. (1997). *Statistical methods for psychology* (4th ed.). Belmont, CA: Duxbury Press.

Huff, D. (1954). *How to lie with statistics*. New York, NY: Norton.

Keith, T. Z. (2006). *Multiple regression and beyond*. Boston, MA: Allyn & Bacon.

Keller, D. K. (2006). *The Tao of statistics: A path to understanding (with no math)*. Thousand Oaks, CA: Sage.

Muenchen, R. A. (2009). *R for SAS and SPSS users*. New York, NY: Springer.

Pyrczak, F. (1999). *Statistics with a sense of humor: A humorous workbook and guide to study skills* (2nd ed.). Los Angeles, CA: Pyrczak.

Salkind, N. J. (2017). *Statistics for people who (think they) hate statistics* (6th ed.). Thousand Oaks, CA: Sage.

Schroeder, L. D., Sjoquist, D. L., & Stephan, P. E. (1986). *Understanding regression analysis: An introductory guide*. Newbury Park, CA: Sage.

Seber, G. A. F., & Lee, A. J. (2003). *Linear regression analysis* (rev. ed.). New York, NY: Wiley.

Singleton, R. A., Jr., & Straits, B. C. (2017). *Approach to social research* (6th ed.). New York, NY: Oxford University Press.

Tabachnick, B. G., & Fidell, L. S. (2013). *Using multivariate statistics* (6th ed.). Boston, MA: Pearson.

Trochim, W. M. K. (2000). *The research methods knowledge base* (2nd ed.). Cincinnati, OH: Atomic Dog. http://www.socialresearchmethods.net/

20

Presenting Research

CHAPTER OBJECTIVES

1. Write discussion sections and abstracts.

2. Differentiate among the three types of conference presentations (paper, poster, and panel).

3. Explain the process one goes through for submitting a paper to a conference.

4. Describe process one goes through for submitting a paper to an academic journal.

5. Explain the three responses an author may receive from a journal editor (accept for publication, publish pending revisions, revise and resubmit, and reject).

6. Summarize some basic rules for data visualization.

This book has taken you on a journey to show how communication researchers conduct quantitative research. In the first three chapters, we introduced you to the basic underlying assumptions in scientific communication research and how to conduct yourself ethically as a researcher. Chapters 4 and 5 discussed how to go about searching for existing literature and then incorporate this literature into a literature review, which enabled you to create a series of arguments that formed hypotheses and research questions in your rationale section. Chapter 6 explained what variables are and how communication researchers utilize variables. Chapters 7 and 8 discussed how we measure variables in communication,

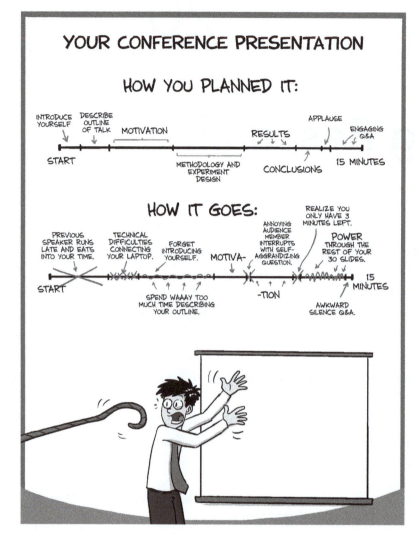

▲ Your Conference
Presentation
Source: Piled Higher and
Deeper by Jorge Cham – www.
phdcomics.com

whereas Chapter 14 explained how mathematics can be used to describe collected variable data. Chapter 9 introduced us to conducting survey research, Chapter 10 introduced content analysis, and Chapter 11 introduced experimental research. Chapter 12 then explained the different types of samples that researchers could use while conducting research. Chapters 6 through 12, along with Chapter 14, provided you with the nuts and bolts of conduct quantitative research, which is the information one generally provides in her or his method section. Chapter 13 introduced you to the theoretical premises behind hypothesis testing before showing you a variety of statistical tests, covered in Chapters 15 through 19. In those chapters, we provided you with many examples of how to write up research results using American Psychological Association (APA) style. The results section of a research paper consists of conducting the most parsimonious tests to answer the hypotheses and research questions you formulated in your rationale section at the end of the literature review. For every hypothesis or research question you posed in your rationale section, you should have a corresponding section in your results section. But we do not stop the research process just because we have written our results.

By this point in your research project, you have completed your data analysis and are probably ready to exhale a huge sigh of relief. But what good are results for a study if an author fails to explain what the information means for the reader? This chapter describes the process of writing the discussion section of a research paper, presenting at conferences, and publishing your research.

Too often, students or authors spend countless hours completing a research project only to have it sit in a file folder. Our purpose in conducting research is to share our knowledge and expand our understanding of phenomena in our discipline. Here, we describe the steps involved in preparing your work for conference presentations and publication. After all, it would be a shame to keep your research findings on a shelf.

Before we can talk about disseminating our research, there are two final parts of the research project we must examine: the discussion section and the abstract. Even then, however, your research task is not complete. After all, has your study contributed to the body of literature on a subject if it remains on your computer or in a file folder? Given the time and energy dedicated to the project, it is important to share the data with others. Several outlets for research exist. These include presenting your research at professional conferences or conventions and submitting your study for publication in an academic journal.

WRITING A DISCUSSION SECTION

The five previous chapters have been dedicated to the data-analysis phase of the research project. Each chapter provided you with information on how to present the findings of your analyses in the results section using APA style format guidelines. But do you recall our instructions to provide "just the facts" in the results section and resist the temptation to engage in any interpretation of the data? There was a reason for that—each research project concludes with a discussion section, and this section provides the author with the opportunity to interpret the findings.

Students often report that they find the **discussion section** to be the most interesting part of a journal article. After all, this is where the author's own voice is heard. The discussion section allows the researcher to create links between the study and previous work, discuss any roadblocks that were encountered during the research process, and provide suggestions for how other scholars can build upon this new information. In essence, the discussion section is like the last chapter in a good book. It provides a conclusion to the research project.

Depending on the type of research method employed, the format of the discussion section will vary. For example, qualitative studies sometimes combine results and discussion sections into one because it is difficult to present findings without simultaneously interpreting them for the reader. This chapter, however, focuses on writing the discussion section for quantitative studies. And as a general rule, there are typically five goals for this section:

1. Summarize the major results or findings of the study.
2. Interpret the findings.
3. Discuss the relationship between the findings and previous research.
4. Acknowledge any limitations of the study.
5. Discuss the implications of the findings, and suggest future research directions.

Summarize the Major Findings

Discussion sections begin with one or two paragraphs summarizing the major findings of the study. In essence, the introductory paragraph serves as an abstract for the discussion section. If the results section is strong, the reader already has the statistical information and knows whether the research questions and hypotheses were supported, so this is not the place to reiterate statistics. Instead, present a clear and succinct summary of the results. Figure 20.1 shows the introductory paragraph from the discussion section of Wrench and Booth-Butterfield's (2003) study on patient compliance. Note how the authors succinctly summarize the major findings of the study and transition into an interpretation of these results.

Wrench and Booth-Butterfield begin the discussion by stating the primary goal for the study. This information creates the foundation for the rest of the section by reminding the reader of the overall purpose for the project. Next, a concise summary of the overall findings is presented. This statement is especially important in studies where extensive data analyses are conducted. It enables the reader, who may not have a strong grasp of statistical analyses, the opportunity to understand the overall results. Wrench and Booth-Butterfield conclude the paragraph with a preview of the information discussed in the section. Previews such as these allow the author to subtly remind the reader what research questions and hypotheses were proposed in the study.

Interpret the Findings

At this point in the research process, you have spent countless hours formulating, examining, and analyzing questions and data. The discussion section of the research report finally provides you with the opportunity to allow your voice to be heard. So a

FIGURE 20.1
Introducing the Discussion Section

The primary goal of this study was to determine how physicians' humor orientation, credibility, and use of compliance-gaining strategies relate to patient satisfaction and compliance. The findings revealed significant relationships suggesting that better physician communication skills were associated with improved patient perceptions of physician credibility and patient satisfaction. The following paragraphs focus on the relationship that a physician's humor orientation has on patient satisfaction and physician credibility, the relationship between patient satisfaction and physician credibility, the relationship of compliance-gaining strategies with physician–patient interactions, and the post hoc analysis of the data sources used.

second goal of the discussion section is to explain the meaning of the results and share insight into why the findings are relevant or important.

Typically, the author will devote a paragraph of discussion for each research question or hypothesis proposed in the study. A good way to start each paragraph is by paraphrasing the question or hypothesis being discussed. Follow this with a concise statement that clearly states the direction of the relationship between the independent and dependent variables. Subsequent sentences focus on the author's interpretation of why the findings are important.

The use of language in interpreting the results is particularly important in this section. Resist the temptation to use definitive language to describe your results. Rather than stating that "results proved" something, consider evaluating results by applying language such as "results suggest" or "indicate."

Review the Wrench and Booth-Butterfield (2003) article, which is available on the textbook's website (https://oup-arc.com/wrench), and note how each paragraph summarizes the research question or hypothesis examined. No statistical information is included in the summaries. Rather, the authors summarize the statistical results using descriptive terms such as "positive relationship," "negative relationship," and "statistically significant." Declarative statements are avoided. Instead, the language used to interpret their findings includes phrases such as "the results appear to show" and "suggest" to avoid making claims that may later need to be defended.

Discuss the Relationship Between Findings and Previous Studies

Remember the review of literature that was completed at the beginning of the research project? Although you may have thought the only purpose of the review was to provide information for formulating the research question or hypothesis, there is one more opportunity to incorporate this information into your paper. One of the primary goals of research is to build a body of knowledge. And because the review of literature serves as the foundation for a research project, it is important to show how the current study builds on the existing knowledge. Therefore, a third goal of the discussion section is to discuss the relationship between the study's findings and previous studies.

How do your findings compare with those of related studies? Discussing the relationship between the current study and previous studies creates a context for the results. If the current study resulted from an idea for future research proposed by a previous study, now is the opportunity to acknowledge this information. Some common phrases used to make connections between studies include "supports the findings of Smith (1998)" or "contribute to the differences found in the current study and those reported by Smith (1998)."

As we mentioned in Chapter 4, one reason many researchers conduct research is to test and extend existing theories. And the discussion section is also where a researcher is able to shed light on the theory he or she is examining based on the results in her or his study. Did the researcher's results support the assumptions of the theory, or did the results negate the assumptions of the theory? Ultimately, clearly showing how one's results impact our understanding of theory is extremely important because your discussion will influence how other people understand the theory.

Wrench and Booth-Butterfield (2003) incorporate previous research findings to provide a rationale for their results. Several references are made throughout the discussion section to previous results in order to demonstrate that a pattern of similar findings exists across studies. This serves to strengthen the conclusions proposed by the authors. Note that references to previous studies are separate from the discussion of the findings. Rather, they are woven throughout the discussion to provide the reader with a "big picture" of the major findings and how they relate to earlier work.

Acknowledge Any Limitations

Every research study is affected by **limitations**. But it is better for the author to identify and address the limitations of the study in the discussion section than to have a reader or reviewer point them out later. You are not claiming that the study was poorly designed by pointing out these flaws; rather, you are sharing the insight gained by looking at the big picture. An author who points out the weaknesses in her or his study will enhance his or her credibility as a researcher.

Besides highlighting limitations, the discussion section provides the author with an opportunity to propose methods for overcoming these flaws in future studies. Examples of limitations often addressed in this section include inappropriateness in the design, population, methods, or instrumentation.

Although the Wrench and Booth-Butterfield (2003) study provides valuable insight for understanding the relationship between physicians' use of humor and patient satisfaction, the study has limitations. The authors highlight these limitations through the use of the subheading "limitations" and devote two paragraphs to addressing the limitations with measurement instruments and sampling methods. Note that they incorporate examples of previous research by other scholars to provide support for their recommendations.

Discuss Implications and Future Directions

The discussion section should conclude with a summary of the theoretical or practical **research implications** of the study and recommendations for **future directions** in research. If the study supports existing theory, it is appropriate to point out the contributions it makes in this section. Perhaps your results offer practical implications for the reader. Use this opportunity to discuss the benefits of the information. In their article, Wrench and Booth-Butterfield (2003) conclude by emphasizing the benefits of the study for enhancing interactions between patients and physicians and potentially decreasing the number of malpractice claims that are filed because of dissatisfaction.

Although the research project answers questions, the end result may actually result in new questions that are unanswered. Some of these questions may evolve because of the findings of your study. The concluding paragraphs of the discussion section provide the author with an opportunity to suggest directions for future research. Reflecting on the current study, ideas are proposed for the next step in research that examines similar variables. Some of these may evolve out of the limitations of the existing study. Others may result from comparing results with similar studies. The future directions provide other researchers with ideas to launch their own research projects.

WRITING THE ABSTRACT

Once you have concluded your discussion section, it is time to write your study's **abstract**. As we discussed in Chapter 5, the 6th edition of the APA style manual says that an abstract should be accurate, self-contained, and concise/specific. To be accurate, an abstract should correctly reflect what occurs in the paper itself. To be self-contained, an abstract should not need any specialized information for the reader to understand what the abstract is communicating. To be concise and specific, the abstract should not retell your entire study, but give enough information so that potential readers understand what you did in your study by discussing any relevant results and conclusions. Many research projects can have 10 or even 20 results or major conclusions, however, so it is usually best to limit your number of conclusions in the abstract to the five most important findings because journals generally vary on how long abstracts can be from 150 to 250 words.

PRESENTING AT CONFERENCES

Now that we have taken you through the world of creating, conducting, and writing quantitative research projects, it is time to talk about how to disseminate your findings to other researchers by both presenting at conferences and (later) publishing. Each professional discipline has its own associations that are designed to promote the research and scholarly activities of its members. In the communication discipline, there are associations at the state, regional, national, and international levels. Depending on your area of specialization, there may even be additional opportunities to network and share research. For example, if you completed a study examining humor in organizations, you could present your research at business conferences (American Management Association-AMA), psychology conferences (American Psychological

Association Convention-APA), or humor conferences (International Society for Humor Studies-ISHS) – instead of more traditional communication conferences. Figure 20.2 lists the communication associations that host conventions or conferences where research is presented.

FIGURE 20.2
Professional
Communication
Associations

INTERNATIONAL
International Communication Association
World Communication Association

NATIONAL
American Communication Association
National Communication Association

REGIONAL
Central States Communication Association
Eastern Communication Association
Southern States Communication Association
Western Communication Association

STATE
Arizona Communication Association
Arkansas Speech Communication
Association
California Speech Communication
Association
Carolinas Communication Association
Florida Communication Association
Georgia Communication Association
Illinois Speech & Theatre Association
Iowa Communication Association
Kansas Speech Communication Association
Kentucky Communication Association
Louisiana Communication Association
Maryland Communication Association
Michigan Association of Speech
Communication
Minnesota, Communication and Theatre
Association
Mississippi Speech Communication
Association
Missouri, Speech and Theatre Association of
Nebraska Speech Communication and
Theatre Association
New Jersey Communication Association
New York State Communication Association
North Dakota Speech and Theatre
Association
North West Communication Association
Ohio Communication Association
Oklahoma Speech Theatre Communication
Association

Oregon Speech Communication Association
Pennsylvania, Speech Communication
Association of
Rocky Mountain Communication Association
South Dakota, Speech Communication
Association
Tennessee Speech Communication
Association
Texas Speech Communication Association
Virginia Association of Communication
Arts and Sciences
Wisconsin Communication Association

SAMPLE OF SPECIALIZED OR
RELATED ASSOCIATIONS
Academy of Management
American Association of Public Opinion
Research
American College of Physicians
American Public Health Association
American Society for the History of Rhetoric
Association for Business Communication
Association for Women in Communications
Association for Education in Journalism and
Mass Communication
Broadcast Education Association
Gerontological Society of America
International Association for Conflict
Management
International Association for Humor Studies
International Association for Intercultural
Communication Studies
International Association for Media and
Communication Research
International Association for Relationship
Research
International Listening Association
International Public Relations Association
Kenneth Burke Society
Media Ecology Association
National Council on Family Relations
Public Relations Society of America
Religious Communication Association
Rhetoric Society of America
Society for Personality and Social Psychology
Society for Risk Analysis

Most associations host annual conferences or conventions that feature research presentations by students and faculty. Some conventions feature special preconferences or coinciding conferences focusing on undergraduate and graduate research. All the regional communication associations (Central [http://www.csca-net.org/], Eastern [http://www.ecasite.org], Southern [http://www.ssca.net/], and Western [http://www.west-comm.org/]) have undergraduate conferences that coincide with those organizations' annual conventions. For example, the Eastern Communication Association (ECA) sponsors the James C. McCroskey and Virginia Peck Richmond Undergraduate Scholars Conference (USC) that coincides with the ECA annual convention. You'll notice that ECA's USC is named after the last two coauthors of this book because McCroskey and Richmond taught generations of communication students how to conduct quantitative research.

Furthermore, there are a number of colleges and universities that sponsor communication conferences targeted for undergraduate research. The best place to find information on these conferences is in either the National Communication Association's (NCA) monthly newsletter *Spectra* or by joining the NCA listserv Communication, Research, and Theory Network (CRTNET; http://www.natcom.org/crtnet/). Deadlines for conference submissions vary, and it is best to consult the organization's website for submission information.

As a student, there are many reasons why a communication conference should be of interest to you. Conferences provide students with an opportunity to meet with and hear from scholars in the field, to learn about new methodologies and applications in research, and to present their own research. Networking and research presentation opportunities are the primary focus of these events. Faculty and alumni from various institutions catch up and share research and teaching ideas. Many schools recruit future graduate students at these events. After all, if an undergraduate student has an interest in presenting research and getting involved in professional associations, this is a good indicator of her or his potential as a graduate student.

Before we continue, it is important to remember that conferences are professional events, so you should always dress appropriately. If you are presenting, you should be in formal business attire, and if you are attending but not presenting, you can go with business casual.

DIVISIONS AND INTEREST GROUPS

An important benefit provided by conferences is the opportunity to network with colleagues who have similar interests. Perhaps the best way to meet other scholars with similar interests is to attend presentations sponsored by specific interest groups or divisions. Most associations provide their members with the opportunity to affiliate with several **academic divisions/interest groups** that represent various communication

FIGURE 20.3
National
Communication
Association—
Divisions, Caucuses,
and Sections

DIVISIONS
Activism and Social Justice Division
African American Communication and
    Culture Division
American Studies Division
Applied Communication Division
Argumentation and Forensics Division
Asian/Pacific American Communication
    Studies Division
Basic Course Division
Communication and Aging Division
Communication and the Future Division
Communication and Law Division
Communication and Sport Division
Communication Assessment Division
Communication as Social Construction
    Division
Communication Ethics Division
Communication and Social Cognition
    Division
Critical and Cultural Studies Division
Economics, Communication, and Society
    Division
Environmental Communication Division
Ethnography Division
Experiential Learning in Communication
    Division
Family Communication Division
Feminist and Women Studies Division
Freedom of Expression Division
Game Studies Division
Gay, Lesbian, Bisexual, Transgender, and
    Queer Communication Studies Division
Group Communication Division
Health Communication Division
Human Communication and Technology
    Division
Instructional Development Division
International and Intercultural
    Communication Division

Interpersonal Communication Division
Language and Social Interaction Division
Latino/Latina Communication Studies
    Division
Mass Communication Division
Nonverbal Communication Division
Organizational Communication Division
Peace and Conflict Communication Division
Performance Studies Division
Philosophy of Communication Division
Political Communication Division
Public Address Division
Public Dialogue and Deliberation Division
Public Relations Division
Rhetorical and Communication Theory
    Division
Spiritual Communication Division
Theatre, Film, and New Multimedia Division
Training and Development Division
Visual Communication Division

CAUCUSES
Asian/Pacific American Caucus
Black Caucus
Caucus on Lesbian, Gay, Bisexual,
    Transgender, and Queer Concerns
Disability Issues Caucus
La Raza Caucus
Women's Caucus

SECTIONS
Communication Centers Section
Community College Section
Elementary and Secondary Education
    Section
Emeritus/Retired Members Section
Master's Education Section
Student Section
Undergraduate College and University
    Section

contexts. The NCA currently has around 50 divisions and sections representing a variety of interests (the 2018 list of NCA divisions can be seen in Figure 20.3). Each of these groups schedules programs of research presentations at an annual convention, so whatever your interests are, there is an outlet for presentation.

Submitting Research for Conference Review

Once you have prepared your research paper for submission to a professional conference, you should consult the call for programs on the organization's website. The call for programs document provides important information on submitting your paper or proposal for review. Typically, the deadlines for convention submissions are six to nine months prior to the actual event. A sample of the **call for papers** for the Organizational Communication Division of Eastern Communication Association (Figure 20.4) illustrates many of the guidelines provided for submissions. Some conferences use e-mail as a way to submit papers and others have submission websites. Please check the individual association's website for more information on how they accept submitted manuscripts.

The call will specify whether the paper should be submitted in electronic format or mailed to the coordinator. Be sure to note what file format is preferred for submissions. Instructions provide guidelines as to page length limitations and deadlines for submission. Specific information on formatting of submissions is included, and often, items

FIGURE 20.4
Sample Call for
Convention Papers

EASTERN COMMUNICATION ASSOCIATION

ORGANIZATIONAL COMMUNICATION DIVISION

Copies of Papers: 1 [in electronic form only; NO hard copies]
Deadline: October 15, 20xx
Specify student papers: yes
Maximum length: 25 pages, excluding title page, abstract, references, tables, and figures

The Organizational Communication Division invites competitive papers and panel proposals on the theory, research, and teaching of organizational communication. The Division embraces all theoretical and methodological approaches to research. The submission of papers and panels pursuing the convention theme, "Insert Theme Here," is strongly encouraged.

Completed Paper Submissions should be emailed with the following:

1. TWO attached Microsoft Word (.doc or .rtf) files:

   • File 1) title page with the paper title and the author name (s)* and contact information (affiliation, mailing address, telephone number, email address) and a statement of professional responsibility (see below).

   • (File 2) text of the paper starting with a one-page abstract. All author identifiers should be removed from the text (excluding previous scholarly works cited in the paper and listed in the reference section). The word "Debut" should be marked on papers by authors who have not presented previously at a regional or national convention.

   • Statement of professional responsibility on the abstract page (see below).

Continued

FIGURE 20.4
Continued

2. The email subject line should include the abbreviation "ECA" and the title of the paper. The email text should include any requests for presentation aids such as overhead projector, TV/DVD player, etc. (see below).

Panel Proposal Submissions should be emailed and include the following:

1. ONE Microsoft Word (.doc or .rtf) file containing:

   - A thematic title for the program
   - Names of the chair and respondents, if any. Please do not have chairs act as respondents.
   - Names, mailing addresses, telephone numbers, email addresses, and institutional affiliations of all participants
   - Titles and abstracts for each paper or presentation
   - A program copy (NO MORE than a 75-word description) as it should appear in the final program
   - A detailed rationale for the program/panel
   - A statement of professional responsibility (see below)

2. The email subject line should include the abbreviation "ECA" and the title of the panel. The email text should include any requests for presentation aids such as overhead projector, TV/DVD player, etc. (see below).

Papers and panels not meeting these submission guidelines will not be distributed for review.

Statement of Professional Responsibility
ALL submissions must include (on either the abstract or the second page of the panel proposal) a statement of professional responsibility that reads:

> "In submitting the attached paper/panel, I/we recognize this submission is a professional responsibility. I/We agree to present this paper/panel if it is accepted and programmed. I/We further recognize that all who attend or present at ECA's annual meeting must register and pay required fees."

ECA Technology Policy
ECA has a Technology Policy (available in full text at http://www.ecasite.org/pdf/technologypolicy042007.pdf). Please note in particular the section that reads, "ECA will not approve requests for the following technology: personal computers, laser printers, satellite links, teleconference equipment, LCD panels and projectors, video data projects, and digital versatile/video disc equipment."

Questions & Additional Information
Please contact the Organizational Communication program planner, **Chair of the Organizational Communication Division**, at chair@genericuniversity.edu if you have any questions. Additional information about the convention, including short courses and other programming, is available on the ECA website, http://www.ecasite.org/.

such as a title page, abstract, key terms, and audiovisual needs are detailed. Some divisions schedule special panels or present awards to the top papers authored by students. To be considered for these, you should include the phrase "student authored" or "student paper" on the title page.

All conference submissions are sent to blind peer review to ensure that the papers are given an equal opportunity for programming. The blind review process requires all authors to remove any identifying information from the text of the paper to ensure that no preferential treatment will be shown in the evaluation. Most of the information that would need to be changed is located in the methods section of the research paper, and changes are often relatively simple. For example, if you initially reported in the paper that participants were students enrolled in classes at Ohio University, the name of the institution could be concealed by changing the description to students enrolled in classes at a large Midwestern university.

TYPES OF CONFERENCE PRESENTATIONS

Presentations take one of three forms at a professional conference: paper presentations, poster presentations, or panel discussions. Scholar-to-scholar presentations, which are like post presentations, will be discussed in this section briefly as well.

Paper Presentations

Paper presentations involve an oral report about the research project, typically followed by a response from a scholar who has conducted research in the area. If time permits, the audience may choose to ask authors questions about the project. Depending on the topic, an average of three to six papers may be scheduled to be presented during the same session. This means that an author can expect to have between 10 and 15 minutes to talk about the research project. That is not a lot of time, so if your paper is selected for presentation, give careful consideration to what you will highlight in your presentation and then rehearse to ensure that your presentation meets the time constraints.

PREPARING YOUR PRESENTATION

If you have only 10 to 15 minutes, how do you condense a 25- to 30-page paper to that short period of time? Here is what we recommend.

TITLE AND BRIEF BACKGROUND
First, start your presentation by introducing your title and giving a short background about how the project was initiated. Did you see a hole in a theory? Did you notice that a communication variable had not been explored

in a new context? Whatever the reasoning for your study, explain why you initiated the project in the first place. This should only take about a minute.

INTRODUCE RESEARCH NECESSARY TO UNDERSTAND VARIABLES Second, introduce the minimal research background necessary for your audience to understand your research variables. If you are dealing with a widely known concept like communication apprehension, you may need to provide a quick definition and a review of one or two studies that set up how you are looking at communication apprehension in your study. On the other hand, if you're dealing with a concept from either outside the communication field or that is emerging within the field, you may need to spend a little more time explaining the new concept and how it plays out within your study. Presenting your study's variables should take only from two to five minutes.

METHODS Third, explain the methods you used in your study. Start by giving a brief overview of how you collected your sample and any important demographics (sex, age, ethnicity, etc.). Next, explain the procedure that you used in your study as briefly as possible. If you conducted a complicated experiment, you may need to allow yourself a little more time to explain your experimental procedures. Then, discuss the instrumentation used in your study. At this point, it is not really necessary to go into detail about alpha reliabilities, means, and standard deviations—just refer your audience to the paper for the specific statistical information. Presenting your methods should take only one to three minutes.

RESULTS AND ANALYSIS Fourth, systematically deliver your results and corresponding analyses. We recommend (1) telling your audience what a specific hypothesis or research question was, (2) explaining how you tested that hypothesis or research question, (3) presenting the general result for the hypothesis or research question, and (4) analyzing briefly what your findings mean. This four-step process should be repeated for each of your major hypotheses and research questions. If, however, your study has many hypotheses and research questions or is overly complex, you may need to break your results into chunks of information that can be easily digested orally by your audience. While presenting your results, you also do not want to get yourself hung up on long strings of numbers that confuse your audience. For example, if you are reporting a regression, just say that the regression was significant, what R^2 was, and whether any beta weights accounted for unique variance. Do not try to read all the numbers in the F test; saying that the regression was statistically significant will cover this in an oral presentation. You can provide a basic interpretation of what each result means as you are discussing each finding. This section may take 2–5 minutes depending on your time limit, so keep it moving steadily.

LIMITATIONS Fifth, explain your limitations briefly (30 seconds at most) and any major future directions you believe this line of research should take. Finally, explain why this research is important and where you see this line of research heading in the future. This last part should be a quick summation of why the overall project was important and how it helps us understand human communication better.

TIPS FOR PRESENTING PAPERS In the event that you are asked to present your paper at a conference or convention, we have some helpful hints for you.

DO NOT READ US YOUR PAPER Okay, we are communication scholars who have taken public speaking. However, many people who present will read their manuscript in a fairly monotone fashion. Instead, we recommend making an outline of notes you can use to deliver your presentation in an extemporaneous fashion—just as you learned to do in public speaking.

WATCH YOUR TIME Make sure you know how much time you will have to present, and then make sure that your presentation can be made in the allotted time frame. Please realize that some speakers will alter their speaking rate once they are in front of an audience. If you know that you are someone who slows down or talks too much in front of an audience, plan your presentation accordingly.

HIT THE HIGHLIGHTS When discussing your literature review, give only the absolutely necessary highlights. People are more interested in your new research than they are in what is already out there. However, if your research involves any complex terms that may not be familiar to a general communication audience, then you should provide definitions so that people will understand the research.

DEALING WITH TECHNOLOGY Do not rely on having technology for your presentation. Increasingly, people want to use PowerPoint or other presentation software systems during a paper presentation. Unfortunately, the cost of such technology is often prohibitive for conferences and conventions. If you want to bring in your own laptop and projector, check with a conference or convention organizer to make sure that this is okay. Many conferences and conventions are held in locations that have strict rules about the use of technology (e.g., conference centers and hotels). Some conference and convention locations allow individuals to bring in outside technology with no extra charge to the conference or convention. Conversely, some conference and convention locations will charge the conference or convention an electricity use fee for any outside technology.

HAVE A BACKUP PLAN Always have a backup plan if you intend to use some kind of technology during your presentation. There is an old presenter's rule that if your technology can break down while presenting, it will. So, again, always have a backup plan. One easy backup plan is to have a handout you can give your audience members. If the technology you wanted to use does not lend itself to a handout, you should think about how you can present without the technology in case something does go wrong. It is always better to have thought out a worst-case scenario before it happens than to come up with a plan during the crisis.

STANDING OR NOT STANDING One of the hardest questions some presenters have to make is whether they should stand or sit during their presentations. There is no standard rule for this issue. On some panels, everyone stands while presenting, whereas on others, no one stands. From a basic public speaking perspective, standing will generally lead to a stronger connection with one's audience, so as a rule, we recommend standing. However, you should do what is most comfortable for you as a presenter.

PAPER RESPONDENTS

After all the presentations are complete, you may have a respondent for your paper. A **respondent** is an academic trained in your area of research who will provide feedback on your manuscript's writing, analysis, and conclusions. The respondent will discuss each person's paper separately, so it is possible that it will feel like you are getting picked on during this process. The respondent is not trying to hurt your feelings or make you feel inferior; he or she really wants to offer you advice on how to strengthen your paper. While listening to the respondent, it is important not to become argumentative even if you think the respondent is wrong. Instead, listen and take notes about what the respondent is saying, and then later decide whether you agree or disagree. If you argue with the respondent, either out loud or inside your head, you may end up missing some useful advice.

After the respondent is finished, the people who are attending the panel session may ask questions as time allows. As researchers, you should be ready for any type of question related to your study. People may ask about why you used specific scales or why you chose your specific statistical analysis. If you are presented with a question that you are not completely sure how to answer, we recommend simply saying that you are not sure, but that you will be glad to find the answer for the questioner if he or she provides an e-mail address at the conclusion of the session.

Poster Presentations

Poster presentations are a great opportunity for individuals just getting their feet wet presenting at academic conferences and conventions. According to Nicol and Pexman (2003a), the goal of a poster "is to summarize findings in a clear, interesting way to facilitate comprehension. Ultimately, the aim is for visitors to the poster to understand what the study was about and what the results were. The more visually appealing, well organized, and informative the poster is, the more likely people are to understand the study and findings" (p. 159).

During a typical poster presentation, an author or group of authors will stand next to their poster, and individuals will walk around the room or hall reading the various posters and talking to the author(s) about the study. One of the nice things about poster sessions is that they are fairly low key and full of energy. You may even want to consider making a handout that summarizes your study for individuals who talk to you about it. You could also have a stack of copies of your actual paper to hand out to individuals during the session.

For undergraduate and graduate students, all the regional communication associations have competitive poster competitions during their conventions. Presenting your original research at a communication conference is a good resume builder whether you plan on entering graduate school or the corporate sector, and poster sessions provide a nonthreatening way to do this even for individuals who have high public speaking anxiety.

SAMPLE POSTER

At this point, you may be asking yourself, "What does a poster presented at a communication conference actually look like?" To give you a general idea of how posters are typically formatted, we have created a simple graphic to help you understand, which is shown in Figure 20.5.

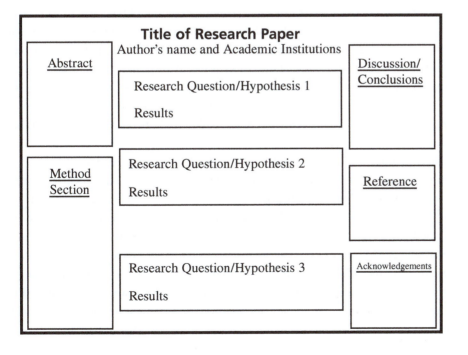

FIGURE 20.5
Sample Poster Format

First, every conference or convention has different requirements for the sizes of the poster, so ensure you find out how large your poster can be before you get there. Furthermore, you will want to know whether your poster should be freestanding (e.g., on a table), displayable on an easel, or tacked to a cork board. The most common size poster is probably the 36- by 48-inch poster. Now it's very important to double-check the individual conference's expectations for posters.

For example, if you are expected to use an easel, then your poster must be thick enough for the poster to stand up on the easel by itself. In these cases, using a foam board (two-sided poster board with about ¼" core of foam between both sides) or a tri-fold cardboard poster (usually made out of corrugated cardboard). Foam board is probably the number one choice for easel displays, whereas trifold posters are great for tabletop displays and easels. The reason we suggest both the foam board and trifold posters is because they tend to have a thickness that allows them to stand up on their own on an easel. If you try to use regular poster board, you will have a lot of problems keeping the poster in place.

However, other conferences will provide you with corkboards to display your posters. In these cases, you'll be using pushpins to attach your poster to the corkboard. Both foam board and trifolds don't work as well on corkboards because pushpins won't hold them very well (or for very long) on the corkboard. In these cases, people are more likely to print their poster on paper or fabric. Depending on whether you are flying or driving, a rolled-up paper poster can be more cumbersome, whereas, a fabric poster can easily fold up into your suitcase or travel bag.

Once you know the basic size of the poster, it is time to determine what information must be put on it. Your poster cannot be a simple retelling of your study. We have all seen lazy poster presenters who literally tack up their entire paper on the poster with no changes at all. As communication scholars, we have all taken public speaking and should know a little about the importance of visual aids, and that is exactly what a poster should be—a visual aid. Remember that the purpose of a poster session is to interact with other people discussing your research study as they walk by your poster. The more interesting the poster is, the more likely people are going to stop and talk to you about your research.

You will note in Figure 20.5 that there are a number of different parts commonly seen on a poster. The first part is the name of your study, centered at the top of the poster, along with the author(s) name(s) and college/university affiliation(s). After the paper title and your name, everything else is more creative. We provided you a simple format you can follow in Figure 20.5, but this is not the only format you could use for your poster. For example, if you have numerous research questions and hypotheses, you may not end up including the references or acknowledgment sections on your poster. If you have too many research questions and hypotheses, you may end up only putting the three or four most important findings on your poster.

The first box you will see on the poster is the abstract box. We think it is a good idea to include your abstract on your poster because it gives a general overview of your paper. People may not stop and ask you questions, but they are more likely to walk by and quickly read your abstract. Abstracts are often great conversation starters with people reading your poster.

The second box included on our sample poster in Figure 20.5 is the method section box. Whether you conducted a qualitative/interpretive, quantitative/scientific, or rhetorical/critical study, people will want to know a little about your methodology. Obviously, you cannot provide all of the intricate details of the method used in your study, but you can provide enough information to quickly explain what it is that you did.

The third, fourth, and fifth boxes are designed for the real heart of your study, or your research questions and/or hypotheses. Some individuals like to clump all of their research questions and/or hypotheses into one box and then their results in another, but we think this ultimately ends up confusing the people examining your poster. We recommend listing a research question or hypothesis, followed by what you found. Ultimately, this helps demonstrate, in a quick and efficient manner, exactly what it is that you found in your study.

The sixth box is for your overall conclusions from your study. We often call this the "So what?" box, or the "Why should we really care about these findings?" box. If you have multiple important conclusions that can be made because of your study, we strongly recommend bulleting them to make them easier to read.

The seventh and eighth boxes contain information that may or may not be overly relevant. The seventh box contains a list of important references or works cited. Obviously, you cannot include all of the references listed or works cited in your manuscript. However, if there are a handful that are important, list those on your poster. The eighth box is one that is technically only necessary if your project was funded by an outside source. Many research projects receive grant funding for the project, and one common requirement of grants is that any presentation made about the study funded by the grant must acknowledge the source of funds. As a quick side note on the issue of grants, some colleges and schools have competitive research grants to students at all levels to help them conduct their research. Consider this as an opportunity to investigate and talk with your faculty research advisor.

TIPS FOR POSTER PRESENTATIONS

So far, we have examined the different parts of Figure 20.5 to help you understand how to organize a top-notch research poster. Now, we want to stress a number of key elements in making a stellar poster:

WORKING WITH COLOR Black and white is boring, so make sure you add color. However, do not go overboard and start "bedazzling" your poster—there comes a point when there is too much flash.

FONT SIZE Twelve-point Times New Roman or Courier New font may look great on the page, but these fonts cannot be read at a distance. When making your poster, stand at least five feet away from all words and see whether you can easily read them. If you cannot read your poster, no one else will even bother trying.

THINKING ABOUT TEXT A poster is a not a research paper, so there is no need to double space text that appears on the poster. On the same subject, do not just take your research paper and paste it onto the poster. Remember, posters are visual aids, so the text should help explain concisely what you did and found.

POSTER JARGON A poster is not an instant message or a text message, so avoid Internet lingo on your poster (unless relevant). Also, make sure you use both upper- and lowercase letters. In fact, any specific jargon or terms that someone would need to know in order to understand your presentation should probably be defined on the poster.

POSTERS ARE VISUAL Too much text on a poster can be boring, so using lists and bullets of information will be appreciated by your readers. Furthermore, graphs, charts, and pictures can help get information across much faster. Again, do not just take your research paper and paste it onto the poster board. Also, don't just throw a bunch of pictures on your poster if they do not relate to the content of the research study conducted.

POSTER HEADINGS Make sure that you use headings for each section of your poster. People get lost easily, so headings help them follow what you are saying.

POSTERS SHOULD ALLOW FOR DISCUSSIONS A poster is a visual aid that should assist you in having a discussion with someone about your research project. The goal of your poster is to help you, not hinder you. Remember, you're the expert on your specific research paper, so enjoy the experience of telling people about the awesome research you conducted.

BE PASSIONATE All of the coauthors of this book have judged many different poster sessions over our careers. One of the easiest ways to stand out in a large sea of posters is through your own passion about your research project. One of our coauthors was recently judging posters and came across three different presenters.

The first presenter had a really cool study on an interesting topic, but the presentation was monotone and the presenter really didn't appear to want to talk about the research. Hands down, this presenter probably had the best designed study in the poster session, but the lack of enthusiasm while presenting really turned all of the judges off.

The second presenter had a poorly designed study that really didn't make sense, but the presenter had so much passion. In fact, most of the judges originally ranked this presenter very high until they started talking about the merits of the study itself. The judges were pretty surprised by how all of them had been taken in by the presenter's passion at first.

The final student had the perfect mix of a solid study and passion, but it was on a topic many of us had heard before. Nothing was necessarily overly new or groundbreaking, but the passion the presenter had for the research really sold the judges. So, having a great study combined with your ability to passionately tell others about your study is what really makes for a great poster session.

Scholar-to-Scholar Posters

Scholar-to-scholar presentations are like poster sessions. The purpose of the scholar-to-scholar sessions is to provide poster presenters with an opportunity to discuss their poster with top-notch scholars in the field of communication. A scholar-to-scholar presentation functions like a poster session, but top scholars whose research relates to that being presented during the scholar-to-scholar sessions are invited to interact with the individuals presenting. Although some scholar-to-scholar presenters still use a traditional poster, others have gone beyond the traditional poster to include audio and video presentations. Either way, scholar-to-scholar presentations provide a great way for you to get feedback about your research study from some of the top minds in the field of communication.

Panel Discussions

Panel discussions are composed of three or more individuals who discuss a common topic in an informal format. Rather than each person delivering a formal presentation, they may be asked to offer their insights or opinions while a facilitator guides the discussion. Audience members are often encouraged to take part during panel sessions as well by asking questions or offering comments.

Although we wish we could say that all presentations are created equally, they really are not perceived this way in academia. Typically speaking, people who are presenting original research on a competitive panel generally are perceived as more prestigious than people presenting posters or sitting on panel discussions. A competitive panel means that all of the papers were reviewed by experts in the field prior to being accepted for the conference. Most of the time, the expert reviewers will not even know who authored a paper while reviewing the study's merits. In fact, some universities will not even count posters or panels as research presentations. We say this not to devalue posters and panels, but to warn that you must know what value your academic institution places on these different presentational formats, especially if you decide to make a career in academia.

Now that you understand the opportunities offered by professional associations for young scholars, we hope that you will consider submitting your research projects for review. After all, the format of a convention paper is nearly identical to the format discussed for research papers in this text.

PUBLICATION

One of the best ways to ensure that your research study contributes to the body of knowledge in the field is to submit it for publication to an academic journal. Articles submitted to academic journals are scholarly in nature. "Scholarly" indicates that the facts and information included in the study are documented by citing the author and date of publication for relevant research. It is important to note that although authors of convention papers often receive feedback in two or three months, the journal review process is considerably longer. It may take anywhere from one to five *years* before an article submitted for review actually ends up in print. To better understand the time required for publishing journal articles, let's inspect the peer review process.

All articles submitted to academic journals are peer reviewed. The **peer review** process for academic journals is similar to that used by professional conventions, but with one notable exception. Feedback provided in a journal article review is much more comprehensive than the comments provided by a convention review panel. Whereas convention reviewers may simply rank papers they think should be presented, the process is much more rigorous when reviewing articles for publication. Journal review board members are often asked to provide one of four recommendations to the editor: (1) publish as is; (2) publish pending revisions; (3) revise and resubmit before a decision is made; or (4) reject the study. If the article is rejected, some editors and reviewers may offer suggestions regarding alternative outlets where the study can be considered again for publication. Whether a study is accepted or rejected, however, authors typically receive extensive feedback from a panel of two or three anonymous reviewers. Let's take a look at the two processes involved in journal publication more closely: the submission process and the review process.

Submission Process

Once you have decided to submit your research for review, the next question often is "Which journal is most appropriate for this study?" There are several options to choose from in determining which outlet is best for your research. Many of the associations listed in Figure 20.2 publish one or more academic journals, and the focus of each journal is unique in terms of the types of methodologies, communication contexts, and length of articles published. To determine which outlet is best suited for your research, review the call for manuscripts for more detailed guidelines. Samples of call for manuscripts are provided in Figure 20.6 for two prominent communication journals: *Communication Education* (CE) and *Communication Research Reports* (CRR).

Each of these samples provides scholars with information on the types of articles that are typically published regarding methodology and contextual focus. In addition, format guidelines are provided, as is information about page length and how to submit articles. One obvious difference in the calls for *CE* and *CRR* is their page length requirements: *CRR* has a limit of approximately 10 pages, whereas *CE* accepts manuscripts

FIGURE 20.6
Call for Manuscripts
for *Communication*
Education **and**
Communication
Research Reports

a) Communication Education (an NCA Journal)

Communication Education invites original, social science research on communication in instructional contexts. These should be methodologically rigorous studies that advance practice and theory in instruction generally, and in communication education specifically. I encourage submissions from well-designed, systematic and programmatic research, theoretically-grounded projects, rigorous literature reviews and meta-analyses. Importantly, these studies must be data-based and have a substantive impact on educational processes.

Sound studies that examine constructs that are important to teaching/learning processes will be emphasized; e.g., teacher/student interaction, verbal/non-verbal interaction in the teaching-learning context, classroom management, information processing, mediated or technology education, educational communication constructs, development and assessment, and learning outcomes will be considered.

One goal is high credibility and visibility of *Communication Education* as a premiere source of the highest level knowledge and information on communication in educational contexts. Therefore, comprehensive, major literature reviews, either empirical or narrative, will be featured. Such reviews should be thorough, detailed, and unbiased, and provide extensive background as well as the latest research on major instructional concepts.

Both new and experienced scholars are encouraged to submit their works, and will receive feedback that is both expedient and helpful. Correspondingly, all authors must submit articles that meet the highest standards of writing, grammar, and mechanics (emphasizing brevity). Authors who need editorial assistance can find support in online proofreading services, such as www.proofreadnow.com.

Given the distinctive missions of each of the NCA journals, book reviews should be submitted to the more appropriate NCA journal, *The Review of Communication*, and articles focusing on teaching practices should be submitted to *Communication Teacher*.

Manuscript Submission

Communication Education has moved to an entirely electronic system for submissions and reviews. To facilitate rapid accessibility and review, manuscripts should be submitted online at Communication Education's ScholarOne site.

New users should first create an account. Once a user is logged onto the site, submissions must be made via the Author Center. Please submit papers formatted in MS Word in a PC-compatible version. To ensure a blind review process, any identifying information is entered during the online submission process where prompted, along with any other relevant information concerning the basis of the study (e.g., a dissertation, grant or paid consulting) and other background (e.g., prior presentations of results, grant support). Please keep all identifying information separate from the attached manuscript.

Manuscripts should be no longer than 25 double-spaced pages (not including tables and references), and must conform to the conventions of the 6th edition of the

Continued

FIGURE 20.6
Continued

Publication Manual of the American Psychological Association. Manuscripts that do not conform to these guidelines will not be reviewed.

Manuscripts submitted to *Communication Education* must not be under consideration in other outlets, or have appeared in any other published form. Upon notification of acceptance, authors must assign copyright to the National Communication Association and provide copyright clearance for any copyrighted material used.

b) *Communication Research Reports* (an ECA Journal)

Communication Research Reports publishes brief empirical articles (approximately 10 double-spaced pages or less excluding tables and references) on a variety of topics of human communication. Empirical studies in the general contexts of interpersonal, organizational, communication traits, intercultural, nonverbal, small group, health, persuasion, mass, political, relational, computer mediated, life-span, and instructional communication are appropriate for submission. Consistent with the mission of the journal, the main portion of submitted manuscripts should focus on the method, results, and interpretation of the results. However, manuscripts must contain a concise theoretical rationale and relevant literature review.

Particular manuscripts may be designated as a Brief Report. At the discretion of the Editor, manuscripts that are designated as such will have gone through the complete review process (as full length manuscripts), provide value for the readership, yet not warrant a full-length article. Brief reports will be no longer than 3 to 5 pages (excluding tables and references) with the focus highlighting a specific finding and implications for the discipline. All sections traditionally included in a manuscript will be required, but must be brief and to the point. All extraneous information must be eliminated. Manuscripts that are submitted as a Brief Report will not be reviewed. The Brief Report designation is a function of editorial decision. Also at the discretion of the Editor will be one manuscript per issue designated as a Spotlight on Method/Analysis piece. These articles will be solicited by the Editor and will be 5–8 pages in length (excluding tables and references) highlighting topics that will range from novel methodological approaches and/or statistical techniques to common misconceptions/issues of contemporary controversy related to method/analysis. Each issue of CRR will contain one such manuscript that will be solicited and/or determined by the Editor.

Review Policy. Manuscripts will be blind-reviewed by at least two experts in the relevant subject matter. These evaluations will constitute the basis for the Editor's decision. *Communication Research Reports* is committed to completing the review process as efficiently and quickly as possible. Manuscripts that do not conform to submission guidelines will not be reviewed. No manuscript submitted for review can be previously published or be under consideration by any other journal at the time of submission.

Submission of Full-Length Manuscripts. *Communication Research Reports* will accept all manuscript submissions electronically via the ScholarOne Manuscripts website located at http://mc.manuscriptcentral.com/crr. For technical support regarding the ScholarOne Manuscripts system, you may contact them at http://scholarone.com/services/support. For all other inquiries, please contact Communication Research Reports at editor@genericuniversity.edu. Submitted

FIGURE 20.6
Continued

manuscripts must be the original work of the author(s) and have all identifiers removed from the document. Authors should submit their files per the submission protocol found on ScholarOne. Manuscripts should be prepared using MS WORD and must conform to the 6th edition of the Publication Manual of the American Psychological Association. All general inquiries about the journal, its policies, or procedures should be directed to Jane Doe, Editor.

Proofs. One set of page proofs will be sent to the designated corresponding author. Proofs should be checked and returned promptly as directed.

Complimentary Policy/Reprints. Each corresponding author will receive 50 complimentary reprints of their article upon registration with Rightslink, our authorized reprint provider. Authors will need to create a unique account and register with Rightslink for this free service. Complimentary reprints are not available past publication. Each corresponding author will also receive one complimentary copy of the issue in which their article appears.

up to 25 pages in length. Another distinction can be found in the research contexts included in the journal: *CE* encourages manuscripts focusing on classroom communication phenomena, whereas *CRR* welcomes manuscripts on a wide variety of topics focusing on human communication. Three basic factors will help guide your decision as to which journal is right for your research: (1) focus on communication context, (2) research methodologies, and (3) page length. To see a list of possible publication outlets for communication scholarship, review the chart of communication-related journals in Figure 4.6 from Chapter 4.

Once you have determined which journal is appropriate for your research, be sure to adhere to all instructions for manuscript preparation detailed in the call. In particular, pay close attention to guidelines for page length, limits on the number of words to be included in the abstract, and preferred style format (APA or Modern Language Association [MLA]). Be sure to carefully edit the manuscript to avoid any embarrassing mistakes. When you submit your paper, it is often a good idea to draft a short cover letter to the editor pointing out the unique contributions of your paper and how it "fits" with the journal content. Some editors may ask that you add a statement confirming that the article has not been published elsewhere and is not being submitted simultaneously for review by another journal.

Review Process

As discussed earlier, the journal review process is lengthy and sometimes frustrating. Once you have reached this point in the process, be prepared to wait. Journal editors will often review the list of references included in your article to identify potential reviewers. Throughout the process, the author(s) and reviewer(s) remain anonymous. However, authors often include information in the manuscript that provides the reviewer with clues as to their identity. To maintain your anonymity, refrain from including too many references to your own work, and be sure to remove any and all identifying information from the manuscript. Citing references from the journal to which you are submitting your article is another way of showing to the reviewers and editor how your research fits with what the journal is already publishing.

Prepare yourself for the feedback you will receive. After all, reviewers often feel obligated to find some issues with your study. Rarely do papers get accepted on the initial submission. In fact, many undergo two to three revisions before they are ready for publication. Editors will send typed comments from the reviewers along with their anonymous recommendation for acceptance, approve with revisions, revise and resubmit, or rejection. If the recommendation from reviewers is to revise and resubmit your article, take heed and be sure to address the concerns identified in their reviews. Once you have made the recommended changes, it is a good idea to draft a letter to the reviewers letting them know that you have made the changes requested in their review. Address each recommendation made by the reviewer, and explain how you responded to it in the revised manuscript. Doing so will communicate to the reviewers and the editor that you are committed to addressing their concerns and value their feedback.

Let's face it: not every manuscript that is submitted to a journal gets accepted. In fact, most communication journals average an acceptance rate of between 10% and 20%. That means that 80% to 90% of the articles are rejected. A summary of the acceptance rates for journals published by NCA, which is shown in Figure 20.7, should provide you with additional insight into journal acceptance rates.

If you decide to submit your research for publication, chances are that you will experience rejections along the way. Although rejection is frustrating, you can

FIGURE 20.7
NCA Journal Acceptance Rates (August 2016 to August 2017)

Journal Name	Acceptance Rate	No. of Submissions
Communication and Critical/Cultural Studies	6%	110
Communication Education	16%	148
Communication Monographs	10%	198
Communication Teacher	38%	175
Critical Studies in Media Communication	38%	236
First Amendment Studies	35%	12
Journal of Applied Communication Research	11%	266
Journal of International and Intercultural Communication	9%	112
Quarterly Journal of Speech	19%	177
Text and Performance Quarterly	25%	72
The Review of Communication	37%	70

Source: https://www.natcom.org/sites/default/files/2017_LA_Binder_Dallas.pdf

adopt a positive view of the process if you use the feedback provided by the reviewers to help revise the paper for submission to a different journal. Ask a colleague or professor to read the paper, and share the feedback provided by reviewers to get his or her suggestions. Although nobody likes being rejected, it is important to remember that it is part of the publication process. Trust us—the satisfaction you will experience on receiving your first acceptance letter will make this entire process worth the effort.

RESEARCH OUTSIDE THE WALLS OF ACADEMIA

Discussions of research abound in the 21st century. We are constantly bombarded with information related to quantitative information, so making the information easy to navigate for those who do not have a background in quantitative research methods is important. For our purposes, we want to discuss two specific aspects of research reporting: writing for business and writing for the general public.

Writing for Business

In Chapter 5, we discussed O'Shea's (1986) nine steps to writing a business research report: (1) executive summary, (2) project background, (3) objectives/scope, (4) methods, (5) analysis, (6) findings/conclusions, (7) recommendations, (8) expected benefits, and (9) implementation guide. Whether you are presenting your research in a written fashion or asked to orally present the information, this nine-step process is good for all basic presentation needs outside academia.

O'Shea (1986) also offers seven keys to writing a readable report that we think should be reiterated here as well.

WRITE SHORT REPORTS

Most people in the business world do not have the time to read long documents, so research reports should be written as shortly and directly as possible.

ARRANGE MATERIAL FOR EMPHASIS

You do not want your biggest finding or your number-one recommendation to get lost because it is buried somewhere in the middle of the report. This is one reason why you should lay out information in a manner that draws attention to the material you want emphasized.

AVOID LONG, COMPLEX PARAGRAPHS AND SENTENCES

As academics ourselves, we know that a gorgeous, flowing, long-winded sentence can be a lot of fun to write. But in the world outside of academia, people want things short and to the point.

AVOID JARGON

Writing about statistics while avoiding jargon can be difficult. If you must use technical ideas and information, ensure that you simply explain the jargon. But if possible, avoid the jargon altogether.

USE ACTIVE VOICE AND CONCRETE WORDS

Use active voice and concrete words rather than euphemisms. Again, you want your reader to actively engage with your writing. If you are writing in a straightforward manner, with direct, descriptive words, people are more likely to read and remember what you have written.

USE PICTURES AND GRAPHS

People like pictures and graphics. We recommend also thinking about strategic use of color as well. However, you do not want to go overboard. We have seen some reports in which every other page is a picture or graph, which can become tedious. Remember, if you try to call attention to everything, you will end up calling attention to nothing. Use pictures and graphs to emphasize pieces of information you want your readers to remember and understand.

USE NUMBERS SELECTIVELY

Obviously, when you are discussing statistics, you will have to use some numbers. However, you need not include every number. For example, one of our coauthors was working on a consulting project that involved correlations. Instead of presenting the correlation coefficients for each relationship in a correlation matrix, he placed a + sign for positive relationships, a − sign for negative relationships, and NR in spaces where no relationship was found. This more visual approach made it easier to understand for readers who were not schooled in quantitative research methods.

Writing for the General Public

When writing up research that will be disseminated to the general public, it is important to remember that most people are functionally numerically illiterate. Any description of statistical analysis and data should be kept short and clear. Admittedly, it is often difficult for researchers to adjust to this type of writing because we get so used to an audience of colleagues who understand the different research methods, statistical tests, and results.

WRITING STATISTICAL STORIES

According to the United Nations Economic Commission for Europe (2009), a statistical story is one that "doesn't just recite data in words. It tells a story about the data.

Readers tend to recall ideas more easily than they do data. A statistical story conveys a message that tells readers what happened, who did it, when and where it happened, and hopefully, why and how it happened" (p. 1). A good statistical story is one where the data can help inform people about various issues that affect them and their environment. The presentation should focus on how the information from a research study can be used by readers while preventing the story from getting bogged down by the researcher's methods and statistics. A good statistical story should accurately represent the research, but the goal of this type of writing is journalistic and designed for a general audience with little to no research background.

According to United Nations Economic Commission for Europe (2009), a successful statistical story contains three primary components: (1) it has a successful headline that grips the attention of readers; (2) it provides the "story behind the numbers in an easily understood, interesting and entertaining fashion" (p. 1); and (3) it shows to both the general public and journalists how statistical information can impact the way that news stories are told. As you can see, statistical storytelling could also be called statistical journalism. Unfortunately, most journalists do not take courses in school related to understanding and handling statistical information. As such, they often rely on others to explain the importance of statistical information.

One common tool that many researchers use is the simple press release. Press releases related to statistical information can help frame how the numbers and the findings get discussed by those in the media. In fact, it is not uncommon that press releases quickly turn into entire stories with little to no editing by news outlets looking for good content.

Historically, the field of communication has done a poor job of expressing the importance of our research to the general public. We have a number of notable public scholars who appear on daytime talk shows, but many of the findings published in our academic journals are read only by those in our own field or in closely related fields. In 2005, the National Communication Association stepped in and created the field's first online magazine devoted to making communication research accessible for those in the general public. *Communication Currents* (http://www.communicationcurrents.com/) takes complicated research and discusses it in a manner that the general public can understand. Many of the articles found in *Communication Currents* are good examples of statistical stories. Other articles approach communication from either a qualitative/interpretive or a rhetorical/critical epistemological perspective.

So how does one write a good statistical story? Figure 20.8 shows the difference between academic and journalistic writing. Academic writing starts off with a broad focus as you investigate your literature review. Over time, your focus narrows as you go into your rationale section, leading to your hypotheses and/or research questions. Ultimately, academic writing gets to its narrowest point during the results and

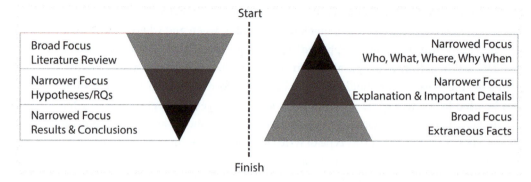

FIGURE 20.8
Academic Versus Journalistic Writing Process

discussion section, where you make sense of what you found. Journalistic writing, on the other hand, is the opposite of academic writing regarding structure. In journalistic writing, you start by focusing on the famous who, what, when, where, and why of the story. You want to get to the important parts of the story first, before you lose your readers' attentions. From there, journalistic writing goes into the supporting information as explanations and important details needed to understand the full scope and context of the introduction. In journalistic writing, the broad part is generally extraneous information, which is left to the end of the article. In fact, most of this extraneous information will eventually get cut by an editor in need of page space.

Although there is a fundamental difference in how academics and journalists approach the writing process, the goal is still to ensure that their readers understand the material being presented. To help with journalistic writing, United Nations Economic Commission for Europe (2009) recommends that when writing about statistical information, writers should use the following:

- Language that people understand;
- Short sentences, short paragraphs;
- One main idea per paragraph;
- Subheadings to guide the reader's eye;
- Simple language: "Get," not "acquire." "About," not "approximately." "Same," not "identical";
- Bulleted lists for easy scanning;
- A good editor. Go beyond Spell-Check; ask a colleague to read your article;
- Active voice. "We found that . . ." Not: "It was found that . . .";
- Numbers in a consistent fashion: For example, choose 20 or twenty, and stick with your choice;
- Rounded numbers (both long decimals and big numbers);

- Embedded quotes (these are sentences that generally explain "how" or "why" and which journalists like to use verbatim in their news stories in quotes);
- URLs, or electronic links to provide your reader with a full report containing further information. (p. 6)

In turn, the United Nations Economic Commission for Europe (2009) recommends that writers should avoid the following:

- "Elevator statistics": This went up, this went down, this went up;
- Jargon and technical terms;
- Acronyms;
- All capital letters and all italics: Mixed upper and lower case is easier to read;
- "Table reading", that is, describing every cell of a complex table in your text. (p. 6)

Although the United Nations Economic Commission for Europe's ideas on writing seem simplistic, their approach to statistical science writing is appropriate to ensure that the general public will understand.

DATA VISUALIZATION

I'm sure we've all heard the phrase "a picture is worth a thousand words." Although not as common in academic research, there is an exploding world of visual statistical data. In 2008, Unwin, Chen, and Härdle wrote, "Data visualization is a new term. It expresses the idea that it involves more than just representing data in a graphical form (instead of using a table). The information behind the data should also be revealed in a good display; the graphic should aid readers or viewers in seeing the structure in the data" (p. 6). Today, the world of data visualization looks at a broad range of tools and tactics to visualize information.

In recent years, substantial statistical information has cropped up visually in books, magazines, and online. An information graphic, or **infographic**, is a visual representation of data, information, or knowledge condensed into a combination of images and text designed to help viewers grasp complex material quickly and clearly. Although the Internet did not create infographics, the Internet has definitely popularized the art form in recent years.

Thankfully, you do not have to be a great artist to create compelling infographics. There are a number of websites where you can buy stock infographics and then reformat them for your own needs (e.g., http://www.vectorstock.org/ and https://www .dollarphotoclub.com/). A few places online also offer free infographic templates that can be used: e.g., http://piktochart.com/ and http://www.freepik.com/). You will need some experience working with a graphics editing software program to use these templates. Two common proprietary software packages used for making infographics come from Adobe, called Photoshop and Illustrator (https://creative.adobe.com/), but you

FIGURE 20.9
Infographic Example

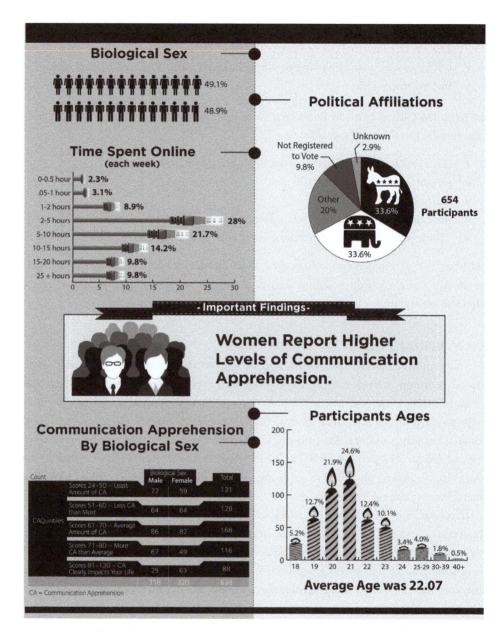

can find free software that is just as effective, such as Gimp (http://www.gimp.org/) and Inkscape (https://inkscape.org/en/).

Figure 20.9 is an example of an infographic based on content found in the dataset collected for this book. Although these data are not necessarily the most conducive for overly creative infographics, the basic gist of the data is easily understood.

CONCLUSION

Throughout this text, we have described the process involved in writing and conducting scholarly research. As you have noticed, this process takes time, and it would be a shame not to share the results of your hard work with others. In this chapter, we have provided information to assist you in writing up the discussion section of your paper. Various elements and suggestions for language use have been provided to interpret results for the reader. We concluded this text with an explanation of the options available and a description of the processes involved in submitting your research for conference presentation or journal publication. As you begin your journey as a communication scholar, we encourage you to share your work with others—after all, you are the future scholars of our field!

KEY TERMS

Abstract p. 567

Academic divisions/interest groups p. 569

Call for papers p. 571

Discussion section p. 563

Future directions p. 566

Infographic p. 591

Limitations p. 566

Panel discussions p. 581

Paper presentations p. 573

Peer review p. 582

Poster presentation p. 576

Respondent p. 576

Research implications p. 566

Scholar-to-scholar presentations p. 581

REFERENCES

American Psychological Association. (2010). *Publication manual of the American Psychological Association* (6th ed.). Washington, DC: American Psychological Association.

Nicol, A. A. M., & Pexman, P. M. (2003a). *Displaying your findings: A practical guide for creating figures, posters, and presentations.* Washington, DC: American Psychological Association.

O'Shea, T. J. (1986). Presentation of results. In S. W. Barcus & J. W. Wilkinson (Eds.), *Management consulting services* (pp. 235–252). New York, NY: McGraw–Hill.

United Nations Economic Commission for Europe. (2009). *Making data meaningful: Part 1—A guide to writing stories about numbers.* [online] Retrieved from http://www.unece.org/stats/documents/writing/MDM_Part1_English.pdf

Unwin, A., Chen, C., & Härdle, W. K. (2008). Introduction. In C. Chen, W. Härdle, & A. Unwin (Eds.), *Handbook of data visualization* (pp. 4–12). Berlin, Germany: Springer.

Wrench, J. S., & Booth-Butterfield, M. (2003). Increasing patient satisfaction and compliance: An examination of physician humor orientation, compliance-gaining strategies, and perceived credibility. *Communication Quarterly, 51,* 482–503.

FURTHER READING

Alexander, A., & Potter, W. J. (Eds.). (2001). *How to publish your communication research: An insider's guide.* Thousand Oaks, CA: Sage.

Kitchin, R., & Fuller, D. (2005). *Academic's guide to publishing.* Thousand Oaks, CA: Sage.

Knapp, M. L., & Daly, J. A. (2004). *A guide to publishing in scholarly communication journals.* Mahwah, NJ: Erlbaum.

McInerney, D. M. (2002). *Publishing your psychology research: A guide to writing for journals in psychology and related fields.* Thousand Oaks, CA: Sage.

Nicol, A. A. M., & Pexman, P. M. (2003). *Presenting your findings: A practical guide for creating tables.* Washington, DC: American Psychological Association.

Glossary

Abstract: Accurate, self-contained, concise description of a research study.

Abstract Variables: Variables that change or differ over time or across situations or contexts.

Academic Divisions/Interest Groups: Groups of people who study a specific area of communication (e.g., organizational, instructional, intercultural, mass mediated).

Accelerated Longitudinal Survey Design: Form of survey design in which a research creates mini age cohorts and studies them over a short period of time to ascertain how changes would occur across age groups over a longer period of time.

Acquiescence: When an individual fakes responses to cooperate with the investigator and give the researcher what he or she wants.

Alternate Forms Reliability: Reliability test in which two measures of the same phenomenon are used to measure the same group at two different times.

Alternative Hypothesis (H_1): Prediction that there is a relationship or a difference that has not occurred by chance or random error.

American Psychological Association Style: Components or features of a research manuscript that dictate how the manuscript should be presented beyond the scope of actual content as dictated by the American Psychological Association's style manual.

Analytical/Explanatory Survey: Type of survey that explains people's attitudes and behaviors by identifying likely causal influences.

Anonymity: When a researcher does not know who participated in a study or which results belong to which participants in a study.

Antecedent: (1) The "if" statement within a logical proof. (2) What happened earlier in time.

Antecedent Variables: Variables that occur prior to the experiment that could impact the way an independent variable or dependent variable functions.

Apparatus: Any appliance or device used in conducting a study.

Appeal to Authority: When people explain a phenomenon by believing that an authority has made it occur.

Appeal to General Empirical Rules: Explaining phenomena through proven scientific facts.

Argument: Set of propositions in which one follows logically as a conclusion from the others.

Assertiveness: Capacity to make requests; actively disagree; express positive or negative personal rights and feelings; initiate, maintain, or disengage from conversations; and stand up for oneself without attacking another.

Attitude: Predisposition to respond to people, ideas, or objects in an evaluative way.

Attributes: Specific values of a variable.

Attrition: Number of participants who left a study since it began.

Audience-Specific Behavior: Behavior exhibited in front of one audience that does not occur in front of other audiences.

Author Search: Database search for an author's name in the author field.

Authorship Credit: Ethical principle that states all researchers involved in a project should receive acknowledgment for their work on a research project.

Axioms: Generally accepted principles or rules.

Backtracking: The process a researcher uses when he or she examines the references of one article in an effort to help her- or himself find other articles and books that may be relevant.

Baseline: Initial score on some variable of interest.

Belief: Perception of reality about whether something is true or false.

Belmont Report: The 1979 report by the National Commission for the Protection of Human Subjects of Biomedical and Behavioral Research that established three basic guidelines for working with human participants: consent, beneficence, and justice.

Beta (β) Weight (regression coefficient): Value in a multiple linear regression that helps explain the degree to which a dependent variable takes varying values and can be interpreted as a correlation.

Bimodal: When two values larger than the other values in a dataset occur at equal frequency within the dataset.

Boolean Logic: Form of symbolic logic created by George Boole that is the basis for electronic search engine technology.

Calculated Value: End result after completion of a mathematical formula related to a specific statistical test.

Call for Papers: Posting that requests scholars send in manuscripts to be considered for a conference/convention or for journal publication.

Categorical/Topical Order: Organizing a literature review by main topics or issues and emphasizing the relationship of the issues to the main problem.

Causation: Ability to determine that an act or agency truly produces an effect.

Cause-and-Effect Order: Literature review organizational pattern used to explain what causes a specific situation and what the effect of that situation is.

Central Limits Theorem: Theoretical idea that the mean of the scores obtained from the probability sample will be equal to the mean of the scores obtained from the population.

Certificate of Confidentiality: Certification granted by the Secretary of Health and Human Services that enables a researcher engaged in biomedical, behavioral, clinical, or other research to protect the privacy of research participants even if the participants are engaged in illicit or illegal behavior.

Channel: Method used to send a message (verbal, nonverbal, or mediated).

Chi-Square (χ^2): Statistical test that evaluates whether the proportions of individuals who fall into categories of two or more nominal variables are equal to hypothesized values.

Chronological Order: Organizing a literature review by historical progression in terms of time.

Citation: When an author gives credit to another individual's thoughts.

Cluster Samples: Samples created by identifying naturally occurring clusters of people with a target variable in a population and then randomly selecting those people to participate in a research project.

Codebook: Book that a researcher creates to explain the operationalization in a clear and succinct way.

Coders: Persons actively involved in the coding process.

Coding: Process that a researcher goes through to group one's variable of interest in a consistent way.

Coding Form: Form that contains all of the information in the codebook in a simple check-off sheet to make it easier for coders to code information quickly.

Cognitive Knowledge: Degree to which someone has actually learned a specific concept or skill.

Cohen's *d*: Effect size test utilized in an independent samples *t* test.

Cohen's Kappa (κ): Statistic used to calculate intercoder reliability for two coders where none of the data is missing.

Common Rule, the: Title 45, Code of Federal Regulations, Part 46, which established a set of guidelines for the rights, welfare, and protection of research participants.

Communication: Process whereby one person stimulates meaning in the mind(s) of another person (or persons) through verbal and nonverbal messages.

Communication Apprehension: Fear or anxiety associated with either real or anticipated communication with another person or persons.

Communication Trait: Hypothetical construct that accounts for certain kinds of communication behaviors.

Communications: Array of mass-mediated technologies people utilize to send messages.

Compare-and-Contrast Order: Organizing a literature review to show how research studies are similar to and different from each other.

Conceptual Equivalence: Issue involved in translating surveys from one language to another that is concerned with whether the basic concept a researcher is attempting to study in one culture even exists within another culture.

Conceptualization: Development and clarification of concepts or your germinal idea.

Concrete Variables: Variables that are stable or consistent.

Concurrent Validity: Form of validity concerned with whether scores taken at the same time are related to each other.

Confederate: Individual who, without the participants' knowledge, is actually part of the experiment being conducted.

Confidence Interval: The degree to which a researcher is certain he or she will accept a true null hypothesis.

Confidence Level: Level of confidence that the results found within a study are generalizable to the population and not a result of chance.

Confidentiality: The treatment of information an individual has disclosed in a relationship of trust with the expectation that it will not, without permission, be divulged to others in ways inconsistent with the understanding of the original disclosure.

Conflict of Interest: When financial or other personal considerations prevent a researcher from abiding by or can give the appearance of compromising scientific and ethical principles.

Confounding Variables: Variables that obscure the effects of your independent variable.

Consequent: The "then" statement within a logical proof.

Construct Validity: Degree to which the survey measures an intended nonobservable trait, which is used to explain observable behavior.

Constructive Replication: When a researcher duplicates a previous study but uses entirely new instrumentation, experimental procedures, and sample and data analysis techniques.

Content Analysis: Summarizing, quantitative analysis of messages.

Control: Process by which an individual both prevents personal biases from interfering with the research study and ensures there are no other explanations for what is seen in the study.

Control Group: Group that the researcher measures without attempting to manipulate in any way.

Convenience Samples: When participants are selected nonrandomly based on availability.

Correlation (r): Statistical test that determines whether two variables are positively, negatively, or not related to each other.

Cramér's Phi (Φ): Effect size test utilized in a chi-square.

Criterion Validity: Form of validity concerned with how accurately a new measure can predict a well-accepted criterion or previously validated concept.

Critical Value: (1) Value of the random variable at the boundary for accepting or rejecting the null hypothesis. (2) Value that a calculated value must be greater than to achieve statistical significance at a calculated confidence level.

Cronbach Alpha Reliability: Scale reliability test that determines how well a set of items measures a unidimensional hypothetical construct.

Cross-Sectional Survey Design: Type of survey design in which a researcher receives information from a group of participants at a given point in time.

Curvilinear Relationship: Relationship between two variables plotted along a curve instead of a straight line.

Data: Collected measures of independent and dependent variables that can be used for statistical calculations.

Data Falsification: Any time one manipulates or alters the data to achieve the results wanted by the researcher.

Data Sharing: Ethical principle by which researchers share their data with other researchers to help further science.

Debriefing: Period following an experiment when a researcher corrects any deception, reaffirms the value of the experiment, and determines whether the answers were changed based on what the participant assumed was occurring.

Decoding: Process a receiver goes through to assign meaning to a source's message.

Degrees of Freedom: Number of participant scores in a sample that can or are free to vary.

Degrees of Freedom Between: In a one-way analysis of variance, number of participant scores in a sample that can or are free to vary between multiple groups.

Degrees of Freedom Within: In a one-way analysis of variance, number of participant scores in a sample that can or are free to vary within a single group.

Deidentify the Data: Making sure the data cannot be linked back to the participants themselves.

Dependent Variable: Measured variable in a study whose changes are determined by changes in one or more independent variables.

Descriptive Statistics: Statistical tests used to describe the shape of a dataset.

Descriptive Survey: Type of survey designed to find out how common a phenomenon is within a given group of people.

Difference: The degree to which one person or a group of people are dissimilar from another person or group of people.

Differences in Kind: Differences that occur when two or more groups do different things associated with their groups.

Differences of Degree: When scores from two or more groups significantly differ from each other.

Diminished Autonomy: When possible participants do not have the ability to intellectually discern for themselves whether participation in a research endeavor is okay.

Directional Research Questions: When a researcher asks whether there is either a positive or a negative relationship or a specific significant difference between two or more variables.

Discussion Section: Section of a research study that appears after the results section to provide an interpretation of the findings, acknowledge limitations, and propose future research.

Dunn–Sidak Test: Statistical test that readjusts the probability level to correct for possible compounded error resulting from multiple pairwise comparisons to help prevent type I error.

Duplicate Data Publication: Publishing the same set of data in two different research publications.

Effect Size: Strength of a relationship or the magnitude of difference occurring between two variables or the degree to which a null hypothesis is false.

Electronic Databases: Computerized systems for searching and retrieving information.

Empirical Generalization: Attempt to describe a phenomenon based on what we know about it at this time.

Empiricism: Belief that science is only acceptable insofar as the phenomenon in question can be "sensed" by average people.

Encoding: Process of creating messages we believe represent the meaning to be communicated and are likely to stimulate similar meaning in the mind of a receiver.

Ends: Outcomes that one desires to achieve.

Epistemology: Way of knowing.

Eta-Square (η^2): Effect size test utilized in a one-way analysis of variance.

Ethical Behavior: When a researcher uses positive means to achieve a positive end.

Ethics: Study of means and ends.

Ethnocentrism: View of one's culture as the center of the universe.

Evoke Empathy: Showing that a phenomenon had good, just, or moral reasons.

Exempt Review: Level of review performed by an institutional review board where a protocol is determined to be exempt from the guidelines established in Title 45, Code of Federal Regulations, Part 46.

Expedited Review: Level of review performed by an institutional review board where a protocol involves no more than minimal risk, does not include intentional deception, does not utilize vulnerable populations, and includes appropriate consent procedures.

Experiment: When a researcher purposefully manipulates one or more variables (independent variables) in the hope of seeing how this manipulation effects change or lack of change in other variables of interest (dependent variables).

Experimental Group: Group that a researcher attempts to manipulate in some clear way.

Experimenter Effects: Effects caused unknowingly by the experimenter on the participants.

Explanation: Attempt to satisfy one's curiosity about an observable event.

Extraneous Variables: Variables not being measured in your study but affecting your results (see intervening and confounding variables).

F Test: Any statistical test that determines whether two population variances are equal.

Face/Content Validity: Form of validity where a researcher determines whether the measure determines the appropriate construct by examining the specific questions.

Factor Analysis: A statistical device that enables researchers to determine whether the responses on a set of scale items actually measure a single construct or multiple constructs.

Factorial Experimental Design: Experimental design that utilizes two or more independent variables.

Faking Responses: Any circumstance in which a respondent to our instrument deliberately attempts to alter the results in some specific way.

Fisher's Least Significant Difference: Post hoc test that is the equivalent of running a series of paired t tests but for which the alpha level is not controlled, so the chance of compounded error is great.

Frequency Distribution: Record of the number of occurrences for each value in the dataset.

Full-Board Review: Level of review performed by an institutional review board where a protocol involves more than minimal risk, uses intentional deception, or uses vulnerable populations.

Future Directions: Subsection of the discussion section in which an author writes about where he or she thinks the research should continue.

General Linear Model: Linear model ($Y = mX + b$) where each object can have multiple measurements. The general linear model underlies many different statistical tests, including one-way analysis of variance and regression.

General-to-Specific Order: Organizing a literature review to examine broad-based research first and then focus on specific studies that relate to the topic.

Generalizability: Notion that the results found from studying a sample can be assumed to be true of the entire population.

Germinal Idea: Spark that causes an individual to realize that something new can be researched or measured.

Hasty Generalizations: Generalizing about something when not enough evidence is available to do so.

Hawthorne Effect: Effect caused when study participants know they are being observed.

Historical Flaw: Threat to a study's external validity that occurs because an historical event has caused a sample to change in a way that is not measurable.

Humor Assessment: Mental measure created by Wrench and Richmond to measure an individual's use of humor in interpersonal interactions.

Hypothesis: Tentative statement about the relationship between independent and dependent variables.

Hypothesis Testing: Process a researcher goes through using inferential statistics to determine whether we reject or accept the null hypothesis.

Illustrations: Generalizable stories that can be applied to a variety of different contexts.

Immediacy: The degree of perceived physical or psychological distance between people in a relationship.

Independent Samples *t* Test: Statistical test that evaluates whether there is a difference between two groups on a dependent variable.

Independent Variable: (1) Variable whose numerical value determines the value of other variables.

(2) Part of the research experiment that is manipulated or changed.

Inferential Statistics: Statistical tests that allow researchers to make inferences about some unknown aspect of a population from a sample.

Infographic: A visual representation of data, information, or knowledge condensed into a combination of images and text designed to help viewers grasp complex information quickly and clearly.

Informed Consent: A person's voluntary agreement, based on adequate knowledge and understanding of relevant information, to participate in research.

Institutional Review Board: Panel of people at institutions that receive federal funds established by Title 45, Code of Federal Regulations, Part 46, which reviews all research proposals for possible risks to research participants and to ensure that all research participants are informed of their rights as research participants.

Instrumental Replication: When a researcher duplicates a previous study by measuring the dependent variable in the same way as the first study, but changes the independent variable to see whether a different operationalization of the experimental procedures will give the same results.

Instrumentation: Section of a literature review where a researcher explains which research measures were used to measure the specific study variables.

Intercoder Reliability: Test to determine whether multiple coders are coding pieces of data in a stable, consistent fashion (most commonly reported as Cohen's kappa or Krippendorff's alpha).

Interval Variables: Variables in which the values of the categories are classified in a logical order that represents equal distances between levels within each category.

Intervening Variables: Variables that intervene between the independent variable and the dependent variable.

Interview Schedule: List of survey questions an interviewer asks an interviewee when conducting an oral survey.

Introduction: The first portion of a paper that contains an attention-getter, a link to the topic, the significance of the topic, an espousal of the credibility of the writer, a thesis statement, and a preview of the main points of the paper.

Isomorphism: Identity or similarity of form.

Item Nonresponse: Form of nonresponse that occurs when an individual participant fails to answer individual or groups of questions on a survey.

Justice: The third ethical standard taken from the Belmont Report that explains that those individuals who take the risks of research should also receive the benefits from that research.

Key Performance Indicators: Quantifiable measures that help organizational decision makers evaluate organizational performance (e.g., meeting or exceeding strategic and organizational goals).

Keyword Search: Database search for a specific keyword or a set of keywords that a researcher is attempting to find.

Known-to-Unknown Order: Organizing a literature review to examine current literature about the problem first and then identify what still is not known.

Kurtosis: The degree of peakedness of a distribution of scores.

Label the Phenomenon: Giving the phenomenon a name.

Language: A system of symbols or codes that represent certain ideas or meanings.

Latent/Hypothetical Variable: Variable that a researcher cannot directly observe, but that can be inferred from other variables that are observable and measured directly.

Likert Scale: Scale in which participants are presented with a declarative statement and then asked to respond to the statement with a range of possible choices: strongly disagree, disagree, neither agree nor disagree, agree, or strongly agree.

Limitations: Subsection in a manuscript's discussion section that highlights the weaknesses of the study, including inappropriateness in the design, population, methods, or instrumentation.

Linear Relationship: Any equation where increasing or decreasing one variable will produce a corresponding change in a secondary variable.

Literal Replication: When a researcher duplicates a previous study keeping the instrumentation, experimental procedures, and sample as similar as possible.

Literature Review: Selection of available documents (published and unpublished) on a given topic that contain information, opinions, data, and evidence written from a particular point of view that aid in a reader's understanding of important concepts and research findings prior to examining the results and discussion in a research study.

Longitudinal Survey Design: Type of survey design in which a researcher gathers information from a group of participants multiple times over a period of time.

Lurker Variables: Variables that explain both the independent variable and the dependent variable.

Machiavellian Ethic: When a researcher uses bad means to achieve a good end.

Major Premise: Premise of a syllogism that contains the major term (which is the predicate of the conclusion).

Manipulation Check: Procedure by which a researcher inserts a quantitative measurement into a study to determine whether different conditions perceive the independent variable differently.

Manipulation of the Independent Variable: Process a researcher goes through to purposefully alter or change an independent variable to see whether this alteration in the independent variable has an effect on the dependent variable during an experiment.

Maturation: Threat to validity that occurs because it is possible that a portion of the estimated change is not a result of independent variable manipulations, but rather a result of the passage of time between the first measure of a dependent variable and follow-up measures of the dependent variable.

Mean: Sum of all of the scores in a sample divided by the number of scores in the sample.

Mean Squares Between: In a one-way analysis of variance, the value calculated by dividing the between sum of squares by the between degrees of freedom.

Mean Squares Within: In a one-way analysis of variance, the value calculated by dividing the within sum of squares by the within degrees of freedom.

Means: Tools or behaviors that one employs to achieve a desired outcome.

Measurement: Process of systematic observation and assignment of numbers to objects or events according to rules.

Measures of Central Tendency: Statistics that help describe the center of a distribution of data (e.g., mean, median, and mode).

Median: Middle value in a list of data.

Mediated Channel: Any channel that uses some kind of mediating device to help transmit information.

Mental Measures: Tools used for the measurement of mental functions like attitudes, beliefs, cognitive knowledge, perceived knowledge, and personality/behavioral traits.

Message: Information the source is stimulating in the mind of the receiver.

Method Section: Section of a research manuscript that discusses participants, apparatuses, procedures, and instrumentation.

Minor Premise: Premise of a syllogism that contains the minor term (the subject of the conclusion).

Mode: Number(s) that occur most frequently within a dataset.

Modified Direct Translation: When someone performs a simple direct translation, which is then given to a panel of experts to decide whether the survey translation is appropriate.

Mono-Operation Bias: Validity flaw related to the single use of an independent variable, cause, program, or treatment in a study.

Multiple Comparison Tests: Statistical tests conducted after a significant difference is noted to ascertain where the significant differences exist statistically among three or more groups (commonly called post hoc tests).

Negative Relationships: When a decrease in one variable corresponds to an increase in the other variable, or vice versa.

Network Samples: Participants are asked to refer researchers to other people who could serve as participants.

Neutral Relationships: When the change of one variable does not correspond with a change in another variable.

Nominal Variable: Qualitative variable in which categories are mutually exclusive, equivalent, and exhaustive and where the categories are not numerically oriented.

Nondirectional Research Questions: When a researcher asks whether there is a relationship between two or more variables or a significant difference occurs between two or more variables.

Nonparametric: Statistical tests that are associated with categories and ordering; these are tests observed at the nominal/ordinal levels.

Nonprobability Sampling: Samples that are not randomly selected.

Nonproportionate Quota Samples: Quota sampling technique by which a researcher recruits volunteers until the determined number of participants has been recruited.

Nonresponse: When a sampled unit does not respond to the request to be surveyed (unit nonresponse) or to particular survey questions (item nonresponse).

Nonresponse Bias: Systematic distortion of a statistic as a result of unit and item nonresponse.

Nonverbal Immediacy: The perceived physical and/or psychological closeness a receiver feels exists between her- or himself and a source that occurs as a result of nonverbal behavior.

Nonverbal Messages: Any communicated messages other than verbal messages.

Normative Equivalence: Issue involved in translating surveys from one language to another language concerned with whether norms or social conventions will influence participants' responses during a survey.

Null Hypothesis (H_0): Hypothesis that predicts that groups will not vary on a dependent variable or that there is not a relationship between two variables.

Objective: The desire to create knowledge by examining facts through the scientific method without distorting one's findings through personal feelings, prejudices, and interpretations.

Observations: The part of the scientific method where a researcher attempts to test the hypotheses created.

One-Tailed Hypothesis: Hypothesis that predicts the specific nature of the relationship or difference.

One-Way Analysis of Variance: Statistical test that evaluates whether there is a difference between two or more groups on a dependent variable.

Operational Replication: When a researcher duplicates a previous study keeping the experimental procedures and sample as similar as possible, but changes the instrumentation or survey.

Operationalization: Detailed description of the research operations or procedures necessary to assign units of analysis to the categories of a variable to represent conceptual properties.

Ordinal Variables: Qualitative variables in which categories are mutually exclusive, equivalent, or exhaustive and where the categories represent clear numerical gradients, which allows rank ordering of the categories.

Outliers: Data points that are far away from the other data points.

Paired *t* Test: Statistical test used to compare two interval/ratio level scores that are taken from the same group at two distinct time periods.

Pancultural: When something is the same across all cultures.

Panel Survey Design: Type of longitudinal survey design used to examine participants who agree to be surveyed periodically over a given period of time.

Panel Discussions: Form of conference presentation by which three or more individuals discuss a common topic in an informal format.

Paper Presentations: Oral reports about the research project typically followed by a response from a scholar who has conducted research in the area.

Parallel Blind Technique: Form of translation by which two translators perform a simple direct translation on the same survey and then compare their translations.

Parameter: A value of a population.

Parametric: Statistical tests that assume the level of measurement that was employed in obtaining the data was at the interval/ratio level.

Paraphrasing: Including another author's ideas in your own words; involves summarizing or highlighting one or two important points.

Parenthetical Citations: Citations used within the text body of a manuscript that enable a reader to know where the information is being taken from—also referred to as internal citations.

Participant Subsection: Subsection of a literature review (under the method section) where a researcher describes her or his participants and any important demographic characteristics.

Peer Review: Process whereby an individual's scholarly work is critiqued by people who also conduct research in a specific area to make sure the new scholarly work is of a quality worthy of publication.

Perceived Knowledge: Degree to which someone believes that he or she has learned a specific concept or skill.

Personality: Total psychological makeup of an individual, which is a reflection of her or his experiences, motivations, attitudes, beliefs, values, and behaviors, derived from the interaction of these elements with the environment external to the individual.

Physical Sciences: Study of the objective aspects of nature.

Pilot Study: Small-scale study a researcher conducts to test the effectiveness of a survey or research procedures.

Plagiarism: Any time a writer does not properly cite or give credit to the source where he or she is getting information.

Population: An entire set of objects, observations, or scores that have some characteristic in common.

Positive Relationships: When an increase in one variable corresponds to an increase in another variable or a decrease in a variable corresponds to a decrease in another variable.

Post Hoc Hypothesis Revision: The revision of hypotheses once an individual receives her or his results.

Poster Presentations: Visual reports about the research project where people mingle and ask questions about research projects that interest them.

Power: Degree to which a researcher is certain he or she can reject a false null hypothesis.

Predictive/Prospective Validity: Form of validity concerned with whether a person's score on a new measure can be used to predict future scores on another measure.

Preview: Point in the introduction when a writer lists the specific sections that he or she is planning to cover in the main body of the literature review.

Primary Sources: Original documents that examine a phenomenon (e.g., poems, diaries, court records, interviews, and research results generated by experiments, surveys, and ethnographies).

Principle of Beneficence: Researchers must ensure that during the research process they maximize possible benefits and minimize possible harms to the research participants themselves.

Privacy: The individual's control over the extent, timing, and circumstances of sharing his- or herself (physically, behaviorally, or intellectually) with others.

Probability: Relative frequency with which a phenomenon is likely to occur.

Probability Level: One minus the percentile confidence level.

Probability Sampling: Randomly selecting participants from a population of interest so that all potential participants have an equal chance of being selected for the sample.

Probability Theory: The score that occurs most frequently in the sample will also be the score that should occur most frequently in the population.

Probability Value (*p* value): Probability of obtaining a result at least as extreme as that calculated, which assumes that the null hypothesis is true (result occurred by chance).

Problem–Cause–Solution Order: Organizing a literature review so that it moves from the problem to the cause to the solution.

Procedure: The sequence of actions or instructions a researcher follows while conducting a study.

Proportionate Quota Samples: Quota sampling technique by which a researcher ensures that the number of volunteers recruited for the study is proportionate or equal to the number of group members in the population.

Proposition: A statement that either confirms something or denies something.

Protected Health Information: Any individually identifiable health information (e.g., demographic data and biological specimens) transmitted or maintained by a covered entity.

Psychological Order: Literature review organizational pattern in which a researcher attempts to demonstrate a logical sequencing of events, or how A leads to B and B leads to C.

Purposive Sampling Participants are nonrandomly picked to be in a study because of a specific characteristic the researcher is investigating.

Quasi-Experimental Design: Looks like an experimental design but likes randomization.

Questionnaire: A form containing a series of questions and mental measures given to a group of people in an attempt to gain statistical information about the group as part of a survey.

Quota Samples: Participants are separated into strata and then nonrandomly selected for participation in the study.

Quotations: Exact use of another author's words in your writing.

R-Squared (R^2): Indicates what proportion of the variability in a dependent variable can be predicted by its relationship with an independent variable(s).

Random Assignment: Procedures experimenters use for placing participants into a research condition that ensures every participant in the sample has an equal chance of being in a research condition.

Random Probe Translation: Form of translation by which a translator performs a simple direct translation and then the researcher pilot tests the translation with a group of bilingual participants to determine whether the researcher's own understanding of the mental measure and that of the participants are the same.

Range: Distance between the largest value and the smallest value in the dataset.

Ratio Variables: Variables in which the values of the categories are classified in a logical order that represents equal distances between levels within each category with the presence of an absolute zero point.

Rationale Section: Section of a research manuscript that explains the fundamental reasons for the hypotheses and research questions posed in the study.

Receiver: Person who interprets a message (decoder).

Reference Page: The page in a document formatted in American Psychological Association style where all of the sources that have been internally cited within the manuscript are referenced.

Regression (R): Statistical test that examines whether an independent variable can linearly account for any of the variance in a dependent variable.

Regression to the Mean: The tendency for extreme scorers on one measurement to move (regress) closer to the mean on a later measurement, causing a change that would normally not happen in the population.

Reinforcer Variables: Variables that enhance the effect of the independent variable on the dependent variable.

Relationships: Correspondences between two variables.

Reliability: Whether a measure produces stable, consistent values.

Replication: Conducting more research on a specific topic to determine whether original results occurred by error or remain consistent.

Research: Investigation or experimentation aimed at the discovery and interpretation of facts, revision of accepted theories or laws, and/or practical application of new or revised theories or laws.

Research Implications: Subsection in discussion section in which an author indicates what her or his findings mean for the larger community of scholars' understanding of the topic.

Research Participant: A living individual about whom a researcher obtains either (1) data through intervention or interaction with the individual or (2) identifiable private information.

Research Question: Explicit question researchers ask about variables of interest.

Respondent: An academic trained in your area of research who will provide feedback on your manuscript's writing, analysis, and conclusions at a conference or convention.

Response Rate: Percentage of surveys returned compared to the percentage of surveys distributed.

Response Set: Any tendency that causes a person to give different responses to test items than he or he would if the items were presented in a different form.

Responsiveness: Capacity to be sensitive to the communication of others, to be a good listener, to make others comfortable in communicating, and to recognize the needs and desires of others.

Results Section: Section of a research manuscript in which a researcher presents her or his empirical findings.

Retrospective/Postdictive Validity: Form of validity by which a researcher attempts to relate a previously taken measure of a phenomenon to a newly designed measure of a phenomenon.

Rhetorical Question: Type of question that asks a listener to think about it without audibly responding.

Sample: People or units that a researcher includes in the study.

Sampling: Selecting people or units for inclusion in a research study.

Sampling Bias: Systematic differences between the population and the sample that result from failing to draw representative cases.

Sampling Error: Degree to which a sample differs with respect to a specific variable from a population.

Sampling Frame: All members of the population accessible to the researcher.

Scalogram: Type of research scale that consists of a set of unidimensional items designed to measure an attitude or opinion where agreement with one item implies agreement with the preceding, less extreme items.

Scheffé: Post hoc test that assumes you wish to test all possible pairs and all possible combinations of means.

Scholar-to-Scholar Presentations: Form of poster presentation in which the researcher has an opportunity to discuss her or his poster with top-notch scholars in the field of communication who specialize in a specific content area.

Science: The study of natural phenomena through quantitative observation, theoretical explanation, and experimentation.

Scientific Method: Empirical process by which a researcher attempts to understand a phenomenon using existing theories to make predictions, empirically observe the phenomenon based on the predictions, and use the observations to make empirical generalizations that then help to refine the original theory.

Screw-You Effect: When a participant either gives a researcher the exact opposite of what the participant believes the researcher wants, or the participant provides a completely random response.

Secondary Sources: Restatements or analyses of primary sources.

Selection Threat: Threat to the validity of an experiment caused by whether the participants who have been selected to participate in an experiment have some characteristic that could slant the findings of the study.

Semantic Differential Scale: Type of research scale that asks respondents to rate their opinion on a linear scale that exists between two endpoints that have opposite meanings (e.g., Good/Bad, Dirty/Clean, Slow/Fast, Weak/Strong, Light/Heavy, Moral/Immoral).

Semantic Equivalence: Issue involved in translating surveys from one language to another concerned with whether scale items are translatable semantically from one language to the next.

Significance Testing: The process to determine whether chance causes a difference or relationship between two or more variables.

Simple Direct Translation: Form of survey translation by which a researcher recruits a bilingual individual who takes the original survey and then translates this survey from the primary language to the secondary language.

Simple Random Samples: Samples created through some means of randomly deciding who in a target population will be asked to participate.

Situational Behavior: Behavior that varies from one situation to another within the same context.

Skewness: The positive or negative direction that an asymmetrical set of data points takes.

Social Desirability Bias: When a participant changes how he or she scores on a measure to be perceived in a "better light" than her or his actual scores would reveal.

Social Sciences: A group of fields that set out to study how humans live and interact.

Socially Desirable Responding: When an individual fakes responses to indicate beliefs that he or she thinks society accepts.

Sociocommunicative Orientation: An individual's trait assertive and responsive communicative behavior.

Sociocommunicative Style: An individual's assertive and responsive communicative behavior as perceived by another individual.

Source: Person who sends the message (encoder).

Specific-to-General Order: Organizing a literature review to try to make sense out of specific research studies so that conclusions can be drawn.

Split-Half Reliability: Scale reliability test in which all of the items are randomly divided into two groups and then a correlation is calculated between the two sets of scores.

Standard Deviation: (1) Measure of the distribution of a set of data points around the mean. (2) Square root of the sum of squares divided by the number of data points minus one.

Statistic: The calculated numerical value that represents a sample or population.

Stratified Random Samples: Samples created by dividing a population into specific strata (group based on a characteristic important to the study) and then randomly selecting participants from each stratem for inclusion.

Student Newman–Keuls: Post hoc stepwise test for ordered means in which the alpha level depends upon the number of "steps apart" each of the means are from each other.

Subject Search: Database search for key terms that the author has submitted to the subject field to describe the article or book.

Subjective Ethic: When a researcher uses good means but achieves a bad end result.

Subscale: A subdivision of a research measure.

Sum of Squares: Sum of all squared values for a set of data points minus the sum of data points squared divided by the number of data points.

Sum of Squares Between: Variation between groups in a study calculated by comparing the mean of each group with the mean of the overall sample.

Sum of Squares Within: Variation within groups in a study calculated by summing the squared deviations between scores on a dependent variable for each group and then summing the group values.

Suppressor Variables: Variables that suppress or reduce the effect of the independent variable on the dependent variable.

Survey: A social scientific method for gathering quantifiable information about a specific group of people by asking the group members questions about their individual attitudes, values, beliefs, behaviors, knowledge, and perceptions.

Syllogism: Form of logical argumentation where the logic deductively flows from a major premise to a minor premise to a conclusion.

Systematic Samples: Samples created by determining the sample size needed from a target population and then picking every nth person from the population for selection.

Test–Retest Reliability: The same measure is administered to the same group on two separate occasions, and the relationship between both measurements is calculated.

Testing Flaw: Threat to a study's validity that occurs because the measurement of a dependent variable at Time 1 affects the measurement of a dependent variable at Time 2.

Theoretical Population: All of the members of a specific population, both accessible and not accessible to the researcher.

Theory: Proposed explanation for how a set of natural phenomena will occur that is capable of making predictions about the phenomena for the future and of being falsified through empirical observation.

Theory of Natural Selection: The process in nature by which only the organisms best adapted to their environment tend to survive and transmit their genetic characteristics in increasing numbers to succeeding generations, whereas those less adapted tend to be eliminated.

Thesis: Short, declarative sentence that explains to a listener the purpose of a paper.

Threshold Effect: When changes in a specific dependent variable are only seen after an independent variable reaches a certain level.

Time Order: Idea that researchers can establish an exact order to when things occur—T_1 occurred, and then T_2 occurred—through experimental procedures.

Title Search: Database search for words included in the title of an article or book.

Trait Behavior: Behavior assumed to be consistent across contexts and specific situations within particular constructs.

Translation/Backtranslation: Form of translation by which a translator performs a simple direct translation, after which another bilingual individual translates the work back to the first language.

Trend Survey Design: Type of longitudinal survey design used to examine different samples of people at different points in time.

Truncation Symbols: Symbols used to ensure that your search looks for every possible version of a word.

Tukey's Honest Significant Difference Test: Post hoc test for pairwise comparisons while controlling for type I error and generating confidence intervals.

Two-Tailed Hypothesis: Hypothesis that predicts a significant relationship or difference but does not indicate the specific nature of the relationship.

Type I (α) Error: When a researcher rejects a null hypothesis based on a sample when the null should be accepted.

Type II (β) Error: When a researcher accepts a null hypothesis based on a sample when the null hypothesis should be rejected.

Unethical Behavior: When a researcher uses bad means to achieve a bad end.

Unit of Analysis: Major phenomenon being analyzed within a study.

Unit Nonresponse: Form of nonresponse when a researcher has a failure to obtain any survey measurements on a sample unit.

Univariate Test: Statistical test with one dependent variable.

Validity: Degree to which the measuring instrument measures what it is intended to measure.

Variable: Any entity that can take on different values.

Variable Attributes: The specific categories of a variable.

Variable Values: The numerical designation assigned to each variable to allow statistical analysis.

Variance: (1) Degree of variability around a mean. (2) Sum of squares divided by the number of data points minus one.

Verbal Immediacy: Use of language to foster an individual's perception of psychological and physical closeness.

Verbal Messages: Use of language to communicate a message.

Volunteer Samples: Participants who choose to be in a study; typically based on some form of reward.

Willingness to Communicate: A person's general level of desire to initiate communication with others.

Index

Page numbers followed by *f* indicate a figure on the designated page

abstract variables, 172–73
abstracts
    APA paper formatting of, 124, 125*f*
    APA style checklist for, 115*f*
    defined, 133
    example of, 134*f*
    as information source, 94
    length of, 134
    purpose of, 132–34
    writing of, 567
academic divisions/interest groups, 569–73, 570*f*
academic fraud, 45
academic theoretical tradition, 19
academic vs. journalistic writing process, 589–90, 590*f*
accelerated longitudinal survey design, 291
acknowledged facts, as attention-getters, 137
Acock, A. C., 426
acquiescence, as type of faking, 276
Adobe Acrobat Reader (software), 112
adolescent alcohol consumption project (1989), 43–44
Adrian, Allyson, 244
advertising, for recruitment of samples, 386
advisors, 313
African American men, untreated disease study.
        See Tuskegee Syphilis Study (1934–1972)
alpha (*a*) value, 402
alpha reliability. *See* Cronbach alpha reliability test
alternate forms reliability, 252
alternative facts, use of term, 22
alternative hypothesis, 395–96, 397
American Psychological Association (APA). *See also* APA
        paper formatting; APA style (citation guidelines)
    on authorship credit ethics, 73–74
    early personality tests, 224
    Publication Manual of the American Psychological Association,
        74–75, 114, 127, 133–34, 412
analysis of covariance. *See* one-way analysis of variance
        (ANOVA)
analytical surveys, 281
anchor, defined, 287
ancient Egyptian science principles, 23
ancient Greek science principles, 2–3, 23, 218
Annals of Improbable Research, 48

anonymity, 51, 284, 286
anonymous sex study (1975), 42
ANOVA. *See* one-way analysis of variance (ANOVA)
ANOVA summary table, 500, 501*f*, 547
antecedent, 27
antecedent variables, 180–81, 339
APA paper formatting
    abstract, 124, 125*f*
    APA style checklist for, 115*f*
    first page of paper, 126, 127*f*
    title page, 122–24, 123*f*
APA style checklist, 114, 115*f*
APA style (citation guidelines), 113*f*, 114–28. *See also* American
        Psychological Association (APA); research paper
        structure
    abstract, 567
    accessible via website, 114
    books, 113*f*
    chi-square (χ^2), test of independence,
        459, 465–66
    correlation, 529, 530, 531–32
    electronic full-text of print journal article, 113*f*
    ethnocentrism, 261*f*
    Generalized Attitude Measure,
        213*f*, 259–60, 262*f*
    Generalized Belief Scale, 213*f*, 262*f*
    .html format articles, 107
    humor assessment scales, 212*f*, 261*f*
    independent samples *t* test, 485
    intercorder reliability, 330
    interviews with people, 113*f*
    Likert scale anchors, 225
    magazine articles, 113*f*
    method section scale elements, 210–12, 212*f*–13*f*
    multiple linear regression, 554
    newspaper articles, 113*f*
    one-way analysis of variance (ANOVA), 510, 511
    p values, 412
    parenthetical citations, 116, 119–20, 119*f*–20*f*
    PRCA-24 results, 212*f*, 261*f*
    preprint publications, 107
    print journal articles, 113*f*
    quotations and paraphrases, 120–22

APA style (citation guidelines) (*continued*)
references and citation of other research, 114, 116, 117*f*–19*f*, 119
regression (*R*), 549, 551, 554, 558
reliability, 259–60, 261*f*–62*f*
statistical tests, 210–12, 212*f*–13*f*
in-text citations, 116, 119*f*
apparatus subsection, in method section, 151, 211
appeal to authority, 25
appeal to general empirical rules, 26
appendices, APA style checklist for, 115*f*
argument, 27–29, 142–43, 149–50
Aristotle, 3, 27
Arnold, W. E., 225
Arthur Guinness & Son, 474
assertiveness, 203, 205, 233
Assessing Organizational Communication (Downs and Adrian), 244
asterisk (*), as truncation symbol, 105
Atkin, C., 412
Atkin, Charles, 43–44
attention-getters, in introduction
acknowledged facts, 137
example of, 136*f*
quotations or acknowledging another source, 138
reference to in conclusion, 159
rhetorical questions, 137
startling statistics or claims, 135, 137
stories/illustrations, 137–38
attitude, defined, 208, 230. *See also* beliefs and attitudes
attitude change, 6
attitudinal research, 5
attributes of variables, 174
attrition, 355
audience-specific behavior, 193
audio recordings, in experimental design, 344–45
author name(s) and affiliation(s), 124
author search, in databases, 102
authority
appeal to, 25
website credentials and, 110
authorship credit, 73–74
axioms, 86

Babbie, E., 20
backtracking, 92, 164
backtranslation, 307–8
Bacon, Francis, 23
Banks, Curtis, 43

Barbato, C. A., 173
Bardhan, N., 380–81
Barker, C., 345
Barraclough, R. A., 306
baseline (score/pretest), 339, 354
BATs. *See* behavioral alteration techniques (BATs)
Beatty, Michael J., 175–76, 192
behavioral alteration techniques (BATs), 535–36
behaviorally oriented trait/state research scales, 229–30
Behling, O., 305–8
belief, defined, 208, 230
beliefs and attitudes, 208–10, 208*f*–9*f*, 230, 277
Bell Curve, 403–4, 404*f*–5*f*, 409*f*
Bell Telephone Company, 9–10
Belmont Report (1979), 42, 47–49
Bem, Sandra L., 203
Bem Sex-Role Inventory (BSRI), 203
beneficence, principle of, 48
Berger, C., 86
Berlo, David K., 6, 9
best fit, use of term, 543
beta (β) weight, 552, 554
bias, types of
hidden, 110
mono-operation, 272
nonresponse, 303
social desirability, 274, 276, 283
Big Data, 536
bimodal datasets, 431–32
Binet, Alfred, 223–24
Binet–Simon scale, 223–24
biological sex
communicative behavior due to, 33
ecological fallacies and, 33–34
nominal measurement, 220
The Biology of Communication (Beatty, McCroskey and Valencic), 192
bipolar scale. *See* semantic differential scales
blind peer reviews, 573
body, APA style checklist, 115*f*
Bogardus, Emory S., 224–25
Bogardus Social Distance Scale, 224–25
Boiarsky, G., 141, 151, 234, 332, 332*f*, 513–14
Book Datasets. *See also* communication study variables; Statistical Package for the Social Sciences 24.0 (SPSS) (software)
accessible via textbook website, 189
chi-square (χ^2), test of independence and, 466, 467*f*
Cronbach alpha reliability test and, 253–56, 255*f*–58*f*, 259–60, 260*f*–62*f*

Generalized Attitude Measure and, 253, 254–55, 255f–58f, 259
independent samples *t* test and, 485–86, 485f
one-way analysis of variance (ANOVA) and, 511, 512f
regression (*R*) and, 550–51, 550f
Book of Optics (Ibn al-Haytham), 23–24
books, APA citation elements for, 113f
Boolean logic, 103–5, 104f
Booth-Butterfield, Melanie, 84, 89, 90, 132, 142, 200, 228, 235, 555–56, 564, 565, 566–67. *See also* Humor Orientation Scale
Booth-Butterfield, Steven, 84, 228, 235. *See also* Humor Orientation Scale
Borisoff, Deborah, 12–13
Brady, R., 344
brainstorming
    Brainstorming Map, 90f
    for stating topic as question, 87
    for topic identification, 84
Bruess, C. J., 382–83
Brummans, Boris H.J.M., 138, 141, 142, 332f, 468–69
Bruner, Gordon, 244
BSRI. *See* Bem Sex-Role Inventory (BSRI)
Buckingham, A., 282–84, 293
Bureau of Applied Social Research, 6
Burgoon, J. K., 205
Buros, Oscar K., 242
Buros Center for Testing, 242
business-related research
    chi-square (χ^2), test of independence applicability, 469
    components of business reports, 167–68, 587
    correlation, 536
    credit scores, 558–59
    data privacy, 316
    guidelines for readable reports, 587–88
    key performance indicators, 514
    length of surveys, 316
    marketing measures, 244
    multiple linear regressions, 558–59
    one-way analysis of variance (ANOVA) and, 514
    study on upselling, 34–35
    writing reports, 587–88

CA. *See* communication apprehension (CA)
Calabrese, R., 86
calculated value, 403, 450–51
call for papers, 570–71, 571f–72f, 573
Campbell, D. T., 353–55
categorical/topical order, in literature review, 146
Cattell, James McKeen, 223, 280

causal relationships, in experimental design, 338
causation, 520–21
cause vs. chance, in experimental design, 339–40
cause-and-effect order, in literature review, 144
Centers for Disease Control and Prevention, 283
central limits theorem, 372
Certificate of Confidentiality, 53
Chan, K., 382
channel, in SMCR model, 11–12
Chen, C., 591
Chesebro, James W., 12–13, 137, 138–39, 142, 262–63, 393, 394, 397
Chesebro, Joe, 534–35
children's science television study (1999), 151, 234, 332, 513–14
chi-square (χ^2), defined, 445–46
chi-square (χ^2), test of independence, 445–70
    (step 1) add totals of rows, 449, 449f
    (step 2) examine expected frequencies, 449–50, 450f
    (step 3) compute sum of equation for each cell, 450, 451f
    (step 4) calculated value, 450–51
    (step 5) calculation of degrees of freedom, 451–52
    (step 6) critical value table, 452–53, 452f
    APA write-up for, 459
    basic assumptions of, 447–48
    biological sex (Dataset), 466, 467f
    Brummans and Miller article, 468–69
    case study introduction, 446–47, 447f
    Cramér's phi (Φ), 457, 458f, 459
    discussion of findings, 460–61, 461f–65f, 464–65
    formula for, 448, 448f
    post hoc APA write-up for, 465–66
    purpose of, 445–46
    statistical significance and, 448
    use of SPSS and, 453–66, 454f–58f, 461f–65f, 467f
Christian, L. M., 387
Christophel, D.M., 306
chronological order, in literature review, 143–44
citations, 116. *See also* APA style (citation guidelines)
claims, as attention-getters, 135, 137
Clement VIII (Pope), 46
Clever Hans (stallion), 32
Clever Hans (the Horse of Mr. Von Osten) (Pfungst), 32
closed-ended questions, 294–95, 302
cluster samples, 376–77, 377f
codebooks, 324, 325f, 327, 330
coder fatigue, 331
coder inattention, 331
coder misinterpretation, 331

coders
    defined, 326
    potential problems in final coding, 331
    retraining of, 331
    training of, 326–30
coding, defined, 324
coding forms, 324, 325f, 326, 327, 328f–29f
coding schemes, in content analysis, 324, 325f, 326
coefficients and reliability/validity, 274–75
cognitive knowledge, 230–31
cognitive-based questions, in surveys, 288
Cohen, J., 330
Cohen's *d* formula, 486–87
Cohen's kappa (κ), 330, 330f, 332, 332f, 513
Collaborative Institutional Training Initiative (CITI)
        training, 63
college students, as overstudied, 365
common knowledge, 18
Common Rule, 49–50, 54, 62, 64, 71
Communication, Affect, and Learning in the Classroom
        (Richmond, Wrench, and Gorham), 107
communication, defined, 9
Communication and Mass Media Complete database
        (EBSCO host), 100, 101f
communication apprehension (CA), 229
    defined, 194
    four subconstructs of, 273
    new measure for during social settings, 266–67
    PRCA-24 and, 194, 195f, 196
    willingness to communicate and, 207
communication associations, 568f, 569
Communication Currents (NCA), 589
Communication Education (NCA)
    call for manuscripts, 582, 583f–84f, 585
Communication Institute for Online Scholarship
        (CIOS), 107
communication journals. *See also specific journals by*
        publisher and name
    abstract, 94
    article title page, 116, 116f
    partial listing of, 96f–97f
    popular magazines vs., 93–95, 95f
    publication process for, 582–87, 583f–85f,
        591–92, 592f
Communication Quarterly, 262, 263f–64f
communication research, introduction, 1–16
    history of social sciences, 2–8
    key philosophers and theorists, 2–6
    nature of communication, 9–12
Communication Research Reports (CRR)

alpha reliabilities for communication articles,
        262, 263f–64f
    call for manuscripts, 582, 584f–85f, 585
    communication articles, 6, 7f–8f
communication study variables, 189–210.
        See also Book Datasets
    age, 209–10
    assertiveness, 203, 205
    audience-specific behavior, 193
    beliefs and attitudes, 208–9, 208f–9f
    biological sex, 189
    communication apprehension, 194–97, 195f, 207
    ethnocentrism and, 197, 198f, 212f
    humor assessment and, 197, 199–200, 199f, 212f, 228–29
    nonverbal immediacy and, 200–201, 202f, 212f
    personality and, 191–94, 194f
    political affiliation, 189–90
    responsiveness, 203, 205
    sociocommunicative orientation, 203, 204f, 213f
    sociocommunicative style, 204–5
    time spent online, 190–91, 213f
    university classification, 190
    willingness to communicate, 205, 206f, 207, 213f
communication trait, 193–94
Communication Trait Continuum, 194f
communications, use of term, 12
compare-and-contrast order, in literature review, 145
Comprehensive Community Health Models Initiative
        (Kellogg Foundation) study (1992), 468–69
computer simulations, in experimental design, 345
concept maps, for identification of key terms, 90
conceptual equivalence, 305
conceptual gaps, in literature review, 85
conceptualization
    in content analysis, 322
    creation of new measures and, 233
    defined, 233
conclusion, 159, 159f
concrete variables, 172–73
concurrent validity, 269–70
confederates, in experimental design, 345, 346, 347f
conference presentations, 567–81
    academic divisions/interest groups, 569, 570f
    CRTNET and, 569
    host communication associations list, 568f
    NCA Divisions, Caucuses, and Sections, 570, 570f
    opportunities for students, 569
    panel discussions, 581
    paper presentations, 573–76
    poster presentations, 576–81, 577f

regional associations, 569
scholar-to-scholar presentations, 581
submission of research papers for review,
    570–73, 571f–72f
confidence interval, 383–84, 400–401, 410f, 411–12, 414, 448
confidence level, 400–401
confidentiality, 52–54, 58–59, 284, 286
conflict of interest, 74
confounding variables
    control of experiments and, 350
    lurker variables, 350
    reinforcer variables, 350
    suppressor variables, 350
consequent, 27
conservative post hoc tests, 507
construct validity, 270–71, 275
constructive replication, 356
content analysis, 319–35
    (step 1) theory and rationale using scientific method, 322
    (step 2) conceptualization, 322–23
    (step 3) operationalization, 323–24
    (step 4) coding schemes, 324, 325f, 326
    (step 5) sampling, 326
    (step 6) training coders and pilot reliability,
        326–31, 328f, 330f
    (step 7) final coding, 331
    (step 8) final reliability, 332, 332f
    (step 9) tabulation and reporting, 332
    applicability of, 320–21
    defined, 319–21
content footnotes, 161
content validity, 268, 275
contextual CA, 196
control, defined, 31
control group, 344
control of experiments, 348–50
    confounding variables and, 350
    experimenter effects and, 348–49
    extraneous variables and, 349–50
    Hawthorne effect and, 349
    intervening variables and, 350
    threshold effect and, 348
controversial questions, in surveys, 287, 288
convenience samples, 379–80
Converse, J. M., 285
Coombs, W. T., 174
Copeland, Peter, 192
copyright permission footnotes, 161
correlation, 517–38. See also Pearson product-moment
        correlation coefficient (r)

(step 1) finding simple descriptive statistics, 523–24, 524f
(step 2) computation of formula above division line, 524
(step 3) computation of formula under division line,
    524–25
(step 4) computation of formula under division line in
    right bracket, 525
(step 5) computations and square root, 525
(step 6) division for r value and practical significance,
    525–26
(step 7) determination of statistical significance
    of r value, 526, 527f
APA write-up for, 529, 530, 531–32
basic assumptions of, 522
case study introduction, 518
formula for, 522, 522f
interpretation of positive/negative, 526
J. Chesebro article, 534–35
Punyanunt article, 535–36
purpose of, 518
reading large tables, 532, 533f
relationship vs. causation, 520–21
relationships among CA/WTC/BELIEF and public
    speaking (Dataset), 530–32, 531f, 533f
spurious discovered correlations, 520–21
types of relationships, 518–20, 519f
use of SPSS and, 527–32, 528f–31f, 533f
correlation (r), 517
Corrigan, Michael W., 142, 179, 287, 344–45, 392–93,
    396–97, 487–89
cover letters, in survey research, 304
Cramér's phi (Φ), 457, 458f, 459
credibility
    espousal of credibility in introduction, 139
    evaluation of websites and, 109–11
    source credibility, 271
    Source Credibility Measure, 239–41
criterion validity, 268–70
critical approach. See rhetorical branch of communication
critical value
    in significance testing, 403–6, 404f–5f
    tables, 452–53, 452f, 499–500, 500f
Cronbach alpha reliability test
    Book Datasets and, 253–56, 255f–58f, 259–60, 260f–62f
    coefficients and, 274–75
Cross-Out Test, 224
cross-sectional survey design, 290
cultural norms
    conceptual equivalence and, 305
    ethnocentrism and, 197
    handling of strangers and, 306

cultural norms (*continued*)
humor and, 200
normative equivalence and, 305–6
styles of expression of ideas, 306
willingness to discuss topics and, 306
curvilinear relationship, 519*f*, 520

Darley, John, 42
Darwin, Charles, 4, 222–23
data, defined, 419–20
data falsification, 71–72
data process and analysis, in survey research, 292
data sharing, 72
data visualization, 591–92, 592*f*
databases. *See* EBSCOhost (databases); electronic
databases; ERIC (Education Resource
Information Center) database
dataset variability, in descriptive statistics, 441, 441*f*–42*f*
De Gail, M. A., 345, 346
debriefing, 352–53
deception
during consent process, 61
expedited review and, 64
in experimental design, 349, 351
Hawthorne effect and, 349
IRB review of, 62, 389
participant debriefing about, 352–53
declarative statements, 565
decoding, defined, 10
degrees of freedom, 451–52, 478, 479
degrees of freedom (df) between, 499–500
degrees of freedom (df) within, 499–500
deidentify the data, 72
Dell Computers, 34–35
demographic questions, 286
dependent variables, 179–80, 312–13, 347–48, 352
Descartes, René, 23
descriptive statistics, 417–44
dataset variability, 441, 441*f*–42*f*
defined, 419
inferential statistics vs., 419–21
measures of central tendency and, 421–34, 425*f*
measures of variability, 435–41, 436*f*–40*f*
descriptive surveys, 281
design of study. *See* experimental research design; study
design, in survey research
differences, in research, 177–78, 178*f*–79*f*
differences and relationships, 177–78, 178*f*–79*f*
differences in kind, 177–78
differences of degree, 178, 178*f*
Dillman, D. A., 300–303, 387

diminished autonomy, 47–48
direct quotations. *See* quotations
directional research questions, 395
Directory of Communication Related Mental Measures, 243
Directory of Open Access Journals (DOAJ), 107
discussion section (of research paper)
defined, 563
example of, 157*f*–58*f*
hypothesis in, 565
implications and future research subsection, 158–59,
566–67
interpretation of findings, 564–65
limitations subsection, 157–58, 158*f*, 566
relationship between findings and previous
studies, 565–66
research questions in, 565
summarization of results/findings, 156–57, 564, 564*f*
disguiser, type of plagiarism, 75–76
DOAJ. *See* Directory of Open Access Journals (DOAJ)
Docear (software), 112
Doescher, T. A., 345–46
double-blind studies, 349
Downs, Cal, 244
Duhigg, Charles, 536
dummy experiments, 349
Dunn–Sidak test, 464–66
duplicate data publication, 72–73
dyad, as unit of analysis, 173

Eastern Communication Association (ECA), 569, 571,
571*f*–72*f*. *See also Communication Research Reports* (CRR)
Eastin, M. S., 344
EBSCOhost (databases)
Communication and Mass Media Complete database,
100, 101*f*
Mental Measures Yearbook, 242
ECA. *See* Eastern Communication Association (ECA)
ecological fallacies, 33–34, 174
.edu (web address), 110
educational assessment, history of, 223–24, 231
Educational Testing Service (ETS), 224, 242
"The Effect of Ambiguity on the Implementation of a Social
Change Initiative" (Brummans and Miller),
468–69
"The Effect of Interest on Recall: An Experiment"
(Weber, Fornash, Corrigan, and Neupauer),
344–45, 487–89
effect size
in hypothesis testing, 408, 409*f*
in independent samples *t* test, 486–87
in significance testing, 408, 409*f*

"The Effects of Humor on Perceptions of Compliance-Gaining in the College Classroom" (Punyanunt), 419, 535–36
electronic databases, 100–105. *See also specific databases by name*
    Boolean logic in searches, 103–5, 104*f*
    functions as index, 100
    listing of, 101*f*–2*f*
    subject searches of, 102–3
    subscriptions to, 100, 107
    truncation symbols in searches, 105
electronic full-text of print journal article, APA citation elements for, 113*f*
Eltinge, J. L., 300–303
e-mail, for recruitment of samples, 387, 387*f*
emotions, and hesitancy to answer surveys, 283–84
empirical generalizations, in scientific method, 33–34
    defined, 31
    ecological fallacies and, 33–34
    exception fallacies and, 34
    hasty generalizations, 33
    refinement of theory, 34
    study limitations, 33
empirical observations, 30
empirical research, 17–38
    empirical generalizations, 31–34
    epistemology and, 18–20
    ordinary vs. scientific knowledge, 20–22
    scientific method and, 23–33, 24*f*
empiricism, 26–27, 30
encoding, defined, 10
end materials
    figures, 162
    footnotes, 160–61
    tables, 161–62
ends, in Ethical Matrix, 45–47
English units, 218
epistemist theoretical tradition, 19
epistemology
    approaches to communication scholarship and, 18–20
    defined, 18
    skepticism and, 19
    sources of knowledge, 18–19
equipment/materials in research, 151
ERIC (Education Resource Information Center) database, 100, 101*f*
errors, in hypothesis testing, 399–400, 402, 409–14, 410*f*, 412*f*
espousal of credibility, in introduction, 136*f*, 139
eta-square (η^2), 505, 506
ethical behavior, 46
Ethical Matrix, 45–47, 45*f*
ethics, defined, 45–47. *See also* research ethics

ethnocentrism, 197, 198*f*, 212*f*, 261*f*
Ethnocentrism Scale, 121*f*, 198*f*, 261*f*
ETS. *See* Educational Testing Service (ETS)
European Union, General Data Protection Regulation (GDPR), 52–53
evaluation apprehension, 274
evoke empathy, 25
ex post facto design, 364
exception fallacies, 34
exempt reviews, by IRBs, 64, 65*f*–67*f*, 67
expectations and compliance study (1994), 345–46
expected frequencies, 449–50, 450*f*
expedited reviews, by IRBs, 62, 64, 68*f*–70*f*
experiment, defined, 338
experimental group, 344
experimental research design, 336–67
    (step 1) introduction of experiment and obtaining consent, 351
    (step 2) random assignment of participants to groups, 340–42, 341*f*–43*f*, 351
    (step 3) manipulation of independent variable, 342–48, 347*f*, 351–52
    (step 4) measurement of dependent variable, 347–48, 352
    (step 5) debriefing of participants, 352–53
    causal relationships and, 338
    control of, 348–50
    determination of cause vs. chance, 339–40
    generalizability and, 365–66
    influence of intervening and antecedent variables, 339
    limits on number of variables, 364
    preexperimental designs, 357–58
    quasi-experimental design, 358–61
    replication and, 356
    ruling out alternative explanations, 339
    threats to validity of experiment, 353–55
    time order and, 336–37, 338
    true experimental designs, 361–64
    use of formulaic characters, 356–57
experimenter effects, 348–49
experimenter expectancies, 274
explanations, 25
explanatory surveys, 281
exploratory research, 282
extraneous variables, 349–50

F test, 499–500
face validity, 268, 275
Facebook
    newsfeed manipulation study, 44
    recruitment of samples via ads on, 386
    survey links on, 298

face-to-face (FTF)
   recruitment of samples, 386
   surveys, 294–95, 296
factor analysis, 240, 275
factorial experiment design, 346, 347f
factorial validity, 271
facts, 22
Fahrenheit system, 221–22
fair use, 161
faking responses, 275–76, 299, 351
fallacy
   ecological, 33–34, 174
   exception, 34
false premises, 27, 238
falsification of theories, 26–27
Family Educational Rights and Privacy
   Act (1974), 52
Fediuk, T. A., 344
field experiments, 365–66
figures, 162
findings and results. *See also* literature review
   of chi-square test, 460–61, 461f–65f, 464–65
   during observation step of scientific method, 31
   results section of paper, 154–55, 155f, 562
   summarization of in discussion section of paper, 156–57,
      564, 564f
Fink, A., steps for conducting surveys, 285–94
first page of paper, APA paper formatting, 126, 127f
Fisher, R. A., 396
Fisher's least significant difference (LSD), 507
fonts, for poster presentations, 580
footnotes, 160–61
forgotten footnoter/referencer, type of plagiarism, 76
"Formal Features in Children's Science Television: Sound
   Effects, Visual Pace, and Topic Shifts" (Boiarsky,
   Long, and Thayer), 151, 513–14
formatting of paper. *See* APA paper formatting
Fornash, Bennie, 138, 179, 344–45, 392–93,
   396–97, 487–89
Fowler, F. J., Jr., 303
frequency distribution
   kurtosis, 433–34, 434f
   skewness, 433–34, 433f–34f
   use of SPSS and, 426–34, 427f–34f
Freud, Sigmund, 4
Frymier, A. B., 267, 273
FTF. *See* face-to-face (FTF)
full-board reviews, by IRBs, 70–71
future research subsection, in discussion section,
   158–59, 566–67

G (group), 495. *See also* one-way analysis of variance
   (ANOVA)
Galileo, 33
Galton, Francis, 222–23
gaps in research, 85, 139
Garramone, G. M., 43–44
Gates, Arthur, 224
general linear model (GLM), 493, 540. *See also* one-way
   analysis of variance (ANOVA); regression (*R*)
generalizability, 284, 326, 365–66, 370
Generalized Attitude Measure, 230
   APA write-up for, 213f, 259–60, 262f
   Book Datasets and, 253, 254–55, 255f–58f, 259
   example of, 209f
   flexibility of, 208–9
   reliability of, 249, 251–52
   scoring of, 250f–51f, 251
   semantic differential items on, 227
Generalized Belief Scale, 230
   APA write-up for, 213f, 262f
   example of, 208f
   flexibility of, 208
general-to-specific order, in literature review, 146–47
germinal idea, 233
ghostwriter, type of plagiarism, 75
Gimp (software), 592
GLM. *See* general linear model (GLM)
glossary, 595–606
The Gods Must Be Crazy (film), 25
Google Scholar (website), 106–7
Gorham, Joan, 107
Gosset, William Sealy, 474
.gov (web address), 110
Graduate Record Exam (GRE), 224
Graham, E. E., 173
Gray, John, 33
group, as unit of analysis, 173–74
Groves, R. M., 300–303
Grunig, L. A., 381
Guéguen, N., 345, 346
Guthery, D., 307
Guttman, L., 5
Guttman scale, 186–87, 187f, 275

Hamer, Dean, 192
handbooks, 98–99
Haney, Craig, 43
Härdle, W. K., 591
Harris, S. R., 21–22
hasty generalizations, 33

Hawthorne effect, 349
Health Insurance Portability and Accountability Act
        (HIPPA) (1996), 52
Heise, D. R., 228
Heraclitus, 9
Hereditary Genius (Galton), 222–23
HHS. *See* US Department of Health and
        Human Services (HHS)
hidden bias, on websites, 110
Hildebrand, D. K., 286
Hippocrates of Cos, 2–3
histograms, 428–29, 431–32, 431*f*–32*f*
historical flaw, 353
Holladay, S. J., 174
Hollander, E. P., 191, 192
Homonegativity Short Form, 183, 184*f*
Hovland, Carl, 6
"How Companies Learn Your Secrets" (Duhigg), 536
"How to Make Our Ideas Clear" (Peirce), 23
HSD. *See* Tukey's honestly significance difference test (HSD)
.html format articles, APA style for, 107
human genetics, personality and, 192
human rights violations, 41–42
human sexuality studies (Kinsey), 295
human subjects, regulations for, 61–63
humor, in interpersonal relations, 197, 199–200, 228
humor assessment
        APA write-up for, 212*f*, 261*f*
        experimental research design and, 343–44, 352
        new scale for classroom settings, 267–68, 273
        use of scales and, 228–29, 235
Humor Assessment Instrument (HA), 199*f*, 261*f*
humor in classroom and compliance study (2000),
        142, 419, 535–36
humor in health-care settings study (2003), 142, 200,
        212*f*, 555–56
humor in preflight safety briefings study (2007), 28–31, 33,
        34, 343–44, 352
Humor Orientation Scale, 228, 235
        APA write-up for, 154*f*
Humphreys, Laud, 42
Hunt, Everett Lee, 4
hypothesis guessing, 274
hypothesis testing, 391–416
        alternative and null hypotheses, 395–97
        case study introduction, 398–99
        defined, 397
        effect size, 408, 409*f*
        95% confidence, 400–405
        research questions and, 394–95

sampling error and, 399–400, 402
significance testing, 401–6, 404*f*–5*f*
testing for power, 406–8, 407*f*
types of hypotheses, 391–94
understanding errors, 409–14, 410*f*, 412*f*
hypothesis/hypotheses. *See also* null hypothesis; one-tailed
        hypothesis; two-tailed hypothesis
        alternative hypothesis, 395–96, 397
        characteristics of well written statements, 392–93
        defined, 143, 391
        in discussion section of paper, 565
        post hoc hypothesis revision, 73
        in rationale section of paper, 149–50
        Research Project Worksheet, 313, 315*f*
        in scientific method, 27–28
hypothetical scenarios, in experimental design, 345–46
hypothetical variables, 225

Ibn al-Haytham, Hasan, 23–24
Ibrahim, F. A., 306
if–then statements, 392–94
Ig Nobel Prizes, 48
illustrations, as attention-getters, 137–38
Illustrator (software), 591
immediacy, 200–201. *See also* nonverbal immediacy
inconsistent data study, 45
"Increasing Patient Satisfaction and Compliance"
        (Wrench and M. Booth-Butterfield), 132, 555–56
independent samples *t* test, 471–91
        (step 1) finding $\Sigma X1$, 474–75, 474*f*–75*f*
        (step 2) computation, 475–76, 475*f*
        (step 3) sum of square calculation, 476–77, 476*f*
        (step 4) complete formula, 477
        (step 5) calculation of big parentheses to right
                of equation, 477
        (step 6) calculations of previous steps, 477
        (step 7) calculation of top of formula, 478, 478*f*
        (step 8) division to compute *t* statistic, 478
        (step 9) calculation of degrees of freedom, 478, 479
        (step 10) critical value table, 479, 479*f*
        APA write-up for, 485
        basic assumptions of, 473
        biological sex and CA (Dataset), 485–86, 485*f*
        case study introduction, 472
        Cohen's *d* formula, 486–87
        effect size and, 486–87
        formulas for, 473, 473*f*, 476
        purpose of, 472
        use of SPSS and, 480–85, 480*f*–85*f*
        Weber, Fornash, Corrigan, Neupauer article, 487–89

independent variables, 179–80, 312, 342–46, 347f, 351–52. *See also* manipulation of independent variable

individual, as unit of analysis, 173

inferential statistics, 277, 397, 419–21, 435

infographics, 591–92, 592f

information sources. *See* sources of information, location of

informed consent, 47–48
    deception during process, 61
    defined, 54
    in experimental design, 351
    legal guardians and, 351
    for medical case studies, 50

informed consent documents, 54–61
    concise summary, 54
    confidentiality, 58–59
    contact information, 57
    costs/payments to participants, 59
    description of participation steps, 57–58
    effectiveness of, 59–60
    example, 54f–57f
    general purpose of study, 57
    length of time in study, 58
    participant rights, 59
    risks, 58
    signatures, 59

Inkscape (software), 592

Institute for Communications Research, University of Illinois, 6

Institutional Review Boards (IRBs), 49–71
    advanced functions of, 63
    annual reviews, 62
    anonymity, 302
    anonymity issues, 51, 286
    Collaborative Institutional Training Initiative (CITI) training requirement, 63
    Common Rule, 49–50
    confidentiality, 52–54, 58–59, 302
    deception during consent process, 61
    diverse membership of, 62
    exempt reviews, 64, 65f–67f, 67
    expedited reviews, 62, 64, 68f–70f
    full-board reviews, 70–71
    informed consent, 54–61
    investigation of adverse events, 62–63
    investigation of protocol violations, 63
    paid participation, 51
    privacy, 51–52
    recruitment of samples, 388–89
    regulations for use of human subjects, 61–63
    research participants, 50
    review of study protocols, 62
    review processes, 64–71
    waivers of consent, 60–61

instrumental replication, 356

instrumentation/measurement subsection, in method section, 151, 153–54, 154f, 211–12

intelligence tests, 223–24

interactional analysis, 323

intercorder reliability, 327–32, 328f–30f

intercultural perspectives taught in public relations courses study (2003), 380–81

interlibrary loan, 165

internal citations. *See* parenthetical citations, APA style for

International Encyclopedia of Communication, 99

Internet-administered surveys, 297–99. *See also* World Wide Web (WWW)

interpretive approach. *See* qualitative branch of communication

interval level questions, in surveys, 287

interval measurement, 188f, 221–22

interval variables
    defined, 183
    Likert scale and, 183–84, 184f
    on questionnaires, 287
    scalograms and, 186–87, 187f
    semantic differential scale and, 184–85, 185f
    Staple scale and, 185–86, 186f

intervening variables, 180, 273, 339, 350

interview schedules, 281, 285, 293

interviews with people
    APA citation elements for, 113f
    as form of operationalization, 234–35

in-text citations, APA style for, 116, 119f

introduction, to research paper, 135–40
    attention-getter element of, 135, 137–38
    defined, 135
    espousal of credibility and, 139
    example of, 136f
    link/transition to topic and, 138–39
    preview and, 140
    significance of topic and, 139
    thesis statement and, 139

IRBs. *See* Institutional Review Boards (IRBs)

isomorphism, 219–20

item analysis, 277

item nonresponse
    defined, 301
    effects of, 303
    institutional requirements and policies, 302
    interview training and, 301

question difficulty and, 302
question structure and, 302
question topics and, 301–2
respondent attributes and, 302–3
survey mode and, 301

Jaffe, David, 43
James, William, 4
James C. McCroskey and Virginia Peck Richmond
    Undergraduate Scholars Conference (USC), 569
jargon, avoidance of, 237, 588
JASP, 254
John Paul II (Pope), 33
Johnson, A. D., 272. *See also* Nonverbal Immediacy
    Scale-Self-Report
Johnson, Aaron, 228–29
journal abstracts, 94
Journal of Applied Communication, on interaction of
    communication researchers and IRBs, 53
Journal of Statistics Education, 282–83
journalistic vs. academic writing process, 589–90, 590*f*
journals. *See* communication journals; publication in
    journals; *specific journals by publisher and name*
Jowett, G. S., 5
justice, as ethical standard, 49

Kellogg Foundation study (1992), 468–69
Kelly, Frederick J., 224
Kelvin scale, 187, 222, 224
Kennamer, J. D., 43–44
key performance indicators, 514
key terms, 89–90, 89*f*
Keyton, J., 323
keyword search, 102, 103–5
Khan, M. N., 75
Kinsey, Alfred, 295
Klein, P., 18, 19
knowledge
    cognitive, 230–31
    common, 18
    epistemology and, 18–19
    ordinary vs. scientific, 20–22
    perceived, 231
known groups, measurement of,
    270–71
known-to-unknown order, 147
Krippendorff's alpha, 332
Kuhn, T., 173–74
Kumblaeus, Johan, 320
kurtosis, 433–34, 434*f*

label the phenomenon, 25
laboratory settings, overreliance on, 365
Lachlan, K., 344
Laine, C., 22
Laing, J. D., 286
languages, number of, 11
Latané, Bibb, 42
latent variables, 225, 350. *See also* intervening variables
Law, K. S., 305–8
Lazarsfeld, P., 6
leading items, 237
Learner Empowerment Scale, 488
Lesser, V., 303
letters/postcards, for recruitment of samples, 386–87
Levene's Test for Equality of Variances,
    482–83, 483*f*, 485, 485*f*
Levine, T. R., 412
liberal post hoc tests, 507
librarians, 93, 100, 108–9
Likert, Rensis, 5, 225
Likert scales
    Homonegativity Short Form, 183–84, 184*f*
    as interval oriented, 222, 287
    Likert-Type Anchors, 225, 226*f*
    measurement by, 225
    writing questions for, 235–39
Likert-Type Anchors, 225, 226*f*
Lime Survey, 299
limitations subsection, in discussion section, 157–58, 158*f*, 566
linear regression. *See* regression (*R*)
linear relationships, 188, 543. *See also* correlation; regression (*R*)
link/transition to topic, in introduction, 136*f*, 138–39
liquor store burglary study (1970), 42
listening style and conversational sensitivity study (1999),
    137, 138–39, 142, 262–63, 393, 397, 534–35
literal replication, 356
literature review, 140–50
    argument, 142–43
    categorical/topical order, 146
    cause-and-effect order, 144
    chronological order for main ideas, 143–44
    common pitfalls in, 166
    compare-and-contrast order, 145
    conceptual gaps in, 85
    defined, 140
    in discussion section of paper, 565–66
    example of, 147, 148*f*, 149
    explanation and rationalization for variables, 141–42
    explanation of terminology, 140–41
    general-to-specific order, 146–47

literature review (*continued*)
  historical context of study and, 141
  known-to-unknown order, 147
  previous findings and further research, 142
  problem-cause-solution order, 145–46
  psychological order, 146
  specific-to-general order, 147
  topic identification, 85
literature review, first draft of, 163–67
  (step 1) topic identification, 163
  (step 2) selection of type of study to conduct, 163
  (step 3) determination of variables, 164
  (step 4) search for primary sources, 164
  (step 5) record full text references, 164
  (step 6) backtracking through references, 164
  (step 7) narrowing list of references, 164–65
  (step 8) organization of references by topics/
    subtopics, 165
  (step 9) review for gaps in references, 165
  (step 10) finding references to fill gaps, 165
  (step 11) creation of outline, 166
  (step 12) writing process, 167
Little, R. J. A., 300–303
Living With Our Genes (Hamer and Copeland), 192
loaded items, 237–38
Long, M., 234
Long, Marilee, 141, 151, 332, 332*f*, 513–14
longitudinal survey design, 290–91
Lonner, W. J., 306
Lowe, B. A., 307
LSD. *See* Fisher's least significant difference (LSD)
lurker variables, 350

Machiavelli, Niccolò, 46
Machiavellian ethic, 46, 61
magazine articles, APA citation elements for, 113*f*
Mahmood, A., 75
Mahmood, S. T., 75, 77
mailed administration, of surveys, 297, 303
major premise, 27–29
Malik, A. B., 75
The Man Who Lied to His Laptop (Nass and Yen), 34–35
Manhattan Project, 47
manipulation check, 352
manipulation into categories, 234
manipulation of independent variable, 342–48, 347*f*, 351–52
marketing scales, 244
Masling, Joseph, 276, 351
Mason, R., 303
mass administration, of surveys, 296–97

mass-mediated communication, 320–21
maturation, as threat to validity, 353–54
McCroskey, James C., 9, 10, 106, 142, 183, 184, 192, 197, 203,
    205, 208, 212, 225, 227, 228–29, 233, 239, 259, 271,
    272, 287, 306, 569. *See also* Ethnocentrism Scale;
    Generalized Attitude Measure; Generalized Belief
    Scale; Nonverbal Immediacy Scale-Self-Report;
    Personal Report of Communication Apprehension–
    24 (PRCA-24); Sociocommunicative Orientation
    Scale; Source Credibility Measure; Willingness to
    Communicate Scale
McNutt, L. A., 59–60
mean, as measure of central tendency, 421–22,
    421*f*–22*f*, 424, 425*f*
mean squares between, 499
mean squares within, 499
means
  effect size and, 408, 409*f*
  in Ethical Matrix, 45–47
measurement, 217–47. *See also* reliability; validity;
    specific tests and scales
  construction of questions, 235–39
  defined, 218
  history of, 218, 222–28, 230–31
  isomorphic numbers and things, 219–20
  levels of, 220–22
  multiple factors/subscales and, 239–41
  procedures and rules, 219
  statistical analysis and, 243–44
measurement in communication studies, 228–43
  beliefs and attitudes, 230, 277
  cognitive knowledge, 230–31
  creation of new measures, 232–35
  Directory of Communication Related Mental Measures, 243
  perceived knowledge, 231
  personality traits/states, 229–30
  resources for, 244
  survey-based research, 241–42
measures, creation of new, 232–35
  conceptualization and, 233
  germinal idea and, 233
  operationalization and, 233–35
measures of central tendency, 421–34
  frequency distribution, 426–34, 427*f*–34*f*
  mean, 421–22, 421*f*–22*f*, 424, 425*f*
  median, 422–24, 425*f*, 426
  mode, 424–26, 425*f*, 431–32
  selection of measures, 425–26
media research, 320–21, 380
median, as measure of central tendency, 422–24, 425*f*, 426

mediated channels, 11–12

mediating variables. *See* intervening variables

medical research, 50, 401, 407

Men Are from Mars, Women Are from Venus (Gray), 33

mental measures, 223, 240, 241–42

    cultural norms and, 305–6

    grouping of anchors for, 287

Mental Measures Yearbook, 242

message, in SMCR model, 10

meta-analysis, 402

method section (of research paper), 150–54

    APA style for, 210–12, 212*f*–13*f*

    apparatus subsection, 151, 211

    instrumentation/measurement subsection,

        151, 153–54, 154*f*, 211–12

    participant subsection, 150–51, 152*f*, 210–11

    procedure subsection, 151, 152*f*, 211

metric system, 218

Microsoft Excel

    chi-square (χ^2), test of independence, 453

    in communications research, 254

    frequency distribution, 426

    random number generation, 374

Milgram, Stanley, 43, 61

Milgram Study (1974), 43, 61

Miller, Katherine, 138, 141, 142, 332*f*, 468–69

Millhouse, B., 343

minor premise, 27–29

misinformer, type of plagiarism, 76

mode, as measure of central tendency, 424–26, 425*f*, 431–32

modified direct translation, 307

mono-operation bias, 272

Morse Code, 11–12

Moser, P. K., 18

multiple administration techniques, of surveys, 304

multiple comparison test, 507–11

multiple linear regression, 551–55, 552*f*–53*f*, 555*f*, 558–59

multiple time-series design, 359–60

mundane realism, 365

Nass, Clifford, 34–35

National Commission for the Protection of Human Subjects

    of Biomedical and Behavioral Research, 42, 47

National Communication Association (NCA), 569, 570. *See*

    also Communication Currents (NCA); *Communication*

    Education (NCA); *Spectra* (NCA newsletter)

    Divisions, Caucuses, and Sections, 570*f*

    journal acceptance rates, 586, 586*f*

    online journal for general public, 589

National Institutes of Health (NIH), 50, 51–52

National Research Act (1974), 42

natural selection, theory of (Darwin), 4

NCA. *See* National Communication Association (NCA)

NCA listserv Communication, Research, and Theory

    Network (CRTNET), 569

negative relationship, 519–20, 519*f*, 526

negative relationships, 175–76, 176*f*

Netflix, 536

Nettler, Gwynn, 25

network samples, 382–83

Neuendorf, K. A., nine steps of content analysis, 319–32

Neuliep, J. W., 197. *See also* Ethnocentrism Scale

Neupauer, Nicholas, 142, 179, 344–45, 392–93,

    396–97, 487–89

neutral relationship, 519*f*, 520

neutral relationships, 177, 177*f*

The New York Times Magazine, on Big Data, 536

newspaper articles, APA citation elements for, 113*f*

Newton, Isaac, 3, 4

Nicol, A. A. M., 576–77

NIH. *See* National Institutes of Health (NIH)

95% confidence interval, 400–405, 448, 452–53

99% confidence, 401, 402, 412, 414

No Child Left Behind (2001), 52

no relationship. *See* neutral relationship

nominal level questions, in surveys, 285–86

nominal measurement, 188*f*, 220

nominal variables, 181–82, 285–86, 471–72

nondirectional research questions, 395

nonparametric tests, 243

nonprobabilty samples, 371, 372, 378–83

    convenience samples, 379–80

    network samples, 382–83

    purposive samples, 380–81

    quota samples, 381–82

    volunteer samples, 380

nonproportionate quota samples, 381

nonquantitative research methods, 12–13

nonresponse, defined, 300

nonresponse bias, 303

nonverbal behaviors displayed in physician–patient

    interactions study (2002), 379–80

nonverbal immediacy, 200–201, 212*f*, 305, 347, 488

Nonverbal Immediacy Scale-Self-Report, 201, 202*f*,

    229–30, 272

    APA write-up for, 212*f*, 261*f*

nonverbal messages

    defined, 11

    new test for during greetings, 267

normative equivalence, 305–6

Notepad (software), 254, 426
null hypothesis, 396–97, 406–14, 494. *See also* significance testing
nuts-to-you response, as type of faking, 276, 299, 351

objective observations, 30–31
observational methods, 282
observations, in scientific method, 29–31
    controlled, 31
    defined, 29–30
    empirical, 30
    objective, 30–31
    reporting results, 31
observer agreement, 275
O'Donnell, V., 5
Office of Human Research Protections (OHRP), 49, 54, 63, 67, 71
OHRP. *See* Office of Human Research Protections (OHRP)
OkCupid, mismatching people study, 44–45
On the Origin of Species (Darwin), 222–23
one-group pretest–posttest design, 357
one-shot case study design, 357
one-tailed hypothesis, 393–94, 406–7, 407*f*
one-way analysis of variance (ANOVA), 492–516
    (step 1) determination of *X* for groups, 495, 495*f*–96*f*
    (step 2) calculation of sum of squares between, 496
    (step 3) computation of G^2/N part of formula, 496
    (step 4) computation of actual value of sum of squares between, 497
    (step 5) calculation of sum of squares within, 497–98, 498*f*
    (step 6) calculation of sum of squares total, 498
    (step 7) computation of degrees of freedom between/within, 499
    (step 8) calculation of mean squares between/within, 499
    (step 9) calculation of *F* tests, 499
    (step 10) critical value table, 499–500, 500*f*
    (step 11) summary table, 500, 501*f*
    APA write-up for, 510, 511
    basic assumptions of, 494
    Bioarsky, Long, Thayer article, 513–14
    case study introduction, 493
    defined, 492
    eta-square (η^2), 505, 506
    formula for, 495, 495*f*
    multiple comparison tests and, 507–11
    political affiliation and humor assessment (Dataset), 511, 512*f*
    post hoc tests, 507, 508*f*
    purpose of, 492–94
    use of SPSS and, 501–11, 501*f*–6*f*, 508*f*, 512*f*
one-way mirrors, in experimental design, 349

online surveys, 297–99
open-ended questions, in surveys, 288–89, 294–96, 302
operational replication, 356
operationalization
    asking people to estimate category, 234
    in content analysis, 233–35
    creation of new measures and, 233–35
    defined, 233, 234
    interviews and surveys as, 234–35
    manipulation into categories, 234
    observation of existing records, 234
opinions, 22
ordinal level questions, in surveys, 286
ordinal measurement, 188*f*, 220
ordinal variables, 182–83, 286
ordinary vs. scientific knowledge, 20–22
.org (web address), 110
organization, as unit of analysis, 174
organization and evaluation of information, 111–13
    maintenance of working bibliography, 111
    source record cards, 112–13, 112*f*, 116
    steps in, 112–13
    sticky-note method, 111–12
    use of Docear (software), 112
organizational ambiguity study (2004), 141, 332*f*, 468–69
organizational orientations theory study (2004), 142, 228–29
organizational patterns
    categorical/topical order, 146
    cause-and-effect order, 144
    chronological order for main ideas, 143–44
    compare-and-contrast order, 145
    general-to-specific order, 146–47
    known-to-unknown order, 147
    problem-cause-solution order, 145–46
    psychological order, 146
    specific-to-general order, 147
Osgood, C. E., 5, 227, 277
O'Shea, T. J., 167–68, 587–88
outliers, 428

p value, 402, 412
page order, APA style checklist for, 115*f*
paired *t* tests, 405, 490
pancultural, 197
panel discussions, 581
panel survey design, 291
paper format. *See* APA paper formatting
paper presentations, 573–76
paper respondents, 576
parallel blind technique, 308
parameter, defined, 243–44, 417–18

parametric tests, 243–44
paraphrasing, 121–22, 138
parenthetical citations, APA style for, 116, 119–20, 119f–20f
participant identify protection, 73
participant subsection, in method section, 150–51, 152f, 210–11
patriotism, 197
Pearson, J. C., 382–83
Pearson correlations, 332
Pearson product-moment correlation coefficient (*r*), 517. *See also* correlation
peer reviews, 126, 573, 582
Peirce, Charles Sanders, 23
perceived knowledge, 231
percentages. *See* descriptive statistics
perfect crime, type of plagiarism, 77
Perse, E. M., 173
Personal Report of Communication Apprehension–24 (PRCA-24)
    APA write-up for, 212f, 261f
    communication apprehension (CA), 194, 195f, 196
    contextual CA, 196
    in correlation study, 518, 522–26, 523f–24f
    criterion validity example and, 268–69
    scoring of, 196, 225, 229
    situational CA, 196
    subscales and, 273
    trait CA, 196
Personal Report of Public Speaking Anxiety (PRPSA), 183, 184
personality, 191–94
    communication trait, 193–94, 194f
    contexts of behavior, 193
    dynamic/consistent aspects of, 192
    external/internal level of, 191–92
    hypothetical constructs and, 229
    situational behavior, 193
    trait behavior, 192–93
personality tests, history of, 224
Pertaub, D. B., 345
Pexman, P. M., 576–77
Pfungst, Oskar, 32
Philosophiae Naturalis Principia Mathematica (*Mathematical Principles of Natural Philosophy*) (Newton), 3
photocopier, type of plagiarism, 75
Photoshop (software), 591
pilot reliability, in content analysis, 326–31, 328f, 330f
pilot study, 293
pilot testing, in survey research, 292–94
    population members and, 293
    post testing interviews, 293–94

sample size, 293
    use of parts of survey, 293
    use of same conditions, 293
plagiarism
    source-cited types of, 76–77
    source-not-cited types of, 75–76, 116
Plagiarism.org, 75–77
Plato, 3
Poole, M. S., 173–74
Popper, Karl R., 24, 26
population, defined, 284, 326, 369–70, 369f, 420
population mean, 421, 421f
positive relationships, 175, 176f, 518–19, 519f, 526
positivism/postpositivism. *See* social scientific branch of communication
post hoc hypothesis revision, 73
postdictive validity, 270
poster presentations, 576–81, 577f
postmodern approach. *See* rhetorical branch of communication
post-structuralist approach. *See* rhetorical branch of communication
potluck writer, type of plagiarism, 75
power, statistical, 406–8, 410f, 413
practical significance, 525–26
Praxis tests, 224
PRCA-24. *See* Personal Report of Communication Apprehension–24 (PRCA-24)
predictions/hypotheses, in scientific method, 27–29
    development of, 27
    formation of arguments, 27–29
    syllogism and, 27–29
predictive validity, 269, 275
preexisting datasets, 282–83
preexperimental designs, 357–58
preprint publications, APA style for, 107
presentation of research, 72–73, 561–94
    to academic divisions/interest groups, 569–70, 570f
    at conferences, 567–81, 568f, 570f–72f, 577f
    panel discussions, 581
    paper presentations, 573–76
    poster presentations, 576–81, 577f
    publication in journals, 582–87, 583f–85f, 591–92, 592f
    scholar-to-scholar, 581
    submission for conference review, 570–73, 571f–72f
    use of technology for, 575
press releases, 589
Presser, S., 285
Pressey, L. W., 224
Pressey, S. L., 224
pretest–posttest design, 358–59, 361–62

preview, in introduction, 136*f*, 140

Prichard, S., 225

primacy concept, 287

primary sources, 91–93

The Prince (Machiavelli), 46

principal researchers, 313, 315*f*

principle of beneficence, 48

print journal articles, APA citation elements for, 113*f*

privacy, 51–52

probability, 397

probability level, 402–3

probability sampling, 372–78

    central limits theorem and, 372

    cluster samples, 376–77, 377*f*

    defined, 371

    simple random samples, 373–75, 374*f*

    stratified random samples, 375–76, 375*f*

    systematic samples, 377–78

probability theory, 372

probability value (*p* value), 402, 412

problem-cause-solution order, in literature review, 145–46

procedural problems, 158

procedure subsection, in method section, 151, 152*f*, 211

professor school undercover study (1005), 44

proportionate quota samples, 381–82

proposition, 27–28

prospective validity, 269, 275

protected health information (PHI), 52

PRPSA. *See* Personal Report of Public Speaking Anxiety (PRPSA)

PSPP (software), 14, 254

psychological order, in literature review, 146

public dissemination, of research, 588, 590*f*

publication in journals, 582–87

    acceptance rates, 586–87, 586*f*

    call for manuscripts example, 583*f*–85*f*

    data visualization, 591–92, 592*f*

    review process, 585–87, 586*f*

    submission process, 582–85

Publication Manual of the American Psychological Association (APA), 74–75, 114, 127, 133–34, 412. *See also* APA style (citation guidelines)

Punyanunt-Carter, Narissa M., 142, 287, 419, 535–36

purchase of samples, 388

purposive samples, 380–81

Pyrrhonian theoretical tradition, 19

qualitative branch of communication, 18–20, 73, 282, 563

Qualtrics (software), 345

quantitative differential psychology, 223

quasi-experimental design, 358–61

questionnaires

    customization of, 285

    defined, 281, 294

    example of, 290*f*

    interval level questions, 287

    sample size, 293

questions for scales, writing of, 235–39. *See also* item nonresponse

    avoidance of double negatives/positives, 238

    avoidance of double questions in one item, 238

    avoidance of emotionally charged items, 237

    avoidance of false premises, 238

    avoidance of hypothetical questions, 238–39

    avoidance of jargon/discipline-specific terminology, 237

    avoidance of leading items, 237

    avoidance of loaded items, 237–38

    avoidance of pronoun references, 239

    avoidance of words "always" and "never," 238

    item analysis, 277

    items reflecting construct, 236

    length of, 236, 265

    recall/memory and, 239

    use of concise/clear/unambiguous wording, 236, 265

    write twice as many as needed, 235–36

quota samples, 381–82

quotations

    citation of, 120–21

    in introductions, 138

random assignment, 340–42, 341*f*–43*f*, 351, 373

random number generator, 341, 373–74, 374*f*

random probe translation, 308

random samples, 373

randomized switching replications, 362–63

range, as measure of variability, 435

rank-order measurement. *See* ordinal measurement

ratio level questions, in surveys, 288

ratio measures, 188*f*, 222

ratio variables, 187–88, 472

rationale section (of research paper), 149–50, 149*f*

R-Commander (GUI), 14

Read, Brock, 111

receiver, in SMCR model, 10

recording errors, in content analysis, 331

recruitment of samples, 385–89

    advertising and, 386

    e-mail, 387, 387*f*

    ethical strategies for, 388–89

    face-to-face (FTF) approach, 386

letters/postcards, 386–87
purchase of samples, 388
snowball technique, 387–88
target population, 385
references
    APA style checklist for, 115*f*
    APA style for, 114, 116, 117*f*–19*f*, 119
    checklist, 160
    in draft of literature review, 164–65
    page formatting, 126–27, 128*f*
regression (*R*), 539–60
    2(step 2) computation of portion of formula, 543–44
    (step 1) finding means of variables, 543
    (step 3) calculation of equation under division line, 544
    (step 4) calculation for means, 544
    (step 5) finding constant, 544
    (step 6) calculation of linear equation, 544
    APA write-up for, 549, 551, 554, 558
    basic assumptions of, 542–43
    beta (β) weight, 552, 554
    bivariate regression, 540, 546, 548–49, 551, 552
    case study introduction, 541–42, 541*f*
    formula for, 542, 542*f*
    linear regression, 543–51
    multiple linear regression, 551–55, 552*f*–53*f*, 555*f*
    relationship between CA and beliefs (Dataset),
        550–51, 550*f*
    Rocca and Vogl-Bauer article, 557–58
    R-squared (*R*2) value, 546–47
    simple linear regression graph, 539–40, 540*f*
    use of SPSS and, 545–55, 545*f*–48*f*, 550*f*, 553*f*
    Wrench and M. Booth-Butterfield article, 555–56
regression to the mean, 354, 355*f*
reinforcer variables, 350
"The Relationship Between Listening Styles and
    Conversational Sensitivity" (J. Chesebro),
    137, 262–63, 534–35
relationships, in research, 175–77, 176*f*–77*f*
relationships and differences, 175–78, 176*f*–79*f*
reliability, 248–65. *See also* validity
    alpha reliabilities for book, 260, 260*f*–62*f*
    alpha reliabilities for communication journal
        articles, 262–63, 263*f*–64*f*
    alternate forms, 252
    APA write-up for, 259–60, 261*f*–62*f*
    archery analogy, 266
    coefficients and, 274–75
    Cronbach alpha, 253–56, 255*f*–58*f*, 259–60, 260*f*–62*f*
    defined, 248–49
    improvement of instruments for, 263, 265

intercorder reliability, 327–32
scalar, 249, 251–59
scores, 259
split-half, 252–53
test-retest, 252
religious identity of speakers study (1994), 344
replication, 356, 402
research, defined, 17
research ethics, 39–80. *See also* Institutional Review
    Boards (IRBs); *specific studies*
    authorship credit, 73–74
    Belmont Report effects on, 42, 47–49
    conflict of interest, 74
    data accuracy, 71–72
    data sharing, 72
    demographic information, 286
    duplicate data publication, 72–73
    Ethical Matrix, 45–47, 45*f*
    ethical scenarios, 40–45
    ethics, defined, 45
    participant identify protection, 73
    plagiarism, 74–77
    post hoc hypothesis revision, 73
    recruitment of samples and, 388–89
    setting significance levels, 448
    survey research and, 67
research implications, 566–67
research librarians, 93, 108–9
research organizations, 107
research paper structure, 131–70. *See also* literature review;
    literature review, first draft of; *specific elements*
    abstract, 132–34, 134*f*
    conclusion, 159, 159*f*
    discussion section, 156–59, 157*f*–58*f*, 564–67, 564*f*
    end materials, 160–62
    introduction, 135–40, 136*f*
    method section, 150–54, 152*f*, 154*f*, 210–12, 212*f*–13*f*
    rationale section, 149–50, 149*f*
    reading and critiquing academic literature, 162–63
    references checklist, 160
    results section, 154–55, 155*f*, 562
    steps in research paper, 133*f*
research papers, for general public, 588, 590*f*
research participants. *See also* informed consent;
    sampling methods
    anonymity, 51, 284, 286
    confidentiality, 52–54
    debriefing of, 352–53
    defined, 50
    identify protection, 73

research participants (*continued*)
    in K–12 educational settings, 52
    maturation threat to validity and, 353–54
    numbers of, 364
    paid participation, 51
    privacy, 51–52
    random assignment of, 340–42, 341*f*–43*f*, 351
    Research Project Worksheet, 312, 314*f*–15*f*
Research Planning Worksheet, 87, 88*f*, 98
Research Project Worksheet, 308–13, 309*f*–10*f*, 314*f*–15*f*
research projects, preliminary steps, 81–130.
        See also specific steps
    (step 1) topic identification, 82–86
    (step 2) research question and key terms, 86–91, 88*f*–90*f*
    (step 3) location of sources of information,
        91–111, 94*f*–97*f*, 101*f*–2*f*, 105*f*
    (step 4) organization and evaluation of information,
        111, 112*f*–13*f*
    (step 5) citation of sources using APA format, 114–28,
        115*f*–20*f*
    APA paper formatting, 122–24, 123*f*,
        125*f*, 126, 127*f*–28*f*
    working with librarians, 108–9
research questions, 86–91
    defined, 143, 394
    directional, 395
    in discussion section of paper, 565
    hypothesis testing and, 394–95
    identification of key terms, 89–90, 89*f*
    identification of synonymous terms, 89*f*, 90–91
    nondirectional, 395
    Research Planning Worksheet, 87, 88*f*
    Research Project Worksheet, 313, 315*f*
    stating topic as question, 87
research reports, non-academic, 167–68
resourceful citer, type of plagiarism, 77
respondent, 576
response rate, in survey research, 299–303
    comparison of techniques and, 294
    defined, 299–300
    improvement of, 303–4
    item nonresponse, 301–3
    nonresponse, defined, 300
    unit nonresponse, 299, 300–301
response set, 276
responsiveness, 203, 205, 233
results section (of research paper), 154–55, 155*f*, 562
retrospective validity, 270
rhetorical branch of communication, 18–20, 282
rhetorical questions, 137

Richmond, Virginia Peck, 6–7, 107, 142, 185, 199, 203, 205,
        228–29, 233, 234–35, 272, 569. *See also* Humor
        Assessment Instrument (HA); Nonverbal Immediacy
        Scale-Self-Report; Sociocommunicative Orientation
        Scale
Riddle, D. L., 379–80
Risk Knowledge Index, 231, 232*f*
rituals in friendships/marriages study (2002), 382–83
Rocca, Kelly A., 142, 153, 173, 290, 395, 557–58
role-playing, in experimental design, 345–46
Rosenthal, H., 286
R.PSPP (software), 14, 254
R-squared (*R*2) value, 546–47
running heads, 122, 123*f*, 124
running heads, on title page, 122, 123*f*, 124
Rutherford, Ernest, 4

sample mean, 422, 422*f*
sample size
    for interview schedules, 293
    null hypothesis and, 407–8
    online calculation of, 385
    in pilot testing of surveys, 293
    for questionnaires, 293
    sampling methods and, 383–85, 384*f*, 407–8
    type II error (β error) and, 408
samples
    in content analysis, 326
    defined, 369–70, 369*f*, 420
    in survey research, 284
sampling, defined, 369
sampling bias, 372, 379
sampling error, 372, 375, 377, 378, 399–400, 402
sampling frame, 371
sampling methods, 368–90
    (step 1) identification of theoretical population, 370
    (step 2) identification of potential participants, 370–71
    (step 3) selection of sample, 371
    determination of sample size, 383–85, 384*f*, 407–8
    nonprobabilty samples, 371, 372, 378–83
    probability samples, 371, 372–78
    recruitment of samples, 385–89
    sampling error, 372, 375, 377, 378
    selection of sampling design, 371–83
Saunders, P., 282–84, 293
scalar reliability, 249, 250*f*–51*f*, 251–59
scales. *See* statistical tests; *specific tests and scales*
scalograms, 186–87, 187*f*, 222, 230, 275
scatterplot graphs, 541, 541*f*
Scheffé (Scheffé), 507–9

scholarly vs. popular sources, 93–95, 95*f*
scholar-to-scholar presentations, 581
Schramm, Wilbur, 6
science, defined, 23
scientific method, 24*f. See also specific steps*
    (step 1) theories, 24–27
    (step 2) predictions/hypotheses, 27–29
    (step 3) observations, 29–31
    (step 4) empirical generalizations, 31, 33–34
    defined, 23
screw-you effect, as type of faking, 276, 299, 351
search engines, 105*f*, 106
secondary sources, 91–93
selection threat, 354
self stealer, type of plagiarism, 76
self-addressed stamped envelope (SASE), 304
self-administration surveying, 296–99
semantic differential scales, 184–85, 185*f*, 222, 227–28,
    277, 286, 287
semantic equivalence, 305
Sextus Empiricus, 26–27
Shannon, Claude, 9–10
Shannon and Weaver Model (SMCR model), 9–10
Sharp, D., 343
Sherblom, J. C., 6–7
shopping behavior studies, 282
shyness, 207
significance testing, 401–9
    (step 1) setting probability level, 402–3
    (step 2) conducting statistical test, 403
    (step 3) comparison of calculated/critical values,
    403–6, 404*f*–5*f*
    defined, 402
    effect size and, 408, 409*f*
    number line, 412*f*
    statistical power and, 406–8, 407*f*
Simon, Theodore, 223–24
Simons, G., 11
simple direct translation, 307
simple random samples, 373–75, 374*f*
situational behavior, 193
situational CA, 196, 229
Skalski, P., 344
skepticism, 19
skewness, 433–34, 433*f*–34*f*
Slater, M., 345
Small, Cathy (aka Rebekah Nathan), 44
SMCR model. *See* Shannon and Weaver Model
    (SMCR model)
smiling and helping behavior study (2003), 345, 346, 347*f*

Smith, Heather, 228–29
Smyth, J. D., 387
snowball technique, for recruitment of samples, 387–88
social desirability bias, 274, 276, 283
social desirability responding, 283
social psychology, 5
social sciences, history of, 2–8
social scientific branch of communication
    epistemology and, 18–20
    limitations of, 29
    upselling study and, 34–35
sociocommunicative orientation, 203, 204*f*, 213*f*
Sociocommunicative Orientation Scale, 203, 204–5,
    204*f*, 233, 261*f*–62*f*
sociocommunicative style, 204–5
Socrates, 230, 239
Solomon four-group design, 363
Songs of Zion, textual analysis of, 320
source, in SMCR model, 10
source credibility, 271
Source Credibility Measure, 239–41, 240*f*
Source Record Card, 112–13, 112*f*, 116
sources of information, location of, 91–111
    backtracking, 92
    citation of secondary sources, 93
    electronic databases, 100–105, 101*f*–2*f*, 104*f*
    Google Scholar, 106–7
    handbooks, 98–99
    how to locate, 95
    overview of information sources, 93–95
    primary sources, 91–93
    research organizational online databases, 107
    scholarly vs. popular sources, 93–95, 95*f*
    secondary sources, 91–93
    subject encyclopedias, 99
    when to use source types, 94*f*
    World Wide Web, 105–6, 109–11
specialty search engines, 105*f*, 106
specific-to-general order, 147
Spectra (NCA newsletter), 569
split-half reliability, 252–53
sports fan perception of fan communication (1999),
    140, 142, 173, 290, 395, 557–58
SPSS. *See* Statistical Package for the Social Sciences 24.0
    (SPSS) (software)
spurious correlations, 520–21
squared metrics, 437
standard deviation, as measure of variability, 437, 438*f*
Stanford Achievement Test (SAT), 224
The Stanford Prison Experiment (film), 43

Stanford Prison Study (1973), 43

Stanley, J. C., 353–55

Stapel, Diederik, 45

Staple, Jan, 185

Staple scale, 185–86, 186f

startling claims, as attention-getters, 135, 137

STATA, 254, 426

state behavior, 229

State Communication Apprehension Measure, 269–70

static group comparisons design, 358

statistic, defined, 417–18

statistical differences, 178, 178f–79f

Statistical Package for the Social Sciences 24.0 (SPSS) (software), 14, 332, 403, 412
   Book Datasets and, 254–55, 255f–58f, 259–60, 260f
   chi-square (χ^2), test of independence, 453–66, 454f–57f, 454f–58f, 461f–65f, 467f
   correlation, 527–32, 528f–31f, 533f
   dataset variability, 441, 441f–42f
   frequency distribution, 426–34, 427f–34f
   independent samples t test, 480–85, 480f–85f
   limitations of, 426
   measures of variability, 439–41, 439f–40f
   one-way analysis of variance (ANOVA), 501–11, 501f–6f, 508f, 512f
   regression (R), 545–55, 545f–48f, 550f, 553f

statistical stories, guidelines for, 588–91

statistical tests. *See also specific tests and scales*
   APA style for, 210–12, 212f–13f
   based on level of variables, 181–88, 188f
   factor analysis, 240, 275
   parametric/nonparametric, 243–44
   selection of, 188f
   well-controlled administration of, 265

statistics
   as attention-getters, 135, 137
   benefits of, 418–19

stereotypes, 34

Stewart, R. A., 344

sticky-note method, 111–12

strangers, culturally-based reactions to, 306

stratified random samples, 375–76, 375f

student interest in college classroom study (2003), 344–45, 392–93, 396–97

student motivation scale, 185

Student Newman-Keuls (SNK), 507–8

Student's t test. *See* independent samples t test

study design, in survey research, 289–91
   cross-sectional, 290
   longitudinal, 290–91

Stumpf, Carl, 32

subject encyclopedias, 99

subject search, in databases, 102–3

subjective ethic, 46–47

subscales, 240–41

Suci, G. J., 227

sum of expected frequencies (Σef) value, 329–30, 329f–30f

sum of squares, 435–37, 436f

sum of squares between, 496–97

sum of squares total, 498

sum of squares within, 497–98

suppressor variables, 350

survey, defined, 294

Survey Monkey, 299, 345

survey research, 280–318
   (step 1) selection of questions, 285–89
   (step 2) creation of clear instructions, 287, 289, 290f
   (step 3) study design, 289–92
   (step 4) data processing and analysis, 292
   (step 5) pilot testing, 292–94
   costs of, 295, 296, 298
   ethics and, 67
   face-to-face surveying, 294–95
   as form of operationalization, 234–35
   generalizability of goal, 284
   grouping of life contexts, 288
   grouping of like questions, 287–88
   hesitancy to disclosure types of information, 283–84
   improvement of response rate, 303–4
   interview schedule, 281
   length of surveys, 304
   marketing measures, 244
   measurement, 241–42
   multiple administration techniques, 304
   order of controversial questions, 287, 288
   populations and samples, 284
   preexisting datasets and, 282–83
   questionnaire, defined, 281
   Research Project Worksheet, 308–13, 309f–10f, 314f–15f
   response rates, 299–303
   self-administration surveying, 296–99
   study goal, 282
   survey, defined, 281
   telephone surveying, 295–96
   timeliness of questions about events, 283
   translation of surveys into other languages, 304–8

Sweeney, Lynn, 286

switching replications design, 360–61

syllogism, 27–29

synonymous terms, 89–91, 89f

systematic samples, 377–78

T (treatment), 495. *See also* one-way analysis of variance (ANOVA)

t test. *See* independent samples *t* test

tables
    APA style checklist for, 115*f*
    inclusion in paper, 161–62

Taichman, D. B., 22

Tamborini, R., 344

Tannenbaum, P. H., 227

Target, 536

technology, in presentations, 575

telephone surveys, 295–96

televangelists and perception of religion study, 398–99

temperature measurement, 221–22

Terman, Lewis, 224

Test of English as a Foreign Language (TOEFL), 224

testing flaw, 354

test-retest reliability, 252

Teven, Jason J., 239. *See also* Source Credibility Measure

Thayer, Greg, 141, 151, 234, 332, 332*f*, 513–14

theoretical population, 370

theories, in scientific method
    appeal to authority, 25
    appeal to general empirical rules, 26
    describes natural phenomenon, 24–25
    evoke empathy, 25
    explanations and, 25
    falsification and, 26–27
    label the phenomenon, 25
    predicting the future, 26

theory, in construct validity, 270

theory of natural selection (Darwin), 4

thesis statement, in introduction, 136*f*, 139

Thomas, C. E., 84, 142

Thomas, William Isaac, 5

Thompson, B., 435

Thorndike, E. L., 224

threats to validity, 272–74, 353–55

threshold effect, 348

time order, 336–37, 338

time-series design, 359

Title 45, *Code of Federal Regulations*, Part 46 (45 CFR 46), 49, 50, 61, 64. *See also* Common Rule

title of paper, 124

title of study, 313, 315*f*

title page, APA paper formatting
    author name(s) and affiliation(s), 124
    example of, 123*f*
    running heads, 122, 123*f*, 124
    title of paper, 124

title page, APA style checklist, 115*f*

title page, of journal, 116, 116*f*

title search, in databases, 102

too-perfect paraphraser, type of plagiarism, 76–77

topic, in introduction, 136*f*, 139

topic identification, 82–86. *See also* research questions
    brainstorming for, 84
    literature review, 85
    purpose of research, 83
    subjects of interest, 83
    theoretically driven questions and, 85–86
    use of personal experiences, 84

topical order. *See* categorical/topical order, in literature review

trait behavior, 192–93, 229

trait CA, 196, 229

"Trait Verbal Aggression, Sports Fan Identification, and Perceptions of Appropriate Sports Fan Communication" (Rocca and Vogl-Bauer), 557–58

translation of surveys, into other languages
    issues of equivalence, 305–6
    methods of, 307–8

translation/backtranslation, 307–8

Traugott, M. W., 303

trend survey design, 291

truncation symbols, 105

Tukey's honestly significance difference test (HSD), 507–9, 508*f*

Turner, L. H., 86

TurnItIn.com, 77

Tuskegee Syphilis Study (1934-1972), 41–42, 49, 50

two-group posttest-only design, 362

two-tailed hypothesis, 393–94, 406, 407*f*

type I error (α error), 410*f*, 413–14, 508

type II error (β error), 410*f*, 413–14
    sample size and, 408
    significance testing and, 403

uncertainty reduction theory (URT), 86

unethical behavior, 46

unit nonresponse, 299, 300–301

United Nations Economic Commission for Europe, guidelines for statistical stories, 588–91

units of analysis
    in content analysis, 323
    dyads, 173
    ecological fallacies and, 174
    groups, 173–74
    individuals, 173
    in interactional analysis, 323
    organizations, 174

Unwin, A., 591
URT. *See* uncertainty reduction theory (URT)
US Census, 419
US Department of Health and Human Services (HHS)
    Office of Human Research Protections (OHRP),
        49, 54, 63, 67, 71
    petition for Certificate of Confidentiality, 53
US Food and Drug Administration, 49
US military, testing of recruits, 224
US Office of War Information, 6
US Public Health Services, 41–42
USA Today, Snapshots statistics, 419
USA.gov, 283

Valencic, Kristin, 192
validity, 265–77. *See also* reliability
    archery analogy, 266
    bad measurement items and, 277
    coefficients and, 274–75
    concurrent, 269–70
    construct, 270–71, 275
    criterion, 268–70
    defined, 266
    employment of multiple approaches, 271
    examples in communication research, 266–68
    face or content, 268, 275
    factorial validity, 271
    faking responses and, 275–76
    measurement of known groups, 270–71
    predictive or prospective, 269, 275
    reliance on theory, 270
    response set and, 276
    retrospective or postdictive, 270
    threats to, 272–74
variability, measures of, 435–41
    range, 435
    standard deviation, 437, 438*f*
    sum of squares, 435–37, 436*f*
    use of SPSS and, 439–41, 439*f*–40*f*
    variance, 437, 437*f*
variable attributes, 174
variable values, 174–75
variables, 171–88. *See also* communication
        study variables
    attributes of, 174
    defined, 172
    levels of, 181–88, 188*f*
    measurement scales and, 183–88, 184*f*–88*f*
    relationships and differences, 175–78, 176*f*–79*f*
    Research Project Worksheet, 312–13, 315*f*
    selection of statistical tests, 188*f*
    types of, 172–73, 179–81
    units of analysis, 173–74
    values of, 174–75
variance, as measure of variability, 437, 437*f*
Vaughan, T. R., 42
Venn diagram, 555*f*
verbal immediacy, 201
verbal messages, defined, 11
video game and hostile thoughts study (2004), 344
video monitoring, in experimental design, 349
video recordings, in experimental design, 344–45
videos, in independent samples *t* test, 487–89
virtual reality, in experimental design, 345
Vogl-Bauer, Sally, 142, 153, 173, 290, 395, 557–58
Volokh, Eugene, 520
volunteer samples, 380
Von Osten, Wilhelm, 32

waivers of consent, 60–61
Wales, Jimmy, 111
Walworth, Janis, 520–21
Wanzer, M. B., 267, 273
Weaver, Warren, 9–10
web address (URL), 110
Weber, Keith, 142, 179, 344–45, 392–93,
    396–97, 487–89
webpages, APA citation elements for, 113*f*
websites. *See also* World Wide Web (WWW)
    Adobe Acrobat Reader, 112
    Annals of Improbable Research, 48
    APA style, 114
    appendices, 12–13
    Belmont Report, 42
    Bruner/Marketing Scales, 244
    Buros Center for Testing, 242
    Centers for Disease Control and Prevention, 283
    Collaborative Institutional Training Initiative (CITI)
        training, 63
    communication associations, 569
    Communication Currents (NCA), 589
    Communication Institute for Online Scholarship
        (CIOS), 107
    CRTNET, 569
    datasets for textbook study, 189
    *Directory of Communication Related Mental
        Measures*, 243
    Directory of Open Access Journals (DOAJ), 107
    Docear, 112
    Educational Testing Service (ETS), 242
    Galton, works of, 223
    Google Scholar, 106

graphic design software, 591–92
International Compilation of Human Research
    Standards, 54
Journal of Statistics Education, 282–83
Lime Survey, 299
mental measures database, 242
online calculation of sample size, 385
Plagiarism.org, 75
random number generator, 341
search engines, 105*f*
Stanford Prison Study, 43
stock infographics and templates, 591
Survey Monkey, 299
TurnItIn.com, 77
US Census, 419
USA.gov, 283
Zoomerang, 299
West, R., 86
West Virginia University (WVU), Department of
    Communication Studies, 12
Western Electric Company, Hawthorne Works, 349
Wheeless, L. R., 10
Wichita Jury Study (1954), 42
Wickersham, J. A., 6–7
Wiener, J. L., 345–46
Wikipedia, 111
Willingness to Communicate Scale, 206*f*
    APA write-up for, 213*f*, 262*f*
willingness to communicate (WTC), 205, 206*f*, 207, 213*f*, 262*f*
Winans, James A., 4

Woodworth, Robert, 224
Woodworth Personal Data Sheet, 224
working bibliography, 111
Workplace Aggression Tolerance Questionnaire, 174
World Wide Web (WWW). *See also* electronic databases;
    websites
    accuracy of site, 110
    authority and credentials of site, 110
    citation elements for webpages, 113*f*
    currency and date of site, 110, 111
    evaluation of credibility of sources on, 109–11
    Internet-administered surveys, 297–99
    limitations of Wikipedia, 111
    objectivity of site, 110
    search engines, 105*f*, 106
    as source of information, 105–6
Wrench, Jason S., 89, 90, 107, 132, 142, 199, 200, 228–29,
    231, 234–35, 287, 292, 308, 343, 352, 555–56, 564,
    565, 566–67. *See also* Homonegativity Short Form;
    Humor Assessment Instrument (HA); Risk
    Knowledge Index
WTC. *See* willingness to communicate (WTC)

Yale University, attitude change study (1953), 6
Yen, Corina, 34–35

Zhang, Q., 305
Zimbardo, Philip, 43
Znaniecki, Florian, 5
Zoomerang, 299

Printed in the USA/Agawam, MA
February 11, 2022

788897.056